RETROSPECTIVE SUPPLEMENT II
James Baldwin to Nathanael West

American Writers
A Collection of Literary Biographies

JAY PARINI
Editor in Chief

RETROSPECTIVE SUPPLEMENT II
James Baldwin to Nathanael West

Charles Scribner's Sons
an imprint of the Gale Group
New York • Detroit • San Francisco • London • Boston • Woodbridge, CT

American Writers, Retrospective Supplement II
Jay Parini, Editor in Chief

Permissions Department
The Gale Group, Inc.
27500 Drake Rd.
Farmington Hills, MI 48331-3535
Permissions Hotline:
248 699-8006 or 800 877-4253, ext. 8006
Fax: 248 699-8074 or 800 762-4058

Since this page cannot legibly accommodate all copyright notices, the acknowledgments constitute an extension of the copyright notice.

LIBRARY OF CONGRESS CATALOGING-IN-PUBLICATION DATA

American writers : a collection of literary biographies / Leonard Unger editor in chief.
   p. cm.
   The 4-vol. main set consists of 97 of the pamphlets originally published as the University of Minnesota pamphlets on American writers; some have been rev. and updated. The supplements cover writers not included in the original series.
   Supplement 2, has editor in chief, A. Walton Litz; Retrospective suppl. 1, c1998, was edited by A. Walton Litz & Molly Weigel; Suppl. 5–7 have as editor-in-chief, Jay Parini.
   Includes bibliographies and index.
   Contents: v. 1. Henry Adams to T.S. Eliot — v. 2. Ralph Waldo Emerson to Carson McCullers — v. 3. Archibald MacLeish to George Santayana — v. 4. Isaac Bashevis Singer to Richard Wright — Supplement[s]: 1, pt. 1. Jane Addams to Sidney Lanier. 1, pt. 2. Vachel Lindsay to Elinor Wylie. 2, pt. 1. W.H. Auden to O. Henry. 2, pt. 2. Robinson Jeffers to Yvor Winters. — 4, pt. 1. Maya Angelou to Linda Hogan. 4, pt. 2. Susan Howe to Gore Vidal — Suppl. 5. Russell Banks to Charles Wright — Suppl. 6. Don DeLillo to W.D. Snodgrass — Suppl. 7. Julia Alvarez to Tobias Wolff — Suppl. 8. T.C. Boyle to August Wilson.
   ISBN 0-684-19785-5 (set) — ISBN 0-684-13662-7
   1. American literature—History and criticism. 2. American literature—Bio-bibliography. 3. Authors, American—Biography. I. Unger, Leonard. II. Litz, A. Walton. III. Weigel, Molly. IV. Parini, Jay. V. University of Minnesota pamphlets on American writers.

PS129 .A55
810'.9
[B]   73-001759

ISBN 0-684-31249-2

Editorial and Production Staff

Project Editor
ALJA KOOISTRA COLLAR

Assisting Editor
MARK DROUILLARD

Copyeditors
JANET L. BADGLEY
JANET BYRNE
LISA DIXON
DIANA GEORGE
GRETCHEN GORDON
ALAN V. HEWAT
JEAN KAPLAN
MARCIA MERRYMAN MEANS
GINA MISIROGLU
CAROL SICKMAN-GARNER
NICOLAS VEROLI

Proofreaders
GRETCHEN GORDON
ANNA SHEETS NESBITT

Permission Researchers
MARGARET CHAMBERLAIN
JULIE VAN PELT

Indexer
KATHARYN DUNHAM

Compositor
GARY LEACH

Publisher
FRANK MENCHACA

Acknowledgments

Acknowledgment is gratefully made to those publishers and individuals who have permitted the use of the following material in copyright. Every effort has been made to secure permission to reprint copyrighted material.

JAMES BALDWIN Excerpts from "Down at the Cross," by James Baldwin. In *The Fire Next Time*. Vantage Books, 1963. Copyright © 1963 by James Baldwin. All rights reserved. Copyright renewed © 1991 by Gloria Baldwin Karefa-Smith, Executrix. Reproduced by permission. Excerpts from "Encounter on the Seine: Black Meets Brown" and "Stranger in the Village," by James Baldwin. In *Notes of a Native Son*. Beacon Press, 1955. Copyright © 1955 by Beacon Press. All rights reserved. Copyright renewed © 1983 by James Baldwin. Reproduced by permission. Excerpts from "Nobody Knows My Name," by James Baldwin. In *Nobody Knows My Name: More Notes of a Native Son*. Vantage Books, 1961. Copyright © 1961 by Vantage Books. All rights reserved. Copyright renewed © 1989 by Gloria Baldwin Karefa-Smith, Executrix. Reproduced by permission.

SAUL BELLOW Excerpts from "The Art of Fiction: Saul Bellow," by Lloyd Harper. *The Paris Review* 9 (1966). Reproduced by permission. Excerpts from "A Conversation with Saul Bellow," by Chirantan Kulshrestha. *Chicago Review* (1972). Reproduced by permission. Excerpts from "An Interview with Saul Bellow," by Joyce Illig. *Publishers Weekly*, 1973. Reproduced by permission.

ELIZABETH BISHOP Excerpts from "The Country Mouse," by Elizabeth Bishop. In *Collected Prose*. Edited by Robert Giroux. Farrar, Straus and Giroux, 1984. Copyright © 1984 by Alice Methfessel. All rights reserved. Reproduced by permission. Excerpts from "Efforts of Affection: A Memoir of Miss Marianne Moore," by Elizabeth Bishop. *Vanity Fair* (May 1983). Reproduced by permission. Excerpts from "Memories of Uncle Neddy," by Elizabeth Bishop. *The Southern Review* 13 (fall 1977). Reproduced by permission of the author. Excerpts from selected letters in *One Art: Letters*. Edited by Robert Giroux. Farrar, Straus and Giroux, 1994. Copyright © 1994 by Alice Helen Methfessel. All rights reserved. Reproduced by permission. Excerpts from "Brazil, January 1, 1502" and "Manuelzinho," by Elizabeth Bishop. In *Questions of Travel*. Farrar, Straus and Giroux, 1965. Copyright © 1965 by Elizabeth Bishop. All rights reserved. Reproduced by permission. Excerpts from "Giant Snail" and "Trouvée," by Elizabeth Bishop. In *The Complete Poems, 1927–1979*. Farrar, Straus and Giroux, 1983. Copyright © 1983 by Elizabeth Bishop. All rights reserved. Reproduced by permission. Excerpts from "Crusoe in England," by Elizabeth Bishop. In *Geography III*. Farrar, Straus and Giroux, 1976.

Copyright © 1976 by Elizabeth Bishop. All rights reserved. Reproduced by permission. Excerpts from interview with Eileen Farley. *University of Washington Daily*, May 28, 1974. Reproduced by permission. Excerpts from "I'm Nobody! Who are you?" by Emily Dickinson. In *The Poems of Emily Dickinson*. Edited by R. W. Franklin. Belknap Press of Harvard University Press, 1976. Copyright © 1976 by the President and Fellows of Harvard College and the Trustees of Amherst College. All rights reserved. Reproduced by permission. Excerpts from "Interlude," by Amy Lowell. In *Pictures of a Floating World*. Macmillan Company, 1919. Copyright © 1919 by the President and Fellows of Harvard College and the Trustees of Amherst College. All rights reserved. Reproduced by permission. Excerpts from "Sand Dunes," by Robert Frost. In *West-Running Brook*. Henry Holt, 1928. Copyright © 1928 by Henry Holt. All rights reserved. Reproduced by permission.

HART CRANE Excerpts from *O My Land, My Friends: The Selected Letters of Hart Crane*. Reprinted by permission of the publisher, from *O My Land, My Friends: The Selected Letters of Hart Crane*. Edited by Langdon Hammer and Brom Weber. New York: Four Walls Eight Windows, 1997. Excerpts from "To Brooklyn Bridge," "The River," "The Dance," "Cape Hatteras," "The Tunnel," and "Atlantis," by Hart Crane. In *The Bridge*. Liveright, 1933. Reproduced by permission. Excerpts from "My Grandmother's Love Letter," "Chaplinesque," "For the Marriage of Faustus and Helen," "Voyages," and "The Broken Tower," by Hart Crane. In *The Poems of Hart Crane*. Liveright, 1986. Reproduced by permission.

RALPH ELLISON Excerpts from "The Art of Fiction," by Ralph Ellison. *Paris Review* 18 (spring 1955). Reproduced by permission. Excerpts from "Study and Experience: An Interview with Ralph Ellison." *Massachusetts Review* 18 (1977). Reproduced by permission. Excerpts from "Richard Wright's Blues," by Ralph Ellison. *Antioch Review* 3 (summer 1945). Copyright © 1945 Antioch Review, Inc. Copyright renewed © 1972 The Antioch Review. Reproduced by permission. Excerpts from "The Charlie Christian Story," by Ralph Ellison. *Saturday Review*, May 17, 1958. Reproduced by permission. Excerpts from "Twentieth-Century Fiction and the Black Mask of Humanity," by Ralph Ellison. *Confluence* (December 1953). Copyright © 1953 by President and Fellows of Harvard College. Copyright renewed © 1981 by Ralph Ellison. Reproduced by permission.

SARAH ORNE JEWETT Excerpts from "The Value of Age in the Fiction of Sarah Orne Jewett," by Susan Allen Toth. *Studies in Short Fiction* 8 (summer 1971). Reproduced by permission. Excerpts from "How Clearly the Gradations of Society Were

List of Subjects

Introduction

In 1834, in his *Journals,* Ralph Waldo Emerson reflected wisely on the notion of genius: "Genius seems to consist merely in trueness of sight, in using such words as show that the man was an eye-witness, and not a repeater of what was told." In a sense, all of the writers reconsidered in this volume of *American Writers* might be considered geniuses, if we use this Emersonian definition. Each has seen things nobody else has seen and managed to speak frankly and truly about the things he or she has seen. The record of their vision, and the evolution of each vision, will be found in these pages.

The idea of reprinting the Minnesota pamphlets occurred to Charles Scribner Jr. (1921–1995). Soon four volumes, titled *American Writers: A Collection of Literary Biographies* (1974), appeared, and it was widely acclaimed by students, teachers, and librarians. The series continues, with volumes added yearly as supplements and retrospectives, such as this one, wherein we revisit major authors, taking into account changing views of their work. The essays in this particular volume embrace the whole career of an important American writer, supplying biographical and cultural context as well as reconsidering the shape of the individual achievement.

The writers of fiction discussed in this collection are, in alphabetical order, James Baldwin, Saul Bellow, Kate Chopin, Theodore Dreiser, Ralph Ellison, Sarah Orne Jewett, Norman Mailer, Flannery O'Connor, Edgar Allan Poe, Isaac Bashevis Singer, Philip Roth, and Nathanael West. The poets are Elizabeth Bishop, Hart Crane, Henry Wadsworth Longfellow, Robert Lowell, Sylvia Plath, and Adrienne Rich. These authors were chosen because of their immense visibility and interest to students and general readers. In each case, a considerable body of secondary literature has grown up around the life and work, although in each of these essays the author attempts to present a fresh reading of the material.

In the past twenty-five years or so, since the advent of post-structuralism, the emphasis in most critical writing has been largely theoretical. What was called "close reading" during the days of the so-called New Criticism—a movement that had its origins in formalist criticism of the 1920s and 1930s, and which reigned supreme in university English departments for several decades—was often immensely useful to students and teachers, who wanted careful and detailed analyses of individual texts. Every effort has been made in these essays to provide useful and patient readings of a writer's works without sacrificing theoretical sophistication. The biographical and historical contexts of each life is presented in ways that bear upon the development of the work itself.

Readers will discover in the course of reading these essays why each writer might be considered, in Emerson's terms, a "genius," someone who possesses a true and honest vision of the world. The essays are written by professional scholars and college teachers, several of whom are writers themselves, and their work is intended to address the concerns of beginning readers and to extend the appreciation and understanding of those who already have some familiarity with the career being reconsidered.

The bibliographies attached to the end of each essay offer a selective guide to further reading.

Our hope is that these essays will encourage readers to return to the fiction or poetry under discussion, thoughtfully, and better informed than they were before. That is, after all, one of the traditional functions of criticism. My own sense is that we have achieved a good deal in this volume and that readers will go away pleased and edified, eager to begin the work of reading or rereading.

——*JAY PARINI*

Contributors

Michael Austin. Chairs the Department of English and Modern Languages at Shepherd College in Shepherdstown, West Virginia. He has published essays on Saul Bellow, Tony Kushner, and Terry Tempest Williams, as well as several studies of religious discourse in seventeenth-century England. SAUL BELLOW

John Canaday. Author of *The Nuclear Muse: Literature, Physics, and the First Atomic Bombs,* a work of criticism, and *The Invisible World,* a book of poems for which he won the Walt Whitman Award from the Academy of American Poets. He teaches poetry writing and playwriting at Harvard's summer and Extension Schools. ROBERT LOWELL

Jane Goldman. Senior lecturer in English and American Literature at the University of Dundee, Scotland. Author of a number of books on modernism and on Virginia Woolf, including *The Feminist Aesthetics of Virginia Woolf: Modernism, Post-Impressionism and the Politics of the Visual.* She has also published essays on Nathanael West (with a view to a book on West and Dada). She is currently writing *Image to Apocalypse: 1910–1945.* NATHANAEL WEST

Tracie Church Guzzio. Assistant Professor of English at the State University of New York at Plattsburgh. Her specialization is African American literature. She teaches courses in multicultural literature, the African American novel, and literary theory. She has written essays on Ishmael Reed and Jean Toomer and is currently working on a study of the writer John Edgar Wideman and a book-length project on the "double" in African American literature and culture. RALPH ELLISON

Philip Hobsbaum. Professor Emeritus of the University of Glasgow and Professorial Re-search Fellow. His many published works include four collections of verse; *Tradition and Experiment in English Poetry; Essentials of Literary Criticism; Metre, Rhythm and Verse Form;* and Reader's Guides to Charles Dickens, D. H. Lawrence, and Robert Lowell. Currently he is at work on a fifth collection of poems, provisionally entitled *North Kelvin.* SYLVIA PLATH, ADRIENNE RICH

Paul Johnston. Chair of the English Department at the State University of New York at Plattsburgh, where he teaches colonial and nineteenth-century American literature. He has published articles on Nathaniel Hawthorne, Susan Cooper and James Fenimore Cooper, and Jonathan Edwards. HENRY WADSWORTH LONGFEL-LOW

Karen L. Kilcup. Professor of American Literature at the University of North Carolina at Greensboro and recently named Davidson Eminent Scholar Chair at Florida International University. Her books include *Native American Women's Writing, c. 1800–1924: An Anthology; Soft Canons: American Women Writers and Masculine Tradition;* and *Robert Frost and Feminine Literary Tradition.* ELIZABETH BISHOP, SARAH ORNE JEWETT

Denise Larrabee. A writer and historian specializing in American women's history and literature. Author of *Anne Hampton Brewster: 19th-century Author and "Social Outlaw"* and editor of *Meridian Bound: Fiction, Essays, Poetry, and More.* Her work has appeared in numerous reference books, anthologies, and publications. KATE CHOPIN

J. Michael Lennon. Emeritus Vice President of Academic Affairs and Professor of English at

xv

Wilkes University. He is the editor or author of five books by or about Norman Mailer, including *Norman Mailer: Works and Days* and *The Spooky Art: A Book About Writing.* He serves as Mailer's archivist and as one of his literary executors. NORMAN MAILER

James A. Lewin. Associate Professor of English at Shepherd College. His publications include an essay on Nelson Algren for the Scribners American Writers series and analyses of Shakespeare's political ghosts. ISAAC BASHEVIS SINGER

Kim Lewis. Ph.D. student of Comparative Literature at the University of Chicago and Professor of Italian at Columbia College, Chicago. She is currently researching postwar French and Italian literature. HART CRANE

Jerome Loving. Professor of English at Texas A&M University. Author of *Walt Whitman: The Song of Himself* and several other books and articles on American literature. He is currently completing a critical biography of Theodore Dreiser. THEODORE DREISER

Tony Magistrale. Professor of English at the University of Vermont. Author of *The Student Companion to Edgar Allan Poe.* Currently writing *Hollywood's Stephen King*, the first book-length analysis of the films that have been made from Stephen King's fiction. EDGAR ALLAN POE

D. Quentin Miller. Assistant Professor of English at Suffolk University. Author of *Re-Viewing James Baldwin: Things Not Seen* and *John Updike and the Cold War: Drawing the Iron Curtain.* He has published on a wide variety of American authors and is a member of the editorial board of the *Heath Anthology of American Literature.* JAMES BALDWIN

Sanford Pinsker. Shadek Professor of Humanities at Franklin and Marshall College. Writes widely about American literature for journals, such as *The Virginia Quarterly, Sewanee Review, Georgia Review,* and *Partisan Review.* Author of *The Comedy That "Hoits": An Essay on the Fiction of Philip Roth.* PHILIP ROTH

Sylvia Bailey Shurbutt. Professor of English, Shepherd College. Author of *Reading Writing Relationships*, articles in *Essays in Literature, Women's Studies, Southern Humanities Review, The Southern Literary Journal, Women and Language, Victorian Poetry,* and chapters and essays on Zelda Fitzgerald, Caroline Norton, Kate Chopin, Matthew Arnold, John Stuart Mill, and Emily Dickinson. FLANNERY O'CONNOR

RETROSPECTIVE SUPPLEMENT II
James Baldwin to Nathanael West

James Baldwin

1924–1987

*I*N THE PREFACE to his first collection of essays, *Notes of a Native Son* (1955), James Baldwin stated his life and career goals with simple eloquence: "I want to be an honest man and a good writer." Through his long and varied career, Baldwin pleased his critics and readers at times for being more than a good writer: a great writer, the spokesman for a generation, a visionary, a prophet. Toward the end of his career, well after he had landed on the cover of *Time* magazine in 1963, his talents and achievements were called into question as his readership declined and his critics accused him of losing his powers, becoming bitter, or being out of touch. The question of his status as a "good writer" has much to do with his goal of being an "honest man," for despite the praise or scorn readers may heap on Baldwin's writings, few dare to accuse him of losing his commitment to honesty. His relentless struggle against the forces that would obscure honesty, in fact, may have been the key factor in determining his literary success. Many "good writers" are actually safe writers or writers who shy away from honesty in favor of telling people what they want to hear. Baldwin never did that. Marked by a shocking frankness about sexuality and race, charged with the apocalyptic rhetoric of the Bible, informed by a deep understanding of history, music, and literature, James Baldwin's writings are as rich, challenging, and energetic as those of nearly any other twentieth-century American author.

The circumstances of his youth did not project this type of success. Baldwin was born in Harlem on August 2, 1924, the oldest of nine children. He grew up under impoverished circumstances during the Great Depression in a community that turned from vibrant to blighted in the first decade of his life. Harlem of the 1930s and 1940s was characterized by violent riots born of overcrowding and poverty, and the young men and women who grew up there tried desperately to escape. In his landmark essay "Down at the Cross" (1963; sometimes referred to as "The Fire Next Time" after the title of the book in which it appears) Baldwin noted that "every Negro boy" who grew up in Harlem came to realize "that he stands in great peril and must find, with speed, a 'thing,' a gimmick, to lift him out, to start him on his way. *And it does not matter what the gimmick is.*" He goes on to say, "it was my career in the church that turned out, precisely, to be my gimmick." Organized religion was as much a part of Harlem in those days as jazz, leftist politics, and street protests. For many Harlemites, religion was the only promise of salvation. Baldwin's stepfather David Baldwin was a preacher who had followed the Great Migration north from his home in New Orleans in the 1920s. Baldwin's mother, Emma Berdis Jones, had moved north from Maryland. James never knew his biological father, and his relationship with his stepfather was contentious, even at times violent. Yet Baldwin himself became a preacher when he turned fourteen, having undergone a religious conversion similar to the one John Grimes, the protagonist of Baldwin's first novel *Go Tell It on the Mountain* (1953), experiences. Before he was twenty Baldwin had left not only the ministry but also the church, and this painful decision energizes many of his early writings, particularly the fictional ones. If the church was a "gimmick" to lift Baldwin out of Harlem, it was clearly just the first one, to "start him on his way." These words from "Down at the Cross" are echoed in the last line of *Go Tell It on the Mountain:* "I'm coming. I'm on my way." The journey for Baldwin was not only out of the church but also out of Harlem and eventually out of the country.

A familiar rite of passage for American writers in the 1920s, such as Ernest Hemingway and F. Scott Fitzgerald, was a period of expatriation in Paris. Baldwin felt compelled to imitate these writers of the Lost Generation in his own quest to become a writer. His writing career began after he graduated from DeWitt Clinton High School in 1942 and left the church at the same time. After a few years of working odd jobs and shuffling around in Greenwich Village, Baldwin began reviewing books, and in 1948 he published his first essay and his first short story. Having discovered finally that his enduring "gimmick" was writing, he entered into his career in earnest but with a conflicted sense of his identity and his mission. He had grown weary of reviewing what he described in the documentary film *James Baldwin—The Price of the Ticket* (1990) as an avalanche of "be kind to Negroes, be kind to Jews" books that came across his desk, and he stated with the restlessness that characterized his life, "I had to go."

BALDWIN IN EUROPE

Baldwin's first trip to Paris was formative as well as frustrating. World War II had ended, and a number of American soldiers were in Paris, many studying on the GI Bill. Paris had long been receptive to American writers and African American artists, and Baldwin was happy to be away from the frenetic drive of New York City. Yet he was experiencing a profound search for identity as he struggled to become a writer while still living a relatively volatile life with many friends but little money.

The final section of *Notes of a Native Son* is comprised of essays about this identity struggle in Paris, where he escaped the racism he encountered in America only to discover a different version of it in Paris. Expatriation was not the same thing as escape, he learned, and he wrote in the essay "Encounter on the Seine: Black Meets Brown" that the black American in Paris "finds himself involved, in another language, in the same old battle: the battle for his own identity." Baldwin saw this identity battle not as unique to black Americans, though, but as an American birthright: "in this need to establish himself in relation to his past he is most American, that this depthless alienation from oneself and one's people is, in sum, the American experience."

Paris afforded Baldwin the opportunity to "establish himself in relation to his past," but it was a complicated past indeed. "Encounter on the Seine" has Baldwin confronting a number of pasts that relate to his own identity. His African past in Paris exists in the form of French people of African descent and Algerian immigrants. Baldwin discovers his kinship with these people, who are connected to him by the color of his skin, yet the French Africans are separate because of their status as colonial subjects rather than American tourists or expatriates. Baldwin attempts to separate the history from the mythology of the African American artist in Paris, which had been established in the jazz age: "The Eiffel Tower has naturally long since ceased to divert the French, who consider that all Negroes arrive from America, trumpet-laden and twinkle-toed, bearing scars so unutterably painful that all of the glories of the French Republic may not suffice to heal them." Baldwin also inevitably confronts his writing past—the myth of the American expatriate writer perpetuated by Hemingway, Gertrude Stein, and others—that Paris is the perfect place for Americans to become writers. Through his confrontation with all of these histories or myths, Baldwin is put in the uncomfortable position of having to disappear in order to develop and to avoid stereotypes:

> The American Negro in Paris is forced at last to exercise an undemocratic discrimination rarely practiced by Americans, that of judging his people, duck by duck, and distinguishing them one from another. Through this deliberate isolation, through lack of numbers, and above all through his own overwhelming need to be, as it were, forgotten, the American Negro in Paris is very nearly the invisible man.

Anticipating Ralph Ellison's extended meditation on invisibility in his novel *Invisible Man* (1952), arguably the most important fictional consideration of racism in the twentieth century, Baldwin's 1950 essay sets up a situation that is painful and uncomfortable: he gradually becomes aware of how racism has been responsible for his identity. His early attempts to become a writer were linked not only to his leaving the church and Harlem but also to his desire to escape the oppression of American racism. The incident that led to his expatriation, which he retold many times in many forms, occurred when a waitress in New Jersey refused to serve him because he was black. He claimed he wanted to kill her, and he hurled a glass at her that shattered a mirror in the restaurant. This murderous anger could only tear him apart or land him in jail, so he left his native country. He came to realize in Paris that racism was going to follow him, that there was, according to one of his favorite Bible passages, "no hiding place."

In "Equal in Paris," another essay in *Notes of a Native Son,* Baldwin tells of how he was arrested and jailed in Paris because one of his friends had stolen a sheet from a hotel and stored it in his room. He felt he was the victim not only of cultural and linguistic misunderstanding but also of racism. He became so despondent that he nearly killed himself in the Paris jail cell over an incident that was so trivial

as to be laughed out of the French courts. If his expatriation was an attempt to escape American racism or to become invisible, he discovered that he could not do either. He went from Paris to a village in Switzerland, Loéche-les-Bains, where the whiteness of the people and the whiteness of the snow made him all the more visible. There he wrote the essay "Stranger in the Village" and completed his first novel, *Go Tell It on the Mountain.*

"Stranger in the Village," published in *Harper's* the same year Baldwin's first novel was published, marked a turning point in his career for a number of reasons. In this essay Baldwin exhibits a keen sense of history and his place in it. He faces the paradoxes of his situation as a black American expatriate in an isolated village, where he is told he is a "sight" yet where the villagers "did not, really, see my smile." Unlike in New York or Paris, Baldwin observes, "Everyone in the village knows my name." Yet at the same time many of them had never seen a black man before, and there was "no suggestion that I was human: I was simply a living wonder." Away from his home and feeling profoundly isolated, Baldwin in Switzerland begins to confront American identity. He writes:

> For the history of the American Negro is unique also in this: that the question of his humanity, and of his rights therefore as a human being, became a burning one for several generations of Americans, so burning a question that it ultimately became one of those used to divide the nation. It is out of this argument that the venom of the epithet *Nigger!* is derived.

Baldwin concludes the essay with the striking sentence, "This world is white no longer, and it will never be white again." The apocalyptic tone of this conclusion marked many of Baldwin's essays from this moment on. Baldwin had successfully integrated the many facets of his life that had been separate before this point: the fiery minister, the victim of racism, the expatriate, and the social critic. After he had written about literary matters, specifically the flaws of protest novels by Richard Wright and Harriet Beecher Stowe, and after he had come to terms with his time in Paris in other essays, Baldwin had arrived at the point where his personal history and the history of the modern world converged. And this point evolved for him in a tiny Swiss village, where he completed his most enduring novel, *Go Tell It on the Mountain.*

In "Everybody's Protest Novel" and "Many Thousands Gone"—his essays on Wright and Stowe—Baldwin had criticized novels that look at American racism through the lenses of Marxism and abolitionism, respectively, and thus fail to penetrate the surface of African American experience, which is richer than any "ism" could convey. He had set himself up for the difficult task of addressing the complexities and difficulties of black American life without making the same mistakes he felt Wright and Stowe had made. *Go Tell It on the Mountain* takes an unusual form with the coming-of-age story of fourteen-year-old John Grimes framing the stories of John's aunt, stepfather, mother, and biological father. At its core the story is a classic bildungsroman, which Horace Porter (1989) and David Leeming (1994) have compared to James Joyce's *Portrait of the Artist as a Young Man.* Yet the weight of the middle section of the book, comprised of the stories of John's parents and aunt, associates the novel with a complex cultural history that is uniquely Baldwin's.

John Grimes's story takes place on his fourteenth birthday. Like Baldwin, who underwent a violent conversion experience at the age of fourteen, John is surprised to find himself on the so-called threshing floor in front of the altar of his church: "He was like a rock, a dead man's body, a dying bird, fallen from an awful height; something that had no power of itself, any more, to turn." Earlier that day John wants desperately to leave his house, and he experiences enormous relief when his mother gives him some birthday

money, which he uses to see a movie. On the way to the movies, he wrestles with the difficulties of his life and his desires for a fate apart from that of his people:

> He did not long for the narrow way, where all his people walked; where the houses did not rise, piercing, as it seemed, the unchanging clouds, but huddled, flat, ignoble, close to the filthy ground, where the streets and the hallways and the rooms were dark, and where the unconquerable odor was of dust, and sweat, and urine, and homemade gin.

The imagery of filth and dust in this passage pervades John's story, and because his last name is "Grimes," it is invariably associated with himself as well as with his home. Like Baldwin, who went to Paris partially to escape the racial persecution of his home country, John Grimes attempts to escape the filth and low station of his home. But dirt follows John just as racism followed Baldwin. John attempts to transcend his circumstances first by mounting a hill in Central Park, then by entering the movie house. In both cases he is lured by fantasies of fame and wealth, the very sins his stepfather Gabriel denounces from the pulpit. John is brought low when he returns home to find that his brother Roy has been stabbed by a gang of white boys. John's individual identity quest is checked by his sense of guilt over his obligations to family. He thus reenters Gabriel's church, and fulfilling everyone's expectations that he will become a minister to compensate for his brother's misbehavior, he prepares himself for conversion.

Before John's conversion in the final section of the book, Baldwin presents the stories, or "prayers of the saints," of his aunt, stepfather, mother, and father. These stories reveal the truth behind the exterior of what John sees: all of the pious elders of the church were once young rebels who left their homes. All of them experienced hope and disillusionment. All were, in fact, rejected by their parents and sought, in their own ways, to define themselves outside the safety of home, despite hostile and alienating surroundings. But the relationship between John's experience and these other stories is far from neat or easily definable. Much silent knowledge passes between John and his aunt and parents when he is undergoing conversion on the threshing floor. If he is becoming aware of his own familial history, it is unconscious, for he has not heard the stories. These stories have somehow created him, yet through his conversion he does not feel a loving connection but rather the murderous power to kill his stepfather Gabriel. His salvation allows him to rise above Gabriel's disapproval and his need for his mother's and his aunt's approval. It is a violent birth not just into the church but into maturity, and the powerful sense of individuality he feels, the reader assumes, will enable him to strike off on his own eventually. Thus the final lines of the novel, as John's parents wait for him to return home from the church, are wonderfully ambiguous. "'I'm ready,' John said, 'I'm coming. I'm on my way.'" In the eyes of the faithful in the novel, John has arrived; but in the eyes of the reader and in his own eyes, John has only begun his journey.

John's journey is continued in the character of David Alexander in Baldwin's 1955 play *The Amen Corner.* In this play David is caught between the ways of the church, represented by his mother Margaret, who is a pastor, and the ways of the world, represented by his father Luke, who is a jazz musician. Margaret has set herself up for a fall. Her flaw is that she has refused to face reality and has tried to separate herself from her past and from her husband, whom she considers unholy and beneath her. When Luke returns, sick and needing comfort, Sister Margaret turns from him. Yet her son David is drawn to his father, and he would rather nurture his musical talent outside of the church than play piano for his mother. Margaret loses her position in the church but arrives at the higher understanding about

what it means to love the Lord. It ain't all in the singing and the shouting. It ain't all in the reading of the Bible. . . . To love the Lord is to love all His children—all of them, everyone—and suffer with them and rejoice with them and never count the cost!

Her son David is not there to witness her transformation; he has run off to explore the same message, not through religion but through art. His conversion is the next logical step after John Grimes's spiritual conversion.

A key development in John's conversion is the approval of Brother Elisha, a boy somewhat older than John who has already been saved and who playfully wrestles with John before encouraging him to think about his soul. Elisha gives John the standard line about the wicked ways of the world, but John does not find Elisha sincere. This is because John is clearly attracted to Elisha, and many readers have interpreted the attraction as sexual. Elisha kisses John on the last page of the novel, and though it is described as "a holy kiss," it is also charged with the sexual tension that has existed between them throughout the novel. Readers would probably not have been tempted to interpret John's attraction to Elisha as physical had it not been for the publication of Baldwin's second novel, *Giovanni's Room* (1956). Between the publication of these two novels Baldwin collected his essays in *Notes of a Native Son,* which remains his best-known collection of essays with the possible exception of *The Fire Next Time* (1963). *Notes* begins with the literary essays on Wright and Stowe and ends with the expatriate essays on Paris and Switzerland. At the center of the collection is a trio of essays on America, including the eponymous essay about his stepfather's death. These essays constitute a personal history that connects to a cultural history. Baldwin had established the tenets of his life and set it down in a masterful prose style that begins to fulfill his goal of becoming "an honest man and a good writer." Yet for all of the honesty of these personal essays, Baldwin does not confront his homosexuality in *Notes* and broaches the subject in only the subtlest way in *Go Tell It*. Baldwin's next novel took on the taboo subject of homosexuality in such an honest way that publishers and readers alike were afraid of it.

Although Baldwin studies homosexuality thoroughly in *Giovanni's Room,* the novel is really about something broader: the refusal to accept oneself, which leads to the impossibility of loving another. Baldwin spent much of his career arguing with labels and never accepted being called "gay." In a 1969 interview published in Fred L. Standley and Louis H. Pratt's *Conversations with James Baldwin* (1989), he claims, "I don't know what homosexual means any more, and Americans don't either." Yet *Giovanni's Room* is widely considered Baldwin's "gay novel," perhaps because it was so unusual in 1956 to read fiction about homosexual experiences described so candidly or perhaps because the narrator David's homosexual experiences pointedly frame the dilemma of the novel. Just as John Grimes is a classic protagonist of a coming-of-age novel, David is a classic protagonist of a modern novel in that his paralysis precipitates tragedy. David is caught between the macho vision of masculinity projected by his father and his own attractions toward men. He becomes someone who is afraid to act on his own desires, and his self-hatred leads to the destruction of everyone who comes close to him.

Giovanni's Room takes place in Paris, and the themes Baldwin initiates in the expatriate essays of *Notes of a Native Son* and continues in his next collection of essays *Nobody Knows My Name: More Notes of a Native Son* (1961) are also evident in *Giovanni's Room*. In contrast to his other novels, *Giovanni's Room* is pointedly not about race or racism; Baldwin did not want to overburden the book's central message with too many issues. David, like Baldwin, came to

Paris both to escape and to find himself. He recognizes that he is in Europe "as we say in America" to "find myself" and remarks, "This is an interesting phrase, not current as far as I know in the language of any other people, which certainly does not mean what it says but betrays a nagging suspicion that something has been misplaced." Here the novel invites us to see David's dilemma in terms that transcend sexuality but that are unique to Americans in general. In his essays, Baldwin often writes about identity quests as struggles or even battles. In these terms, a war is being fought within David, and like so many wars, there is devastation but no real progress.

The war is especially evident in Giovanni's room. David's lover Giovanni brings him to his room to reveal to him the nature of human love that he has been avoiding. Giovanni's room is characterized by a strange beauty and security but also by chaos and disorder. It is dirty, cramped, and isolated, yet it is the site of the most sublime love David will ever know. David tries in vain to straighten and clean the room, then he escapes from it and returns to the arms of his neglected fiancée Hella. He turns his back on Giovanni largely because Giovanni represents to him a tormented soul, a chaotic and difficult force in contrast to the safety of a predictable, heterosexual, middle-class life. David's urge for safety and his refusal to accept his own desires are deep flaws. In the eyes of the European Giovanni, David is a stereotypical American type who cannot handle the dirt of a lover's room or the stink of a lover's body—who in short is unwilling to face any unpleasant reality. When David turns his back on him, Giovanni disintegrates, becomes the subject of a scandalous murder trial, and is executed in the old French way—by guillotine. David ends his story as he begins it, staring at his own reflection in a window-turned-mirror, looking out at the world only to see himself and to come to terms with his identity in a profoundly private and guilty way. His attempts to move on with his life are futile. As he tears up a letter in hopes of leaving the past behind, the wind blows the bits of paper back, and some of them stick to him.

Baldwin again attempts to create a deeply affecting psychological narrative about facing reality and about the responsibility of the individual to care for others in his most famous short story "Sonny's Blues" (1957), published the year after *Giovanni's Room*. These works of fiction are strikingly similar in theme, yet "Sonny's Blues" has nothing to do with homosexuality. At this point in his career, Baldwin was clearly reaching for an enduring humanistic message, and he chose the tremendous difficulties of love or, as David puts it, "to say Yes to life." In *Giovanni's Room* the impediments to love stem from David's attempts to seek safety, to avoid suffering, and to believe that love should be clean and tidy. The narrator of "Sonny's Blues" is similarly deluded, and his attempt to escape reality takes the form of ideology: he believes that leading an upright, middle-class existence will allow him to avoid suffering. Just as Giovanni causes David to see life from another point of view, the narrator's brother Sonny causes the narrator to revise his own safe viewpoint. But "Sonny's Blues" ends in transcendence rather than tragedy.

Just like David, the narrator of "Sonny's Blues" begins his story looking out a window that turns into a mirror. The stories of the downtrodden always bring Baldwin's characters back to themselves and invite them to consider what their roles are. The narrator was told about his proper role as Sonny's big brother early in life: his mother said to him before her death, "you got to let him know you's *there*." But the narrator believes the role of an older brother is to tell a younger brother what to do, not to listen to him. When Sonny declares he wants to be a jazz musician, the narrator scowls and suggests he find a more respectable, more reliable job.

When Sonny is jailed for heroin use, the situation confirms the narrator's suspicions, and he turns his back on his younger brother. Yet Sonny can teach his schoolteacher brother something: Sonny has suffered and has experienced the world that the narrator has tried to avoid. Sonny reenters his brother's life and teaches him about suffering, about the value of individuals of all types, and about how to listen. In the story's profound conclusion, the narrator hears Sonny for the first time, not through his words, which are often inadequate and halting, but through his music.

"Sonny's Blues" is the first contact most readers have with Baldwin's work, and it stands at the center of his career in many senses. Here is a brilliant illustration of Baldwin's theory of the "gimmick" elaborated in "Down at the Cross." Sonny's gimmicks are heroin and music; the narrator's gimmick is teaching. Baldwin's message is a difficult one for many readers to grasp: "it does not matter what the gimmick is." Sonny tells his brother: "*Everybody* tries not to [suffer]. You're just hung up on the *way* some people try—it's not *your* way!" The message could apply to David in *Giovanni's Room,* to Sister Margaret in *The Amen Corner,* or to John Grimes in *Go Tell It*. Yet Baldwin's message was about to have a different, more political and racially charged context on the eve of the turbulent 1960s. The American South was on fire. The civil rights movement had begun, and it needed guidance. Baldwin had to come home from Europe to step up as a spokesperson. In 1957, after the publication of "Sonny's Blues," Baldwin journeyed to the American South to witness firsthand how the promise of America was failing and to provide hope for its renewal.

BALDWIN AND THE SOUTH

Baldwin's first collection of essays had gained him some notoriety, and it is no accident that he subtitled the second collection *More Notes of a Native Son.* Yet the tone of the essays in *Nobody Knows My Name* is somewhat different from the tone of the earlier essays. Although they do not reach the burning crescendo of *The Fire Next Time,* they are somewhat angrier and less carefully crafted than Baldwin's first essays. The elaborate sentences modeled after Henry James, one of Baldwin's favorite authors, gave way to terser observations. In his ongoing quest to become an honest man and a good writer, he discovered a slightly different voice, which had much to do with his trip south. In the title essay Baldwin writes of a parallel between his earlier situation as an American expatriate and his current situation as a

> Northern Negro in the South [who] sees himself as he was before he was born, perhaps; or as the man he would have become, had he actually been born in this place. He sees the world, from an angle odd indeed, in which his fathers awaited his arrival, perhaps in the very house in which he narrowly avoided being born. He sees, in effect, his ancestors, who, in everything they do and are, proclaim his inescapable identity.

In this essay he makes explicit his revised observation of America: "I am very often tempted to believe that this illusion is all that is left of the great dream that was to have become America; whether this is so or not, this illusion certainly prevents us from making America what we say we want it to be."

Baldwin's purpose in "Sonny's Blues" was to expose the human failure to listen, and in his essays of the same period he compounds that message by revealing the failure to see. This message is specifically true with regard to American myths about African Americans. In "A Fly in Buttermilk" he writes that segregation in the South "has worked brilliantly" in that "it has allowed white people, with scarcely any pangs of conscience whatever, to *create,* in every generation, only the Negro they wished to see." Here again we see Baldwin attempting to

reveal reality and to do away with the mythology that would keep us safe and secure, but the essays on the South have an urgency to them. He described freedom in *Giovanni's Room* as "unbearable, once one has it," but freedom in "Nobody Knows My Name" is "the fire which burns away illusion." The difference has to do with the courage "to look reality in the face," especially if that reality is unpleasant or something one does not want to accept.

This concept can be applied to the last short story Baldwin ever published, "Going to Meet the Man" (1965), which gave the title to his only collection of stories. "Going to Meet the Man" is a vicious story filtered through the viewpoint of a racist white sheriff named Jesse, whose manhood ritual had been to witness the lynching and castration of a black man. Our ability to hate Jesse is tempered by our pity for him. As a child he had become friends with a black boy, but his parents separated them and forced him to witness the ritual lynching and castration. Jesse is sick and poisoned, and it is apparent that his racism has been instilled in him not only by his parents but by the whole segregated, racist society around him. He cannot have sex with his wife without imagining the lynching scene. Baldwin wanted to illustrate the connection between sexual violence and racism, and the story reads like a stomach-turning parable.

Baldwin's fictional rhetoric changed as a result of his political involvement in the South in the early 1960s. His 1964 play *Blues for Mister Charlie* coincided with the onset of the Black Arts movement. At the same time, it was another traditional blues piece rendered into writing, like "Sonny's Blues" and like the title of his poetry collection *Jimmy's Blues* (1983, 1985). In 1964 Baldwin demonstrated his knowledge of the blues as a kind of reality in an essay called "The Uses of the Blues." In his 1964 play his blues are played for "Mister Charlie"—a derogatory term for white American men. *Blues for Mister Charlie,* like "Going to Meet the Man," reads like a race parable. Based loosely on the infamous 1955 murder of Emmett Till, *Blues for Mister Charlie* illustrates with fiery intensity the connection Baldwin perceived between racial violence and sexual mythology. It also dramatizes the possibilities for violent or nonviolent reactions to racial injustice. Richard Henry, who is murdered at the outset of the play, gives a gun to his father Meridian in the first act of the play. And although Meridian does not fire it in the third act, he is carrying it under his Bible at the play's conclusion, as if to signal the potential danger to come.

The play, set in the fictional Plaguetown, does not seek solutions to racial violence as much as it reveals the depth and complexity of the problem. The main conflict appears to be personal animosity between Richard, who is young and black and who left the South to be educated in the North, and Lyle Britten, who is aging, white, and associated with the Old South. Lyle, like Jesse in "Going to Meet the Man," is a despicable racist, yet Baldwin makes clear that he has been shaped by his sexual anxiety and his personal history. The archetypal natures of these characters are reinforced through the presence of two choruses, Blacktown and Whitetown, that comment predictably on the trial of Lyle Britten. The focal characters of the play are Parnell James, the white editor of the local paper, and Juanita, a student who had been involved with Richard. These two characters, as the intermediaries between the two separated worlds, offer the hope for reconciliation. Both are thoughtful and wise, and both could teach the residents of Plaguetown something that might help their collective illness, yet the fact that they are not fully accepted by their peers reinforces the difficulty of the situation and makes it more likely that Meridian's gun will be fired after the play's conclusion.

BALDWIN THE CELEBRITY

The trajectory of Baldwin's writing clearly changed as a result of his involvement in the civil rights movement and his witnessing the racial violence of the 1950s and 1960s. Yet he did not stay in the American South or even in America for long. His two novels of the 1960s were written partially in Istanbul, and his tendency to travel out of the country is evident in both novels, which are bigger and more ambitious than his 1950s novels. *Another Country* (1962) and *Tell Me How Long the Train's Been Gone* (1968) are notable departures for Baldwin. They are sprawling novels that range over time and space in a way his earlier works do not. They are perhaps sloppier novels, decentered and fraught with confusion. They involve large casts of characters. Baldwin's readers had to make adjustments and to prepare to revise their opinions of the author if they were to follow these challenging books. Many were not willing to do so, and although *Another Country* was successful in terms of sales, its publication marked a turning point in Baldwin's reputation, especially as a novelist. The following year Baldwin appeared on the cover of *Time* magazine (May 17, 1963) the week the Birmingham riots reminded Americans that the struggle for racial equality was an actual battle, not just a philosophical one. The *Time* article pointedly downplays Baldwin's novels in favor of discussing his essays and his powers as a public speaker. The distinct critical trend was to appreciate Baldwin as either an essayist or a novelist, and in the years following the publication of *The Fire Next Time,* which was a nonfiction best-seller, his reputation as an essayist was clearly greater. This was a matter of great disappointment to Baldwin, not only because he worked long and hard on his novels but because he did not want his modes of writing to be seen as separate or separable.

Although its reviews were not universally laudatory, *Another Country* pleased many readers and critics in 1962, and it is one of Baldwin's greatest literary achievements in terms of its daring experimentation and its engagement with human despair, American identity, and the complexity of sexual and racial relationships. It begins with the final, desperate days of Rufus Scott, a despondent black New Yorker who has been damaged and marginalized by society. He has no outlet for the bitterness and poison that fills him, though he attempts to eradicate it through an abusive, misogynistic relationship with a southern white woman named Leona. When he realizes the futility of this attempt either to love or to hate, Rufus feels he has no alternative but to commit suicide by jumping off the George Washington Bridge. All of Baldwin's novels from this point on follow the pattern of beginning with tragedy and examining in great detail its aftermath. To recall Sonny's message in "Sonny's Blues," there is no way to avoid suffering. But much can be learned in Baldwin's novels from the way characters cope with suffering, or try to avoid it, or attempt to understand those who have suffered deeply, like Rufus.

What may have confused Baldwin's readers is the Dickensian sweep that frames his passionate honesty in his third novel. It is difficult to name with certainty the protagonist of *Another Country,* whereas his two earlier novels centered around single characters. Even the title is ambiguous, for the novel begins and ends in America with a relatively brief episode in France near the novel's center. Yet the title suggests the theme of the book, which is largely about the willingness to cross boundaries or to inhabit a place outside safe homes. Much like Baldwin's life, the novel crosses invisible borders between uptown and downtown Manhattan, between men and women, between black and white Americans, between North and South, and between Europe and America. If people are alive and aware of the need for one another, they are constantly entering another country.

David Leeming has demonstrated how all of the main characters of *Another Country* represent some facet of Baldwin's experience. The suicidal Rufus is familiar from Baldwin's despairing incident in the French prison. Rufus's sister Ida struggles desperately for self-understanding in a series of relationships with black and white men and concludes that none of them finally understands her because each is unwilling to see her for who she is. Like her author, she is ultimately angry and alienated as the spokesperson for black America to a sympathetic but naive white audience. Her lover and Rufus's good friend Vivaldo is a struggling writer who, unlike his friend Richard, wants to stay true to his art rather than produce a commercial success that will bring him fame and wealth. Richard's wife Cass has chosen a safe, comfortable life, yet she has become dissatisfied with her husband's treatment of her and with her thankless role in the shadow of his fame. She initiates a relationship with Eric, the southern expatriate actor who has discovered a seemingly Edenic relationship with a male European lover named Yves.

Characters in *Another Country* are largely confused by the meaning of their sexual encounters even as they hold onto them as a kind of salvation. As in *Giovanni's Room,* the sexual relationships in this novel provide a kind of refuge from the harsh realities of the world, but many of the relationships fail because the characters use sex to avoid suffering. Vivaldo, for instance, believes his relationship with Ida will help heal the racial strife that poisoned Rufus and will help alleviate his personal guilt over having neglected Rufus. Cass believes her relationship with Eric will deliver her from Richard. Yet Ida and Eric have no intentions of having permanent, monogamous relationships. They become, in different ways, messengers who deliver the knowledge of the meaning of love. Ida angrily tells Vivaldo the same thing Eric gently tells Cass: they are people who grow and learn, sometimes painfully. Eric and Vivaldo have a one-night affair, and Vivaldo realizes the central message of the novel as they are parting the next morning: "What can we really do for each other except—just love each other and be each other's witness?" Even this will not bring Rufus back, but it is the first step toward alleviating guilt over his tragic death.

The characters in *Another Country* drink too much, sleep with a variety of people, and are occasionally selfish and unlikable. The same could be said of other classic American novels like *The Sun Also Rises* and *The Great Gatsby*, and *Another Country* is Baldwin's attempt to enter the American canon, to demonstrate the range of his understanding of literary masterpieces as well as human nature. At the same time the novel has a supercharged feeling that reveals the intensity of the times. *Another Country* was born of the racial strife exploding in the American South, and Ida's message to both Cass and Vivaldo resonates with the same kind of prophecy that characterizes Baldwin's essays. She tells Cass: "life is a *bitch,* baby. It's the biggest hype going. You don't have any experience in paying your dues and it's going to be rough on you, baby, when the deal goes down." The novel is at once a product of its times and its bohemian Greenwich Village milieu and an attempt at an expansive literary vision that could encompass a nation.

Like *Another Country, Tell Me How Long the Train's Been Gone* explores nearly all of the themes associated with Baldwin's work: the conflicted role of the artist, the tense relationship between brothers, the church's oppression and possibilities for redemption, the difficulty of self-acceptance, and the inability of contemporary America to deal with its race problems. The novel is the story of Leo Proudhammer, a stage and film actor of great renown, who suffers a heart attack and who uses his convalescence to reflect upon his life. Like *Another Country, Tell Me* is a sprawling, restless narrative with a large cast of characters and no conventional center, or no contrived shape. It is simply Leo's story, and it is about nothing less than the struggle to survive.

Love is both the reward for this struggle and the cause of it. Leo observes, "Everyone wishes to be loved, but, in the event, nearly no one can bear it." Leo has reached this conclusion through personal experience: he struggles throughout his narrative to understand the consequences of love, whether from friends, male and female lovers, family, or the public. He is a victim in the sense that he occasionally loses control of his life and is forced to be what others want him to be. He is exhausted by everyone's demands, and his doctor warns him that if he does not take care of himself he will suffer another heart attack. Baldwin was clearly projecting a side of himself in the character of Leo. Americans in the 1960s demanded so much, vocally, and a public figure like Baldwin was constantly called upon to speak, to act, and to perform. It would be natural to want to retreat or to collapse.

After his collapse, Leo helps himself recuperate by telling his story, making himself vulnerable in a way actors typically do not. From the public's perspective, his story is the classic rags-to-riches theme, made more poignant because he grew up poor and black. In the novel's final pages, a white character holds him up as an example of how anyone of any race can succeed in America. Leo grows angry and silent, but he knows he must respond. He says:

> You can't imagine my life, and I won't discuss it. . . . Negroes of this country are treated as none of you would dream of treating a dog or a cat. . . . If you don't want to believe it, well, that's your problem. And I don't feel like talking about it anymore, and I won't.

Leo's desire to remain silent on issues of race is surprising, given the fact that he has just exposed his life in great detail, just as Baldwin revealed his life in autobiographical essays. But the point is that Leo (like Baldwin) tells his story on his own terms, in his own way. He is tired of role-playing for others and of being used as an example of this or that. If his audience cannot see or hear him for what he is, that is its problem.

Leo's story and the stories of those around him are not necessarily heroic or designed specifically to delight and instruct. Baldwin's aesthetic was to capture a kind of dense realism as a way of fulfilling his original goal of honesty. Leo is thus impossible to categorize. He has suffered racial discrimination at the hands of ignorant rural folks, police, and well-intentioned white liberals, yet it would be reductive to call him a victim. He sleeps with men and women, white and black yet would resist any label about his sexual or racial preferences. In short, he is an actor who is impossible to typecast, and he attempts to be comfortable with that status. Yet the sense is that he is occasionally lost, that he does not fit in anywhere. In the novel's final line he finds himself "standing in the wings again, waiting for my cue."

Something about this conclusion is a little unsettling, for it implies that Leo is still being controlled by others. His life has included a number of voices (or directors): his embittered father, his plaintive lover Barbara, the critical director Saul San-Marquand, his Christian older brother Caleb, and finally the militant activist Black Christopher. This swirl of voices and forces pulls Leo in many different directions, and the comparison can be drawn again to *Invisible Man,* a comparison Lynn Orilla Scott makes in her 2002 study of Baldwin's later fiction. But unlike the narrator of Ellison's novel, Leo Proudhammer finishes his story in the public eye without having had a long period of hibernation to determine his proper role. Despite his success, there is a strong indication that, in the absence of a clear direction, he may spiral downward.

DISILLUSIONED AND DISCOURAGED

The seething anger that characterizes the play and two novels Baldwin published in the 1960s can be seen in his essays of the same period, which like Baldwin's novels tended to be longer and more ambitious than his earlier efforts. The messages of these works are evident in his fictional works as well, but the subjects of his 1960s essays were much more topical. To be black during that decade invariably meant being asked to choose between two distinct forces: the radical, militant rhetoric famously associated with Malcolm X and the Black Muslims and the peaceful, nonviolent rhetoric famously associated with Martin Luther King Jr. The assassinations of both of these leaders left black America confused, discouraged, and more divided than ever. Baldwin had been friends with both Malcolm X and King, but he was not directly allied with either of their movements. As someone who resisted labels and who never stayed in America long, he found himself left behind or left out of the debates he had contributed to so frequently in the early 1960s.

Baldwin was also the victim of a vicious homophobic attack by the black militant Eldridge Cleaver in his 1968 memoir *Soul on Ice.* Cleaver's vitriolic voice spoke directly to the teeming masses of angry black youths who needed a dose of something strong in the wake of the assassinations. In his celebrated essay on Elijah Mohammed, "Down at the Cross," Baldwin had already distanced himself from the Black Muslims though not from Malcolm X. He agreed to write a screenplay about Malcolm's life, but the project was scrapped due to profound differences between what he felt to be the honest version he wrote and the tame version Columbia Pictures wanted. Although a version of the script Baldwin co-wrote served as the basis (along with *The Autobiography of Malcolm X*) for Spike Lee's 1992 film *Malcolm X,* few people associate Lee's movie with Baldwin's screenplay. Baldwin was disillusioned with Hollywood and discouraged by the deaths of Malcolm X, King, and other black leaders, such as Medgar Evers, all of whom he counted among his friends. He published his version of the Malcolm X screenplay as *One Day, When I Was Lost: A Scenario Based on Alex Haley's "The Autobiography of Malcolm X"* in 1973, yet his book-length essay *No Name in the Street* (1972) was a more comprehensive attempt to come to terms with the turbulence of race relations in contemporary America. In this ambitious and wide-ranging essay, Baldwin tried to demonstrate his anger in such a way that he might regain the readers who had turned their backs on him in favor of revolutionary voices like Cleaver's. Baldwin had evidently become a victim of the confusion of the times, and like Leo Proudhammer, his relentless pace, his self-destructive lifestyle, and the demands of his public were taking a toll on him.

No Name in the Street begins, like "Down at the Cross," with a consideration of Baldwin's autobiography. Yet Baldwin moves decidedly out of his personal history into a chronicle of the history of the times, focusing around certain figures like Malcolm X, King, and a friend of Baldwin's named Tony Maynard, who was in prison in Germany on a murder charge. The essay eventually discusses other notable black leaders and movements. The Black Panthers and Huey Newton become part of Baldwin's careful study, and Baldwin even tips his hat to Cleaver, who "very much impressed" him despite the fact that Baldwin "didn't like what [Cleaver] had to say about [Baldwin] at all" in *Soul on Ice*. This surprising generosity reveals how Baldwin had changed as a result of the tumultuous 1960s. In the wake of the assassinations and riots, he comes across in this essay as a wandering soul whose need to justify the rage of black Americans to white Americans had never been more pressing. The style of the book is less erudite than his early essays. The sentences are not as complex, and the raw material, though occasionally philosophical, has one foot firmly planted in the contemporary world. More than anything else, *No Name in the Street* signals Baldwin's need to counter the perception that he was an outsider.

No Name in the Street ends on a familiar note of prophecy: "I think black people have always felt this about America, and Americans, and have always seen, spinning above the thoughtless American head, the shape of the wrath to come." This wrath derives at least partially from one of the most pervasive injustices in contemporary America, the systematic police brutality and wrongful imprisonment that defined African American experience in the post–civil rights era. Baldwin's central figure in the essay is not Malcolm X or King, who take up a good percentage of its space, but Tony Maynard, Baldwin's one-time driver and bodyguard who swore upon his soul that he did not commit the murder of which he was accused. Baldwin makes Maynard's case his personal project and draws strong conclusions about the law that sound decidedly like Henry David Thoreau: "I do not claim that everyone in prison here is innocent, but I do claim that the law, as it operates, is guilty, and that the prisoners, therefore, are all unjustly imprisoned." Baldwin treated the idea fictionally in his next novel, *If Beale Street Could Talk* (1974). Like *No Name in the Street*, this novel is markedly different from Baldwin's earlier work in terms of its vernacular style. Tish Rivers, the novel's narrator, is a streetwise nineteen-year-old black girl, a character type virtually absent from Baldwin's previous novels. Echoing Baldwin's situation with Maynard, Tish and her family are motivated by the need to prove the innocence of her boyfriend Fonny, who has been wrongfully charged with rape. The situation is urgent, though, as she is carrying Fonny's baby.

If Beale Street Could Talk was yet another departure for Baldwin, a marked contrast to his first two novels about spiritual experience and the paralysis of a homosexual American in Paris and his next two novels, which were sprawling narratives about struggling artists and bohemians in a hostile and occasionally racist world. Baldwin's attention had turned to injustice on the street. The title refers to the street in Memphis where the blues were born, but the novel takes place in New York. It is yet another blues story, and its joy and pain are evident throughout. Tish and Fonny represent an ideal version of love as Baldwin has defined it. Their love is far from sappy, though; their relationship begins when they are children and Tish hits Fonny with a nail-spiked board. Although their love is not characterized by this violence, neither is it without pain. Their first sexual encounter is described from Tish's point of view, and her loss of virginity, though tender, is a sloppy and uncomfortable event. Yet they are good to one another, and they offer themselves to each other when necessary and leave each other alone when necessary. Fonny is an artist, a sculptor, and this vocation demands his time and attention. Yet he does not neglect Tish. Thus the fact that he is not there for her during her time of greatest need—her pregnancy—is an example of how society's unreasonable forces can weaken the sacred bond of human love. And that is the subject of this version of Baldwin's blues.

Tish must rely on her family to help her in her plight, and her family's unquestioning support helps balance the ills of social injustice. Fonny's family is less supportive, though. They have apparently been poisoned, like Rufus in *Another Country,* to such a degree that they cannot recover, and Fonny's father's bitterness leads to his suicide. The baby, whose wail dominates the novel's conclusion, is the ambiguous hope for the future. To be born in the wake of such strife is far from ideal, yet the baby's crying is like the blues: a certain relief and joy coexists with grief and despair.

NEGLECTED FINAL WORKS

It is curious that Baldwin, having tried to reconnect with the younger and perhaps more militant segments of his black readership in *No Name* and *Beale Street,* departed in his next book, an extended essay on American cinema called *The Devil Finds Work* (1976). On one hand, it is more evidence that he refused to be categorized and that he was never content with one literary mode or style. On the other hand, it helps explain why Baldwin's reputation has never been fixed, as he continued to baffle readers and critics throughout his career. The American cinema had long been part of Baldwin's perspective and was visible in his writings from *Go Tell It on the Mountain,* when John experiences both epiphany and overwhelming guilt in the movie theater, to *No Name in the Street,* which examines Baldwin's disillusionment with Hollywood in its attempted manipulation of the Malcolm X script. *The Devil Finds Work* is not merely film criticism, though; it is an outlet for Baldwin's reflections on contemporary America and on his place in it.

Baldwin accepted a couple of college teaching posts just before his final novel, *Just above My Head* (1979), was published. He was still a public figure, but he somehow found the time to write his longest novel despite his other projects and public appearances and despite his deteriorating health. The novel begins with tragedy, the premature death of the gospel singer Arthur Montana. Arthur's story is narrated by his brother Hall, and their relationship is reminiscent of earlier brothers in Baldwin's fiction: Sonny and the narrator of "Sonny's Blues" and Leo and Caleb in *Tell Me. Just above My Head* has a huge cast of characters and covers the range of Baldwin's travels from New York to Paris to the American South. Again the characters do not automatically "say yes to life" and are confused by their own sexual attractions in the face of society's taboos. Again Baldwin expresses the tremendous need for strong, functional families as supports for the individuals. Yet among all of these familiar Baldwin motifs is the central struggle of Hall, the narrator who is a witness to his brother's life. He says, as he introduces the final section of the book, "You have sensed my fatigue and my panic, certainly, if you have followed me until now, and you can guess how terrified I am to be approaching the end of my story." Fatigue, panic, and terror are all related to Baldwin's ever-changing sense of his own role as a writer and storyteller. They are the price of the honesty he sought when he became a writer. They are the emotions of Sonny when he faces his blues solo. Yet they precede an enormous relief; Hall achieves clarity and understanding through his narrative. It is the same emotion readers experience at the end of all of Baldwin's novels. The struggle to confront despair and to understand tragedy cannot erase them, but it can make life more bearable.

In his final years Baldwin published his collected poems in a slim volume called *Jimmy's Blues* that was initially rejected by his American publisher and was published first in England in 1983. The volume did not receive much attention; no one seemed prepared to think of Baldwin as a poet at this point in his career. The poems in the collection were written at various points throughout his life. They are distilled versions of the blues theme he tried to communicate all along, and the themes of blindness, invisibility, the burden of the witness, and the difficulties of loving are once again evident. The long opening poem, "Staggerlee Wonders," is a striking example of Baldwinian prophecy rendered into simple verse, and though it has been largely neglected along with Baldwin's other poetry, it would be a useful entry point for a study of Baldwin's work.

Baldwin's last work, *The Evidence of Things Not Seen* (1985), was similarly neglected and is similarly important. It can be seen as Baldwin revisiting the South that was the basis for his most famous essay, "Down at the Cross." During this trip south, Baldwin investigated a series of child murders that began in Atlanta in 1979. He ended up writing about the murders as evidence of something more widespread in America: the racism, lack of faith, and lack of vision that plagues the nation and prevents its vaunted dream. The book reflects what Baldwin had been doing his entire life: it exposes the truth beneath the surface of American society. The Atlanta murders provided a final opportunity to meditate on his nation, to expose its shortcomings and predict its future. His final book is as layered and as penetrating as any essay he had published. Unfortunately, fewer of his compatriots were listening now. Two decades earlier he was an apt spokesman, but at the end of his career he was largely unnoticed, echoing the title of his last book.

Baldwin died in southern France in 1987 from esophagus cancer. His death was marked by a tremendous celebration of his life at the Cathedral of St. John the Divine in New York, and celebrations thereafter have focused on his literary achievements and his wisdom. A tribute book, *James Baldwin: The Legacy*, edited by Quincy Troupe with contributions by some of the most famous writers and critics of the time, was published in 1989. Baldwin's name and his words were frequently invoked after the Rodney King riots and debates over black English in California in the 1990s. Toni Morrison edited two volumes of Baldwin's writings for the esteemed Library of America series. Amid a resurgence of Baldwin studies, five books of criticism on his writings were published between 1999 and 2002. Although healthy debate over what Baldwin should be remembered for continues, no one doubts that he will be remembered as one of the most important American writers of the late twentieth century. Certainly no one doubts that he achieved the goal he set for himself at the beginning of his career: to be an honest man and a good writer.

Selected Bibliography

WORKS OF JAMES BALDWIN

NOVELS AND SHORT STORIES

Go Tell It on the Mountain. New York: Knopf, 1953.

Giovanni's Room: A Novel. New York: Dial, 1956.

Another Country. New York: Dial, 1962.

Going to Meet the Man. New York: Dial, 1965.

Tell Me How Long the Train's Been Gone: A Novel. New York: Dial, 1968.

If Beale Street Could Talk. New York: Dial, 1974.

Just above My Head. New York: Dial, 1979.

James Baldwin: Early Novels and Stories. Edited by Toni Morrison. New York: Library of America, 1998.

ESSAY COLLECTIONS

Notes of a Native Son. Boston: Beacon, 1955.

Nobody Knows My Name: More Notes of a Native Son. New York: Dial, 1961.

The Fire Next Time. New York: Dial, 1963.

No Name in the Street. New York: Dial, 1972.

The Devil Finds Work: An Essay. New York: Dial, 1976.

The Evidence of Things Not Seen. New York: Holt, Rinehart and Winston, 1985.

The Price of the Ticket: Collected Nonfiction, 1948– 1985. New York: St. Martin's, 1985.

James Baldwin: Collected Essays. Edited by Toni Morrison. New York: Library of America, 1998.

PLAYS AND POETRY

The Amen Corner: A Play. New York: Dial, 1968. (First produced in 1955.)

Blues for Mister Charlie: A Play. New York: Dial, 1964.

Jimmy's Blues: Selected Poems. London: Michael Joseph, 1983; New York: St. Martin's, 1985.

Gypsy and Other Poems. Northampton, Mass.: Gehenna Press, 1989. (A limited edition of 325 copies; never reprinted.)

OTHER WORKS

Nothing Personal. Photographs by Richard Avedon. New York: Atheneum, 1964.

A Rap on Race. With Margaret Mead. Philadelphia: Lippincott, 1971.

One Day, When I Was Lost: A Scenario Based on Alex Haley's "The Autobiography of Malcolm X." New York: Dial, 1973.

A Dialogue. With Nikki Giovanni. Philadelphia: Lippincott, 1973.

Little Man, Little Man: A Story of Childhood. Illustrated by Yoran Cazac. New York: Dial, 1976.

BIBLIOGRAPHY

Standley, Fred L., and Nancy V. Standley. *James Baldwin: A Reference Guide.* Boston: G. K. Hall, 1980.

CRITICAL AND BIOGRAPHICAL STUDIES

Balfour, Lawrie. *The Evidence of Things Not Said: James Baldwin and the Promise of American Democracy.* Ithaca, N.Y.: Cornell University Press, 2001.

Bobia, Rosa. *The Critical Reception of James Baldwin in France.* New York: Peter Lang, 1997.

Bloom, Harold, ed. *James Baldwin.* New York: Chelsea House, 1986.

Campbell, James. *Talking at the Gates: A Life of James Baldwin.* New York: Viking, 1991.

Chametzky, Jules, ed. *A Tribute to James Baldwin: Black Writers Redefine the Struggle.* Amherst, Mass.: Institute for Advanced Study in the Humanities, 1989.

Eckman, Fern Marja. *The Furious Passage of James Baldwin.* New York: M. Evans, 1966.

Harris, Trudier. *Black Women in the Fiction of James Baldwin.* Knoxville: University of Tennessee Press, 1985.

Harris, Trudier, ed. *New Essays on* Go Tell It on the Mountain. New York: Cambridge University Press, 1996.

Kinnamon, Keneth, comp. *James Baldwin: A Collection of Critical Essays.* Englewood Cliffs, N.J.: Prentice-Hall, 1974.

Leeming, David. *James Baldwin: A Biography.* New York: Knopf, 1994.

McBride, Dwight A., ed. *James Baldwin Now.* New York: New York University Press, 1999.

Miller, D. Quentin, ed. *Re-Viewing James Baldwin: Things Not Seen.* Philadelphia: Temple University Press, 2000.

Nelson, Emmanuel S. "Critical Deviance: Homophobia and the Reception of James Baldin's Fiction." *Journal of American Culture* 14, no. 3:91–96 (1991).

Porter, Horace A. *Stealing the Fire: The Art and Protest of James Baldwin.* Middletown, Conn.: Wesleyan University Press, 1989.

Pratt, Louis H. *James Baldwin.* Boston: Twayne, 1978.

Scott, Lynn Orilla. *James Baldwin's Later Fiction: Witness to the Journey.* East Lansing: Michigan State University Press, 2002.

Shin, Andrew, and Barbara Johnson. "Beneath the Black Aesthetic: James Baldwin's Primer of Black American Masculinity." *African American Review* 32, no. 2:247–261 (1998).

Standley, Fred L., and Nancy V. Burt, eds. *Critical Essays on James Baldwin.* Boston: G. K. Hall, 1988.

Sylvander, Carolyn Wedin. *James Baldwin.* New York: Frederick Ungar, 1980.

Thorsen, Karen, and Douglas K. Dempsey. *James Baldwin—The Price of the Ticket.* Produced and written by Karen Thorsen and Douglas K. Dempsey, directed by Karen Thorsen. Maysles Films and WNET, New York, 1990. (Film based on the life of James Baldwin.)

Troupe, Quincy, ed. *James Baldwin: The Legacy.* New York: Simon & Schuster, 1989.

Weatherby, W. J. *James Baldwin: Artist on Fire.* New York: Dell, 1989.

INTERVIEWS

Standley, Fred L., and Louis H. Pratt, cds. *Conversations with James Baldwin.* Jackson: University Press of Mississippi, 1989.

—D. QUENTIN MILLER

Saul Bellow

1915–

*I*N 1976, WHEN Saul Bellow became the seventh American writer to win a Nobel Prize in literature, his career was already hailed by commentators for its remarkable longevity. By this time, Bellow had published important novels in four successive decades and had been regarded as one of America's most important authors for more than twenty years. In addition to the Nobel Prize, he had earned a Pulitzer Prize, an International Literary Prize, and an unprecedented three National Book Awards. What no one could have guessed in 1976, however, was that the sixty-one-year-old Bellow was only a little more than halfway through with his writing career. Twenty-four years later, in 2000, the eighty-five-year-old Bellow published the novel *Ravelstein* to widespread critical acclaim. He accomplished something few American writers ever have: the publication of a major work of literature in each of seven successive decades. From his first novel, *Dangling Man* (1944), through *Ravelstein,* Saul Bellow has accumulated a body of work that places him in the first rank of American novelists alongside his fellow Nobel Laureates William Faulkner, Ernest Hemingway, and John Steinbeck.

Though his career as a writer has been both long and distinguished, Bellow's literary output has been fairly modest: ten novels, four novellas, two collections of short stories, a Broadway play, a travel memoir, and the usual assortment of essays, reviews, interviews, and occasional writings one would expect after more than half a century in the public eye. Conspicuously absent in Bellow's fiction is any single book that scholars consider either his best or his most representative work. By general critical consensus, his most important novels are *The Adventures of Augie March* (1953), *Henderson, the Rain King* (1959), *Herzog* (1964), and *Humboldt's Gift* (1975), with both *Mr. Sammler's Planet* (1970) and the novella *Seize the Day* (1956) following closely behind. But even these six works taken together do not represent the full range of their author's concerns. In his nearly sixty years as a writer, Bellow has grown, developed, evolved, forgotten things, and on a number of occasions, changed his mind. The rebellious young Trotskyite who wrote *Dangling Man* in 1944 saw the world differently from the aging conservative cultural warrior who wrote the preface to Allan Bloom's *The Closing of the American Mind* in 1987. It is possible, though, to trace through Bellow's fiction the development of a certain combination of strong character development, loose plot development, digressive narrative structure, stylistic flair, metaphysical humor, and guarded optimism found so often in Bellow's mature fiction that critics describe it with the single eponymous adjective "Bellovian."

"A YOUNG WRITER FROM CHICAGO"

Solomon Bellow was born on June 10, 1915, in Lachine, Quebec, to Abram and Lescha Bellow, whose name had been changed from its original "Belo" only two years earlier, when they emigrated from Russia to avoid the persecution of Jews. Bellow lived in this quiet Canadian community with his parents, two older brothers, and one older sister until his father's business failures forced the family to move to Chicago in July 1924. The Chicago of the early twentieth century—Carl Sandburg's "City of Big Shoulders," with its stockyards, factories, business districts, immigrant neighborhoods, and relentless American optimism—left an indelible impression on Bellow and his fiction. He painted a vivid portrait of the city and its people in his third novel, *The Adventures of Augie March,* and eventually set about half of his works wholly or partially in the neighborhoods he knew in his youth. "In Chicago, things were done for the first time, which the rest of the world later learned and imitated," Bellow remarked in an interview with Joyce Illig. "Capitalist production was pioneered in the stockyards, in refrigerator cars, in the creation of the Pullman, in the creation of farm machinery, and with it also certain urban and political phenomena which are associated with the new condition of modern democracy."

Upon graduating from high school in 1933, Bellow enrolled at the University of Chicago, but after two years he transferred to Northwestern University, where he studied anthropology and received his degree in 1937. His first inclination was to pursue graduate studies in anthropology, but after one semester at the University of Wisconsin, where, he later admitted, he spent much more time reading novels than studying assigned texts, he dropped out and announced to his family that he intended to become a writer. In 1938 he married Anita Goshkin, and he subsequently worked for the Works Progress Administration (WPA) Writers' Project, a New Deal program that gave aspiring writers a salary to work on various government-defined writing projects. He initially had little luck submitting fiction to national magazines, but in 1941 his short story "Two Morning Monologues" was accepted by the small but highly influential literary magazine the *Partisan Review,* which described him only as "a young writer from Chicago." The next year he published a second story in the same magazine and began working on the manuscript that eventu-

ally became his first novel, *Dangling Man,* which was published shortly before the birth of his first child, Gregory Bellow, in 1944.

Dangling Man is a short, well-constructed, semi-autobiographical book modeled consciously on Rainer Marie Rilke's *Journal of My Other Self* but that also resonates with clear echoes of Franz Kafka, Albert Camus, and Fyodor Dostoyevsky. The novel presents, in journal form, the meditations of its protagonist, Joseph (no last name is ever given, but the name strongly suggests "Joseph K.," the protagonist of Kafka's novel *The Trial*), who has been drafted into the army but is prevented from actually serving because of issues arising from his Canadian citizenship. As the novel opens, Joseph has been "dangling" for seven months, supported by his wife and unable to get a permanent job because of his draft status. Joseph's journals alternate between interior meditations on his condition and self-justifying descriptions of his descent into a Hobbesian state of nature. As the novel progresses, he becomes increasingly abusive to his family, violent toward his friends, and suspicious of everybody. Like the antiheroes of European existential literature upon which he is based, Joseph cannot function as a free human being in the absence of institutional structures. Freed from these structures, he searches desperately, but unsuccessfully, for an intellectual framework capable of giving meaning to his existence. In the process, he loses the ability to interact with his fellow human beings—all of whom exist within the institutional structures he has abandoned or, more precisely, have abandoned him. When he is finally eligible to join the army, he willingly surrenders freedom for structure. "I am no longer to be held accountable for myself; I am grateful for that," Joseph writes in his final journal entry. "I am in other hands, relieved of self-determination, freedom cancelled."

Though *Dangling Man* was well received and well reviewed by New York book critics, it sold fewer than two thousand copies in hardcover and disappeared quickly from the bookshelves. In many ways, it is Bellow's least characteristic work, lacking the distinctive style and aggressive character development for which he became famous. In later interviews, he referred to it as an apprenticeship novel in which he consciously imitated themes and forms from the great writers whose ranks he hoped to join. His second novel, *The Victim* (1947), was more original in its theme, but it was no more innovative in its writing style. "I was restrained, controlled, demonstrating that I could write 'good,'" Bellow later remarked in an interview with Maggie Simmons. "I didn't understand that if you came from the streets of Chicago, to write 'good' was to write in a foreign language. So *Dangling Man* was my M.A. and *The Victim* my Ph.D."

Published in 1947, *The Victim* tells the story of two men, Asa Leventhal, a Jewish copywriter for a New York trade journal, and Kirby Allbee, a former magazine writer who blames Leventhal for his personal and financial ruin. Years before the novel opens, Leventhal had unknowingly caused Allbee to lose his job and begin a long spiral into depression and alcoholism that ended with the death of his wife. Allbee accuses Leventhal of deliberately sabotaging his career to punish him for his anti-Semitism. Though he initially rejects Allbee's claims, Leventhal is haunted by guilt and doubt and allows himself to become drawn into Allbee's life. Allbee moves into Leventhal's apartment and takes increasingly bolder liberties with his privacy and property, culminating in an attempt to kill both himself and Leventhal by releasing gas into the apartment from Leventhal's oven.

Perhaps the most important thing about *The Victim* in the context of Bellow's overall work is that it is his first attempt to grapple with his own experiences and perspectives as a Jewish writer. Joseph in *Dangling Man* had come from a Jewish home, but the narrative mentions this fact only in passing. Leventhal, however, cannot escape his Jewish identity. His colleagues, his friends, and his family constantly remind him of it, and when Allbee finally accuses him of having conspired, as a Jew, to ruin his life, he is only extending the conspiratorial, anti-Semitic logic of other characters in the novel. Some engagement with these issues was probably inevitable, given the fact that Bellow wrote *The Victim* at precisely the time that Americans were becoming familiar with the events of the Holocaust. Critics later saw in *The Victim* a more nuanced portrayal of a Jewish identity in America than can be found in any other novel of the first half of the twentieth century. Bellow does not gloss over Leventhal's Jewishness, but neither does he make it a defining characteristic or turn him into a caricature. Bellow resists the temptation to make *The Victim* a struggle of archetypes—"Jew" versus "anti-Semite"—and instead makes it a struggle between two fully realized and developed characters in which issues of Jewishness and anti-Semitism are important but ultimately less important than the overall human issues their relationship raises.

From *The Victim* on, the position of the Jewish intellectual in contemporary American society has pervaded Bellow's fiction. As one of the first major American writers not to come from the Protestant majority, Bellow has often been seen as a voice for Jewish America—a label he himself has always rejected while, at the same time, never minimizing the importance of his heritage. "I think of myself as a person of Jewish origin—American and Jewish—who has had a certain experience of life, which is in part Jewish," he told Chirantan Kulshrestha in an interview. "Proportions are not for me to decide. I don't know what they are: how much is Jewish, how much is Russian, how much is male, how much is twentieth century, how much is midwestern." Nevertheless, Bellow's enormous critical and popular success definitely paved the way for a new generation of Jewish writers— including such important twentieth-century literary figures as Bernard Malamud, Philip Roth (who considered Bellow a mentor and used him as the model for the fictional Felix Abravanel in *The Ghost Writer*), and Isaac Bashevis Singer (whose work was first brought to national attention when Bellow translated his Yiddish story "Gimpel the Fool" into English for the *Partisan Review*).

"A SORT OF COLUMBUS"

Between 1946 and 1953, Bellow secured a string of temporary teaching appointments at the University of Minnesota, New York University, Princeton University, and Bard College as well as a Guggenheim Fellowship that allowed him to spend a full year writing in Paris. During most of this time, however, his chief occupation was the manuscript of a new book, *The Adventures of Augie March*. Bellow understood that, to be genuinely successful as a writer, he would have to radically alter the course his fiction had taken in his first two novels. Both *Dangling Man* and *The Victim* were well-crafted, intelligent novels, but they did little to distinguish their author from the crowd of New York intellectuals writing literary fiction in the 1940s. Bellow knew that, to make his mark as a great writer, he had to find a completely unique narrative voice—one that incorporated his Jewish heritage, his midwestern upbringing, his love of classical literature, and his status as an immigrant to America— into a kind of fiction that did more than imitate the masters or fit in with contemporary tastes. That he had found such a voice was evident from the first lines of *The Adventures of Augie March:*

> I am an American, Chicago born—Chicago, that somber city—and go at things as I have taught myself, free-style, and will make the record in my own way: first to knock, first admitted; sometimes an innocent knock, sometimes a not so innocent. But a man's character is his fate, says Heraclitus,

and in the end there isn't any way to disguise the nature of the knocks by acoustical work on the door or gloving the knuckles.

Like Bellow's earlier novels, *The Adventures of Augie March* has its precursors. In its picaresque hero can be found traces of Tom Jones, David Copperfield, Huckleberry Finn, and even Stephen Dedalus. But the book is nonetheless breathtakingly original. Told in an exuberant first-person narrative, *The Adventures of Augie March* chronicles the life of its hero from his childhood and youth in the same Chicago neighborhoods Bellow knew as a boy, through a series of comic adventures in Mexico, to his service on a battleship in World War II, and on to his postwar life as an American businessman living in Paris. Throughout his adventures, Augie wears many hats. Among other things, he is a professional textbook thief, an accomplice to armed robbery, a personal caretaker to a powerful Chicago businessman, the manager of a prize fighter, a smuggler of immigrants, an eagle trainer, a soldier, a lover, and a vernacular philosopher extraordinaire. Yet Augie's strongest impulse in the novel is to resist both commitment and classification. Always the optimist, he keeps his options open, and though he does many things, he cannot truly be said to be anything at all. Augie is best at avoiding other people's plans for him and refusing to fit into categories not of his own making. As soon as his commitment to any course of life threatens to become an identifying label, Augie somehow finds a way to move on.

What impressed critics most about *The Adventures of Augie March* was not its plot— which is incomplete, far-fetched, and often rambling—but its narrative voice, which combines Augie's street-smart Chicago vernacular with an identifiably Yiddish idiom and a wealth of classical and biblical allusions that add a sense of mythic importance to the hero's day-to-day life. Above all, though, *The Adventures of Augie March* is a comic novel in which Bellow replaces the gloomy existentialism of *Dangling Man* with a more optimistic response to the same basic problems. While any effort to find meaning and transcendence in the modern world may be doomed to failure, the author of *Augie March* suggests, the journey itself can be spiritually satisfying or, at the very least, fun.

In his closing summation of his own life, Augie acknowledges the groundbreaking nature of his own story.

> Why I am a sort of Columbus of those near-at-hand, and believe you can come to them in this immediate *terra incognita* that spreads out in every gaze. I may well be a flop at this kind of endeavor. Columbus too thought he was a flop, probably, when they sent him back in chains. Which didn't prove that there was no America.

These references to Columbus are particularly apt, as they point to both the pioneering nature of Augie's narrative and to the fact that it is, ultimately, a uniquely American story. Bellow later acknowledged that he was overwhelmed by the sense of discovery he felt when writing his third novel. "When I began to write *Augie March*," he told interviewer Gordon Lloyd Harper, "I took off many . . . restraints. I think I took off too many, and went too far, but I was feeling the excitement of discovery. I had just increased my freedom, and like any emancipated plebeian I abused it at once."

The "abuses" Bellow refers to were largely matters of length and focus. *The Adventures of Augie March* is Bellow's longest single work. It moves through dozens of characters and scores of scenes as it chronicles its hero's life from early childhood through middle age. Perhaps in response his own misgivings, Bellow's next major work, a novella entitled *Seize the Day,* was a model of restraint, representing only about four hours in the life of its protagonist, a middle-aged schlemiel named Tommy Wilhelm. As the novel opens, Tommy has recently walked out on his wife and his children and has quit his high-paying sales job. Down to his last $700, he makes an appeal for assistance to his father, a wealthy retired doctor, who flatly denies him. In the absence of a caring father, Tommy has transferred his affections to an obvious con man, Dr. Tamkin, a self-professed psychologist and financial guru who promises to turn Tommy's last few dollars into a fortune by speculating in the commodities market. Dr. Tamkin is a famous example of the class of characters that Bellow refers to, in an interview with Sanford Pinsker, as "Reality Instructors"—people who "think they know the score. You don't. They're going to teach you." Tamkin, like all reality instructors, always has easy solutions to complex problems and preaches a gospel made up of tricks, maneuvers, and shortcuts. In presenting himself as both a psychologist and a "scientific" speculator, Tamkin pretends to have two things completely figured out: human nature and the Chicago commodities exchange. Tommy accepts his authority in these areas precisely because his opinions are so simple. Unfortunately, as Tommy must eventually learn, neither human beings nor pork bellies respond well to simplistic formulations.

As the novel builds to its conclusion, all of Tommy's relationships with other people deteriorate. Tamkin loses his $700 and disappears, his father refuses a direct plea for emotional support, and his wife (who is modeled on Bellow's first wife, Anita, whom Bellow was in the process of divorcing when *Seize the Day* was written) calls to harangue him about a postdated child-support check. Emotionally battered and unable to turn to anyone for help, Tommy wanders around in a daze until he comes to a funeral parlor during a service and begins to cry uncontrollably. Here the novel comes to its famous climax:

> The flowers and lights fused ecstatically in Wilhelm's blind, wet eyes; the heavy sea-like music came up to his ears. It poured into him where he had hidden himself in the center of a

crowd by the great and happy oblivion of tears. He heard it and sank deeper than sorrow, through torn sobs and cries toward the consummation of his heart's ultimate need.

Perhaps no single passage in Bellow's fiction has been the subject of more analysis than this final scene in *Seize the Day,* and understanding it is crucial to understanding much of Bellow's later fiction. Many critics have read it as Bellow's great affirmation of the power of love, which literally baptizes the protagonist into a superior existence. Others see it has a moment of bitter irony in which Tommy once again falls for a simple-sounding cliché and confuses crying over an unknown dead man with having a relationship. Still others see it as a deus ex machina ending in which Bellow himself becomes a Tamkinesque reality instructor by offering a simplistic solution ("all you need is love") to the complicated relationship problems he raises in the novel. But all agree that similar scenes recur with great frequency in Bellow's fiction and that, whether or not Tommy is actually redeemed by his tears, Bellow believes meaningful human connections hold at least the abstract possibility of redemption.

In 1956 Bellow, who had recently divorced his first wife, married Sondra Tschacbasov, a twenty-three-year-old Bennington College graduate whom he had met in New York three years earlier. A year later, his second son, Adam Abraham Bellow, was born in Tivoli, New York, where the couple had purchased a dilapidated farmhouse. Bellow's second marriage, however, lasted only three years, during which time he juggled temporary teaching appointments at the University of Minnesota, Northwestern University, and the New School for Social Research in New York while working on an unlikely manuscript about a New England pig farmer who puts his life on hold to take a trip to the wilds of Africa. When *Henderson, the Rain King* first appeared in 1959, reviewers did not know what to make of it. It was unlike any book Bellow or anyone else had ever written. Its plot was farfetched, its characters were cartoonish, and its portrayal of Africa was, at best, inaccurate. Reviews at the time were largely negative, but history has reversed that judgment. The more scholars have studied *Henderson, the Rain King,* the more its literary reputation has grown, and it is considered one of Bellow's major works. The influential Modern Library poll of the "100 Best Novels of the Twentieth Century" included *Henderson, the Rain King* at number twenty-one. The only other Bellow novel to make the list, *The Adventures of Augie March,* came in sixty places later at number eighty-one.

Though often grouped with *The Adventures of Augie March* as a "comic novel," the predominant mode in *Henderson, the Rain King* is satirical, and like any good satire, it aims at a variety of targets. One of its targets is the reigning American novelist of the day, Ernest Hemingway, who shared his tough-guy attitude, his enormous physical prowess, his fondness for guns, his penchant for African safaris, and his initials with Bellow's hero, Eugene Henderson. But Hemingway was a minor, if highly visible, object of attack. *Henderson, the Rain King* satirizes human nature, literary pretension, and more specifically, the large body of romantic quest literature that presents the external journey as a metaphor for inner discovery. In creating Eugene Henderson, Bellow freely adapted character traits from the classic texts in the satiric tradition: *Gargantua and Pantegruel, Rasselas, Gulliver's Travels,* and perhaps most of all, *Don Quixote.*

A millionaire by inheritance, Henderson has never had to work and, as a consequence, has accomplished little in his life. The first four chapters of the novel portray his general malaise and his alienation from his family. He is plagued with an inner voice that keeps repeating "I want, I want" without identifying any object of desire. He does not know what he wants, only that he does not have it. Spurred on by this unnamed desire and horrified at his abusive and irrational treatment of his friends and family, Henderson travels to Africa, first in the company of friends and then with only an English-speaking guide, Romilayu, to take him deep into what he hopes will be the Conradian "Heart of Darkness." The remainder of the narrative is split between the two decidedly un-Conradian tribes Henderson encounters, the Arnewi and the Warari—both of whom are led by English-speaking chieftains with European educations.

Henderson stays only briefly with the peaceful Arnewi, who treat him so generously he decides to help them with their biggest problem. Their water supply is infested with frogs they cannot kill because of their pacifist beliefs. However, his efforts turn into a disaster when, to kill the frogs, he also destroys the water supply. Disgraced, Henderson leaves the Arnewi village and spends most of the remaining two-thirds of the book with the more aggressive Warari and their remarkable chief, King Dahfu. Dahfu is Bellow's perfect synthesis of thought and action. He is both educated and intelligent, but he does not allow education and intelligence to paralyze him. He is, in Henderson's words, a "Be-er," whereas Henderson himself is a perpetual "Becomer." When Henderson moves a heavy statue during a tribal ritual, he becomes the tribe's "Rain King," and Dahfu becomes his friend and philosophical mentor. When the king is killed trying to capture his father's spirit (which, the tribe believed, resided in the spirit of a lion), Henderson learns that being a "Rain King" makes him the successor to the throne. He also discovers that the simple, idyllic African tribe he came so far to find has as much Machiavellian intrigue as any European court or American city hall. Afraid for his life, Henderson leaves the village and sets out for home, carrying with him the lion cub that was thought to host Dahfu's spirit.

On the plane back to the United States, Henderson seems a changed man. Bellow even contrives to have Handel's *Messiah* playing in the background as he tells a stewardess how much he loves his wife and children and cannot wait to return to them. The change in Henderson is overly sentimental, and nothing in the novel seems to justify it. But this is part of the satire. Henderson has undertaken a highly symbolic journey to a distant location, studied "being" under a charismatic master, and stared death in the face. "How could he not come back a changed man?" Bellow seems to be saying in the background, tongue firmly in cheek, "he has followed all the rules." Like many great satires, however, *Henderson, the Rain King* manages to transcend its original function as a parody. Henderson's "quest" is absurd, to be sure, and its absurdity is a direct stab at the entire genre of the "quest hero." But Henderson, like Don Quixote and Gulliver before him, becomes a fully realized character whose absurd quest for some kind of significance cannot be dismissed as a joke. His quest, with all of its attendant absurdity, really does come to represent everybody's absurd but absolutely necessary quest for higher meaning. Perhaps this is why, despite the fact that Henderson seems less like his author than almost any other character in the Bellow canon, Bellow himself, when asked by an interviewer, Nina Steers, which of his characters he most resembled, replied without qualification, "Henderson—the absurd seeker of high qualities."

AMERICA'S GREATEST LIVING NOVELIST

In the early 1960s critics regularly referred to Saul Bellow as the best novelist of his generation and the heir apparent to Hemingway and Faulkner. Writing had made him famous, but it had not made him rich. Already in his late forties at the time, Bellow had never made a living wage from his fiction and had to support himself with temporary writer-in-residence positions at universities. In 1960 Bellow went to the University of Puerto Rico for his last temporary appointment. A year later, he returned to the United States and married Susan Glassman. In the fall of 1962 he accepted a permanent position as a member of the Committee on Social Thought at the University of Chicago. This new job had the double effect of providing him with a steady income while he wrote and bringing him back to the city that had always been at the center of his fiction.

Back in Chicago, Bellow celebrated the birth of his third son, Daniel Oscar Bellow, in March 1964. That same year, he saw two projects he had been working on for years come to fruition: a play about psychoanalysis and a novel based partly on his divorce from Sondra. The play, which was originally called *Bummidge* and later was changed to *The Last Analysis,* was Bellow's first real foray into drama (A one-act play, "The Wrecker," had been included in the volume *Seize the Day,* but it had never been performed). The action of *The Last Analysis* centers around an aging television comic, Philip Bummidge, who invents a method of self-psychoanalysis that he believes will bring the benefits of Freud to the masses. Throughout the play, Bummidge has his friends and family members help him act out various childhood sexual traumas, which are broadcast on closed-circuit TV to a gathering of distinguished psychologists. The play competently satirizes the excesses of psychoanalysis: its preoccupation with sex, its tendency to explore every corner of one's past, and even its vogue among the wealthy. But the play also suffered, as Bellow conceded in the preface to the published version, from a "cluttered and inconsequent plot which puzzled the audience (and even the playwright)." In late 1964 *The Last Analysis* ran briefly on Broadway with Sam Levine in the roll of Bummidge, but it was both a commercial and a critical failure.

Bellow's big Broadway flop, however, came right on the heels of the greatest commercial success of his career, the novel *Herzog.* One of Bellow's most difficult books, *Herzog* did not seem to have the makings of a popular bestseller. The story of a literature professor, Moses Herzog, negotiating his way through a complex personal life is one of Bellow's most confessional books. The story's main conflict—Herzog's discovery that his ex-wife had been having an affair with his best friend while the two were still married—exactly parallels Bellow's own discovery that his wife Sondra had been having an affair with one of his good friends in the years before their divorce. But *Herzog* is not a story about an affair, which happens offstage and well before the action in the novel begins. The novel, in fact, is not really "about" any external event; it is a compelling portrait of a man trying to understand the chaos in his life and find the words to explain it. Herzog, the first of Bellow's heroes to be a professionally trained academic, is the author of a well-regarded intellectual history and an expert in the great ideas of Western civilization. Herzog's tragedy, though, is that his lifelong engagement with great ideas has not made him a great man.

Like Joseph, Augie March, and Eugene Henderson, Herzog is searching for the answer to the question, "How should I live?" Presumably, his liberal education should give him an advantage, since he has read so many other answers to the same question. But Herzog's education turns out to be his greatest stumbling block. He has become, as another character tells him, "sick with abstractions." Even erotic attachment, as represented in the novel by Herzog's sexually sophisticated girlfriend Ramona, becomes another abstract ideology that competes with literature, philosophy, history, and politics for his intellectual allegiance. "What this country needs," Herzog tells himself, unable to make connections among all of the knowledge he has, "is a good five-cent synthesis." Herzog's desire to cope with conflicting ideologies drives him to write a series of letters to politicians, philosophers, writers, professors, world leaders, and finally, God.

Herzog never finds any concrete answers. At the end of the novel, he is exactly as confused, as alienated, and as burdened by his ideas as he is at the beginning. What is crucial, though, and what ultimately makes *Herzog* a comedy and not a tragedy, is that he does not give in to what he calls "the void." For Herzog, as for Bellow, nihilism, relativism, and despair—three pillars of modern intellectual life—are cop-outs. They are easy formulations designed to relieve people of the moral responsibility to keep looking for meaning, even when it is not easy to see. "There are moral realities . . . as surely as there are molecular and atomic ones," Herzog writes to a famous professor in one of his letters. And in his final letter, which he writes to God, he reports: "How my mind has struggled to make coherent sense. I have not been too good at it. But have desired to do your unknowable will." This desire, rather than any extraordinary action or discovery on his part, makes Herzog a memorable character. And it is this quality in Bellow's fiction that the Swedish Academy singled out when it awarded him the Nobel Prize in literature:

> The awareness of a value . . . gives man freedom, thereby responsibility, thereby a desire for action and a faith in the future. That is why Bellow, never one to look through rose-coloured spectacles, is at heart an optimist. It is the light of that conviction which makes the facets of his writing sparkle. His "anti-heroes" are victims of constant disappointment, born to defeat without end, and Bellow (it cannot be over-emphasized) loves and is able to transform the fate they find worthwhile into superb comedies. But they triumph nonetheless, they are heroes nonetheless, since they never give up the realm of values in which man becomes human.

Herzog made Bellow a celebrity. The novel spent nearly a year on the *New York Times* bestseller list, going all the way to number one, and earned Bellow a second National Book Award, solidifying his reputation as the greatest living American novelist—Hemingway and Faulkner having died in 1961 and 1962, respectively. Bellow followed *Herzog* with a well-received collection of short fiction entitled *Mosby's Memoirs and Other Stories* (1968). The book was somewhat superfluous, as three of the six pieces had already been collected in *Seize the Day,* but it was well received. Two of the stories in it ("Leaving the Yellow House" and "Looking for Mr. Green") are standard anthology pieces that have introduced two generations of nonspecialists to Bellow's fiction.

One unavoidable consequence of Bellow's new celebrity was that his private life suddenly became newsworthy. When his third marriage ended after only three years, the resulting court battles, which went on for more than ten years, became front-page news. Another consequence, and one that had a greater effect on his fiction, was that people expected him to have opinions about many of the chaotic events that gripped America during the 1960s: the civil rights movement, the Vietnam War, campus unrest, and women's liberation, to name only a few. Like most intellectuals who came of age during the 1920s and 1930s, Bellow had once considered himself a communist and had always leaned toward the left. It was expected, therefore, that he would share the liberalism of most other writers and intellectuals of the day. But Bellow was not one for toeing lines. In 1965 he angered much of the New York literary community when he accepted Lyndon Johnson's invitation to a White House artistic festival after the poet Robert Lowell had organized a boycott of the event to protest the Vietnam War. Because of his increasingly conservative public stands and his status as a "great writer" in the Western tradition, Bellow became a target for student protesters whenever he gave readings at college campuses. His experiences with students, his opinions about national and world events, and his distress over the state of American culture in the late 1960s all found their way into his next novel, *Mr. Sammler's Planet.*

Mr. Sammler's Planet follows the loose narrative structure of *Herzog* with its highly introspective viewpoint character, its lengthy flashbacks, and its numerous philosophical digressions. Unlike Moses Herzog, though, who spends most of his time analyzing and trying to explain his own life, Mr. Artur Sammler is a detached observer trying to make some sense of the world in which he lives. A cultivated Jewish intellectual, he escaped the Nazi death camps by hiding in a mass grave and killing a German soldier. When Sammler is finally brought to New York City by his late wife's nephew, he is something of an oddity who observes life from the margins. And what he observes is a profound moral decay. Two short scenes toward the beginning of the novel set up its main themes. In the first of these scenes, a black pickpocket chases Sammler down, corners him, and shows him his penis. In the second, Sammler himself is invited to lecture at Columbia on his memories of H. G. Wells, whom he had known in London before the war. Instead of being treated with enthusiasm or even respect, Sammler is shouted down by a student protester, as Bellow himself was shouted down at San Francisco State University a year before writing the novel. The cumulative effect of these two scenes is to impress on Sammler and on the reader both the immaturity and the irrationality of young Americans' responses to events that should seem trivial when compared to Sammler's experiences as a Holocaust survivor. "Who had raised the diaper flag?" Sammler wonders to himself as these events are unfolding. "Who had made shit a sacrament? What literary and psychological movement was that."

Like *Herzog, Mr. Sammler's Planet* is a critique of many of the ideas at the heart of modern thought. For Herzog, though, the ideas had simply been confusing; for Mr. Sammler,

they have become dangerous. Bellow's loose narrative structure allows him to turn parts of *Mr. Sammler's Planet* into long essays in which he marshals his arguments not only against the sexual and cultural turmoil of the sixties but also against Marx, Freud, Nietzsche, and even his Committee on Social Thought colleague Hannah Arendt, whose book *Eichmann in Jerusalem* (1963) had infuriated Bellow by suggesting that the Holocaust could be blamed largely on the banal bureaucratic efficiency of ordinary Germans rather than the exceptional human evil of Hitler and other Nazi leaders. Like Herzog, however, Sammler ultimately refuses to give into nihilism and despair—despite having much better reasons to do so. In his lengthy conversation with other characters and occasionally with himself, Sammler gives the clearest available outline of what has been referred to in Bellow's work as the "God-pervaded condition" of humanity—the inability to disbelieve in higher truths, even when disbelief would be preferable to belief, because of a persistent "sense of God," "strong impressions of eternity," and "an inclination to believe in archetypes of goodness."

Though it attracted the wrath of its intended targets—feminists, minorities, war protesters, and radicals of every stripe—*Mr. Sammler's Planet* won the National Book Award in 1971, making Bellow an unprecedented three-time winner of one of America's most prestigious literary prizes. From 1970 to 1975 he served as the chair of the University of Chicago's Committee on Social Thought. In 1974 he married Alexandra Ionescu Tulcea, a Romanian-born professor of mathematics at Northwestern. One year later, at the age of sixty, Bellow published his seventh novel, *Humboldt's Gift.*

Humboldt's Gift is the story of two writers. The first, the narrator Charlie Citrine, is the author of a successful Broadway play and several serious works of history, biography, and social commentary. Charlie's works have been both popular and critically acclaimed, and he has won Pulitzer Prizes for both drama and biography (the ease with which the narrator seems to win a Pulitzer Prize every time he dabbles in a new genre is almost certainly a jab at the prize committee itself, which ignored Bellow's work completely until he published *Humboldt's Gift*). As the novel opens, however, Charlie's career has stalled. His most recent book has sold poorly, and he has been unable to write anything since. A protracted divorce has cost him most of the money he has ever made, and though he remains intellectually active and committed to various projects, his intellectual energy has become too diffuse to bear fruit. Citrine is also haunted by his persistent, intrusive memories of the novel's title character, Von Humboldt Fleisher, Citrine's former friend and mentor who died years before but who has remained a towering figure in the narrator's life. Bellow based the character of Humboldt largely on Delmore Schwartz, the archetypal American *poète maudit*—the damned poet who is too devoted to art and beauty to survive the harsh realities of the real world. Schwartz burst onto the American literary scene in 1938 and, for a brief time, was a celebrity. Never able to recapture the success he experienced in his twenties, Schwartz descended further and further into alcoholism, drug addiction, paranoia, and insanity, until he died penniless in a squalid Times Square hotel in 1966. Bellow saw Schwartz's fate, which he reproduced faithfully through the character of Von Humboldt Fleisher, as the inevitable consequence of being a great poet in a country that did not value great poetry.

Both Humboldt and Citrine have the makings of tragic heroes, but *Humboldt's Gift* is one of Bellow's most comedic productions. By the end of the novel, Charlie has been abandoned by his girlfriend, who, tired of waiting for Charlie to propose, runs off with a wealthy mortician on the very day Charlie he decides that he wants to marry her. Charlie is living alone and in poverty, hiding from his ex-wife in Europe, and is in more than a little danger of ending up exactly like Von Humboldt Fleisher. Past and present come together through the device named in the title: Humboldt's "gift." Long after Humboldt's death, Charlie discovers that his friend had left him an inheritance of two movie scenarios—one they had worked on together and shopped around to studios and one Humboldt wrote himself. When Charlie is at his lowest point, he discovers that their coauthored scenario has been stolen by a major studio and turned into a successful movie. Humboldt's gift (which, amazingly enough, he had the forethought to copyright by mailing it to himself in a sealed envelope) redeems both poets, solving Charlie's financial problems and giving Von Humboldt Fleisher the adoration that he craved for most of his life. That both Citrine's fortunes and Humboldt's recognition must come from Hollywood and moviegoers, rather than from educated readers of great poetry, provides the novel's final satiric commentary on the state of intellectual and cultural life in America.

Humboldt's Gift became a national best-seller and in 1976 was awarded the Pulitzer Prize—the same award Von Humboldt Fleisher had referred to as "a dummy newspaper award given by crooks and illiterates." Bellow followed this success up with a nonfiction book, *To Jerusalem and Back* (1976), a travelogue and extended meditation on modern Israel that he wrote while accompanying his wife on a visiting lectureship at Hebrew University. Though a new genre for Bellow, the book was widely praised and helped to establish his credentials as a world-class intellectual. In his thirty-year career, Saul Bellow had become one of the most recognizable writers in the world, and in October 1976, he received the highest recognition the literary world has to offer: the Nobel Prize in literature.

A LITERARY ELDER STATESMAN

Bellow was keenly aware that the Nobel Prize was often a career-ending honor for major writers. According to Hemingway, who won the prize in 1953, "No son of a bitch that ever won the Nobel Prize ever wrote anything worth reading afterwards." For a time, it appeared Bellow might not provide the exception. For six years after winning the Nobel Prize, his only publication was a brief short story in *The New Yorker* entitled "The Silver Dish" (1978). However, he soon regained his stride and, during the 1980s, wrote and published more than he had during any previous ten-year period in his career—two full-length novels, two shorter novellas, and a major collection of short fiction—putting to rest the speculation that the most prestigious award in the literary world had claimed another victim.

Bellow's first major post-Nobel work, like almost all of his previous fiction, had its genesis in the events of his own life. In December 1978 Bellow traveled to Romania with his wife, whose mother—a former government minister who had incurred the disfavor of the Ceausescu regime—was dying in a Bucharest hospital. The trip lasted for only a few weeks, but it exposed Bellow for the first time to day-to-day life behind the Iron Curtain. In *The Dean's December* (1982) the details of this trip are reproduced in the life of Albert Corde, a journalist and unlikely dean of students at an unnamed Chicago university, and his wife Minna, a world-famous astronomer. Corde's focus in the novel, though, is only partially on the plight of his wife and mother-in-law. Before leaving Chicago, the dean had become involved in the prosecution of a black man charged with killing a white graduate student and had been severely criticized by campus radicals and college administrators for the political incorrectness of his involvement.

The larger story of *The Dean's December* is how ideologies have destroyed or are destroying the novel's two principal cities: Bucharest and Chicago (and, by extension, the entire American and Soviet spheres of influence). Reaching back to some of the themes he explored in *Mr. Sammler's Planet,* Bellow presents the psychological gap between white and black Americans as the inevitable result of a liberal ideology that minimizes individual responsibility and, therefore, the importance of individuals. "A tender liberal society has to find soft ways to institutionalize harshness and smooth it over compatibly with progress," Corde tells a colleague. "When people are merciless, when they kill, we explain that it's because they're disadvantaged, or have lead poisoning, or come from a backward section of the country, or need psychological treatment." The denial of individuality implied by this position is, as Bellow presents it, closely tied to the collectivist logic that led to the Stalinist purges.

In several magazine articles written before his trip to Bucharest, Corde presented the problems of the inner city as moral problems and suggested that a solution might lie in strengthening people's souls with great literature. "Perhaps only poetry," he wrote, "ha[s] the strength to rival the attractions of narcotics, the magnetism of TV, the excitements of sex, or the ecstasies of destruction." It is no coincidence that this same suggestion eventually became a central argument in Allan Bloom's controversial best-seller *The Closing of the American Mind,* as Bellow and Bloom were close friends and colleagues on the Committee on Social Thought. Both believed that the cultural relativism that grew out of the 1960s was both intellectually and spiritually flawed, and both insisted that a strong education in the classical and European traditions was essential to the moral health of American democracy.

Unlike most of Bellow's earlier novels, *The Dean's December* is not written in either a comedic or a satiric mode. Bellow does not place his characters in the hilarious situations that characterize *The Adventures of Augie March* and *Henderson, the Rain King,* nor does he give them the steady stream of witty, self-deprecating rejoinders and comedic observations he provides in such abundance for Moses Herzog, Mr. Sammler, and Charlie Citrine. Two years after publishing *The Dean's December,* though, Bellow returned to his familiar comic mode with his collection *Him with His Foot in His Mouth and Other Stories* (1984). One of the most compelling comic creations in all of Bellow's short work is Herschel Shawmut, the hero of the title story, who frames the story as a letter of apology to a fragile librarian he had offended thirty-five years earlier by making a cruel joke at her expense. Most of the other stories in this collection exhibit the same exuberant comic spirit, as does Bellow's second major novel of the decade, *More Die of Heartbreak* (1987).

Even by Bellow's standards, *More Die of Heartbreak* is a loosely plotted book. It concerns the relationship between the narrator Kenneth Trachtenberg, a professor of Russian literature at an unnamed midwestern university, and his uncle Benn Crader, a world-famous botanist with a penchant for attracting needy, desperate, and manipulative women. The book's title is taken from Benn's statement to a reporter who interviewed him after the Chernobyl disaster: "More people die of heartbreak than of radiation." What plot there is in the novel revolves around Benn's romantic entanglements with women: with Della Bedell, his spinster neighbor who demands (and gets) a sexual encounter by shouting, "what am I supposed to do with my sexuality"; with Carolyn Bunge, a widow who seduces and plans to marry Benn but is left at the alter as he escapes to a scientific conference in Tokyo; and finally, with Matilda Layamon, Benn's young wife with expensive tastes who involves her husband in a complicated web of conspiracy, intrigue, and blackmail in order to afford an expensive apartment. Kenneth, too, has problems with women. He is in love with a diminutive woman named Treckie, the mother of his daughter, who refuses to marry him precisely because he is not sufficiently abusive.

The most important relationship in the book, though, is the relationship between Kenneth and Benn. Kenneth, a French citizen by birth, immigrates to the United States specifically to care for his uncle, with whom he feels a strong, spiritual connection. This kind of connection, in either its presence or its absence, has always been important to Bellow. In *More Die of Heartbreak* he begins to describe it in self-consciously Platonic terms. Like Plato in the *Symposium,* which Kenneth quotes from directly in a vital passage, Bellow presents his protagonists as incomplete, fractured beings looking for completion. The "heartbreak" that more die of closely resembles the phenomenon Plato describes as erotic longing—the intense desire one soul feels for its absent other that can only be temporarily assuaged by the counterfeit connection of sexual relations. *More Die of Heartbreak* is an extended analysis of how two basically sympathetic characters attempt to deal with what the narrator describes as "the ordeal of desire." It is also a work that shows the continuing influence of Bloom on Bellow's mature work. "Souls without Longing" was Bloom's working title for *The Closing of the American Mind,* and Bloom's posthumously published book *Love and Friendship* (1993), based on ideas about erotic longing that Bellow and Bloom developed for their joint literature class at the University of Chicago, provides a precise vocabulary for understanding the many unsuccessful relationships Kenneth and Benn have with women—as well as the one successful relationship they ultimately have with each other.

As Bellow was completing the manuscript for *More Die of Heartbreak* in 1986, his wife filed for a divorce. Three years later, in 1989, he married Janis Freedman, a thirty-one-year-old former graduate student of the Committee on Social Thought. That same year, Bellow published two original novellas, *A Theft* and *The Bellarosa Connection.* In the first of these, Bellow offers his first female protagonist since Hattie Waggoner in "Leaving the Yellow House" (1958): Clara Velde, a successful fashion executive living in Manhattan with her fourth husband. After Clara hires an Austrian nanny named Gina to care for her daughter, she discovers that an expensive ring—given to her by a former lover to whom she feels a stronger connection than to any of her husbands—has been stolen, and she blames the girl's Haitian boyfriend. Clara turns Gina out but immediately regrets doing so. The ring eventually turns up by Clara's bedside. When she finally reconnects with Gina and hears how the girl arranged for the ring's return, Clara, in a moment of transcendence almost identical to Tommy Wilhelm's in *Seize the Day,* breaks into uncontrollable tears while walking down a Madison Avenue sidewalk.

A Theft made only a few small ripples when it was published and subsequently failed to engage scholars. Bellow's second novella of 1989, however, has attracted a substantial amount of critical attention and may well turn out to be the most important work of his post-Nobel career. The narrator of *The Bellarosa Connection* is a minor character narrator whose name is never mentioned but who, readers know, is an expert on memory and the founder of a successful memory-training institute. Using his impeccable memory to revive facts and details buried for thirty years, the narrator recounts the attempts of the story's hero, Harry Fonstein, to meet and thank the famous Broadway producer Billy Rose (an actual historical figure), who saved him from the Nazi death camps by financing a secret rescue operation in fascist Italy before the war. Rose flatly refuses to talk to Harry and rebuffs every attempt at a meeting. When Fonstein's American wife Sorella obtains documents that could damage Rose's reputation, she tries to blackmail him into a meeting, but he still refuses. The narrative then shifts to the present to recount the

narrator's attempt to regain contact with Harry and Sorella Fonstein only to discover that they both died in a car accident six months earlier.

The fact that the narrator of *The Bellarosa Connection* is a memory expert is crucial to the book's central theme. It is a story about memories and, more specifically, about memories of the Holocaust. The novella accepts as its fundamental premise the centrality of the Holocaust as the defining experience for Judaism in the twentieth century and grapples with the issue of how this experience should be remembered. Fonstein, a survivor, feels a compulsion to have his memories and his experiences acknowledged openly. Billy Rose, however, aggressively resists the memory of his own role in the Holocaust, even though the role was a heroic one. Billy prefers to see himself as a powerful, successful American rather than as a helpless victim of the twentieth century's greatest crime. The narrator, too, is a forgetter. He does not actively reject Fonstein's memories, as Billy does, but he does not actively remember them either. Caught up in the American business of making a fortune from his mnemonic abilities, he conspicuously does not use his most important natural gift to honor the Fonsteins and their Holocaust experiences, allowing them to slip away from him until it is too late. In the closing paragraph readers learn that *The Bellarosa Connection* itself is the narrator's attempt to atone for his sin of forgetfulness.

Throughout the 1990s, Bellow remained an active writer and teacher. In 1991 he published *Something to Remember Me By,* a largely repackaged collection that included *A Theft, The Bellarosa Connection,* and the story "Something to Remember Me By." The next year, he left the University of Chicago after thirty years on the faculty and took a position at Boston University, where he edited *It All Adds Up: From the Dim Past to the Uncertain Future* (1994), a collection of nonfiction essays and occasional pieces published during the course of his career. In 1997 Saul Bellow was back before readers with *The Actual,* a new novella about an aging antique dealer named Harry Trellman who, after living a chaotic, alienated life, is given a second chance to connect with his one great love, a woman named Amy Wustrin, whom he had briefly dated in high school forty years earlier. In *The Actual* Bellow returns to his well-known fascination with the theme of human connection and to the Platonic musings of *More Die of Heartbreak.* Trellman's longing for Amy goes far beyond (but does not entirely discount) sexual attraction; it is an "actual affinity" that has been the source of both pain and desire for much of his life. The final scene, in which Harry finally confesses his feelings to Amy and makes a marriage proposal (that readers assume will be accepted) contains Bellow's strongest affirmation to date that the profound but abstract spiritual connections he has been gesturing toward for most of his career might actually be obtainable in the world of fact.

In 1999 the eighty-four-year-old Saul Bellow astounded his friends and family when his wife gave birth to his fourth child and only daughter, Naomi Rose Bellow. A year later, he astounded the world when he published *Ravelstein,* his tenth full-length novel and his first since *More Die of Heartbreak* thirteen years earlier. Several months before the publication of *Ravelstein* word leaked out that it was to be an account of Bellow's relationship with his friend Bloom, who had died in 1992. The same sources also indicated that Bellow's book would reveal two things about Bloom that were not widely known outside of intellectual circles: that America's most influential cultural conservative had been a homosexual and that he had died of AIDS. However, those who read *Ravelstein* to see how Bellow reconciled his ideology and his sexuality were disappointed. The narrator, a Bellow-esque writer named Chick, reveals Abe Ravelstein's homosexuality as a passing fact, like his nervous chain smoking, his taste for

flashy clothing, his passion for basketball, and his conservative politics, which Chick simply dismisses: "He had views of his own on political and moral matters. I am not interested in presenting his ideas."

Chick is, however, interested in presenting Ravelstein's ideas on love and friendship—ideas Bellow introduced in nascent form in *More Die of Heartbreak* and developed further in *The Actual.* In *Ravelstein* they become a full-fledged, systematic philosophy of erotic longing and Platonic love. Chick rehearses Ravelstein's erotic theories so often they become part of the narrative's essential fabric:

> People are beaten at last with their solitary longings and intolerable isolation. They need *the* right, *the* missing portion to complete themselves, and since they can't realistically hope to find that they must accept a companionable substitute. . . . The marriage of true minds seldom occurs. Love that bears it out even to the edge of doom is not a modern project. But there was, for Ravelstein, nothing to compete with this achievement of the soul. . . . The best we can hope for in Modernity is not love, but a sexual attachment—a bourgeois solution, in bohemian dress. . . . Ravelstein taught that in the modern condition we are in a weak state. The strong state—and this is what he learned from Socrates—comes to us through nature. At the core of the soul is Eros.

But even these ideas, which are featured prominently throughout the book, are ultimately less important than the book's portrayal of the friendship between Ravelstein and Chick. The real protagonist of *Ravelstein* is neither the narrator nor the title character but the relationship between them: a long-term, emotionally healthy, intellectual friendship between two cultivated individuals. It is precisely the kind of nonsexual, Platonic friendship Bloom himself, in *Love and Friendship,* attributes to Prince Hal and Falstaff in Shakespeare's *Henry IV:* "They are soul mates, and without any touch of solemnity, they prove the possibility of a purely spiritual association. . . . It is really an erotic relationship, the attraction based on the potential for shared insight." But *Ravelstein* is a tragic story as well, and the tragedy is not just that Ravelstein dies or even that he dies of AIDS but that the very force that created such great beauty in his life—insatiable erotic longing—ultimately brings about his demise.

It is impossible to know whether *Ravelstein* will be Saul Bellow's last novel, but the chances are good that it will not. Bellow's track record so far suggests he will be working on something and probably several things as long as he has the physical capacity to do so. *Ravelstein* is, however, a fitting work to use to focus the career of one of the most important American writers of the twentieth century. It is much more than an elegiac memoir about an old friend. It provides a powerful sense of resolution to issues that have been present in Bellow's major fiction for more than fifty years, such as the nature of friendship, the power of memory, the connection between philosophy and life, and perhaps most importantly, the possibility that connections with others can produce genuine spiritual meaning. The philosophy of erotic desire that Bellow articulates in *Ravelstein* provides a vocabulary to explain Henderson's constant cries of "I want, I want" and to interpret the inarticulate sobbing at the end of both *Seize the Day* and *A Theft.* The same vocabulary helps explain why Asa Leventhal endures Allbee's endless manipulations in *The Victim,* why Charlie Citrine cannot resolve his obsession with Von Humboldt Fleisher in *Humboldt's Gift,* why Kenneth Trachtenberg immigrates to America to care for his Uncle Benn in *More Die of Heartbreak,* and even why poor Herschel Shawmut apologizes for a thirty-five-year-old insult in "Him with His Foot in His Mouth." What makes Bellow's fiction tragic at times is that most of these characters never find the spiritual meaning they are so desperately searching for; what ultimately makes it great is that they never give up the search.

Selected Bibliography

WORKS OF SAUL BELLOW

NOVELS
Dangling Man. New York: Vanguard, 1944.
The Victim. New York: Vanguard, 1947.
The Adventures of Augie March: A Novel. New York: Viking, 1953.
Henderson, the Rain King: A Novel. New York: Viking, 1959.
Herzog. New York: Viking, 1964.
Mr. Sammler's Planet. New York: Viking, 1970.
Humboldt's Gift: A Novel. New York: Viking, 1975.
The Dean's December: A Novel. New York: Harper & Row, 1982.
More Die of Heartbreak. New York: Morrow, 1987.
Ravelstein. New York: Viking, 2000.

NOVELLAS AND SHORT STORY COLLECTIONS
Seize the Day, with Three Short Stories and a One-Act Play. New York: Viking, 1956.
Mosby's Memoirs and Other Stories. New York: Viking, 1968.
Him with His Foot in His Mouth and Other Stories. New York: Harper & Row, 1984.
A Theft. New York: Penguin, 1989.
The Bellarosa Connection. New York: Penguin, 1989.
Something to Remember Me By: Three Tales. New York: Viking, 1991.
The Actual. New York: Viking, 1997.
Collected Stories. Preface by Janis Freedman Bellow. New York: Viking, 2001.

UNCOLLECTED SHORT FICTION
"Two Morning Monologues." *Partisan Review* 8:230–236 (May–June 1941).
"The Mexican General." *Partisan Review* 9:178–194 (May–June 1942).
"Sermon by Dr. Pep." *Partisan Review* 16:455–462 (May–June 1949).
"Dora." *Harper's Bazaar,* no. 18:188–190, 198–199 (November 1949).

"The Trip to Galena." *Partisan Review* 17, no. 8:779–794 (November–December 1950).

"By the Rock Wall." *Harper's Bazaar,* April 1951, pp. 135–205, 207–208, 214–216.

"Address by Gooley MacDowell to the Hasbeens Club of Chicago." *Hudson Review* 4:222–227 (summer 1951).

PLAYS

"The Wrecker." *New World Writing* 6:271–287 (1954).

The Last Analysis: A Play. New York: Viking, 1965.

"A Wen." *Esquire,* January 1965, pp. 72–74.

"Orange Souffle." *Esquire,* October 1965, pp. 130–136.

NONFICTION

To Jerusalem and Back: A Personal Account. New York: Viking, 1976.

It All Adds Up: From the Dim Past to the Uncertain Future: A Nonfiction Collection. New York: Viking, 1994.

BIBLIOGRAPHIES

Cronin, Gloria L., and Blaine H. Hall. *Saul Bellow: An Annotated Bibliography.* New York: Garland, 1987.

Field, Leslie, and John Z. Guzlowski. "Criticism of Saul Bellow: A Selected Checklist." *Modern Fiction Studies* 25, no. 1:149–170 (1979).

Nault, Marianne. *Saul Bellow, His Works and His Critics: An Annotated International Bibliography.* New York: Garland, 1997.

Noreen, Robert G. *Saul Bellow: A Reference Guide.* Boston: G. K. Hall, 1978.

Sokoloff, B. A., and Mark E. Posner. *Saul Bellow: A Comprehensive Bibliography.* Norwood, Pa.: Norwood Editions, 1973.

CRITICAL AND BIOGRAPHICAL STUDIES

Atlas, James. *Bellow: A Biography.* New York: Random House, 2000.

Bach, Gerhard, ed. *The Critical Response to Saul Bellow.* Westport, Conn.: Greenwood Press, 1995.

Bach, Gerhard, and Gloria L. Cronin, eds. *Small Planets: Saul Bellow and the Art of Short Fiction.* East Lansing: Michigan State University Press, 2000.

Bloom, Harold, ed. *Saul Bellow.* New York: Chelsea, 1986.

Bradbury, Malcolm. *Saul Bellow.* London: Methuen, 1982.

Braham, Jeanne. *A Sort of Columbus: The American Voyages of Saul Bellow's Fiction.* Athens: University of Georgia Press, 1984.

Clayton, John Jacob. *Saul Bellow: In Defense of Man.* Bloomington: Indiana University Press, 1968.

Cohen, Sarah Blacher. *Saul Bellow's Enigmatic Laughter.* Urbana: University of Illinois Press, 1974.

Cronin, Gloria L. *A Room of His Own: In Search of the Feminine in the Novels of Saul Bellow.* Syracuse, N.Y.: Syracuse University Press, 2000.

Cronin, Gloria L., and L. H. Goldman, eds. *Saul Bellow in the 1980s: A Collection of Critical Essays.* East Lansing: Michigan State University Press, 1989.

Dutton, Robert R. *Saul Bellow.* New York: Twayne, 1971.

Fuchs, Daniel. *Saul Bellow: Vision and Revision.* Durham, N.C.: Duke University Press, 1984.

Goldman, L. H. *Saul Bellow's Moral Vision: A Critical Study of the Jewish Experience.* New York: Irvington, 1983.

Harris, Mark. *Saul Bellow: Drumlin Woodchuck.* Athens: University of Georgia Press, 1980.

Hyland, Peter. *Saul Bellow.* New York: St. Martin's, 1992.

Kiernan, Robert F. *Saul Bellow.* New York: Continuum, 1989.

Malin, Irving. *Saul Bellow's Fiction.* Carbondale: Southern Illinois University Press, 1969.

Malin, Irving, comp. *Saul Bellow and the Critics.* New York: New York University Press, 1967.

McCadden, Joseph F. *The Flight from Women in the Fiction of Saul Bellow.* Lanham, Md.: University Press of America, 1981.

McConnell, Frank D. *Four Postwar American Novelists: Bellow, Mailer, Barth, and Pynchon.* Chicago: University of Chicago Press, 1977.

Miller, Ruth. *Saul Bellow: A Biography of the Imagination.* New York: St. Martin's, 1991.

Newman, Judie. *Saul Bellow and History.* New York: St. Martin's, 1984.

Opdahl, Keith M. *The Novels of Saul Bellow: An Introduction.* University Park: Pennsylvania State University Press, 1967.

Pifer, Ellen. *Saul Bellow against the Grain.* Philadelphia: University of Pennsylvania Press, 1990.

Porter, M. Gilbert. *Whence the Power? The Artistry and Humanity of Saul Bellow.* Columbia: University of Missouri Press, 1974.

Rodrigues, Eusebio, L. *Quest for the Human: An Exploration of Saul Bellow's Fiction.* Lewisburg, Pa.: Bucknell University Press, 1981.

Rovit, Earl. *Saul Bellow.* Minneapolis: University of Minnesota Press, 1967.

Scheer-Schäzler, Brigitte. *Saul Bellow.* New York: Frederick Ungar, 1972.

Trachtenberg, Stanley, comp. *Critical Essays on Saul Bellow.* Boston: G. K. Hall, 1979.

INTERVIEWS

Boyers, Robert. "Moving Quickly: An Interview with Saul Bellow." *Salmagundi* 106–107:32–53 (spring–summer 1995).

Brans, Jo. "Common Needs, Common Preoccupations: An Interview with Saul Bellow." *Southwest Review* 62:1–19 (1977).

Cronin, Gloria L., and Ben Siegel, eds. *Conversations with Saul Bellow.* Jackson: University Press of Mississippi, 1994. (Reprints twenty-nine interviews given between 1953 and 1994, including interviews by Gordon Lloyd Harper, Joyce Illig, Chirantan Kulshrestha, Sanford Pinsker, Maggie Simmons, and Nina Steers.)

Dudar, Helen. "The Greying of Saul Bellow." *Saturday Review,* January 1982, pp. 16–20.

Roudané, Matthew C. "An Interview with Saul Bellow." *Contemporary Literature* 25, no. 3:265–280 (fall 1984).

Singh, Sukhbir. "Meeting with Saul Bellow." *American Studies International* 35, no. 1:19–31 (February 1997).

FILM BASED ON A WORK OF SAUL BELLOW

Seize the Day. Written by Ronald Ribman, directed by Felder Cook, starring Robin Williams as Tommy Wilhelm. Distributed by Merrimack Films, 1986.

—MICHAEL AUSTIN

Elizabeth Bishop

1911–1979

*I*N HER AUTOBIOGRAPHICAL prose narrative "The Country Mouse" (published in *The Collected Prose* in 1984, several years after her death), Elizabeth Bishop tells the powerful and troubling story of her paternal grandparents' Boston bull terrier named Beppo. She describes him with affection and sympathy:

> He was a clever dog; he wore a wide collar with brass studs, which was taken off every night before he went to bed. Every morning at eight o'clock he would come to my door with the collar in his mouth, and bang it against the door, meaning for us to get up and dressed and start the day together.

Bishop notes that he "had a delicate stomach; he vomited frequently" and that "when he was 'bad,' he was punished by being put in a large closet off the sewing room and left there . . . for half an hour." One day when he had been playing with young Elizabeth, Beppo disappeared and would not respond to her calls:

> Finally he was found, seated gloomily by himself in the closet, facing the wall. He was punishing *himself*. We later found a smallish pile of vomit in the conservatory. No one had ever before punished him for his attacks of gastritis, naturally; it was all his own idea, his peculiar Bostonian sense of guilt.

Bishop's account of Beppo's "transgression" and self-punishment resonates with several qualities of her work more generally: meticulous attention to detail, vivid imagination, profound sympathy, moral acuity, and wry humor. Though the strength of her poetry was recognized early on, Bishop has acquired an increasingly strong reputation since her death, with interest growing in both her prose and her massive collection of letters, which was published in 1994. Like much of her work, "The Country Mouse" combines the perspectives of child and adult viewer that simultaneously complicate and enable readers' appreciation of this intense, powerful, and sometimes enigmatic writer.

IN THE BEGINNING: CONTEXTS

Bishop's story of Beppo gains additional poignancy from its context, an account of her travel from the modest Nova Scotian home of one set of grandparents to that of her wealthy paternal grandparents in Worcester, Massachusetts, outside of Boston. Born on February 8, 1911, in Worcester to William Thomas Bishop and Gertrude Bulmer (often written as "Boomer") Bishop, Elizabeth Bishop lost her thirty-nine-year-old father to Bright's disease when she was only eight months old. The writer's widowed mother never recovered from this blow and wore mourning clothes for five years, presaging the full-blown mental illness that would eventually emerge. Indeed, in a characteristic gesture of self-protectiveness, Bishop later revealed that as a child she confused "mourning" with "morning." This early experience rendered the idea of "home" an important theme in her writing, as a complex experience intensely desired yet feared.

A year after Gertrude's first recorded mental attack in 1914, she and young Elizabeth returned to Gertrude's birth home, Great Village, Nova Scotia, to live with Elizabeth's grandparents. The period between their arrival and Gertrude's commitment to an institution in 1916 were disturbing both to Elizabeth and to the rest of the family. Her mother's erratic behavior, and the family's response to it, sparked the confusion, guilt, shame, fear, and loss that Bishop recounts in her narrative "In the Village," which opens, "A scream, the echo of a scream, hangs over that Nova Scotian village. . . . Its pitch would be the pitch of my village. Flick the lightning rod on top of the church steeple with your fingernail and you will hear it." The pain from this early experience emerges also in "Primer Class," where she notes, "My father was dead and my mother was away in a sanatorium. Until I was teased out of it, I used to ask Grandmother, when I said goodbye [for school], to promise me not to die before I came home."

In spite of this painful period, Bishop was fortunate to have devoted grandparents and other relatives in Great Village, a farming community overlooking the Bay of Fundy. Her grandmother's sense of humor was significant for the writer's development, and her grandfather, a hardworking and kind man, fostered her impeccable manners and sensitive perspective. He insisted, for example, that when they came to a hill in their wagon, the passengers walk to lighten the horse's work. Others in her extended family contributed variously to her development, with her Aunt Mary (who was twelve years older) accompanying her to the village school for her first year. Bishop describes Mary with affectionate impatience in "Primer Class," for her aunt typically waited until the last possible moment to leave the house, and when they arrived one day in the middle of the Lord's Prayer, although Bishop herself was tearful, her "awful aunt was still *laughing*."

Bishop's Uncle Arthur, who appears as "Uncle Neddy" in the fictionalized prose narrative "Memories of Uncle Neddy," had a tinsmith shop where the writer was fascinated by the manifold shapes and forms of the tinsmith's art:

Night descends as one walks back, then daylight grows as one reaches the dirty windows above the workbench. This night sky of Uncle Neddy's is

hung with the things he makes himself: milk pails, their bottoms shining like moons; flashing tin mugs in different sizes; watering pots like comets, in among big dull lengths of stove pipe with wrinkled blue joints like elephants' legs dangling overhead.

Uncle Arthur also provided another, less appealing kind of model: a lifelong alcoholic, he was a binge drinker and an embarrassment to his Baptist family. Bishop regretfully regarded him as evidence for the hereditary alcoholism that troubled her own life. In "Memories" she concludes, speaking from the adult's perspective that alternates in the narrative with the child's, "I realize only now that he represented 'the devil' for me, not a violent, active Devil, but a gentle black one, a devil of weakness, acquiescence, tentatively black, like the sooty mildew."

After three years of this life that was by turns wonderful and painful (or perhaps, to borrow from her poem "The Bight," "awful but cheerful"), Bishop's wealthy American grandparents came to Great Village to return her to their home in Worcester. In "The Country Mouse," Bishop evinces her distinctive attention to detail, here focused on the body, as she describes new scenes of shame: she is sick on the train; her paternal grandparents' bodies discomfit her; and she notes, "Yesterday's white socks were very dirty. 'And she only has one pair, John,' said Grandma." By referring to her uncleanliness, her grandmother implicitly casts aspersions on Elizabeth's beloved Bulmer grandparents' care and appears to disparage their poverty. Although the well-meaning, generous Bishops willingly assumed responsibility for Elizabeth, their elite lifestyle and perspective would often puzzle and embarrass her. She observes, "I had been brought back unconsulted and against my wishes to the house my father had been born in, to be saved from a life of poverty and provincialism, bare feet, suet puddings, unsanitary school slates, perhaps even from the inverted *r*'s of my mother's family." As shown in this narrative probably written in 1961, Bishop's resentment sizzles almost forty-five years after the actual move to Worcester. The instability of her early family life would lend resonance to her developing idea of "home" and, paradoxically, spark an intense, lifelong interest in traveling.

In spite of her new home's many shortcomings, there were some compensations, among them kindly servants, new friends, a caring teacher, and a rambling house to explore. Best of all, perhaps, was her grandfather's unexpected and memorable gift of three golden bantams, two hens and a rooster: "They were reddish, speckled, with tiny doll-like red combs; the rooster had long tail feathers. They were *mine.* . . . I could scarcely bear to leave my little poultry." Bishop would later proffer readers a devastating commentary on patriarchal gender relations in her poem "Roosters," where she describes cocks with "protruding chests / in green-gold medals dressed, / planned to command and terrorize the rest"; but these childhood poultry, in contrast, seem to represent unambiguous evidence of love.

Her home with the elder Bishops was destined to be short-lived, for within less than a year Bishop became ill with a variety of allergies, including asthma and eczema, which necessitated her move to the working-class Revere, Massachusetts, home of her Aunt Maud and Uncle George Sheperdson. Although she still was often ill with asthma, Bishop enjoyed reading and visiting the nearby Boston museums with her Aunt Maud. While she was in her early teens, both her Bishop grandparents died, leaving her Uncle Jack Bishop, whom Elizabeth never liked, to administer the funds left for her care. During this time, she attended summer camp on Cape Cod and then a girls' boarding school, Walnut Hill, which would prove an important influence: she met friends whom she kept throughout her life and developed the in-

tellectual foundation for her later studies in music and literature at Vassar College. One of her friends at Walnut Hill later recalled her sense of "her own rightness, or of her being at the center of her own world and being able to find her way through it" (quoted in *Remembering Elizabeth Bishop*). Her friend also emphasized a trait that would become important in Bishop's work:

> Elizabeth had such funny and original ways of looking at things and people. On the one hand, Elizabeth was a bit amused by a lot of things. She had a sort of general attitude of amusement toward the foibles of the human race. She was more than anything else amused, but not in an unkindly way.

Bishop's sense of humor stood her in good stead at Vassar, at that time still a women's college, where she wrote for the school newspaper and, with several friends, founded an alternative literary journal, *Con Spirito*. The critic Bethany Hicok observes that "In a limited sense . . . *Con Spirito* allowed Bishop to 'come out' as both a writer and, perhaps much more provisionally, a lesbian."

Perhaps the pivotal point of her Vassar experience, however, was meeting her lifelong friend and mentor, the poet Marianne Moore, who, as Brett C. Millier asserts, "was without a doubt the most important single influence on Elizabeth Bishop's poetic practice and career." From Moore, Bishop learned the importance of the significant detail; Moore's poetry also provided a model of aesthetic restraint, whose contours Bishop would tactfully and gracefully test throughout her writing career. Another milestone was the death of Bishop's mother in a mental institution at the end of Bishop's senior year. In some sense, she lived Emily Dickinson's odd and poignant assertion, "I never had a mother." Travel in Europe with her Vassar friends after graduation fostered the writer's development and provided her with one of the central metaphors for her writing. Indeed, the tension between "travel" and "home," the familiar and the strange, would inflect virtually all of the writer's subsequent work.

"CHOOSING NOT CHOOSING": BISHOP THE POET

Best known as a poet, Bishop is enjoying a renaissance of interest that Thomas Travisano describes as "The Elizabeth Bishop Phenomenon." Some early critical work on the poet tended to underestimate her. David Kalstone observes in his *Five Temperaments:* "Critics have praised her descriptive powers and treated her as something of a miniaturist. As mistakenly as with the work of Marianne Moore, they have sometimes asked if Bishop's is poetry at all." As readers had done with such predecessors as Walt Whitman and Robert Frost, Bishop's critics were often unable to see beyond the surface details, but as Charles Mann notes, "Bishop's work, like Robert Frost's best, has an apparent simplicity that belies a greater depth beneath." Nevertheless, Bishop's poetry has almost always been treated with respect. Although critics agree that her overall aesthetic method—meticulous attention to detail, refined prosody, and terse diction—did not change radically over the course of her career, they also agree that her poems gradually move toward greater personal revelation and substantive openness. Her putative simplicity has generated accounts of Bishop's poetics as variously symbolist, surrealist, classicist, modernist, transcendentalist, romantic, anti-romantic, feminist, postmodernist, regionalist, devotional, political, and lesbian. Her wide-ranging subjects include time, geography, gender, loss, place, paradox, vision, travel, art, home, and memory, and she is praised for her restraint, precise description, and visual artistry.

Perhaps most characteristic of her poetry is the balancing that Sharon Cameron identifies in Emily Dickinson's work, which Cameron denominates "choosing not choosing"; that is,

like her New England predecessor, Bishop frequently proposes a problem or a conflict for which there are multiple "correct" perspectives. In this "objective" stance Bishop underscores her generosity toward the reader and at the same time affirms the reader's responsibility. Like Whitman, who explicitly urged readers to seek their own meanings in his poems rather than through the poet or other readers, Bishop challenges her readers to investigate the multiple perspectives articulated and elicited by her austere, elegant, and luminous verse. Bonnie Costello suggests that although Bishop "concerned herself, throughout her career, with questions of mastery—artistic, personal, and cultural," she nevertheless "forces herself and her reader to encounter the mess of life, at times even to exhilarate in it." Bishop's "Poem," about a painting "about the size of an old-style dollar bill, / American or Canadian," figures the necessary commitment by the reader to "this little painting (a sketch for a larger one?)": readers must invest their own imaginations to flesh out the contours and colors of the "sketch."

Bishop couples this attitude of challenge and respect with a disarming humor that reverberates throughout her work. Citing a letter to a friend, Marilyn May Lombardi describes the poet's perception in *The Body and the Song:* "A poem must be kept aloft . . . like a balloon, a bubble, defying gravity with ebullience and laughter." The poet's wry and often dark wit, which emerges in various forms, illuminates her vision from the beginning of her career. Although she has been compared with an enormous range of poets, from her beloved George Herbert, whose clarity and plainness she admired, to Gerard Manley Hopkins and Wallace Stevens (both of whom she studied with interest in college), one of the most appropriate touchstones for her work is Robert Frost; as Robert Lowell asserts in "Elizabeth Bishop's *North & South,*" "in her marvelous command of shifting speech tones, Bishop resembles Robert Frost." Like her elder contemporary, Bishop believed in formal control, and her work embodies his concept of poetry as "a momentary stay against confusion." Bishop would likely have acknowledged some truth in Frost's remark, "I own any form of humor shows fear and inferiority. Irony is simply a kind of guardedness. So is a twinkle. It keeps the reader from criticism" (quoted in *The Letters of Robert Frost to Louis Untermeyer*), and she would certainly have agreed with his view that "We shall be judged finally by the delicacy of our feeling of where to stop short" (quoted in *Selected Letters of Robert Frost*).

Bishop's first book, *North & South,* published in 1946, opens with a poem titled "The Map," in which she inaugurates a delicate strand of humor with the questions concluding the first stanza:

. . . does the land lean down to lift the sea from
  under,
drawing it unperturbed around itself?
Along the fine tan sandy shelf
is the land tugging at the sea from under?

The bright, ostensibly cheerful comedy of the personified land's actions pairs with the undertow of the image in a rhetorical gesture that both expresses the poet's delight and evokes drowning. In a similarly paradoxical manner, "Chemin de Fer" deploys rhythm and rhyme to convey the poet's double vision:

Alone on the railroad track
  I walked with pounding heart.
The ties were too close together
  or maybe too far apart.

Here Bishop recalls a Robert Frost poem, such as "Sand Dunes," in which the narrator wryly notes:

Sea waves are green and wet,
But up from where they die,

Rise others vaster yet,
And those are brown and dry.

The simple language and apparent indecisiveness of each narrator highlights the chronically skeptical vision of the poets, a vision undergirded by a confidence in humor to provide a durable compensation for the fragility of life and love, an important subject in each of these poems.

North & South, for which Bishop won the Houghton Mifflin Poetry Fellowship, was published just after World War II; critics have recognized the (often coded) alliances among the poet's perspective, her work, and the theme of war. Bishop worried about readers' apprehension of the apparent distance of her work from the crisis of the war and wrote to her editor and publisher Ferris Greenslet (reprinted in *One Art,* 1994):

The fact that none of these poems deal [*sic*] directly with the war, at a time when so much war poetry is being published, will, I am afraid, leave me open to reproach. . . . I think it would help some if a note to the effect that most of the poems had been written, or begun at least, before 1941, could be inserted at the beginning. . . .

However separate from the war the poems of *North & South* may have been in origin, many nevertheless resonate with conflict. The most obvious example, "Paris, 7 A.M.," veers from the whimsy of the "ornamental urns / set on the mansard roof-tops where the pigeons / take their walks" and "The childish snow-forts, built in flashier winters" to the violence of "the ammunition, the piled-up balls / with the star-splintered hearts of ice." "Introspection . . . or retrospection" yields such images of simultaneous self-protection and aggression that extend far beyond childhood, as the clocks that guard the entrance to and exit from the poem provide no answer and no consolation. The humor in the images of childhood, augmented by the geometric shapes that provide the poem's bones, mutates into a "dead" sky, "or the sky from which a dead one fell"—all the more frightening because of this vision's naive origins in youth. Violence lurks in many of the poems in Bishop's first volume: in the beautiful hidden menace of "The Imaginary Iceberg," in the burning, loving boy of "Casabianca," in the bladed chariot and warriors of "Wading at Wellfleet," and in the comic explosions of "Love Lies Sleeping."

Bishop was not alone in her apparent elimination of the war from her poetic vision. From the black comedy of "The Witch of Coös" and "The Pauper Witch of Grafton"—poems about murder, lost love, and betrayal—to the war-era poems of *Steeple Bush* and *A Masque of Reason* and *A Masque of Mercy,* Robert Frost, like Bishop, combines the wry, the whimsical, and the dangerous in poems that appear to have no immediate relevance to their historical moment. He was sharply criticized for his apparently disengaged attitude toward the war, though like Bishop, he wrote a number of these poems well before the war. His work, too, explores the tensions and rifts of the age in indirect and artful ways that are often more powerful than didacticism or direct discussion. With its invocation of "the children's house of make-believe" located "back out of all this now too much for us," "Directive" parallels the "introspection" and "retrospection" of "Paris, 7 A.M.," which was published only a year earlier. For both Bishop and Frost, time engenders distance and decay; at the end of his poem Frost plays with the redemptiveness of the prophet-poet's vision but, like Bishop, suggests that loss is at best counterbalanced by invented will.

At its conclusion "Directive" mockingly advises the reader to "drink and be whole again beyond confusion," while in "The Man-Moth," Bishop's reprise on a newspaper misprint, the narrator suggests that a similar redemption is available from drinking the eponymous hero's singular, palmed tear: "If you watch, he'll hand it over, / cool as from underground springs and pure enough to drink." Invoking the myth of the Holy Grail, a chalice reputed to contain the blood of the crucified Christ, both poets emphasize the diminishment of faith and its consolations in the modern era. This emphasis emerges in large part via the poems' use of whimsy. The image of the Man-Moth—which juxtaposes the gigantism of "mammoth" with the miniaturism of a moth—situates the hero both visually and aurally in an interstitial zone where his skewed perspective generates images both comic and frightening ("He thinks the moon is a small hole at the top of the sky, / proving the sky quite useless for protection"; "He has to keep / his hands in his pockets, as others must wear mufflers").

Like many other images, Bishop's "mufflers" reverberate in multiple directions. First, the image translates the weird hero into human terms, as he suffers from the childlike vulnerability that her writing repeatedly explores. At once larger than life and smaller than life, the Man-Moth possesses a vision of survival that includes both an avoidance of "the third rail, the unbroken draught of poison," and the need to keep his hands warm. In addition, "mufflers" possesses a comic sound, and ending the penultimate stanza here disarms the sententiousness of the poem's earlier stanzas and prepares the reader for the mock-heroic ending. Finally, "mufflers" suggests the silencing, even secrecy, that structures the writer's life and art; the poet's narrative itself ironically performs a kind of exposure of the surreal underpinnings—the Man-Moth is at "home" in the subway—of modern life.

Other poems in this first volume reiterate the themes of duality, of hidden realities, and of beauty and terror in conversation. "Seascape," for example, flashes and spins with imagery in the opening lines, inviting the reader to transcendent reflection and exquisite joy, describing

> . . . the beautiful pea-green back-pasture
> where occasionally a fish jumps, like a wild-flower
> in an ornamental spray of spray.

Balancing this vision, however, is the "skelctal lighthouse standing there / in black and white clerical dress" who "knows that heaven is not like this":

> Heaven is not like flying or swimming,
> but has something to do with blackness and a
>   strong glare
> and when it gets dark he will remember something
> strongly worded to say on the subject.

Brought down to earth by the clerical lighthouse, readers are terrified, amused, and warned of the dangerous delights in visions of earthly heaven. In retrospect, however—a stance that Bishop insists readers assume throughout her work—from the beginning of the poem she suggests that the heaven itself is a figment of our imaginations: "This celestial seascape, with white herons got up as angels" reminds us that self-deception is at once beautiful ("celestial") and comical ("got up" is amusingly casual). Similarly, the "bright green leaves" of "the weightless mangrove island" are "edged neatly with bird-droppings." Even the poem's concluding image undermines itself, with the incongruity of the lighthouse saying "something / strongly worded" when literally it cannot speak at all. As with many of her poems, including "Florida," "The Unbeliever," "Large Bad Picture," "Roosters," and "A Miracle for Breakfast," Bishop leaves room for the reader, asking us to consider whether or not humor provides necessary consolation, especially during trying times, or if it only augments the terror of clear-eyed vision.

North & South, which includes poems inspired by Bishop's childhood and young womanhood, such as "Large Bad Picture" and "Wading at Wellfleet," also contains works elicited by the poet's residence in Florida (including "Florida," "Cootchie," "Jerónimo's House," and her famous "The Fish"). After leaving Vassar, spending some time working in New York (which she details wittily in her prose piece "The U.S.A. School of Writing"), and traveling in Europe, Bishop moved in 1938 to Key West, where she maintained a residence for nearly ten years. Key West provided numerous benefits to the impecunious young writer: it was inexpensive, colorful, historic, and casual, a place where unconventional perspectives and social differences were welcomed. Although she had had and would continue to have warm friendships with men, by this time it was clear that Bishop's principal emotional and physical relationships would be with women. Her senior-year college roommate had been an early infatuation, and she had had intense friendships, including an intimate relationship with her wealthy former classmate Louise Crane, since Vassar. After separating from Crane, with whom she had bought a house on Key West, she took up residence with Marjorie Stevens on the island in mid-1941.

In an intensely homophobic era, this homoerotic affiliation necessitated for Bishop a stringent sense of privacy, which is reflected in a remark made near the end of her life to her friend, the poet Richard Howard. After a visit from the lesbian poet Adrienne Rich, in which Rich had urged the elder woman to be more explicit about her sexuality, Bishop (in a characteristically oblique reference to her new home at Lewis Wharf in Boston) laughingly asserted, "You know what I want, Richard? I want closets, closets, and more closets" (quoted in *Remembering*). This personal philosophy also informs the aesthetic of much of her poetry, which endorses the merit of Emily Dickinson's statement "Tell all the truth but tell it slant— / Success in Circuit lies" while it resists the "confessional" mode made famous by the poet Robert Lowell.

In early 1947, shortly after Bishop's *North & South* and Lowell's *Lord Weary's Castle* were published, Bishop met Lowell through Randall Jarrell, the influential poet-critic who became one of her strongest supporters. By this time, Marianne Moore's influence on Bishop's work had begun to wane, as the younger poet increasingly trusted her own voice. Bishop and Lowell's ensuing friendship provided each of the young poets with intelligent and challenging criticism, and they met regularly over the next two years. Lowell would over time encourage the shy Bishop to participate in the public side of poetry, such as giving readings, and he recommended Bishop for numerous honors. He later remembered one period early in their relationship when he wanted to marry her. In spite of periodic disagreements and numerous personal difficulties, including Lowell's hospitalization for mental illness, the pair conducted an energetic and caring correspondence for essentially the rest of their lives.

During her time in Key West, where she enjoyed fishing, socializing with local people, and making a home, Bishop fell victim to the alcoholism that would shadow her whole life. Although she often drank to excess—and to the severe detriment of her health, with her many allergies—this behavior escalated when the intensely private Bishop was placed in situations requiring performances of one kind or another. When she was awarded a prestigious residency at Yaddo writer's colony in Saratoga Springs, New York, and shortly afterward assumed the position of Consultant in Poetry to the Library of Congress—an office now referred to as Poet Laureate—in September 1949 (thanks to Lowell's recommendation), the pressure to binge was enormous and often irresistible. Although friends like Stevens, Lowell, Moore, and May Swenson worried about Bishop's behavior, there was little they could do to help.

By this time much admired in literary circles, Bishop shunned the public eye, and the Library of Congress position proved to be a trial. After this stint in Washington, she returned to Yaddo for the fall and winter of 1950 and 1951 and then lived for several months in New York City, where her drinking almost killed her. In spite of recognition of her professional stature, such as an American Academy of Arts and Letters award, Bishop was profoundly adrift.

In late fall 1951 the writer embarked on a small freighter for South America. An allergic reaction during a stop in Brazil would transform her life: Lota de Macedo Soares, an affluent Brazilian woman whom Bishop had met briefly in New York and who would become her beloved companion and friend for fifteen years, assumed her care and—most importantly—gave her a home. Even as she was recovering from her illness, Bishop wrote to her friend and doctor in New York, Anny Baumann, "Aside from my swelled head and the asthma I feel fine & although it is tempting Providence to say so, I suppose, happier than I have felt in ten years." Her delight in Brazil, and the painterly perspective that colors and shapes virtually all of her work, emerges in a letter about her birthday, when she received a toucan from friends of Lota: "He has brilliant, electric-blue eyes, gray-blue legs and feet. Most of him is black, except the base of the enormous bill is green and yellow and he has a bright gold bib and bunches of red feathers on his stomach and under his tail." The humor representative of Bishop emerges here, too, in a hyperbolic description: "He eats six bananas a day. I must say they seem to go right through him & come out practically as good as new—meat, grapes—to see him swallowing grapes is rather like playing a pinball machine." Her letter concludes, "I have been so happy that it takes a great deal of getting used to."

Bishop's happiness fostered her creativity, and soon she began assembling poems for a new book, *A Cold Spring,* which was published by Houghton Mifflin with the earlier *North & South* in 1955; this volume won the Pulitzer Prize for poetry in 1956. Bishop was also at work translating the diary of a Brazilian girl, eventually published as *The Diary of "Helena Morley"* in 1957, and writing a picture-and-text volume (heavily edited, much to her dismay), *Brazil,* for Time-Life, published in 1962.

Though brief, *A Cold Spring* contains several poems that are among her best and most famous, including "Over 2,000 Illustrations and a Complete Concordance," "The Bight," and "At the Fishhouses." The title poem expresses an optimism that seems less guarded than in many of the poems in her first volume, and although there are, as always, gestures that balance the narrator's delight ("the after-birth, / a wretched flag" seen after a calf's birth; the dogwood blossom petals "burned, apparently, by a cigarette-butt"), hope vibrates down the lines, again most evident in the poet's quiet amusement:

Four deer practised leaping over your fences.
The infant oak-leaves swung through the sober
 oak.
Song-sparrows were wound up for the summer,
and in the maple the complementary cardinal
cracked a whip, and the sleeper awoke,
stretching miles of green limbs from the south.

"The Bight" balances—even synthesizes—ugliness and beauty, with the "sheer" "water" of the opening line supported by "white, crumbling ribs of marl [that] protrude and glare." Bishop's ability to construct startlingly oblique metaphors from comically ordinary experience offers the reader stunning surprises: "the frowsy sponge boats keep coming in / with the obliging air of retrievers." Like the messiness of life itself, "All the untidy activity continues, / awful but cheerful."

Bishop's ability to deflate pomposity—including, as in "The Bight," poets' own

tendency to high-flown images—reemerges in "View of the Capitol from the Library of Congress." Skewing the apparent orderliness of the literal image, the poet invites readers to share a vision of power disrupted by art, or by nature—readers are left to choose whether or not the music of the Air Force Band is captured by "giant trees":

I think the trees must intervene,

catching the music in their leaves
like gold-dust, till each big leaf sags.

The closing stanza vibrates with ambiguity marked by a whimsical yet deadly wit:

Great shades, edge over,
give the music room.
The gathered brasses want to go
boom—boom.

Are the first two lines here descriptive or imperative? Is the poet addressing the "giant trees" or the ghosts of the country—Washington, Jefferson, Lincoln? The "gathered brasses," ostensibly an image of authority and providing authority's sound, deflates the "boom[ing]," florid speeches in the Capitol with the sound made by a child who describes falling down: *"boom—boom."* Bishop's narrator recalls Emily Dickinson's childlike assertion,

I'm Nobody! Who are you?
Are you—Nobody—too?
Then there's a pair of us!

and delicately and deliberately enlists the reader in comic diminishment of the powers that be; the critic Langdon Hammer states that "The artist's relation to the world is the ground for an intersubjective relation—an intimacy—between artist and audience."

Bishop's unpublished work reveals her struggling to negotiate her feelings in a manner adequate to her stern aesthetic, and, as Marilyn

May Lombardi acknowledges, the poet "offers only rare glimpses of love or sexuality in print." Perhaps the most intimate poem in the new volume is "The Shampoo," which forecasts the more open and increasingly autobiographical nature of some of her later writing and suggests the influence of Robert Lowell. In "The Shampoo" Bishop again defies sententiousness by juxtaposing powerful, gorgeous images with the comically mundane title; but, as in so much of the poet's work, the humor here augments rather than undercuts the encounter she describes. The poem incorporates themes of love and mortality and suggests the beautiful violence of life, opening with

> The still explosions on the rocks,
> the lichens, grow
> by spreading, gray, concentric shocks.

No stranger to "shocks," Bishop mourns the inevitable loss of her beloved in the last stanza while she celebrates her presence:

> The shooting stars in your black hair
> in bright formation
> are flocking where,
> so straight, so soon?
> —Come, let me wash it in this big tin basin,
> battered and shiny like the moon.

Evoking the many precursor love poems that call upon the image of the moon, Bishop familiarizes and humanizes the poem's incipient romanticism with the "battered" "big tin basin."

Although her published letters do not mention Amy Lowell, it would be surprising if Bishop was not familiar with her famous predecessor, her close friend Robert Lowell's cousin, whom Van Wyck Brooks described in 1940 as "the prime minister of the republic of poets." Lowell, an overtly lesbian poet feared and admired by her male counterparts, composed and published many love poems in an earlier (and in some ways more open) era. "Interlude" powerfully anticipates "The Sham-

poo" with its quiet admiration, undercurrent of regret and loss, and recourse to the moon as an image of love. Near the end of the poem, Lowell's narrator affirms:

> If the sun is beautiful on bricks and pewter,
> How much more beautiful is the moon,
> Slanting down the gauffered branches of a plum-
> tree;
> The moon,
> Wavering across a bed of tulips;
> The moon,
> Still,
> Upon your face.
> You shine, Beloved,
> You and the moon.
> But which is the reflection?

More straightforward about her love and desire than Bishop, Lowell nevertheless participates in a vigorous American lesbian poetic tradition that includes such diverse precursors as Margaret Fuller, Sophie Jewett, Katharine Lee Bates, and Bishop herself.

Bishop dedicated her next volume of poetry, *Questions of Travel* (1965), to Lota. The opening poem, "Arrival at Santos," offers a typically humorous and self-deprecating voice, inviting the reader to participate in self-reflection. Upon arrival, the reader is greeted by "impractically shaped and—who knows?—self-pitying mountains" and "warehouses, / some of them painted a feeble pink, or blue." The tourist requires too much of the new (in several senses):

> . . . Oh, tourist,
> is this how this country is going to answer you
>
> and your immodest demands for a different world,
> and a better life, and complete comprehension
> of both at last, and immediately,
> after eighteen days of suspension?

The mock address to the "boy" unloading luggage, whose "boat hook" has "caught Miss Breen's / skirt!" deconstructs the romance of travel and travelers; readers learn that "Miss

Breen is about seventy, / a retired police lieutenant, six feet tall," whose "home, when she is at home, is in Glens Fall / s, New York." Bishop's wit again extends to the poet's art: the singular "s," which lands both on a new line and a new page (Bishop was famously fastidious about the production and layout of her books), delays the reader's comprehension and pokes fun at the poet herself. The poem's conclusion, however, vibrates with the ambiguity for which Bishop is well known: "We are driving to the interior." Given the images of Miss Breen and of the generic "tourist," readers are led to interrogate this "drive" to self-examination as the narrator directs her doubt toward herself and us.

As her stories and letters also reveal, the poet was concerned with social issues such as poverty, class structure, and racism, both institutionalized and individualized. Bishop's "Brazil, January 1, 1502," a profoundly serious poem about the "discovery" and rape of the New World by Portuguese explorers, undermines (and again reinforces) its intensity with personification—"in the foreground there is Sin: / five sooty dragons near some massy rocks"— and with oxymoronic images (the rocks are "threatened from underneath by moss / in lovely hell-green flames"). Green and red counterbalance each other in this poem: "lovely" nature emerges in the ironic image of a female lizard, "her wicked tale straight up and over, / red as a red-hot wire." Assuming a perspective that both acknowledges her collaboration in the exploitation by the "hard as nails" Portuguese and subverts their imaginations of "an old dream of wealth and luxury" "plus a brand-new pleasure," the poet unveils their hypocrisy and violence:

Directly after Mass . . .
. . . .
they ripped away into the hanging fabric,
each out to catch an Indian for himself,—
those maddening little women who kept calling,
calling to each other (or had the birds waked up?)
and retreating, always retreating, behind it.

"Brazil, January 1, 1502" recalls poems ranging from Lydia Sigourney's "Indian Names" to Frost's "The Vanishing Red" and severely critiques history's conquerors without shunning the poet's own implication in the violence and loss perpetrated on the indigenous peoples of the Americas—or allowing the European American reader to do so. But unlike many of her predecessors, Bishop resists representing the native inhabitants entirely as victims.

Questions of Travel reveals a stern and unrelenting (if indirect) investment in social issues, whether in such Brazilian poems as "Squatter's Children," "The Burglar of Babylon," and "Questions of Travel" or in such poems (from the second portion of the volume) as "From Trollope's Journal" and "Visits to St. Elizabeths." In the same collection there are also poems that would allow critics to categorize Bishop as a regionalist poet. Just as some of Frost's early critics unfairly used the label of "regionalist" to diminish his achievement, so many of Bishop's more overtly activist contemporaries confused a focus on place with a lack of interest in "larger" human matters. Bishop's work is often more effective in rebutting such criticisms (and is less defensive) than Frost's, and it consistently takes an oblique approach to social commentary.

The poem "Manuelzinho," for example, conducts a dispassionate scrutiny of the local with the distance of an affectionate visitor. The speaker is "a friend of the writer," but frequent snippets of dialogue by Manuelzinho intervene; the writer and the reader negotiate the difference between these perspectives. Local color suffuses this poem with life, but unlike some precursor late-nineteenth-century writing, this local color emphasizes the genial humor of the insider rather than the disparaging distance of the outsider. Manuelzinho is "the world's worst gardener since Cain"; seduced by beauty, he grows flowers in the vegetables, and when the rains destroy all, he returns to his supposed landlord (the narrator) for more seeds. The result is that

> . . . eventually you bring me
> a mystic three-legged carrot, ,
> or a pumpkin "bigger than the baby."

Wonder is Manuelzinho's customary attitude, and although the narrator observes,

> . . .You starve
> your horse and yourself
> and your dogs and family.

and disaster recurs repeatedly ("Your cow eats 'a poison grass' / and drops dead on the spot / Nobody else's does"), his innocence and optimism overwhelm the narrator, poet, and reader. Reflecting a different kind of mystery than the surreal poem "The Riverman," "Manuelzinho," like many of Bishop's dramatic poems, concludes with a pledge (here by the narrator, an alter ego for both the poet and the reader):

> You helpless, foolish man,
> I love you all I can,
> I think . . . .
> . . . .
> Again I promise to try.

Bishop's letters from this period reflect her happiness in Brazil and her love for the people, even when they are frustrating or impractical; in a letter to Moore in July 1955, she notes,

> The [cook's] baby is marvelous. Her mother dresses her, now that it's cold, in bright rose or yellow flannel garments, with bright green or yellow socks—the father helps crochet them. They are so proud of her that we have to fight every Sunday to keep them from taking her on grueling long bus trips to show her to all their relatives.

Not everyone has regarded Bishop's attitude toward the Brazilian people as uniformly affirmative; echoing Robert Lowell, the poet Frank Bidart (her younger friend), believed Bishop to be influenced by Lota's oligarchic attitude and saw a diminishment in her social consciousness, particularly reflected in "Manuelzinho," which he regards as condescending. However, many of Bishop's later poems, written after she left Brazil, indicate a strong social conscience. For example, "12 O'Clock News" renders a bitter indictment of the Vietnam War; and her last completed poem, "Pink Dog," published in 1979, offers a vicious assessment of the Brazilian class system, suggesting that she never strayed far from her earlier attitude of social critique developed at Vassar. Although Bishop was frequently accused of being apolitical, she expresses her views clearly in a 1956 interview in Brazil: "Every good writer takes into account the social problems of his times . . . and in one way or another, all good poetry reflects those problems" (quoted in *Conversations with Elizabeth Bishop*). In another Brazilian interview in 1964, she praises her adopted country for its racial harmony and expresses optimism for the United States. But while discussing "the Marxist '30s" in a 1966 interview with Ashley Brown of *Shenandoah,* she complicates her stance on the relation of politics and aesthetics: "I was always opposed to political thinking as such for writers"; that is, unlike such contemporaries as Muriel Rukeyser and Edna St. Vincent Millay, Bishop believed that poetry should not represent explicit comments on political issues. As John Palattella observes, "During the thirties she suggested in shades and shadows the political necessity of avoiding the prisons of doctrinaire perspective and masculine heroism." Given her interest in travel and her profound concern with cultural difference, Bishop is beginning to be considered in the context of postcolonial theory; Mary Louise Pratt's observation in *Imperial Eyes: Travel Writing and Transculturation* that affluent women's most important goal when traveling was not, like their male counterparts, to acquire objects but "first and foremost to collect and possess themselves" applies well to Bishop.

In the time between the publication of *Questions of Travel* in 1965 and *Complete Poems* in April 1969, Bishop continued her meandering lifestyle, which included teaching for a semester at the University of Washington in Seattle—her first such attempt, a necessary vocation for the impecunious private poet—traveling to Europe a second time with Lota, and again taking up residence briefly in New York. It was there that one of the most tragic events in a life scarred by tragedy occurred: Lota's death, possibly a suicide, from a drug overdose. For a variety of reasons, including Lota's political work in Brazil (which had made her physically and psychologically ill) and Bishop's new love relationship with a much younger woman in Seattle, the pair had been growing apart. Bishop would feel the trauma of Lota's death for the rest of her life, and soon realizing that she could no longer live in Brazil, she decided to settle in San Francisco with Suzanne Bowen (a pseudonym commonly used for Bishop's Seattle lover). She arrived there on Christmas morning of 1967. Fortunately for Bishop, Bowen handled all of the details of daily life, from finding an apartment to doing the writer's taxes, with ease and without fuss.

Bishop's first *Complete Poems* (1969), for which she was awarded the National Book Award, offers several new poems, including a series of prose poems. Indicating a willingness to be somewhat more personally revealing, "Giant Snail" suggests the writer's continuing vulnerability and self-protectiveness when the snail (the narrator) avers,

> I give the impression of mysterious ease, but it is only with the greatest effort of my will that I can rise above the smallest stones and sticks. And I must not let myself be distracted by those rough spears of grass. Don't touch them. Draw back. Withdrawal is always best.

In conclusion the snail envisions himself from both the inside and the outside and makes assertions that could as easily refer to the poet herself:

> I know my shell is beautiful, and high, and glazed, and shining. I know it well, although I have not seen it. Its curled white lip is of the finest enamel. Inside, it is as smooth as silk, and I, I fill it to perfection.
>
> My wide wake shines, now it is growing dark. I leave a lovely opalescent ribbon: I know this.
>
> But O! I am too big. I feel it. Pity me.

Again Bishop's self-deprecating humor underlies these lines; like many of her friends, the poet Robert Duncan highlights this strength: "She was the sort of person who had the twinkle of humor always in her eyes and [loved] an amusing situation." But in public Bishop never asked for pity, and Duncan remarks about this time in her life (quoted in *Remembering*):

> There never was any letting down of Elizabeth's hair, no self-exposure [at her parties]. . . . There had to be this amused sharing of knowing looks and the kind of indirect jokes. Elizabeth's form of humor is one that I always associated with people that ride through a really hard life.

This tough, tragic vision appears again and again in her poems, from "House Guest," where no one can "cheer" the "sad seamstress" protagonist, not even with "a dress, a drink, / roast chicken, or fried fish—" to "Trouvée," which describes a hen run over "on West 4th Street / in the middle of summer." Relishing the disjunction of a hen in the city (and playing on the pretentiousness of the title, which suggests a gallery display of found objects), the narrator moves to characteristic gallows humor: "She was a white hen / —red-and-white now, of course."

After a brief return with Bowen to the house she had purchased and restored in Brazil during happier times, Bishop separated from her new lover and moved to the Boston area, where, with the recommendation of Robert Lowell, she taught at Harvard for several years and continued to travel, on various trips visiting, among other places, Ecuador, the Galápagos Islands, Peru, Sweden, Finland, Russia, Norway, Portugal, and Maine. During this time she also coedited *An Anthology of Twentieth-Century Brazilian Poetry* (1972), won several more awards for her poetry, including the Neustadt International Prize for Literature (the first American and first woman to do so), and published her acclaimed *Geography III* (1976). This volume of poetry contains some of her finest work, including "In the Waiting Room," "Crusoe in England," "The Moose," and "One Art." One of her most discussed poems, the first of these synthesizes actual experience with imagination to describe a child's coming to self-knowledge:

> . . . you are an *I,*
> you are an *Elizabeth,*
> . . . .
> I scarcely dared to look
> to see what it was I was.

At the same time, the poem gestures unmistakably toward the reader and the process of reading, and it invites the reader to understand the uses of the "figure" of woman in the poetic enterprise and to resist facile, literal readings that conflate "inside" with "outside."

Reemphasizing her interest in both inner and outer travel, in *Geography III* Bishop again explores the geography of the psyche. In "Crusoe in England" humor again underscores the complexity of the definition of "home." In discussing his own "self-pity," Crusoe reflects:

> . . . I told myself
> "Pity should begin at home." So the more
> pity I felt, the more I felt at home.

Similarly, in a sardonic passage that echoes Bishop's own grinding experience with alcohol-

ism, Crusoe resorts to making "home-brew," which inspires him to "whoop and dance among the goats" and to contemplate, "Home-made, home-made! But aren't we all?" This question gains poignancy in the context of Bishop's troubled (and often absent) home life as both a child and an adult, encouraging readers to consider the contingency of experience and the contingent (rather than refined or polished) quality of daily life. Even her masterpiece "One Art" reflects the philosophy of making do, of the willed revision of experience ("the art of losing isn't hard to master") into "art," and suggests Frost's "momentary stay against confusion" and Dickinson's assertion that "After great pain, a formal feeling comes—." Without such "mastery," Bishop repeatedly suggests, comes "disaster."

Soon after *Geography III* was published, Bishop retired from teaching at Harvard, although she taught one more semester at New York University. These last few years were difficult ones for the poet, in part because of personal losses. Moore died in 1972 after a series of incapacitating strokes. Bishop also became temporarily estranged from Lowell, whose death in 1977 devastated her, as her moving elegy, "North Haven," suggests. At the same time, her alcoholism, always a problem, intensified, although she was fortunate to have the devotion of Alice Methfessel, whom she met when the younger woman was working at Harvard, and the poet Frank Bidart, who became her literary executor.

On October 6, 1979, Bishop died from a cerebral aneurysm at her home at Lewis Wharf in Boston. Richard Wilbur, poet laureate of the United States between 1987 and 1988, recalls a conversation shortly before her death about Christianity, in which Bishop asked him about his beliefs and "began mentioning points of Christian doctrine that she thought it intolerable to believe" (quoted in *Remembering*). He concludes that she was left with "the questions, if not the answers, of a person with a religious temperament." The day after her death Bishop was scheduled to give a benefit reading for a Boston literary magazine, and her friends decided that the most fitting memorial was for them each to read a selection of their favorite poems by the writer. Robert Pinsky, who would become laureate during the period 1997–2000, recalls the "quality of celebration" at the reading, where "there was laughter" and "people . . . just read these incredibly beautiful and amusing poems." Unlike other poets, whose work, he says, is often elevated by the power of their personality and whose reputation diminished after their deaths, Bishop has "a pure reputation based upon the quality of her work, and so when the personality is withdrawn, no artificial support is withdrawn" (quoted in *Remembering*). This reputation has been enhanced by the publication of *The Complete Poems: 1927–1979* (1983), *The Collected Prose* (1984), and *One Art* (1994), her selected letters.

MORE THAN ONE ART: BISHOP'S OTHER VOICES

Although some of the essays and stories were published much earlier, including some in *The New Yorker,* the prose works in *Collected Prose* reveal a previously unseen side of Bishop. Hammer maintains that Bishop's prose suggests her interest in the "mixing of discourses" and the "generic hybrid" that also characterize her verse. Not unlike her poetry, the prose is suffused with humor and takes on a variety of subjects ranging from travel to family, art, and politics. The prose narratives, however, reveal much more about this uncommonly private writer's personal history and her attitude toward it. Moving from what Lorrie Goldensohn identifies as the "metaphors of shell, skin, screen, or mask" in her poetry, in her prose Bishop explores the delight and pain she felt in the experiences that provide

the basis for "Primer Class," "The Country Mouse," and "Gwendolyn." "Gregorio Valdes," "Mercedes Hospital," "To the Botequim & Back," and "The Diary of 'Helena Morley'" (her introduction to the Brazilian text she translated) demonstrate extraordinary skill in regionalist narrative. The first of these stories, a memorial to the eponymous painter, combines witty descriptions of the paradoxes in his life and art with a delicate poignancy. Never sentimental—Bishop acknowledges that "Gregorio was not a great painter at all"—she nevertheless appreciates, and conveys to the reader, the painter's gift: "Surely anything that is impossible for others to achieve by effort, that is dangerous to imitate, and yet, like natural virtue, must be both admired and imitated, always remains mysterious." Similarly, in a terse, precise, and paradoxical sentence she illuminates the "saintly qualities" of Miss Mamie in "Mercedes Hospital": "It is the absence of tenderness that is the consoling thing about her."

Bishop's prose might be placed in the tradition of New England regionalism emblematized in the precursor fiction of Sarah Orne Jewett, Rose Terry Cooke, and Mary Wilkins Freeman, which also deployed humor (often gallows humor, as in Cooke's "Freedom Wheeler's Controversy with Providence"), pictorial imagery (as in Jewett's *The Country of the Pointed Firs*), and an understanding of human experience as fundamentally "awful but cheerful"— that is, as contingent and mixed but amenable to moments of illumination and joy. Bishop acknowledges her regionalist strain in letters to friends, writing that (as quoted in *Elizabeth Bishop's Poetics of Intimacy,* by Victoria Harrison) although Sarah Orne Jewett's work was "dated," it is

still sometimes marvellous stuff and worth reading. . . . I was appalled when I recently read a whole book—I'm sure anyone who read my story ["In the Village"] would think I was imitating her shamelessly—whole phrases, even—it is very strange; I had really never laid eyes on the ones that are like mine.

Although her feelings about this resemblance were ambivalent and she tried to distinguish herself from Jewett, she recognizes her predecessor's power.

Another kind of pleasure emerges in one of her most moving essays, "Efforts of Affection: A Memoir of Marianne Moore," which was written between 1969 and 1979 but first published in the May 1983 issue of *Vanity Fair,* after the deaths of both writers. The title is taken from a Moore poem; in the narrative Bishop begins by recalling their initial meeting, arranged by the Vassar College librarian, Miss Borden, who had known Moore since childhood. Bishop speaks of her mentor with both reverence and amused appreciation as she recounts how their meeting was scheduled for "the bench at the right of the door leading to the reading room of the New York Public Library." Miss Borden had arranged several such meetings that "had somehow failed to please," and Bishop says, "I learned later that if Miss Moore really expected *not* to like would-be acquaintances, she arranged to meet them at the Information Booth in Grand Central Station—no place to sit down, and, if necessary, an instant getaway was possible." Bishop captures Moore's eccentricity and gentle self-assertiveness in a description of how, when the two next met for a day at the circus, Moore persuaded her young friend to distract the adult elephants with bread while with "strong nail scissors" she snipped off some hairs of a baby elephant ("As I probably knew, elephant hairs grow only on the tops of the heads of very young elephants"). Moore needed the hairs to repair a bracelet given to her by her brother.

Bishop describes Marianne's mother, Mrs. Moore, with equal insight, fondness, and humor and provides background for her mentor's aesthetic: "Her manner toward Marianne was that of a kindly, self-controlled parent who felt that she had to take a firm line, that her daughter [by that time in her late forties] might be given to flightiness or—an equal sin, in her eyes—mistakes in grammar." Mrs. Moore and her daughter were both, in Bishop's phrase, "overfastidious"; several novels of the period, including one by Bishop's Vassar classmate Mary McCarthy, "were taken down to the cellar and burned in the furnace." Bishop's account also proves to be self-revealing and characteristically self-deprecatory:

I published a very bad short story a year or two after I knew the Moores and I was reprimanded by both of them for having used the word "spit." (Two or three years later I was scolded for having used "water closet" in a poem, but by then I had turned obstinate.)

Reflecting on later feminist critics of Moore who seemed ungenerous, Bishop comes to her friend's defense:

One of [these writers] described her as a "poet who controlled panic by presenting it as whimsy." Whimsy is sometimes there, of course, and so is humor (a gift these critics sadly seem to lack). Surely there is an element of mortal panic and fear underlying all works of art? Even so, one wonders how much of Marianne's poetry the feminist critics have read.

In all, Bishop appreciates—in the best and most complex sense of the word—the friendship, advice, and (though she never uses the word) love she received from the Moores.

As her response to feminist critics' views of Moore suggests, Bishop possessed a complex relationship to feminism. On the one hand, she claimed in an interview with Joan Zyda, "I've always considered myself a strong feminist" and was nettled by suggestions to the contrary. Bidart observes, "She was passionately feminist, and could be bitter about how the world had treated her because she was a woman" (quoted in *Remembering*). In spite of angering many feminists, Bishop said that her feminism dictated that she not appear in "woman-only" anthologies and that such segregation reinforced women's second-class status; in part, this stance may have been a reaction to her concern about being denominated "sentimental" ("feminine") in an American poetic tradition that by the time she was writing had become insistently masculine. Although she was also critical of the privilege of many middle-class women poets, in a 1974 interview (quoted in *Conversations*) Bishop lashes out at sexist criticism of women writers:

> You read a very favorable review of a writer, saying she is very clever and talented and you think this writer must be wonderful. Then, at the end, it says, "Best book written by a woman," and all that has gone before loses its value. . . . I like my anthologies, all the arts, mixed: sexes, colors, and races. Art is art and should have nothing to do with gender.

Bishop's friend James Merrill points out in "Elizabeth Bishop (1911–1979)," the poet's "instinctive, modest, lifelong impersonations of an ordinary woman." As critics have emphasized and the poet herself acknowledged, gender framed both her experience and her art in important ways. In an interview with George Starbuck in 1977, she admits, "Sometimes I think if I had been born a man I probably would have written more. Dared more, or been able to spend more time at it."

On the other hand, Bishop was a deeply closeted lesbian who negotiated (more or less successfully at various times) the profound misogyny and homophobia of her cultural moment. Grouping Bishop with Gertrude Stein and Adrienne Rich in her recent book about the lesbian tradition in American poetry (which, she argues, is fundamentally based in the subjects of love, war, and place), Margaret Dickie highlights the need of the lesbian poet "to confront a culturally encouraged silence." Such a cultural censorship, she says, prompted literary experimentation in a particular form: "The hiding and secrecy were part of the pleasure of the expression, part of the pains they took in their poetry. Thus, these poets learned to write in code, to create texts with powerful subtexts, even to create the illusion of a common language." Being a lesbian to Bishop meant that she would, as Hammer notes, "create a relation (different from the one in confessional poetry) in which it would be possible for poet and reader to be alone together, safe from public exposure." Thus, Bishop's terse originality, her reticence, emerged not only from her family background of mediated silence and from her alcoholism, but also from the cultural milieu requiring, at least, transformation of "different" and potentially subversive erotic perspectives. During her lifetime Bishop kept private a wide range of materials—letters, diaries, notebooks, drafts of poems—that are now available and that have shed increasing light on the life and work of this complex writer, including the untitled lesbian poem that begins, "It is marvellous to wake up together."

Merrill underscores "Bishop's preference for the happy ending, or the ruefully cheerful one." In spite of the tragedies of her life, Bishop's later years in particular reflected an undercurrent of optimism about the future. A 1970 interview, "Poetry As a Way of Life," relates this perspective forcefully. Speaking about gendered reception of poetry by women, in an interview with Regina Colônia (quoted in *Conversations*) Bishop affirms her confidence and expresses an abiding understanding:

> There are those still who judge us prejudicially along those romantic lines. Yet one must take those persons with a touch of humor because, if not, one will embitter life itself. . . . In the United States the younger generation has already achieved equality between the sexes. . . . And all over the whole world . . . there is the tendency to transcend such prejudice.

Here and elsewhere, Bishop emerges as a poet of the world, not merely of a region or nation, in a time that needed such global perspectives. Bishop's observation about her beloved village of Ouro Prêto in this interview further gestures toward her ethically informed aesthetic and her social principles: "What matters is durability—here things last."

Selected Bibliography

WORKS OF ELIZABETH BISHOP

POETRY

North & South. Boston: Houghton Mifflin, 1946.

Poems: North & South—A Cold Spring. Boston: Houghton Mifflin, 1955.

Poems. London: Chatto and Windus, 1956.

Brazil. New York: Time, 1962. (In Life World Library Series.)

Questions of Travel. New York: Farrar, Straus and Giroux, 1965.

Selected Poems. London: Chatto and Windus, 1967.

The Complete Poems. New York: Farrar, Straus and Giroux, 1969.

Geography III. New York: Farrar, Straus and Giroux, 1976.

The Complete Poems, 1927–1979. New York: Farrar, Straus and Giroux, 1983.

COLLECTED WORKS

The Collected Prose. Edited by Robert Giroux. New York: Farrar, Straus and Giroux, 1984.

One Art: Letters. Selected and edited by Robert Giroux. New York: Farrar, Straus and Giroux, 1994.

Exchanging Hats: Paintings. Edited by William Benton. New York: Farrar, Straus and Giroux, 1996.

OTHER WORKS

The Diary of "Helena Morley." Translated by Elizabeth Bishop. New York: Farrar, Straus and Cudahy, 1957; reprinted with new foreword, New York: Ecco Press, 1977.

An Anthology of Twentieth-Century Brazilian Poetry. Edited by Elizabeth Bishop and Emanuel Brasil. Middletown, Conn.: Wesleyan University Press, 1972.

MANUSCRIPT PAPERS AND CORRESPONDENCE

Papers, 1925–1979. Elizabeth Bishop Collection. Vassar College Libraries, Poughkeepsie, N.Y.

Bishop–Marianne Moore Correspondence, Papers of Marianne Moore. Series V: Correspondence. Rosenbach Museum and Library, Philadelphia, Pa.

Bishop–Robert Lowell Correspondence. 1947–1970. Robert Lowell Papers. Houghton Library, Harvard University, Cambridge, Mass.

CRITICAL AND BIOGRAPHICAL STUDIES

Bidart, Frank. "On Elizabeth Bishop." In *Elizabeth Bishop and Her Art.* Edited by Lloyd Schwartz and Sybil P. Estess. Ann Arbor: University of Michigan Press, 1983. Pp. 214–215.

Brooks, Van Wyck. *New England: Indian Summer, 1865–1915.* New York: E. P. Dutton, 1940.

Cameron, Sharon. *Choosing Not Choosing: Dickinson's Fascicles.* Chicago: University of Chicago Press, 1992.

Colwell, Anne. *Inscrutable Houses: Metaphors of the Body in the Poems of Elizabeth Bishop.* Tuscaloosa: University of Alabama Press, 1997.

Costello, Bonnie. *Elizabeth Bishop: Questions of Mastery.* Cambridge, Mass.: Harvard University Press, 1991.

Dickie, Margaret. *Stein, Bishop, & Rich: Lyrics of Love, War, & Place.* Chapel Hill: University of North Carolina Press, 1997.

Diehl, Joanne Feit. *Elizabeth Bishop and Marianne Moore: The Psychodynamics of Creativity.* Princeton, N.J.: Princeton University Press, 1993.

Doreski, C. K. *Elizabeth Bishop: The Restraints of Language.* New York: Oxford University Press, 1993.

Edelman, Lee. "The Geography of Gender: Elizabeth Bishop's 'In the Waiting Room.'" *Contemporary Literature* 26, no. 2:179–196 (1985).

Erkkila, Betsy. *The Wicked Sisters: Women Poets, Literary History, and Discord.* New York: Oxford University Press, 1994.

Ferry, Anne. "The Anthologizing of Elizabeth Bishop." *Raritan* 19, no. 3:37–64 (winter 2000).

Fountain, Gary, and Peter Brazeau. *Remembering Elizabeth Bishop: An Oral Biography*. Amherst: University of Massachusetts Press, 1994.

Franklin, R. W. *The Poems of Emily Dickinson*. Variorum edition. 3 vols. Cambridge, Mass.: Belknap Press of Harvard University Press, 1998.

Frost, Robert. *The Letters of Robert Frost to Louis Untermeyer*. Edited by Louis Untermeyer. New York: Henry Holt, 1963.

———. *Selected Letters of Robert Frost*. Edited by Lawrance Thompson. New York: Henry Holt, 1964.

———. *Collected Poems, Prose, & Plays*. Edited by Richard Poirier and Mark Richardson. New York: Library of America, 1995.

Gardner, Thomas. *Regions of Unlikeness: Explaining Contemporary Poetry*. Lincoln: University of Nebraska Press, 1999.

Gilbert, Roger. "Framing Water: Historical Knowledge in Elizabeth Bishop and Adrienne Rich." *Twentieth Century Literature* 43, no. 2:144–161 (summer 1997).

Goldensohn, Lorrie. *Elizabeth Bishop: The Biography of a Poetry*. New York: Columbia University Press, 1992.

Harrison, Victoria. *Elizabeth Bishop's Poetics of Intimacy*. Cambridge: Cambridge University Press, 1993.

Hicok, Bethany. "Elizabeth Bishop's 'Queer Birds': Vassar, *Con Spirito,* and the Romance of Female Community." *Contemporary Literature* 40, no. 2:286–310 (1999).

Jarrell, Randall. "Poets." In his *Poetry and the Age*. New York: Knopf, 1953. Pp. 234–235.

Kalstone, David. *Five Temperaments: Elizabeth Bishop, Robert Lowell, James Merrill, Adrienne Rich, John Ashbery*. New York: Oxford University Press, 1977.

———. *Becoming a Poet: Elizabeth Bishop with Marianne Moore and Robert Lowell*. Edited by Robert Hemenway. Ann Arbor: University of Michigan Press, 2001.

Kilcup, Karen L. *Robert Frost and Feminine Literary Tradition*. Ann Arbor: University of Michigan Press, 1998.

Lentricchia, Frank. *Modernist Quartet*. New York: Cambridge University Press, 1994.

Lombardi, Marilyn May, ed. *Elizabeth Bishop: The Geography of Gender*. Charlottesville: University Press of Virginia, 1993.

———. *The Body and the Song: Elizabeth Bishop's Poetics*. Carbondale: Southern Illinois University Press, 1995.

Lowell, Amy. "Interlude." In her *The Complete Poetical Works of Amy Lowell*. Boston: Houghton Mifflin, 1955.

Lowell, Robert. "Thomas, Bishop, and Williams." *Sewanee Review* 55, no. 3:493–503 (July–September 1947).

———. "Elizabeth Bishop's *North & South*." In *Robert Lowell: Collected Prose*. Edited by Robert Giroux. New York: Farrar, Straus and Giroux, 1987. Pp. 76–80.

Mann, Charles Edward. "Elizabeth Bishop and Revision: A Spiritual Act." *American Poetry Review* 25, no. 2:43–50 (March/April 1996).

McCabe, Susan. *Elizabeth Bishop: Her Poetics of Loss*. University Park: Pennsylvania State University Press, 1994.

Menides, Laura Jehn, and Angela C. Dorenkamp, eds. *"In Worcester, Massachusetts": Essays on Elizabeth Bishop*. New York: Peter Lang, 1999.

Merrill, James. "Elizabeth Bishop (1911–1979)." *The New York Review of Books,* December 6, 1979, p. 6.

———. "Afterword." In David Kalstone, *Becoming a Poet: Elizabeth Bishop with Marianne Moore and Robert Lowell*. Ann Arbor: University of Michigan Press, 2001. Pp. 251–262.

Millier, Brett C. *Elizabeth Bishop: Life and the Memory of It*. Berkeley: University of California Press, 1993.

Moore, Marianne. "Archaically New." In *Trial Balances*. Edited by Ann Winslow. New York: Macmillan, 1935. Pp. 82–83.

Morris, Timothy. *Becoming Canonical in American Poetry*. Urbana: University of Illinois Press, 1995.

Oliveira, Carmen L. *Rare and Commonplace Flowers: The Story of Elizabeth Bishop and Lota de Macedo Soares*. New Brunswick: Rutgers University Press, 2002.

Palattella, John. "'That Sense of Constant Readjustment': The Great Depression and the Provisional Politics of Elizabeth Bishop's *North & South*." *Contemporary Literature* 34, no. 1:18–43 (1993).

Paz, Octavio. "Elizabeth Bishop; or, The Power of Reticence." *World Literature Today* 61, no. 1:15–16 (winter 1977).

Pratt, Mary Louise. *Imperial Eyes: Travel Writing and Transculturation.* London: Routledge, 1992.

Roman, Camille. *Elizabeth Bishop's World War II– Cold War View.* New York: Palgrave, 2001.

Schwartz, Lloyd. "One Art: The Poetry of Elizabeth Bishop, 1971–1976." *Ploughshares* 3, nos. 3–4:30–52 (1977).

Schweik, Susan. *A Gulf So Deeply Cut: American Women Poets and the Second World War.* Madison: University of Wisconsin Press, 1991.

Travisano, Thomas. "The Elizabeth Bishop Phenomenon." *New Literary History* 26, no. 4:903–930 (autumn 1995).

———. *Midcentury Quartet: Bishop, Lowell, Jarrell, Berryman, and the Making of a Postmodern Aesthetic.* Charlottesville: University Press of Virginia, 1999.

Unterecker, John. "Elizabeth Bishop." In *American Writers.* Supplement 1, Part 1. New York: Scribners, 1979. Pp. 72–97.

Vendler, Helen. "Domestication, Domesticity, and the Otherworldly." *World Literature Today* 61, no. 1:23–28 (winter 1977).

Wolosky, Shira. "Representing Other Voices: Rhetorical Perspective in Elizabeth Bishop." *Style* 29, no. 1:1–17 (spring 1995).

REVIEWS

Ashbery, John. Review of *The Complete Poems. New York Times Book Review,* June 1, 1969, pp. 8, 25.

Bloom, Harold. "Books Considered." *New Republic,* February 5, 1977, pp. 29–30. (Review of *Geography III.*)

Davison, Peter. "Sandpiper Poetry." *The Atlantic,* May 1983, p. 101. (Review of *The Complete Poems, 1927–1979.*)

Hammer, Langdon. "Useless Concentration: Life and Work in Elizabeth Bishop's Letters and Poems." *American Literary History* 9, no. 1:162–180 (spring 1997). (Review of *One Art: Letters.*)

Hardwick, Elizabeth. "The Perfectionist." *New Republic,* March 19, 1984, pp. 32–35. (Review of *The Collected Prose.*)

Lehman, David. "The 'Unerring Muse.'" *Newsweek,* March 14, 1983, p. 72. (Review of *The Complete Poems, 1927–1979.*)

McClatchy, J. D. "Letters from a Lonely Poet." *New York Times Book Review,* April 17, 1994, pp. 1, 22–23. (Review of *One Art: Letters.*)

Moore, Marianne. "A Modest Expert." *The Nation,* September 28, 1946, p. 354. (Review of *North & South.*)

Moss, Howard. "A Long Voyage Home." *The New Yorker,* April 1, 1985, pp. 104–112. (Review of *The Collected Prose.*)

Oktenberg, Adrian. "The Letter and the Spirit." *Women's Review of Books* 11, nos. 10–11:27–29 (July 1994). (Review of *One Art: Letters.*)

Pinsky, Robert. "Geographer of the Self." *New Republic,* April 4, 1983, pp. 24–28. (Review of *The Complete Poems, 1927–1970.*)

Schwartz, Lloyd. "One Art: The Poetry of Elizabeth Bishop, 1971–1976." *Ploughshares* 3, nos. 3–4:30–52 (1977).

Shetley, Vernon. "On Elizabeth Bishop." *Raritan* 14, no. 3:151–163 (winter 1995). (Review of *One Art: Letters.*)

INTERVIEWS

Monteiro, George, ed. *Conversations with Elizabeth Bishop.* Jackson: University Press of Mississippi, 1996. (Includes interviews by Ashley Brown, Regina Colônia, George Starbuck, and Joan Zyda.)

—*KAREN L. KILCUP*

Kate Chopin

1850–1904

KATE CHOPIN SPENT the first half of her life preparing to write and the second half making up for lost time. In a literary career that spanned no more than fourteen years, Chopin produced three novels, more than a hundred short stories, and numerous poems, essays, and translations. She started writing at the age of thirty-nine, when her husband died, drawing primarily on her life in Louisiana. As a result, she was labeled a southern regionalist early in her career with the publication of *At Fault* (1890), her first novel. Despite the literary fame she achieved, Chopin grew to dislike the designation of regionalist as she developed into an artist with her own personal vision, incorporating psychological realism into stories on unconventional subjects, such as adultery, featuring strong, defiant women. Chopin, an emotionally reserved person, wrote daring fiction, exploring human relationships fully and honestly. Her characters survived unhappy marriages and spoke to each other uncivilly when angry, but they also cherished their children and loved with abandon. Ironically, her best work, *The Awakening* (1899), precipitated the decline of her literary career—critics could not accept a female protagonist with two lovers and no sense of guilt. For many years after her death, scholars ignored Chopin, only to revive her later as a southern regionalist in the 1930s after the publication of Donald Rankin's *Kate Chopin and Her Creole Stories* (1932). Subsequently, scholars have discovered a multitude of literary influences in her work, including romanticism, realism, naturalism, feminism, and transcendentalism. *The Awakening*'s theme of a woman's innate yearning for self-realization brought

Chopin posthumous fame as a pioneer feminist. As scholarship reveals the universality of her characters and the themes she explores in her fiction, Chopin takes her place as a major figure in American literature.

EARLY LIFE AND THE CIVIL WAR

Kate O'Flaherty Chopin was born on February 8, 1850, in St. Louis, Missouri, the daughter of Eliza Faris and Thomas O'Flaherty. Eliza Faris was only sixteen when, in 1844, she married O'Flaherty, a widower twenty-three years her senior and the father of a young boy named George. O'Flaherty, ambitious and hard working, had emigrated from Ireland in 1823 and since become a well-established businessman, owning a boat store and real estate holdings. Together they had two children who lived to adulthood: Thomas Jr. and Kate.

The O'Flahertys, a Catholic, bourgeois family, lived in a large, attractive home with Chopin's grandmother, numerous young aunts and uncles, and several slaves. Critics surmise that Chopin had a good relationship with her father, who encouraged her innate curiosity and laid the foundation for her free and rebellious spirit. Her mother, though not well educated, was confident and poised. She spoke with a Creole accent that would later make it easy for her daughter to incorporate Creole dialect in her fiction. Chopin's father died in a railroad accident in 1855 when she was five years old, leaving her mother a young widow with a large estate. She never remarried because widows were generally respected, and she was financially secure. The O'Flaherty household became a matriarchy, run by several confident, independent widows: Chopin's mother, grandmother, and great-grandmother, Victoire Charleville.

Chopin attended the St. Louis Academy of the Sacred Heart through the 1850s and 1860s, sometimes boarding and never spending a full year at school until she was ten. When at school, the nuns held her to rigorous standards as they emphasized literature, writing, science, and needlework. With her fellow student and closest friend, Kitty Garesché, Chopin developed into a voracious and discerning reader. According to Garesché, some of the books they enjoyed together were *Grimm's Fairy Tales, Dickens for Little Folks, Queechy, The Wide Wide World, Zaidee,* and *Pilgrims Progress.* When at home, she was taught by her great-grandmother, and Chopin learned to love music, speak French, and delight in colorful stories of local and family history. Victoire Charleville exposed Chopin to the personal foibles and follies of men and women in a nonjudgmental fashion, which may account for the characteristic realism of Chopin's fiction writing as an adult.

When the Civil War broke out in 1861, Chopin was eleven years old. The O'Flahertys supported the Confederacy, and Chopin's half-brother, George, joined the Confederate troops. In a city torn between secessionists and unionists, violent outbursts were not uncommon and people lived in constant fear, particularly Confederate sympathizers. Like many people, Chopin suffered traumatic losses during the war. The family of Kitty Garesché was banished by Union authorities, Chopin's great-grandmother died, and her half-brother succumbed to typhoid fever as he was making his way home to St. Louis after his discharge. The tremendous impact of the war on Chopin is most evident in her short stories, which frequently concern young men futilely sacrificing their lives to war while their loved ones mourn them. In "The Return of Alcibiade," an old man waits for his long-dead son to return from the war; a widow

in "A Lady of Bayou St. John" spends her life mourning the death of her husband, a Confederate soldier. It is worth noting that Chopin never romanticizes the brutality and grief of that time.

A LITERARY DEBUTANTE

Chopin graduated from Sacred Heart in June 1868. During her last years there, Madam Mary O'Meara of the Sacred Heart nuns encouraged her to write about death in order to work through her grief. This gifted teacher stressed the importance of literature to all her students and cultivated Chopin's literary leanings and ironic sense of humor. Under Madam O'Meara's influence, Chopin began keeping a commonplace book in 1867 in which she copied passages from history books and wrote essays on such topics as "Reigning Sovereigns of Europe" and "Christian Art." She also took notes on books she was reading, such as Henry Wadsworth Longfellow's *Hyperion,* Edward George Bulwer's *The Novel,* Anna Brownell Jameson's *Sketches of Art,* and Lady Blessington's *Conversations with Byron.* In this last book Chopin focused on the discussion of Madame de Staél's strong, passionate female characters. In her critiques, Chopin insisted on clarity in other writers, a standard to which she held herself when she began writing professionally.

Despite her Catholic upbringing and education at Sacred Heart, Chopin had very little to do with religion once she graduated. She also had less to do with literature than she would have preferred. In 1868 she entered St. Louis society as a debutante, and her commonplace book became primarily a diary for recording her personal thoughts. She continued to read women authors, copy passages, and record her literary opinions, but in her diary she complains of too little time for reading and writing: "parties, operas, concerts, skating and amusements ad infinitum have so taken up all my time that my dear reading and writing that I love so well have suffered much neglect." In her later fiction, Chopin would revisit this conflict between a woman's desires and her obligations, along with the issue of women's prescribed role in society.

In 1869, after a three-week trip to New Orleans with family and friends, Chopin wrote what is believed to be her earliest surviving story, "Emancipation. A Life Fable." It was inspired by her trip to New Orleans, where Chopin started smoking cigarettes, experienced the sensuality of a warm southern climate, and discovered the joy of solitude. The story focuses on an unidentified animal living in a cage with all of its needs met. One day, when the door of its cage opens accidentally, the animal flees and discovers a full life of joy and suffering. The story illustrates Chopin's view of young women entering society, protected and prevented from living a full life.

MARRIED LIFE

During her debutante season, Chopin met her future husband, Oscar Chopin of Louisiana, a handsome and ambitious young man of French descent. True to her reserved nature, nothing is mentioned about their courtship in her diary, but it appears to have been a marriage of love: she describes Oscar as the "right man" and her wedding day as "the happiest in my life." After their honeymoon, to Germany, Switzerland, and France, the Chopins lived in New Orleans, also the home of Oscar's widowed father, Dr. Jean Baptiste Chopin, who died soon after the young couple set up housekeeping. Oscar worked as a cotton factor and commission agent, and the newlyweds lived in the not-so-prestigious neighborhood known as "the Irish Channel." Later, they moved to a better address uptown.

The Chopins had few friends in New Orleans, so they traveled often by boat to Natchitoches ("Nak-i-tush") Parish to visit Oscar's relatives. Chopin also visited her mother numerous times

in St. Louis. In fact, two of her children were born there. She spent summers at Grand Isle while Oscar worked in New Orleans. He visited his family on weekends, an arrangement that was common among Creoles at the time. Many years later, Chopin would draw on these years when writing *The Awakening,* which takes place in New Orleans and Grand Isle. It was also not uncommon for Chopin to take long walks alone in New Orleans smoking cigarettes, an activity considered improper for women. She recorded her observations during these walks, particularly the hustle and bustle along the riverfront and Canal Street.

Despite her obvious inclination to write, the next ten years were consumed with the domestic responsibilities of raising children and managing a home. Chopin gave birth to six children between 1871 and 1879: Jean Baptiste, Oscar Charles, George Francis, Frederick, Felix Andrew, and Lélia. All of her children lived to adulthood. Marriage and motherhood opened up new ways of feeling and being for Chopin that she apparently welcomed. Unlike her most famous female protagonist, Edna Pontellier in *The Awakening,* Chopin always put her children first, without resentment. She even took a sensual, almost primal, delight in the birth of her first child, Jean. In 1894 she wrote in her diary, "The sensation with which I touched my lips and my fingertips to his soft flesh only comes once to a mother. It must be the pure animal sensation: nothing spiritual could be so real—so poignant."

Oscar prospered in his business until the late 1870s, when cotton crops were repeatedly poor. This probably came as no surprise to Chopin, who, unlike most wives, was privy to information about Oscar's business. In 1879 the Chopins moved to Cloutierville ("Cloochyville"), a small town in Natchitoches Parish, where Oscar and his family owned land. There Oscar bought and operated a general store while managing his share of the family property. Chopin described

Cloutierville in her story "For Marse Chou-choute" as "two long rows of very old frame houses, facing each other closely across a dusty roadway." It was simple and bland, but the surrounding countryside of plantations, forests, and grass was appealing and provided the local color, which would later put Chopin on the national literary map as a regionalist.

Chopin's life in what is also known as Cane River country consisted of caring for children, running a household with several servants, visiting at the general store, playing cards, riding her horse, and attending local dances and parties. She found time to study her new interests—anthropology and biology—reading Charles Darwin, Thomas Huxley, and Herbert Spencer. Chopin also enjoyed observing people at close range, finding her neighbors and their personal dramas intriguing. She seemed to make the most of her time there, and all these diversions would provide her with material for her future stories—the dances teemed with romance and the general store exuded gossip. Nevertheless, biographers believe Chopin never fully enjoyed living in what she called the "little French village."

She remained an outsider with what many considered strange ways. Although she was Catholic, spoke French, and could claim some local cousins as relatives on her mother's side, she rode her horse astride rather than sidesaddle, wore fashionable clothes in loud colors (lavender was a favorite), and smoked. And it did not help that the locals still despised Oscar's father for running off to France with his family during the Civil War and prospering financially. Still, Oscar and his brother, Lamy, were generally well liked, and the Chopins developed a social circle of family and neighbors.

In the fall of 1882, after living in Cloutierville for only three years, Oscar developed malaria and died on December 10, 1882, leaving Chopin a widow with six children. Biographers speculate that the mourning of Thérèse Lafirme in Chopin's first novel, *At Fault,* may reveal the author's feelings on losing her husband: "Of course Thérèse had wanted to die with her Jérôme, feeling that life without him held nothing that could reconcile her to its further endurance. For days she lived alone with her grief; shutting out the appeals that came to her from the demoralized 'hands,' and unmindful of the disorder that gathered about her."

Chopin inherited $12,000 of debt from Oscar, including taxes, doctors' bills, real estate payments, and more. In December 1883 she sold $8,100 worth of land and all the property that she could spare, paying off a portion of the debt. She kept Oscar's business and some of the plantations inherited from his father and managed them on her own. Like the widows who raised her, Chopin was determined to live independently and bring up her children, ranging in age from three to eleven. She worked during the day while childcare was provided by servants, relatives, and neighbors. Numerous men in the small town offered to help the attractive widow, making Chopin the target of gossip. One man in particular stood out—Albert Sampite, a handsome, charming, and successful planter. While he may have been an attractive lover for Chopin, he was a cruel husband to his wife, Loca, and known for his violent temper.

Evidence abounds that Chopin and Sampite did, indeed, have a romance, possibly begun before Oscar died. There were frequent and long trips Chopin made to St. Louis that could indicate some marital problems between her and Oscar, and biographers cite numerous stories passed down through the Sampite family and the families of their neighbors in Cloutierville. Of course, there is also Chopin's fiction, in which she would often use the name Alcée for passionate, male characters she modeled after Sampite. These characters often participate in illicit affairs, such as those of Calixta and Alcée Laballière in "The Storm" and Edna Pontellier and Alcée Arobin in *The Awakening.* Chopin's reserved nature prevents biographers from determining whether or not she truly loved Sampite. Regardless, Chopin moved to St. Louis in 1884, at her mother's urging. She left some of her sons (biographers are unclear which ones) with her brother-in-law Lamy, a common practice for widows with many children.

LAUNCHING A LITERARY LIFE

Chopin initially lived with her mother in St. Louis, but the house soon proved too small, and she moved across the street. About a year later, Chopin's mother died. Chopin had been very close to her mother, and the death left Chopin grief-stricken. As she did when faced with tragic loss as a child, Chopin began writing, this time at the suggestion of a friend, Dr. Frederick Kolbenheyer, who had helped deliver two of her sons. He presented her with descriptive letters she had sent him from Louisiana as proof she was talented enough to write for publication. He also knew that she needed money, though not desperately, as she inherited real estate holdings in Louisiana and St. Louis.

Despite her lifelong literary inclinations, it took several years of encouragement from her friends, as well as a visit to Natchitoches Parish, before Chopin began writing seriously in 1888. Although she is best known for her fiction, Chopin's first published work was a poem, "If I Might Be." It appeared in January 1889 in *America,* a respected literary and political journal. She took her poems seriously enough to submit them to periodicals but would ultimately write more poetry than she published— approximately forty-five poems in all. Her verse is conventional in diction and meter and is generally considered average by critics.

For the next four years (1889–1893) Chopin focused on learning how to write well and finding periodicals that would publish her work. Besides needing money, she longed to make her mark on the American literary scene. Her first published short story, "A Point at Issue!" appeared in the *St. Louis Post-Dispatch* nine months after the publication of "If I Might Be." Like much of Chopin's fiction, "A Point at Issue!" explores marriage, and the characters experiment with its boundaries. The couple in the story live separately in order to pursue their own intellectual interests, but jealousy leads them to reunite under one roof. Significantly, it is the wife who gives up her life in Paris studying French to rejoin her husband in America. "A Point at Issue!" maintains that marriage prevents a woman from retaining her individuality, and it resembles another early Chopin story, "Wiser Than a God," in which a woman refuses to marry so that she might pursue her career as a pianist.

From the start, Chopin was not afraid to tackle controversial subjects, and from her diligent records it is clear that she had difficulty placing some of her stories in magazines. Her first story of 1891, "Mrs. Mobry's Reason," focuses on venereal disease and the ensuing mental illness that can be passed from one generation to the next. The story was rejected by fourteen literary magazines before being accepted by the *New Orleans Times-Democrat* in 1893. "A Shameful Affair" was rejected by nine magazines before it, too, found a home in the *Times-Democrat.* It is about a woman on holiday who has a romantic interlude with a farmhand. "The Christ Light," originally entitled "The Going and Coming of Liza Jane," was rejected by twelve magazines before being placed with the American Press Association for syndication at Christmas 1892. It is the story of a wife who, under the influence of her novel reading, leaves her provincial husband to seek a more cultured life.

Although most of Chopin's fiction is intended for an adult audience, she wrote a number of children's stories, usually for *Youth's Companion* and *Harper's Young People.* Her first was "With the Violin," written in 1890. This was also her first Christmas story, and tells the story of an orphan whose life is transformed by the generosity of a violinist. It, too, was rejected four times before being published by the *St. Louis Spectator.* Driven by what she called her "commercial instinct," Chopin persisted in writing children's stories because they were one of the surest means to literary success for a woman in the nineteenth century.

AT FAULT

Chopin was what the mainstream media of the nineteenth century termed a New Woman. She was independent, intellectual, and supported herself financially, but she rejected the roles of suffragist and social reformer. This has been attributed to her skepticism of progress. Her son, Felix, described her as a "lone wolf" when it came to social issues. Chopin moved in intellectual circles among men and women who supported women's rights, but she never explicitly recorded her opinions on these and other social issues. She refrained from taking a stand, holding herself apart as an observer, as she believed a serious artist ought to do.

Chopin began her first novel, *At Fault,* in July 1889 and finished it in April 1890. She offered the manuscript to *Belford's Monthly* in Chicago, a journal that printed one novel per issue. When *Belford's* rejected it, Chopin, forty years old and eager for literary recognition, published it on her own. She was well organized and determined in this endeavor. Her records indicate that she sent 250 copies to a distributor and numerous copies to libraries and editors of magazines and newspapers in St. Louis, New Orleans, Boston, and New York.

At Fault, set in the Cane River country of Louisiana, follows the development of two relationships. The first involves Thérèse Lafirme, a Creole widow in love with the St. Louis businessman David Hosmer. He has divorced his alcoholic wife, Fanny, but Thérèse believes David has abandoned her. Somewhat self-righteous, Thérèse convinces David that the honorable thing to do is remarry Fanny, which he does. When Fanny drowns in a flood, David and Thérèse are married.

The second relationship concerns Thérèse's nephew, Grégoire Santien, a passionate, hotheaded Creole, and David's sister Melicent, an elitist flirt. She is one of several urban women in this novel whom Chopin creates to satirize what she referred to as "club women"—those women who have too much leisure time and not enough sense to know what to do with it. While Grégoire falls in love with Melicent quickly, she is slow to warm up to him, and her affection for him is forced. When Grégoire kills an Acadian man who has set fire to David's sawmill, Melicent is indignant and uses the episode as an excuse to end her relationship with him. Grégoire leaves for Texas, where he is killed in a fight. When Melicent learns of his death, she eagerly wears mourning and basks in the attention it brings.

Modern critics, while noting Chopin's facility with local color, often find the plot artificial, the language stilted, and the characters wooden, but they attribute this to Chopin's lack of writing experience. Thematically, *At Fault* has more merit. In this novel Chopin begins her exploration of a theme she will revisit in most of her fiction: love, autonomy, and a sense of belonging are essential to a happy, fulfilled life. Melicent, whose personal growth is stifled, serves as a foil for Thérèse, the consummate self-realized woman. In fact, all of the women in this novel except Thérèse are incomplete. But the book operates on more than one level. In his essay "Landscape Symbolism in Kate Chopin's *At Fault,*" Robert D. Arner maintains that the main characters symbolize a union of the past, present, and future. Grégoire dies because he lives in the shadow of the Civil War, ruled by the past and Southern guilt over slavery. Melicent lives in the present, constantly seeking attention and stimulation. Thérèse and David ultimately accept the responsibilities of the present, relying on the strength of traditions and institutions in order to move forward. Arner calls the novel "a wedding of South and North, agrarianism and industrialism, pastoralism and history, tradition and innovation."

Overall, *At Fault* received positive reviews that praised Chopin's portrayal of characters and setting and initiated the long-held view of her as a regionalist. The *New Orleans Daily Picayune* described the novel as charming, and *The Nation,* the only national periodical to review the book, commended Chopin's skill with dialect and characterization. St. Louis newspapers happily noted that the main characters were from St. Louis, and they applauded Chopin's realism and humor, her moral compass, and the strength of the plot.

Negative reviews of *At Fault* objected to Chopin's subjects—divorce and alcoholism—and her truthful portrayal of everyday life. As the reviewer for the *St. Louis Post-Dispatch* wrote, "One shudders at hearing Hosmer tell his wife to 'shut up,' and we protest against Melicent's five engagements. If she really was engaged five times it ought not to be mentioned." Chopin bristled at the negative reviews and sent letters to the *St. Louis Republic* and the *Natchitoches Enterprise* correcting the reviewers' misconceptions. Still, criticism of her unvarnished subject matter would only increase for Chopin as years passed.

Chopin was a prolific writer, despite her late start, or perhaps because of it. Throughout her first four years as a professional writer, she completed eight poems, fifty-two short stories, a one-act play, an essay on German music, eight translations of French articles and stories into English, and two novels. She produced such a large number of manuscripts in part because she attempted little or no revision of her writing. Accounts verify that she thought of an idea for a story, wrote it out fervently on an old lapboard, copied it legibly with few corrections,

and sent it off to a periodical. Chopin wrote in an early version of an essay that appeared in the *Atlantic Monthly* in 1896, "I am completely at the mercy of unconscious selection. To such an extent is this true, that what is called the polishing process has always proved disastrous to my work, and I avoid it, preferring the integrity of crudities to artificialities." This process undoubtedly made it easier for Chopin to fulfill her domestic and parental responsibilities.

THE RELUCTANT REGIONALIST

At Fault's numerous reviews increased Chopin's exposure and elicited considerable praise, but the author still longed for broader literary recognition. As she searched for an audience, she attempted writing in different genres, including historical fiction, which was popular at the time. The short story "The Maid of St. Phillippe" is a tale of a young woman who rejects marriage and is the only time Chopin drew on the stories her great-grandmother related to her about St. Louis history. Although "The Maid of St. Phillippe" was easy to publish, the process of writing it proved difficult, and Chopin never attempted historical fiction again. She came to believe that a writer should draw on her own experience and that one who does so "attains . . . somewhat to the dignity of a philosopher." Because local color stories were popular in the late nineteenth century, Chopin began setting her stories in rural Missouri and Louisiana. Local color, with its ties to realism, came naturally to Chopin. She found stories set in Louisiana, with its unique cultural heritage, much more popular than those set in Missouri, and stories featuring Cajun and Creole cultures often sold on first submission. These tales first appeared in such periodicals as *Vogue, Youth's Companion, Two Tales,* and *Harper's Young People.*

Chopin demonstrated an exceptional confidence operating within the literary business world when she attempted to sell a collection of these and other Louisiana stories. In May 1893 she traveled to New York and Boston with the manuscript of *Young Dr. Gosse and Théo* and a separate collection of twenty-three stories under her arm. She visited numerous publishers and by June received rejection letters from each one. In fact, Chopin would submit *Young Dr. Gosse and Théo* to magazines and publishers for several years, but after numerous rejections, she destroyed it in 1894. (Friends who read the manuscript said it represented Chopin's strongest work to date.) A copy of the story collection, however, was accepted by Houghton, Mifflin and Company in Boston, who titled the collection *Bayou Folk* and published it in March 1894.

Bayou Folk is a unified collection of short fiction: all of the stories, a mixture of adult and children's tales, take place in Louisiana, and Chopin incorporates the various dialects among the Creoles and Cajuns living in Natchitoches Parish. She drew on her own experiences in these Louisiana stories, as well as gossip she had heard when she lived in Cloutierville and stories her family sent her in letters. In "A Rude Awakening," an irresponsible father named Sylveste is based on Sylvère DeLouche, a Cloutierville drunk. Characters based on Chopin's former lover, Albert Sampite, appear in "Désirée's Baby" and "At the 'Cadian Ball." "Ma'ame Pélagie" is the story of three generations of Cane River women, the oldest of whom longs to rebuild the plantation home of her youth, burned in the Civil War. Here, Chopin drew on her knowledge of the Hertzog mansion ruins in Cloutierville.

Many of the stories in this collection move beyond local color to present defiant female characters making their own life choices. Romantic stories abound, and several include women utilizing their power during courtship, power they may or may not relinquish through marriage. In "A No-Account Creole," a woman named Euphrasie commits herself to Placide

Santien, only to discover later that she is in love with Offdean. Placide, once he learns of Euphrasie's true feelings, releases her. In "At the 'Cadian Ball," Alcée Laballière is rejected by Clarisse one day and loses his rice crop to a cyclone the next. When he shows up at the 'Cadian Ball with whiskey on his breath, he draws the attention of Calixta, a "Spanish vixen." As soon as Alcée shows interest in Calixta, Clarisse takes him away from the ball and tells Alcée she will marry him. Disappointed, Calixta accepts the proposal of the awkward Bobinôt, who has been lovestruck by her sensual ways from the start. Romantic stories such as this, in which the men are passionately foolish and the women sensible, are common among Chopin's Cane River stories.

Several of Chopin's *Bayou Folk* stories examine the prolonged effects of the Civil War. In "The Return of Alcibiade" a delusional father still waits after thirty years for his son to return home from the war. In "Old Aunt Peggy" a freed slave is unable to fully embrace freedom and withdraws from life. Freed slaves who need to feel they belong somewhere after emancipation illustrate a recurring theme in Chopin's fiction. In "The Bênitou's Slave" Uncle Oswald, who belonged to the Bênitou family for fifty years, does not rest until he is reunited with the two other remaining Bênitous, a milliner and her daughter.

The collection received over one hundred reviews, varying in length, but almost always describing the book as "charming." Chopin most often received praise for her use of local color and clever characterization, as in a review from the *Boston Beacon* in which her stories were described as "very charming in their delicacy of portraiture and felicity of coloring." This warm reception of her work is not surprising considering that the stories in *Bayou Folk* are well written and fairly conventional, despite Chopin's strong female characters and their challenges to societal norms. Primitive passions may be explored, but "bad" characters are punished and "good" ones rewarded. For example, in "At the 'Cadian Ball," Calixta is saddled with Bobinôt as a husband after she flirts with Alcée, and Clarisse wins Alcée by remaining proper and aloof.

For Chopin, the label of regionalist became entrenched with the reviews of *Bayou Folk* and followed her to the grave and beyond. She is regarded, along with George Washington Cable, as being responsible for the introduction of Louisiana Cajun culture into American fiction. But Chopin did not try, as most regionalists, to develop the sense of place beyond what was needed to tell the story. Many Southern regionalists sentimentalized slavery and tried to re-create the pre–Civil War South. Chopin, while stereotyping blacks on occasion, usually presented these characters in her stories with dignity, concentrating on the interior life of the individual rather than slavery as a social issue. Her portrayal of black women, particularly mothers, was sympathetic. Further, she was more interested in the emotional life of her characters than their locale or cultural trappings. As Per Seyersted wrote in *Kate Chopin: A Critical Biography* (1969), "Though the local color of Kate Chopin's Louisiana stories is unmistakable, they could be set almost anywhere."

Chopin, while pleased with the reception of *Bayou Folk,* expressed disappointment that so few reviewers understood her plots and even fewer seriously discussed her writing. "I am surprised at the very small number which show anything like a worthy critical faculty," she wrote in her diary. Chopin would have liked reviewers to comment on her use of literary techniques, such as ironic plot reversal, and the unmistakable influence of Guy de Maupassant, whom Chopin had begun reading and studying around 1888. He became her new literary model, and his influence is best illustrated in one of Chopin's most popular short stories, "Désirée's Baby." In this story, Armand marries Désirée, whose family background is a mystery. She had been left on the doorstep of the Valmonde family, who raised her. Armand and Désirée live happily until she gives birth to their first child, whose skin is dark. Armand sends Désirée away in racist anger, and the last time readers see her, Désirée is walking toward the bayou with her baby. In the end, Armand learns that his own mother, who died when he was a child, was black.

Modern critics frown upon Chopin's repeated use of such ironic twists in her short fiction, which they believe manipulate the reader and compromise the artistic strength of the story. In her defense, it has been suggested that Chopin suppressed her artistic inclinations early in her career and used irony and local color to place stories in popular, commercial magazines and establish herself as a writer. More important, this first collection of short stories illustrates that Chopin was already exploring the theme of woman in search of her true self. Already, the influence of Darwin, Huxley, and Spencer was making its way into Chopin's fiction, as she challenged societal mores and ethical constraints.

A NIGHT IN ACADIE

After the publication of *Bayou Folk,* Chopin became a literary celebrity. She was invited to speak before women's groups and sought out by novice writers for advice and encouragement. She even held an informal literary salon in her home—Chopin's answer to the tradition of women holding a regular reception day, which she disliked. (Edna, in *The Awakening,* develops a disdain for this ritual as well.) Visitors included the translator Thekla Bernays, the journalist Florence Hayward, the newspaper editor George Sibley Johns, the editor and writer Billy Reedy, and Rosa Sonneschein, the founding editor of *The American Jewess.* While Chopin did not revel in celebrity, her "commercial instincts" led her to make the most of it. She was happy to be featured in articles in St. Louis publications and beyond, such as *Southern Magazine,* where she was one of its "representative Southern Writers" in 1894.

Chopin continued writing at an industrious pace. From 1895 to 1897 she completed twenty-five short stories and published eighteen in such periodicals as *Vogue,* the *Criterion,* and the *St. Louis Mirror.* As she presented more controversial subjects in her work the *Century* stopped publishing her stories. Genteel magazine editors of the nineteenth century routinely rejected tales about wives who desire men other than their husbands, question the choices they have made, or run off to New Orleans alone. *Vogue,* however, was one magazine that Chopin could count on to publish her most daring stories.

Near the close of 1897 Chopin published her second collection of short stories, *A Night in Acadie,* with Way & Williams in Chicago. The collection contains twenty-one of Chopin's stories, half of which had been written since the publication of *Bayou Folk.* All take place in Louisiana, but only a few feature Cajuns, and all had been published before, except the title story. This collection contains several tales featuring children who influence the lives of adults in significant ways, such as "Mamouche," in which a waif who descends on an unmarried doctor one rainy night gives the grown man an opportunity for a more fulfilling life. The fourteen-year-old title character in "Polydore" confesses to his guardian, Mamzelle Adelaide, that he feigned illness to avoid work, filling her with the warmth of maternal love for the first time.

Once again, most of the tales examine romantic relationships between men and women, with assertive female characters actively searching for what is missing in their lives. "A Respectable Woman" explores Mrs. Baroda's attraction to her husband's best friend, and "Athénaïse" tells the story of a newly married woman who leaves her much older widower husband. She ends up in New Orleans, where she meets an unmarried newspaperman, Gouvernail, who falls in love with her. When Athénaïse discovers she is pregnant by her husband, she happily returns home, as impending motherhood transforms her feelings about marriage. "A Night in Acadie" features a sensuous girl named Zaïda, who is planning to marry a violent drunk named André Pascal. The afternoon before the wedding, Zaïda meets Telèsphore, who is mesmerized by her: "his brain was not so occupied with her as his senses were." Telèsphore takes Zaïda to the justice of the peace, where she tells André, "You might stan' yere till the day o' judgment on yo' knees befo' me. . . . I ain't neva goin' to marry you." André and Telèsphore fight while Zaïda looks on, refusing to interfere, letting these men determine her destiny. Telèsphore wins the fight and takes Zaïda, who is now quiet and submissive, home, although whether or not they marry remains unclear.

Chopin changed the ending of "A Night in Acadie" in order to publish it in the *Century.* She wrote the editor, R. W. Gilder, "I have made certain alterations which you thought the story required to give it artistic or ethical value. . . . The marriage is omitted, and the girl's character softened and tempered by her rude experience." Chopin rarely compromised her art in this manner.

From the beginning of her career, Chopin asserted herself in print, and many of the stories in *A Night in Acadie* feature strong, unconventional women like those mentioned above. But the influence of Maupassant on Chopin's writing went a step further once she began translating his stories from French into English in 1894. (She completed eight but published only three.) In 1896 she wrote in the manuscript version of the essay "In the Confidence of a Story-Writer":

> I read his stories and marvelled at them. Here was life, not fiction; for where were the plots, the old fashioned mechanism and stage trapping that in a

vague, unthinking way I had fancied were essential to the art of story making. Here was a man who had escaped from tradition and authority, who had entered into himself and looked out upon life through his own being and with his own eyes; and who, in a direct and simple way, told us what he saw.

Chopin credits Maupassant with launching her "real growth" as a writer, as she developed more self-confidence and dared to give full reign to her own personal vision. Chopin gave up strict control of her plot, allowing her characters to progress naturally toward an end not meant to teach a moral lesson. Her writing style evolved into a clear, sharp, psychological realism that complemented her subjects, which were antithetical to traditional views of acceptable literary topics.

A Night in Acadie received fewer reviews than *Bayou Folk* in part because Way & Williams did not have Houghton, Mifflin and Company's distribution and promotion network. Overall, reviews were positive, but critics still overwhelmingly perceived Chopin as a regionalist. Reviews coming out of St. Louis were numerous and mostly positive, celebrating one of their own. Chopin's friend Billy Reedy of the *St. Louis Mirror* applauded her "delicious" style and her commitment to writing about "grand passion." He also had a response to those who criticized "Athénaïse" that clarifies Chopin's views on marriage: "It is not the man she hates, although she makes the mistake that many wives do of thinking it is, but it is the institution."

The *St. Louis Globe-Democrat,* however, was not so kind. Chopin's story "Miss McEnders" was published in St. Louis eight months before *A Night in Acadie.* Ellen McKee, the owner of the *Post-Dispatch,* perceived that story as a personal attack on herself and her father, who made his fortune skimming taxes off illegally brewed whisky. The story involves an elitist female philanthropist who is ignorant of her father's illegal activities and treats those she is

dedicated to helping with indifference. Featuring an unmarried woman who gives birth to a child, it took five years for Chopin to publish "Miss McEnders," and when she did, it appeared under the pen name "La Tour." But it was no secret in St. Louis who wrote the story, as Chopin's disdain for "club women" and reformists was well known. Ellen McKee could not ignore the publication of *A Night in Acadie,* but her newspaper's review dismissed Chopin as just another sentimental regionalist.

Outside of St. Louis, newspapers generally praised the collection. However, *The Critic* in New York did not like what it called the "coarseness" of "Athénaïse." Further, it criticized Chopin's uncommon literary structure, in which she would let the story unfold naturally without obvious authorial control. The reviewer wrote: "She is never very exciting or dramatic; there is even a slight feeling after reading about six of the stories, that one has read something very like the seventh before." This reviewer was critical of the very literary techniques that Chopin was so eager to develop and that she believed were indicative of her growth as an artist.

THE CALM BEFORE THE STORM

Chopin wrote her next novel at the suggestion of H. E. Scudder, an editor at *The Atlantic Monthly,* who told her that the chance of success with a novel was greater than with collections of short stories. She began *A Solitary Soul* in the summer of 1897 and finished it about eight months later, in January of 1898. Way & Williams, publishers of *A Night in Acadie,* accepted it almost immediately and changed its name to *The Awakening.* They also accepted another collection of stories, *A Vocation and a Voice.*

While waiting for the publication of *The Awakening,* Chopin wrote numerous short stories and poems. One in particular stands out.

"The Storm," written in the summer of 1898, is a sequel to "At the 'Cadian Ball." The characters in this story have been married for five years, Alcée Laballière to Clarisse and Bobinôt to Calixta. A heavy rain leaves Bobinôt and his young son stranded at the village store; Calixta is at home sewing. When she stops to close the windows and doors, she notices Alcée riding up. He asks to wait out the storm and she invites him inside. It is not long before the former lovers embrace:

> They did not heed the crashing torrents, and the roar of the elements made her laugh as she lay in his arms. She was a revelation in that dim, mysterious chamber; as white as the couch she lay upon. Her firm, elastic flesh that was knowing for the first time its birthright, was like a creamy lily that the sun invites to contribute its breath and perfume to the undying life of the world. . . .
>
> When he touched her breasts they gave themselves up in quivering ecstasy, inviting his lips. Her mouth was a fountain of delight. And when he possessed her, they seemed to swoon together at the very borderland of life's mystery.

After the storm dies down, Alcée rides away. He is happy, Calixta laughs, Bobinôt and his son make their way home, and that night Alcée writes his wife, Calixta, encouraging her to stay another month in Biloxi with their children, as she has been eager to do. "The storm passed and everyone was happy," Chopin writes. Obviously, the storm in this tale refers not only to the rain that traps Bobinôt in the general store with his son but to the passions that have been suppressed within Calixta and Alcée. Modern critics praise Chopin for her description of the physical act of making love, which reveals just enough so that the reader actually feels what happens between the lovers. In this regard, Chopin foreshadows the sexual explicitness of D. H. Lawrence and Ernest Hemingway.

In the hands of another writer, the issue of adultery would be resolved. But "The Storm" is not about adultery; it is about the special connection Calixta and Alcée share, so delightfully natural that it brings happiness, not misery, to themselves and their spouses. However, Chopin was realistic enough to know that "The Storm" stood little chance of ever seeing print, and she never attempted to publish it.

In November 1898 Chopin gained a new publisher for *The Awakening.* Way & Williams dissolved their three-year-old business earlier that year, and Herbert S. Stone & Company took over their books and assets. Stone formally accepted *The Awakening* and *A Vocation and a Voice,* scheduling the novel to appear in the spring of 1899.

THE AWAKENING

Although it was harshly reviewed upon its publication, today *The Awakening* is considered Chopin's masterpiece. Here she explores, with psychological realism, the emotional, creative, and sexual awakening of a married woman with children, who questions the ability of any woman to develop into an independent, fulfilled self within the confines of marriage and motherhood.

Edna Pontellier, a twenty-nine-year-old wife and mother of two sons, Raoul and Etienne, lives in New Orleans with her Creole husband, Léonce. Originally from the Midwest, Edna feels like an outsider among the Creoles with whom she and her husband socialize, although no one treats her unkindly. Like their friends, Edna and the children spend the summer on Grand Isle, and Léonce visits by boat on the weekends. Edna develops several relationships on Grand Isle: Robert Lebrun, who teaches Edna to swim, rekindles her dormant sexual desires; Adèle Ratignolle, a devoted wife and mother, leads Edna to question her own domestic life; and Mademoiselle Reisz, the musician, reawakens latent artistic passions in Edna. All of these characters represent aspects of her self that Edna cannot reconcile because she is a woman living within the confines of marriage. Edna's life is dictated by biology, and so self-fulfillment, which she comes to desire, is impossible to obtain.

Edna's marriage to Léonce is satisfactory to her at the start of the novel. He is kind and devoted, but cannot acknowledge Edna as an autonomous person. Having married her husband for security and in rebellion against her Presbyterian family, Edna is vulnerable to Robert's attentions, believing the young Creole sees her as an individual. When Robert teaches Edna to swim, it initiates her sexual awakening: "A feeling of exultation overtook her, as if some power of significant import had been given her to control the working of her body and her soul. She grew daring and reckless, overestimating her strength. She wanted to swim far out, where no woman had swum before." Once he realizes that he is falling in love with Edna, Robert leaves abruptly for Spain, believing his behavior is honorable.

Adèle Ratignolle also plays a significant role in initiating Edna's sexual awakening with her warm and physically affectionate Creole manner. More important, she exemplifies the submissive wife and "mother-woman":

> The mother-women seemed to prevail that summer at Grand Isle. It was easy to know them, fluttering about with extended, protecting wings when any harm, real or imaginary, threatened their precious brood. They were women who idolized their children, worshiped their husbands, and esteemed it a holy privilege to efface themselves as individuals and grow wings as ministering angels.

Modern critics contend that Adèle is insecure in her role as mother, despite her apparent fulfillment, citing Adèle's incessant need for attention concerning her pregnancy, or "condition." Adèle also lacks insight into other aspects of life beyond motherhood and domesticity, illustrating the limitations of a person who does not evolve, even willingly, into an autonomous person. Edna, despite her affection for Adèle, objects to the narrow existence of her friend.

Upon returning to New Orleans, Edna refuses to perform many of her domestic duties, such as spending time with her children and receiving visitors on Thursdays. She moves into a small house around the corner from her home with Léonce, takes long walks, and paints. Before long, Edna has an affair with a rogue named Alcée Arobin, though she still longs for Robert and what she considers real love. Throughout this period, Mademoiselle Reisz has been receiving letters from Robert, which she shares with Edna, thus facilitating a long-distance relationship between the two. Mademoiselle Reisz has the independence that Edna wants but lacks love and any sensuousness in her life beyond music. Like Adèle, she is half-formed and confirms Edna's resolve to fashion a complete and fulfilling existence for herself.

When Robert returns to New Orleans, he and Edna admit their love to each other one evening in Edna's home. They are interrupted when Adèle, who is giving birth to her fourth child, summons Edna for help. Adèle, whose pregnancy progresses alongside Edna's personal growth, illustrates the powerful and natural connection between a woman's self-identity and her role as mother. Edna feels obligated to leave but asks Robert to wait for her. Upon her return, Edna finds Robert has gone, leaving a note, which reads, "I love you. Good-by—because I love you." Edna spends a sleepless night despairing over her loss. But during their visit earlier that evening, Edna had to remind Robert, "I am no longer one of Mr. Pontellier's possessions to dispose of or not. I give myself where I choose." She had put all her hopes for a complete life in Robert, only to learn that he, too, cannot see her as an autonomous person. The next day, Edna travels to Grand Isle.

From the start of the novel, Chopin creates a sensual world on Grand Isle, and the sea becomes the symbol of freedom—the full, powerful, uncompromising essence of life. The sea, where life originated, is the sight of Edna's rebirth or awakening. It is where Edna learns to swim and where she eventually dies, when she realizes she cannot fully realize her newfound freedom or return to the traditional life she led before.

> She walked out. The water was chill, but she walked on. The water was deep, but she lifted her white body and reached out with a long, sweeping stroke. . . .
>
> She went on and on. . . . She did not look back. . . .
>
> Her arms and legs were growing tired. . . .
>
> Exhaustion was pressing upon and overpowering her.
>
> . . . the shore was far behind her, and her strength was gone.

It is only through death on her own terms that Edna believes she can be completely free. All other life choices—motherhood, marriage, art—require Edna to compromise her autonomy, and she has reached the point where she cannot compromise, even for her children: "I would give up the unessential; I would give my money, I would give my life for my children; but I wouldn't give myself."

Edna's suicide is central to an understanding of her character and the theme of the novel, and interpretations vary. Comparisons to Gustave Flaubert's *Madame Bovary,* another famous literary suicide figure, are common. But while there are similarities, Chopin's Edna is self-determined and cannot reconcile herself with the consequences of exercising her newly discovered sexual and artistic freedom. Flaubert's Bovary is a romantic character, manipulated by plot, who becomes disillusioned by the realities of love.

Some critics view Edna as drifting aimlessly into death, as she seems to drift throughout the novel, in and out of sleep. Others label her selfish, maintaining that the whole novel chronicles her regression into irrational, childlike rebel-

lion. But most critics affirm Edna's suicide. They celebrate the heroic grandeur and spiritual emancipation of this, her final act of absolute freedom, or they interpret it as the act of a courageous woman who will not give up her life for her children, but will die for them so that they will not have to bear the consequences of her rebellious behavior. Critics identifying a transcendentalist theme in Chopin's novel maintain that Edna's suicide is the logical result of her realization of her innate solitary nature. Other scholars believe that Edna had no choice but to commit suicide, for to live the free, sensuous life she desires is impossible, given the consequences. Although it is Edna's suicide that draws considerable critical attention today, it was the novel's acts of adultery that generated considerable discussion at the time of its publication.

The Awakening was officially issued in April 1899, and the first notice of its publication to appear in print was by Lucy Monroe in the March issue of *Book News.* Monroe described the book as one "so keen in its analysis of character, so subtle in its presentation of emotional effects that it seems to reveal life as well as to represent it." Two other equally favorable notices appeared in the *St. Louis Republic* and *The Book Buyer.*

Along with her admirers in St. Louis, Chopin had enemies. She had satirized prominent people of her hometown in past fiction, and there are strong similarities between the plot of *The Awakening* and the summer romance of a local St. Louis socialite at the time. *The Republic,* with ties to prominent local citizens, ran an influential and scathing review of *The Awakening* on April 30, despite its favorable notice in March. The reviewer dismissively summarized the plot of the novel as the story of a woman who wants everything her own way and, when she cannot have that, drowns herself. Over the next month, *The Awakening* received negative reviews in several St. Louis publications, including the *Mirror,* edited by Chopin's friend Billy Reedy. This review, by the conservative writer and critic Frances Porcher, found the book morally unacceptable. Like many critics of the nineteenth century, Porcher assumed writers had a moral obligation to their readers, while Chopin was critical of didactic literature.

Nationally, *The Awakening* did not fair much better. *The Chicago Times-Herald* declared that "it was not necessary for a writer of so great refinement and poetic grace to enter the overworked field of sex fiction," and *Literature* called the novel "an essentially vulgar story." Even Willa Cather, writing for the *Pittsburgh Ledger* under the name of "Sibert," wrote, "I shall not attempt to say why Miss Chopin has devoted so exquisite and sensitive, well-governed a style to so trite and sordid a theme." A few reviews were less harsh, but most praised the writing and condemned the plot.

Chopin publicly responded to these and other critics in July with a short piece in the *Book News,* where she wrote satirically:

Having a group of people at my disposal, I thought it might be entertaining (to myself) to throw them together and see what would happen. I never dreamed of Mrs. Pontellier making such a mess of things and working out her own damnation as she did. If I had had the slightest intimation of such a thing I would have excluded her from the company. But when I found out what she was up to, the play was half over and it was then too late.

Always reserved, the general consensus is that Chopin told no one how she truly felt about the criticism of *The Awakening.* Emily Toth in *Kate Chopin* documents a "severe spell of illness" that Chopin refers to in a personal letter, which could have been depression. But, Chopin's family, friends, and admirers were supportive. Chopin continued to socialize enough that her debutante daughter, Lélia, came out successfully that year in St. Louis society, she was invited to lecture at local women's groups, and her books sold in St. Louis bookstores. Records indicate that she continued writing and completed two short stories, an essay, and a couple of poems that year. She continued to publish and collect royalties. The *Century* printed her poem "I Opened All the Portals Wide," and in September, the *Saturday Evening Post* published the story "A Family Affair." In addition, her national literary reputation remained secure—*Youth's Companion* recommended her new story "A Little Country Girl" as being one of the best for girls.

This difficult year ended on a positive note when the *Post-Dispatch* published an illustrated article about Chopin along with an essay by her on writing. The newspaper reported her history and praised her fiction, describing her as much more than a local colorist: "she appeals to the universal sense in a way not excelled by any other American author. She is not sectional or provincial, nor even national, which is to say that she is an artist, who is not bound by the idiosyncrasies of place, race, or creed."

In her essay Chopin erroneously noted, concerning the availability of *The Awakening,* "The libraries! Oh, no, they don't keep it." Thus began the legend of the novel being banned or withdrawn from library shelves. Chopin's son, Felix, Clarence E. Miller, a former librarian of the St. Louis Mercantile Library, and early biographers helped perpetuate this story. Emily Toth maintains that *The Awakening* was never banned and documents that the St. Louis Public Library and the Mercantile Library each bought several copies of the novel in 1899. Further, no records exist at either library indicating they removed the books from their shelves for any reason other than that the books were worn, a common practice in libraries. In addition, Billy Reedy, Orrick Johns, and other contemporary writers in St. Louis who were quite outspoken concerning censorship never wrote about the banning of *The Awakening.*

LITERARY DECLINE

Chopin wrote relatively little—eleven short stories, four poems, and two essays—in the five years between publication of *The Awakening* and her death. She published the essays and sold most of the short stories, but only three of the latter were published: "The White Eagle," "The Wood-Choppers," and "Polly." In addition, Herbert S. Stone & Company reduced the number of books on its publication list and deleted Chopin's *A Vocation and a Voice.*

A Vocation and a Voice tackles many subjects, including spirituality, the power of nature, suicide, disillusionment, and sexuality, but the overriding theme is once again that autonomy, love, and belonging are essential to self-fulfillment. The title story features a homeless boy with no known name who is "adopted" by a gypsy couple, Suzima and Gutro. With this couple he feels a sense of belonging that has always eluded him. As he grows into manhood, he and Suzima become lovers, which results in an explosive fight between the boy and Gutro. The boy is appalled at his own capacity for violence and enters a monastery. There he goes by the name of Brother Ludovic and dedicates his life to building a wall around the grounds. One day, while working on the wall, he hears a woman splashing in a nearby pool, singing. The sexual attraction he feels is overpowering and he jumps the wall to follow the voice wherever it leads, realizing there are aspects of himself he will never completely understand but must accept and experience fully.

Another story, "The Story of an Hour," finds Mrs. Mallard, a woman with heart trouble, learning that her husband has been killed. She weeps for him, but then a new feeling overcomes her.

> What was it? She did not know. . . . But she felt it . . . reaching toward her through the sounds, the scents, the color that filled the air. . . . she was striving to beat it back with her will. . . . When she abandoned herself a little whispered word escaped her. . . . She said it over and over under her breath: "free, free, free!"

Mrs. Mallard's husband was kind and loving, but also overbearing, and Mrs. Mallard is eager to develop her autonomous self. Chopin's attraction to the ironic twist, however, has Mr. Mallard surprise his wife—he is alive after all—and the shock kills her immediately. The story supports the theme Chopin returns to time and again in her fiction: love cannot compensate for a lack of self realization.

Chopin never tried to find another publisher for *A Vocation and a Voice,* despite needing the money and positive publicity. Biographers intimate that, had she attempted to find another publisher for this collection, she stood a good chance of success and may have regained the ground she had lost in her literary career due to *The Awakening.* Her characters are better developed than in earlier stories, and she delves more deeply into their interior lives. As it stands, Chopin was largely ignored after her death until the 1930s, when Daniel Rankin published his study of her.

Toward the end of her life Chopin lived with four of her grown children: Jean, Oscar, Felix, and Lélia. Her public persona was maintained by such publications as *Who's Who in America* (its first edition) and the *Republic,* which featured her in an article on St. Louis writers and asked her to recommend books to readers. Her essay "Development of the Literary West" recommends works by such writers as Mary Hallock Foote, Ambrose Bierce, Owen Wister, A. B. Frost, Bret Harte, and Hamlin Garland—fairly conventional choices that indicate an attempt by Chopin to repair her literary reputation.

By 1903 Chopin often felt weak and tired; biographers suspect she was suffering from diabetes or emphysema. Before long she moved out of the home in which she had lived her entire writing career and into a house around the corner from her son Jean, who, with his wife, was expecting a child. Four of her children joined her: Felix, Fred, Oscar, and Lélia. Financial concerns may have prompted the move; Chopin's last earnings from writing, recorded in 1902, reflect only $3.35 in royalties for *Bayou Folk* and a total of $105 for three stories. There were no royalties recorded for *A Night in Acadie* or *The Awakening*.

TRUE LITERARY GENIUS

On Saturday, August 20, 1904, Chopin visited the St. Louis World's Fair and came home very tired, complaining of severe pain in her head. She apparently suffered a cerebral hemorrhage and died on August 22 with her children nearby. Obituaries appeared on the front pages of the *Post-Dispatch* and the *Mirror* and, not surprisingly, on page thirteen of the *Globe-Democrat*. Most paid tribute to her writing and her skill as a regionalist, favoring *At Fault, Bayou Folk,* and *A Night in Acadie* over *The Awakening*.

Billy Reedy wrote a personal remembrance of Chopin that appeared in the *Mirror* and supports the idea that she was able to achieve what Edna Pontellier could not—the fusion of motherhood and an artistic life. It probably would not been possible had Oscar lived. "She was a remarkably talented woman," Reedy wrote, "who knew how to be a genius without sacrificing the comradeship of her children. . . . her contributions to fiction, though few, showed that she possessed true literary genius."

Selected Bibliography

WORKS OF KATE CHOPIN

NOVELS AND SHORT STORIES

At Fault. St. Louis: Nixon-Jones Printing Co., 1890. Reprint, with an introduction by Bernard Koloski. New York: Penguin, 2002.

Bayou Folk. Boston: Houghton, Mifflin and Co., 1894.

A Night in Acadie. Chicago: Way & Williams, 1897. Reprinted as *Bayou Folk and A Night in Acadie.* Edited with an introduction and notes by Bernard Koloski. New York: Penguin, 1999.

The Awakening. Chicago & New York: Herbert S. Stone & Company, 1899. Reprint, edited by Margaret Culley. New York: W. W. Norton & Co., 1976. (There are numerous reprints of *The Awakening;* this contains an excellent collection of critical essays.)

A Vocation and a Voice: Stories. Edited and with an introduction and notes by Emily Toth. New York: Penguin, 1991.

COLLECTIONS

The Complete Works of Kate Chopin. 2 vols. Edited and with an introduction by Per Seyersted. Foreword by Edmund Wilson. Baton Rouge: Louisiana State University Press, 1969.

A Kate Chopin Miscellany. Edited by Per Seyersted and Emily Toth. Oslo and Natchitoches: Universitetsforlaget and Northwestern State University Press, 1979.

JOURNALS, CORRESPONDENCE, AND MANUSCRIPTS

Kate Chopin's Private Papers. Edited by Emily Toth and Per Seyersted. Bloomington: Indiana University Press, 1998.

The personal papers and manuscripts of Kate Chopin are housed at the Missouri Historical Society and the Cammie Henry Research Center of the Eugene Watson Library at Northwestern State University of Louisiana.

BIBLIOGRAPHIES

Bonner, Thomas, Jr. "Kate Chopin: An Annotated Bibliography." *Bulletin of Bibliography* 32:101–105 (July–September 1975).

Green, Suzanne Disheroon, and David J. Caudle. *Kate Chopin: An Annotated Bibliography of Critical Works.* Westport, Conn.: Greenwood Publishing Group, 1999.

Potter, Richard. "Kate Chopin and Her Critics: An Annotated Checklist." *Missouri Historical Society Bulletin* 26:306–317 (July 1970).

Seyersted, Per, and Emily Toth, eds. *A Kate Chopin Miscellany.* Oslo and Natchitoches: Universitetsforlaget and Northwestern State University Press, 1979. Pp. 201–261. (Includes a listing of Chopin's novels, stories, poems, essays, play, and private papers, as well as a briefly annotated list of books, dissertations, articles, and selected reviews of writings about Chopin.)

Toth, Emily. *Kate Chopin.* New York: William Morrow and Company, Inc., 1990. Pp. 413–421. (An adaptation and updating of Seyersted's bibliography in *A Kate Chopin Miscellany,* including all of Chopin's known writings—published, unpublished, and those recorded in her account notebooks but now destroyed or lost.)

CRITICAL AND BIOGRAPHICAL STUDIES

Arner, Robert D. "Landscape Symbolism in Kate Chopin's *At Fault.*" *Louisiana Studies* 9:142–153 (fall 1970).

Bloom, Harold, ed. *Kate Chopin: Modern Critical Views.* New York: Chelsea House Publishers, 1987.

Bonner, Thomas, Jr. "Kate Chopin's *At Fault* and *The Awakening:* A Study in Structure." *Markham Review* 7:10–15 (fall 1977).

———. *The Kate Chopin Companion, with Chopin's Translations from French Fiction.* Westport, Conn.: Greenwood Publishing Group, 1988.

Culley, Margaret, ed. *The Awakening: An Authoritative Text, Contexts, Criticism.* New York: W. W. Norton, 1976.

Ewell, Barbara C. *Kate Chopin.* New York: Ungar, 1986.

Garietta, Anthony Paul. "The Critical Reputation of Kate Chopin." Ph.D. thesis, University of North Carolina, 1978.

Koloski, Bernard, ed. *Approaches to Teaching Chopin's* The Awakening. New York: Modern Language Association, 1988.

———. *Kate Chopin: A Study of the Short Fiction.* New York: Twayne Publishers, 1996.

Lattin, Patricia H. "Kate Chopin's Repeating Characters." *Mississippi Quarterly* 33:19–37 (1979–1980).

Petry, Alice Hall, ed. *Critical Essays on Kate Chopin.* New York: G. K. Hall & Co., 1996.

Potter, Richard. "Negroes in the Fiction of Kate Chopin." *Louisiana History* 12:41–58 (winter 1971).

Rankin, Daniel. *Kate Chopin and Her Creole Stories.* Philadelphia: University of Pennsylvania Press, 1932.

Seyersted, Per. *Kate Chopin: A Critical Biography.* Baton Rouge: Louisiana State University Press, 1969.

Showalter, Elaine. "Tradition and the Female Talent: *The Awakening* as a Solitary Book." In *New Essays on* The Awakening. Edited by Wendy Martin. Cambridge: Cambridge University Press, 1988. Pp. 33–35.

Skaggs, Peggy. *Kate Chopin.* Boston: G. K. Hall, 1985.

Taylor, Helen. *Gender, Race, and Region in the Writings of Grace King, Elizabeth McEnery Stuart, and Kate Chopin.* Baton Rouge: Louisiana State University Press, 1989.

Thornton, Lawrence. "*The Awakening:* A Political Romance." *American Literature* 52:50–66 (1980).

Toth, Emily. "Kate Chopin and Literary Convention: "Désirée's Baby." *Southern Studies* 20:201–208 (1981).

———. *Kate Chopin.* New York: William Morrow and Company, Inc., 1990.

Walker, Nancy A. "Feminist or Naturalist: the Social Context of Kate Chopin's *The Awakening.*" *Southern Quarterly* 17:95–103 (1979).

———. *Kate Chopin: A Literary Life.* New York: Palgrave Macmillan, 2001.

Wymand, Eleanor B. "Kate Chopin: Her Existential Imagination." *Southern Studies* 19:373–384 (1980).

FILMS BASED ON THE WORKS OF KATE CHOPIN

The End of August. Screenplay by Anna Thomas and Gregory Nava, based on *The Awakening* by Kate Chopin. Quarter Films, Inc., 1982.

Kate Chopin's "The Story of an Hour." Ishtar, 1982.

The Grand Isle. Screenplay by Hesper Anderson. Directed by Mary Lambert. 1991.

—DENISE LARRABEE

Hart Crane

1899–1932

Harold Crane was born in Garrettsville, Ohio, on July 21, 1899. Early the previous year, on a trip to Ohio from Chicago, Grace Edna Hart had met Clarence Arthur (known as C. A.) Crane, and after a brief but intense courtship they were married in June 1898. The Crane family remained in Garrettsville only until 1901, when Crane's grandfather agreed that, at the age of twenty-nine, it was time for his son to establish his own distribution branch of the family's already well-established maple syrup business. This he did, in Warren, Ohio, where Crane was to live until 1908. Crane's father was a born entrepreneur and inventor. Beginning with the economically practical corn syrup–maple syrup blend, with which he immediately expanded the family business and riches in Warren, he later moved into the candy business, concerning himself with the making and, more importantly, the selling of fine chocolates. He even invented a certain hard candy with a hole in the middle that is now known as the Lifesaver. Crane's father's insistent immersion in the world of business and profits was to plague his relationship with his less economically minded son for the rest of both their lives.

The marriage between Crane's parents was turbulent at best. In 1908 Crane was sent to live with his mother's parents in Cleveland, where his previously separated but temporarily reconciled parents soon joined him. In Cleveland his mother embraced the religion of the Christian Scientists that she was to adhere to for much of her life but that Crane was to leave behind as soon as he was old enough to leave home (claiming to not have ever been particularly af-

fected by it, but to have objected to its avoidance of suffering). Though Crane's parents were soon back on the same marital roller coaster, the family managed to remain in Cleveland until 1916 when his mother, in the midst of rumors of her husband's blatant infidelity, filed for divorce. By the end of that year, Crane was to leave Cleveland for New York.

Though few details about his youth have survived, it is clear that life was not easy for the sensitive Crane, who demonstrated early on a tendency to become severely physically ill as a result of his parents' quarrels, of his own often neglected position in the middle of them, and perhaps in response to various other social and personal pressures. His allegiance through the years seems to have been consistently to his mother, who was to continue to inspire and to drain her son's creativity, love, attention, and energy for the rest of his life. Together with his physical weakness, he was often kept out of school by his travels with her. The devoted son often accompanied his mother on trips to both American coasts and, most notably, to the Hart family plantation on the Isle of Pines, off the coast of Cuba, where Crane was to return years later to experience some of the most creative months of his poetic career. Incessantly plagued by his parents' instability, the depression of Crane's teenage years culminated in two suicide attempts during a long vacation from his father with his mother on the Isle of Pines in February 1915. Not long after, Crane left Ohio's confusions for the perhaps less anguished confusion of New York City, but his parents' and in particular his mother's instability continued to disturb and frustrate even the grown man until he finally broke with his mother completely in October 1928. His poetry contains few direct references to his childhood, and the few traces that appear are melancholy and brief.

Despite sporadic attendance in school, the teenage Crane was not disliked by teachers or students. The high school friends that were to maintain some importance in his life included George Bryan and William Wright, the latter of whom would be one of Crane's most significant correspondents. He apparently had a girlfriend and, perhaps more importantly to his later preferences, he also had his first homosexual encounter in those years with an unknown though likely older man. Despite being bright enough, Crane's frequent absences left him labeled a mediocre student. Though he was to continue the avid reading and pursuit of poetry that began in his tower room in Cleveland, he never finished high school. Upon striking out for New York in December 1916, his intention was to hire tutors to prepare him for the entrance exams to Columbia University, but financial difficulties and poetic distractions left this plan abandoned. Crane took his mother's maiden name, "Hart," as his first name in early 1917, after having published his first few poems.

Thus Crane's formal education is highly unimpressive on paper. His correspondence, however, reveals his lifelong pursuit of a sort of self-education, concentrated on the great works of literature that he deemed relevant or interesting to his own writing, and on most anything created by his contemporaries. He studied a minimum of Latin and German in high school, French and Spanish afterward, but he was never able to read in any foreign language without heavy use of a dictionary. This did not prevent him from reading rather extensively, but far from systematically, works in translation from such classic writers as Dante, Cervantes, Dostoyevsky (with whom he was enthralled), Rabelais, Apuleius, Petronius (Satyricon), Baude-laire, Rimbaud, and others. He shared an interest in French literature with other American modernist poets and journals of that time.

His knowledge of British literature was somewhat more complete, first manifesting itself in a fascination with Oscar Wilde, about whom in 1916 he wrote and published his first poem "C 33" (thirty-three being Wilde's prison cell number). Most worthy of mention, however, is the constant influence of the English Romantics, particularly William Blake, attested to by his letters and noted by critics of Crane's work both in his time and after. He was also formally fascinated with the Elizabethan masters, in particular Christopher Marlowe, and he claimed, in *O My Land, My Friends* (1997) to seek to recover in his own work the "interior form" of other beloved poets like Ben Jonson, Michael Drayton, and John Donne, "a form so thorough and intense as to dye the words themselves with a peculiarity of meaning, slightly different maybe from the ordinary definition of them separate from the poem." It was an observation that would have a great influence upon Crane's own ideas of what he would call "the logic of metaphor."

American literature from Walt Whitman to the most contemporary, however, is at the heart of Crane's own poetic output and autodidactic pursuits. He dedicated three of his poems to perhaps three of the most important nineteenth-century American writers: Emily Dickinson, with "To Emily Dickinson"; Herman Melville, with "At Melville's Tomb" (it was a *third* reading of Melville's *Moby-Dick* that, during a particularly horrible experience of being stranded on the mosquito- and disease-infested island of Grand Cayman, "saved my mind," Crane wrote to the American poet and critic Yvor Winters in January 1927); and Walt Whitman, with the fourth section of *The Bridge*, "Cape Hatteras," which addresses the ever-present (to Crane) father of American poetry:

Walt, tell me, Walt Whitman, if infinity
Be still the same as when you walked the beach
Near Paumanok—your lone patrol—and heard the
  wraith
Through surf, its bird note there a long time
  falling . . .

In all three poems Crane sees the pieces of his heritage as an American poet, and his own attempts at the (re)creation of a myth of America necessarily include their echoes and address their experiences.

In this way Crane situates himself as something of a bridge between the poets of the past and the numerous others that keep him in the present. Crane's letters are a catalog of his opinions about the work and the philosophies of poets of his own time. They partially fill the gap left by Crane's lack of critical essays and relative silence in the debate that would surround contradicting reviews of his work for most of his life. Besides a few more personal correspondents such as William Wright, his mother, and his Aunt Sally from the Isle of Pines, Crane's main letter exchanges were with other writers and with people who often passed in and out of his life as friends and critics, but whose support, feedback, and presence was essential to his vision of himself and his work. Despite his lack of a formal education, and the all too frequent lack of employment or professional respect that was to plague Crane in almost all the years that followed that first trip to New York in 1916, he was to become and remain an integral part of the American poetry scene both in the journals and socially throughout the 1920s. His letters to the writers and journal editors Gorham Munson, Allen Tate, Malcolm Cowley, Waldo Frank, Winters, and others are readers' only source of insight into Crane's goals, insecurities, and trials and tribulations as a poet and as a man—which for Crane perhaps more than for many were one and the same.

ON THE WAY TO *WHITE BUILDINGS*

This description of Crane, written in a memoir about him by Cowley in his *A Second Flowering: Works and Days of the Lost Generation* (1973), perhaps best explains his reputation and his frenzied existence both in his writing and in his life:

> Hart excused himself for a moment, I suppose to visit the hidden bottle. When he returned, he was in the second phase, that of brilliant monologue. Everything reminded him of something else: landscapes, of musical compositions; poems, of skyrockets or waterfalls; persons, of birds, animals, or piles of grimy snow; he could abstract the smile from a woman's face and make us see it in the design of the mantelpiece. His now immense eyes glowed in the first lamplight; they seemed to have burned the vitality from his other features and turned his hair to ashes. Soon he was launched on a stream of words repeated more for their sound than for their meaning.

To many who were to meet Crane, he was a man driven to write, to drink, and to love by what Munson called in Crane's poetry "divine madness." Crane's bouts of writing, drinking, and loving, however, increasingly led to periods of complete artistic stagnation. When he was able to write, Crane did so in spurts, in daylong, weeklong, and once even a summerlong span of devoted typewriter clicking. He spent years embellishing and revising the images and ideas that, when he was not writing, still obsessed him to the point of constant distraction from any of the various careers that life, his father, and his friends had to offer him.

For this reason, to say that *White Buildings*, written in 1926, was his first book and *The Bridge* his second (published in January 1930) would be misleading. The idea for a long poem with a bridge as its central image appears as early as February 1923 in a letter to Munson and was to be a continuation and development of the ideas he was working on then in the poem

"For the Marriage of Faustus and Helen." Thus Crane wrote many of the poems for *White Buildings*—capturing the attention of the American poetry universe with formidable pieces such as "At Melville's Tomb," "Repose of Rivers," and the sequence of "Voyages"—at the same time that he was pondering and often struggling with the longer piece for which admirers now know him.

White Buildings emerged not as a cohesive whole but as a collection of Crane's major poems from 1919 to 1926, all previously published in poetry journals such as *The Dial, The Little Review,* and *Secession.* The title of the collection was originally a poem that he split into two poems, "Possessions" and "Recitative," and it refers apparently to many things. To his mother, he claimed the title was a reference to a Giorgio De Chirico painting. To Winters, however, he writes that it "has two symbolic meanings, or connotations, its primary one being metaphysic-mechanical: it is only secondarily 'Woolworthian.'" By saying the title is "Woolworthian," Crane is alluding to the highly visible white Woolworth's building in New York; calling the title "metaphysic-mechanical" means that his poems are the white buildings, the constructions of the imagination whose "abstract 'life' of course, is dependent on organic correspondences to Nature."

The poems up to and including "For the Marriage of Faustus and Helen" reflect a poet who has found his calling but who has not yet discovered the direction in which it compels him. Crane's first trip to New York ended as both a financial disaster and a poetic beginning. *The Pagan* published over a half dozen of his early poems, but he was forced to return to Ohio by his own poverty and his mother's emotional crisis (Crane's father had remarried). There he made an attempt at the straight and narrow plan of a steady career as, among other things, a cub reporter for the *Cleveland Plain Dealer.* By early 1919, however, Crane had decided once again that his place was in New York, and he managed to stay for most of the year publishing, thanks to the growing interest of Munson and a few increasingly intriguing pieces, some of which were to be included in *White Buildings.*

Finally, in November 1919, with the beginnings of "My Grandmother's Love Letters" already in the works, but with dwindled economic possibilities in New York, Crane again headed back to Cleveland to work for his father's chocolate business. "My Grandmother's Love Letters," published in *The Dial* in March 1920, brought Crane ten dollars, his first major acclaim as a poet, and his first experiences of the anxieties that were to afflict him after each success, the fear that his next endeavor might not match up. The poem addresses in simple and melancholic tones two of Crane's major preoccupations: the ability of writing to capture and communicate, in some way, any truth of human existence, and his own capacity to rescue not just the past but also traces of his own heritage and to make them ring out in the present.

> "Are your fingers long enough to play
> Old keys that are but echoes:
> Is the silence strong enough
> To carry back the music to its source
> And back to you again
> As though to her?"

Already the poet imagines the transformation of words into music and the journey of the music back again into the words of his own poem. Already he envisions his work as seeking to bring not just the echoes but also the very source of the echoes, that which brought the love letters into existence, into his own present tense, with or in between the words of his own poem.

Three years later Crane attempts this same quest in the jazz rhythms of "For the Marriage of Faustus and Helen," which he later refers to as a "kind of bridge" between the past and the present. He struggles to build this bridge by giving the myths of the past the language and the images of the present, with images of Helen on a modern-day bus and of modern-day war devastation that is perhaps the result of a new version of the same Faustian (failed) quest for progress, rather than for the more elusive knowledge of those like the poem's speaker, who do not inhabit the clockwork world of the day. *"There is the world dimensional for / those untwisted by the love of things / irreconcilable . . ."* and the speaker is twisted by just such a love, by just such a perhaps impossible desire to bring traces of the past to the present, and to create hope in a present tense that otherwise appears irreversibly fragmented and bleak. After the "eternal gunman," reminiscent of T. S. Eliot's "eternal footman" of death has fired down upon the city, "The imagination spans beyond despair," the speaker has survived

> And will persist to speak again before
> All stubble streets that have not curved
> To memory . . .

"For the Marriage of Faustus and Helen," as with those to follow, rails against the pessimism of Eliot at the same time that it echoes his words, his structures. With a hostility for the world that materially overcomes him time and time again, Crane had written to the American poet Wilbur Underwood in 1922, "Life is meagre with me. I am unsatisfied and left always begging for beauty. I am tied to the stake—a little more wastefully burnt every day of my life . . ." Yet, even as Crane sees the ruins of the present tense, and the danger of technology, his burden as a poet is not to lament such decay, but to uncover a vision less immediately perceived but that exists beside the despair to which Eliot had lent so much beauty:

> I take Eliot as a point of departure toward an almost complete reverse of direction. His pessimism is justified, in his own case. But I would

apply as much of his erudition and technique as I can absorb and assemble toward a more positive, or (if [I] must put it so in a sceptical age) ecstatic goal. . . . After this perfection of death—nothing is possible in motion but a resurrection of some kind. . . . All I know through very much suffering and dullness . . . is that it interests me to still affirm certain things.

As in the poem "Chaplinesque," written two years before, Crane the poet is to be seen as both the exiled and suffering kitten seeking shelter from a hostile world, and part of the "we" that

> . . . can still love the world, who find
> A famished kitten on the step, and know
> Recesses for it from the fury of the street

Even as Crane sees himself (perhaps, his friends sometimes thought, too self-indulgently) as the battered victim of his age's frenzied quest for material wealth and professional recognition, he also sees himself as the bearer of the message that will save his age. Though not as developed as his later work, "For the Marriage of Faustus and Helen" is Crane's first highly complicated attempt to exorcise from poetry the death-obsessed erudition of Eliot with what many readers would come to view as his own brand of mysticism. It is a command to move on past the destruction, to thresh the heights not with the diabolical power of technology, but with the imagination.

CRANE IN LOVE

"For the Marriage of Faustus and Helen" brought Crane's genius to light and lifted him to a new level of literary recognition with editors such as Munson, Frank, Tate, Slater Brown, and Jean Toomer. By the spring of 1923, he was again in New York, this time with copy-writing experience gained in Ohio to lead him to employment. Crane was, however, clearly not ever cut out for the long hours of writing ads that left him mentally exhausted and drained of creativity at the end of most days. His letters complain of his inability to concentrate enough to get the poems that he has already conceived down on paper. He envisions himself as something of a Christ figure (writing "Lachrymae Christi," which is also the name of a delicate, white Italian wine). The now often intoxicated Crane feels himself hung and withering on the cross of the daily grind and a world obsessed with money and material progress.

In April 1924 Crane met the man who was to re-inspire his writing and introduce a whole new aspect to his poetry. Though Emil Opffer was one of many sailor lovers that Crane would have in his life, he was by far the most important to the poet, if not to the man as well. He wrote to Frank:

> For many days, now, I have gone about quite dumb with something for which "happiness" must be too mild a term. At any rate, my aptitude for communication, such as it ever is!, has been limited to one person alone, and perhaps for the first time in my life (and, I can only think that it is for the last, so far is my imagination from the conception of anything more profound and lovely than this love). . . . I have seen the Word made Flesh. I mean nothing less, and I know now that there is such a thing as indestructibility.

Crane's experience with Opffer was to inspire most of the "Voyages" sequence in *White Buildings,* though the first part of the sequence had been written three years before. The six poems make up a sea journey, which the voyager envisions simultaneously as a journey through love, with a lover that he possesses and then loses in the course of his wandering. The experience of love is a search for communication that merges, upon the sea, with the quest for language, as the voyager seeks an answer to an unasked question (of mortality? of God?), an eternal communication that finally materializes in the eternal communication of the "imaged Word" at

the end of "Voyages VI." It is perhaps not the "Word made Flesh" described in his letters about Opffer, but it is nevertheless made possible only because of the love that began the journey.

From this voyage on, the sea is simultaneously an image of love in motion, whose "undinal vast belly moonward bends," a place of eternally passing and yet unmarkable time ("Mark how her turning shoulders wind the hours"). The sea is the being whose depths contain answers that she writes only upon the transient waves of the night that envelopes the second section of this poem: "Take this Sea, whose diapason knells / On scrolls of silver snowy sentences."

The voyager who cannot be bound in time, who cannot freeze an instant of the waves in motion, may only find the truth upon the bottom of the sea, in the shell scraps with which the children in "Voyages I" are playing or in the wreckage of voyages past. Crane indicates them in "At Melville's Tomb" (written in late 1925):

> And wrecks passed without sound of bells,
> The calyx of death's bounty giving back
> A scattered chapter, livid hieroglyph,
> The portent wound in corridors of shells.

Knowing this, the voyager pleads with the sea (and simultaneously with love) to allow this voyage to continue until a vortex may allow him to find his answers and his grave at the bottom of the sea:

> Bequeath us to no earthly shore until
> Is answered in the vortex of our grave
> The seal's wide spindrift gaze toward paradise.

The solution is not as simple as death, however, for the ship pulls into a bay harbor and, as the water calms in "Voyages V," the beloved slips away. The voyager can no longer keep his lover's hand, nor follow his gaze into the apparent death that has enthralled him. "There's / Nothing like this in the world," the other tells him, but the voyager can no longer understand what he sees, his "breath sealed by the ghosts I do not know."

As dawn breaks the voyager is left with Belle Isle (incidentally, a small island just off the coast of northern France with no connecting bridge to the mainland). In the island of the sixth section of the poem he receives the answer he sought in the vortex of the first section:

> The imaged Word, it is, that holds
> Hushed willows anchored in its glow.
> It is the unbetrayable reply
> Whose accent no farewell can know.

As Harold Bloom describes in the introduction to *The Complete Poems of Hart Crane* (2000), the sequence of poems is a "journey to a covenant that yields up the tally in return for 'the imaged Word'" that trades erotic loss for poetic gain. The "Belle Isle" section of the poem is its voyager's extraordinary movement toward a hope that does not depart, toward an eternal answer to be found not at the bottom of the sea but upon the ground, after the voyage is complete.

Crane will hold on to the imagery of "Voyages" and to the image of himself as the voyager seeking answers in the poems that he writes after "Voyages." From this point on, the persona of his poems seeks the sea, flows with rivers on the way to the sea, but never again is there to be any such glowingly simple answer as Belle Isle. Ever increasingly it becomes the embarking upon the journey itself that is important for Crane, the poem leading the speaker to the sea, but no longer upon the turbulent shimmering of this love poem from 1924. The grown child who reaches the sea in "Repose of Rivers" is to glory in the sound of the "wind flaking sapphire," but the poem leaves him at the edge of the sea, not upon it. Columbus in the "Ave Maria" section of *The Bridge* has reached his destination, has found a sort of truth, but again has embarked upon the sea and is left behind by the poem,

still fearing that he may never be able to convey his truth, to carry it back into actual reality. Even Crane's glorious bridge can only indicate answers, can put one in position to be swept up into one's contemplation, but it is not an answer in itself.

As his letters indicated, perhaps Crane himself began to suffer from the fear of his own Columbus: that he would not be able to bring his imagined poems into reality. Even if he were able to do so to his own satisfaction, the world might not understand them. His poetry might not be capable of any communication, any sort of bridge at all. Crane articulated these doubts in a letter to Frank in June 1926, just before embarking upon the three most intense months of writing that Crane was ever to experience again. "Emotionally I should like to write the bridge; intellectually judged the whole theme and project seems more and more absurd. A fear of personal impotence in this matter wouldn't affect me half so much as the convictions that arise from other sources. . . ."

Such dejection was partially a result of Crane's material and personal dilemmas. Given two thousand dollars by the banker Otto Kahn in December 1925 for the purposes of finishing *The Bridge* that had been more or less abandoned since 1923, Crane was able to leave work and the city to devote himself full-time to the writing of that poem. He went to Patterson, New Jersey, where he had spent time on and off for the past two years with the Tates in the space they rented from a woman named Addie Turner. It was a part of the country into which Crane and his friends had often escaped the summers and the spending temptations of New York. Crane's poor style of financial management, however, ate away at his funds at a rate much quicker than expected. A falling-out with the Tates over living conditions in the crowded house soon added to feelings of alienation that had begun the year before when Crane's refusal to adhere to any particular poetic philosophy led to his break with Munson. More or less encouraged to leave Patterson, Crane eventually left New York to head for the calm and economically feasible Hart family plantation on the Isle of Pines in May 1926, feeling detached from the poetry world that had until recently seemed to support him.

The hostility Crane perceived was not a result of only personal difficulties, but also of an increasing resistance on the part of critics to his work. Crane's poetry was perceived as *too* difficult, too convoluted, for the readership of most of the journals in which he was forced to publish. He departed for Cuba in the midst of complications regarding the publication of *White Buildings,* which had finally been accepted by Boni & Liveright (after rejections elsewhere) on the grounds that Eugene O'Neill would write an introduction to the book that he was apparently reluctant to write. Publication stalled until Allen Tate eventually composed the introduction that got the book into publication. Crane had also had a number of disputes with Marianne Moore of *The Dial* in 1925 over his poem "The Wine Menagerie," which Moore had accepted only on the condition that she could rewrite parts of it for better clarity and rename it "Again." The then impoverished Crane had been forced for a pitifully meager sum to accept her conditions. He had published "At Melville's Tomb" with similar difficulties at the beginning of 1926 in *Poetry,* under the stipulation that he write a prose explanation to accompany the poem. Crane's mixed metaphors and complicated structures seemed forced and nonsensical to readers, including those who were perhaps already predisposed against him because of his homosexuality, his irresponsible behavior, and his growing reputation as a drunk. (Winters was eventually to pass over into one of these readers, as Munson had less forcefully done before.)

Crane, however, was attempting to advance in his poetry ideas that the simple intellect seeking rational constructions might not necessarily understand. His theory and use of metaphor is one of the subjects that still most fascinates and frustrates his critics. Crane was more interested in the immediate and often irrational effects of words upon the consciousness, of sensations and instinctual associations that lead to metaphor, than he was in the rigid and logical significations of words in their everyday definitions. Even as he stayed within the confines of fairly traditional forms, Crane wanted to break away with his language from the logic and rationality that confined him, that would not allow him to describe the almost indescribable sensations and concepts that he seeks in "Voyages" and that did not perhaps, he felt, have words in common speech. Only through the juxtaposition of words and slightly off-kilter reinterpretations could Crane write of the imagined realm of which he wished to write, a communication that spans time and space in the way that the poetic bridge "For the Marriage of Faustus and Helen" had already sought to do.

He responded in print (a rare gesture for Crane) to the objections of Harriet Monroe, editor of *Poetry,* who had asked him for the prose interpretation of his poem after criticizing the overly intellectualized and forced obscurity of the poem's language. He wrote:

The logic of metaphor is so organically entrenched in pure sensibility that it can't be thoroughly traced or explained outside of historical sciences, like philology and anthropology. This "pseudo-statement," as I. A. Richards calls it in an admirable essay touching our contentions in last July's *Criterion,* demands completely other faculties of recognition than the pure rationalistic associations permit.

Crane then went on to say that "the *rationale* of metaphor belongs to another order of experience than science, and is not to be limited by a scientific and arbitrary code of relationships either in verbal inflections or concepts." Perhaps then, like human relationships themselves, Crane's poetry asks for a small act of faith on the part of his reader, a momentary suspension of the rational desire to explain that will result, instead, in an ability to understand the very immaterial and inexplicable concepts and experiences with which he concerns himself. He wanted to address a level of comprehension that perhaps existed only before the logic of language took hold, and he attempts to touch with his images an intuition that, like the traces of the past he is forever uncovering, may not have been lost in the changes of modernity.

As Malcolm Cowley describes in the passage quoted above, Crane the drunken ranter can make one see a woman's face in the mantelpiece, and Crane the poet gives readers the "dice of drowned men's bones he saw bequeath / An embassy." It is perhaps the quality responsible for Munson's description of Crane's poems as "divine madness," for the hypnotic frenzy that Winters first describes and then critiques in Crane's work. It is the genius that prompts Tate's defense of the poetry in the introduction to *White Buildings* when he says that "the *poetical* meaning is a direct intuition, realized prior to an explicit knowledge of the subject-matter of the poem. The poem does not *convey;* it *presents;* it is not topical, but expressive." The importance of this expression is left subjected to the reader's capacity of understanding. As Allen Grossman describes the "siren song" that is Crane's poetry in his 1982 article, "Hart Crane and Poetry: A Consideration of Crane's Intense Poetics with Reference to 'The Return,'" the "difficult" poem such as Crane's "situates the reader internal to the poem, and assigns him the task of completing rather than deriving significances." Crane's poetry has no and yet all possibility of relation to the world, but it is up to his reader to create or reject that possibility.

The obscurity and convolution of many of Crane's metaphors and poems as a whole are perhaps best seen as (what else?) a bridge between poet and reader. Like the love story behind his grandmother's love letters, Crane wants the reader to understand his own wordless experiences and workings of imagination that lie behind the words on the page. Even more than *White Buildings, The Bridge* requires this capacity on the part of poet and reader to meet in unconventional, anti-rational descriptions of such ineffable material as the passing and the meeting of the times, the history of a nation, and the presence of hope in the otherwise bleak present tense. Dejected by the apparent lack of connection between himself and the world, and unable as he often was as a result to embody his poem in written words, Crane wrote to Waldo Frank:

> These "materials" were valid to me to the extent that I presumed them to be (articulate or not) at least organic and active factors in the experience and perceptions of our common race, time and belief. The very idea of a bridge, of course, is a form peculiarly dependent on such emotional convictions. It is an act of faith besides being a communication. The symbols of reality necessary to articulate the span—may not exist where you expected them, however. By which I mean that however great their subjective significance to me is concerned—these forms, materials, dynamics are simply non-existent in the world, I may amuse and delight and flatter myself as much as I please—but I am only evading a recognition and playing Don Quixote in an immorally conscious way.

The act of faith, that the image of joined hands best describes, is Crane's poetic attempt at a communication that is perhaps not meant to be any less intuitive, illogical, mystical, and overwhelming than that which overcame him when he met Opffer. Perhaps less Quixotic than it might have appeared given the persistence of criticism of Crane's poems that followed along the lines of the early comments by Monroe, Crane was finally able to overcome his darker moments of fear that there was no common ground at all to support his poetic communication. With the last of Otto Kahn's assistance funds, Crane managed to pass three months of frenzied creation late in the summer of 1926 in the tranquility of his family's Isle of Pines plantation, far from the temptations and the distractions of city life and worries.

BUILDING *THE BRIDGE*

When Crane left for Cuba, he had already written the first and last sections of what was to become the book-length poem *The Bridge*. Crane had already begun "Atlantis," the last section of the poem and the first part finished, when he left Cleveland for New York again in March 1923, and he began "To Brooklyn Bridge," the poem's proem, shortly thereafter. He realized early on the enormity of his project, but the nearly seven years that it would take him to finish went beyond even his own worst expectations. He ended up putting the project aside for the next three years and picking it up again in late 1925, writing the following plan for its structure in a progress report to Kahn the following spring:

> There are so many interlocking elements and symbols at work throughout *The Bridge* that it is next to impossible to describe it without resorting to the actual metaphors of the poem. Roughly, however, it is based on the conquest of space and knowledge. . . .
>
> I Columbus—Conquest of space, chaos
>
> II Pokahantus—The natural body of America-fertility, etc.
>
> III Whitman—The Spiritual boy of America (A dialogue between Whitman and a dying soldier in a Washington hospital; the infraction of physical death, disunity, on the concept of immortality)
>
> IV John Brown (Negro porter on Calgary Express making up berths and singing to himself (a jazz form for this) of his sweetheart and the death of John Brown, alternately)

> V Subway—The encroachment of machinery on humanity; a kind of purgatory in relation to the open sky of the last section
>
> VI The Bridge—A sweeping dithyramb in which the Bridge becomes the symbol of consciousness spanning time and space

The final version of the poem clearly departs from this early layout. There is the addition of the sections "Cutty Sark" and "Quaker Hill," a rather radical transformation of "John Brown" into "Three Songs," and the elimination of any direct dialogue between Whitman and anyone but the poet himself. The skeleton of Crane's plan remains, but the final poem is even more fragmented than the original, and according to some critics it is in fact so fragmented that the image of the bridge at the beginning and end falls short of unifying the time and space that Crane wishes to envelop. The critic Margaret Dickie, for example, attributes this failure (as many saw and continue to see it) to the fact that Crane himself no longer held to his own image of unity, conceived so many years before the body of the poem. She writes, "As he wrote various sections of the poem, Crane moved away from his ending, and his vision of the bridge as an icon faded in the process. . . . Far from leading up to the ending, the poem was written away from it."

Whether or not they make up parts of a coherent whole, however, the parts of *The Bridge* developed in Cuba during Crane's long awaited creative breakthrough in the late summer of 1926 include, along with the opening and closing he had already written, the strongest sections of the poem. He worked on "Powhatan's Daughter," "The Tunnel," "Cutty Sark," "Three Songs," and "Cape Hatteras" (which he finally completed in the fall of 1929) simultaneously, moving from one to the other constructing, as he wrote, the bridge from both ends at once. During that time, he also wrote the poems that were to make up the volume *Key West,* but which were not published as such during Crane's lifetime. His productivity came to an end on October 18, 1926, when a hurricane destroyed the house that he and his aunt inhabited.

Crane headed back to New York, back out to Patterson, and back to New York again, but he was never able to find the peace and ease with which he had worked on the Isle of Pines. He was once again struggling financially, despite further loans from Kahn and his father and an inheritance from the death of his grandmother on the Hart side (hard won from Hart's mother, who tried to use the money to make him stay with her in California). In the hope of finding inspiration outside of New York, Crane began to travel. An odd job as a personal assistant to Herbert Wise, a rich and ailing dilettante of sorts, enabled him to get to Hollywood for the early months of 1928. His grandmother's money provided a trip to London, Spain, and France, where he met Eugène Jolas (editor of *transition,* a Paris-based journal that had published many of Crane's poems in 1927) and the French luminaries Gertrude Stein, Philippe Soupault, and Louis Aragon. Neither trip, however, led to much in the way of poetry as Crane found it difficult to resist the temptation of foreign adventures and erotic encounters and was suffering from increasingly violent alcoholism.

The trip to France did, however, bring Crane into contact with Caresse and Harry Crosby, whose Black Sun Press was to be the first to publish *The Bridge* in January 1930, in a limited edition dedicated to Kahn that included three Walker Evans photos of the Brooklyn Bridge. It seems to have been Harry's tragic double suicide with a lover on a visit to New York in December 1929 that prompted a depressed and fragmented Crane to finally get Caresse the final drafts of the last two and, according to most critics, weakest sections of *The Bridge:* "Indiana" and "Quaker Hill."

TIME, SPACE, AND BRIDGING

In an attempt to explain the all-consuming task of creating a vision of his time in *The Bridge,* Crane writes to Winters in 1926 (reprinted in *O My Land, My Friends*): "But what is 'mythical' in or rather, of the twentieth century is not the Kaiser, the sinking of the *Titanic,* etc. Rather it is science, travel (in the name of *speed*)—psychoanalysis, etc. With, of course, the eternal verities of the sea, mountain and river still at work." These are the elements that dominate Crane's America. The bridge is an almost too perfect image to encompass them all in the sort of weaving that Crane hoped to accomplish in his long poem, which was a colossal combination of many of the themes that he had introduced in the poems of *White Buildings.* Its most important philosophical antithesis and structural model was Eliot's *The Waste Land* (1922); Crane's overarching quest with *The Bridge,* however, was entirely different: to re-create something of the myth of America, of its original spirit and inhabitants, of its European discoverers, of its early pioneers, of its poets, and of its land and rivers. He sought to illuminate the traces of this mythic past in the present day and, while still emphasizing the all too obvious crumbling of his own time, to create a new myth out of the present tense itself. Even if trains, planes, bridges, and technology had become material and practical means to material and practical ends, they could still be viewed in the light of humanity's eternal search for new territory, new knowledge, and perhaps even some kind of spiritual understanding. Even as Crane alternately embraced and rejected a negative vision of a world in shambles, unable to understand itself, he nevertheless also envisioned a continuous motion toward knowledge, toward a future, that was perhaps no less possible in Crane's time than it was, for example, in Whitman's: "Yes, Walt," Crane answers his own question in "Cape Hatteras" ("if infinity / Be still the same . . . ?").

Afoot again, and onward without halt,—
Not soon, nor suddenly,—No, never to let go
    My hand
            in yours,
                    Walt Whitman—
                            so—

The eight parts of *The Bridge* are carefully structured and labeled pieces of what is intended to be viewed as a whole, and they often read like a narrative of certain events in the history of America. However, any attempt to paraphrase or summarize the entire work would not merely be futile but would lock the poem into the very coherence that it carefully avoids. Like its opening epigraph from the Book of Job, "From going to and fro in the earth, / and from walking up and down in it," the poem does not move in a single purposeful direction but often shuttles among its many themes and images. Crane propels the reader from one place to another, one time to another, with the intuitively associative logic of his metaphors, making his reader labor to figure out where and when he is, as well as why he has gone there. As is almost always the case with Crane's voyagers, it is not the purposeful *user* of the bridge with a planned trajectory from point to point who reaches an understanding of the unbrokenness of time and space, of the connection between divine and mortal. Rather it is the traveler—like his modern Faustus, who is willing to forget his way and to succumb to a dreamlike flow between places, times, and images—who arrives at such revelation. With this in mind, it would seem that the first key image to understanding *The Bridge* is the often explored water that it spans.

The river under the bridge is Crane's vision of the presence of history in even the modern-day city. "The River" begins with the roar of the train in New York:

        . . . whistling down the tracks
    a headlight rushing with the sound—can you
    imagine—while an EXPRESS makes time like
    SCIENCE . . .

The train heads west toward Ohio, moving at the same time through images of the past tense of the poet.

            Behind
    My father's cannery works I used to see
    Rail-squatters ranged in nomad raillery,
    The ancient men—wifeless or runaway
    Hobo-trekkers that forever search
    An empire of wilderness of freight and rails.
    Each seemed a child, like me, on a loose perch,
    Holding to childhood like some termless play.

The poet feels himself tied to the rail voyagers, to their wandering that is in fact a search. They and the poet himself "touch something like a key perhaps," and have access to a knowledge of their land that turns, in the next stanza, into the body of a woman that soon becomes the body of a Native American woman.

At this point the poet's own wandering, however, becomes musings of the imagination. His wandering is a midnight trodding within a dimly lit room, where he has "dreamed beyond the print that bound her name." He knows her beyond the story that her name evokes, though the other destination-less travelers (those "who have touched her, knowing her without name") also know her in a sense more intimate than the factual or historical. For Crane, names, like words themselves, are humans' failed attempt at playing immortal over all that is mortal around them. With words, people pin things to a definition and maim them in the process. Crane writes in "A Name for All": "Names we have, even, to clap on the wind; / But we must die, as you, to understand." Crane does not name the Woman of the South in "Southern Cross," saying, "It is / God—your namelessness." Likewise, the woman in "The River" still remains nameless and obscure, the embodiment of the mythical Native American past that Crane wishes to establish beneath the feet (or the trains) in this section of the poem.

The woman does receive a name in the narrative of "The Dance," the next section of the poem. She is Pocahontas, the bride of the dancing Maquokeeta, who enthralls the willing poet into the past, into his rhythm whose frenzy the poem itself mimics. "Medicine-man, relent, restore— / Lie to us,—dance us back the tribal morn!" the poet pleads with him, as he watches Maquokeeta transformed into part of the night sky where he will gaze through all time at his bride who is transformed into the earth below him.

> And saw thee dive to kiss that destiny
> Like one white meteor, sacrosanct and blent
> At last with all that's consummate and free
> There, where the first and last gods keep thy tent.

Maquokeeta, whom Crane refers to as the "snake that lives before," is the lizard that becomes "pure serpent, Time itself," and is present already in the vision of the woman in "The River." In the poet's nights of dreaming and wandering, he says:

> . . . But I knew her body there
> Time like a serpent down her shoulder, dark,
> And space, an eaglet's wing, laid on her hair.

Here time is the Native American prince, presiding eternally in the night sky over the expanse of the body of his bride, Pocahontas, who is the space of the America that Crane is re-creating. Both are therefore present even in the city, above and on either side of the Brooklyn Bridge.

The train voyage continues, however, onto the bridge over where the Ohio River meets the Mississippi River, and then in rhyming quatrains the poet takes readers upon the river itself. The modern train meets the ancient river, symbol of time eternally passing, slowly, silently, and taking everyone eventually into its flow (though they joke and smile and sniff, unaware of the significance of the river they cross).

> You will not hear it as the sea; even stone
> Is not more hushed by gravity . . . But slow,

> As loth to take more tribute—sliding prone
> Like one whose eyes were buried long ago

> The River, spreading, flows—and spends your dream.
> What are you, lost within this tideless spell?
> You are your father's father, and the stream—
> A liquid theme that floating niggers swell.

The river, unlike the sea, is tideless and timeless (without waves to mark the hours). It is the meeting place of all that has come before and all that comes now, still alive. "Tortured with history, its one will—flow!" unceasingly toward the sea, toward the voyage that yields Belle Isle or, as this poem indicates, toward the graveyard of remnants at the sea bottom. It is the water that flows over the land that is Pocahontas and reflects the sky where Maquokeeta gazes.

The river is what the bridge in the middle of New York City spans. Martin Heidegger's description of a bridge in "Building, Dwelling, Thinking" (in *Poetry, Language, Thought,* 1971) seems to aptly describe the sort of bridge that Crane wishes to glorify:

> The bridge *gathers* the earth as landscape around the stream. Thus it guides and attends the stream through the meadows. Resting upright in the stream's bed, the bridge-piers bear the swing of the arches that leave the stream's waters to run their course. The waters may wander on quiet and gay, the sky's floods from storm or thaw may shoot past the piers in torrential waves—the bridge is ready for the sky's weather and its fickle nature. Even where the bridge covers the stream, it holds its flow up to the sky by taking it for a moment under the vaulted gateway and then setting it free once more. . . . The bridge *gathers* to itself in *its own* way earth and sky, divinities and mortals.

On its simplest level, the poem-bridge perhaps signifies the act of communication between past and present (of the nation and the individual), between the poet of the past and the poet of the present, and between the poet and the reader of all times. More importantly, though, the bridge, like the poem, is that which draws humankind out of the nearly skyless rushing ahead of the city. The bridge rises up in the space created by the river and, while allowing one to look down upon that river, draws the eye upward. It lifts the observer up into the same night sky and questions that the voyager contemplates from his ship. In its infinitely practical purpose of aiding humanity's conquest of space, the bridge does nothing more than move man faster, but no closer to any notion of God. Beside and enveloping that notion of the bridge, however, is the one that Crane re-creates, harp and altar created by man that gathers all time and space to itself.

> . . . Here by the River that is East—
> Here at the waters' edge the hands drop memory;
> Shadowless in that abyss they unaccounting lie.
> How far away the star has pooled the sea—
> Or shall the hands be drawn away, to die?
>
> Kiss of our agony Thou gatherest,
> O Hand of Fire
> gatherest—

Crane's bridge, though it may appear solid and immobile, is only an illusion of stillness.

> O Sleepless as the river under thee,
> Vaulting the sea, the prairies' dreaming sod,
> Unto us lowliest sometime sweep, descend
> And of the curveship lend a myth to God.

The bridge is as sleepless as the river flowing through time. Its cords and curves are in constant song. The "Tall Vision-of-the-Voyage" pulls the eyes upward (into contemplation, the up and down of Job's walking). Crane had explored this sense of flight in "For the Marriage of Faustus and Helen"; the flight of the intellect does not destroy and does not crash, unlike literal, technological means of flight, such as the airplane in "Cape Hatteras":

> down gravitation's
> vortex into crashed

. . . dispersion . . . into mashed and shapeless debris. . . .

like that at the bottom of Melville's sea. Instead, the music of the bridge, with those that it uplifts, flows eternally upward in an Icarian flight that, in this recreation of Atlantis, is not doomed to failure:

> . . . upward, upward ring
> With silver terraces the humming spars,
> The loft of vision, palladium helm of stars.
>
> Sheerly the eyes, like seagulls stung with rime—
> Slit and propelled by glistening fins of light—
> Pick biting way up towering looms that press
> Sidelong with flight of blade on tendon blade
> —Tomorrows into yesteryear—and link
> What cipher-script of time no traveller reads
> But who, through smoking pyres of love and death,
> Searches the timeless laugh of mythic spears.

Only the voyager who seeks the overcoming of time and space that is God (never a defined Christian God for Crane, but a god, an eternal answer, an Everpresence) can have access to this vision of Crane's bridge-poem. These searchers alone undergo a sort of transformation into seagulls, that in the proem circle up and up out of sight.

Crane's "Atlantis" is meant to be a resurrection of any and all lost promised lands, including that of his Columbus whose Cathay turned into Crane's America. Most importantly it is the realization of all humanity's Atlantis, where humans reach or even become God, where all time and space are condensed into one man-made image. The Hand of Fire that gathered is now the "One Song, one Bridge of Fire!" The poem finishes by asking if this image of the bridge is in fact the promised land.

> . . . Is it Cathay
> Now pity steeps the grass and rainbows ring
> The serpent with the eagle in the leaves . . . ?

Crane's Bridge responds with its antiphonal whispers.

THE BROKEN TOWER

The Black Sun Press edition of *The Bridge* was followed three months later in April 1930 by a Liveright trade edition that, despite America's economic depression, sold all one thousand of its printed copies by September of that year. Reviews were mixed, from the usual complaints of Crane's obscurity to Cowley's praise and Tate's guarded approval that situated Crane at the end of an exhausted age of romanticism. Winters' lambasting of the poem in *Poetry* came as the biggest surprise to Crane, who believed he had the support of his longtime correspondent, despite their many poetic differences. Winters found the poem to be too emotional and anti-intellectualist, a failed epic lacking framework, feigning elevation into a realm with which Crane could not possibly be familiar. Crane responded in a rather indignant letter to Winters in June 1930 with a dig at Winters' own poetry. "The results have not been as satisfactory as I had hoped for; but I believe that such 'wreckage' as I find remaining, presents evidence of considerably more significance than do the cog-walk gestures of a beetle in a sand pit."

Crane was still living in New York with his usual financial and health problems at the time of the publication of *The Bridge*. In the summer of 1930 he went back to Patterson, only to be thrown out by his landlord who was weary of his violent and now almost constant intoxication. Back in New York again, Crane found himself still unable to write and still unable to find work, with growing fears that he had in fact lost or, worse, destroyed his poetic talent. He applied for a Guggenheim award to go to Europe, and headed back to Cleveland until the Guggenheim came through in March of the following year. Attempting to avoid the sort of artistic stagnation that had afflicted him on his last trip to Europe, Crane decided at the last minute to go to Mexico instead.

He spent the next year living in a house outside Mexico City. Having gone with the rather vague idea that he had first mentioned in 1926 of writing "a blank verse tragedy of Aztec mythology," Crane did little more than dabble in the subject while he was in Mexico. He managed to spend some time in Tepotzlán with the archaeologist Milton Rourke, where he participated in an Aztec festival ceremony, but his serious poetic pursuits dwindled quickly. For the most part, he seems to have drunk a lot and written very little of significance. He had only sporadic and often unpleasant contact with fellow Guggenheimers living outside Mexico City. Despite a general lack of connections with the Mexican literary scene, with Frank's letters of introduction Crane met the Mexican poets Genaro Estrada and Léon Felipe Camino. Word of Crane's apparently inappropriate behavior with the two men got back to Frank who, exasperated with his friend's inability to keep promises of sobriety, joined the ranks of those friends who had already stopped writing to Crane.

Crane's last months in Mexico were drastically changed by the arrival of Peggy Cowley, who was soon to become Malcolm's ex-wife. She became perhaps Crane's one and only serious heterosexual love. "You can give me many things besides—if time proves me fit to receive them: the independence of my mind and soul again, and perhaps a real wholeness to my body," he wrote to her in January 1932. Shortly thereafter, he wrote "The Broken Tower," perhaps the only poem of great interest that he had written since *The Bridge,* and one that despite its traces of a love that revives seems highly aware of the poet's demise.

The bells, I say, the bells break down their tower;
And swing I know not where. Their tongues engrave
Membrane through marrow, my long-scattered score
Of broken intervals . . . And I, their sexton slave!

Crane committed suicide on April 27, 1932. He and Peggy had set sail for New York, with plans to marry as soon as her divorce was finalized. Crane was already distraught, having, in a drunken state, twice attempted suicide a few weeks before. He had sent "The Broken Tower" to *Poetry* only to receive no response, apparently furthering his fears of poetic failure and feelings of isolation. (It was later discovered that Crane's submission never arrived—see the letter from the editor Morton Zabel in John Unterecker's biography.) As the story goes, a missed meeting with Peggy during a layover in Havana started Crane drinking. He drank through the night, had a run-in with some of the sailors, and was locked in his cabin but, still drinking, managed to get himself out the next morning. His now well-known last statement to Peggy was, "I'm not going to make it, dear. I'm utterly disgraced." He walked up on deck, removed his coat, and jumped into the ocean, never to be found.

Selected Bibliography

WORKS OF HART CRANE

POETRY

White Buildings: Poems by Hart Crane. New York: Boni & Liveright, 1926. (Contains an introduction by Allen Tate.)

The Bridge: A Poem. Paris: The Black Sun Press, 1930; New York: Liveright, 1930.

The Collected Poems of Hart Crane. Edited by Waldo Frank. New York: Liveright, 1933.

Complete Poems of Hart Crane. Edited by Marc Simon. New York: Liveright, 2000. (Contains an introduction by Harold Bloom.)

LETTERS

O My Land, My Friends: The Selected Letters of Hart Crane. Edited by Langdon Hammer and Brom Weber. New York: Four Walls Eight Windows, 1997.

BIBLIOGRAPHIES AND CONCORDANCES

Landry, Hilton, and Elaine Hilton. *A Concordance to the Poems of Hart Crane*. Metuchen, N.J.: The Scarecrow Press, 1973.

Schwartz, Joseph. *Hart Crane: A Descriptive Bibliography*. Pittsburgh: University of Pittsburgh Press, 1972.

———. *Hart Crane: A Reference Guide*. Boston: G. K. Hall, 1983.

CRITICAL AND BIOGRAPHICAL STUDIES

Arpad, Joseph J. "Hart Crane's Platonic Myth: The Brooklyn Bridge." *American Literature* 39:75–86 (March 1967).

Bennett, Maria F. *Unfractioned Idiom: Hart Crane and Modernism*. New York: Peter Lang Publishing, 1987.

Blackmur, R. P. "New Thresholds, New Anatomies: Notes on a Text by Hart Crane." In his *The Double Agent: Essays in Craft and Elucidation*. Gloucester, Mass.: P. Smith, 1962.

Bloom, Harold, ed. *Hart Crane: Modern Critical Views*. New York: Chelsea House, 1986.

Brunner, Edward. *Splendid Failure: Hart Crane and the Making of* The Bridge. Urbana: University of Illinois Press, 1985.

Butterfield, R. W. *The Broken Arc: A Study of Hart Crane*. Edinburgh: Oliver & Boyd, 1969.

Clark, David R., ed. *Critical Essays on Hart Crane*. Boston: G. K. Hall, 1982. (Contains Allen Grossman, "Hart Crane and Poetry: A Consideration of Crane's Intense Poetics with Reference to 'The Return,'" 1982; and John T. Irwin, "Hart Crane's 'Logic of Metaphor,'" 1975.)

Combs, Robert. *Vision of the Voyage: Hart Crane and the Psychology of Romanticism*. Memphis: Memphis State University Press, 1978.

Cowley, Malcolm. *A Second Flowering: Works and Days of the Lost Generation*. New York: The Viking Press, 1973.

Dembo, L. S. "The Unfractured Idiom of Hart Crane's *Bridge*." *American Literature* 27:203–204 (May 1955).

Dickie, Margaret. *On the Modernist Long Poem*. Iowa City: University of Iowa Press, 1986.

Edelman, Lee. *Transmemberment of Song: Hart Crane's Anatomies of Rhetoric and Desire*. Stanford, Calif.: Stanford University Press, 1987.

Fisher, Clive. *Hart Crane: A Life.* New Haven, Conn.: Yale University Press, 2002.

Frank, Waldo. "The Poetry of Hart Crane." *The New Republic* 50:116–117 (March 16, 1927).

Friedman, Paul. "*The Bridge:* A Study in Symbolism." *Psychoanalytical Quarterly* 21:49–80 (1952).

Giles, Paul. *Hart Crane: The Contexts of* The Bridge. Cambridge, Mass.: Cambridge University Press, 1986.

Hammer, Langdon. *Hart Crane and Allen Tate: Janus-faced Modernism.* Princeton, N.J.: Princeton University Press, 1993.

Hanley, Alfred. *Hart Crane's Holy Vision:* White Buildings. Pittsburgh: Duquesne University Press, 1981.

Heidegger, Martin. *Poetry, Language, Thought.* New York: Harper & Row, 1971.

Horton, Philip. *Hart Crane: The Life of an American Poet.* New York: W. W. Norton, 1937.

Lewis, R. W. B. "Days of Wrath and Laughter." In his *Trials of the Word: Essays in American Literature and Humanistic Tradition.* New Haven, Conn.: Yale University Press, 1965.

———. *The Poetry of Hart Crane, A Critical Study.* Princeton, N.J.: Princeton University Press, 1967.

Liebowitz, Herbert A. *Hart Crane: An Introduction to the Poetry.* New York: Columbia University Press, 1968.

Mariani, Paul. *The Broken Tower: The Life of Hart Crane.* New York: W. W. Norton, 1999.

Martin, Robert K. "Hart Crane." In his *The Homosexual Tradition in American Poetry.* Austin: University of Texas Press, 1979. Pp. 115–163.

Moss, Howard. "Disorder as Myth: Hart Crane's *The Bridge.*" *Poetry* 62:32–45 (April 1943).

Munson, Gorham. *The Awakening Twenties: A Memoir-History of a Literary Period.* Baton Rouge: Louisiana State University Press, 1985.

Norton-Smith, John. *A Reader's Guide to Hart Crane's* White Buildings. Lewiston, N.Y.: The Edwin Mellen Press, 1993.

Parkinson, Thomas. *Hart Crane and Yvor Winters: Their Literary Correspondence.* Berkeley: University of California Press, 1978.

Paul, Sherman. *Hart's Bridge.* Chicago: University of Illinois Press, 1972.

Pease, Donald. "Blake, Crane, Whitman, and Modernism: A Poetics of Pure Possibility." *PMLA: Publications of the Modern Language Association of America* 96:64–85 (January 1981).

Riddel, Joseph. "Hart Crane's Poetics of Failure." *Journal of English Literary History* 33:473–496 (December 1966).

Shapiro, Lindsay Stamm. "William Lescaze and Hart Crane: A Bridge between Architecture and Poetry." *Syracuse University Library Associates Courier* 19:25–28 (spring 1984).

Smith, Ernest. *The Imaged Word: The Infrastructure of Hart Crane's* White Buildings. New York: Peter Lang Publishing, 1990.

Sundquist, Eric. "Bringing Home the Word: Magic, Lies, and Silence in Hart Crane." *Journal of English Literary History* 44:376–399 (summer 1977).

Trachtenberg, Alan, ed. *Hart Crane: A Collection of Critical Essays.* Englewood Cliffs, N.J.: Prentice-Hall, 1982.

Unterecker, John. *Voyager: A Life of Hart Crane.* New York: Farrar, Straus and Giroux, 1969.

Uroff, Margaret Dickie. *Hart Crane: The Patterns of His Poetry.* Urbana: University of Illinois Press, 1974.

Weber, Brom. *Hart Crane: A Biographical and Critical Study.* New York: The Bodley Press, 1948.

Winters, Yvor. *In Defense of Reason.* Athens: Swallow Press/Ohio University Press, 1987.

Wolf, Jack C. *Hart Crane's Harp of Evil: A Study of Orphism in* The Bridge. Troy, N.Y.: Whitston Publishing Company, 1986.

Yannella, P. R. "Toward Apotheosis: Hart Crane's Visionary Lyrics." *Criticism* 10:313–333 (fall 1968).

Yingling, Thomas E. *Hart Crane and the Homosexual Text: New Thresholds, New Anatomies.* Chicago: University of Chicago Press, 1990.

Zeck, Gregory R. "The Logic of Metaphor: 'At Melville's Tomb.'" *Texas Studies in Literature and Language* 17:673–686 (fall 1975).

—KIM LEWIS

Theodore Dreiser

1871–1945

THEODORE DREISER GENERALLY is accorded the title "Father of American Realism," even though realism in this context is a misnomer for naturalism. Realism better describes the work of Henry James and William Dean Howells, writers of the previous generation who viewed their literary characters more or less through the lens of Social Darwinism, the belief that humankind could rise above the deterministic forces of heredity and environment. In *The Rise of Silas Lapham* (1885) by Howells, for example, the main character falls financially but rises morally. Dreiser's lens is decidedly naturalistic because his major characters (usually the lower class or "foreigners," who were ignored by the Social Darwinists as genetically weak) view the world as a place where duty wars against desire. They are fully the products of heredity and environment, who seek out creature comforts and sexual pleasure instead of following the higher roads of morality and social justice. For example, George Hurstwood of *Sister Carrie* (1900) and Clyde Griffiths of *An American Tragedy* (1925), Dreiser's two greatest novels, are driven to their dooms by their love of sex and money. The origin of literary naturalism is the French nineteenth-century novelist Émile Zola, but Dreiser, who never read Zola's works, was influenced directly by his compatriot, Honoré de Balzac. Balzac taught him to pile up minute and realistic details in his novels. Zola, of course, was as much a passive force in the intellectual marketplace as Darwin. Dreiser also was influenced strongly by the deterministic writings of the English philosopher Herbert Spencer, the British biologist Thomas Huxley, and the British physicist and popularizer of science John Tyndall.

The broader use of "realism" to describe the area of Dreiser's literary achievement stems from the fact that the schools of realism and naturalism were reacting against the sentimental fiction of the 1850s. This means not merely the domestic fiction of the "feminine fifties" (though anything a woman wrote then usually was dismissed as "sentimental") but more generally the eleventh commandment of American society in the Victorian age that life be depicted as it ought to be rather than as it was. Walt Whitman had tried to tell the truth in poetry between 1855 and the 1880s. He was largely reviled by the literary establishment, and the 1882 edition of *Leaves of Grass* became the first book to be "banned in Boston." James, and especially Howells, had sought to tell the same truth without Whitman's candor. Dreiser, however, came from the same side of the tracks as Whitman. He also learned to write as a newspaper reporter. In this profession, particularly as a police reporter in Pittsburgh, he noted the disparity between what newspapers beholden to big business and city hall reported and what was the often sordid truth about American society as well as the individuals propelled by it.

Herman Theodore Dreiser was born in the smoky industrial town of Terre Haute, Indiana, on August 27, 1871, the twelfth of thirteen children of John Paul Dreiser and Sarah Maria Schänäb. His father was a German immigrant, and his mother came from a family of Mennonite farmers in Ohio. Dreiser became the first major American writer who was not descended from English stock. He was born next to the river immortalized in Paul Dresser's "On the Banks of the Wabash," the most famous song of his eldest brother (after the early deaths of the first three children). Paul is the other famous Dreiser (who changed his surname to avoid the discrimination experienced at that time by the children of German immigrants). He wrote many Tinpan Alley songs, including the equally famous "My Gal Sal," and his celebration of the Wabash River became the official state song of Indiana. Another of his songs, "Just Tell Them That You Saw Me," is about a prostitute in the big city ashamed to visit her small hometown and beloved mother; its pattern of the virgin ensnared by the wiles of the city anticipates the tale of Carrie Meeber (of *Sister Carrie*). Both brothers—along with trouble-destined sisters (two the models for leading Dreiser characters) and male siblings headed either for jail or the stage—fled their father's stern Catholicism and rigid morality. The victim of a mill accident, John Paul Dreiser tithed his meager earnings to the church while his children went without shoes in winter and were forced to steal lumps of coal from railroad cars to heat their home. Their father, whom Dreiser later came to both pity and admire, also was frequently unemployed.

When Theodore was eight or nine, the family split up to make ends meet. Sarah took the three youngest children first to southern Indiana and later to Warsaw in the northeast corner of the state, making her living by taking in borders and laundry. Dreiser dropped out of high school at age sixteen and took the train to Chicago (as does his heroine in *Sister Carrie* when she sets out for the big city). He worked there first as a dishwasher and later as a stock boy in a hardware store. An early reader of the European eighteenth- and nineteenth-century writers Voltaire, Henrik Ibsen, Johann Wolfgang von Goethe, and Arthur Schopenhauer, he was whisked away from his blue-collar fate by a former

schoolteacher from Warsaw who provided the means for him to spend a year at Indiana University (1889–1890). Although he later belittled the importance of this one year of college, it gave him a perspective on life that transcended the anger and self-pity of several of his brothers and sisters, whose bitter memories of their early poverty had marked them for failure in life. Upon returning to Chicago to find his mother dying, he became a newspaper reporter first in Chicago and later in St. Louis and Pittsburgh, as he gradually worked his way to New York City.

Assisted by Paul Dresser, whom he later eulogized in "My Brother Paul" in *Twelve Men* (1919), Dreiser eventually became a magazine editor and later a frequent contributor. By the late 1890s he had published more than a hundred magazine articles. In December of 1898 he married Sara Osborne White, a teacher in St. Louis. Soon he began *Sister Carrie,* ultimately suppressed by the publisher because of its uncompromising depictions of working-class America. As a result, the novel was a commercial failure, sending Dreiser into a three-year funk and depression, until Paul, by then a successful Broadway songwriter, rescued him and sent him to a sanitarium for a month in 1903. Dreiser recovered to manage the production of a trio of women's magazines but did not return to writing fiction until 1910. By that time his marriage had fallen apart in the wake of Dreiser's infatuation with a teenage girl, Thelma Cudlipp. Dreiser and his wife, whose strait-laced Midwestern background made her particularly unsuited to Dreiser's Bohemian ways, never divorced, though they lived apart until Sara's death in 1942. He restarted his literary career with the publication of *Jennie Gerhardt* (1911); like his first novel, it was based on the life of a wayward sister. He followed this up with a travel book and then the first and second volumes of his Trilogy of Desire, *The Financier* (1912) and *The Titan* (1914). Another novel, *The "Genius"* (1915), was closely modeled on his own life. Its candor eventually led to its suppression by the forces of the American reformer Anthony Comstock and his successor, John Sumner. Since the 1870s Comstock's Society for the Suppression of Vice had sought to stamp out the kind of "profanity" already found in the Bible, Shakespeare, and the classics.

In late 1919 Dreiser met and fell in love with his second cousin Helen Patges Richardson and followed her to Hollywood, where she played bit parts in silent movies, including *The Four Horsemen of the Apocalypse* (1921). It was during this nearly three-year period before returning to New York that Dreiser, after failing as a screenwriter, began *An American Tragedy*. He had thought of writing such a "crime novel" for many years—indeed, as far back as the days following *Sister Carrie*—and had investigated up to fifteen actual murder cases over the years, before settling upon the 1906 murder of Grace Brown by Chester Gillette. Most of the crimes that he considered were poisoning cases, but the drowning of the pregnant Brown by her lover, Gillette, in the lake country of upstate New York so that he could marry a rich girl finally won the day. Possibly it reminded Dreiser of the lakes around Warsaw, Indiana, where his own dreams of women and wealth had crystallized. Common to all the cases Dreiser examined was the inversion of the American Dream, in which sex and money proved to be a deadly dose.

An American Tragedy became an immense box-office and critical success, ultimately earning Dreiser hundreds of thousands of dollars, especially when he sold the novel to Hollywood. Dreiser had spent almost three solid years on the book, and the achievement quite exhausted his talent. Afterward, he exchanged literary celebrity for the life of a not-so-celebrated social activist whose causes were connected closely to the Communist Party in America in the 1930s. Most of his literary work after *An American Tragedy* consisted of either reworkings or reis-

sues of earlier labors (such as the shortened version of *The Financier* in 1927 or *A Gallery of Women* in 1929). He tried to finish *The Bulwark,* a novel he had begun around 1912, and *The Stoic,* the third volume of his planned Trilogy of Desire, but his heart was no longer in either project.

His head was turned toward social reform mainly by an extended visit to the Soviet Union on the tenth anniversary of the Bolshevik Revolution. Invited there along with numerous world-famous writers and speakers, Dreiser went as a confirmed individualist and returned as a converted Communist, mainly because of the influence of a young woman, an American expatriate who served as his secretary, traveling companion, and lover during the visit. (Ever since his separation in 1910 Dreiser had become a lifelong philanderer.) The memory of his impoverished youth also contributed to his conversion. Once the stock market crash of October 1929 ushered in the Great Depression, he was fully persuaded that capitalism was a failed economic system kept in place to exploit the poor. He published *Tragic America* in 1931, a cobbled-together screed condemning American capitalism as well as the influence in America of the Catholic Church. During the 1930s he attracted national attention for his involvement with the American writer John Dos Passos in the coal miners' strike in Harlan, Kentucky, and for his public efforts to aid the communist-inspired campaign to save the Scottsboro Boys, nine young black men falsely accused of raping a white woman in Alabama. In 1936 he endorsed the reform writer Upton Sinclair in his unsuccessful bid for the governorship of California.

As Dreiser's political activities increased, his literary reputation steadily declined. Its slide was well under way by the time Sinclair Lewis, whose literary achievement today is considered inferior to Dreiser's, became the first American to win the Nobel Prize in literature in 1930. Many in America believed that it should have gone to Dreiser (complaining that Lewis had won in the eyes of the Swedes merely because his books made fun of America). He also took up hackwork at top dollar in the magazines, especially after the stock market collapse had claimed half of his financial worth. In 1938 he returned permanently to Southern California, where he published yet another diatribe inspired by his communism, *America Is Worth Saving* (1941). Its notoriety earned him a greatly lengthened FBI record, a file first established after the publication of *Tragic America*. The book also underscored his isolationist policies before the entry of the United States into World War II. In this respect, Dreiser was for once in the majority because most Americans before the attack on Pearl Harbor wanted nothing to do with a European war after the failure of World War I to bring about a permanent peace in Europe. He was a vocal part of the America First campaign, an isolationist movement spearheaded by the American aviator Charles Lindbergh. Dreiser also disapproved of Great Britain, or, more specifically, its upper class, which he dismissed as horse-riding snobs; his scorn stemmed not only from what he saw as their superciliousness but also from England's opposition to Russian socialism. He was run out of Canada in 1942 for making anti-British remarks to the press.

Finally, a few years before his death, Dreiser finished both *The Bulwark,* a tale of tragedy in a Quaker family caught up in the modern age, and *The Stoic,* the final volume of his Trilogy of Desire. These novels, clearly Dreiser's weakest, were published posthumously in 1946 and 1947, respectively. They lacked his penchant for detail if not his natural-born ability as a storyteller (as evidenced at least in the last part of *The Bulwark*). In fact, Dreiser did not return to these novels for literary reasons at all, but for religious ones. By 1938, as a result of extended studies in natural science (selections of which were published in 1974 in *Notes on Life*), Drei-

ser the determinist became a latter-day transcendentalist, or one who believes that God acts through nature in a manner in which apparent evil is found to be ultimately good in the larger context of life. One of the catalysts for his transition may have been his study of the works of the transcendentalist Henry David Thoreau in the late 1930s—he took up the study of Thoreau to write the introduction for a book of his selected works. Dreiser also had read the transcendentalist Ralph Waldo Emerson in his youth.

As a result of Dreiser's eleventh-hour conversion, both novels conceived with a determinist theme concluded on a positive religious note. The daughter of the Quaker patriarch cries at his funeral not for his death but for life in general, in which good and evil must vie with each other in the unfolding of the drama of human experience. Following the death of the ruthless financier in *The Stoic,* his mistress discovers the meaning of life in Hinduism. This denouement in either case was ultimately nothing new for Dreiser, for he was always fascinated by the beauty and terror of life. Dreiser began and ended in protest over the contradictions, and, indeed, many have wondered how this determinist also could have been a social reformer. But such contradictions and ironies followed this champion of the oppressed all the way to the grave. Dreiser died of a heart attack on December 28, 1945, in Los Angeles. His burial was delayed for three days because of a gravediggers' strike.

SISTER CARRIE

Although *Sister Carrie* is one of the world's greatest naturalistic novels, it has no obvious precursor either abroad or at home. Not only had Dreiser not read Zola, (nor even Flaubert's *Madame Bovary* by 1900), he had not even read "the American Zola," Frank Norris, or his masterpiece, *McTeague* (1899), when he wrote

Sister Carrie. If there is any direct model, it may be the American writer Stephen Crane in *Maggie: A Girl of the Streets* (1893), for Dreiser took some of his models from Crane's Bowery journalism in early newspaper sketches. Crane's sketches of urban despair, such as "An Experiment in Misery," strongly influenced Dreiser's 1899 essay entitled "Curious Shifts of the Poor," which was first published in *Demorest's Magazine* before eventually being absorbed into *Sister Carrie*. This magazine piece later was adapted to sketch out Hurstwood's last days on skid row. Mainly, *Sister Carrie* was a spontaneous creative act emerging out of a decade in which Dreiser saw the Darwinian scheme of "survival of the fittest" acted out in the American 1890s. He wrote the novel at the urging of his friend Arthur Henry, who also had been a journalist in the Midwest before coming to New York. Along with his wife, Sara, Dreiser spent the summer with Henry and his spouse at their home on the Maumee River in northwestern Ohio. There, Dreiser wrote four or five short stories, including "Nigger Jeff," his most important short fiction, based on a black lynching he had reported outside St. Louis in the early 1890s. (Unfortunately, this sympathetic treatment of the plight of the African American at the height of the lynching era is kept out of college anthologies today because of the pejorative in its title.) Coincidentally, his friend Henry had written one of the earliest Klan novels in 1890, but Dreiser never knew of its existence.

Henry wrote stories, too, and by the time the two friends returned to New York City in the fall of 1899, he began to "ding-dong about a novel," as Dreiser told his friend and champion the editor and satirist H. L. Mencken in 1916. Henry was writing a romance entitled *A Princess of Arcady* (1900), while Dreiser was writing a gloomy tragedy along deterministic lines. Doubleday published both in the same year. Later Dreiser claimed to have written the final

chapter of *A Princess of Arcady,* but, in fact, Arthur Henry may have penned the final paragraphs of *Sister Carrie,* where Carrie, financially sated, rocks in her chair and wonders what remains missing from her life. Although Dreiser had a definite romantic streak, these paragraphs were added at the behest of one of his editors. The manuscript that Dreiser initially submitted to his publisher ends with the suicide of Hurstwood.

Dreiser apparently began the novel, which was dedicated to Arthur Henry, with no preconceived plan or plot. He simply took out a sheet of yellow paper and wrote down at random the words "Sister Carrie." This was the story of his sister Emma, who, like Carrie, became involved with a married man who worked in an upscale saloon in Chicago. Threatened by his wife's efforts to publicize his infidelity and cost him his job, L. A. Hopkins stole $3,500 from his employers' safe and fled with Emma to New York by way of Canada in the winter of 1886. By the time Dreiser arrived in New York at the height of the economic depression in 1894 to live briefly with his sister, she and Hopkins had fallen on hard times. Eventually, Dreiser helped his sister and her two children desert the failing Hopkins, who, like his fictional counterpart, may have worked in a run-down hotel in the Bowery before dying from exposure. Dreiser testified that the idea for Hurstwood was born on the cold winter day on which he lost his job at the *New York World* and observed homeless men and vagrants shifting about in a public park in the freezing temperatures.

The plot of the novel involves essentially three characters. Carrie Meeber leaves her Wisconsin homestead for Chicago at the age of eighteen to live with her sister and brother-in-law. On the train to Chicago she meets a traveling salesman, or "drummer," named Charles Drouet, who later seduces her when she is out of work in Chicago. While living as Drouet's "wife," Carrie falls for George Hurstwood, the manager of a fancy Chicago saloon, who outshines Drouet. Rather than face his outraged wife, who soon discovers the affair, Hurstwood steals $10,000 from the saloon and flees to New York by way of Canada. As Hurstwood stands before his employers' safe, Dreiser makes it clear that he has no free choice but is led by instinct and circumstance. It is at this point that Hurstwood begins his long decline. As he fails over the next seven years, Carrie rises, eventually leaving him as she had abandoned Drouet in Chicago and succeeding on the popular stage. Drouet, the old butterfly, concludes at around the same level he began, neither rising nor falling. Like leaves in the wind, these three characters are blown this way and that by cosmic gales.

One complaint about the novel is that the title is not representative because the story is about two major characters and not one woman, like the one in Balzac's *Cousine Bette* (1847), a book that may have suggested Dreiser's use of "Sister" in his title. Mencken, who reviewed most of Dreiser's novels, considered it a major flaw that the novel opened with one main character and concluded with another. In fact, its original ending, as already noted, featured Hurstwood instead of Carrie. Structurally, Mencken might have been correct, but the decline of Hurstwood in the Bowery contrasts with Carrie's ascent and is one of the most poignantly gripping sequences in American literature. The reader follows the former saloon manager as he loses his apartment and finally his money to become a Bowery bum. Dreiser, whose early poverty made him always a worrier about money, conveys this fear fully to the reader through the pathetic figure of Hurstwood.

There is a fourth, though minor, figure, Bob Ames, a young inventor/engineer. His role was larger in the holograph (available in the historical edition of *Sister Carrie*), and he faintly resembles the young Thomas Edison, whom Dreiser once interviewed in the 1890s for a magazine called *Success*. Ames tries in vain to persuade Carrie to pursue more serious stage roles. He also gets her to read Balzac. This is clearly the author himself entering his own fiction to urge Carrie to rise above her circumstances somehow. Dreiser was always of two minds in his worldview, fascinated with both the mystery and the melancholy of life. He also was influenced by Spencer's thesis about the gradual amelioration of the human race. Dreiser, in an aside in the eighth chapter of *Sister Carrie* about "the forces which sweep and play throughout the universe," sees "untutored man" as only halfway perfected, "his free-will not sufficiently developed to replace his instincts."

This kind of naïveté, the fruit of Social Darwinism, whose romantic theory of progress generally was restricted to the white and middle-class male, is one of the very few exceptions to Dreiser's relentlessly grim portrayal of American life between 1889 and 1897, the time line of the novel. It caught America on the threshold of the twentieth century, still immersed in much of the superstition of the Victorian age yet already exposed to the modern world of the American city. This was largely a decade of economic depression, in which Coxey's Army of unemployed (a group brought together by the politician and businessman Jacob Selcher Coxey) marched east to Washington, D.C., to demand assistance from Congress, only for its leaders to be arrested for walking on the grass. It was also the age in which the department store emerged. Dreiser had interviewed the merchant Marshall Field, founder of the eponymous dry-goods store that grew to be the largest in the world, in Chicago in 1898 for a magazine article. It is to there, in the third chapter, that Carrie turns unsuccessfully for work, but not without first becoming dazzled by its store windows "filled with rarest gems and gaudiest trifles" (in *Theodore Dreiser's Ev'ry Month,* 1996). Earlier, Dreiser had penned a Whitmanesque catalog of Broadway's elaborate window displays. As a young man, he had absorbed everything around him, and it all went into the furnishings for *Sister Carrie.*

One invaluable source for the types of the rich and famous who patronize Fitzgerald and Moy's Saloon in Chicago, where Hurstwood is manager, was Dreiser's brother Paul, who, as a successful songwriter in the 1890s, introduced his shy younger brother ("the writer") to his pals and cronies up and down Broadway. As Ellen Moers writes, "In the background of *Sister Carrie* . . . the figure of Paul is an important if invisible presence, for the novel takes place in a social world to which Paul gave Theodore access but to which Theodore never truly belonged . . . traveling salesmen, Elks, chorus girls, and ladies set up in cozy flats." Paul, who weighed almost 300 pounds, had friends on every corner. He was the first and only family member to believe in his brother's talent and to encourage him as a writer.

Dreiser's writing has always been criticized for its awkward style, but most of the critics making this complaint nevertheless have to admire his great power as a storyteller. At his death, the *New York Herald Tribune* (December 30, 1945) described him as "the great writer who didn't know how to write." Contemporary critics also complained that *Sister Carrie* featured a class of Americans not worthy of dramatizing. Dreiser's "divine average," like Whitman's, worked for a living and spoke the vernacular of the day, which was generally not found in American novels before 1900. American readers (mostly women) did not want to read about skirt-chasing salesmen such as Drouet or girls next door like Carrie, who trade their virginity for fine clothes. They did not want to read about middle-aged men such as Hurstwood, who lusts after a woman half his age and abandons his wife and family. "It reeks of life's sordid endeavor," complained the *Louisville Times* (November 20, 1900). The *Chicago Chronicle* (January 14, 1901) declared that there

was "little art in the book." Mainly, it was seen as merely a photograph of life and one taken from the wrong angle. The story of *Sister Carrie* came directly from life, indeed, from Dreiser's own past as he grew up watching his elder siblings get into trouble. An American classic today, it took almost a decade after its initial publication to become recognized as such.

Although the principal characters in *Sister Carrie* are intellectually shallow, they are well rounded as realistically depicted literary characters. Drouet, the slick salesman, is like a moth drawn to a light in terms of his desire for the feminine. Hurstwood's concupiscence is even stronger than that of the less ambitious Drouet. It draws him all the way to his death by suicide. Carrie, the small-town girl on the lam, loves absolutely no one but herself—not her sister, Minnie, who provides her first shelter in Chicago; not Drouet, who saves her from a life on the streets of Chicago; and not Hurstwood, who gives up everything for her physical beauty and youth. As Dreiser writes of Carrie in the first chapter, no doubt thinking of his sister Emma, "Self-interest with her was high, but not strong. It was, nevertheless, her guiding characteristic." It is not that Carrie is atypically selfish; it is that she is humanly selfish and thus a survivor in the Darwinian jungle. Carrie, Dreiser writes, "was a fair example of the middle American class—two generations removed from the emigrant." Before Dreiser, who was only one generation removed from the feudalism of Europe, and other naturalistic writers at the turn of the century, the main characters of American fiction were typically ladies and gentlemen.

JENNIE GERHARDT

Jennie Gerhardt presents a similar kind of female, one whose resistance to exploitative men is only slightly stronger than Carrie's but also one whose heart is stronger than her appetite for creature comforts. *Jennie* was based on the early life of Mame, Dreiser's eldest sister, who became a "saint" to family members. Dreiser had resented Mame in his youth but eventually came around to view her as a saint as well. After being seduced in Terre Haute by a man whom Dreiser dubbed "Colonel Silsby" in his autobiography, Mame had a stillborn child. She married Austin Brennan, who hailed from a wealthy family in Rochester, New York, solidly opposed to the lower-class Mame. In the novel, Jennie is made pregnant by George Sylvester Brander, a U.S. senator many years her senior who dies suddenly, before he can marry her. She keeps the identity of her daughter a secret. As a maid in an upscale home, she meets Lester Kane, a man closer to her age and the heir, with his brother, to their father's prosperous carriage factory. They fall in love and secretly live together because his wealthy parents would not approve of his marrying someone from such a lower station in life. When ultimately faced with financial ruin orchestrated by his brother, Lester leaves Jennie for a woman of his own social class. When he dies, Jennie, faithful to the end, manages to be at his side.

Not only is Jennie a loving mother but she also adopts two children after the early death of her daughter; they become the main purpose of her life once she has given up all illusions about romantic love. Jennie concludes as a maternal figure who, after making mistakes in her own life, dedicates herself to helping others. One of Dreiser's literary models for this novel was Thomas Hardy's *Tess of the D'Urbervilles* (1891)—a tale about a woman who has sinned but is still basically good. Jennie gives herself to the senator because he is helping her family, and she essentially surrenders to her second lover for the same reasons, even though she loves him.

Like that of *Sister Carrie,* the plot of *Jennie Gerhardt* came primarily from Dreiser's family life. Jennie's life is based primarily on Mame's and so is her German family, in which the patriarch often speaks German in response to his children's English. One of Drieser's finest portraits is that of old Gerhardt, who resembles Dreiser's own father. Whereas John Paul Dreiser was fanatically Catholic, William Gerhardt is devotedly Lutheran. Rigidly moralistic, he refuses to allow Jennie to remain in the family home once he discovers that she is pregnant, but he finally is softened by the presence of his granddaughter, whom he cares for in Jennie's absence. John Paul Dreiser became emotionally attached to Carl Dreiser, the bastard son of his daughter Sylvia, who also served as a partial model for Jennie. Jennie also has a brother named Sebastian, based on Rome Dreiser, who initially tries to help his sister.

As a work of naturalism, this novel is not as successful as *Sister Carrie,* certainly not as "purely" deterministic; the human emotions are shown to rise up against, if not conquer, the relentless adversity of life. As a "story" about life and love, it is, of course, much more satisfactory, for in *Sister Carrie* nobody loves anybody else. Jennie is something of the earth, naturally good despite the circumstances and certainly not ruthless and selfish like Carrie. As a result, more idealistic, perhaps younger, readers prefer Jennie to Carrie. At the end of the story, of course, life grinds on, and Jennie must endure the privations and indignities of the human condition. Dreiser even thought of giving the novel a happy ending, but fortunately he was talked out of it. Here Dreiser also flirted with melodrama. This is especially true of the Brander section, in which the senator's lust is partly explained away as a component of his affection for Jennie and her family. It was, in the words of Donald Pizer, the model for the "classic" sentimental novel.

In the Lester Kane section, however, Jennie comes to life as an unselfish person whose love for her man and her child rivals the love of Hester Prynne for Arthur Dimmesdale and Pearl in Nathaniel Hawthorne's novel *The Scarlet Letter*

(1850). (It is interesting to note that one of the last magazine pieces Dreiser wrote before becoming a novelist with the writing of *Sister Carrie,* which also bears a faint resemblance to *The Scarlet Letter,* was a magazine article titled "Haunts of Nathaniel Hawthorne.") Jennie is neither a helpless maiden nor a gold digger but a woman who rises to the challenges of life in helping those she loves, including the man who finally, if reluctantly, spurns her. Lester Kane is the portrait of the reluctant financier who is torn between social classes and cursed by being born rich. As a result of his unearned affluence, he is never able, in the manner of Jennie, to commit himself unselfishly to anyone or anything.

TRILOGY OF DESIRE

The Financier, the first volume of Dreiser's Trilogy of Desire, which includes *The Titan* and *The Stoic,* marks an important departure for Dreiser, as he turned away from his family as the bedrock for his fiction. He also was finished for a long period with women as principals in his fiction. His next two novels were based on the real-life exploits of Charles Tyson Yerkes, the Philadelphia-born financier whose empire quickly vanished after his death in 1905. Dreiser had considered the lives of several such moguls as models for his financial superman, having interviewed some of the biggest for magazines in the 1890s. Nonetheless, he chose Yerkes as the model for Frank Cowperwood (pronounced "Cooperwood"), mainly because of the easy access to his biographical record in nearby Philadelphia, where he had lived in 1902. The details of Yerkes' flamboyance and shady dealings were readily available in all the newspapers throughout the first decade of the twentieth century, as his widow and his last mistress, along with many creditors, fought over his diminished estate.

Dreiser did not invent the "business novel" in America, of course. The first one to do that was probably William Dean Howells with *The Rise of Silas Lapham.* In that novel the successful businessman was still depicted idealistically as an ethical creature. With the rise of the robber barons in the 1890s and their exposure by muckraking journalists, however, that image all but disappeared. Such investigative journalists as Ida Tarbell and Lincoln Steffens attacked business and industry for its corruption in highly publicized exposés. These writings led to the anti-business novel, first developed by Frank Norris, David Graham Phillips, and Robert Herrick. The image of the entrepreneur became so tarnished during the first and second decades of the twentieth century that universities began to develop colleges of business to stress the need for ethics in commerce. Dreiser came somewhat late to this field of fiction, but he told the tale more dramatically and with much greater detail than did any of his predecessors. He also endowed his hero with a Nietzschean sense of power and confidence as well as an appetite summed up in Cowperwood's motto, "I satisfy myself."

All his life Dreiser had pitied and sympathized with the poor, but he also admired the "big brain," as he later referred to the strong who ruled their environments. His Tamerlane of American business was as much a product of the natural order as the weak were part of the Darwinian equation. Life was a struggle in which morality played no part. The central idea of the Cowperwood novels is suggested in the first chapter, when young Frank observes the defeat of a squid by a lobster in the window of a local fish market and concludes: "That's the way it has to be." Originally, Cowperwood's entire tale was to be told in one volume, before Dreiser realized that he would need at least one more and then, finally, two more separate books to cover all the territory of his epic. The volumes of the trilogy follow Cowperwood's adventures in Philadelphia, Chicago, and London. *The Financier* traces Frank's rise as a financier who makes his fortune in the evolving traction, or streetcar, lines that begin to cover the city in the wake of the Civil War.

Cowperwood of Philadelphia is Franklinesque not only in his financial rise but also in his sexual escapades. Because Dreiser could not "research" the intimate adventures of the noted philanderer Yerkes, he fell back on his own sexual encounters following his separation from his first wife. Cowperwood's philandering, which involves only one illicit lover in *The Financier,* increases exponentially in *The Titan* (where at least one of Dreiser's lovers can be identified). In *The Financier* he marries a widow and has children; he eventually abandons them all for Aileen Butler, his second wife in *The Titan.* Aileen is the daughter of a powerful Philadelphia politico who feels betrayed by Frank's secret acquisition of his daughter while pretending to be his friend. The portrait of Edward Butler, a semi-illiterate Irishman who rose from a job as a slop peddler, is one of the most powerful in the Dreiser canon. Butler is out to get Cowperwood and seizes the opportunity during the financier's illegal business dealings with the city treasurer. After the great Chicago fire of 1871, Philadelphia's loans are suddenly called in. Cowperwood, along with the city's treasurer, is exposed and eventually put on trial for embezzlement. He is convicted and sent to the infamous Eastern District Penitentiary of Pennsylvania in Philadelphia, not far from where Dreiser had once lived. *The Financier* contains a hauntingly accurate description of this prison, which is today a historical site and museum. Once released, Cowperwood starts over in Chicago.

To write *The Financier* and its sequels, Dreiser researched his subject prodigiously, also mastering the complex world of high finance. Indeed, at times the literary-minded reader becomes lost in the details of Cowperwood's manipulations of stocks and bonds. Yet the figure who finally emerges from this portrait, which is almost detailed and accurate enough to be called a biography, is not Yerkes but Dreiser himself. Despite the fact that he went outside his family for the basis of his fiction, the personal side of the portrait is Dreiser in all his "varietism" for women as well as his romantic vision of feminine beauty. Dreiser resembled Edgar Allan Poe, one of his favorite writers, in his excitement over "the loss of a beautiful woman." For Poe, that woman disappeared again and again and most memorably in the sonnet "To Helen." In 1944 Dreiser finally married Helen Richardson, who, like Poe's young wife, was her husband's second cousin. Cowperwood shares Dreiser's love of the feminine, which is realized not only in endless seeking after young women but also in art, which the financier collects in earnest. For Cowperwood, as for Dreiser, the woman was also an art object to be possessed. In his autobiography Dreiser confessed that "for the second, third and fourth decades of my life . . . there appeared to be a toxic something in form itself—that of the female of the species where beautiful—that could effect veritable paroxysms of emotion and desire in me."

THE "GENIUS"

The "Genius," the most blatantly autobiographical of Dreiser's novels, naturally focuses on this aspect of human nature. It does not, however, mark Dreiser's return to himself as the basis for fiction, because it was composed before *The Financier.* Today, *The "Genius"* is possibly Dreiser's most unread novel, after *The Bulwark* and *The Stoic.* Several of his friends, including Mencken, disliked the book intensely and tried to dissuade Dreiser from publishing it. When it was released, many of its frank details had to be either removed or modified. The story strikes the reader of today as rankly egotistical, despite the quotation marks around the word "Genius" in the title. Yet the verist (from "verism," the theory that rigid representation of truth and reality is essential to art and literature) is at work here as much as anywhere else in the Dreiser canon. Eugene Witla is a painter who moves in the art world around the turn of the century—the Ashcan School, which revealed the bleak side of city life, especially in and around New York. In the middle 1890s Dreiser knew many of these painters through his work as editor of *Ev'ry Month,* a magazine connected to his brother Paul's sheet music company. Even though the protagonist is modeled on Dreiser the writer, his painter model may have been William Louis Sonntag, the artist at *Ev'ry Month.* Other models for Dreiser's self-doting protagonist include the artists George Luks, John Sloan, Robert Henry, Everett Shinn, William Glackens, and Alfred Stieglitz.

The plot of the novel is patterned on Dreiser's life for the first forty years. Eugene comes out of Illinois instead of Indiana and goes to Chicago and, ultimately, New York City. His early love affairs parallel Dreiser's love life during this period, discussed in his autobiography. Eugene marries Angela Blue, whereas Dreiser married Sara White. Dreiser even exploits the fact that during his courtship he became attracted to Sara's sister. As in the case of Dreiser and Sara, who were separated in 1910, Eugene and Angela experience marriage problems because Angela does not adopt the emancipated spirit of the art world of Greenwich Village. Here the "Genius" finds success as a painter, but his career is eventually derailed by a disabling depression, the way Dreiser suffered "neurasthenia" after the commercial failure of *Sister Carrie.*

After recovering in a sanitarium and working outdoors for his health, Eugene reenters the world of art as a newspaper artist and eventually becomes a highly paid advertising manager of a magazine conglomerate (as Dreiser, following his own recovery in a sanitarium, became general editor of three magazines for the Butter-

ick Corporation around 1908). At this corporate height, Eugene falls in love with Suzanne Dale, the teenage daughter of an employee (modeled on Dreiser's infatuation with Thelma Cudlipp in 1910). The affair costs him both his marriage and his lucrative position. In a desperate effort to save their marriage, Angela becomes pregnant while Suzanne's mother spirits her daughter off to Canada so that Eugene cannot see her. In the end, he becomes a Christian Scientist through the efforts of his sister and a widower who now dotes on his daughter. (Dreiser briefly flirted with Christian Science but never had any children.) Years later he encounters Suzanne on Fifth Avenue, but they pass each other without saying a word.

Dreiser's unabashed use of the details from his own life as well as those around him is remarkable as a measure of his belief that nothing was finally embarrassing or immoral. His motto here (also the refrain about the sex offender in Dreiser's only full-length play *The Hand of the Potter, 1919*) is "I didn't make myself." This is also the excuse Dreiser offers to George Hurstwood, Jennie Gerhardt, Frank Cowperwood, and other literary creations. Eugene's name comes from the Greek word for "wellborn." He had been born an artist, but he just as well could have been born a failure. Dreiser always insisted that he was in no way responsible for his talent as a writer. His family of ten surviving siblings served as a microcosm for the world at large. He and Paul became successes, whereas several of the others from the same gene pool were utter failures. Just as Eugene ends his tale on a philosophical note, so Dreiser was obsessed with the beauty of the world that lay even behind the terror and confusion. He was also superstitious, but this tendency in Dreiser has been exaggerated, for he lived, or grew up, in an age in which Madame Blavatsky, the organizer of the occult Theosophical Society, and other spiritualists were headlined in newspapers and discussed in the intellectual journals of the day. Dreiser later claimed to have undergone two mystical experiences. In the words of Richard Lehan, "Eugene's story, in fact, is written in the stars, or so Dreiser would like us to believe when a fortune teller predicts the catastrophic events in his life, her words hanging over him as they do the heroes of Greek tragedy."

AN AMERICAN TRAGEDY

An American Tragedy is the second high point in Dreiser's career, coming after a ten-year period in which he published no novel. This was not a dry period for Dreiser, however, as he wrote a number of one-act plays and *The Hand of the Potter: A Tragedy in Four Acts*. These works show the influence of Sigmund Freud as well as an original flair for the kind of experimentation later found in the works of the American playwrights Eugene O'Neill and (even later) Edward Albee. He also wrote *A Hoosier Holiday* (1916; his second travel book), *Free, and Other Stories* (1918), *Twelve Men* (his strongest book of nonfiction), *Hey Rub-a-Dub-Dub: A Book of the Mystery and Wonder and Terror of Life* (1920; a book of philosophical essays), *A Book about Myself* (1922; reissued in 1931 as *Newspaper Days*), and *The Color of a Great City* (1923; sketches old and new). He was basically trying to survive as a writer, living exclusively on his meager royalties and commissions. He also was preoccupied with court battles over the alleged obscenity of *The "Genius,"* which was finally reissued uncut in 1923. This book had been one of his best moneymakers until it was initially withdrawn, and it posted one of his highest royalty totals upon reissue.

During this decade Dreiser injected his fiction with the ideas of the German-born American biophysiologist and behaviorist Jacques Loeb's mechanistic theories and the writings of Sigmund Freud. Loeb suggested that life was a series of tropisms, or predetermined and interrelated responses to physical stimuli—a tropistic tango in which we are drawn to our fates much the way a caterpillar is drawn irresistibly up a branch toward the sun. This was the "equation inevitable," as Dreiser called it in an essay of the same name in *Hey Rub-a-Dub-Dub*. Freud, of course, suggested a psychological dynamic that is responsible for Clyde Griffiths' interior monologues in *An American Tragedy*. Also, in the climactic scene in which Clyde allows his girlfriend Roberta to drown, Dreiser describes his actions and reactions in sentence fragments, to suggest the dreamlike helplessness of Clyde's situation. Clyde's inaction as a result of a catatonic trance seals his fate in the same way that Hurstwood's theft dictates his outcome. In both cases Dreiser implicitly asks, "Did he do it?" and the answer is invariably no.

But *An American Tragedy* is much more than the result of Dreiser's reading of behavioral science and psychology. For one thing, Poe is as much an influence as Freud in terms of the main character's interior monologues as he is torn between hope and fear. This epic novel of the tragic reversal of the American dream also packs into its narrative Dreiser's experiences dating back to the 1890s as a newspaper reporter. During this era society pages of newspapers kept the public abreast of the doings of the rich, whose sons and daughters often were married off to minor European royalty. Dreiser himself hoped in his wilder dreams to marry a wealthy woman. It was certainly one way for the poor and middle class to realize the American dream of becoming rich in a country filled with first-generation immigrants.

As early as 1892 in St. Louis, Dreiser became interested in a certain crime of "passion" in which the male suitor violently disengaged himself from a poor girl to marry a rich one. The first case to draw his attention concerned a young perfume dealer who had poisoned his girlfriend so that he could free himself to marry into one of the old French families of the city. In 1894 he became fascinated with the trial of Carlyle Harris, a young medical student in New York who poisoned his lover to be with a wealthy one. Then there was the case of Roland Molineaux at the turn of the century, another more sensational poisoning case in which the wrong person was murdered, along with the intended victim. During the winter of 1915–1916, Dreiser wrote six chapters of an unfinished novel, "The Rake," based on this case, as well as "Her Boy," an uncompleted short story based on a Philadelphia crime. He also began another unfinished novel using the Clarence Richeson case of 1911; it concerned a minister who poisoned his sweetheart to marry another parishioner. Dreiser makes reference to many of these cases in the *Hey Rub-a-Dub-Dub* essay "Neurotic America and the Sex Impulse" and the serialized "I Find the Real American Tragedy" for *Mystery Magazine* in 1935.

It was the Chester Gillette and Grace Brown murder case of 1906, however, that finally produced *An American Tragedy*. Dreiser had been drawn to the case even before he moved to Hollywood. He wrote approximately the first twenty chapters of his novel in Southern California, though they later underwent significant change. The novel opens with a street scene featuring Clyde's missionary parents in Kansas City, which may have been inspired by one of Dreiser's Hollywood landlords, who greeted him every morning with "Praise the Lord!" It also harks back to Dreiser's own pietistic father, whom he had given up trying to reflect in *The Bulwark,* the novel he was then under contract to write.

An American Tragedy consists of three books, or parts, in the manner of *The "Genius."* The novel is more than 400,000 words long, and it has been estimated that the original draft of the novel approached a million words. This is probably an exaggeration, but Dreiser needed a large

canvas: the 1912 edition of *The Financier* and *The "Genius"* are almost as long as the printed version of *An American Tragedy.* He also required editors willing and able to reduce his almost obsessive use of detail. Dreiser followed the court records of the Gillette trial for the second and third parts of his novel (sometimes so closely that critics at the time of its publication questioned its status as fiction), but he relied on his own background in the first part, where Clyde is reared in a religious family with little means. He escapes from this dreary life by landing a job as a bellhop in a large hotel. There his growing sense of materialism is whetted by the rich clientele and his association with other bellboys from poor homes also bent on the hedonistic life. There is a hit-and-run automobile accident during a night of joyriding, in which a small child is killed. Clyde manages to escape from the scene and runs away to Chicago.

There he meets Samuel Griffiths, his father's estranged brother, while working in another hotel. His uncle owns a collar factory in upstate New York. Feeling guilty because he helped cheat his eccentric brother out of the family inheritance, Samuel Griffiths offers Clyde a job. In Lycurgus (Cortland, New York) he encounters his uncle's family, including a look-alike cousin who becomes his immediate superior in the factory. But despite this unexpected opportunity, life there becomes frustrating to Clyde. Although he enjoys the status of the Griffiths name at work, he is not included in the social activities of his cousins, who are members of the American social scientist Thorstein Veblen's "leisure class." To fill up his idle social hours, he becomes romantically involved with Roberta Alden, a farmer's daughter who works under him in the factory. Despite her declarations of love, she views Clyde as a means to social advancement in the same way that Clyde covets the world of his cousins and their friends. Eventually, Clyde wins the affection of Sondra Finchley, whose mere name rings with money, but at this juncture the impoverished Roberta announces that she is pregnant with Clyde's child.

Clyde thus finds himself in the same quandary of several Dreiser protagonists, but most dramatically that of George Hurstwood, who is forced to choose between duty and desire, the drab obligations of a wife and children who have ceased to love him and the exciting prospect of running away from Chicago with a beautiful eighteen-year-old woman. Like Hurstwood, Clyde cannot legally extricate himself from his predicament. Roberta will not willingly go away, and if Sondra or any of her class discovers that he has made Roberta pregnant, he will lose his chance of marrying money and winning the beautiful Sondra in the bargain. On a bogus honeymoon trip upstate to Big Bittern Lake (Big Moose Lake in New York, where Grace Brown drowned), Clyde takes Roberta out in a boat to tell her that he cannot marry her. As she suddenly stands up in the boat and approaches him beseechingly, he accidentally strikes her with a heavy camera he happens to be holding (a tennis racket in the Gillette-Brown case). The blow knocks her into the water, at which point Clyde fails to assist her (not a crime in itself long before the days of the Good Samaritan laws), and she drowns.

Soon after he flees the scene, he is arrested and charged with her murder. A long trial ensues, which ends with Clyde's conviction and sentence of death. Some readers feel that the trial is too long for the novel, but this section fairly sparkles with character analyses of the various players in the sealing of Clyde's fate. These include the sexually repressed district attorney, who envies Clyde his sexual freedom with Roberta (even while decrying it as an outrage); additionally, he secretly hates Clyde because of his seemingly wealthy status. Clyde dies in Auburn State Prison, in the same death house where Chester Gillette was executed in 1906. Such is a bare-bones outline of a most complex story, one whose hard facts Dreiser studied intensely and used liberally in his novel (including nearly verbatim accounts of several of Grace Brown's pathetic letters to Chester). Dreiser brings up numerous current social issues in his novel, among them, the difficulty of disseminating birth-control information and the illegality of abortion. This acquaintance and admirer of the birth-control advocate Margaret Sanger, this brother of so many sisters who started out life as unwed mothers, this twelfth of thirteen children implies in his novel that the murder would not have occurred if society had not forbidden the publication of information concerning birth control.

For Clyde it all comes down to class difference. One of his attorneys recalls to himself that as a youth he had been in the same dilemma but had had the funds and the social connections to arrange an abortion. The doctor known to do abortions for the right people and price clearly discriminates against Roberta, telling her that she has a moral duty to bear the child regardless of her marital status. This was doubtless the same advice that Dreiser's sisters received. To promote the novel as well as to call attention to the social issues it embraced, Dreiser's publisher sponsored a national contest to choose the best essay to answer the question "Was Clyde Griffiths guilty of murder in the first degree?" The winner, a young liberal law professor, won by arguing that Clyde is morally guilty of Roberta's death but legally and socially innocent. And even here the moral obligation to save a drowning person is undercut by the fact that Clyde did not make himself but rather is a product of poverty and ignorance kept in place by society itself.

The question of Clyde's legal culpability is complicated further by the fact that he set out for Big Bittern Lake with the intention of murdering Roberta, backed out of the deed at the last minute, and then fled as if he had murdered her. Because Clyde has no eyewitness to this fact (except the reader), circumstantial evidence convicts him of first-degree murder. His pragmatic lawyers realize that no jury would acquit him of the charge of premeditated murder with such a story. Instead, they concoct one in which Clyde is branded a "moral coward" but not a cold-blooded killer. They have him testify that although he set out to murder her, he suffered a change of heart at the last minute and was prepared to marry Roberta if she refused to release him. It was in her joy at this news, his attorneys argue, that she stood up in the boat and was accidentally struck by the camera. In the real-life case, Chester Gillette (who never admitted to murder, even when facing execution) claimed that Grace stood up precariously after he threatened to inform her parents of her pregnancy. Chester also had not won the heart of any rich girl in his uncle's society (though he became a heartthrob to many young women who lined the streets as he was taken from a local jail to the death house).

Ultimately, Clyde is convicted of a criminal offense for a moral crime. This was an important distinction for Dreiser. While he is on death row, Clyde is visited by his mother and the Reverend Duncan McMillan, an itinerant clergyman who ministers to Clyde during the appeal of his death sentence. Both come to suspect that Clyde is morally guilty of murder, and McMillan, at least, is reluctantly persuaded, like the jury, that such guilt warrants the death penalty. All his life and especially since his newspaper days, Dreiser believed that morality was a weapon the hypocritical rich used against the poor to oppress them financially. Those with money, for example, might get an abortion and avoid the necessity of murder. In Roberta's case, though interestingly not in Grace Brown's or any of the cases Dreiser studied, the pregnant woman is willing to undergo the abortion. Far worse for Roberta than breaking the law forbidding abortion—and here Dreiser makes another of his favorite points—is the shame of unwed motherhood. Society by the turn of the century had so demonized the unwed mother that a single pregnant woman would do almost anything to escape her predicament, certainly beg and finally threaten with exposure the father of her child until he is desperate enough to murder her. Dreiser himself bitterly recalled in his autobiography the shame he felt as a boy when neighbors would gossip about one or another of his wayward sisters.

Except for the fact that there is no conclusive evidence that she would have accepted an abortion as a way out of her crisis, this was exactly the situation Grace Brown faced in the spring of 1906. In *An American Tragedy,* Roberta Alden is equally ashamed and afraid. Both are barely out of a century where parents of their lower socioeconomic class (as Crane dramatized in *Maggie: A Girl of the Streets*) disowned their daughters as fallen women. Roberta reacts like a woman of Grace's time, not the 1920s, the era of the New Woman as well as the flapper. *An American Tragedy* was published in 1925, the same year as F. Scott Fitzgerald's *Great Gatsby,* when the shadow of the failure of the Great War hangs over the lives of its characters. Both Nick Carraway and Jay Gatsby in Fitzgerald's novel have served in World War I (while Tom Buchanan apparently has not), but nobody in *An American Tragedy* seems to have ever heard of it—or Prohibition either, for that matter. In *An American Tragedy,* while he depended on the facts of an actual crime, Dreiser deliberately blurred the historical moment so that, at times, we hear actual songs from the twenties and at others the sights and sounds of an earlier era. For the problem dramatized in his novel does not belong exclusively to the 1920s or to 1906 but to Dreiser's last thirty or so years, when he first became conscious of the painful contrast between wealth and poverty in America.

In its relentless verisimilitude, *An American Tragedy* set the precedent for Richard Wright's *Native Son* (1940), Truman Capote's *In Cold*

Blood (1965), E. L. Doctorow's *Ragtime* (1975), and Norman Mailer's *Executioner's Song* (1979). It generally is considered Dreiser's best novel, though many prefer *Sister Carrie* or consider it a tie between the two. Its publication marked not only Dreiser's first novel in ten years but also essentially his last, because *The Bulwark* and *The Stoic* are so weak compared with the rest of his work. In those novels, he tried to take his protagonists away from the reality of life, mainly through religion, but it was not much different from the kind of romance in which Crane's Henry Fleming immerses himself at the end of *The Red Badge of Courage* (1895) as a way to accept the carnage of war—and of life. Of course, Henry Fleming's successor, Frederic Henry in Ernest Hemingway's *A Farewell to Arms* (1929), rejects the same carnage, only to be slain (in the death of his pregnant lover, with whom he has fled World War I) by the fact that one cannot run away from the realities of life. After writing *An American Tragedy,* Dreiser essentially turned away from fiction to embrace the dreams of a utopianist and the life of social reform. This shift, ironically both abrupt and long in coming, was accelerated by his three-month stay in the Soviet Union in 1927. Shortly before his death in 1945, he formally became a member of the Communist Party of the United States.

In accepting the Nobel Prize, Sinclair Lewis conceded that Dreiser had "cleared the trail from Victorian, Howellsian timidity and gentility. . . . Without his pioneering I doubt that any of us could, unless we liked to be sent to jail, express life, beauty and terror" (*New York Times,* December 13, 1930). Lewis, the son of a doctor in Minnesota, had been America's "rebel from Main Street," as the subtitle of one biography of the author of *Main Street* (1920) and *Babbitt* (1922) suggests, showing up the petty hypocrisies of small-town life and the boosterism of the business class. Dreiser, on the other hand, had come from the wrong side of the tracks, nowhere near Main Street in the economically depressed towns of Indiana. As a mature novelist, however, he realized the world both as a place of beauty and a place of terror. His characters are immediately swept up by the world's beauty (the beautiful woman of Poe, for example). Hurstwood must have Carrie, Kane must have Jennie, and Cowperwood and Witla must have every beautiful young woman. Clyde, it may be assumed safely, would have tired of Sondra eventually. At the same time, all these worshippers at the feet of beauty move in a perilous world run by a "Creative Force," which, in a real Emersonian sense, must sacrifice the parts or individuals for the harmony of the whole. In *Hey Rub-a-Dub-Dub,* Dreiser even tried to excuse God by suggesting that the Deity was somehow subordinate to a higher, meaner god. By the end of his life, he was no longer angry with God for the indignities of the human condition. Even in *An American Tragedy* there is a glimmer of this acceptance in Clyde's death-row scenes, and in *Sister Carrie* Carrie, now rich and famous, vaguely senses a higher meaning as she sits in her rocking chair.

Selected Bibliography

WORKS OF THEODORE DREISER

NOVELS

Sister Carrie. New York: Doubleday, Page, 1900. (An edition based on the original manuscript is edited by John C. Berkey, Alice M. Winters, James L. W. West III, and Neda Westlake. Philadelphia: University of Pennsylvania Press, 1981. The preferred modern edition of the Doubleday version is edited by Donald Pizer. New York: Norton, 1991.)

Jennie Gerhardt. New York: Harper & Brothers, 1911. (See also *Jennie Gerhardt: Theodore Dreiser.* Edited by James L. W. West III. Philadelphia:

University of Pennsylvania, 1992. Unfortunately, this historical edition is the only one available in paperback.)

The Financier. New York: Harper & Brothers, 1912. Revised, New York: Boni & Liveright, 1927.

The Titan. New York: John Lane, 1914.

The "Genius." New York: John Lane, 1915; New York: Boni & Liveright, 1923. (The latter edition was published following suppression and court battles over the first edition.)

An American Tragedy. New York: Boni & Liveright, 1925.

The Bulwark. New York: Doubleday, 1946.

The Stoic. New York: Doubleday, 1947.

SHORT STORIES

Free, and Other Stories. New York: Boni & Liveright, 1918.

Twelve Men. New York: Boni & Liveright, 1919.

The Color of a Great City. New York: Boni & Liveright, 1923.

Chains: Lesser Novels and Stories. New York: Boni & Liveright, 1927.

A Gallery of Women. New York: Horace Liveright, 1929.

PLAYS

Plays of the Natural and the Supernatural. New York: John Lane, 1916.

The Hand of the Potter: A Tragedy in Four Acts. New York: Boni & Liveright, 1919. Revised, New York: Boni & Liveright, 1926.

POETRY

Moods, Cadenced and Declaimed. New York: Boni & Liveright, 1926. (Limited edition of 550 signed copies.)

Moods, Cadenced & Declaimed. New York: Boni & Liveright, 1928.

Moods: Philosophic and Emotional, Cadenced and Declaimed. New York: Simon & Schuster, 1935.

TRAVEL BOOKS

A Traveler at Forty. New York: Century, 1913.

A Hoosier Holiday. New York: John Lane, 1916.

Dreiser Looks at Russia. New York: Horace Liveright, 1928.

AUTOBIOGRAPHIES

A Book about Myself. New York: Boni & Liveright, 1922. Republished as *Newspaper Days.* New York: Horace Liveright, 1931.

Dawn. New York: Horace Liveright, 1931.

POLITICAL AND PHILOSOPHICAL WRITINGS

Hey Rub-a-Dub-Dub: A Book of the Mystery and Wonder and Terror of Life. New York: Boni & Liveright, 1920.

Tragic America. New York: Horace Liveright, 1931.

America Is Worth Saving. New York: Modern Age Books, 1941.

Notes on Life. Edited by Marguerite Tajder and John J. McAleer. Tuscaloosa: University of Alabama Press, 1974.

LETTERS AND DIARIES

Letters of Theodore Dreiser: A Selection. 3 vols. Edited by Robert H. Elias. Philadelphia: University of Pennsylvania Press, 1959.

Theodore Dreiser: American Diaries 1902–1926. Edited by Thomas P. Riggio and James L. W. West III. Philadelphia: University of Pennsylvania Press, 1983.

Dreiser-Mencken Letters: The Correspondence of Theodore Dreiser and H. L. Mencken, 1907–1945. 2 vols. Edited by Thomas P. Riggio. Philadelphia: University of Pennsylvania Press, 1986.

COLLECTED WORKS

Selected Magazine Articles of Theodore Dreiser. Edited by Yoshinobu Hakutani. Rutherford, N.J.: Fairleigh Dickinson University Press, 1985. (Includes "Haunts of Nathaniel Hawthorne," among other works.)

Theodore Dreiser: Sister Carrie, Jennie Gerhardt, Twelve Men. Edited by Richard Lehan. New York: Library of America, 1987.

Theodore Dreiser's Ev'ry Month. Edited by Nancy Warner Barrineau. Athens: University of Georgia Press, 1996. (A collection of Dreiser's writing for this music magazine.)

The Collected Plays of Theodore Dreiser. Edited by Keith Newlin and Frederic E. Rusch. Albany, N.Y.: Whitston, 2000.

JOURNALS, CORRESPONDENCE, AND MANUSCRIPTS

The University of Pennsylvania is the trustee of the Dreiser estate. The Annenberg Rare Book and Manuscript Library at the university houses a collection of unpublished writings, letters, photographs, and other memorabilia. The library holdings can be perused online, (http://www.library.upenn.edu/special/mss/dreiser/dreiser.html).

BIBLIOGRAPHY

Pizer, Donald, Richard W. Dowell, and Frederic E. Rusch. *Theodore Dreiser: A Primary Bibliography and Reference Guide,* 2d ed. Boston: G. K. Hall, 1991.

CRITICAL AND BIOGRAPHICAL STUDIES

Dudley, Dorothy. *Forgotten Frontiers: Dreiser and the Land of the Free.* New York: Harrison Smith and Robert Haas, 1932.

Elias, Robert Henry. *Theodore Dreiser: Apostle of Nature,* emended ed. Ithaca, N.Y.: Cornell University Press, 1970.

Fishkin, Shelley Fisher. *From Fact to Fiction: Journalism and Imaginative Writing in America.* Baltimore: Johns Hopkins University Press, 1985. Pp. 85–134.

Gerber, Philip L. *Theodore Dreiser Revisited.* New York: Twayne, 1992.

Griffin, Joseph. *The Small Canvas: An Introduction to Dreiser's Short Stories.* Rutherford, N.J.: Fairleigh Dickinson University Press, 1985.

Hussman, Lawrence. *Dreiser and His Fiction: A Twentieth-Century Quest.* Philadelphia: University of Pennsylvania Press, 1983.

Lehan, Richard. *Theodore Dreiser: His World and His Novels.* Carbondale: Southern Illinois University Press, 1969.

Lingeman, Richard. *Theodore Dreiser.* Vol. 1, *At the Gates of the City, 1871–1907.* New York: Putnam, 1986. Vol. 2, *An American Journey, 1908–1945.* New York: Putnam, 1990.

McAleer, John J. *Theodore Dreiser: An Introduction and Interpretation.* New York: Holt, Rinehart, and Winston, 1968.

Moers, Ellen. *Two Dreisers.* New York: Viking, 1969.

Pizer, Donald. *The Novels of Theodore Dreiser: A Critical Study.* Minneapolis: University of Minnesota Press, 1976.

Salzman, Jack, ed. *Theodore Dreiser: The Critical Reception.* New York: David Lewis, 1972.

Shapiro, Charles. *Theodore Dreiser: Our Bitter Patriot.* Carbondale: Southern Illinois University Press, 1962.

Swanberg, W. A. *Dreiser.* New York: Scribners, 1965.

—JEROME LOVING

Ralph Ellison

1914–1994

*F*ᴇᴡ ᴡᴏʀᴋs ᴏꜰ American literature inspire the word "epic," but Ralph Ellison's masterpiece, *Invisible Man* (1952), certainly belongs to that category. Fifty years after its publication, it remains amazingly contemporary, controversial, dynamic, stunning, and, in retrospect, prophetic about life in post–World War II America. Ellison was also a painstaking stylist, a writer who lingered over his prose, ever fearful of what he called a "failure of eloquence." Trained as a classical composer and a musician (his instrument was the trumpet), Ellison treated his writing process as if he were practicing scales or perfecting a piece. His true love was jazz—a subject he often wrote about—and he once proposed in an interview with Ishmael Reed, Quincy Troupe, and Steve Cannon, that being a writer was like being "a jazz musician who creates his own style out of the styles around him, I play it by ear." Whenever he could not find the words, according to his wife, Fanny, he would go and play the trumpet, and in his writing one can still hear the rhythm of his thoughts and the chorus of the multiple "styles" that engendered his art.

Many critics point out, however, that Ellison never became a "great American writer" because *Invisible Man* was the only novel that appeared in his lifetime. (*Juneteenth,* his second novel, was published posthumously in 1999.) Still, in the span of his writing career, he produced more than seventy-five reviews, essays, published lectures, and interviews. His essays on American literature, the writer Richard Wright, jazz, and African American culture are considered by many to be some of the most eloquent and incisive written by an American writer. Ellison

was the rarest of people—a true American "Renaissance man." He was a philosopher, musician, writer, painter, sculptor, photographer, and intellectual—feats that are the more remarkable because Ellison came from such difficult and humble beginnings.

One of his obsessions was the celebration of African American art and culture. He worked through his writing and through his stewardship of magazines, journals, and artistic and educational foundations to illuminate the contributions of African Americans to the American historical and cultural fabric. In his eyes, the African American was seen by society as the penumbra of the American experience. In an early interview with Alfred Chester and Vilma Howard, Ellison stated that "the history of the American Negro is a most intimate part of American history. . . . We may identify ourselves with it and recognize it as an important segment of the larger American experience—not lying at the bottom of it, but intertwined, diffused in its very texture." Ellison attempted in his art to bring African American life and culture out from the shadows, up from the "bottom of it." Consequently, shadows, the interplay of light and dark, and even invisibility are common motifs in Ellison's writing.

While Ellison's novels and short stories are not generally considered "historical fiction," each could be said to possess a historical consciousness. In his work, Ellison transforms the material of the past into something both usable and profound. Countering the "official history" of the United States that pushes African Americans to the margins, Ellison embraced the vernacular of his people—the blues, jazz, folklore, the sermon, and the "dozens" (a verbal, ironic, often rhyming joust, peppered with insults—twelve "censures" in all—popular in African American culture). The oral story of African Americans registers a different and more diverse vision of America. The tragedy and the ironic humor found in much of Ellison's fiction is the blues itself—a result of the realization that someone else (historians, sociologists, journalists) is always telling one's story and getting it horribly wrong. Ellison tried to strike a complex chord, a sounding that obliterated the simple and usually negative stereotypes of African American existence.

Ellison often admitted that classical, European, and American literature was responsible for the formation of his aesthetic but that it was the voices of his childhood and of his "folk" that gave his work its spirit. Yet Ellison's artistic project drew criticism from members of the Black Arts movement in the 1960s because of its lack of political content and because Ellison himself was not at the forefront of civil rights causes. During a college lecture tour stop at Oberlin, an audience member called Ellison an "Uncle Tom," an indictment he heard from other young writers, students, and radicals throughout the era. Many did not know that he had been actively involved in the Communist Party as a young man (though he was never an official member). As early as 1954 Ellison addressed such criticism in an interview with Chester and Howard when he announced: "I recognize no dichotomy between art and protest." African American vernacular (which he tried to capture and celebrate in his fiction) by its very nature was a political argument against essentialist notions of African American identity. At the heart of "The World and the Jug" (Ellison's response to Irving Howe's "Black Boys and Native Sons") is Ellison's fight against a world that sees African Americans as symbols or types. As he put it in "The World and the Jug," "Evidently Howe feels that unrelieved suffering is the only

'real' Negro experience." Ellison's battlefield was not the streets of Detroit or Watts or Montgomery; it was the American consciousness. Civil rights could not be achieved until America saw African Americans as complex humans, sometimes noble and sometimes flawed. What history, sociology, and other studies had not achieved was evident in the stories and the music of the African American people, which his writing fought to bring to light.

Within a few years even the voices of the Black Arts movement would change their tune about Ellison. Larry Neal, once a strident critic of *Invisible Man* and Ellison, pronounced that he had been wrong in his analysis and that Ellison's aesthetic was "not that far removed from the ideas of some of the best black writers and intellectuals working today." Ellison had presented a "nascent, loosely structured form of black nationalism and cultural theory." Other critics (such as Howe) who believed that *Invisible Man* and its author "violated" the reality of African American life might have been surprised to discover that the novel was chosen in 1972 in a poll of literary critics, professors, and writers as the "most likely to endure." (This is a hallmark reiterated by many critics in their lists of important works of the twentieth century.) Robert O'Meally states that on the occasion of the novel's thirtieth anniversary, a *Washington Post* critic declared, "*Invisible Man* has as much claim to being that mythical, unattainable dream of American literature, the 'great American novel,' as any book in our literature."

That Ellison did not follow up the success of *Invisible Man* with another novel published in his lifetime is likely a testament to personal and professional forces that scholars can only guess at. A fire destroyed the manuscript of the second novel (which would become *Juneteenth*), but the lack of another text of the magnitude of *Invisible Man* has not abbreviated the interest in Ellison or his work. There is more than a generous amount of academic criticism available, and more continues to be written today. Recent critics have investigated *Invisible Man* with a poststructuralist lens, seeing in this modernist novel the beginnings of postmodernism. Cataloguing the novel's dialogic nature, jazz-influenced style, dazzling hybrid form, and intertextuality, scholars are once again revisiting and rethinking one of the most "engaging" novels and writers of the twentieth century.

BIOGRAPHY AND CRITICAL OVERVIEW

In 1942 the journal *New Masses* reported Ralph Ellison's birthday as March 1, 1914. This date was never disputed by Ellison and has always been taken by scholars as the accurate date. A recent biography by Lawrence Jackson, however, suggests that the year might have been 1913. Birth records were not kept at the turn of the twentieth century in Oklahoma City, where Ellison was born. Oklahoma had been ratified only recently as a state, and it was still considered by many to be what Ellison called it in later years, the "territory." It was clear from the beginning that Ellison was meant for a life beyond what his father, Lewis, had known. Lewis Alfred and Ida Millsap Ellison named their son Ralph Waldo Ellison in honor of the poet and philosopher Ralph Waldo Emerson. Believing that a name certified one's destiny, Lewis Ellison christened his son after his favorite writer with the hope that his child would someday become a famous poet.

It was a mighty dream for the future, especially in light of the Ellisons' past. Lewis' father, Alfred, had been born a slave, and Ida's parents had been sharecroppers. Deeply frustrated by the Jim Crow laws of the South, Lewis had left and joined the Twenty-fifth U.S. Colored Infantry. Before he left to fight in the Philippines, he had spent some time in the western territory. Upon his release from the military in 1901, Lewis married and later returned to the "territory," Oklahoma, where Jim Crow had yet to crush the spirits of African American families. That would change in the years to come, as Oklahoma politicians began to fashion their new state in the image of the South, longing to become a "Little Dixie."

The young Ralph Ellison often accompanied his father to work. Lewis delivered ice for a living and hired the teenage Jimmy Rushing, who later would make his mark as a jazz musician and singer, to help him. One day, while making deliveries, a block of ice fell, slicing through Lewis Ellison's stomach. Doctors told Ida that her husband's ulcers had hemorrhaged in the accident and advised experimental surgery to correct the problem. Lewis never recovered; he died on July 19, 1916. His death certificate further substantiates Ralph Ellison's birth date as 1913; the writer stated several times that he was three years old when his father died. Ida was left to care for two young boys—Ralph and his one-month-old brother, Herbert.

Ida Ellison worked as a domestic to support her sons, but the family remained in poverty for many years, moving from rented room to rented room. As a young woman, Ida had attended school, probably with the intention of becoming a teacher. Even though the children often had to be left alone (with young Ralph watching his brother), Ida prepared them for a brighter future. The ticket was enlightened education. Ida brought home discarded magazines and journals, such as *Vanity Fair* and *Literary Digest,* as well as classical music recordings. She took her boys walking through rich, white neighborhoods so that they would see what else life had to offer. In 1919 they lived at the parsonage of Avery Chapel of the African Methodist Episcopal Church (A.M.E. Chapel), where Ida worked. The chapel had a large library, where Ellison most likely was first exposed to a wide array of reading material. In the spirit of her husband's dreams for his son, Ida presented five-year-old Ralph with a toy typewriter and desk for his birthday.

Even though the Ellisons were poor, Ida made certain to introduce the boys to a variety of people and experiences. The editor of Oklahoma City's *Black Dispatch* was a family friend, and Ida knew a small group of intellectuals and activists through her own political involvement. Despite their impoverished state, Ida Ellison provided her boys with a rich learning environment. She was a formidable parent and teacher, indoctrinating her children in every way conceivable, but her greatest gift to her eldest son may have been her social conscience married to strong-minded, ironic humor that saw the absurdity in the darkest moments.

Ellison began Frederick Douglass Elementary School in 1919. The walk to school through a gauntlet of warehouses, crime, and prostitutes was a learning experience in itself, but it also enveloped Ellison in the sounds of the streets at the time: blues and jazz. It was in elementary school that Ellison's introduction to and apprenticeship in music began. The segregated Oklahoma schools were unusual because the African American community developed and controlled their curriculum. Young students were exposed to the literature of Langston Hughes, Countee Cullen, and James Weldon Johnson. In 1918 the district hired Zelia Breaux to conduct the music studies in the black schools. Breaux turned out to be one of Ellison's earliest mentors, revealing to him the musical opportunities that his community had to offer. By 1922 Ellison's mother had purchased for her young son his first instrument, a cornet.

In addition to a growing interest in music, Ellison also blossomed into a voracious reader. A local pool hall in Ellison's neighborhood had been converted into a public library. Before clerks had the opportunity to classify reading material for adults, Ellison already had picked up works by Theodore Dreiser and Shakespeare. At the same time, an interest in art developed through his childhood friend, Frank Meade, who

was a budding artist and whose father taught Ellison to play his recently acquired cornet.

In 1924 Ida remarried. James Ammons, Ellison's new stepfather, gave the family stability for the first time. This stability lasted only briefly, however: Ammons died a year after the marriage, plunging the family deeper into economic hardship. In 1925 Ellison began junior high school, where he played in the band. Music teachers struggled to keep their students' interest away from the popular jazz of the day; Ellison succumbed, however, and started playing with jazz musicians outside school, including Eddie Christian, the brother of the legendary jazz guitarist Charlie Christian. Still, Ellison sought out any musical venue, including going to the symphony, hearing choral groups and marching bands, and even seeing the jazz trumpeter Louis Armstrong when he came to town. Ellison was struck by Armstrong's ability to dislocate segregation in the city through his personality and his art.

At this time, Ellison also took private music lessons, which he received in exchange for taking care of a lawn. His love of reading grew as well, working beyond the requirements of his English classes, but math and Latin proved difficult. His struggling in these subjects kept him from graduating with his class. Though Ellison had done well in most of his course work (while he was working odd jobs and perfecting his music), he did not finish school until he was nineteen. The late matriculation also affected his chance at a scholarship. Nonetheless, in 1933, through the help of Breaux, he was offered a music scholarship to Tuskegee Institute in Alabama. Since his mother had remarried in 1929 (to John Bell), Ellison felt free finally to pursue his dream of becoming a musician and composer. The family did not have enough money to pay his passage to Alabama, however, so Ellison rode the freight trains as a "hobo." Two hundred miles outside Tuskegee, white railroad detectives assaulted Ellison and beat him with their gun butts. When he reached Tuskegee, he was sent to the school infirmary for treatment of head wounds.

From the beginning, Ellison seemed to have ideological differences with Tuskegee's educational, artistic, and political philosophy. His music flourished under the tutelage of the pianist Hazel Harrison and the orchestra director Captain Frank Drye (who had played in the Tenth U.S. Calvary), but he found working with the composer and professor William Dawson frustrating. Along with many of the other teachers, Dawson insisted that students pay less attention to jazz and swing and more to classical composition. Ellison's performance in one of Dawson's music classes kept him from being on the dean's list.

Slowly, Ellison's enthusiasm for his music studies turned to other pursuits and classes. He enrolled in watercolor and sculpture courses with Eva Hamlin, and he employed a great deal of his artistic and intellectual energy in Morteza Sprague's English literature classes. As Ellison's biographer Jackson notes, Sprague encouraged him to realize the "importance of an authentic black voice." Through his extracurricular activities, Ellison met and fostered relationships with trustees, students, and alumni who shared his interest in art and literature. These relationships afforded him the opportunity to visit people's homes and their personal libraries—by this time he had read many of the major literary works available in the Tuskegee collection. By the beginning of his junior year, Ellison was no longer enrolled in music courses.

He was, however, enrolled in Sprague's senior literature class and several sociology courses, and he was still the student band conductor. It was during his senior year that Ellison discovered T. S. Eliot's *The Waste Land*. Ellison detected in the poem a merging of his many interests: poetry, jazz, classical literature, myth, folklore, and history. The poem so excited his emerging artistic and intellectual sensibilities that he began reading literary criticism and spent hours after class discussing the poem with Sprague, who saw, even if Ellison did not, that he was in the presence of a blossoming writer and critic. In his junior year Ellison met the band leader Duke Ellington, a boyhood hero, who personified the grace, intelligence, and artistic success that Ellison desired. Ellison also met the Howard University professor and "New Negro" scholar Alain Locke, who was to be instrumental in changing the route of Ellison's career. In the spring semester of 1936, Ellison left Tuskegee for New York City to study sculpture with Augusta Savage. He would not return to complete his studies.

In New York, particularly Harlem, Ellison found the creative and stimulating environment that he had hungered for in Alabama. A day after he arrived in Harlem he ran into Locke at the YMCA annex. Locke introduced him to the acquaintance with whom he was conversing, the poet Langston Hughes. Hughes took Ellison under his wing and conducted him around New York. He reintroduced Ellison to Ellington, who remembered the young musician from Tuskegee. Ellington invited Ellison to rehearse with his band but then had to cancel the invitation because he was already booked. This may have been a turning point in Ellison's life; he seems never again to have seriously considered a career as a musician. Instead, Ellison, at Hughes's prompting, chose to study sculpture with Richmond Barthé. For almost a year Ellison worked but also committed himself to reading and studying, even after deciding not to return to Tuskegee.

It was during this time that he first encountered the work of Richard Wright. Ellison asked Hughes for an introduction, and in 1937, the two young men met. Ellison finally had found an intellectual equal who had similar interests in art and in politics. Both men admired Ernest Hemingway and the French writer André Malraux. Wright suggested that Ellison read Henry James's prefaces (collected in *The Art of Fiction*) to learn about the craft of fiction. Ellison visited Wright at the Communist Party office, and although he was interested in their social agenda, he never officially joined the Party (though he often wrote for their journals and newspapers). Wright also encouraged Ellison to write his first book review and to work on short stories.

Ellison's "workshopping" was brought to a halt when news arrived that his mother was ill. Ida (then living in Ohio) had cracked her hip, and tuberculosis had set in. The day after Ellison returned home, his mother died. He published his first review, "Creative and Cultural Lag," in *New Challenge* while he was in Ohio. Not having enough money to return, Ellison stayed for seven months, first with his aunt and then in an abandoned car with his brother.

By 1938 Ellison was able to return to New York and qualified for relief as a writer. Working as a writer for the Federal Writers Project, he collected folklore, urban stories, and histories of prominent African American men and women of New York. His research took him to the Schomburg Collection (later the Schomburg Center for Research in Black Culture of the New York Public Library), where he immersed himself in African American history, literature, and cultural studies. His work through the project kindled the desire to celebrate the literature and culture of the folk as well as to support them politically. His research and political interests also prompted him to write on racism and violence in New York City for *New Masses.*

In the fall of 1938 Ellison married Rose Aramita Poindexter, a dancer. His friend Richard Wright followed suit, marrying Dheema Meidman; Ellison served as best man. But Ellison and Wright's relationship was strained when Wright and his wife began to have marital problems. Ellison and Rose were stuck in the middle of the difficulties. The tension between Wright and Ellison was exacerbated after Ellison showed Wright a draft of his new story. Wright accused Ellison of writing in his style. Ellison clearly was hurt by the accusation and decided never to show Wright his fiction again. Later, when critics sought to emphasize Wright's "fatherly" role in his career, Ellison countered in a 1976 interview with Robert B. Stepto and Michael S. Harper: "I had no desire, or need, to cast Wright or anyone else, even symbolically, in such a role."

Ellison published two short stories, "Slick Gonna Learn" and "The Birthmark," back to back in 1939 and 1940. Wright's masterpiece, *Native Son,* was published in 1940 to commercial and critical success, but in some areas, especially the corridors of the Communist Party, Wright's book was vilified. Ellison vigorously defended the book and wrote a review for the Federal Writers Project (under the editorship of Kenneth Burke) titled "Richard Wright and Recent Negro Fiction." Wright was pleased with the review, which helped mend the rift between the two. The success of *Native Son* also catapulted Ellison (because of his known association with Wright) into a new intellectual and elite circle composed of writers, artists, and thinkers. Critical work today on the two writers suggests that Ellison's friendship and insight had a significant impact on the development of Wright's novel.

Ellison's stature as a writer and critic grew in the early 1940s. In 1942 he became managing editor of *Negro Quarterly* and, through the journal, established the Negro Publication Society of America. There were considerable personal changes in his life as well. He separated from his wife (whom he divorced by 1945) and was drafted into the army. He opted to serve in the Merchant Marine (between 1943 and 1945) as a cook and baker aboard ship. During his tour of duty he maintained his editorial responsibilities and continued to write. Two of his most celebrated short stories were influenced by his years in the service and were written and published before the end of the war. The two short works, "King of the Bingo Game" and "Flying Home," emerged from Ellison's growing anger and frustration over the discrepancy between the American "dream" and reality.

In August 1943 a black serviceman was shot and killed by police in New York City. The incident ignited the "Harlem riot." At the time, Ellison was stationed at home in Harlem, so he reported on the story. The lasting effect of the serviceman's death and the riot would be felt in "Flying Home" and *Invisible Man.* The success of "Flying Home" brought a proposal from Henry Volkening, who offered to be Ellison's agent. The publishing houses Harcourt and Reynal and Hitchcock both tendered Ellison book contracts. Even though Ellison was receiving a steady paycheck as a stereo technician, he needed money and thus chose Reynal and Hitchcock's advance offer.

Langston Hughes introduced Ellison to Fanny McConnell Buford in 1944. Fanny was a writer and had worked for the Urban League. She also had run a people's theater in Chicago and worked as James Weldon Johnson's secretary. The two immediately connected through their love of literature, their politics, and their dedication to art. Ellison presented Fanny with a copy of Herman Melville's *Moby-Dick* (a favorite of his), and in the years to come (following their marriage in 1946) Fanny would become an integral part of Ellison's writing process. Although he was hard at work on a novel (not yet the one that would become *Invisible Man*), Ellison took time out to read and review *Black Boy.* Wright's autobiographical work occasioned Ellison's essay "Richard Wright's Blues," published in the summer 1945 issue of the *Antioch Review,* which is considered one of the most lucid and definitive readings of Wright's work. The essay also championed Ellison's own theoretical foundations for art and writing and

affirmed his philosophy of history, humanity, and tragedy. Wright was touched by the work, admitting that the essay went "way beyond the book." In 1945 Ellison won a Rosenwald Committee fellowship and traveled to Vermont, where one morning, on a friend's farm, he scribbled the words, "I am an invisible man."

Ellison worked diligently on the novel, formulating, writing, and revising based on the work of Kenneth Burke (with whom Ellison had worked and whom he greatly admired). Burke's philosophy of history and his ideas of dramatic structure, rhetoric, and symbol served as the basis for Ellison's organizational pattern of the novel. While he was working on *Invisible Man,* he spent time with his friends and fellow writers Chester Himes and Hannah Arendt, but his political activism suffered; it took time away from the novel, and Ellison had started to embrace the idea that art must precede political action. It also was becoming increasingly dangerous to make public statements about connections to the Communist Party. Besides, Ellison was dissatisfied with the Party's treatment of Wright and of their abandonment of poor African Americans. Ellison did support urban programs that ministered to the sick and destitute, including a clinic that treated the mentally ill. Ellison's involvement with the clinic led to a deepening interest in psychology, especially the ways in which traumatic events affect the psyche—this interest transformed into one of his most common literary investigations of individual identity and tragedy.

Ellison's editor, Albert Erskine, left Reynal and Hitchcock for Random House, and Ellison soon followed. Erskine worked with Ellison to trim the manuscript of *Invisible Man* and suggested Louis Armstrong, rather than Buddy Bolden, as the central jazz figure of the book. In 1952 Random House released the novel. A portion of it already had been published (the section that later became known as the "Battle Royal") as "Invisible Man" in *Horizon,* and the prologue had appeared in *Partisan Review*. Reviews praised the novel's daring and virtuosity. Some critics heralded it as a significant event in American literature. Most negative or critical reviews came from the liberal left, who were outraged over the portrayal of the "Brotherhood" (a radical organization resembling the Communist Party), and from some African Americans, who were distressed, generally, over the negative portrayals of blacks. Nevertheless, the novel won the National Book Award in 1953, the first time an African American had ever garnered the prize. In his acceptance speech, "Brave Words for a Startling Occasion," Ellison noted that his purpose in writing the book was to "return to the mood of personal moral responsibility for democracy which typified our best of our nineteenth-century fiction."

Ellison envisioned writing a novel as a political act in and of itself. He spent his writing life after the birth of *Invisible Man* discussing the interrelationship of art, culture, and democracy and laboring over his second novel, which he began as early as 1953. In the same year, he published the essay "Twentieth Century Fiction and the Black Mask of Humanity." In the essay, Ellison wrestles with American literature and culture's depiction of African Americans. In a critical analysis that prefigures Toni Morrison's theoretical observations of American fiction in *Playing in the Dark* (and echoes Frantz Fanon's *Black Skin, White Masks*), Ellison argues that

> whatever else the Negro stereotype might be as a social instrumentality, it is also a key figure in a magic rite by which the white American seeks to resolve the dilemma arising between his democratic beliefs and certain antidemocratic practices, between his acceptance of the sacred democratic belief that all men are created equal and his treatment of every tenth man as though he were not. Thus on the moral level I propose that we view the whole of American life as a drama acted out upon the body of a Negro giant, who, lying trussed up like Gulliver, forms the stage and the scene upon which and within which the action unfolds.

Ellison's writings in the years proceeding this statement address these very issues and enumerate the artistic contributions (through music, through the vernacular) of African Americans to American culture.

Ellison received the Rockefeller Foundation Award in 1954, followed by the Prix de Rome Fellowship in 1955. He lived in Rome for two years and worked on the second novel, during which time he continued to publish short fiction and essays, including the memorable "Society, Morality, and the Novel." Ellison dedicated much of his time to teaching, taking several significant postings in his career. The first was between 1958 and 1961 at Bard College, where he taught Russian and American literature (and shared a house with the novelist Saul Bellow). In the same year that he began teaching at Bard he wrote "Change the Joke and Slip the Yoke," a response to Stanley Edgar Hyman's reading of *Invisible Man* and African American folklore. Ellison was disappointed in Hyman's reading, especially because Hyman was a friend and a white man that Ellison felt he had educated regarding African American culture. Once again, Ellison was compelled to analyze the image of blackness in the white mind: "out of the counterfeiting of the black American's identity there arises a profound doubt in the white man's mind as to the authenticity of his own image of himself."

The appearance of two short pieces, "And Hickman Arrives" and "The Roof, the Steeple, and the People" in 1960 seemed to signal that the second novel was on its way, since both were segments of the yet untitled work. Ellison continued teaching, taking the position in 1961 of Alexander White Visiting Professor at the University of Chicago. Between 1962 and 1969 he was a visiting professor at Rutgers University and a Visiting Fellow of American Studies at Yale (1962–1964). In 1963 he published a revised version of a story that had been part of *Invisible Man,* called "Out of the Hospital and

Under the Bar." That was the same year that he received an honorary doctorate from Tuskegee Institute (where he returned after a thirty-year absence to accept the honor).

The essay "The World and the Jug" also appeared in 1963. In 1964 it was published in Ellison's first collection of essays, lectures, and interviews, *Shadow and Act.* Most of the included work focused on African American culture, music, and writing and American literature. The collection served as another attempt to remove African Americans from the "shadow" of American life. Based on a poll of two hundred critics, the *New York Herald Tribune Book Week* in 1965 chose *Invisible Man* the most distinguished novel written after World War II. That same year he published the story "Juneteenth" (which would later become the title of his posthumous novel) and became a charter member of the National Council of the Arts. In the following year he received an honorary doctorate from Rutgers University. For the next two years, Ellison served on the Carnegie Commission on Educational Television (a forerunner of the Public Broadcasting System). He continued his commitment as a public servant when he was asked to be a witness for a U.S. Senate subcommittee hearing on urban issues.

Ellison continued his patronage of the arts in 1967 when he became a vice president of the National Institute of Arts and Letters. That year he was awarded two more honorary doctorates, from the University of Michigan and Grinnell College, but 1967 proved to be ominous in Ellison's literary life. A fire at his summer home in the Berkshires destroyed 360 pages of the second novel; Fanny had to be restrained by firefighters when she tried to retrieve the pages. At first Ellison seemed confident that the lost work could be replicated, but in the years to come he confessed that the manuscript that had been burned had to be considered irretrievable.

In 1969 President Lyndon B. Johnson bestowed on Ellison the Medal of Freedom, and in the following year André Malraux (one of Ellison's heroes) presented him with the Chevalier de l'Ordre des Arts et Lettres from France. This prestigious honor rarely is given to a foreign writer. Between 1970 and 1979 Ellison served as the Albert Schweitzer Professor in the Humanities at New York University. He became professor emeritus at the university in 1979. Over the course of his career, Ellison received over thirteen doctorates from some of the most prestigious universities in the country, including Harvard, Rutgers, and the College of William and Mary.

In 1973 another short piece that had been part of the destroyed manuscript of the second novel was published. Titled "Cadillac Flambé," the work proved to be one of Ellison's most controversial, and one wonders if the dominating motif of fire was an allusion to the fire that destroyed the original text of the novel. In 1975 Ellison became a member of the American Academy of Arts and Letters, and in 1979 Brown University held a Ralph Ellison Festival, celebrating the man and his work. In 1986 Random House released another collection of essays, *Going to the Territory.* On April 16, 1994, shortly after his eightieth birthday, Ellison died of pancreatic cancer. He lived in Harlem until his death, never leaving permanently since he arrived in 1936.

Following his death, the journal *Callaloo* released an issue entitled "Remembering Ralph Ellison," and John F. Callahan, Ellison's literary executor, collected and edited the work Ellison had left behind. With the help of Ellison's wife, Callahan published *The Collected Essays of Ralph Ellison* (1995) and *"Flying Home" and Other Stories* (1996). He also edited what was available of Ellison's work in progress, the never finished second novel, which was published as *Juneteenth* in 1999. In 2000 Callahan and Albert Murray, Ellison's close friend, published *Trading Twelves,* a selection of letters between Murray and Ellison that captures an easygoing and relaxed aspect of Ellison's character and details their "lifelong dialogue about life, literary craft, and American identity." The collection illustrates to readers a writer and thinker who, even in his lightest and most quotidian moments, never stopped playing the dozens, never stopped practicing his craft, never stopped wrestling with America.

INVISIBLE MAN

When *Invisible Man* first appeared, Richard Wright wrote to Ellison, praising the accomplishment: "I think you can be proud of what you turned in, Ralph. You entered the ranks of literature with your book, and there is no doubt about it." Other friends and colleagues weighed in as well. Langston Hughes wrote a favorable review, and Kenneth Burke considered the novel "epoch-making." Even though the book did have many detractors, it immediately precipitated critical and scholarly discussion. Whatever anyone thought about the novel, it was clearly what the critic Robert Stepto later called a new narrative development in African American literature.

Ellison's philosophical reflection on African American identity and history initiated a blues and jazz style in novelistic discourse. As Albert Murray asserts,

Invisible Man was par excellence the literary extension of the blues. It was as if Ellison had taken an everyday twelve bar blues tune (by a man from down South sitting in a manhole up North in New York singing and signifying about how he got there) and scored it for full orchestra.

The blues and spirituals are heard throughout the text. There are references to Mahalia Jackson, Buddy Bolden, and Jimmy Rushing. Mary Rambo, the narrator's landlady, sings "Backwater Blues." When the narrator's friend and fellow organizer, Tod, is killed, he is eulogized at the funeral by mourners who sing "Many Thousand Gone," an old African American spiritual. Peetie Wheatstraw, a character in the novel, is also the name of a blues singer. *Invisible Man* is a meta-narrative of the blues: it is the long, sad song of a people and their condition in America, and it is the long, sad song of its main character, a man who, by the end of the novel, is transformed into a blues hero. By sharing his pain and suffering, he confirms the human connection to his audience. He becomes a spokesperson, whose account of tragedy invites us to share and release our suffering as well. When he asks, "Who knows but that, on the lower frequencies, I speak for you?" the narrator involves us in this process. It is a call-and-response moment that initiates discussion beyond the closing of the text. The narrator opens up a space for new stories to be told, especially for those people and would-be storytellers who have gone unheard in the past. It is an open-ended work, but as Ellison reminds us in the essay "Remembering Jimmy," blues is the "art of ambiguity."

The blues is also a powerful meditation on the forces of history and society. When the narrator hears the blues playing from a record shop, he wonders if "this is the true history of the times, a mood blared by trumpets, trombones, saxophones, and drums, a song with turgid, inadequate words." Blues acts as a counterforce to the prevailing notions of African Americans in history and illustrates more truthfully the reality of African American life than "official history" does. Ellison compares the blues to existentialism, thereby expressing the tragic and absurdist elements of the human drama.

This is most memorably realized in the character of Jim Trueblood and his blues tale. Trueblood's tale reveals the "ritual use" of the blues. He is able to transform the painful incident with his daughter that has destroyed his family into a story of understanding, contrition, survival, and even bitter irony—this is the essence of the blues. Trueblood manages to expel some of his pain every time he tells his tale; it becomes a way for him to control the tragic event (the "accidental" incestuous liaison with his daughter) and his participation in it. In hearing it, Norton, the white patron of the narrator's college, is made to contemplate his own pain and sin—the implied incestuous feelings he has had for his own dead daughter.

Houston Baker's study of blues in African American literature devotes considerable space to the Trueblood episode. He points out that the novel is fluid, improvisational, and multivocal, resembling the character of jazz as well as the blues. The text is redolent with the sounds and flavor of jazz. It digresses, it swings, it riffs, and it improvises on other texts and songs. Even Ellison's position as a writer is linked to jazz. Seeking to meld African American vernacular with the novelistic tradition, Ellison attempts to contribute something of his own voice to the voices that have gone before him. In his essay "The Charlie Christian Story," this is what he has claimed that jazz musicians do:

> For true jazz is an art of individual assertion within and against the group. Each true jazz moment (as distinct from the uninspired commercial performance) springs from a contest in which each artist challenges all the rest; each solo flight, or improvisation, represents (like the successive canvases of a painter) a definition of his identity: as individual, as member of the collectivity and as a link in the chain of tradition.

Ellison revises and repeats the stories of African American culture and European and American novelistic discourse. One can feel the influence of Fyodor Dostoyevsky's *Notes from Underground,* Malraux's *Man's Fate,* the *Odyssey,* Herman Melville's *Moby-Dick* and *The Confidence-Man,* Mark Twain's *Huckleberry Finn,* James Joyce's *Ulysses,* Eliot's *The Waste Land,* and Wright's "The Man Who Lived Underground." But the novel also imbricates

within its pages slave narratives, sermons, and folklore as well as jazz and blues. Everything is here, including elements of popular culture, such as film.

The hybrid nature of the novel has led recent critics to reconsider its modernist style. J. Lee Greene contends that *Invisible Man* "emerges as a matrix of intertextuality that installs, parodies, rereads, and interfaces texts of various kinds from various disciplines, from different cultures and from different historical periods." Elliot Butler-Evans concurs, suggesting that the novel "appropriates . . . discourses of the other." It is clear that Ellison was concerned with polyphony and heteroglossia (or a text composed of many different voices, sounds, languages, and discourses), benchmarks of what might be considered a postmodern text. Even critics who do not consider the novel postmodern suggest that Ellison is critiquing modernism and naturalism. Other scholars believe that the novel represents an early postmodern sensibility or, at the very least, marks the end of one tradition and the beginning of another.

Whether the novel is a modernist or postmodernist text likely will continue to be debated. Whatever its designation, the work is one of the most comprehensive allegories of African American life. The historical matrix of the novel recapitulates an individual on a quest for his identity, a picaresque novel. On a larger scale, however, this is the story of the quest for African American identity, free from slavery or racism. The underground in which the invisible man resides is a symbol for the history of African Americans in this country. Despite the narrator's belief that hard work and good fortune will ensure his part of the American dream, he cannot fathom the words of his dying grandfather, "to overcome 'em with yeses, undermine 'em with grins, agree 'em to death and destruction, let 'em swoller you till they vomit or bust wide open." Readers do not see this scene firsthand. It is an echo of the narrator's past—a voice from the past that still haunts this family, the narrator, and African Americans.

Ellison's tropological revision of African American texts and signs addresses and attempts to rewrite the burdens of that past in a way that is able to overcome its pain while embracing the strength, humor, and resiliency that enabled African American culture to survive in the cauldron of slavery. One such trope that Ellison tackles is the importance of naming. Throughout the slave narratives and African American autobiographies, from the abolitionist Frederick Douglass to the civil rights leader Malcolm X, naming has been a right assumed by the captors. In *Invisible Man,* the narrator constantly is being given an identity by others. The Brotherhood provides him with a new name, and when the narrator receives electric shock treatment, he is unable to remember his name. Readers never discover it. It is not until the narrator is able to name his own experience, to define his own life, that he will be able to create his identity. The act of storytelling and naming himself connects him to a larger African American tradition to which Ellison wants to allude. Here, however, the name is withheld until the time when he discovers who he is; then he will "be free" to forge his own life.

Ellison also embeds in his novel the folkloric trickster figure. There are multiple tricksters throughout the book: Dr. Bledsoe, Lucius Brockway, Rinehart, Trueblood. Even the narrator resembles folklore figures: Brer Bear and Brer Rabbit. He could be said to be hibernating like a bear and living in a hole like a rabbit. The Brer Rabbit image is also invoked during the scene in which the narrator receives electric shock treatment. When the doctors ask the narrator who he is and then who Brer Rabbit is, the narrator comes back from the brink. The folktale connects him to his past and to his identity.

Even the image of a yam works to represent identity in the novel. The narrator takes a bite of the yam he has purchased from a cart and realizes, "I yam what I am!" The yam serves as an iconographic image, a symbol of identity and African American history. It links the narrator to the South, to Africa, to all the people of the diaspora. Unlike the southern meal that he tries to avoid for breakfast, the narrator begins to relish his past in the act of hungering for and enjoying this food.

Other icons of African American identity can be found in the briefcase that the narrator carries with him throughout the work. It represents the "cultural baggage" that African Americans must still carry with them. The Sambo doll, the racist caricature of the bank, the chain, the letters—these historical and cultural artifacts symbolize what the narrator most hold on to, what he must discard, and what is difficult to get rid of. These negative, stereotypical images of African Americans contained in the narrator's briefcase, as well as the historical items that he possesses that verify the enslavement of the past, each carry a different, metaphorical weight in the consciousness of African American identity.

The narrator moves within the historical stream of African American life. Slavery, miscegenation, Reconstruction, the frontier, the migration north, a shift from rural to urban culture, the involvement with communism, the experience of returning World War I and II veterans—the landscape is epic in scope but focuses on the effects of this weighty past on the consciousness of an individual. It forces invisibility upon him despite the very real presence of African Americans in America. At the Liberty Paints factory the narrator is told the company slogan: "If It's Optic White, It's the Right White," but he is surprised to find that the whiteness is achieved by adding drops of black paint. The white cannot exist without the black, and, consequently, American history and what Americans value most in that history ("liberty") is possible because of "blackness." This theme is prominent in nearly all of Ellison's work—American culture is what it is because of the African American experience.

Ellison emphasizes this by drawing attention to the vernacular. The narrator tells one of the white members of the Brotherhood that if he really wants to understand African American life, he should ask his wife to take him "around to the gin mills and the barber shops and the juke joints and the churches, Brother . . . and the beauty parlors. . . . A whole unrecorded history is spoken then." This truth is there, underground (like the narrator), waiting to be found, to be told, to be understood, to be celebrated.

THE ESSAYS

In his review of Ellison's *Going to the Territory,* John Edgar Wideman submits that "great writers are always teaching us to read them" and that Ellison's essays help us do just that. In his two essay collections (the other being *Shadow and Act*), Ellison visits the landscape of American literature, history, and culture to discover and reveal the ubiquitous presence of African Americans. In an interview with Robert B. Stepto and Michael S. Harper, Ellison describes that presence:

In my class I get raised eyebrows by pointing out that race is always at the center of our uneasy preoccupation with American identity. It is as abiding as our concern with the principles of freedom and equality. Thus, when you read American literature and fail to see the words "Black" or "Negro" or "Afro-American" in a given work, it doesn't mean that they are not operating there symbolically.

Ellison's fiction negotiates this presence, but his essays speak directly to this idea. By focusing his attention on jazz and blues musicians, such as Charlie Parker, Jimmy Rushing, Duke El-

lington, Charlie Christian, and Mahalia Jackson, at the same time that he considers the work of Hemingway, Twain, and Stephen Crane, Ellison democratizes art and literature. The storytelling and artistry of African Americans receives the same weight and consideration as the "canonical" American writers. If social equality is still a battle for African Americans, artistic equality is achieved in the collections of Ellison's essays and lectures. He states in "The World and the Jug" that writing is "a social action in itself."

As Wideman points out in his review of *Going to the Territory,* however, one of the salient features of the essays is the gaze they provide into Ellison's work. In "The Little Man at Chehaw Station," the readers understand the process and diligence of Ellison's writing, performing at his best for every audience. The essay "The Art of Romare Bearden" focuses on this Harlem Renaissance artist's style, the way that jazz permeates it. Ellison locates the improvisation and masking in Bearden's work, and, through his musings, alert readers see into the workings of Ellison's artistic consciousness.

"What America Would Be Like without Blacks" again clarifies Ellison's project in his fiction: to re-inscribe African American presence in literature and culture. The essay is critical of the infamous "Moynihan Report," which typifies African American life as pathological. Critics of *The Negro Family: The Case for National Action,* written in 1965 by Daniel Patrick Moynihan, who was later a U.S. senator from New York, claimed that instead of alerting readers to a social crisis, the report blamed the victims of America's social ills. In "What America Would Be Like without Blacks," Ellison cautions readers to realize that "whites are culturally part Negro American without realizing it" and that if African American life is stigmatized, the foundations of American society will continue to be chiseled away. These ideas are explored further in "Society, Morality, and the Novel." One of Ellison's most celebrated essays, this work discusses the craft of the novelist but also examines the novel's place in forging, maintaining, and developing American identity and conscience: the "novel is bound up with the notion of nationhood." This is the theme of "The Novel as a Function of American Democracy" as well. Examining nineteenth-century American writers, Ellison argues that it is in these great works of American literature that democracy is best realized. Ellison implies in many of the essays, however, that our novelistic tradition, like our country, has not yet met the promise of its fiction, of its own myth.

The significance of jazz in Ellison's life and its impact on his style is better understood by analyzing any of his numerous essays on music. "Blues People," a review of LeRoi Jones's (Amiri Baraka) book of the same name, argues that Jones sees blues in a limited scope. Ellison feels that the blues was forged in the American experience, that the blues exist because they "speak to us simultaneously of the tragic and the comic aspects of the human condition and they express a profound sense of life shared by many Negro Americans." This description of the blues could apply easily to *Invisible Man*, as could the well-respected review of Wright's *Black Boy* (titled "Richard Wright's Blues"), where Ellison describes the blues implicit in African American life and literature:

> The blues is an impulse to keep the painful details and episodes of a brutal experience alive in one's aching consciousness, to finger its jagged grain, and to transcend it, not by the consolation of philosophy but by squeezing from it a near-tragic, near-comic lyricism. As a form, the blues is an autobiographical chronicle of personal catastrophe expressed lyrically.

The essays signify much more, of course, than blueprints to understanding Ellison's artistic agenda. Ellison's essays culminate in one of the most significant and elegant conversations that a writer has ever had with America.

THE SHORT STORIES

Several pieces of Ellison's short fiction were collected and edited in the form of the novel *Juneteenth*. Other works were collected in *"Flying Home" and Other Stories*. A few others have not yet been collected in a single volume. Several stories that appear in *"Flying Home"* had not been previously published, including "A Party Down at the Square," "The Black Ball," "Hymie's Bull," "Boy on a Train," "A Hard Time Keeping Up," and "I Did Not Learn Their Names." Several of the stories in the collection have been anthologized elsewhere and have garnered a great deal of attention. One of the earliest works in *"Flying Home"* is "Mister Toussan," one of the several "Buster and Riley" stories about two boys testing themselves against the world.

"Mister Toussan" takes place as Buster and Riley try to figure out a way to gather some of their white neighbor's cherries. Even though the birds are eating the fruit, the boys are forbidden to take any. They wait for an opportunity to grab some of the cherries and, in the meantime, play the dozens, talk about school, and so on. They essentially play a storytelling game, trying to outdo each other, extending and adding details to the line that the other one has just spoken. They wonder where they would go if they could fly (a motif in many of Ellison's works) and consider what they learned in school. Their geography book tells them that Africans are lazy, but Riley's father tells them otherwise. Here, the oral story carries more weight than what is written. It has to because the written word tries to offer them a negative picture of themselves. They also learn about the Haitian slave revolt of the late eighteenth century led by Toussaint Louverture, who emancipated the slaves and briefly established Haiti as a black-governed French protectorate. Taking the little bit of history they have learned about the event, they add their own details. In doing so, they create and control their own story and make history theirs. It is a way for them to subvert the authority of the educational system that neglects the contributions to the world by people who look like them.

"King of the Bingo Game," also collected in *"Flying Home,"* foreshadows the surrealism found in sections of *Invisible Man.* In this story a man has gone to a movie house to watch a film that he has apparently seen before, which he realizes when he notes that the scenes of the film do not change because "everything was fixed." Readers discover that he is really at the theater to play a bingo game because he needs money to pay for a doctor for his ailing wife. (The bingo wheel is brought out between shows, and moviegoers are encouraged to play.) The man is a recently arrived immigrant from the South, who has come to the "promised land" of depression-era Harlem only to discover things are not any better up north. The North is an illusion of freedom, in the same way that films are an illusion of life. When he wins the chance to spin the wheel, he suddenly feels, for the first time, that he is in control of his life because he is in control of the wheel: "He was running the show, by God!" By this point he has forgotten his name. Like the "invisible man," he has no identity and no power. He feels as if "his whole life was determined by the bingo wheel," and he cannot let go. The button is controlled by electricity, a trope for power that appears again in *Invisible Man.* This Kafkaesque tale ends when uniformed white men beat the man, wrest the control button from him, and take him away.

The story "Flying Home" also echoes the themes that later would be developed in *Invisible Man.* The story "responds" to several other texts embedded in the narrative, for example, the folktales "All God's Children Had Wings" and "Colored Man in Heaven," as well as Lionel Hampton's jazz piece "Flying Home." "All God's Children" is a warning not to forget the past or where one has come from; otherwise one might not be able to get back. Todd, the

pilot in "Flying Home," has forgotten the stories of his past and of his people—hence the title of the story. Todd needs to return to his past, to what it was like growing up as a black man in the segregated South: "The memory sickened him and he wanted to remember no more." As Ellison indicates in the story, however, one cannot forget the horrors of the past without also forgetting the ways to overcome and survive them.

Todd is one of the Tuskegee Airmen, asked to fly for America in World War II but continually grounded by racism. His plane crashes when it runs into "jim crow," an ironic allusion to the segregation that ruled the South and, in this story, even manages to control borders in the sky, although "flight" usually signifies freedom. The bird "knocks him back a hundred years," signaling that segregation is like living in "second slavery." Todd, however, believes that flying is the "only dignity" he has. He decides that if he exhibits patriotism and courage, white Americans finally will value his humanity. When white men come for him with a straitjacket, convinced that a black man trying to fly must be crazy, Todd discovers that this is not the case. This scene reverberates in the Golden Day episode of *Invisible Man,* where veterans are institutionalized not because of shell shock or battle fatigue but because of the treatment they received when they returned home. The psychological effects of racism, as Ellison learned when he worked closely with a clinic in Harlem, destroyed the men's self-image.

Jefferson, the old sharecropper who comes to Todd's aid after the plane crash, tells him a story, a rendering of the folktale "Colored Man in Heaven." Jefferson's version is meant to be instructional and edifying for Todd, a man who has also fallen out of the sky. Todd has missed the true dignity in his life, the connection to his past, to his stories, to his people. He hears Jefferson's voice "with gratitude," understanding that the tale is a blues rendition of how far the black man soars despite his burdens. It comforts the pilot, and in the last scene, though readers are uncertain of what his fate may be, the "jim crow" is transformed into a bird "of flaming gold."

JUNETEENTH

Very little scholarly work exists on the novel *Juneteenth*. The work, which was published after his death, became Ellison's lifelong work in progress. In his conception of the novel, Ellison admitted that he was trying to revisit and extend the themes of *Invisible Man* (like a jazz musician playing a certain song in a new way each night). As James Allen McPherson states in the book's introduction: "I think he was trying to Negro-Americanize the novel form, at the same time he was attempting to move beyond it." In 1967, at the time the original manuscript of the novel was destroyed, it was 360 pages in length. Several of the chapters already had been published. Before Ellison's death, eight sections had appeared in print: "Juneteenth," "And Hickman Arrives," "The Roof, the Steeple, and the People," "It Always Breaks Out," "Night-Talk," "A Song of Innocence," "Backwacking: A Plea to the Senator," and "Cadillac Flambé." Following Ellison's death, his literary executor John Callahan reworked some of the sections, using some of Ellison's notes, and fit the sections together. A scholarly edition of *Juneteenth* is in preparation and should enlighten interested readers about the choices that Callahan made when editing the novel. Of course, Ellison's plan for the sections left behind may never be known.

The novel centers on two characters, Reverend Hickman and Senator Sunraider, who was known as "Bliss" when he was a child. Hickman is a former trombone player turned preacher (an allusion to James Weldon Johnson's poetry collection *God's Trombones: Seven Negro Sermons in Verse*). Bliss's mother, a white woman, had falsely accused Hickman's brother of rape and had abandoned Bliss. Hickman's mother and brother die in the aftermath of the false accusation of rape, and the abandoned child, Bliss, comes under Hickman's care, in an act of compassion and forgiveness for what Bliss's mother brought upon this family.

The story is told in a series of dreamlike flashbacks (reminiscent at times of *Invisible Man*), following the attempted assassination of Senator Sunraider. Turning his back on his past and his race, the senator has transformed himself into a "race-baiting" politician. He has passed for white for several years, but Hickman comes to warn him that there is going to be an attempt on his life. Arriving too late to preempt the act, Hickman is called to the senator's bedside. Hickman consoles him: "I'm still with you. I'll never leave now." The comment is also a reflection of the importance of the past in each of our lives. No matter how far Bliss has run from his identity, it is always something he cannot negate. This could characterize America as well; who we are as a country is who we *were*. The past is always echoed in the present, especially in terms of race and equality. The novel is a cultural allegory of these relationships. Juneteenth is the "day" (an unknown date in June) when Union troops arrived in Texas, announcing to slaves that they were free—nearly four years after President Abraham Lincoln had signed the Emancipation Proclamation. When the Reverend declares at the Juneteenth celebration that "there's been a heap of Juneteenths before this one and I tell you there'll be a heap more before we're truly free," the reader is reminded of just how far there still is to go in fulfilling the promise of democracy.

As Hickman sits at the senator's bedside, the man remembers his days as Bliss. The conversations, fragmented and elusive, bring him back to the site of memory, a place to which he has not wanted to return. Just as he has turned his back on his collective memory, or his racial past, he also has forgotten his individual identity. The disease of American racism has fostered in him a fear of who he really is and what the future holds for him. Unable to reconcile his mixed heritage, he made a choice. Again, the character of Bliss and his background easily could be read as a comment on America and the historical relationship to African Americans. It is through the call-and-response passages with Hickman, where he falls easily back into their partnership in the church, that the past is remembered. The oral history renews his spirit, if not his actual life.

Readers are confronted with the process of remembering as well. The audience is forced to connect the links of time and space, in a sense they are "re-membering" the pieces of the novel. They must make meaning from the flashes, digressions, fragments—put it together in order to understand it, no matter how messy it may be. It is the same relationship that Americans must have with the still confounding and haunting pieces of the American past. Reverend Hickman's Juneteenth "Dry Bones" sermon embellishes this idea further:

> divided and scattered, ground down and battered into the earth like a spike being pounded by a ten-pound sledge, we were on the ground and in the earth and the earth was red and black like the earth of Africa. And as we moldered underground we were mixed with this land. We liked it. It fitted us fine. It was in us and we were in it. And then—praise God—deep in the ground, deep in the womb of this land, we began to stir.

Like the movie that Hickman takes Bliss to as a young man, which was "marvelous" at the same time that it was "terrible," the past must be acknowledged and illuminated. Hickman tells Bliss not to be afraid of the shadows in the movie: "They're only dangerous if you believe in them." Although the movie is not named, there are clues that it is *Birth of a Nation*. This infamous silent film, depicting the Ku Klux Klan as rescuers of white women and heroes of the South, is certainly a "shadow" that is "dangerous" if its images are accepted. The problem is Bliss does believe in the illusions and shadows of the film, and even more deeply the negative stereotypes applied to African American males. The actress Mary Pickford, who plays a white woman in distress in the film, replaces Bliss's own mother in his mind, and Bliss later leaves Hickman in search of his white identity. By failing to understand the past fully, Bliss becomes its victim. Bliss then embraces the life of a con artist, telling young women that he is a moviemaker. He has followed the shadows rather than the more difficult path to knowledge.

As with other Ellison works, *Juneteenth* emphasizes that life is composed of the terrible and the marvelous and that one must accept both to overcome suffering. Horace Porter's book *Jazz Country: Ralph Ellison in America* (2001) includes one of the few treatments of *Juneteenth*. In this work, he argues that Ellison stresses the marvelous in the novel "as a corrective to the overwhelming emphasis by journalists, statisticians, politicians, and certain intellectuals on blacks as criminals or victims." This could be said of nearly any of Ellison's artistic or critical projects. In *Juneteenth*, however, it is clear that the marvelous is found in Hickman's music or his sermons. The vernacular culture is able to battle social forces that seek to define and control African American life.

In his eulogy for Ralph Ellison, John Callahan related one of Ellison's statements: "If we laugh at each other, we won't kill each other." Like the most profound writers before him (and since), Ellison seeks to explain the mysteries of who we are and where we are going. In America this has been a uniquely difficult task. The tensions of our identity threaten to rip the fabric of the culture. Perhaps where Ellison has had the most success is in providing his readers with art that both transcends and embraces that tension in the name of knowledge and freedom. He extols the sacred and profane in us, like his character in *Invisible Man,* who claims that "in order to get some of it down I *have* to love . . . so I denounce and I defend and I hate and I love." He proposes "infinite possibilities," not as a naive optimist offering a panacea but as a blues man who refuses to believe that he cannot conquer the suffering in his life. As Larry Neal suggests,

> Where Wright, in *Black Boy,* saw black life "void of hope" and bare of tradition, Ellison countered with a very positive vision of Afro-American life. For Ellison, black people did not exhibit a tradition void of hope, memories, and personal attachments. They were, instead, profoundly human and blessed with a strong, spiritually sustaining culture.

Ellison may never have marched a single mile in the hope of making the American dream a reality for African Americans, but his legacy on the page was ultimately as powerful. His style and his words helped memorialize the ways and the spirit of the men and women who survived the horrors of American slavery and racism though their folk wit, their blues resistance, and their soulful song.

Selected Bibliography

WORKS OF RALPH ELLISON

NOVELS
Invisible Man. New York: Random House, 1952. (This essay cites the Vintage Books edition, 1989.)
Juneteenth: A Novel. Edited by John F. Callahan. New York: Random House, 1999. (Published posthumously.)

COLLECTED ESSAYS AND SHORT STORIES
Shadow and Act. New York: Random House, 1964. (Includes "The Charlie Christian Story," "Remembering Jimmy," and "Richard Wright's Blues.")

Going to the Territory. New York: Random House, 1986. (Includes "Society, Morality, and the Novel.")
The Collected Essays of Ralph Ellison. Edited by John F. Callahan. New York: Modern Library, 1995. (Published posthumously. Includes "Brave Words for a Startling Occasion," "Change the Joke and Slip the Yoke," "What America Would Be Like without Blacks," and "The World and the Jug," among other essays.)
"Flying Home" and Other Stories. Edited by John F. Callahan. New York: Random House, 1996. (Published posthumously.)
Living with Music: Ralph Ellison's Jazz Writings. New York: Modern Library, 2001. (Published posthumously; includes fiction, letters, interviews, and essays.)

UNCOLLECTED ESSAYS AND FICTION
"Judge Lynch in New York." *New Masses* 33:15–16 (August 15, 1939).
"Slick Gonna Learn." *Direction* 2:10–11, 14, 16 (September 1939).
"The Birthmark." *New Masses* 36:16–27 (July 2, 1940).
"Out of the Hospital and under the Bar." In *Soon, One Morning: New Writing by American Negroes, 1940–1962.* Edited by Herbert Hill. New York: Knopf, 1963. Pp. 242–290.
"Harlem's America." *New Leader* 49:22–35 (September 26, 1966).
"Cadillac Flambé." *American Review* 16:249–269 (February 1973).

MANUSCRIPTS AND CORRESPONDENCE
Ralph Ellison asked that upon his death his wife, Fanny Ellison, and his literary executor, John F. Callahan, collect and donate his papers to the Library of Congress's Manuscript Division. They are housed there as the "Ralph Ellison Papers."
Trading Twelves: The Selected Letters of Ralph Ellison and Albert Murray. Edited by Albert Murray. New York: Modern Library, 2000.

BIBLIOGRAPHIES

Benoit, Bernard, and Michel Fabre. "A Bibliography of Ralph Ellison's Published Writings." *Studies in Black Literature* 2, no. 3:25–28 (1971).

Covo, Jacqueline. *The Blinking Eye: Ralph Waldo Ellison and His American, French, German, and Italian Critics, 1952–1971.* Metuchen, N.J.: Scarecrow Press, 1974.

CRITICAL AND BIOGRAPHICAL STUDIES

Baker, Houston. *Singers of Daybreak: Studies in Black American Literature.* Washington, D.C.: Howard University Press, 1974.

———. *Blues, Ideology, and Afro-American Literature: A Vernacular Theory.* Chicago: University of Chicago Press, 1984.

Bell, Bernard. *The Afro-American Novel and Its Tradition.* Amherst: University of Massachusetts, 1987.

Benston, Kimberly W., ed. *Speaking for You: The Vision of Ralph Ellison.* Washington, D.C.: Howard University Press, 1987.

Blake, Susan. "Ritual and Rationalization: Black Folklore in the Works of Ralph Ellison." *PMLA* 94, no. 1:121–135 (1979).

Bloom, Harold, ed. *Ralph Ellison.* New York: Chelsea House, 1986.

Busby, Mark. *Ralph Ellison.* Boston: Twayne, 1991.

Butler, Robert J., ed. *The Critical Response to Ralph Ellison.* Westport, Conn.: Greenwood Press, 2000.

Butler-Evans, Elliot. "The Politics of Carnival and Heteroglossia in Toni Morrison's *Song of Solomon* and Ralph Ellison's *Invisible Man:* Dialogic Criticism and African American Literature." In *The Ethnic Canon: Histories, Institutions, and Interventions.* Edited by David Palumbo-Liu. Minneapolis: University of Minnesota Press, 1995. Pp. 117–139.

Callahan, John F. "Chaos, Complexity, and Possibility: The Historical Frequencies of Ralph Waldo Ellison." *Black American Literature Forum* 11, no. 4:130–138 (1977).

———. "'Riffing' and Paradigm-Building: The Anomaly of Tradition and Innovation in *Invisible Man* and *The Structure of Scientific Revolutions.*" *Callaloo* 10, no. 1:91–102 (1987).

———. *In the African-American Grain: Call-and-Response in Twentieth-Century Black Fiction.* Middletown, Conn.: Wesleyan University Press, 1988.

———. "Frequencies of Memory: A Eulogy for Ralph Waldo Ellison." *Callaloo* 18, no. 2:298–320 (1995).

Crouch, Stanley. "How Long? So Long." *Partisan Review* 61, no. 4:367 (1994).

Dickstein, Morris. "Ralph Ellison, Race, and American Culture." *Raritan* 18, no. 3:30–50 (1999).

Fabre, Michel. "The Narrator/Narratee Relationship in *Invisible Man.*" *Callaloo* 8, no. 3:535–543 (1985).

Ford, Douglas. "Crossroads and Cross-currents in *Invisible Man.*" *Modern Fiction Studies* 45, no. 4:887–904 (1999).

Gates, Henry Louis, Jr. *The Signifying Monkey: A Theory of Afro-American Literary Criticism.* New York: Oxford University Press, 1988.

Greene, J. Lee. *Blacks in Eden: The African-American Novel's First Century.* Charlottesville: University Press of Virginia, 1996.

Hersey, John, ed. *Ralph Ellison: A Collection of Critical Essays.* Englewood Cliffs, N.J.: Prentice Hall, 1974.

Jackson, Lawrence. *Ralph Ellison: Emergence of Genius.* New York: John Wiley and Sons, 2002.

Lee, Kun Jong. "Ellison's *Invisible Man:* Emersonianisms Revised." *PMLA* 107, no. 2:331–344 (1992).

Lyne, William. "The Signifying Modernist: Ralph Ellison and the Limits of Double Consciousness." *PMLA* 107, no. 2:319–330 (1992).

McSweeney, Kerry. *Invisible Man: Race and Identity.* Boston: Twayne, 1988.

Marvin, Thomas F. "Children of Legba: Musicians at the Crossroads in Ralph Ellison's *Invisible Man.*" *American Literature* 68, no. 3:587–608 (1996).

Murray, Albert. *The Omni-Americans: New Perspectives on Black Experience and American Culture.* New York: Outerbridge and Dienstfrey, 1970.

Nadel, Alan. *Invisible Criticism: Ralph Ellison and the American Canon.* Iowa City: University of Iowa Press, 1988.

Neal, Larry. "Ellison's Zoot Suit." In *Speaking for You: The Vision of Ralph Ellison.* Edited by Kimberely Benston. Washington, D.C.: Howard University Press, 1990. Pp. 105–124.

Nichols, Charles. "The Slave Narrators and the Picaresque Mode: Archetypes of Modern Black

Personae." In *The Slave's Narrative.* Edited by Charles T. Davis and Henry Louis Gates Jr. New York: Oxford University Press, 1985. Pp. 283–298.

O'Meally, Robert G. *The Craft of Ralph Ellison.* Cambridge, Mass.: Harvard University Press, 1980. (Includes a comprehensive bibliography of Ellison's published and unpublished work in the appendix.)

———, ed. *New Essays on* Invisible Man. Cambridge: Cambridge University Press, 1988.

———. "On Burke and the Vernacular: Ralph Ellison's Boomerang of History." In *History and Memory in African-American Culture.* Edited by Geneviève Fabre and Robert O'Meally. New York: Oxford University Press, 1994. Pp. 244–260.

Parr, Susan Resneck, and Pancho Savery, eds. *Approaches to Teaching Ellison's "Invisible Man."* New York: Modern Language Association, 1989.

Porter, Horace A. *Jazz Country: Ralph Ellison in America.* Iowa City: University of Iowa Press, 2001.

Reilly, John M., ed. *Twentieth Century Interpretations of* Invisible Man: *A Collection of Critical Essays.* Englewood Cliffs, N.J.: Prentice Hall, 1970.

Rowell, Charles H., ed. "Remembering Ralph Ellison." Special Issue of *Callaloo* 18, no. 2:249–320 (1995). (The issue was dedicated to Ellison following his death in 1994. It includes essays, poems, and remembrances about Ellison's life and work.)

Schor, Edith. *Visible Ellison: A Study of Ralph Ellison's Fiction.* Westport, Conn.: Greenwood Press, 1993.

Schultz, Elizabeth. "The Illumination of Darkness: Affinities between *Moby-Dick* and *Invisible Man.*" *CLA Journal* 32, no. 2:170–200 (1988).

Scott, Nathan A., Jr. "Ellison's Vision of 'Communitas.'" *Callaloo* 18, no. 2:310–318 (1995).

Skerrett, Joseph. "Ralph Ellison and the Example of Richard Wright." *Studies in Short Fiction* 15, no. 2:145–153 (1978).

Steele, Meili. "Metatheory and the Subject of Democracy in the Work of Ralph Ellison." *New Literary History* 27, no. 3:473–502 (1996).

Stepto, Robert B. *From behind the Veil: A Study of Afro-American Narrative.* Urbana: University of Illinois Press, 1991.

Sundquist, Eric J., ed. *Cultural Contexts for Ralph Ellison's* Invisible Man. Boston: Bedford Books of St. Martin's Press, 1995.

Watts, Jerry Gafio. *Heroism and the Black Intellectual: Ralph Ellison, Politics, and Afro-American Intellectual Life.* Chapel Hill: University of North Carolina Press, 1994.

Wideman, John Edgar. "What is Afro, What is American." *New York Times Book Review,* August 3, 1986, p. 15.

Wolfe, Jesse. "'Ambivalent Man': Ellison's Rejection of Communism." *African American Review* 34, no. 4:621–637 (2000).

INTERVIEWS

Graham, Maryemma, and Amritjit Singh, eds. *Conversations with Ralph Ellison.* Jackson: University Press of Mississippi, 1995. (Includes interviews with Ishmael Reed, Quincy Troupe, and Steve Cannon; Alfred Chester and Vilma Howard; and Robert B. Stepto and Michael S. Harper.)

—TRACIE CHURCH GUZZIO

Sarah Orne Jewett

1849–1909

*"T*HERE IS A golden hospitality of the heart that makes it a pleasure to be a stranger and go knocking at certain gates. But alas! Some homes show no hospitality and seem to give no welcome even to those who live in them altogether, and find them houses, but no homes." Published in the St. Louis, Missouri, *Republic* in 1892 and subtitled "Decide on Your Own Style and Don't Change Your Noon Dinners for Guests," Jewett's popular advice essay "About Hospitality" anticipates several of the writer's central concerns, among them, traveling, home, gender, friendship, family, the stranger, empathy, and hospitality.

CONTEXTS

Born in the coastal New England village of South Berwick, Maine, on September 3, 1849, Sarah was the second of three daughters of Caroline Perry Jewett and Theodore H. Jewett. The Jewetts were an affluent family; Theodore Jewett's father was a wealthy sea captain and shipowner whose success in the West India trade enabled his consumptive son to become a country doctor, whom the young Sarah, suffocated and made unhappy by conventional schooling, accompanied in his buggy on visits to local families. Her father, who would become the model for the generous and kind Dr. Leslie in her novel *A Country Doctor* (1884), was much appreciated by the region's families for his modesty, dedication to service, and rare ability to listen; "from her father," says her biographer Paula Blanchard, Jewett "gained her emotional poise, the sensitive balance of compassion and humor with which she viewed the human scene around her." A prominent physician in Maine and an intellectual, he valued study and provided a model of seriousness and a zest for formal, systematic study that Sarah admired but could rarely achieve. Nevertheless, with her father she explored a wide range of reading in literature, history, science, and religion. In the essay "Looking Back at Girlhood" (collected in *Novels and Stories,* 1994) she affirmed the importance to her later life of her father's library and interest in books: "He gave me his first and best knowledge of books by his own delight and dependence upon them, and ruled my early attempts at writing by the severity and simplicity of his own good taste." Her father also provided her with a valued dictum, "Don't try to write *about* people and things, tell them just as they are!" This assertion resonates in her numerous evocative sketches of daily life and "ordinary" people in New England, in which she emphasizes character traits, such as responsibility, stoicism, industry, and kindness over plot.

The daughter of the doctor who trained Dr. Jewett, the writer's mother seems to have followed the expected pattern of domesticity for women of her class and era; in particular, unlike the writer's father, she enjoyed the numerous visits of female relatives and was a generous and gently formal hostess. Jewett wrote and spoke little of her mother, apparently feeling closer to her after her death, but her mother's family, especially Jewett's grandfather William Perry, were formative influences. William Perry was a farm boy from Rehoboth, Massachusetts, who had gone to Exeter, New Hampshire, when he was twenty-six years old and there had married into the elite Gilman family, which was full of prominent statesmen, bankers, and public servants. Jewett prized her grandfather's seriousness, generosity, and supportiveness. She wrote later that "it was he . . . who was proudest and most sympathetic at any flicker of success" among his grandchildren, whether male or female. Another important relative in Jewett's life was her paternal grandmother, Mary, the third wife of Captain Jewett and a stern, principled woman who demanded focus and success of her grandchildren. Jewett tells the poignant story of how, as a young girl, she enthusiastically picked a rosebud from one of her grandmother's prized bushes and brought it to her with delight, only to be reprimanded for her thoughtlessness.

Although she explores the town history with warmth and enthusiasm in "The Old Town of Berwick," as her essay "River Driftwood" documents and her poem "A Farmer's Sorrow" suggests, by the time Sarah reached maturity, South Berwick, like many New England villages, was in decline. In the case of Berwick, the losses incurred in the Civil War, the construction of the railroads as an alternative to sea transport, and the migration of younger people to industrialized cities and to the West all played a role. However, this situation also meant that many towns were like a time capsule to the past, representing ways of life quickly being lost elsewhere. Jewett's fiction and nonfiction (including "Fair Day," "Going to Shrewsbury," "A Native of Winby," and "A Plea for Front Yards") amply document, with considerable appreciation and nostalgia, the strengths in the older men and—particularly—women left behind by time and "progress"; as Richard Cary observes in his *Appreciation of Sarah Orne Jewett,* "[her] fiction abounds with self-sufficient, self-reliant New England women, speckled products of the Protestant ethic, Emersonian optimism, and indestructible heredity." At the same time that she affiliated herself with country

life, she was able to see both the benefits and disadvantages of city life and industrialization. Works such as "The Gray Mills of Farley," "The Two Browns," "A Business Man," "The Failure of David Berry," "Tom's Husband," "Every-Day Work," "A Lonely Worker," "An Every-Day Girl," "The Growtown Bugle," and "The King of Folly Island" variously explore the growing distinctions between manual and intellectual labor, the treatment of factory workers, the participation of women in the formal workplace and in a consumer culture that fostered economic disparities, and the spiritual drain of modern business affairs.

As a member of the privileged class in Berwick, Jewett enjoyed respect from the villagers, an affluent lifestyle, and a variety of educational opportunities in her childhood. The most formal influence was Berwick Academy, which she attended beginning in 1861; her father and uncles had studied at this excellent preparatory school, which included among its graduates one scholar who had gone on to become a dean of Harvard and others who became eminent in the academic life of nineteenth-century Maine as presidents of Bowdoin, Bates, and Colby Colleges and the University of Maine. Formal education, however, was not her strength, for she was easily bored. Her 1871 children's story "The Boy with One Shoe" reflects this attitude, with its protagonist Tommy playing "hookey" due to spring fever:

> Tommy waked up one morning, raised himself on his elbow, and looked out of the window; and laid down again, feeling very perverse and unsteady. It was pleasanter than it had been any day that spring; and he remembered the long sums at school, and thought how much he should like to wander about and do nothing.

In addition, early on and throughout her life, Jewett suffered from rheumatoid arthritis, which caused her serious pain and numerous absences from school, although she was able to graduate with her friends in 1865 by studying at home.

Like her mother, whose eventually fatal illness emerged during Sarah's childhood, the young Sarah was expected to participate in as many family activities as possible and to regard her illness more as an inconvenience than as a disability, an attitude that served her well during later recurrences.

Other forms of education were regular if less organized. Paula Blanchard writes that Sarah Orne Jewett grew up hearing the conversation of

> a more or less constant assembly of retired sea captains and their wives, along with an assortment of physicians, lawyers, judges, editors, and politicians. . . . Each came from that generation of two wars [the Revolutionary War and Civil War], and each carried around enough personal history to fill a novel. The wives were no less interesting than their husbands.

Another important part of her education as a writer was the informal schoolrooms offered by her visits to the local country store (owned by her grandfather and great-uncle Thomas) and to the homes of community members with her father. In "Looking Back on Girlhood" she appreciates her "contact with the up-country people as well as with the sailors and shipmasters. . . . I used to linger about the busy country stores, and listen to the graphic country talk. I heard the greetings of old friends, and their minute details of neighborhood affairs, their delightful jokes." This "country talk" would delight her readers in periodicals ranging from the *Atlantic Monthly* to the *Boston Globe* and *The Congregationalist*. In her travels with her father on his house calls, she learned to appreciate "the quiet village life, the dull routine of farming or mill life, [which] early became interesting to me. I was taught to find everything that an imaginative child could ask, in the simple scenes close at hand." In the same essay Jewett offers important advice to the reader: "I believe that we should know our native towns much better than most of us do, and never let

ourselves be strangers at home." The theme of the complicated relationship between "stranger" and "native" emerges repeatedly in Jewett's oeuvre, from *Deephaven* to "The King of Folly Island," "The Life of Nancy," and "The Foreigner."

The Civil War erupted during Jewett's years at Berwick Academy, a national cataclysm that would change lives across the nation in ways large and small. For the Jewetts, the tangible results of the war were less personal than for most families. They were fortunate to have lost none of their men in the war, and the Jewett fortunes continued to flourish. Berwick (which began as one community but was eventually divided into two towns, although Sarah always referred to her home community as Berwick) emerged after the war as a flourishing commercial center that also included two large textile mills. Linked by rail and steamer to the great resorts of the New Hampshire mountains and lake country, the bustling city of Portsmouth, New Hampshire, and Boston, Berwick flourished in ways both exciting and alarming to many, including Jewett herself, who could see early on the potential for social and cultural loss in these transformations. With some prescience, she anticipated the eventual decline of villages like Berwick as the century moved toward its conclusion. In "River Driftwood" she documents in particular the diminishment of the river's importance as a life-giving thoroughfare.

Other transformations, such as marriage, could be avoided, and with the variety and sophistication offered by her extended family circle and friends, Jewett found little need—and apparently had little inclination—to seek romantic male attachment. Even if she had been so inclined, the losses of the Civil War seriously diminished the number of eligible partners. To a certain degree, Jewett enjoyed and extended her idyllic childhood, which would become an important resource for her writing. Paula Blanchard observes, "The sense of seeing everyone and everything with a fresh eye, the playfulness, the absolute honesty and lack of pretense that we associate with the characteristic Jewett style, all belong to her childhood self and are typical of the voice heard in the earliest available letters and diaries." An early uncollected story, "Grown-Up," which appeared in the popular, liberal, religiously inflected newspaper *The Independent* in 1872, blends adult and child perspectives, and the narrator imagines herself transforming from adult to child, noting, among other things, that "I found coasting [sledding] when you are grown up has great advantages, the chiefest of which, is that one may stay out as long as one likes, and not hear a disagreeable bell-ringing or an indignant voice coming faintly across the wintry waste." In spite of her attitude toward play and appreciation for a carefree childhood, however, she gained a sense of ambition from her family. This perspective emerges explicitly in "The Hiltons' Holiday" (collected in *Novels and Stories*), in which a boyish farmer, talking to his wife about exposing their two daughters to the wider world, affirms that satisfaction with one's life is not sufficient: "Contented ain't all in this world; hopper-toads may have that quality an' spend all their time a-blinkin'. I don't know's being contented is all there is to look for in a child. Ambition's somthin' to me."

Jewett's own childhood included her two sisters, Mary and Caroline (two years older and six years younger, respectively), with whom she shared a close relationship throughout her life. Even as a girl, Jewett's closest extrafamilial affiliations were with girls and women. She records in her diaries a crush on a girl that she met during a trip to Cincinnati in the winter of 1868–1869; these youthful feelings would culminate later in a long-term relationship with the Bostonian Annie Adams Fields. From early on, Jewett manifested both anxiety about and disparagement of marriage. Her first novel, *Deephaven* (1877), addresses this subject

indirectly, exploring the close relationship between two young women, Kate Lancaster and Helen Denis, during their summer vacation in a Maine community. *A Marsh Island* (1885) seems uncertain about the desirability of the heroine's prospective marriage to either of her two suitors; Jewett wrote to Fields that "I know I could write a better story without a lover in it!" (quoted in Blanchard). In *The Country of the Pointed Firs* (1896) the closest relationships are between and among women; older women are presented as contented widows; and the most poignant figure, "Poor Joanna," who has been betrayed and rejected by her fiancé, is secretly admired for her independent and harmonious single life on Shell-heap Island. Jewett's first published story, "Mr. Bruce" (1869 in the *Atlantic Monthly*), appears to celebrate marriage, but it also investigates the ways in which both men and women negotiate the marriage market and unveils the social hierarchies of class structure in the putatively egalitarian United States. Later stories, such as "The Taking of Captain Ball," "All My Sad Captains," "A Second Spring," and "The Courting of Sister Wisby," show older women in positions of relative power in relation to suitors and husbands, often with affectionate humor.

As Jewett concluded her teen years, she entered into a religious crisis, much as her predecessor, Emily Dickinson, had done much earlier. But unlike Dickinson's departure from Mount Holyoke Female Seminary under the duress of conversion pressures—and her lifelong balance between skepticism and skeptical belief—Jewett's self-searching culminated in her departure from the Congregational faith of her family and her confirmation at St. John's Episcopal Church in Portsmouth, New Hampshire. This conversion was due in part to her exposure to the charismatic preaching of Phillips Brooks of Boston and strengthened by her friendship with the Harvard professor and Swedenborgian author Theophilus Parsons, who encouraged her professional writing career through his personal admonitions and through the prescriptions of his faith, which included personal responsibility and an active role in seeking and advancing divine purpose. The effect of these religious influences on her early writing, including her collection of children's stories, *Play Days* (1878), was a relatively greater emphasis on moral messages than in her mature work. Like her later work, *Deephaven* reflects her continuing interest in spiritualism and communication between the dead and the living, an interest that Paula Blanchard attributes to Parsons' (and, though less directly, Ralph Waldo Emerson's) influence and one that was shared by many nineteenth-century literary people and intellectuals. Jewett could be wickedly witty about sham or hypocritical religion, however, as in "The Courting of Sister Wisby" and "The Guests of Mrs. Timms."

In her twenties, increasingly lonely in Berwick with the departure of friends and classmates for marriage and family, Jewett began to travel extensively, visiting friends and family across the New England region and outside it in Canada, Philadelphia, and the American West. Probably the most difficult event of her life to that point was the sudden death of her father in 1878, in spite of her sense of an enduring spiritual connection with him. His continuing influence was affirmed also by her ascendancy in periodicals such as the elite *Atlantic,* which fostered acquaintances, and eventually friendships, with publishers, writers, editors, and intellectuals, from William Dean Howells to Charles Eliot Norton and Julia Ward Howe. But her most important meeting was with the wife of the publisher James T. Fields, Annie Adams Fields—a poet, social reformer, and patron of the arts, who held famous literary salons in Boston attended by such luminaries as Charles Dickens, William Makepeace Thackeray, and Emerson. Annie shared with Sarah the traits of modesty, a strong sense of humor, and apprecia-

tion for traditional manners and morals, coupled with a strong social conscience.

Soon after James Fields's death in 1881, Annie Fields and Jewett began an enduring relationship and partnership. The pair traveled together, going to Europe several times and visiting friends that included Henry James, Alfred, Lord Tennyson, and the respected French literary figure Marie Thérèse Blanc. When they were in the United States, Jewett divided her time equally between the family residence in Berwick and Fields's homes in Boston and Manchester, Massachusetts, finding it easier to create in the rural environment that she loved but gaining intellectual stimulation in the atmosphere of the urban intellectual elite. This pattern continued until Jewett's death from a stroke in 1909. Beginning in the late twentieth century, an important discussion focused on the nature of her relationship with Fields, in particular, on its erotic component. The critic Lillian Faderman describes the Jewett-Fields relationship as an example of what she calls a "Boston marriage": two women who

> are generally financially independent of men, either through inheritance or because of a career. They were usually feminists, New Women, often pioneers in a profession. They were also very involved in culture and in social betterment, and these female values, which they shared with each other, formed a strong basis for their life together.

In considering Jewett's intimate friendships, Blanchard suggests, it is difficult for early-twenty-first-century Americans "to distinguish among the shades of sexual, nonsexual, and semisexual passion that the nineteenth century accepted as part of the normal spectrum of human emotions." In addition to providing companionship, love, and support, Jewett's relationship with Fields, who had servants, coupled with her sister Mary's assumption of household responsibilities while Jewett stayed in Berwick, freed her from many of the ordinary burdens of most women, allowing her time and leisure to write.

Beyond her relationship with Annie, Jewett enjoyed many other close friendships with women. She corresponded regularly with her fellow countrywoman, the poet and nature writer Celia Thaxter, whose own literary salons on the Isles of Shoals off the coast of Portsmouth drew famous visitors such as the painter Childe Hassam and the writer Nathaniel Hawthorne; Jewett helped Thaxter complete her signature volume, *An Island Garden* (1894). Beginning in the 1880s, another important friend was the artist and designer Sarah Wyman Whitman, who created the cover art for most of Jewett's volumes. A much briefer friendship, but one important in American literary history, was her mentoring relationship with Willa Cather, who met Jewett in 1908 when she was working for *McClure's* magazine. With Annie Fields, Jewett provided the young lesbian writer with crucial encouragement and advice, as well as modeling an affirmative intimate relationship between women.

Cather paid tribute to Jewett in various ways, including dedicating her first significant work, *O Pioneers!* (1913), to her mentor, and in 1925 publishing an expanded edition of *The Country of the Pointed Firs* at a time when Jewett was in danger of being forgotten. Although this edition radically changed Jewett's text by incorporating three later Dunnet Landing stories ("A Dunnet Shepherdess," "The Queen's Twin," and "William's Wedding"), Cather's important preface articulated a view of the book's power and importance that would reemerge in feminist criticism of the writer beginning in the 1970s: "If I were asked to name three American books which have the possibility of a long, long life, I would say at once, *The Scarlet Letter, Huckleberry Finn,* and *The Country of the Pointed Firs.* I can think of no others that confront time and change so serenely." Cather's tribute underscored a literary career distinguished both by

quantity and quality: although she wrote little following a disabling carriage accident in Berwick in 1902, at the time of her death seven years later Jewett had published five adult and two children's novels; dozens of short stories and poems for both adults and children; and essays, sketches, and advice writing.

REGIONALISM AND GENDER

Jewett's work is best understood in the context of the critical frameworks that have both illuminated and, at times, limited our understanding. Although Jewett has been one of the writers who has benefited most from the feminist rediscovery of nineteenth-century writers that began in the mid-1960s, unlike such counterparts as Rose Terry Cooke, Mary Wilkins Freeman, and Grace King, she never disappeared from view. For more than a century, from the earliest appearance of her sketches, Jewett's "significance" has generated much discussion. Her contemporaries valued her principally as a realistic writer who accurately reproduced the cultural milieu of rural New England. The first reviews of her work expressed both admiration and criticism; for example, according to a *Nation* reviewer, a sketch published in the 1873 *Atlantic Monthly* that would later become part of her first novel, *Deephaven,* was not just "very agreeable reading," but "more like talk than reading, and talk of a very fresh, unaffected kind." A *New York Times* reviewer, however, judged *Deephaven* itself to be slight and naive, concluding severely, "it is by some mistake, doubtless, that it got into print at all" (quoted in Cary, *Appreciation*). This mingling of perspectives emerged perhaps most famously in Henry James's miniaturizing assessment of Jewett's masterpiece as a "beautiful little quantum of achievement." Perhaps her women readers understood her best or appreciated her most: for example, her fellow New Englander and writer Alice Brown observed, "No such beautiful and perfect work has been done for many years;

perhaps no such beautiful work has ever been done in America."

Among her supporters in the first part of the twentieth century, Jewett emerged as a regional writer with a nostalgic (and at times, perhaps, even sentimental) perspective; their own "tributes" to her are, ironically, themselves sentimental in tone. F. O. Matthiessen and Van Wyck Brooks, two of Jewett's most influential early critics, published appreciative biographies that emphasize the idyllic rural elements of her early life. Matthiessen describes the writer's journeys with her father in terms that evoke nostalgia for an earlier period and echo Jewett's own work: "They stopped at one or two other places farther along. Sarah observed how almost every house had plots of gay flowers out front, carefully hedged with barrel staves to keep out miscreant hens. Calves were tethered in shady spots, and puppies and kittens were adventuring from doorways." Brooks describes Jewett's childhood from a similar perspective:

> she had grown up in a world of square, white houses, picket fences,—some of them ornamental, with high posts and urns—and yards overflowing with larkspurs, petunias and asters, with hollyhocks and borders of box. When the fences were torn down, and the old reserve went with them, she felt that she belonged to an age that was passing.

To see Jewett in these terms is not necessarily incorrect. Her work, beginning even with the earliest published stories, indeed possesses a tinge of nostalgia and reverence for the past. In *Deephaven* Kate and Helen's exploration of the Brandon house, where they stay and where Kate enjoyed an imaginative childhood, reveals its alluring antiquity and suggests to the reader, as well as to the girls, the stories it holds:

> The chairs looked as if they had been put, at the furnishing of the house, in their places, and there they meant to remain. . . . It is a house with great possibilities. . . . There are four very large rooms on the lower floor, and six above, a wide hall in

each story, and a fascinating garret over the whole, where were many mysterious old chests and boxes, in one of which we found Kate's grandmother's love-letters. . . .

Helen, the narrator, invokes the past via Kate's childhood:

> The carpets were particularly interesting, and I remember Kate's pointing out to me one day a great square figure in one, and telling me she used to keep house there with her dolls for lack of a better play-house, and if one of them chanced to fall outside the boundary stripe, it was immediately put to bed with a cold.

The Brandon house echoes the elegance and refinement of Jewett's own home in Berwick.

Similarly, Jewett explores the resonances of the past in *Old Friends and New* (1879), as the collection's title suggests. Many of the protagonists are older people, particularly older women, whom Jewett describes with subtle admiration. In "A Sorrowful Guest" a brother and sister are reunited in their childhood home after many years of separation, and they comfort a man haunted by the ghost of a cousin who is supposedly dead. "A Late Supper" tells of the impecunious Miss Catherine Spring, who, in a series of amusing accidents, comes to have agreeable boarders who help pay her bills and in the process enable her to help a little orphan girl. In "A Lost Lover" readers learn about Miss Horatia Dane, an elderly woman whose lover had been many years earlier lost at sea, and who "stood in the position, not of an unmarried woman exactly, but rather of having spent most of her life in a long and lonely widowhood." Jewett's gentle humor and strong appreciation for her characters for the most part prevent her stories from becoming cloying or preachy, although they sometimes stray toward what Richard Cary affectionately describes (in his introduction to a 1971 collection of Jewett's stories) as a "beguiling sentimentality." This emphasis upon an empowering past—at least for some members of the community—reappears regularly in her writing, including such Civil War stories as "Decoration Day," which explores a village's conception of its history and its treatment of its veterans, and "A War Debt," which romantically imagines reconciliation between the families of Northern and Southern white soldiers.

Although critics in the first half of the twentieth century increasingly disparaged the potential for sentimentalism in Jewett's work (and the propensity for sentimentalism among women writers more generally), feminist critics of the last thirty years have underscored the gender bias in this charge, recuperating the reputations of Jewett and other writers who provide affirmative models of feminine community. One important emphasis has been upon Jewett's positive portraits of elderly women (and men) and the communities in which they participate:

Old women, rather than men, seem to have acquired this feeling for the rituals of everyday life, perhaps because they have lived closest to the center of family and household life. Among women, Miss Jewett chose to write about spinsters or widows, for they are the ones who concentrate with singlemindedness on maintaining and celebrating the bonds of community, whether attending a reunion or preparing a tea-table

writes Susan Allen Toth. From Mrs. Kew and Mrs. Patton to Mrs. Bonney, *Deephaven* is full of older women who possess a profound understanding of connections between humans and those between humans and nature. In "The Town Poor," from *Strangers and Wayfarers* (1890), Mrs. William Trimble and Miss Rebecca Wright visit two elderly sisters, "the Bray girls," who have "gone on the town" because they have no means of support after the death of their improvident father. The visitors find the sisters remaining courageous and generous in deplorable circumstances—the town selectmen have in effect farmed out their care to the lowest bid-

der—and, outraged, determine to have them returned to their family home in town. Here Jewett emphasizes the power of older women to restore community; as Josephine Donovan has observed in *New England Local Color Literature* (1983), "Sarah Orne Jewett created a symbolic universe which expressed the longing of late-nineteenth-century women that the matriarchal world of the mothers be sustained. . . . Hers is perhaps the last fully female-identified vision in women's literature." "The Queen's Twin" (1899), a Dunnet Landing story that includes Mrs. Todd and the narrator of *The Country of the Pointed Firs,* suggests the links between and among women, even when they are widely separated by status and place.

In spite of such positive representations of women and rural community in Jewett's work, feminist critics have also observed that Jewett, along with such realist-regionalist writers as her famous New England contemporaries Rose Terry Cooke and Mary E. Wilkins Freeman, wrote in part to contradict their predecessors' (including Harriet Beecher Stowe's) representations of rural life as simply utopian and serene. Like Freeman's powerful "A Mistaken Charity," in which two sisters are sent to the poorhouse by a well-meaning but thoughtless neighbor, "The Town Poor" underscores the partial responsibility of wealthier women to attend to the psychic as well as physical needs of their poorer counterparts. Similarly, in "The Passing of Sister Barsett," from *A Native of Winby, and Other Tales* (1893), Jewett suggests that the affluent Mrs. Mercy Crane is insufficiently attentive to the situation of the impoverished Sarah Ellen Dow, who is obliged to circulate among the families in her village doing nursing work because she has no home. They commiserate on the putative death of Sarah Ellen's latest charge, Sister Barsett, over tea:

The two women sat down to deep and brimming cups of tea. Sarah Ellen noticed with great gratification that her hostess had put on two of the best tea-cups and some citron-melon preserves. It was not an every-day supper. She was used to hard fare, poor, hard-working Sarah Ellen, and this handsome social attention did her good.

In many of Jewett's stories, including "Miss Tempy's Watchers" (first collected in *The King of Folly Island, and Other People,* 1888), a more affluent woman is educated by an impoverished but wiser counterpart. "The Flight of Betsey Lane" (from *A Native of Winby, and Other Tales*), however, shows how one indigent woman is able to dream beyond the boundaries of the narrow experience shared by her fellow residents in the town poorhouse.

Like many of Jewett's stories, "The Town Poor" and "The Passing of Sister Barsett" contain strong elements of humor, whereas other narratives reveal that assertions of her affirmative and nostalgic view are overstatements. Perhaps her most searing vision of the hardships endured by country people, "In Dark New England Days" (collected in *Strangers and Wayfarers*) offers a grim portrayal of the grinding poverty of the Knowles sisters who, after their miserly father dies, discover a fortune in gold in his trunk, only to have it stolen the same night. The chilling curse that Betsey Knowles places on Enoch Holt, the man accused of the theft, and his descendants reverberates throughout the community and undercuts the traditional values of cooperation and trust that enable country people to survive. Even *The Country of the Pointed Firs,* with its relatively utopian vision, intimates the hardships and complexities of rural life: Captain Littlepage, a retired sea captain, offers the writer-narrator a haunting vision of an interstitial world between life and death, inspiring the protagonist, Mrs. Todd, to remark upon his "spells"; rejected by her fiancé, "Poor Joanna" exiles herself to an island; Elijah Tilley mourns the loss of his wife for years. In "A Dunnet Shepherdess," from *The Country of the Pointed Firs,* the subject is a long-delayed romance between Mrs. Todd's brother, William, and Esther Hight, who each care for an aging mother, as Jewett gently suggests the costs of duty and patience.

Many feminist accounts of Jewett's work have contended that her affiliation with regionalism, retrospectively constructed as feminine and overly nostalgic, enabled dominant male critical accounts to diminish the power and importance of her work: "suggestions that Jewett's work is fine but slight are usually linked to her regional subject matter and often (at least by implication) to her status as a woman writing mostly about women," June Howard has suggested (in her introduction to a collection of essays on *The Country of the Pointed Firs*), an assertion that finds concurrence in the work of a number of scholars, including Judith Fetterley, Marjorie Pryse, Stephanie Foote, Josephine Donovan, Donna Campbell, and Michael Bell. Fetterley and Pryse have argued that regionalism as practiced by many women writers differs from that of their male counterparts in that the former represent the perspective of a sympathetic observer who participates in the community, rather than the view of a critical outsider. Marcia McClintock Folsom has explored the way Jewett models this perspective in many of her characters, including Mrs. Blackett of *The Country of the Pointed Firs.* A more suspicious view of the writer, and of regionalism more generally, has been put forth by Richard Brodhead, suggesting that Jewett, like many authors, sought to provide affluent readers with the equivalent of literary tourism—a visit to a remote or vanishing community from a secure and unchallenging distance. These conflicting critical perspectives explicitly indicate that one subtext of this disagreement is the question of Jewett's status as a "major" or "minor" writer, a judgment frequently based on a small sample of her elite work in such venues as *The Atlantic,* rather than on a comprehensive overview that includes her newspaper or children's writing.

In the search to understand Jewett's aesthetic, feminist critics have also proposed that she creates a different model for fiction, emphasizing her reinvention of the "sketch," which indicates a narrative focused on character and place rather than plot. Elizabeth Ammons has argued that for some of Jewett's longer work, a model of writing structured as circular or as a web, versus a conventional linear, developmental narrative with a definitive climax and conclusion, seems to be more appropriate. In *The Country of the Pointed Firs* the narrative consists of a series of linked episodes with one of the most "important," the narrator's visit to Green Island with Mrs. Todd, occurring relatively early, in chapter 8. Another effort at recuperating Jewett's complexity positions her within the genre characterized by Sandra A. Zagarell as "narrative of community." Much of this aesthetic criticism, however, has centered upon Jewett's masterpiece, *Country,* although her other work is receiving increased attention for its skill with structure. For example, as Betty Powell has shown, there is a developmental narrative—a "narrative unity"—tying together the individual sketches of *Old Friends and New:* "Jewett's circuitous narrative strategy connects the various chapters of the text into a unified whole by allowing the disparate female voices throughout the work to 'speak to one another.'" Similar arguments could probably be constructed for some of her other collections.

As gay and lesbian critics have sought to recover a homoerotic literary tradition in the United States, another strand emerging from the feminist interpretation of Jewett has been her recuperation as a lesbian writer—that is, as a writer with significant lesbian themes in her work. This component is perhaps most apparent in *Deephaven,* which serves as a precursor text to *The Country of the Pointed Firs.* Protagonists Kate and Helen spend the summer in an idyllic female-centered world in which their relationship is central. This relationship represents a prelapsarian connection prior to the social expectation for them of "adult" marriage and its concomitant heterosexuality; as Kate notes, urging Helen to accompany her,

> It might be dull in Deephaven for two young ladies who were fond of gay society and dependent upon excitement, I suppose; but for two little girls who were fond of each other and could play in the boats, and dig and build houses in the sea-sand, and gather shells, and carry their dolls wherever they went, what could be pleasanter?

Although *Country* has moments of intense intimacy between women, including Mrs. Todd's sharing of her favorite pennyroyal plot with the narrator, the lesbian theme is much less overt.

It reemerges, however, in the 1897 story first collected in *The Queen's Twin, and Other Stories* (1899), "Martha's Lady." Young Helena Vernon, the cousin of Miss Harriet Pyne, comes from Boston to visit her older relative in Ashford, who employs the unpromising Martha as her new maid. Of a "tall, ungainly shape," Martha is "dull and indifferent to everyone else" but "showed a surprising willingness and allegiance to the young guest." As Helena helps Martha to overcome her shyness and inexperience, the latter falls in love with her affluent counterpart, who eventually leaves, marries, and returns to the village after many years. Her return culminates in her recognition of Martha's love and devotion even in her absence: "'Oh, my dear Martha!' she cried, 'won't you kiss me goodnight? Oh, Martha, have you remembered like this, all these long years!'" Jewett's crossing of boundaries (including those of class and sexuality) in this story suggests not only the complexity of her themes, but also of her aesthetic more generally. As with many of her stories, "Martha's Lady" also recapitulates the relationship between "foreigner" and "native." Other stories, such as "An Autumn Holiday" (collected in *Country By-Ways,* 1881), in which the elderly Captain Dan'el Gunn unwittingly crossdresses as a woman; "Tom's Husband" (collected in *The Mate of the Daylight, and Friends Ashore,* 1884), in which the hero takes on a domestic role and his wife Polly assumes the lead in business matters; and *A Country Doctor,* in which the solitary Nan Prince affirms that she is made for something different than marriage and motherhood, suggest Jewett's investment in both negotiating and deconstructing boundaries of gender and sexuality.

RACE, ETHNICITY, AND CLASS

Given the radical changes occurring in United States culture at the end of the nineteenth century—including the arrival of a substantial number of immigrants, the culmination of the western Indian wars in the Wounded Knee Massacre, the emergence of the robber barons and unrest by labor unions, and the instability of the economy—it is not surprising that Jewett's work both encompasses and seeks respite from these cultural stresses. In partial reaction to what they regarded as the idealization of Jewett's work during the early 1980s, many later critics have interrogated her vision of community more carefully, focusing most particularly on her views of race, ethnicity, region, and class. These reappraisals tended to critique what they assert is the writer's relatively narrow vision of community. In *Deephaven,* for example, readers encounter Mrs. Bonny, an older woman who lives alone in the woods and of whom the narrator observes, "There was something so wild and unconventional about Mrs. Bonny that it was like taking an afternoon walk with a good-natured Indian." This depiction has negative resonances; it echoes the dominant culture's fear of the masculinization of women in the ostensibly savage wilderness: "she wore a man's coat, cut off so that it made an odd short jacket, and a pair of men's boots much the worse for wear." This representation of the potential transformation of woman to "savage" recurs.

Mrs. Bonny is (to Helen and Kate) an uncomfortably lax housekeeper who offers Kate a distressingly filthy drinking glass. Ambiguous, stereotypical, or negative portraits of American Indians also emerge in Jewett's children's poem "York Garrison, 1640" (published in 1886 in *Wide Awake,* a children's magazine) and in *The Country of the Pointed Firs.* In "Tame Indians," an early children's story published in *The Independent* in 1875, the writer explores similarly stereotypical perspectives, as the narrator describes a visit to the Oneida tribe in Wisconsin (as Jewett herself had done in the 1870s, during an intense period of Indian wars in the United States) to the younger brother and sister of a Boston friend. Responding to the children's romantic conceptions of Native Americans, she advises that they read a book about the history of the Jesuits in North America as a source of information about old Indian tribes. "They were so horribly cruel," she says, adding, "Though I suppose in these days we only know the worst side of the story."

As her problematic depiction of emancipated slaves in "A War Debt" and "The Mistress of Sydenham Plantation" demonstrates, other racial or ethnic groups, including the privileged Normans, emerge in Jewett's work. During the earliest feminist reappraisal of Jewett's work in the 1970s and 1980s, scholars often portrayed the Bowden family reunion in *The Country of the Pointed Firs* in idealized terms, as a culminating moment of community for the narrator. Later critical responses emphasize the emergence of ethnic preferences, for example in the narrator's affirmation that

> I had said to myself before that Mrs. Blackett was plainly of French descent . . . but this is not surprising when one has learned how large a proportion of the early settlers on this northern coast of New England were of Huguenot blood, and that it is the Norman Englishman, not the Saxon, who goes adventuring to a new world.

On the same subject, Mrs. Todd comments "modestly," "They used to say in old times . . . that our family came of very high folks in France." From one angle, this sensibility suggests the construction of a national identity on the foundation of privileged ethnic differences. In this vein, more disturbingly to some readers, in talking to Mrs. Todd, Mrs. Caplin observes that "Somebody observed once that you could pick out the likeness of 'most every sort of a foreigner when you looked about you in our parish. . . . I always did think Mari' Harris resembled a Chinee." One could, however, read the racialized diction of this passage more affirmatively, as a celebration of difference, a reading supported by the immediate response of Mrs. Blackett, whom Jewett presents as an ideal mother-woman and who arrives "to see . . . that we were out of mischief": "Mari' Harris was pretty as a child, I remember." In this reading, Mrs. Todd's subsequent observation that "Mari' was one o' them pretty little lambs that make dreadful homely old sheep" serves more to highlight Mrs. Todd's human frailty than to undermine Mrs. Blackett's authority (and Jewett's openness to difference).

This reading may also be supported by Jewett's later Dunnet Landing story, "The Foreigner." Readers learn of how Mrs. Captain Tolland, a woman from Jamaica who has married one of the town's sea captains, is ostracized by the community. Although Mrs. Tolland is ostensibly of French descent and arrived in the Caribbean with her first husband, who died (with their child) of yellow fever, she appears to the villagers as culturally ambiguous by virtue of her residence in Jamaica; moreover, she is Catholic, another oddity in Dunnet. Mrs. Todd tells the narrator an amusing story about the villagers singing and dancing delightedly in the church vestry in response to Mrs. Tolland's enthusiasm; Mrs. Todd affirms, "There wa'n't one of 'em but enjoyed it." The following day, however, the townspeople soberly consider these events "an awful scandal." The story as a whole reflects upon the closed-mindedness of Dunnet residents and on Mrs. Todd's learning acceptance and appreciation of difference from her mother, Mrs. Blackett.

Jewett's complicated views toward race and ethnicity have also been studied in the context of her Irish stories, which, although they are often ethnographically inaccurate and sometimes sentimentalize Irish life, reveal considerable sympathy with the exploited Irish workers of nineteenth-century America. In the introduction to *The Irish Stories of Sarah Orne Jewett* (1996), the editors Jack Morgan and Louis A. Renza maintain that these pieces, written after Jewett visited Ireland with Annie Fields in 1882, "serve to undo the 'Paddy' stereotype of the Irish favored in nineteenth-century Yankee discourse"; critics have also indicated the way Jewett's views compare favorably with the much greater ethnocentrism of such writers as Nathaniel Hawthorne, Ralph Waldo Emerson, and Henry David Thoreau. In "The Luck of the Bogans," for example, she invites readers to understand the homesickness shared by many Irish immigrants, and she appreciates how they left behind "a life in the open air under falling showers and warm sunshine, a life of wit and humor, of lavishness and lack of provision for more than the passing day—of constant companionship with one's neighbors, and a cheerful serenity." Reflecting Jewett's concern throughout her work for the enduring values of community and an appreciation for the natural world, the Irish stories also reflect her interest in oral storytelling and dialect, which frequently provide a sensitive barometer of social, ethnic, and gender differences.

Although in the past, accounts of the writer's work have tended to diverge between the celebratory and the historical, current criticism seems to be reaching toward a more balanced and carefully historicized account of Jewett's attitudes toward difference, particularly ethnic and class difference. For example, although over time Jewett revised *Deephaven* to conform to her developing practice of regionalism, early versions of this first novel reveal a rehearsal of the contradictions between cosmopolitanism and regionalization, representing a form of what Zagarell identifies as "self-questioning regionalism." Jewett's storytelling, Jacqueline Shea Murphy states in "Replacing Regionalism," "not only recognizes her own historical position of relative privilege in place, but also leaves space for other continuing storytelling practices in and of that place."

In addition to discussion of race and ethnicity, critics have begun to consider in more detail the role of social class, an important theme for the writer. In contrast to critics in the early 1900s—who frequently depicted Jewett as an aristocrat engaged in the process of constructing a normalized national identity with a racist and hierarchical perspective that represents considerable anxiety about immigrants and the working class—later twentieth-century views resisted linking Jewett with some regionalist counterparts for whom this view is more accurate. Alison Easton has illuminated the way both Jewett's complicated personal history and the agrarian society of rural Maine more generally suggest the fluidity of social class boundaries in her experience. In addition, as such stories as "The Passing of Sister Barsett," "The Town Poor," and "Martha's Lady" suggest, her work regularly explores the problematics of class distinction. In "The Town Poor" not only do the Bray sisters fall from self-sufficiency and gentility and suffer pinched living circumstances, but an even more menacing and grinding form of poverty is revealed, embodied in Mrs. Trimble's and Miss Wright's cryptic references to the village of Parsley that frame the narrative.

As "Mr. Bruce," her first published story in an elite outlet, the *Atlantic Monthly*, demonstrates, the writer's interest in class differences appeared early in her career. Indicating the complexity residing underneath the surface of her work, the narrative embeds a letter within a story within a story within a story; its subjects include, in addition to love, family, and mistaken identity, class differences. When Kitty Tennant's father brings several business associates home for dinner, the maid is away on family business, and Kitty determines, for a lark, to take her place serving dinner. One of the guests is Mr. Bruce from London, who later meets Kitty at the home of a Baltimore relative. She does not recognize him, but he believes her to be the serving-girl that she earlier impersonated who has in the interim received an education. Mr. Bruce also believes her to be concealing her "true" identity which, the reader knows, is accurate, although not in the way he believes. Although the mistake is eventually cleared up and the two marry, in the intervening narrative Jewett surveys for readers the indistinct boundaries between social classes and suggests the potential role of education and cultured society to diminish or destroy these boundaries.

Conveyed indirectly, this message is made more palatable by form and tone. The frame narrator, an older woman representative of many heroines in Jewett's oeuvre, highlights the elements of tricksterism and wry humor that often appear in her work. Speaking about an older "maiden lady" friend, the narrator observes that "all the young ladies of her acquaintance . . . are her devoted friends; and she often gives them dinners and tea parties, takes them to plays and concerts, matronizes them in the summer, takes them to drive in her handsome carriages, and is the repository of all their joys and sorrows." With the sly substitution of "matronizes" for the usual "patronizes," Jewett deploys the witty voice, embedding social criticism in a covert and graceful manner, that characterizes much of her writing. In "The Dulham Ladies" (collected in *A White Heron*, 1886), although she is appreciative of the refined, elderly Dobin sisters, her sympathy for their dilemma of losing their hair erupts into high comedy at their purchase of mismatching and unfashionable wigs, suggesting her simultaneous impatience with merely superficial gentility.

Class differences emerge as a repeated concern. In *Deephaven* Helen and her friend Kate are subtly divided by class distinction, with Kate being the more affluent and educated. In one scene, where Kate substitutes for the local woman, Mrs. Kew, in showing visitors around her lighthouse, a shop girl mistakes Kate, whose "celebrated Lancaster complexion was rather darkened by the sun," for a working girl and invites her to come to Boston, live with her, and work in her shop. Kate's response transforms the meeting into a study of good manners, but the novel pursues the question of class difference more anxiously and directly in the chapters that follow, especially in "Deephaven Society," which opens with the assertion that "it was curious to notice, in this little fishing-village, how clearly the gradations of society were defined." In *Deephaven* as a whole, Jewett comes to few conclusions about class difference, although she provides her urban elite readers a series of evocative and wrenching portraits of rural poverty. Similarly, in "The Life of Nancy," the writer uses the motif of a Boston visitor to revisit social difference, this time between Nancy and her urban counterpart, Tom. In this story, however, travel is bidirectional, with Nancy visiting Boston as well as Tom visiting Maine, as class proves once again to be more fluid than might have been entirely comfortable for Jewett's city readers.

One of the most radical handlings of the subjects of social class surfaces in the 1898 story "The Gray Mills of Farley." As Alison Easton observes, "The tale's message is clearly that workers have the right to share the profits of their own labor." In this lengthy narrative, readers learn of the clash between the Corporation and its "operatives," who "were at first eager young men and women from the farms near by, these being joined quickly by pale

English weavers and spinners . . . then came the flock of Irish families, poorer and simpler than the others but learning the work sooner, and gayer-hearted; now the Canadian-French contingent furnished all the new help." Not only are the latter described as "quicker-fingered," but, more tellingly, they "were willing to work cheaper than any other workpeople yet." An important strand of Jewett's narrative is the antagonism between and among the remnants of these various groups; the Irish workers, for example, see their French Canadian counterparts in much the same way that their more affluent employers might have done, as "thrash [trash]" who "ain't folks at all, 'tis but a pack of images they do be, with all their chatter like birds in a hedge." Another concern for Jewett is the convergence of ethnicity and class with gender, for women constituted the bulk of American millworkers in the nineteenth century. Finally, in this story, the writer represents social class as fluid: orphaned at the age of three, the mills' agent comes from a working-class family and serves not merely as the intermediary between owners and workers but also as the latter's advocate. Although she avoids a direct call for labor intervention when the mills start to lose money, Jewett offers a scathing portrait of corporate greed and blindness to working conditions.

Easton suggests that Jewett's last novel, *The Tory Lover* (1901), "makes best sense if placed in the context of Jewett's earlier explorations of class. Here current issues of class are displaced sideways onto Loyalist/Patriot tensions." Class and race intersect at the opening of the novel with the representation of Maine's black servants. In contrast to "The Gray Mills of Farley" and her other stories concerned with divisions between capital and labor, *The Tory Lover* displays the more complicated—and again, fluid and interactive—class relations that emerge, for example, in *Deephaven,* as well as in some of the short fiction. Unlike some of the earlier texts, however, the last novel negotiates between classes and between and among individuals of different classes, in an ambiguous (and perhaps ambivalent) manner. As she does in *The Country of the Pointed Firs* and elsewhere, Jewett writes approvingly of elites, yet Easton notes "a rhetoric of republican equality confusingly cuts across this" approval. But, even in *Country,* Jewett embeds the tension (or at least the difference, in this relatively egalitarian narrative) between classes: the narrator is an urbanite, a paying summer guest who can afford to rent the empty schoolhouse for a writing studio when she finds herself distracted by Mrs. Todd's business.

Class emerges as well, and more problematically, in some of Jewett's children's stories. *Betty Leicester's Christmas* (1899) shows the young Betty demonstrating to Warford, the heir to a great English estate, how to be appreciative of his inheritance (in all senses). Nevertheless, as was true for Jewett's earlier counterparts such as Lucy Larcom and Alice Cary, the genre of children's writing seems sometimes to enable a more candid assessment of the problems of relationships between people of different classes than in "adult" fiction. "The Best China Saucer" (in *Play Days*) is probably the finest (and most shocking) example of how the working classes possess the potential to disturb middle-class comforts and pretensions. At the beginning of the narrative, Mrs. Willis warns her daughter Nelly not to play with their neighbor, Jane Simmons, whom she observes is "a very naughty girl, and always teaches you bad words and bad manners, and tries to make you disobey me." Nevertheless, when Jane appears, looking "unusually dirty that morning and very naughty," Nelly is faced with a middle-class dilemma, put to her by Jane herself: "You're p'lite, ain't you. . . . See me coming and made believe you didn't see." Although her mother has instructed her to avoid Jane, she has also taught Nelly that politeness is a virtue, especially politeness toward Jane ("Mamma said I must always be kind to her"), and at this juncture it is an alluring virtue, for it enables her disobedience.

At the center of the story is the girls' engagement in a pretend tea party, to which Jane also brings her little brother, known only as "The Baby." (Because Jane's mother has to work and has no household help, The Baby is left to the care of Jane.) Clearly an object of neglect (Jane claims that before he could tell on her, she often tied her brother to a lilac bush and abandoned him for the day), The Baby is disgusting to Nelly: "He had the dirtiest face you ever saw, and it always seemed to be the same dirt."

But dirt is not the only problem with Jane and her brother: they have not had enough to eat, and Jane frightens Nelly into looking for food in the house. In the process of the tea party, Jane robs one of Nelly's dolls of her undergarments and, because of her neglect, The Baby breaks one of Nelly's mother's best china saucers and the cream pitcher to her own doll's tea set. Jane's true barbarism, however, is revealed by her "jewelry": "a necklace of flies, on a long piece of white thread, to which the needle was still hanging. . . . Some were dead, but others faintly buzzed." In her essay on the story, Sarah Way Sherman points out that whereas Nelly has only to deal with "the boredom of leisured gentility" and is responsible only for her expensive doll, Jane has to care for a real baby, whom the narrator describes as wearing his mother's old shawl trailing on the ground, with "some little sticks and several burdock burrs tangled into the fringe." Jane and her brother's necessary investment in bodily functions cannot be ignored—indeed, as Jewett presents these characters, they are refreshing and humorous antidotes to the overrefined sensibilities of Nelly and her mother. Jewett underscores this perspective with the explicit "moral" that begins the story: "Mind your mother,—unless, of course, you are perfectly sure she is a foolish and unwise woman, and that you are always the more sensible of the two." In addition to "The Best China Saucer," Jewett wrote numerous children's stories for publications ranging from *Our Young Folks* to *St. Nicholas* and *The Independent.*

Coupled with concern about gender identity, social class emerges indirectly but significantly in Jewett's second novel, *A Country Doctor.* Although her dying mother's spirit energizes her determination to become a physician, Nan Prince is an orphan, able to rely only briefly on her grandmother before she becomes the ward of the paternal Dr. Leslie, who provides her medical training. In moving from the rural agrarian class to the professional class of doctors, Nan forms part of an emerging group of women in medicine; Judith Bryant Wittenberg discusses the novel in light of the statistic that "by the late nineteenth century, seventeen medical colleges for women had been established in the United States, and the number of women physicians increased to a total of nearly 2,500 by 1880." By this time, three women doctors had acquired national fame: Harriot K. Hunt, Elizabeth Blackwell, and Marie Zakrzewska; of the three, Hunt and Blackwell both published autobiographies before the appearance of Jewett's novel, notes Wittenberg. Jewett's contemporary, Elizabeth Stuart Phelps, had published a novel about a woman doctor, *Dr. Zay,* in 1882. Although relations between Mrs. Todd and the Dunnet Landing doctor in *The Country of the Pointed Firs* are cordial, in "The Courting of Sister Wisby" Jewett registers the tension between traditional herbalists, often female, with their male medical counterparts, in the disgust of the herbalist Mrs. Goodsoe about "young doctors, bilin' over with book-larnin', that is truly ignorant of what to do for the sick."

Nan crosses both class and gender boundaries in her development as a doctor. A tomboy as a young girl, she feels frustrated by household duties; nor, later on, is she interested in romance and marriage. Married to her profession, she rejects the advances of the alluring George Gerry—despite the encouragement of her affluent aunt for her connection with Gerry—creating her own category of independent and self-actuated female life. At the same time, like Jewett's real-life contemporaries, the character Nan presents herself not as a social reformer but as an individual with extraordinary gifts, asserting that she is "very far from believing that every girl ought to be a surgeon." Similarly, Nan conforms to some of the expectations for women (such as piety) that help to mute the novel's social criticism and make it more palatable for the readers of Jewett's era.

BEYOND BORDERS

Anticipating Robert Frost's affirmation that "good fences make good neighbors," Jewett observes in "From a Mournful Village" (collected in *Country By-Ways*) that "people do not know what they lose when they make away with reserve, the separateness, the sanctity of the front yard of their grandmothers. It is like writing down the family secrets for anyone to read." In spite of this affirmation, as the preceding accounts of Jewett's representations of gender, race, ethnicity, nation, sexuality, and class suggest, the writer's work regarded as a whole avoids simplistic, either-or perspectives. Although individual stories seem to present a single-minded attitude, other stories counter that attitude. As Marjorie Pryse has observed, "Her work seems to resist the very concept of category. . . . her fiction . . . does shift the reader's focus away from social and cultural categories to the fluid, permeable movement *across* and *between* borders."

This movement is represented literally in the humorous narrative "The Confession of a House-Breaker," from *The Mate of the Daylight, and Friends Ashore,* which opens, "This confession differs from that of most criminals who are classed under the same head; for whereas house-breakers usually break into houses, I broke out." Departing from her house just at daybreak, the narrator is enabled to suggest to readers a new and different perspective: "One never knows the grace and beauty of white petunias until they have been seen at night, or, like this, early in the morning." More menacingly, she reports,

A bat went by me suddenly, and at that I stood still. I had not thought of bats, and of all creatures they seem most frightful and unearthly,—like the flutter of a ghost's mantle, or even the wave and touch of its hand. A bat by daylight is a harmless, crumpled bit of stupidity, but by night it becomes a creature of mystery and horror, an attendant of the powers of darkness.

As it progresses, the narrative offers a spiritual meditation on the transformations attendant upon death, as well as upon the ways in which "we [are] bound to the conventionalities of existence."

The natural images of these passages suggest the affiliation between Jewett's work and the emergent traditions of women's nature writing and ecofeminism. One of her most famous works, "A White Heron," juxtaposes the perspective of a young girl, Sylvia (a refugee from "a crowded manufacturing town," whose name suggests the woods), living in rural Maine with her grandmother, to that of a young male hunter-ornithologist, who seeks a rare white heron to add to his collection, which contains "stuffed and preserved [birds], dozens and dozens of them." Jewett concludes the story with the image of Sylvia climbing a huge pine tree to find the bird's home; the vision the girl acquires provokes her resistant silence in the face of the hunter's desire for knowledge. Jewett published this story when the craze for bird plumage on women's hats was at a peak; like her friend Thaxter, who protested against such despoiling in an important essay, "Woman's Heartlessness," for the premier issue of *Audubon* magazine, Jewett proposes that the value of the heron (and

nature) lies elsewhere than in commerce. As Josephine Donovan has observed in her book, in Jewett's work, "The world of rural Maine, the land of the pointed firs . . . emerges as a place on the edge of historical time; it is an almost timeless female realm that stands as a counter-reality to the encroaching male world of modern technology."

The theme of nature's value and presence saturates Jewett's writing. In *The Country of the Pointed Firs* Mrs. Todd stops on the way to the Bowden family reunion to talk of a tree as if it were a person, whereas "A Winter Drive" expresses the writer's own similar feelings of affinity with trees. In "River Driftwood" Jewett makes explicit her perspective on the relationship between humans and the natural world:

it is but seldom, as yet, that people really care much for anything for its own sake, until it is proved to have some connection with human-kind. We are slow to take an interest in the personality of our neighbors who are not men, or dogs, or horses, or at least some creature who can be made to understand a little of our own spoken language. Who is going to be the linguist who learns the first word of an old crow's warning to his mate, or how a little dog expresses himself when he asks a big one to come and rout his troublesome enemy?

Affirming that "it is easy to say that other orders of living creatures exist on a much lower plane than ourselves; we know very little about it, after all. They are often gifted in some way that we are not; they may even carry some virtue of ours to a greater height than we do," Jewett anticipates that "the day will come for a more truly universal suffrage than we dream of now, when the meaning of every living thing is understood, and it is given its rights and accorded its true value." Having emerged in more balanced critical perspectives as a writer whose work is postmodern in its ability to cross borders and invested in a holistic vision of the world and its citizens, Jewett speaks as resonantly to many readers in the early twenty-first century as she did to those in her own era.

Selected Bibliography

WORKS OF SARAH ORNE JEWETT

NOVELS AND UNCOLLECTED STORIES
Deephaven. Boston: J. R. Osgood, 1877.

A Country Doctor. Boston: Houghton, Mifflin and Co., 1884; New York: Bantam Books, 1999. (The modern edition includes an introduction by Paula Blanchard.)

A Marsh Island. Boston: Houghton, Mifflin and Co., 1885.

"About Hospitality." *St. Louis Republic,* February 14, 1892, p. 25.

The Country of the Pointed Firs. Boston: Houghton, Mifflin and Co., 1896. (Modern editions have been published by Norton, 1968; Penguin, 1995; Oxford University Press, 1996; and the University Press of New England, 1997.)

The Tory Lover. Boston: Houghton, Mifflin and Co., 1901.

An Empty Purse: A Christmas Story. Boston: privately printed, 1905.

COLLECTIONS (FICTION AND NONFICTION)
Old Friends and New. Boston: Houghton, Osgood, 1879.

Country By-Ways. Boston: Houghton, Mifflin and Co., 1881.

The Mate of the Daylight, and Friends Ashore. Boston: Houghton, Mifflin and Co., 1884.

A White Heron, and Other Stories. Boston: Houghton, Mifflin and Co., 1886.

The King of Folly Island, and Other People. Boston: Houghton, Mifflin and Co., 1888.

Tales of New England. Boston: Houghton, Mifflin and Co., 1888.

Strangers and Wayfarers. Boston: Houghton, Mifflin and Co., 1890.

A Native of Winby, and Other Tales. Boston: Houghton, Mifflin and Co., 1893.

The Life of Nancy. Boston: Houghton, Mifflin and Co., 1895.

The Queen's Twin, and Other Stories. Boston: Houghton, Mifflin and Co., 1899.

The Uncollected Short Stories of Sarah Orne Jewett. Edited and with an introduction by Richard Cary. Waterville, Maine: Colby College Press, 1971.

Novels and Stories. Edited by Michael Bell. New York: Library of America, 1994.

The Irish Stories of Sarah Orne Jewett. Edited by Jack Morgan and Louis A. Renza. Carbondale: Southern Illinois University Press, 1996.

The Sarah Orne Jewett Text Project. Edited by Terry Heller, Coe College (http://www.public.coe.edu/~theller/soj/sj-index.htm). (This relatively comprehensive on-line collection of Jewett's work includes much uncollected and difficult-to-obtain writing.)

POETRY
Verses: Printed for Her Friends. Boston: Merrymount Press, 1916; Cleveland: American Weave Press, 1949.

The Complete Poems of Sarah Orne Jewett. Forest Hills, N.Y.: Ironweed Press, 1999.

CHILDREN'S WRITING
Play Days: A Book of Stories for Children. Boston: Houghton, Osgood, 1878.

The Story of the Normans, Told Chiefly in Relation to Their Conquest of England. New York: G. P. Putnam's, 1887.

Betty Leicester: A Story for Girls. Boston: Houghton, Mifflin and Co., 1889.

Betty Leicester's Christmas. Boston: Houghton, Mifflin and Co., 1899.

"Uncollected Pieces for Young Readers." The Sarah Orne Jewett Text Project. Edited by Terry Heller, Coe College (http://www.public.coe.edu/~theller/soj/sj-index.htm). (Includes "The Boy with One Shoe.")

LETTERS
The Letters of Sarah Orne Jewett. Edited by Annie Fields. Boston: Houghton Mifflin, 1911.

Letters. Edited by Richard Cary. Waterville, Maine: Colby College Press, 1956; enl. and rev. ed., 1967.

MANUSCRIPT COLLECTIONS

Maine Women Writers Collection, Westbrook College of the University of New England, Portland, Maine.

Manuscripts and Special Collections Library, Maine Historical Society, Portland, Maine.

Sarah Orne Jewett Collection, Dimond Library, Special Collections, University of New Hampshire, Durham, New Hampshire.

Sarah Orne Jewett Collection, Miller Library, Special Collections, Colby College, Waterville, Maine.

Sarah Orne Jewett Papers, 1877–1903. Hawthorne-Longfellow Library, Special Collections, Bowdoin College, Brunswick, Maine.

Sarah Orne Jewett Papers, the Houghton Library, Harvard University, Cambridge, Massachusetts.

Society for the Preservation of New England Antiquities Library and Archives, Boston, Massachusetts.

CRITICAL AND BIOGRAPHICAL STUDIES

Alaimo, Stacy. *Undomesticated Ground: Recasting Nature as Feminist Space.* Ithaca, N.Y.: Cornell University Press, 2000.

Ammons, Elizabeth. "Going in Circles: The Female Geography of Jewett's *Country of the Pointed Firs.*" *Studies in the Literary Imagination* 16, no. 2:83–92 (fall 1983).

Blanchard, Paula. *Sarah Orne Jewett: Her World and Her Work.* Reading, Mass.: Addison-Wesley, 1994.

Brodhead, Richard. *Cultures of Letters: Scenes of Reading and Writing in Nineteenth-Century America.* Chicago: University of Chicago Press, 1993.

Brooks, Van Wyck. *New England: Indian Summer, 1865–1915.* New York: Dutton, 1940.

Brown, Alice. Review of *The Country of the Pointed Firs* (1897). In *Critical Essays on Sarah Orne Jewett.* Edited by Gwen L. Nagel. Boston: G. K. Hall, 1984. P. 39.

Campbell, Jennifer. "'The Great Something Else': Women's Search for Meaningful Work in Sarah Orne Jewett's *A Country Doctor* and Frances

E. W. Harper's *Trial and Triumph.*" *Colby Library Quarterly* 34, no. 2:83–98 (June 1998).

Cary, Richard, ed. *Appreciation of Sarah Orne Jewett: Twenty-nine Interpretive Essays.* Waterville, Maine: Colby College Press, 1973. (Includes essays by Thérèse Bentzon [Marie Thérèse Blanc], Edward M. Chapman, Edward Garnett, Horace Scudder, Charles Miner Thompson, and Susan Allen Toth.)

Cather, Willa. Preface to *The Country of the Pointed Firs, and Other Stories.* New York: Anchor Books, 1956.

Church, Joseph. "The Healing Arts of Jewett's Country Doctor." *Colby Library Quarterly* 34, no. 2:99–122 (June 1988).

Davis, Cynthia J. "Making the Strange(r) Familiar: Sarah Orne Jewett's 'The Foreigner.'" In *Breaking Boundaries: New Perspectives on Women's Regional Writing.* Edited by Sherrie A. Inness and Diana Royer. Iowa City: University of Iowa Press, 1997. Pp. 88–108.

Donovan, Josephine. *New England Local Color Literature: A Women's Tradition.* New York: F. Ungar, 1983.

———. "Women's Masterpieces." In *Challenging Boundaries: Gender and Periodization.* Edited by Joyce W. Warren and Margaret Dickie. Athens: University of Georgia Press, 2000. Pp. 26–38.

Easton, Alison. "'How Clearly the Gradations of Society Were Defined': Negotiating Class in Sarah Orne Jewett." In *Jewett and Her Contemporaries: Reshaping the Canon.* Edited by Karen L. Kilcup and Thomas S. Edwards. Gainesville: University Press of Florida, 1999. Pp. 207–222.

Faderman, Lillian. *Surpassing the Love of Men: Romantic Friendship and Love between Women from the Renaissance to the Present.* New York: Morrow, 1981.

Fetterley, Judith. "Reading *Deephaven* as a Lesbian Text." In *Sexual Practice/Textual Theory: Lesbian Cultural Criticism.* Edited by Susan J. Wolfe and Julia Penelope. Cambridge, Mass.: Blackwell, 1993. Pp. 164–183.

———. "'Not in the Least American': Nineteenth-Century Literary Regionalism as Un-American Literature." In *Nineteenth-Century American Women Writers: A Critical Reader.* Edited by Karen L. Kilcup. Malden, Mass.: Blackwell, 1998. Pp. 15–32.

Fetterley, Judith, and Marjorie Pryse. Introduction to *American Women Regionalists, 1850–1910.* New York: Norton, 1992. Pp. xi–xx.

Folsom, Marcia McClintock. "'Tact Is a Kind of Mind-Reading': Empathic Style in Sarah Orne Jewett's *The Country of the Pointed Firs.*" *Colby Library Quarterly* 18, no. 1:66–78 (1982).

Foote, Stephanie. "'I Feared to Find Myself a Foreigner': Revisiting Regionalism in Sarah Orne Jewett's *The Country of the Pointed Firs.*" *Arizona Quarterly* 52, no. 2:37–61 (1996).

Goheen, Cynthia J. "Editorial Misinterpretation and the Unmaking of a Perfectly Good Story: The Publication History of *The Country of the Pointed Firs.*" *American Literary Realism* 30, no. 2:28–42 (1998).

Heller, Terry. "Speaking Softly to Be Heard: Jewett's Feminist Reform Contributions to *The Congregationalist,* 1882–1884." *Colby Quarterly* 36, no. 3:209–225 (2000).

Howard, June, ed. *New Essays on* The Country of the Pointed Firs. Cambridge: Cambridge University Press, 1994. (Includes an introduction by Howard. See also the essays by Michael Bell, Susan Gillman, and Sandra A. Zagarell.)

———. "Unraveling Regions, Unsettling Periods: Sarah Orne Jewett and American Literary History." *American Literature* 68, no. 2:365–384 (1996).

James, Henry. "Mr. and Mrs. James T. Fields." *Atlantic Monthly* 116:30 (July 1915).

Johanningsmeier, Charles. "Sarah Orne Jewett and Mary E. Wilkins (Freeman): Two Shrewd Businesswomen in Search of New Markets." *New England Quarterly* 70, no. 1:57–82 (1997).

Kaplan, Amy. "Nation, Region, and Empire." In *Columbia Literary History of the United States.* Edited by Emory Elliott. New York: Columbia University Press, 1988. Pp. 240–266.

Kilcup, Karen L., and Thomas S. Edwards, eds. *Jewett and Her Contemporaries: Reshaping the Canon.* Gainesville: University Press of Florida, 1999. (Includes essays by Donna M. Campbell, Alison Easton, Melissa Homestead, Priscilla Leder, Marcia B. Littenberg, Paul Petrie, Marjorie Pryse, Ann Romines, Carol Schachinger, Mitzi Schrag, Sarah Way Sherman, and Patti Capel Swartz.)

McMurry, Andrew. "'In Their Own Language': Sarah Orne Jewett and the Question of Non-Human Speaking Subjects." *Isle: Interdisciplinary Studies in Literature and Environment* 6, no. 1:51–63 (1999).

Matthiessen, Francis Otto. *Sarah Orne Jewett.* Boston: Houghton Mifflin, 1929.

Murphy, Jacqueline Shea. "Getting Jewett: A Response to Sandra A. Zagarell, 'Troubling Regionalism.'" *American Literary History* 10, no. 4:698–701 (1998).

———. "Replacing Regionalism: Abenaki Tales and 'Jewett's' Coastal Maine." *American Literary History* 10, no. 4:664–690 (1998).

Oakes, Karen. "'All That Lay Deepest in Her Heart': Reflections on Jewett, Gender, and Genre." *Colby Library Quarterly* 26, no. 3:152–160 (1990).

———. "'Colossal in Sheet-Lead': The Native American and Piscataqua-Region Writers." In *A Noble and Dignified Stream: The Piscataqua Region in the Colonial Revival, 1860–1930.* Edited by Sarah L. Giffen and Kevin D. Murphy. York, Maine: Old York Historical Society, 1992. Pp. 165–176.

Powell, Betty J. "Speaking to One Another: Narrative Unity in Sarah Orne Jewett's *Old Friends and New.*" *Colby Library Quarterly* 34, no. 2:150–171 (June 1998).

Pryse, Marjorie. "Sex, Class, and 'Category Crisis': Reading Jewett's Transitivity." In *Jewett and Her Contemporaries: Reshaping the Canon.* Edited by Karen L. Kilcup and Thomas S. Edwards. Gainesville: University Press of Florida, 1999. Pp. 31–62.

Renza, Louis A. *"A White Heron" and the Question of Minor Literature.* Madison: University of Wisconsin Press, 1984.

Sherman, Sarah Way. *Sarah Orne Jewett: An American Persephone.* Hanover, N.H.: University Press of New England, 1989.

———. "Introduction." *The Country of the Pointed Firs and Other Stories.* By Sarah Orne Jewett. Hanover: University Press of New England, 1997.

———. "Party out of Bounds: Gender and Class in Jewett's 'The Best China Saucer.'" In *Jewett and Her Contemporaries: Reshaping the Canon.* Edited by Karen L. Kilcup and Thomas S. Edwards. Gainesville: University Press of Florida, 1999. Pp. 223–248.

Silverthorne, Elizabeth. *Sarah Orne Jewett: A Writer's Life*. Woodstock, N.Y.: Overlook Press, 1993.

Toth, Susan Allen. "The Value of Age in the Fiction of Sarah Orne Jewett." In *Appreciation of Sarah Orne Jewett: Twenty-nine Interpretive Essays.* Edited by Richard Cary. Pp. 255–263.

Thorp, Margaret Farrand. "Sarah Orne Jewett." In *American Writers,* vol. 2. Edited by Leonard Unger. New York: Scribners, 1974. Pp. 391–414.

Wider, Sarah Ann. "Books and Their Covers: Sarah Orne Jewett and Sarah Wyman Whitman through *My Daughter's Eyes.*" *Colby Library Quarterly* 34, no. 2:172–194 (June 1998).

Wittenberg, Judith Bryant. "Challenge and Compliance: Textual Strategies in *A Country Doctor* and Nineteenth-Century American Women's Medical Autobiographies." In *Jewett and Her Contemporaries: Reshaping the Canon.* Edited by Karen L. Kilcup and Thomas S. Edwards. Gainesville: University Press of Florida, 1999. Pp. 123–136.

Zagarell, Sandra A. "Narrative of Community: The Identification of a Genre." *Signs: Journal of Women in Culture and Society* 13:498–527 (1988).

———. "*Country's* Portrayal of Community and the Exclusion of Difference." In *New Essays on* The Country of the Pointed Firs. Edited by June Howard. Cambridge: Cambridge University Press, 1994. Pp. 39–60.

———. "Crosscurrents: Registers of Nordicism, Community, and Culture in Jewett's *Country of the Pointed Firs.*" *Yale Journal of Criticism* 10, no. 2:355–377 (1997).

———. "Response to Jacqueline Shea Murphy's 'Replacing Regionalism.'" *American Literary History* 10, no. 4:691–697 (1998).

———. "Troubling Regionalism: Rural Life and the Cosmopolitan Eye in Jewett's *Deephaven.*" *American Literary History* 10, no. 4:639–663 (1998).

—KAREN L. KILCUP

Henry Wadsworth Longfellow

1807–1882

O<small>N</small> D<small>ECEMBER</small> 5, 1824, at the age of seventeen, Henry Wadsworth Longfellow, already a senior at Bowdoin College, wrote to his father to express his hopes for his future. "The fact is," he wrote, working up his courage, "I most eagerly aspire after future eminence in literature; my whole soul burns most ardently for it, and every earthly thought centers on it." Following his death nearly sixty years later, at the age of seventy-seven, his bust was placed in Westminster Abbey in London, in the Poet's Corner, joining the company of Geoffrey Chaucer, Edmund Spenser, William Shakespeare, and John Dryden, the first American poet so honored. Yet within two generations his reputation among literary critics had fallen considerably, and his readership, now largely dependent on his inclusion in school curricula, has since steadily withered. What literary eminence remains attached to his name is difficult to say: he was enormously popular, he has since become neglected, yet his name and certain fragments of his poetry—the village smithy under the spreading chestnut tree, the forest primeval, the wigwam of Nokomis by the shores of Gitche Gumee and her grandchild Hiawatha, the bold yet gentle demand of Priscilla that her proxy lover speak for himself, the midnight ride of Paul Revere, the poet in his study surprised by his loving daughters—persist in American consciousness.

Henry Wadsworth was born the second of eight children of Stephen Longfellow and Zilpah Wadsworth Longfellow on February 27, 1807, in Portland, Maine. His father, a graduate of Harvard, was a well-respected lawyer in the seaport town, then still a colony of Massachusetts. His mother too was well educated, a descendent of the *Mayflower* settlers at Plymouth. Henry's early reading included all the important English poets, and his first published poem appeared in the *Portland Gazette* when he was thirteen. He enrolled at Bowdoin College in Brunswick, Maine, where his father was a trustee, the following year. Among his classmates was Nathaniel Hawthorne. He graduated fourth in his class of thirty-eight. He was among the small group of graduates chosen to speak at his commencement in September 1825, and he delivered a seven-minute oration on "Our Native Writers," having been advised by his father that his original choice of subject, the English poet Thomas Chatterton, was too specialized for the occasion. In his commencement oration, Longfellow declared that the aspiring American poet must be willing to undergo "an utter abandonment of everything else" if he is to succeed in a young nation primarily dedicated to the practical. But practical concerns nevertheless remained for a young man without wealth or patronage, and his father continued to encourage him toward the study of law. Following his graduation, however, his father presented him with another possibility, one that determined the course of his future life. A new chair of modern languages was to be established at Bowdoin, and the trustees wanted their own new graduate to fill it, with the stipulation that he first spend time in Europe acquainting himself with the languages and literatures it would be his responsibility to teach. Longfellow eagerly accepted and in April 1826 he set sail for Europe, where he would spend the next three years traveling, studying, and living in France, Spain, Italy, Austria, and Germany. It was a transforming experience for the provincial young man who in his first nineteen years had ranged little beyond the small towns and seacoast of Maine. Though he would always remain a proponent of a new American literature, he would do so with a cosmopolitan European sensibility foreign to—or rejected by—many of his mid-nineteenth-century American contemporaries.

PROFESSOR AND MAN OF LETTERS

Following the death of his sister Elizabeth in May 1829, Longfellow returned to America and began teaching at Bowdoin in September. The life of a professor promised a more suitable life for one with literary ambitions than did the life of a lawyer. Yet despite having published some forty poems by the time he had graduated from Bowdoin, he would not publish his first book of poems, *Voices of the Night* (1839), for another ten years. His duties as the first professor of foreign languages at Bowdoin, and among the first anywhere in America, required much of his time in preparing not only lectures but also textbooks for his students. He continued to read widely in French, Spanish, and Italian literature, extending his studies to the literature of the Middle Ages. Following appointment in 1834 to a comparable position as professor of modern languages at Harvard, Longfellow returned to Europe, focusing his studies and travels in this second visit on northern and central Europe—Germany, Denmark, Sweden, Finland, Holland, Switzerland, Austria. While in Rotterdam, his wife Mary, traveling with him, succumbed to an infection that had resulted from a miscarriage earlier in the trip. Longfellow did not return to America immediately but continued on in

Europe for another year, during which time he met the young woman, Frances (Fanny) Appleton, who would become his second wife seven years later. Upon his return to America in 1836, Longfellow took up residence in Cambridge, Massachusetts, first in a house near the Harvard campus and then in the historic Craigie House, which had served as the headquarters of George Washington during one stage of the Revolutionary War.

As part of his teaching Longfellow often had need of translations of European poetry, which he sometimes undertook himself. In 1833 he published a translation of the fifteenth-century Spanish poet Jorge Manrique's *Coplas por la muerte de su padre* ("Stanzas for the death of his father"), together with translations of a handful of Spanish sonnets, his first published book of verse. Longfellow continued to translate poetry throughout his career; he included sections of translations in many of his subsequent volumes of poetry and eventually published a translation of Dante's *Divine Comedy* (1865–1867). His translations ranged broadly: his *Complete Poetical Works* (1886) includes nearly a hundred translations of poems originally written in Spanish, Swedish, Danish, German, French, Italian, and Portuguese, as well as in Latin and Anglo-Saxon; a small handful are from non-European languages.

These translations display a great deal of technical skill in prosody. As he would throughout his career in his own poetry, Longfellow shows himself to be the master of a variety of verse forms, chosen in these instances not as expressions of his own poetic sensibility but in response to the verse forms of the original poems. Longfellow's original poetry too comes in a remarkable variety of verse forms—in the *Tales of a Wayside Inn* (1863), to cite but one example, not only does each tale have its own distinct verse form and diction, but the single long tale "The Saga of King Olaf" varies in form from section to section. This interest in mastering a variety of meters without developing a characteristic metrical form of his own links Longfellow with the other "Fireside Poets"—William Cullen Bryant, James Russell Lowell, Oliver Wendell Holmes, John Greenleaf Whittier—with whom he is commonly grouped. But it also separates him from those of his contemporaries—Walt Whitman, Emily Dickinson, even Ralph Waldo Emerson—whose poetic voices are more distinctively individual and whose reputations eclipsed his with the coming of modernism.

Among Longfellow's favorite poets was the Swedish poet Esaias Tegnér (1782–1846), a Lutheran priest whose poetry combines the drinking and battling of northern European medieval skaldic poetry with his own often sentimental Christian piety. The influence of Tegnér in particular and Scandinavian poetry in general on Longfellow's own poetry was considerable. In translating Tegnér's long poem "The Children of the Lord's Supper," Longfellow retained Tegnér's revival of the dactylic hexameters of Homer, a verse form he would return to with both success and controversy in *Evangeline* (1847) and *The Courtship of Miles Standish* (1858). "The Saga of King Olaf" is directly evocative of Tegnér's "Frithiof's Saga," and the meter of "The Song of Hiawatha" (1855) is borrowed from the Finnish epic *Kalevala*. Much of the best imagery of Longfellow's poetry—its northern seacoasts, hemlock forests, winter winds, and crackling firesides—is the imagery alike of northern Europe and his native Maine.

In addition to developing his own poetic powers, Longfellow's translations had the important effect of introducing much of his readership to the culture of the Europe that their ancestors had left behind in coming to America. Partly due to the influence of Puritanism, which had rejected both the folk culture and high culture of Europe, and partly due to the demands of making a commercial society where none had previously existed, Americans only a generation or two removed from Europe had little knowledge of either the poetry or the culture of Europe. Longfellow's role in restoring to American awareness its European heritage—to the extent that it was restored in the nineteenth century—cannot be overstated. In addition to his foreign language textbooks and grammars and his translations, Longfellow also edited four collections of poetry—two slender volumes, *The Waif* (1845) and *The Estray* (1846); the 770-page (later expanded to more than a thousand pages) *The Poems and Poetry of Europe* (1844), for which he also wrote extensive introductory passages; and, at the end of his career, the thirty-one volume *Poems of Places* (1876–1879).

Not just Europe's poetry, but its culture and its intellectual ideas appear in Longfellow's first two books of prose, *Outre-Mer* (1835) and *Hyperion* (1839). In the first of these, published just as he is leaving Bowdoin for Harvard, he declares that in his youthful imagination "the Old World was a kind of Holy Land, lying far off beyond the blue horizon of the ocean." In saying so, and in writing with such evident fondness of both the peasant countryside and the cities of Europe, Longfellow went very much against the American grain that Emerson was soon to articulate so forcefully in "The American Scholar," "Self-Reliance," and other lectures and essays in which the influence of Europe is rejected in favor of new thoughts and new men. Longfellow's sensibility, on the other hand, is attuned to the traditional and the timeless, found for him not among the pumpkin fields of America, though these were dear to him, but in our inheritance from Europe.

ongfellow's original plan for *Outre-Mer* included a fictional narrator, a village schoolmaster, that he eventually dropped in favor of simply an anonymous first-person narrator. *Hyperion* not only creates a fictional central character, the heartsick Paul Flemming, but creates him in the third person, thus creating something closer to a work of fiction, though

Hyperion otherwise satisfies few expectations of a novel. Published after Longfellow's second extended visit to Europe, in preparation for his professorship at Harvard, *Hyperion* shifts in scene from the southern Europe of *Outre-Mer*—France, Spain, and Italy—focusing instead on Switzerland, Austria, and, most importantly, Germany. Its slight fictional framework allows Longfellow to explore not only the places, ideas, and poetry of his second visit but also the two events of that visit that affected him deeply: the death of his first wife, which is only vaguely alluded to in the introduction of the central character as one who has suffered "the setting of a great hope," and his meeting Fanny Appleton, daughter of a wealthy Boston merchant.

In *Hyperion,* Longfellow's thinly disguised failed courtship of Fanny is developed at a length that was embarrassing to Fanny when it appeared in print. Paul Flemming's fictionalized courtship of Mary Ashburton consists largely of reciting German poetry to her and discussing with her the intellectual ideas then current in Europe, discussions that have the flavor of the lectures Longfellow gave in his classroom but that very likely also represent something of the flavor of his actual attempts at courtship, which may in part explain Fanny's long delay in saying yes. These passages, together with other slightly fictionalized discussions with other characters, also constitute an important introduction for American readers to German intellectual and literary currents, including a conflicted discussion of Goethe and even a chapter on the German ideas that would give rise to American transcendentalism, though Longfellow shows himself skeptical of the ideas that would possess his more adventuresome contemporaries, from Emerson to Herman Melville.

Longfellow returned to a fictional schoolmaster in *Kavanaugh* (1849), his third and last work of sustained prose. Much more satisfactory as a work of fiction, if more confined, *Kavanaugh* is a portrait of small-town New England in the mid–nineteenth century, an early example of the local color novel that would be more fully developed by Harriet Beecher Stowe, Sarah Orne Jewett, and others. The title character is the new pastor, with whom two girls, themselves close friends, fall in love. The schoolmaster, Mr. Churchill, is in some aspects a portrayal of the author, or at least of his temperament and perhaps frustrations; he is always hoping to write a romance, but the everyday demands of teaching and his own procrastination combine to continually frustrate his intentions. Meanwhile, the love story unfolds gently. Mild but not trivial discussions of religion and New England character are intermixed with greater ease than they are in the more heated *Hyperion;* in chapter 20, in which Mr. Churchill is invited to contribute to a new journal, Longfellow presents both sides of the argument over a national literature for the new country, though the side that would eventually become manifest in the poetry of Whitman—"We want a national drama in which scope enough shall be given to our gigantic ideas, and to the unparalleled activity and progress of our people!" the editor-to-be enthusiastically declares, "we want a literature altogether shaggy and unshorn, that shall shake the earth, like a herd of buffaloes thundering over the prairies"—comes off the worse for its provincialism and naiveté. But Longfellow cannot altogether dismiss the idea of a national epic that shall correspond to the size of the country, for in *Evangeline,* completed just before he began writing *Kavanaugh,* Longfellow had already written such an epic, though to be sure a quiet and unassuming epic, for all its scope.

EVANGELINE

Longfellow had been a classmate of Nathaniel Hawthorne at Bowdoin, and though they had not been close friends then, they became and remained friends when both had established themselves as writers living in the towns around Boston, Longfellow in Cambridge and the more itinerant Hawthorne in Concord and Salem. After Longfellow's marriage to Fanny Appleton in 1843, Fanny's father purchased for the couple the Craigie House, an easy walk from the Harvard campus, in which Longfellow had been living as a boarder. Longfellow would live there for the remainder of his life. He had published four volumes of his own poetry—*Voices of the Night, Ballads and Other Poems* (1841), *Poems on Slavery* (1842), and *The Belfry of Bruges and Other Poems* (1845)—when he set to work on the story he got from Hawthorne's friend, the Reverend Horace L. Conolly, who came to dinner with Hawthorne one evening at the Craigie House. Conolly related to Longfellow the story of an Acadian couple separated on their wedding day by the British military, who met again only when the groom-to-be lay on his deathbed many years later. Hawthorne suggested to Longfellow that he use the story for a poem, assuring him that he did not himself want it for a story. Though Longfellow had not then written a poem of any similar length, he immediately set to work, choosing for his meter the dactylic hexameter of Tegnér's "Children of the Lord's Supper," and completed the poem in February 1847.

Nova Scotia had been settled by both French and English immigrants in separate communities. Struggle for control of the region persisted throughout the seventeenth and eighteenth centuries in the series of conflicts that culminated in the French and Indian War. At the time of this final conflict, the French settlers in Nova Scotia—the Acadians of Longfellow's poem—declared themselves to be neither English nor French but neutral. The British, though, who had taken political control of the area, did not trust their neutrality and in 1755 forcibly expelled the Acadians from their homes and farms and villages, carrying them by ship to various regions of North America, from New

England to Louisiana, where a remnant of those who were expelled, referred to now as "Cajuns," a corruption of "Acadians," continue to retain their heritage.

Evangeline is divided into two parts. The first part describes the village of Grand Pré—its landscape, its culture, and its inhabitants—as it existed just prior to the expulsion. The main characters of the story are all introduced: the young Evangeline; her father Benedict Bellefontaine, a prosperous farmer; her lover Gabriel Lajeunesse and his father Basil, a blacksmith; and Father Felician, the village priest. Preparations are underway for the wedding day of Evangeline and Gabriel; at the same time British ships ride at anchor in the harbor of the village and a command has been given that all the men are to gather in the church that same day for an announcement from the British government. Thus, Gabriel and Evangeline are separated, as the men are kept sequestered under armed guard in the church while the British oversee the removal to the seaside of their belongings by the women. The first section ends with the loading of the ships, the separation of the Acadians as they are forced onto separate ships with separate destinations, the burning of the Acadian homes, and the death of Evangeline's father on the shore.

The second section tells the story of Evangeline's search for her lover, a feminine *Odyssey* following the first book's gentle *Iliad*. Longfellow first follows Evangeline to the bayous of Louisiana, where Gabriel's father has become a rancher, then to the western prairies, where Gabriel is thought to be hunting and trapping, then to the forests of Michigan, and finally to the city of Philadelphia. Together with the pathos of Evangeline's fruitless quest stand out the descriptions of the landscape and character of these different regions of what had by Longfellow's day become states and territories of the United States of America. The languid scenes of the Mississippi and the bayous and rivers of Louisiana, particularly of the Atchafalaya River, where Evangeline and Gabriel pass in the night, are particularly beautiful. Beautiful too are the native stories told to Evangeline on the prairie by a young Shawnee widow, Evangeline's native counterpart in grief, stories of Mowis, the bridegroom of snow who melts into air, and of Lilinau, the maiden who marries a phantom and disappears following him into the forest.

Longfellow did not visit either the bayous or the prairies; rather, he drew on his reading, on his imagination, and, for his descriptions of the Mississippi, on painted panoramas he saw on exhibit in Boston. Similarly, his descriptions of the landscape and culture of Grand Pré and Nova Scotia derive as much from his travels in rural France and his reading of Swedish literature as from his knowledge of maritime Canada. The famous description of "the forest primeval" with its murmuring pines and hemlocks is a more accurate description of the Maine of his childhood than of the farming communities of eighteenth-century Acadia. Yet the inaccuracies that result do not detract from Longfellow's poetic achievement. Years before Whitman was to attempt to capture the expansiveness of America with his catalogue recitations of place names and geographical names, Longfellow had already infused this same expanse with the tender feeling, quiet courage, human longing, and poignant sadness of Evangeline's story. French America, Spanish America, immigrant America, the America of its native peoples, the America of Catholics and Quakers, the America of farm and village and city, of rivers and prairies and forests, all these were rendered in language of great beauty at a time when Longfellow's New England compatriots often displayed an imagination bound by New England and even, particularly in Hawthorne and Henry David Thoreau, by the environs of Boston and Concord. Thoreau's mind may have been more adventuresome than Longfellow's,

but its field of view at times hardly takes in more than the little pond where he built a cabin, whereas Longfellow's Evangeline travels to the far-flung regions of the young nation.

At its deepest, *Evangeline* is an American poem of loss, a loss that its readers continue to respond to without being aware of what it is they have lost. The world of part 1 is nominally the world of eighteenth-century Acadia, but it is really the world of old Europe, and the removal of its inhabitants to the United States parallels the coming of Europeans to America. The world left behind is largely Catholic, a world of community and tradition, a world of vivacity and beauty and simple pleasures, a world even of gaiety, the world of thatched roofs and nut-brown ale and dancing to the tunes of Michael the fiddler. The British Protestants put an end to all of this just as the Puritan immigrants to New England sought to put an end to the folk culture, so heavily influenced by Catholicism, of their own native homeland. (Though Longfellow does not mention it in his poem, he surely was aware that the Acadians were replaced by settlers from his own Puritan New England.) The world of part 2, the new world of America, is a world of opportunity and new beginnings, but even more it is a world of displacement and rootlessness and loss. The final reunion of the lovers is felt not so much as a recovery of that which has been lost but as a recognition, in the dying Gabriel, that that which has been lost cannot be recovered.

The hexameters Longfellow chose for his meter evoked both admiration and criticism. Those who attacked Longfellow's choice objected that the metrical form of Homer, based as it is on the length of syllables, cannot be imitated in English verse that is based rather on accentuation. In this view, an English dactyl—an accented syllable followed by two unaccented syllables—is not the equivalent of a long syllable followed by two short syllables. The two accented syllables that form the final foot of the classical hexameter would have to find their equivalent in two accented final syllables, that is, in a trochee, of which English provides few candidates. The line itself, seventeen syllables long, is always in danger of turning to awkward prose, particularly as necessity dictates the use of irregular feet. But other readers have found Longfellow's handling of the meter the finest that English has to offer and completely appropriate to the gentle pace of the poem. Longfellow himself gracefully and self-deprecatingly acknowledged the difficulty and the danger of his choice when he wrote Hawthorne a note thanking him for a favorable review of *Evangeline* that Hawthorne had published in a Salem newspaper: "This success I owe entirely to you, for being willing to forego the pleasure of writing a prose tale which many people would have taken for poetry, that I might write a poem which many people take for prose." Longfellow would subsequently return to hexameters again, in a poem even closer to Hawthorne's accustomed subject matter, *The Courtship of Miles Standish.*

THE SONG OF HIAWATHA

A reader coming to *Evangeline* with no prior knowledge of its subject might easily form a wrong impression from its opening eight lines:

This is the forest primeval. The murmuring pines
　and the hemlocks,
Bearded with moss, and in garments green,
　indistinct in the twilight,
Stand like Druids of eld, with voices sad and
　prophetic,
Stand like harpers hoar, with beards that rest on
　their bosoms.
Loud from its rocky caverns, the deep-voiced
　neighboring ocean
Speaks, and in accents disconsolate answers the
　wail of the forest.
This is the forest primeval; but where are the
　hearts that beneath it
Leaped like the roe, when he hears in the wood-
　land the voice of the huntsman?

An elegiac opening that speaks of a people no longer found where they once lived beneath the forest might well be taken for the opening of a poem about the Indians, the native inhabitants of a land of which they have been dispossessed. And just as Longfellow sympathized with the dispossessed Acadians, so too does he sympathize with the dispossessed Indians of North America. It was perhaps inevitable that he would write a poem on the subject equal to or even greater in scope than *Evangeline*. But he would not undertake *The Song of Hiawatha* for another seven years. In the intervening years he continued to lecture on European writers, particularly on those closer to the Middle Ages. He also worked on *The Golden Legend* (1851), a verse drama set in the Middle Ages that was to be the second of a three-part dramatic poem on the history of Christendom, one of Longfellow's most cherished projects. He also worked on a translation of Dante's *Purgatorio*, itself the middle section of a three-part epic Christian poem, as well as on shorter poems of his own. Two years after the publication of *Evangeline* appeared his collection *The Seaside and the Fireside* (1850), which included "The Building of the Ship" and "The Fire of Drift-Wood," the former ending with its famous exhortation on the looming national crisis as sectional differences, primarily over slavery, threatened to tear asunder the Union, the latter among Longfellow's most successful poems on a private, rather than public, subject.

In 1835 the Finnish poet Elias Lönnrot (1802–1884) published his epic poem *Kalevala,* composed from material found in Finnish oral tradition. An expanded version appeared in 1849, which Longfellow read in 1854 in a German translation, shortly after resigning his professorship at Harvard. Inspired both by its pre-Christian stories of mythic heroism and by its striking unrhymed tetrameter, Longfellow set to work that summer on his own "Indian Edda," as he described *The Song of Hiawatha* in an introductory note when it was published the following year.

As was so often the case, Longfellow wrote *The Song of Hiawatha* not primarily from personal acquaintance with its subject matter but from his reading. His most important source was the ethnologist Henry Rowe Schoolcraft, whose accounts of Ojibway and Plains Indian legends form the basis of Longfellow's poem. Longfellow drew on other sources as well, as his notes to the poem indicate. He also borrowed, perhaps unwittingly, some of the substance of his poem, as well as its meter, from Lönnrot's *Kalevala,* leading some to accuse him of plagiarism, a charge often made against him, most famously by Edgar Allan Poe. Longfellow denied that the stories themselves came from the *Kalevala,* declaring instead that similarities were due to the universality of mythic stories.

That Longfellow strove for a different kind of universality, not just of primitive myths but of human hearts at all times and places, is evident in the poem's introduction, in which he addresses the poem to readers "Who believe, that in all ages / Every human heart is human." This approach gives Longfellow's poem many admirable strengths, but it also opened it to criticism. *The Song of Hiawatha* was an advance over other portrayals of Indians that came before it, whether positive, negative, or a mixture of the two, in that it treats Indians as multifaceted human beings, rather than as the creatures of the forest and prairie that they are even in James Fenimore Cooper's work. Hiawatha brings to his people the secrets of agriculture, of medicine, of picture-writing. He is a friend to Chibiabos and Kwasind, a rival to Pau-Puk-Keewis, and lover to Minnehaha. He wrestles his father, the West-Wind, out of real passion, but can only fight him to a draw. Yes, he has magic moccasins and magic mittens, but he is also a craftsman, building the first canoe as canoes were built by the Indians, with cedar framing and birch skin sewn together with tamarack roots

and made watertight with balsam resin. He is generous with guests, even when they come as strangers uninvited to his wigwam, as Famine and Fever do in the darker latter passages of the poem. The myths and stories in large part are not the myths Europeans imposed upon the Indians but the myths and stories of the Indians themselves, as best that Longfellow could determine them from his sources. At the same time, Longfellow, in emphasizing their human hearts just like his readers' own hearts, at times makes them too much like his readers, or at least like his readers' good opinions of themselves, nowhere more so than in his portrayal of Minnehaha, the only figure in the poem of Longfellow's own invention, as she peeps from behind a curtain at her handsome suitor. But even this picture does not remain entirely pretty; she dies of famine while Hiawatha, wild with despair, hunts futilely in the woods for game.

Longfellow's Indians, then, are a combination of a people as they were, as ethnology had recovered them, and as Longfellow wished them to be. But though this latter element brought the poem criticism almost immediately, anthropology has come to recognize that such projection is unavoidable. All ethnological descriptions reflect in part the wishes of the ethnologist. In Longfellow's case, this tendency is relatively benign, diminishing recognition of the Native American propensity for cruelty, for instance, while privileging their harmonious relationship to nature. In these and other ways, Longfellow can be seen to have anticipated attitudes that have since become respectable. Regarding the Native American relationship to nature, Longfellow's portrayal might be the more realistic in fact, showing Hiawatha both as intimate with nature's creatures and at the same time their adversary.

The poem's final cantos move from myth and story into the world of history, as the white man, represented by the Jesuit missionaries, comes to the land of Hiawatha, signaling his departure to the land of the Hereafter. Modern readers may object to the positive manner in which Longfellow portrays this transition, but the poem's religious point of view is finally not a simple one. At the same time Longfellow wrote *The Song of Hiawatha* he also had in mind what he hoped would be a greater poem on the history of Christianity, his three-part *Christus* (1872) of which he had only completed the middle part. Yet throughout *The Song of Hiawatha* the pantheism of the Indians is given to the reader as something to enjoy and in part it represents Longfellow's own feelings. Even the medicine men are portrayed benignly, a radical departure from the Puritan point of view, and at the end the reader feels more loss in Hiawatha's departure than hope in the arrival of the white man. The Indian response to the Jesuits is the welcome of the Hurons, rather than the torture of the Iroquois, but this is in keeping with the overall spirit of the poem, as well as the actual experience of the Jesuits who originally pushed west into the region of *The Song of Hiawatha* before relations soured. The poem is, finally, a kind of resetting of John Milton's "The Morning of Christ's Nativity" in the land of Lake Superior, in which paganism gives way to the advent of Christ. But all the pleasures of the poem are the pleasures of the vanquished pagan world, as they are in Milton's poem, and one cannot help but feel that Longfellow achieved greater success with *The Song of Hiawatha* than he did with *Christus: A Mystery* because the poet in him felt the world of Hiawatha more deeply.

THE COURTSHIP OF MILES STANDISH

In 1856 the manuscript of William Bradford's account of the first years of the Pilgrims, *Of Plymouth Plantation,* was published by the Massachusetts Historical Society, some two hundred years after its completion. Two years later Longfellow published his own treatment of the Puritan Pilgrims at Plymouth, *The Courtship of Miles Standish.* It is difficult to imagine two treatments of the same subject more different in tone and effect. Bradford's tone is serious, severe, pious, self-righteous—in a word, Puritan. Longfellow's tone is surprisingly playful. Longfellow had a natural interest in the story he tells; its two main characters, the young lovers Priscilla Mullins and John Alden, were ancestors of Longfellow on his mother's side. The title character, Miles Standish, the chief military officer of the Puritan colony, turns out to be a secondary character, and Longfellow's treatment of him is gently but unambiguously comic.

The bind John Alden finds himself in, forced to choose between the love he feels for Priscilla and the duty he feels toward the Puritan stalwart Miles Standish, reflects the deeper opposition at the heart of *The Courtship of Miles Standish:* the opposition between Puritanism's denial of life's earthly impulses and the heart's yearning for earthly pleasure and fulfillment. This opposition has its fullest development in the moment when Alden stands poised to step into the boat that would carry him to the *Mayflower* as it prepares to depart for England. Above him a cloud seems to point toward England—a portent of the kind taken seriously by the Puritans as signals of God's will—while the hand of Priscilla beckons him to stay. Alden's choice, to reject the Puritanical duty that is a denial of life and accept an earthly embrace, is clear:

> Float, O hand of cloud, and vanish away in the ether!
> Roll thyself up like a fist, to threaten and daunt me; I heed not
> Either your warning or menace, or any omen of evil!
> There is no land so sacred, no air so pure and wholesome,
> As is the air she breathes, and the soil that is pressed by her footsteps.

Meanwhile, Miles Standish has gone off to do battle with the Indians. In the confrontation with

Pecksuot and Wattawamat, Longfellow shows Standish to be a stalwart leader after all, despite his comic bluster. Yet Longfellow links his military prowess as much to personal pique and hot temper as to God's will for his chosen people. Standish fills the rattlesnake skin with powder and shot while still angry with John Alden, and he strikes Pecksuot dead after Pecksuot insults him. The Indian warriors too fight as much from vanity and love of fighting as from any morally defensible motive, yet in death "the brave Wattawamat" "fell with both hands clutching the greensward, / Seeming in death to hold back from his foe the land of his fathers." Longfellow's own point of view, represented by Priscilla, the feminine alternative to the martial masculinity of Miles Standish, is evident, if mildly stated, when Standish sends back to Plymouth the head of their foe:

> And as a trophy of war the head of the brave Wattawamat
> Scowled from the roof of the fort, which at once was a church and a fortress,
> All who beheld it rejoiced, and praised the Lord, and took courage.
> Only Priscilla averted her face from this spectre of terror,
> Thanking God in her heart that she had not married Miles Standish;
> Shrinking, fearing almost, lest coming home from his battles,
> He should lay claim to her hand, as the prize and reward of his valor.

The values Longfellow affirms, then, are not the values affirmed by the Puritans themselves. This had also been true in *Evangeline*. The Puritans were staunchly anti-Catholic; a common Puritan epithet for the Anglicans from whom the Pilgrims at Plymouth had separated, in Bradford and elsewhere, is "papists," in that the Puritans felt the Church of England had not sufficiently eliminated the superstitions and holidays and sensuousness of the Catholic Church. Yet in *Evangeline* the revelry and music and nut-brown ale of the Catholic Acadians are

put forward positively, and in *The Song of Hiawatha* the superstitious pantheism of the Ojibways is presented not only without criticism, but with much pleasure. In William Bradford's *Of Plymouth Plantation* the natural world of colonial Massachusetts is presented, when it is acknowledged at all, as harsh and threatening, the dark abode of Indians and devils, a trial to test the faith of the elect. In *The Courtship of Miles Standish,* the natural world is part of the human world and vice-versa, full of life and beauty. At the poem's conclusion, Alden accompanies Priscilla, who rides a white bull, as they approach the home they will share together as husband and wife:

> Pleasantly murmured the brook, as they crossed the ford in the forest,
> Pleased with the image that passed, like a dream of love, through its bosom,
> Tremulous, floating in air, o'er the depths of the azure abysses.
> Down through the golden leaves the sun was pouring his splendors,
> Gleaming on purple grapes, that, from the branches above them suspended,
> Mingled their odorous breath with the balm of the pine and the fir-tree,
> Wild and sweet as the clusters that grew in the valley of Eschol.

TALES OF A WAYSIDE INN

The Puritans of Massachusetts had wished to found a new society with a single people, believers like themselves, God's chosen saints. But though a new society was eventually to emerge from the British colonies of North America, its inhabitants would not be a single people, even in Massachusetts. Just as the natural world of the developing nation presented a great diversity of forest and plains, mountains and rivers, so too did its people. Appreciation for this diversity had already appeared in *Evangeline,* with its Catholic farmers and French trappers and Spanish ranchers, with its Quakers and Germans, with the Shawnee spirit-sister of Evangeline, herself a wandering refugee of the wars of Europe's capitals.

The small group gathered at the Sudbury Inn outside of Boston, in *Tales of a Wayside Inn,* also exhibit this diversity. The landlord, to be sure, is of solid English stock, descendent of those who fought at Concord for liberty and independence from their mother country. Among the others, though, are a young Sicilian, an olive-skinned Spanish Jew, and a Norwegian master of the violin, as well as three others who round out the diversity of interests and vocations that also characterizes the group. This group, in addition to representing the growing diversity of American society, represents as well different facets of Longfellow himself. The Sicilian is deeply steeped in the literature of Renaissance Italy, the student in the literature of the Middle Ages. The theologian hopes to build a Universal Church in which right living will matter more than sectarian creeds. The musician plays the music of northern Europe:

> The scream of sea-birds in their flight,
> The rumor of the forest trees,
> The plunge of the implacable seas,
> The tumult of the wind at night,
> Voices of eld, like trumpets blowing,
> Old ballads, and wild melodies
> Through mist and darkness pouring forth,
> Like Elivagar's river flowing
> Out of the glaciers of the North.

The poet—modeled on a fellow translator of Dante—is given the briefest description in the "Prelude," perhaps because the becoming attributes Longfellow gives him—talent, modesty, generosity—are those he wished attributed to himself.

Tales of a Wayside Inn was published in three parts, the second and third parts published in response to the great success of the original set, which remains the portion most widely known and read. The first part opens with the landlord's tale of "Paul Revere's Ride." Though the collection as a whole does not focus on America, as had the major poems that precedes it, "Paul Revere's Ride" establishes the American setting for the telling of the tales to follow. Written as the United States was entering the Civil War, "Paul Revere's Ride" is a memorable call to arms from a poet who elsewhere shows himself distressed at war. Longfellow's great hope, expressed repeatedly, was that an age of peace will one day succeed the great ages of war. Priscilla turns her face from the severed head of Wattawamat in *The Courtship of Miles Standish. The Song of Hiawatha* opens with the making of the peace pipe, and Hiawatha's mission, above all others, is to make peace among the warring Indian nations. Yet Longfellow, like his friend and fellow poet John Greenleaf Whittier, a pacifist and Quaker, opposed slavery. As it did for Whittier, the war to end slavery thus posed special challenge for the otherwise pacifist Longfellow, bringing violence in the name of justice even as it threatened to sunder the Union that Longfellow loved. At the same time, in the early months of the war, occurred the tragedy of Longfellow's mature life, the death of his wife Fanny in his arms as the dress she had been wearing while sealing envelopes with sealing wax caught fire. The beard Longfellow wore in later life was result of his inability to shave, so badly scarred was he by the flames.

Longfellow answers both the challenge of the war and the challenge of personal grief, at least in part, with "Paul Revere's Ride." The fate of a nation, the landlord declares, rode with Paul Revere that night. Now, as that nation's fate once again hung in the balance, Longfellow, in perfectly realized verse, evoked that stirring ride again, the waiting horse and impetuous rider, the signal in the belfry tower, the spark from the hoof, the cry in the night through every Middlesex village and farm, told now so that

> In the hour of darkness and peril and need,
> The people will waken and listen to hear

The hurrying hoof-beats of that steed,
And the midnight message of Paul Revere.

It is a call to vigor and action, as "A Psalm of Life" had been in his first volume of poetry, a call to greatness.

Though "Paul Revere's Ride" is the best known, the centerpiece of the first part of *Tales of a Wayside Inn* is "The Saga of King Olaf." Written in twenty-two cantos and nearly as long as *The Courtship of Miles Standish*, "The Saga of King Olaf" retells the coming of Christianity to Norway. Its opening canto, "The Challenge of Thor," written separately some years earlier, presents the war god Thor's challenge to Christ for dominion of the world. Olaf, in the cantos that follow, is Christ's champion and in his triumph the old pagan days come to an end. Yet the story Longfellow tells is itself as violent as any tale of the Vikings, and Olaf gives little indication that it is the Prince of Peace he fights for. In the canto "Iron-Beard," Olaf, like the British ruler in *Evangline,* summons all the farmers of Drontheim to gather in the pagan temple. The farmer Iron-Beard, reminiscent of the Catholic farmers of *Evangeline,* would rather ignore the summons and not confront Olaf,

> But he loved the freedom of his farm,
> His ale at night, by the fireside warm,
> Gudrun his daughter, with her flaxen tresses.

> He loved his horses and his herds,
> The smell of the earth, and the song of birds,
> His well-filled barns, his brook with its water-cresses.

King Olaf answers his defiance, declaring, "I command / This land to be Christian land," and smiting the graven images of the old Norse gods. In the struggle that ensues, Iron-Beard is killed, and Olaf addresses the wailing crowd.

> King Olaf from the doorway spoke,
> "Choose ye between two things, my folk,

> To be baptized or given up to slaughter!"

> And seeing their leader stark and dead,
> The people with a murmur said,
> "O King, baptize us with thy holy water."

> So all the Drontheim land became
> A Christian land in name and fame,
> In the old gods no more believing and trusting.

> And as a blood-atonement, soon
> King Olaf wed the fair Gudrun;
> And thus in peace ended the Drontheim Hus-Ting!

The concluding exclamation point, if nothing else, sounds the note of astonished irony that is the chief response called for throughout this poem of Christian heroism.

A different kind of irony, darker and more chilling, pervades the theologian's tale, "Torquemada." A tale of familial horror and religious fanaticism, that of Catholic Spain during the Inquisition, "Torquemada" is the closest Longfellow comes to the morbidity of Edgar Allan Poe, all the more effective for its abnormality. More typical of Longfellow is the poet's tale, "The Birds of Killingworth." An ecological fable that warns against man's destruction of nature, "The Birds of Killingworth" recounts the story of a New England town that, to protect its farmers' crops, declares a bounty on all the town's birds, which leads to "A slaughter to be told in groans, not words, / The very St. Bartholomew of Birds!"

> The Summer came, and all the birds were dead;
>   The days were like hot coals; the very ground
> Was burned to ashes; in the orchards fed
>   Myriads of caterpillars, and around
> The cultivated fields and garden beds
>   Hosts of devouring insects crawled, and found
> No foe to check their march, till they had made
> The land a desert without leaf or shade.

"The Birds of Killingworth" concludes the first part of the *Tales of a Wayside Inn,* though not on so bleak a note, as the following year the birds are restored. The poems of the second and third parts are generally lighter fare, tales of knights and ladies, monks and kings, lovers and heroes and scoundrels. Longfellow's powers of versification and narrative still produced much that is pleasing in these tales. Taken as a whole, *Tales of a Wayside Inn* is a tour de force of poetic narrative and of metrical variation, handled always with ease and a sure touch unrivaled by other American poets.

DRAMATIC POEMS

Longfellow's interest in verse drama was manifest as early as his junior year at Bowdoin, when he wrote "The Poor Student, A Dramatic Sketch." Among his earliest published volumes is *The Spanish Student* (1843), a three-act play that was his first extended work in verse, published four years before *Evangeline*. He returned to drama again four years after *Evangeline*, publishing *The Golden Legend* in 1851. *The Golden Legend*, the story of a medieval prince who seeks a cure for his mortal illness through the sacrifice of a maiden willing to give her life for him, came to be the second part of *Christus: A Mystery*, the work that Longfellow hoped would be the crowning achievement of his career. The third part, *The New England Tragedies* (1868), two plays dealing with religious intolerance in colonial New England, was published shortly after the Civil War. The first part, *The Divine Tragedy* (1871), a dramatic presentation of episodes from the life of Christ, was the last to be published. The three separate pieces were brought together in a single volume the following year. "The Masque of Pandora" (1875), modeled loosely on the Elizabethan court masque, is Longfellow's only extend treatment of classical subject. "Judas Maccabaeus" (1872), the last work in dramatic form published in Longfellow's lifetime, retells a story from Jewish history. After Longfellow's death, the manuscript of "Michael Angelo: A Fragment" was found among his papers.

The Spanish Student is very much the product of Longfellow's travels in Spain at the age of twenty and should be considered alongside *Outre-Mer* and his early translations of Spanish poetry. The story, taken from Cervantes, involves gypsies, lovers, jealousy, revelations of true parentage, and other stock elements of light romantic comedy. Songs are scattered throughout, many of which are translations by Longfellow of songs he had heard traveling in Spain. *The Spanish Student* is not a serious work of poetry, even of light comic poetry; nevertheless, it captures something of the flavor of Longfellow's experience of Spain, pleasant if not profound.

The three parts of *Christus: A Mystery* are very much intended to be serious poetry; they are at best uneven, not least in relation to each other and to Longfellow's intended design. The three parts were to represent the spirit of Christianity in the Apostolic, Medieval, and Modern eras; at the same time they were to represent the Christian virtues of faith, hope, and charity. That this project did not come easily to Longfellow can be seen by the awkwardness of the result. The three parts do not form a poetic whole. *The Divine Tragedy*, the last part to be completed though first in the scheme, is written as spoken parts, but can hardly have been conceived for the stage. Its twenty-four scenes simply present successive episodes in the life of Christ, with no effort made at dramatic continuity. The characters of one episode—John the Baptist and a priest in the first episode, for instance—are simply replaced by the characters of the next—Lucifer and Christ as Christ is tempted in the wilderness in the second—who are in turn replaced by those in the next—the wedding party at Cana, and so forth. *The Golden Legend*, on the other hand, tells a story with narrative continuity from one scene to the next, as Prince Henry and Elsie move toward fulfillment of their destinies at Salerno. Still, *The Golden Legend* is not really conceived as a play. *The New England Tragedies* consists of not just one but two real plays, "John

Endicott" and "Giles Corey of the Salem
Farms." That the Puritan persecutions of Quakers and witches in colonial New England can
stand for the spirit of Christianity in the modern
era, much less for the quality of charity (except
by highlighting the consequences of the absence
of charity), seems questionable, even if Longfellow had been a more pessimistic Christian
than he was. Rather, it seems more likely that
Longfellow was drawn to these two persecutions as poetic subjects suitable for dramatic
treatment and simply forced them into his *Christus* in the absence of anything else more suitable to his scheme.

Each part of *Christus: A Mystery,* though,
when considered separately, has its merits as
well as its weaknesses. Where *The Divine Tragedy* stays close to the Gospels, there is little that
Longfellow can do to match the English of the
King James Bible, except paraphrase and repeat
it. He does much better, however, when he
ventures out on his own, as he does in the
development of characters beyond the scope
given to them in the Gospels. Manahem the Es-
senian, developed by Longfellow from the mer-
est suggestion in Acts, presents a purer form of
Judaism than do the worldly priests who
persecute Christ, providing another, more intellectual, perspective on Christ. Pontius Pilate,
disturbed by what he sees as Jewish fanaticism,
is given a worldly soliloquy in which he laments a religious movement that makes the
divine so distant and so masculine:

Incomprehensible, fanatic people!
Ye have a God, who seemeth like yourselves
Incomprehensible, dwelling apart,
Majestic, cloud-encompassed, clothed in darkness!
One whom ye fear, but love not; yet ye have
No Goddesses to soften your stern lives,
And make you tender unto human weakness,
While we at Rome have everywhere around us
Our amiable divinities, that haunt
The woodlands and the waters, and frequent
Our households, with their sweet and gracious
 presence!

I will go in, and while these Jews are wrangling,
Read my Ovidius on the Art of Love.

In *The Divine Tragedy* Longfellow, as if answering this soliloquy, seeks to emphasize the gentle
and the feminine in the new religion of Christ.
Christ himself is described as "manly yet
womanly" and throughout the poem female
characters are given prominence. Christ's
mother figures prominently, as does the woman
at the well. Mary Magdalene has a strong
soliloquy and her counterpart, Helen of Tyre,
who gives herself not to Christ but to the false
magician Simon Magus, is a figure of genuine
pathos.

Longfellow's sympathy with women, his
tendency toward privileging the feminine, gives
strength to much of his best poetry. Priscilla,
in *The Courtship of Miles Standish,* is the
strongest manifestation of this tendency in
Longfellow, speaking firmly to her lover about
the wrongs men do women, deciding for herself
who her husband should be, rejecting the
masculinity of Miles Standish that everyone
else admires. Though more modest in her
desires, Evangeline is also an admirable figure.
Minnehaha, on the other hand, is given less to
do, though Nokomis is a figure of real force
and her daughter Wenonah, Hiawatha's mother,
is clearly wronged by the faithless West-Wind,
Mudjekeewis, Hiawatha's father. Elsie, however,
in *The Golden Legend,* shows Longfellow's
tendency at its worst. Though central to the
poem's meaning—it is her willingness to
sacrifice herself that finally redeems Henry
when he realizes the injustice of what he is
about to accept—the very eagerness with which
she embraces self-sacrifice makes her a somewhat repellent figure. Yet Longfellow is much
at home in the Middle Ages, and *The Golden
Legend* gives him his most extended opportunity
to develop this affinity. An interpolated miracle
play, depicting Jesus as a child, it is more successful than is the whole of *The Divine Tragedy*
in conveying a poetic sense of Christ.

"John Endicott" is the more successful of the two plays that constitute *The New England Tragedies.* Longfellow invents a son for the stern Puritan governor, whom he uses both to bring out the severity of Endicott while at the same time making him a figure of human interest. The persecuted Quaker maiden, Edith, is a figure of courage beyond Longfellow's other heroines, as she is more directly threatened by harm and yet stands firm, setting an example for young John Endicott, who would be her lover, rather than depending upon him. Other characters, both major and minor, are well developed, including the unbending minister John Norton, who, unlike Governor Endicott, has no pangs of conscience, declaring, "There is no room in Christ's triumphant army / For tolerationists." In the companion play, "Giles Corey of the Salem Farms," the witch trials are presented as a second instance of Puritan intolerance. The title character, sentenced to death by pressing, and his wife are forcefully presented as simple people of courage, but the play as a whole is less dynamic than "John Endicott." Taken together, though, they challenge New England's Puritan heritage more forcefully than does the more playful *Courtship of Miles Standish.*

"The Masque of Pandora" retells the familiar story of the title character. Its chief interest lies in its embrace of dryads and oreads and other figures of classical pastoral, pantheistic poetry. While common in the European poetic heritage, such overt pastoralism is rare in Puritan-influenced American poetry. Longfellow may have chosen the subject of "Judas Maccabaeus"—the confrontation between the heroic title character, the champion of Judaism, and his enemy Antiochus Epiphanes, the Syrian King who is determined to convert the Jews to pagan Hellenism—as an opportunity to balance his tendency to side with even pagan sensibility when it is faced with a sternness and purity that is in the end life denying. If so, his tendency undermines his intention, as his handling of the story gives little scope for the strength of Judas Maccabaeus to become manifest. More successful is Longfellow's portrayal of a different kind of strength, the strength of an artist who perseveres in his dedication to his art, in his unfinished dramatization of Michaelangelo. "Michael Angelo: A Fragment" is written, like the *Divine Tragedy,* as a series of episodes rather than as a play, but in this case Longfellow does not have to compete, as he did in the earlier poem, with the language of the King James Bible, and he captures much of the character of the great artist. Longfellow, like the Michaelangelo he portrays, is now an old man near the end of his life, no longer concerned with the trivialities of the youthful *Spanish Student* but mindful of the more profound matters of life and death.

SHORTER POEMS

In 1879, on the poet's seventy-second birthday, the children of Cambridge presented Longfellow an armchair carved from the chestnut tree made famous by the poem "The Village Blacksmith." A more fitting tribute to Longfellow's poetry can hardly be imagined. Throughout his career Longfellow had celebrated children; he had also celebrated the good, solid things of life, such as "the spreading chestnut tree" and the village smithy who worked beneath it. Craftsmanship was also a frequent subject of his poetry, the kind of craftsmanship—like that of Hiawatha building his canoe or of the potters from around the world in "Kéramos" or of the shipmaster in "The Building of the Ship"—that had produced his own poems. Fitting too is the chair as a symbol of a passing time, carved from a tree cut down in the transition of Cambridge from village to modern suburb, for even as the chair was given to Longfellow the era of his predominance in American poetry was passing.

In addition to the major poems already discussed, Longfellow produced shorter poems, such as "The Village Blacksmith," throughout his career, beginning with those collected in *Voices of the Night,* in which he struck some of his characteristic notes. The night as a time of refuge from the glaring cares of the day is an image he returns to throughout his career, a time of beauty and rest rather than of melancholy. "A Psalm of Life," much admired in Longfellow's day and much criticized afterward, struck the note of optimism that persists as the public's chief perception of Longfellow's poetry despite the abundance of poetry in other moods that he produced. His second volume, *Ballads and Other Poems,* established Longfellow as a popular storyteller. In it are "The Skeleton in Armor," a story of Vikings coming to America invented by Longfellow in response to the archaeological discovery of its title, and "The Wreck of the Hesperus," a vigorous tale of determination and love of children gone awry, as the dead daughter of the determined sea captain is found lashed to the mast the morning after the storm. The closing quatrain alone should dispel any overemphasis on Longfellow's optimism:

> Such was the wreck of the Hesperus
> In the midnight and the snow!
> Christ save us all from a death like this,
> On the reef of Norman's Woe!

The title poem of *The Belfry of Bruges and Other Poems* presents Longfellow's love of medieval Europe, still present in the medieval churches and castles he visited. Its celebration of medieval heroes and battles contrasts with Longfellow's rejection of war in "The Arsenal at Springfield" and "The Occultation of Orion." This rejection of war sprang from the same social conscience that led him to write *Poems on Slavery.* Though embraced by abolitionists, this volume did little else for Longfellow's reputation at the time and has since been criticized for being thin and lacking in sufficient

indignation. By the late twentieth century, however, these poems had helped begin the recovery of Longfellow's reputation, as morally earnest poetry on such social themes has come to be admired regardless of its actual poetic force.

The Seaside and the Fireside, published after *Evangeline,* identifies two characteristic moods found in Longfellow's poetry: the domestic warmth and romantic glow of the fireside and the more brisk and active world of the ocean and its shores. A kind of melancholy and profundity also characterizes the ocean in its depths and storms, in its eternal tides, and in the waves coming to the shore. (Longfellow felt the regular slow heave and withdrawal of the waves was the original inspiration for the classical hexameter line he used in *Evangeline* and elsewhere.) "The Building of the Ship" reflects the vigor of the sea, even in its famous call for national unity in the years leading up to the Civil War—"Thou, too, sail on, O Ship of State! / Sail on, O UNION, strong and great!"— whereas "The Fire of Driftwood," capturing the inevitable separation of young friends and perhaps the finer poem, evokes the depths and melancholy of the ocean, as well as the poignancy of the fireside, here not in a warm domestic setting but rather in an abandoned farmhouse by the sea.

A poignant sense of loss is also captured in "My Lost Youth," included among the "Birds of Passage" of *The Courtship of Miles Standish and Other Poems.* Longfellow's hometown of Portland—"the beautiful town / That is seated by the sea"—is recalled, as is the Lapland song that haunts the poet's memory. Its refrain, repeated at the end of each stanza—"A boy's will is the wind's will / And the thoughts of youth are long, long thoughts"—provided the title in the next century for Robert Frost's first book of poems, *A Boy's Will.* Subsequent volumes that, like *The Courtship of Miles Standish and Other Poems,* are divided between a longer poem and shorter poems also group the shorter poems under the heading "Birds of Passage," eventually numbering five "flights" in all. Longer poems stand on their own in the volumes they appear in: "The Hanging of the Crane," in *The Masque of Pandora and Other Poems,* which uses the ceremonial hanging of the swinging arm in the hearth of a newly wedded couple as the starting point for a meditation on the successive stage of happy domestic life; "Morituri Salutamus: Poem for the Fiftieth Anniversary of the Class of 1825 in Bowdoin College," in the same volume, which uses the familiar salutation of the gladiators to Caesar— "We who are about to die salute you!"—to address the halls of Bowdoin and surrounding meadows and ocean; "Kéramos," which alternates an address to the spinning potter's wheel with celebratory descriptions of the world's pottery, from Delft and Tuscany to Egypt, China, and Japan. The variation in Longfellow's achievement can be seen in these longer poems as well as in the more than two hundred shorter poems he published. If the sentimentality of "The Hanging of the Crane" has become too cloying, the forthright acknowledgment of aging and death in "Morituri Salutamus" remains impressive, even in its closing image, which returns to Longfellow's appreciation of night and its darkness:

> For age is opportunity no less
> Than youth itself, though in another dress,
> And as the evening twilight fades away
> The sky is filled with stars, invisible by day.

Among Longfellow's shorter poems are many tributes to his friends, as well as to fellow writers both living and dead. These poems are characterized both by Longfellow's great generosity of spirit and by his thoughtfulness, as he finds the perfect evocation of each. "Hawthorne" recalls the day of his classmate's funeral, where the poet wanders the meadow of the Old Manse on the banks of the Concord River, home at different times to both Haw-

thorne and Emerson, and the hillside graveyard not far away:

> Now I look back, and meadow, manse, and stream
> Dimly my thought defines;
> I only see—a dream within a dream—
> The hill-top hearsed with pines.
>
> I only hear above his place of rest
> Their tender undertone,
> The infinite longing of a troubled breast,
> The voice so like his own.

For Whittier's seventieth birthday celebration he wrote "The Three Silences of Molinos," using the teaching of a seventeenth-century Spanish priest to capture the spirituality of the Quaker poet. "The Three Silences of Molinos" is written as sonnet, a form Longfellow returned to throughout his career. Critics who have nothing good to say about "A Psalm of Life" or "Excelsior" or "The Wreck of the Hesperus" nevertheless acknowledge Longfellow's achievement with the sonnet. In this most imitative of poetic forms, Longfellow rarely imitates, declining to write of eros or romantic love, the subject matter of the traditional sonnet, in favor of meditations on his reading, the worlds he loved, his own quiet emotional life. In "The Broken Oar" he gives a surprising image of a poet wandering a lonely seashore who finds carved on a wooden oar the words "Oft was I weary, when I toiled at thee":

> And like a man, who findeth what was lost,
> He wrote the words, then lifted up his head,
> And flung his useless pen into the sea.

Longfellow's health began to fail in the months following the publication of *Ultima Thule* in 1880. On a chilly March day in 1882, he was stricken by peritonitis while taking an afternoon walk on his veranda. He died in his bed on March 24. Found among his papers was a sonnet he had written some years before his death. "The Cross of Snow" expresses Longfellow's response to the death of his second wife, and it is among his finest achievements as a poet.

> In the long, sleepless watches of the night,
>   A gentle face—the face of one long dead—
>   Looks at me from the wall, where round its head
>   The night-lamp casts a halo of pale light.
> Here in this room she died; and soul more white
>   Never through martyrdom of fire was led
>   To its repose; nor can in books be read
>   The legend of a life more benedight.
> There is a mountain in the distant West
>   That, sun-defying, in its deep ravines
>   Displays a cross of snow upon its side.
> Such is the cross I wear upon my breast
>   These eighteen years, through all the changing scenes
>   And seasons changeless since the day she died.

CRITICAL ESTIMATE

If the chair given him by the schoolchildren of Cambridge was a fitting tribute to Longfellow's achievement, his bust in the Poet's Corner of Westminster Abbey clearly was not. Longfellow's achievement is not commensurate with that of the greatest poets of the English language, and it is not surprising that a reaction against such praise soon followed. The reputations of his two great contemporaries, Walt Whitman and Emily Dickinson, less recognized in their own day, have deservedly eclipsed his own. Their genius, so different from each other but alike in their individuality and in their modernism, was greater than Longfellow's. Their best is superior to Longfellow's best and their worst retains their distinctive voices. Yet Longfellow possessed strengths Whitman and Dickinson do not; to banish him utterly, as twentieth-century critical opinion threatened to do despite the demurrers of those who have read him closely, would be to banish much from American poetry that is not elsewhere so abundantly found.

Longfellow was a poet of more wide-ranging interests than either Dickinson or Whitman, a poet more at ease with his neighbors and more conversant with the world. One comes to know Dickinson and Whitman more intimately than Longfellow when reading their poetry, but in reading Longfellow one comes to know other people, not in their conjectural existence but in their daily lives. There are two sexes, and relationships between them vary; sometimes they are easy, sometimes difficult, sometimes happy, and sometimes not. In capturing a fuller range of human types and experiences, Longfellow is more akin to the great poets honored in the Poets Corner—Chaucer, Shakespeare, Spenser, even Dryden—than are his more modern contemporaries.

Longfellow's tendency to moralize, to make each poem a sermon, certainly goes against modernist taste, however much it was necessary in order to bring to poetry middle-class readers unused to poetry but used to sermons. But poetry in the latter part of the twentieth century has developed its own moral didacticism in its concern for the marginalized and the oppressed, and a poem such as "The Revenge of Rain-in-the-Face," written following the battle of Little Big Horn in 1876, depicting an Indian warrior holding aloft the "brave heart" of General Custer and ending

> Whose was the right and the wrong?
> Sing it, O funeral song,
>   With a voice that is full of tears,
> And say that our broken faith
> Wrought all this ruin and scathe,
>   In the Year of a hundred Years.

seems now surprisingly modern.

Like his moralizing, Longfellow's sentimentality is at odds with modernist taste. But it is possible that modernism went too far in denying the validity of the sentimental; certainly postmodern irony has come to seem more clever than profound. In reading "Killed at the Ford," the modern reader can admire the skill with which Longfellow depicts the almost casual death of "the beautiful youth" shot in the darkness by an unseen sniper. But when the same bullet, in the poet's vision, speeds north to the youth's home town and kills as well his sweetheart, that same reader will be tempted to smile and think, with Hemingway's Jake Barnes, "Isn't it pretty to think so." Yet the cynic is not always right, and a certain poetic truth and poetic force remains in the reader's mind. And modernism, like cynicism, remains a taste after all. "The Hanging of the Crane" will never please some readers, but for others, for whom the expression of the ideals they strive for is more important than sophistication, its expression of domestic happiness will be meaningful. Those put off by it can instead turn to "A Dutch Picture" and read of the old buccaneer consigned to the quiet of domestic life, who hears voices calling him once more to the sea, until

> . . . he thinks he shall take to the sea again
> For one more cruise with his buccaneers,
> To singe the beard of the King of Spain,
> And capture another Dean of Jaen
> And sell him in Algiers.

If "A Dutch Picture" comes as a surprise, the fault is partly due to Longfellow's admirers, who tended to make him tamer than he was. The Fireside Poets—Longfellow, Whittier, Bryant, Holmes, Lowell—were once the staples of American classrooms, and thus enjoyed a conservative status that ultimately does not serve them well. Their limitations became easily discerned; their virtues suprisingly less so. In deemphasizing them or even removing them from the curriculum, educators no doubt have sought to give students a better poetry, but this has not necessarily been the result. Rather, the average American knows no poetry at all. Longfellow's most successful poems, both those once well known—*Evangeline, The Courtship of Miles Standish,* "My Lost Youth," "The Village Blacksmith," even "The Wreck of the Hesperus," "Paul Revere's Ride," and *Hiawatha*—as well as those not so well known—"The Fire of Driftwood," "The Saga of King Olaf," "Morituri Salutamus," "The Cross of Snow," and many others—could change that if restored to their rightful place in the classroom. With the recent issue of new collections of Longfellow's writing, that restoration may be under way.

Selected Bibliography

WORKS OF HENRY WADSWORTH LONGFELLOW

POETRY

Voices of the Night. Cambridge, Mass.: John Owen, 1839.

Ballads and Other Poems. Cambridge, Mass.: John Owen, 1841.

Poems on Slavery. Cambridge, Mass.: John Owen, 1842.

The Spanish Student: A Play in Three Acts. Cambridge, Mass.: John Owen, 1843.

The Belfry of Bruges and Other Poems. Cambridge, Mass.: John Owen, 1845.

Evangeline: A Tale of Acadie. Boston: Ticknor, 1847.

The Seaside and the Fireside. Boston: Ticknor, Reed, and Fields, 1850.

The Golden Legend. Boston: Ticknor, Reed, and Fields, 1851. (Verse drama.)

The Song of Hiawatha. Boston: Ticknor and Fields, 1855.

The Courtship of Miles Standish and Other Poems. Boston: Ticknor and Fields, 1858. (Includes poems collected under the general heading "Birds of Passage.")

Tales of a Wayside Inn. Boston: Ticknor and Fields, 1863. (Also includes "Birds of Passage: Flight the Second.")

Flower-de-Luce. Boston: Ticknor and Fields, 1866.

The New England Tragedies. Boston: Ticknor and Fields, 1868. (Includes verse dramas "John Endicott" and "Giles Corey of the Salem Farms.")

The Divine Tragedy. Boston: James R. Osgood, 1871. (Verse drama.)

Christus: A Mystery. Boston: James R. Osgood, 1872. (Brings together *The Divine Tragedy, The Golden Legend,* and *The New England Tragedies,* with additional introductory, connecting, and concluding passages.)

Three Books of Song. Boston: Ticknor and Fields, 1872. (Includes "Tales of a Wayside Inn, Second Day"; "Judas Maccabaeus," verse drama; and "A Handful of Translations.")

Aftermath. Boston: James R. Osgood, 1873. (Includes "Tales of a Wayside Inn, Third Day" and "Birds of Passage: Flight the Third.")

The Masque of Pandora and Other Poems. Boston: James R. Osgood, 1875. (Also includes "The Hanging of the Crane," "Morituri Salutamus," "Birds of Passage: Flight the Fourth," and "A Book of Sonnets.")

Kéramos and Other Poems. Boston: Houghton, Osgood, and Company, 1878. (Also includes "Birds of Passage: Flight the Fifth" and a second "Book of Sonnets.")

Ultima Thule. Boston: Houghton, Mifflin and Co., 1880.

In the Harbor: Ultima Thule Part 2. Boston: Houghton, Mifflin and Co., 1882. (Published posthumously.)

PROSE

Outre-Mer: A Pilgrimage Beyond the Sea. 2 vols. New York: Harper and Brothers, 1835.

Hyperion: A Romance. 2 vols. New York: Samuel Colman, 1839.

Kavanaugh: A Tale. Boston: Ticknor, Reed, and Fields, 1849.

TRANSLATIONS AND ANTHOLOGIES

Coplas de Don Jorge Manrique, Translated from the Spanish with an Introductory Essay on the Moral and Devoitonal Poetry of Spain. Boston: Allen & Ticknor, 1833. (Translations of Manrique's *Coplas por la muerte de su padre* and seven Spanish sonnets.)

The Poems and Poetry of Europe. Philadelphia: Carey and Hart, 1844. (Expanded edition published by Porter and Coates, Philadelphia, 1871. Includes translations by Longfellow as well as by others.)

The Waif: A Collection of Poems. Cambridge, Mass.: John Owen, 1845.

The Estray: A Collection of Poems. Boston: Ticknor, 1846.

The Divine Comedy of Dante Alighieri. 3 vols. Boston: Ticknor and Fields, 1865–1867.

Poems of Places. 31 vols. Vols. 1–19, Boston: J. R. Osgood and Company; vols. 20–31, Boston: Houghton, Osgood, and Company, 1876–1879.

COLLECTED WORKS

Prose Works of Henry Wadsworth Longfellow. 2 vols. Boston: Ticknor and Fields, 1857. (Vol. 1, *Outre-Mer, Drift-Wood;* vol. 2, *Hyperion, Kavanaugh.* Collects Longfellow's miscellaneous prose writings under the title *Drift-Wood* for the first time. Arrangement of texts continued in subsequent Houghton Mifflin complete editions.)

The Works of Henry Wadsworth Longfellow with Bibliographical and Critical Notes. 11 vols. The Riverside Edition. Edited by Horace E. Scudder. Boston: Houghton, Mifflin and Co., 1886. (Vols. 1–6, poetry; vols. 7–8, prose; vols. 9–11, translation of Dante's *Divine Comedy.*)

Complete Poetical Works. 6 vols. The Riverside Edition. Boston: Houghton, Mifflin and Co., 1886. (The six poetry volumes from the *Works.*)

The Works of Henry Wadsworth Longfellow with Bibliographical and Critical Notes and His Life with Extracts from His Journals and Correspondence, Edited by Samuel Longfellow. 14 vols. The Standard Library Edition. Edited by Horace E. Scudder. Boston: Houghton, Mifflin and Co., 1891. (Same as Riverside Edition, with Samuel Longfellow's *Life* in three volumes.)

Complete Poetical Works. The Cambridge Edition. Boston: Houghton, Mifflin and Co., 1893. (The texts of the six-volume *Complete Poetical Works* with new headnotes and biographical sketch.)

Complete Poetical Works. The Household Edition. Boston: Houghton, Mifflin and Co., 1902. (Illustrated.)

The Complete Writings of Henry Wadsworth Longfellow with Portraits, Illustrations, and Facsimiles. The Craigie Edition. Edited by Horace E. Scudder. Boston: Houghton, Mifflin and Co., 1904. (Same as the Riverside Edition, with illustrations.)

The Works of Henry Wadsworth Longfellow. 10 vols. Edited by Charles Walsh. New York: Davos Press, 1909. (Vols. 1–3, prose; vols. 4–6, poetry; vols.

7–10, Dante's *Divine Comedy*. An alternative to the Houghton Mifflin editions, containing some prose pieces not collected elsewhere.)

Longfellow's Boyhood Poems. Edited by R. W. Pettingill. Saratoga Springs, N.Y., 1925. (Privately printed.)

SELECTED EDITIONS

Henry Wadsworth Longfellow: Representative Selections. Edited by Odell Shepard. New York: American Book Company, 1934. (Excellent introduction and annotated bibliography.)

The Poems of Henry Wadsworth Longfellow. Edited by Louis Untermeyer. New York: The Heritage Press, 1943. (Good introduction and commentary. Also issued by the Easton Press in a deluxe edition.)

Longfellow. Edited by Howard Nemerov. New York: Dell, 1959. (Good introduction by a twentieth-century American poet.)

Henry Wadsworth Longfellow: Evangeline and Selected Tales and Poems. Edited by Horace Gregory. New York: New American Library, 1964. (Contains commentary by Van Wyck Brooks and Norman Holmes Pearson and an affectionate parody of *Hiawatha* by Lewis Carroll, as well as the editor's own thoughtful introduction.)

Henry Wadsworth Longfellow: Selected Poems. Edited by Lawrence Buell. New York: Viking Penguin, 1988. (A worthy attempt, after a long lapse, to once again restore Longfellow to serious appreciation.)

Henry Wadsworth Longfellow: Poems and Other Writings. Edited by J. D. McClatchy. New York: Library of America, 2000. ("Note on the Texts" is a thorough, useful bibliographical essay. The "Chronology" of Longfellow's life is similarly thorough.)

LETTERS, JOURNALS, AND MANUSCRIPTS

No scholarly or popular edition of Longfellow's journals has yet been published. Portions can be found in Samuel Longfellow's *Life*. The main body of Longfellow's manuscripts is in the Special Collections of Harvard Library. Important material is also housed in the Special Collections of the Bowdoin College Library.

Mrs. Longfellow: Selected Letters and Journals of Fanny Appleton Longfellow (1817–1861). Edited by Edward Wagenkecht. New York: Longmans, Green, 1956. (Presents Longfellow's second wife as an interesting figure in her own right, with a sensibility more wry than her husband's.)

The Letters of Henry Wadsworth Longfellow. 6 vols. Edited by Andrew Hilen. Cambridge, Mass.: Harvard University Press, 1966–1982.

BIBLIOGRAPHY

Livingston, Luther Samuel. *A Bibliography of the First Editions in Book Form of the Writings of Henry Wadsworth Longfellow*. New York, 1908. (Privately printed.)

CRITICAL AND BIOGRAPHICAL STUDIES

Aaron, Daniel. "Introduction." In *Henry Wadsworth Longfellow, The Song of Hiawatha*. London: J. M. Dent, 1992.

Allen, G. W. *American Prosody*. New York: American Book Company, 1935. (Chapter 6 is devoted to Longfellow.)

Arms, George. *The Fields Were Green*. Stanford, Calif.: Stanford University Press, 1948. (A study of the "Fireside Poets"—Longfellow, Bryant, Lowell, Holmes, Whittier—with an incisive chapter on Longfellow.)

Arvin, Newton. *Longfellow: His Life and Work*. Boston: Little, Brown, 1962.

Brooks, Van Wyck. *The Flowering of New England, 1815–1865*. New York: Dutton, 1936.

Charvat, William. "Longfellow" and "Longfellow's Income from His Writing." In *The Profession of Authorship in America, 1800–1870*. Edited by Matthew Bruccoli. Columbus: Ohio University Press, 1968.

Crowinshield, Clara, and Andrew R. Hilen, eds. *Diary: A European Tour with Longfellow, 1835–1836*. Seattle: University of Washington Press, 1956.

Derbyshire, John. "Longfellow and the Fate of Modern Poetry." *New Criterion* 19, no. 4:12–20 (2000).

Ferguson, Robert. "Longfellow's Political Fears: Civic Authority and the Role of the Artist in *Hiawatha* and *The Courtship of Miles Standish*." *American Literature* 50:187–215 (1978).

Fiske, Christabel F. "Mercerized Folklore." *Poet Lore* 31:538–575 (1920). (On *The Song of Hiawatha*.)

Fletcher, Angus. "Whitman and Longfellow: Two Types of the American Poet." *Raritan* 10, no. 4:131–145 (1991).

Gioia, Dana. "Longfellow in the Aftermath of Modernism." In *The Columbia History of American Poetry*. Edited by Jay Parini. New York: Columbia University Press, 1993.

Gorman, H. S. *Longfellow: A Victorian American.* New York: Doran, 1926. (Representative of the unfavorable reaction against Longfellow's reputation forty years after his death.)

Haralson, Eric L. "Mars in Petticoats: Longfellow and Sentimental Masculinity." *Nineteenth-Century Literature* 51, no. 3:327–356 (1996).

Hilen, Andrew. *Longfellow and Scandinavia: A Study of the Poet's Relationship with the Northern Languages and Literature.* New Haven, Conn.: Yale University Press, 1947.

Jones, Howard Mumford. "Longfellow." In *American Writers on American Literature*. Edited by John Macy. New York: H. Liveright, 1931.

Kennedy, William Sloane. *Henry W. Longfellow: Biography, Anecdote, Letters, Criticism.* Cambridge, Mass.: Moses King, 1882.

Longfellow, Samuel. *Life of Henry Wadsworth Longfellow.* 2 vols. Boston: Ticknor, 1886. (Contains excerpts from journals and correspondence and previously unpublished poems. Subsequently published in three volumes, with the inclusion of *Final Memorials*.)

———. *Final Memorials of Henry Wadsworth Longfellow.* Boston: Ticknor, 1887.

Matthews, J. Chesley, ed. *Henry W. Longfellow Reconsidered: A Symposium.* Hartford, Conn.: Transcendental Books, 1973.

Milward, Celia, and Cecelia Tiche. "Whatever Happened to Hiawatha?" *Genre* 6:315–332 (1973).

Osborn, Chase S., and Stellanova Osborn. *Schoolcraft-Longfellow-Hiawatha.* Lancaster, Pa.: Jacques Cattell, 1942.

Papers Presented at the Longfellow Commemorative Conference. Washington, D.C.: Government Printing Office, 1982.

Poe, Edgar Allan. *Essays and Reviews.* Edited by G. R. Thompson. New York: Library of America, 1984. (Contains Poe's reviews and attacks accusing Longfellow of both plagiarism and bad poetry.)

Scramm, Wilbur L. "Hiawatha and Its Predecessors." *Philological Quarterly* 11:321–343 (October 1932).

Seelye, John. "Attic Shape: Dusting off *Evangeline*." *Virginia Quarterly Review* 60:21–44 (1984).

Smeaton, Oliphant. *Longfellow and His Poetry.* London: G. Harrap, 1919.

Thompson, Lawrance. *Young Longfellow (1807–1843).* New York: Macmillan, 1938.

Tucker, Edward L. *The Shaping of Longfellow's "John Endicott": A Textual History including Two Early Versions.* Charlottesville: University Press of Virginia, 1985.

Wagenknecht, Edward. *Longfellow: A Full-Length Portrait.* New York: Longmans, Green, 1955.

———. *Henry Wadsworth Longfellow: Portrait of an American Humanist.* Oxford: Oxford University Press, 1966. (Revision of *Longfellow: A Full-Length Portrait*.)

———. *Henry Wadsworth Longfellow: His Poetry and Prose.* New York: Ungar, 1986.

Ward, Robert S. "Longfellow's Roots in Yankee Soil." *New England Quarterly* 41:180–192 (1968).

Williams, Cecil B. *Henry Wadsworth Longfellow.* New York: Twayne, 1964.

—PAUL JOHNSTON

Robert Lowell

1917–1977

ROBERT LOWELL HAS been called the most important American poet since World War II. Even during his lifetime, Lowell was widely regarded as *the* major poet of his generation. Though time has tempered this judgment with a more balanced critical estimation of Lowell in relation to contemporaries such as Elizabeth Bishop and John Berryman, he remains one of the most accomplished and influential poets of the twentieth century.

The poets in Lowell's generation seemed to suffer with unusual frequency from alcoholism and mental illness, and Lowell was no exception. Throughout his adult life he struggled with manic depression, for which he was hospitalized many times. Yet Lowell's personal difficulties did not prevent him from producing a large and varied body of work. Though he is primarily remembered as a poet, having published twelve collections of poetry during his lifetime, he is also the author of two volumes of poetry in translation, eight plays, and a wide range of critical and autobiographical writing.

Lowell was a great public poet, and yet he is also remembered as one of the first and most influential confessional poets in America. For Lowell, there was no separation between the personal and the political, and though he was not a politician himself, at various points in his life he was an active and influential voice in the political arena. Sometimes in formal verse and sometimes in freer lines, his poems cast a critical and unflinching eye on human failures and limitations, both personal and social. But whether they struggle for transcendence or wrestle with acceptance, his poems never stop searching for new ways to make art out of human experience, and in the process Lowell became famous for repeatedly reinventing himself as a poet.

LOWELL'S LIFE

Robert Traill Spence Lowell IV was born on March 1, 1917, in Boston, to Charlotte Winslow and Robert Traill Spence Lowell III. Both his parents claimed descent from New England nobility. The first Winslows had arrived on the Mayflower; both Edward Winslow and his brother John were governors of Plimouth Plantation. The Lowell family had arrived in the New World only a few years later, in 1639; among the descendents of the first Lowells were the poets James Russell Lowell and Amy Lowell. Lowell's father, however, belonged to a branch of the family that had lost most of its wealth and relied on pedigree for its social status. The elder Robert was an unambitious officer in the navy, more interested in tinkering with radios than advancing his career. Lowell's mother, on the other hand, was the daughter of a self-made millionaire, Arthur Winslow, and had inherited his drive and forceful character. She was dissatisfied with her marriage and did not enjoy being a mother. She exerted considerable pressure on those around her, as though by bending them to her will she could reshape her own. Lowell, an only child, struggled against his mother's attempts to direct and reshape him throughout his life.

Lowell's family moved several times during his childhood, following his father's naval career: from Boston to Philadelphia in 1919, back to Boston in 1921, to Washington in 1923, and then finally to Boston in 1925. At this point, Lowell's parents enrolled him at the Brimmer School. He was not happy there or at home. In his dissatisfaction, he became a schoolyard bully, a role he never entirely outgrew. As a young man, in particular, his forceful personality and his uncommon size and strength allowed him to impose his will on those around him.

During this time, Lowell developed a fictive character—half companion, half alter ego—that would play an active role in his imagination and in his relationships throughout the rest of his life. This character, "Arms of the Law," was a bear (or a "bert," as Lowell liked to call him) who could act at times like a tough, belligerent Irishman and at others like an upper-class Bostonian. He had many of Lowell's own characteristics, including immense physical strength, and he provided a medium for Lowell to externalize troubling emotional conflicts. Arms of the Law also became a means of interacting with other people, and Lowell liked to invent bear characters for each of his friends.

When Lowell was eleven, he transferred to the Rivers School for two years. At Rivers his skirmishes became so violent that he broke his arm, yet this made him feel proud rather than discouraged. In 1930 he began boarding at St. Mark's, a prep school outside Boston. In his first years there, he was a below-average student, and his continuing belligerence earned him the nickname "Cal," a combination of Caligula and Caliban, which he relished for the rest of his life. At this point, however, he began to apply his tremendous energy and determination in more constructive ways. He made two lifelong friends, Frank Parker and Blair Clark; his grades improved; and he began a program of intellectual self-improvement, in which he insisted Parker and Clark join him. He also tried to write poetry, with some guidance from Richard Eberhart, a poet and teacher at St. Mark's. After graduating in 1935, Lowell and his friends spent the summer on Nantucket, living in a small cottage, eating eels supplied by local fishermen, and following a rigorous program of reading and discussion designed by Lowell.

In the fall, the three friends entered Harvard University together, where Lowell's cousin, A. Lawrence Lowell, was president. Lowell disliked Harvard even before he arrived, feeling that his parents had pushed him to follow a conventional path, disregarding his own ambitions. He enrolled only in English classes and soon stopped going to classes altogether. He began to devote all his time to preparing himself for a career as a poet, insisting at the same time that Parker must become a painter and Clark a musician or philosopher.

In May of 1936, at the end of his first year at Harvard, Lowell met Anne Dick, a cousin of Parker's. On their fourth meeting he kissed her and from that point on considered himself engaged. He began to direct her education along with Parker's and Clark's. Lowell announced the engagement in June before leaving for a second summer on Nantucket and on his return took Anne to meet his parents. They were not pleased and did everything they could to discourage the match, which only confirmed the rebellious Lowell in his choice. That Christmas his father wrote a scolding note to Anne's father, accusing Anne of impropriety in her visits to Lowell's room at Harvard. When Anne showed Lowell the note, he went home and knocked his father down.

Lowell's mother turned for help to a psychiatrist and poet named Merrill Moore whom she had been seeing for the past few years. He convinced Lowell to apologize to his father and then arranged for him to attend Vanderbilt, where John Crowe Ransom and Allen Tate were teaching. When Lowell arrived in Nashville, he drove out to Tate's house, expecting to find a room there. Tate tried to brush him off, saying he had no room. With typical chutzpah, Lowell pitched a tent in Tate's yard and stayed for three months, while sitting in on Ransom's classes. At the end of the academic year, Ransom left Vanderbilt for Kenyon, and Lowell decided to follow him.

At Kenyon, Lowell shared a room in Ransom's house with Randall Jarrell, who was working on his master's degree. Lowell spent the year studying English and classics and writing poetry. By this time, his relationship with Anne Dick had fizzled. He began to write frequent and passionate letters to Jean Stafford, whom he had met over the summer at a writers' conference in Colorado. In the fall of 1938, she wrote Lowell to meet her in Cleveland where she would be stopping on her way to Boston. Lowell went and asked her to marry him, and she said she would if he bought her another drink. Lowell took her seriously and followed her to Boston a few weeks later during his Thanksgiving break. Her letters at this time referred to Lowell as a "monster," yet when he returned to Boston that Christmas, she agreed to see him. While driving her home from a nightclub, Lowell crashed the car, breaking Stafford's nose and fracturing her skull. Yet she continued to respond to Lowell's advances, and in 1940, during spring break of Lowell's final year at Kenyon, they were married, without telling Stafford's parents and over the objections of Lowell's.

By this time, Lowell had published some poems in the college literary magazine and one in Ransom's new *Kenyon Review*, confirming him in his desire to be a poet. In 1940 he graduated summa cum laude, Phi Beta Kappa, valedictorian, and class speaker, and then he and Stafford moved to Louisiana State University, where Lowell had been offered a junior fellowship. Lowell did little in Baton Rouge other than read, and his reading began to focus on Catholic theology. He began a course of study, under the guidance of Father Shexnayder, that soon led to his conversion. Typically, Lowell plunged himself—and everyone around him—

into his new enthusiasm with fanatical intensity. As Stafford put it, he became for several years "more Catholic than the church." As Lowell became more obsessive, Stafford drank more heavily, and their uneasy relationship grew more tense, erupting in frequent fights and once—on a trip to New Orleans—physical violence, when Lowell hit Stafford and broke her nose a second time.

In September 1941 Lowell and Stafford moved to New York City where Lowell began working for the Catholic publisher Sheed and Ward. Since his move to Louisiana, Lowell had written almost no poetry. Stafford meanwhile had been working on a novel, *Boston Adventure,* and now entered into negotiations with Robert Giroux at Harcourt, Brace. When she received an advance, she and Lowell decided to combine it with the income from a small trust of Lowell's in order to spend a year living with Tate and his wife, Caroline Gordon, in Monteagle, Tennessee. In May 1942, after eight months in New York, they headed south again.

Though all four writers felt claustrophobic in their new domestic arrangement, each was prolific during this time. Lowell began the year working on a biography of Jonathan Edwards, but this project did not proceed far. Soon he was writing more poems, and by the summer of 1943 he had begun publishing in periodicals again, with poems appearing in *Sewanee Review, Partisan Review,* and *Kenyon Review.* At Tate's urging, he sent a collection of his poems to Cummington Press in Massachusetts, under the title *Land of Unlikeness.* The editors accepted it enthusiastically.

Following the United States' entry into World War II, Lowell not only registered for the draft but also tried more than once to enlist; however, he was rejected because of his poor eyesight. In September 1943, he was called to appear again before the draft board in New York City. By this time, however, he believed that the war had shifted from defensive to aggressive. He wrote a letter to President Franklin Delano Roosevelt expressing his opposition and refusing to serve. His refusal earned him a year and a day in the Federal Correctional Center in Danbury, Connecticut—a light sentence, possibly the result of his Lowell pedigree. On his way to Danbury, he spent a few days at New York's West Street Jail, where Murder, Incorporated's Louis Lepke was also imprisoned (see "Memories of West Street and Lepke" in Lowell's *Life Studies*, 1959).

Lowell served five months of his sentence and was then released on parole on March 15, 1944. He spent the next seven months cleaning floors at St. Vincent's Hospital in Bridgeport, Connecticut, while living with Stafford in Black Rock, a largely Hungarian neighborhood within sight of St. Stephen's Church. He began writing again during this time with great energy and produced some of his first great poems, such as "Colloquy in Black Rock" and "The Quaker Graveyard in Nantucket." In September *Land of Unlikeness* was published in an edition of 250 copies. Stafford's *Boston Adventure* appeared the same month, and by April had sold 400,000 copies and had been nominated for a Pulitzer Prize. If Lowell found his wife's greater success hard to take, he enjoyed the money it brought in, and his own book received a large number of reviews for so small a printing—thanks largely to Lowell's growing network of friends and acquaintances in the literary world, which by this time included Marianne Moore, Delmore Schwartz, Robert Frost, and e. e. cummings, in addition to Ransom, Tate, Jarrell, and Eberhart.

During the summer of 1945, Lowell and Stafford rented a cottage in Boothbay Harbor, Maine, in which they lived while Stafford worked on a new novel and Lowell wrote new poems. These poems, combined with those he had written in Black Rock along with some revised poems from *Land of Unlikeness*, would make up his next book, *Lord Weary's Castle*.

By the end of the summer they had bought a house in Damariscotta Mills. They remained there through January 1946, when they went down to Cambridge to stay with Delmore Schwartz. Though their ménage began well, it ended with Schwartz implying he had had an affair with Stafford and Lowell swinging at him. Lowell and Stafford retreated to Maine, where the next summer brought an excess of guests, including John Berryman. Lowell and Stafford had been increasingly at odds with one another, spurred on by Stafford's drinking and Lowell's mania—including an incident in which he tried to force himself on her. When Gertrude Buckman, Schwartz's former wife, visited, her attentions to Lowell completed Stafford's alienation. They left their Maine house for good on September 20 and moved to New York, to separate apartments.

In New York, Lowell stopped going to church and started seeing Buckman. *Lord Weary's Castle* was published in the fall of 1946, and that winter, Lowell met Elizabeth Bishop, who was just publishing her own first book. In April, Lowell received a Guggenheim Fellowship, a grant from the American Academy of Arts and Letters, and a Pulitzer Prize for *Lord Weary's Castle*. He was then invited to his publisher's offices to meet T. S. Eliot, with whom he began a lifelong friendship.

Lowell spent the summer of 1947 at Yaddo, where he worked on "The Mills of the Kavanaughs" and befriended Theodore Roethke. He and Roethke traveled to the Bread Loaf School of English to read and meet with Frost. In September, Lowell moved to Washington, where he became the Consultant in Poetry to the Library of Congress. While in Washington, Lowell regularly visited Ezra Pound at St. Elizabeth's Hospital, where Pound was incarcerated as a mental patient. He also traveled to Rutherford, New Jersey, to meet William Carlos Williams. He began dating Carley Dawson, a wealthy divorcée and amateur writer seven years his senior, and soon asked her to marry him, but the relationship did not last long.

In September 1948 Lowell returned to Yaddo and stayed for five months working on the ever-expanding "Mills of the Kavanaughs." There he got to know the novelist Elizabeth Hardwick, whom he had first met a few years earlier at parties for the *Partisan Review*. At first the relative solitude agreed with him and his writing went well—but soon his drinking began to increase, and rumors began to circulate in New York that he was becoming manic. When the FBI arrived at Yaddo in February 1949 to investigate its administrator, Elizabeth Ames, and her connection to suspected Communists, Lowell's mania flared. Despite the fact that Ames had been kind to him—letting him remain long past the end of his two-month official stay—he called a meeting of Yaddo's board of directors to demand her removal. His reasoning was disjointed, and Ames was eventually exonerated, but Lowell roared on, headed toward his first breakdown.

Lowell became convinced he was on a divine mission, seeking guidance from Robert Fitzgerald and Flannery O'Connor in New York, and then at the end of March 1949 traveling out to visit Tate in Chicago. A few days after his arrival he handed Gordon a list of Tate's lovers and then held Tate out a second-floor window while reciting "Ode to the Confederate Dead" in the voice of Arms of the Law. Tate called the police, but though it took four of them to wrestle Lowell into submission as he cried out for them to cut off his balls, Tate talked them out of arresting him. Instead he let Lowell take a train down to Bloomington, Indiana, to visit his friend, the writer Peter Taylor. That evening Lowell went on another rampage, running through the streets cursing homosexuals and beating up police officers who tried to subdue him. His mother and Moore flew in the next day and took him, foaming at the mouth, to Baldpate, a small hospital north of Boston,

where he was put in a padded cell, given shock treatments, and medicated.

On the eve of his release, in July 1949, after three months at Baldpate, Lowell wrote Hardwick asking her to marry him. Though his parents disapproved of the relationship, the couple was married in a small ceremony at his parents' house on July 28. By then Lowell was entering a deepening depression, and two weeks later he checked into the Payne Whitney Clinic in New York where he was diagnosed as manic-depressive. Once again he was hospitalized for three months. During this time he finally left the Catholic Church. When he was released in December, he felt like a new man. He accepted a job at the University of Iowa, where W. D. Snodgrass would be among his students, and he and Hardwick moved in January 1950. At the end of August, they were about to set sail for a year in Italy when Lowell's father died. Lowell felt numb, writing to Bishop that "the death seems almost meaningless, as is perhaps always the case when the life has long resigned itself to a terrible dim, diffused pathos."

Lowell and Hardwick settled in Florence in early October 1950. In November they traveled to Rome where Lowell at last met George Santayana, with whom he had been corresponding for four years. Back in Florence, Lowell's writing stalled. *The Mills of the Kavanaughs* was published in the spring of 1951 to mixed reviews, and he was eager to move on to something new, but nothing presented itself. Then Lowell suddenly decided he wanted to move to Amsterdam and sent a reluctant Hardwick ahead to find an apartment, which she finally managed to do at the end of September 1951.

They lived in Amsterdam, writing a little, mostly reading, with very little social life until May 1952, when they headed south to Brussels, Paris, Vienna, and finally Salzburg, where Lowell taught for six weeks at F. O. Mathiessen's Seminar in American Civilization. At the end of the course, Lowell had another manic attack, falling in love with Giovanna Madonia, an Italian music student. Eventually, American military police were called in, and Lowell was taken first to an army hospital in Munich and then to the Binswanger Sanatorium in Kreuzlingen, Switzerland. After ten days he was ready, in mid-September, to travel to Rome, where he and Hardwick settled for three months. At last Lowell began writing again, feeling he was finding the new style for which he had been searching. On January 9, 1953, they sailed home.

Lowell taught at the University of Iowa that spring and the next fall, and at Ransom's School of Letters during the summer. He then accepted the chair of poetry at the University of Cincinnati for the spring of 1954. They had barely settled in when a telegram arrived from Italy where Lowell's mother was traveling: she had suffered a stroke. Lowell reached his mother in Rapallo barely an hour after she died of a second stroke, on February 14. Lowell responded with a mixed sense of loss and relief. Her death left him newly his own man— financially and emotionally—and he quickly headed into a new explosion of mania.

While settling his mother's affairs, Lowell met Madonia and rekindled his affair with her. On March 11 he returned to Cincinnati to announce jauntily that his marriage was over. On April 8 he was committed to the Jewish Hospital, and then after a few weeks was moved to Payne Whitney, where he was treated with Thorazine. He was not released until mid-September. During these outbreaks, Lowell sometimes directed a great deal of anger at Hardwick, as though she were responsible for locking him up, while at other times he was contrite.

Lowell and Hardwick then moved to Boston where Lowell began writing prose reminiscences, partly as a form of therapy. With summer, they spent time in Castine, Maine, where Lowell's cousin Harriet Winslow had a summer house. In the fall they bought a house in Boston at 239 Marlborough Street, a block from Lowell's birthplace. Lowell began teaching at Boston University, and on January 4, 1956, their daughter Harriet was born. In March, Lowell embarked on a West Coast reading tour. This trip had an important effect on his style: he began simplifying lines, adding syllables, and glossing phrases in foreign languages. His prose work likewise pulled his poetry away from a strict adherence to meter.

In December 1957, after a particularly productive fall, Lowell's mania began to resurface, and he was hospitalized again for a month. While in the hospital, Lowell met Ann Adden, a young psychiatric fieldworker. Typically, Lowell's mania focused on Adden. After he was discharged in mid-January, he spent a week shuttling between a room in Harvard Square and Marlborough Street, trying to decide whether to stay with Hardwick or run off with Adden. Finally, he moved back to Marlborough Street, but he was still sick and after a week had to be admitted to McLean's Hospital, where he stayed until the middle of March. His poem "Waking in the Blue" describes his time there, drugged with massive doses of Thorazine, surrounded by other men wrestling with their private demons.

Lowell completed *Life Studies* during the summer of 1958 as he recuperated from his mania. Hardwick, Harriet, and he continued to move back and forth between Castine and Boston. *Life Studies* was published in the spring of 1959. By May Lowell was back in McLean's, where he remained until June. Reviews of *Life Studies* on both sides of the Atlantic were mixed, and his writing stalled again. He turned to translations—of Eugenio Montale, Ranier Maria Rilke, Charles Baudelaire, Johann Wolfgang von Goethe, and Boris Pasternak, among others—while teaching at Boston University and Harvard summer school, where his students now included Anne Sexton and Sylvia Plath.

In September 1960 Lowell and Hardwick moved to New York, on a grant from the Ford Foundation to study opera. Lowell's interest had been turning toward drama, and during the previous summer he had translated Jean Baptiste Racine's *Phèdre* and begun a stage adaptation of Herman Melville's story "Benito Cereno." Lowell and fellow grantee William Meredith sat in on rehearsals and performances at the Metropolitan Opera. In February 1961 Lowell's mania began to resurface, again centering around his enthusiasm for a young woman, Sandra Hochman. This time his psychiatrist, Viola Bernard, did not discourage his manic intentions. But by March 3 even Hochman thought he should be hospitalized. He spent four weeks in the locked ward of the Neurological Institute at the Columbia-Presbyterian Medical Center. When he was released, he set up an apartment with Hochman, so Hardwick took Harriet back to Boston. This seems to have shocked Lowell out of his mania. He left Hochman and joined Hardwick in Boston, where they sold their house and headed to Castine.

The summer of 1961 was restorative and productive. Lowell finished *Benito Cereno* and wrote dramatic adaptations of two stories by Nathaniel Hawthorne: "Endicott and the Red Cross" and "My Kinsman, Major Molineux." Back in New York in the fall, he began once again to write poems. In November he published a collection of his loose translations, which he called *Imitations*. Lowell did well through the winter. In June 1962 he flew to South America with Hardwick and Harriet on an extended trip sponsored by the Congress for Cultural Freedom. They spent the summer of 1962 in Brazil, and then Lowell headed on alone to Buenos Aires on September 4. Lowell was by then drinking heavily, unable to sleep, and gearing up for a major attack of mania. In Buenos Aires he insulted the general who was about to become president of Argentina and then insisted on climbing every equestrian statue in the city.

It eventually took six men to wrestle Lowell into a straitjacket. Blair Clark flew to Buenos Aires to escort Lowell to the Institute for Living in Hartford, Connecticut, where he was committed for six weeks.

Lowell spent the rest of the fall and early winter writing. In February 1963 he began commuting from New York to Harvard twice a week to teach two classes. At the same time he helped start the *New York Review of Books*. That fall, on November 22, President Kennedy was assassinated, one more in a series of dramatic deaths, that included Frost, Plath, Williams, and Roethke. Two weeks later Lowell suffered another attack and was once more committed to the Institute for Living. He came home in January 1964, and was well for most of the year, working on more translations, including a version of the Oresteia. *For the Union Dead* was published and received glowing reviews. In the fall, Jonathan Miller directed *Benito Cereno* and *Major Molineux,* collectively titled *The Old Glory.* At the end of the year Lowell met Vija Vetra, a young Latvian dancer. Soon he was gadding about town with her, introducing her as his fiancée. They rented an apartment together until, on January 25, 1965, Clark and Vetra drove Lowell up to the Institute for Living. After a few weeks he returned home, and his lawyers contacted Vetra and demanded she vacate the apartment.

Early in 1965 President Lyndon Johnson approved bombing raids in Vietnam. Lowell responded as he had to the bombing of German cities during World War II. When he was invited to attend the White House Festival of the Arts on June 14, he sent a letter to Johnson declining the invitation on the grounds that he could "only follow our present foreign policy with the greatest dismay and distrust." He sent a copy to the *New York Times*, which ran the story on the front page. The event turned into a publicity fiasco for the enraged president. In August

Lowell addressed a rally against the war in Washington and was invited to meet Ted Kennedy.

This was not his first meeting with a Kennedy: he had been invited to John F. Kennedy's inauguration, where the new president revealed that he had read *Life Studies*. Then, on the first anniversary of John F. Kennedy's death, Lowell had given Jackie Kennedy inscribed copies of some of his books. On the second anniversary, in 1965, he gave her *The Old Glory*, which had just been published. The book was dedicated to Jarrell, but before Lowell had a chance to send it to him, Jarrell was hit and killed by a car in what may have been a suicide. Lowell was heartbroken. His mania resurfaced, and he spent a brief time at McLean's, returning home in January 1966.

During 1966, his relationship with the Kennedys deepened: he had Jackie to dinner, attended her birthday party, corresponded with Robert, and, when his mania flared up again, called them both to share his ideas on how the government should be run. Over the summer he worked on an adaptation of Aeschylus' *Prometheus Bound* for Peter Brook of the Royal Shakespeare Company and proofed galleys of *Near the Ocean*, which would be published in the spring of 1967.

On Christmas Day 1966 Lowell's mania reached a pitch that again required police intervention. He was taken to McLean's where he stayed until February 1967. His doctors recommended that he switch from Thorazine, which he had by then been taking for twelve years, to lithium carbonate. In June Lowell began with characteristic intensity to write his own poems again after a lull of two years. These were loose "sonnets"—largely unrhymed, unmetered, but more regular than the poems in *For the Union Dead*. At the same time he found himself increasingly called on to perform as a public figure. In September he received an invitation to take part in a protest against the Vietnam War in Washington. One of his com-

panions, Norman Mailer, wrote an account of the experience, published as *Armies of the Night*, which Lowell thought was "one of the best things ever written about me."

That winter Lowell missed what had become his annual breakdown. The lithium seemed to be evening out the highs and lows as it was supposed to, but it did not stop his philandering. He continued to have affairs with younger women in Cambridge and with an assistant of Ivan Illich's at his Center for Intercultural Documentation in Cuernavaca, Mexico, which he visited in January 1968. These affairs were not, however, accompanied by manic proposals of marriage; they were more typical of a middle-aged man attempting to recapture his youth.

During the spring of 1968, Lowell became a traveling companion of Eugene McCarthy during his campaign for the Democratic nomination. McCarthy's primary support, at least initially, came from young idealists, and Lowell joined this "children's crusade" with little hope of success but with real admiration for McCarthy. But Robert Kennedy's assassination in June, the Soviet invasion of Czechoslovakia in August, and the violence-ridden Democratic convention in Chicago later that month left Lowell depressed and frustrated—confirmed in his jaundiced view of American politics.

Lowell once again avoided a winter breakdown, but in March 1969, while traveling in Israel for two weeks, he suffered what at the time he thought was a stroke but which was more likely a by-product of his excessive drinking or of the thyroid medicine he was taking to counteract the effects of the lithium. In April, he and Hardwick and Harriet headed to Maine for their regular summer in Castine, and in June he published *Notebook 1967–68*. That fall Lowell began revising his *Notebook* poems, with Frank Bidart's assistance, as he continued writing new ones.

In April 1970 Lowell moved to Oxford for two months at All Souls College. Soon after he arrived, he accepted a two-year teaching position at the University of Essex. Hardwick and Harriet were to join him as soon as he could find an apartment for them all in London. But before he had even begun looking, he renewed an acquaintance with Lady Caroline Blackwood, a thirty-eight-year-old Irish aristocrat of the Guinness clan, and they quickly fell in love. At first Lowell kept the affair secret; by the time Hardwick found out, she had given up her job at Barnard and Harriet's place in school for the following year.

Hardwick was furious, though she guessed that Lowell was having another attack of mania. In fact it soon became apparent, even to Blackwood who did not yet know Lowell well, that despite the lithium he was in the midst of another breakdown. Lowell was admitted to Greenways Nursing Home in London on July 9. Blackwood was unnerved and departed for Ireland, writing Lowell that she loved him but could not assume responsibility for him. By the time he was released a month later, Blackwood was back in London but would not let him stay with her in the complex of three apartments she shared with her estranged second husband, the composer Israel Citkovitz, and their three daughters. Lowell rented an apartment nearby, and in October he began teaching two days a week at Essex.

Through the new year Lowell continued to waffle in letters to Hardwick over whether he was coming back to her. Then in February 1971 his future was decided by default when Blackwood learned she was pregnant. Lowell welcomed the prospect of a new child as though it justified his leaving Hardwick and helped ease his sense of lost connection with Harriet. Throughout this time he was recording his feelings and experiences in daily fourteen-line poems as he left one family and began another. That spring he visited the London Dolphinarium and found the symbol that would bind these

poems into a book, *The Dolphin*. His son, Sheridan Lowell, was born on September 28, 1971.

When Hardwick heard, through friends who had seen the manuscript, what Lowell's new collection of poems was about, she wrote him to express her distress. He answered that the book need not be published, yet he invited Frank Bidart to visit in January 1972 to help him sort through the mass of poems he had accumulated. When Bidart left six weeks later, Lowell had the manuscripts of three books: *History, For Lizzie and Harriet,* and *The Dolphin.* By September, he had committed to publish *The Dolphin* in July 1973.

In October 1972 Lowell and Blackwood flew to New York—where he signed a divorce settlement with Hardwick—and then on to Santo Domingo, where they divorced their respective spouses and married each other. The next eight months were a lull before the storm that followed the publication of his three books in the summer of 1973. *The Dolphin* in particular was criticized in the United States as insensitive and even cruel in its use of biographical materials, particularly Hardwick's letters and telephone conversations. Its publication led Hardwick to write Lowell that she never wanted to speak to him again—though Harriet was still in London visiting Lowell when the most severe reviews appeared. Lowell had signed his trust fund over to Hardwick, along with the 67th Street apartment; he kept his royalties and $141,000 from the sale of his papers to the Houghton Library at Harvard. Though his financial situation was not desperate, he felt he had to keep teaching, and in the fall he returned to Harvard with his new family.

At the beginning of 1974, they all returned to Milgate, Blackwood's country house an hour outside London. In April *The Dolphin* won Lowell his second Pulitzer, despite the negative reviews. In July Ransom died. W. H. Auden had died the previous September and Pound in November. Lowell was increasingly concerned about his health, which led him to try to give up alcohol. That summer Blackwood had an extended nervous breakdown. In late September Lowell fainted at a party, perhaps because he accidentally drank orange juice with vodka in it. Four months later, in the spring of 1975, back in the United States for another semester teaching at Harvard, Lowell collapsed again while on a trip to New York. At Mount Sinai Hospital it was determined that, fearing a manic attack, he had overdosed on lithium.

Back in England during the summer of 1975, Lowell worked on the free verse poems that would make up *Day by Day* (1977) and put together his *Selected Poems* (published in the spring of 1976). Then in November 1975 the manic attack Lowell had been fearing hit, and he was admitted to the Priory, a private hospital south of London. After two weeks he checked himself out and at Blackwood's suggestion began acupuncture treatments. For the next two months he was alternately at Blackwood's London apartment, where he was attended by nurses twenty-four hours a day; at Greenways; and at St. Andrew's Hospital north of London. By February 1976 he was himself again, but his marriage was in trouble. Blackwood had been severely shaken by Lowell's latest attack, and she herself soon became ill. As they were about to leave for a semester at Harvard, Lowell had another attack and was admitted to Greenways, where he stayed for six weeks. Blackwood, unable to help or bear standing by, fled to Boston.

By the time Lowell joined her in November, it was clear the marriage was in a shambles. Blackwood was drinking heavily, and the tension in their house pushed Lowell into a mild heart attack. Blackwood returned to England with the children, and Lowell waited until mid-December to follow her. They enjoyed a quiet Christmas in Scotland, and then Lowell was back in Cambridge by January 17, 1977, to teach. But in the middle of his second night there, he woke Bidart, with whom he was stay-

ing, saying he had to get to the hospital immediately. He spent ten days at Massachusetts General hospital with congestive heart failure before being released. He resumed teaching, then flew to Dublin, where Blackwood had relocated, to spend spring break with her. The visit was a failure, and he returned to Cambridge with the sense that the marriage was finished.

By this time, Lowell's relationship with Hardwick had improved, through letters, a few brief meetings, shuttling Harriet between them, and now almost-daily phone calls. Hardwick generously offered to let him come and live with her in New York and Castine when the semester ended. Blackwood was upset by this arrangement and tried to convince Lowell to return to her. Though torn, Lowell refused, saying only that he would come for a visit in September. In July he traveled with Hardwick to Moscow for ten days. *Day by Day* was published that summer, to a rave review by Helen Vendler. On September 2 Lowell arrived in Dublin, as he had promised, for a visit of two weeks. But Blackwood was deep in depression and left for London on September 11. Lowell flew back to New York the next day and, in a cab on his way from the airport to West 67th Street, he fell asleep and never woke up. He was buried in his family's graveyard in Dunbarton, New Hampshire.

LOWELL'S WRITING

Lowell's first book, *Land of Unlikeness,* was published in 1944 by Cummington Press in Massachusetts in an edition of only 250 copies. Not unexpectedly, given Lowell's youth—he was only twenty-seven—the poems are uneven: a mishmash of ancient history, Christian imagery, and musings on war. Lowell had converted to Catholicism in 1941, and the poems center around religious iconography and explorations of the role of Catholic doctrine in a world torn apart by war. Reflecting Lowell's training in classics at Kenyon and his extensive reading in literature and history, the poems are also full of historical and literary allusions, as can be seen in this passage from "On the Eve of the Feast of the Immaculate Conception: 1942":

> Six thousand years
> Cain's blood has drummed into my ears,
> Shall I wring plums from Plato's bush
> When Burma's and Bizerte's dead
> Must puff and push
> Blood into bread?

The poems express a tremendous longing for transcendence, and they exhibit Lowell's willingness to tie himself and his verse in knots in the name of redemption, yet they are products of a sensibility that is too bitter, too cynical, to believe in the possibilities for which they strain.

This tension produces poems that seem to pull themselves apart, embodying, as William Doreski points out in *Robert Lowell's Shifting Colors,* the social disintegration they would seem to have been written to heal. Yet this tension is also crucial to these poems, and crucial to most of Lowell's later work as well, which almost obsessively explores ways in which human beings are caught between irreconcilable and inescapable forces in society and in themselves. Though in *Land of Unlikeness* he had not yet learned to turn these disruptive energies to the work's advantage, he can be seen beginning to tackle a number of issues that would prove fruitful in later poems.

Chief among these issues is an intense interest in history and politics. Throughout his work, Lowell demonstrates a conviction that poetry offers a powerful and effective means of addressing important historical and political themes. A number of important critical books address this public, performative side of Lowell's poetry, including, in addition to Doreski, Alan Williamson's *Pity the Monsters* and Patrick Cosgrave's *The Public Poetry of Robert Lowell.* At the same time, however, Low-

ell was also a very self-involved man, and his work therefore also exhibits a more personal, introspective strain. With the publication of *Life Studies,* in fact, he would be credited with initiating a new trend toward confessional poetry.

Although the public and the personal strains appear to be opposed—a looking outward and a turning inward—they coexist in all of Lowell's work, and both are evident in *Land of Unlikeness.* In the selection quoted above, for instance, a line like "Shall I wring plums from Plato's bush" directs the reader's attention to the historical figure of Plato in the same breath in which it foregrounds the speaker as an actor in the poem and posits the speaker's dilemma as its central question. This juxtaposition is typical of Lowell's work, for he consistently treats historical figures as if they were contemporaries and portrays his speaker as caught up in historical struggles and doubts. Lowell's poems view the historical in personal terms and recognize in the personal the ongoing processes of history.

Formally, the poems in *Land of Unlikeness* demonstrate an intense attention to craft, a reliance on structural devices such as meter and rhyme, and a mastery of the techniques of formal verse. At the same time, however, there is a subtle but persistent resistance to formal constraint in these poems, in two senses. First, the rhythms of Lowell's lines strain against their meter, rejecting the fluidity and polish of the Romantics and assuming a roughness beyond even the more turbulent lines of William Butler Yeats or the colloquial rhythms of Frost. Second, Lowell's diction often suggests an affinity for direct speech and a mistrust of typically "poetic" language, as can be seen in the reference to "Burma's and Bizerte's dead."

The development of Lowell's verse is sometimes characterized as a movement away from regular form in favor of free verse, and indeed his later poems tend to be "freer" than his earlier ones; but the movement is not a simple one.

After *The Mills of the Kavanaughs* (1951), Lowell did turn to freer verse in his next two books, *Life Studies* (1959) and *For the Union Dead* (1964); yet even these poems are exhaustively crafted. The poems in his next book, *Near the Ocean* (1967), were written in a meter borrowed from Andrew Marvell, and the five books after that—*Notebook 1967–1968* (1969), *Notebook* (1970), *History* (1973), *For Lizzie and Harriet* (1973), and *The Dolphin* (1973)—were all written in loose sonnet form. Only in his last book, *Day by Day* (1977), did he turn to free verse in its conventional sense. Therefore, it is more useful to think of Lowell's verse as the product of a tension between his belief in the aesthetic potentials of form and his desire for direct expression unmediated by aesthetic concerns. Throughout his career, he explored different ways of responding to this tension without, not surprisingly, ever resolving it.

Lowell recognized the limitations of his first book almost immediately, and freely plundered it in the process of preparing his second book, *Lord Weary's Castle* (1946), using a few poems from the earlier volume with minor revisions, heavily revising others, incorporating pieces of the old poems in new ones, and abandoning the rest. He never made any effort to reprint *Land of Unlikeness*, and years later when he assembled his *Selected Poems*, he included no poems earlier than *Lord Weary's Castle*. Because of this, and the book's small initial press run, the poems in *Land of Unlikeness* are hard to find, and for all practical purposes, *Lord Weary's Castle* stands as Lowell's first mature volume. It earned him his first Pulitzer Prize.

Most of the poems in *Lord Weary's Castle* are written in a style that accentuates the thickness of language: that is, they call attention to words instead of attempting to focus primarily on meaning. They do this in a number of ways. First, they emphasize metaphoric rather than literal language, requiring the reader to pause often to consider which connotations of a given word should be followed and which should be set aside. Second, they stress the sounds of the words they use, incorporating many heavily stressed words with thick consonantal clusters. Third, they incorporate foreign words and phrases, primarily from Latin. Fourth, the poems are all strictly metered and rhymed, though in some of them Lowell allows himself the flexibility of uneven line length. In the first section of "The Quaker Graveyard in Nantucket," the most famous poem in *Lord Weary's Castle*, for instance, the lines vary from two feet (four syllables) to five feet (ten syllables).

Like a number of the other poems in *Lord Weary's Castle*, "The Quaker Graveyard" is based on incidents in Lowell's family history—in this case, the death by drowning of his cousin Warren Winslow, a young naval officer—which Lowell fuses with a wide range of literary and historical sources. The result is a poem that embodies the breadth of Lowell's concerns during this period. For instance, its elegiac form pays homage to John Milton's famous elegy "Lycidas" (which, during one of his manic episodes, Lowell was convinced he had written), suggesting Lowell's deep immersion in the work of his literary forebears as well as his desire to emulate their achievements. In addition to its secular sources, "The Quaker Graveyard" is also full of allusions to the Bible and to Catholic doctrine, reflecting Lowell's recent conversion to Catholicism and his struggle to reconcile his new faith with his rational, literary, and historical sensibilities. In addition, the poem incorporates themes, incidents, and images from Herman Melville's novel *Moby-Dick*, indicating Lowell's abiding fascination with the two-sided coin of transcendental experience: the sublime and the apocalyptic.

The central importance of *Moby-Dick* in "The Quaker Graveyard" also points to the extensive use Lowell made of prose sources. The sixth section of "The Quaker Graveyard" ("Our Lady of Walsingham"), for example, is "an adaptation of several paragraphs from E. I. Watkin's *Catholic Art and Culture*," as Lowell tells us in an introductory note to *Lord Weary's Castle*. Likewise, "Mr. Edwards and the Spider" is based on the writings of Jonathan Edwards, the eighteenth-century American theologian, as is "After the Surprising Conversions." Other poems, such as "The Exile's Return," rely on additional prose sources, as Hugh Staples discusses in *Robert Lowell: The First Twenty Years*.

One of the most significant effects of Lowell's use of prose sources is that it introduces a colloquial tone into some of his poems. "Mr. Edwards and the Spider," for instance, begins and ends with striking images rendered in a flatter, more conversational tone than is usual in most of the poems in this volume:

> I saw the spiders marching through the air,
> Swimming from tree to tree that mildewed day
>   In latter August when the hay
>   Came creaking to the barn. . . .
> . . . .
> . . . this is death,
> To die and know it. This is the Black Widow,
>   death.

Compare these lines with the following more typical passage from "Winter in Dunbarton":

> This winter all the snowmen turn to stone,
> Or, sick of the long hurly-burly, rise
> Like butterflies into Jehovah's eyes
> And shift until their crystals must atone
>
> In water.

While "Mr. Edwards and the Spider" discusses death and eternal damnation, these lines describe a far more mundane occurrence—a snowman melting—yet in far more elevated, grandiose language.

In part, the prose source of "Mr. Edwards and the Spider" may have helped to tamp down Lowell's rhetoric. Another important factor,

however, is that Edwards' own writing already incorporates the encounter with forces that are sublime, or apocalyptic, or both, that Lowell seems to long for and to fear in each poem in *Lord Weary's Castle,* and this may have freed him from the sense that his own poem needed to strain quite so hard. But as the lines from "Winter in Dunbarton" make clear, even the most everyday experience becomes, in *Lord Weary's Castle,* a stage on which archetypal forces struggle and create the possibility of sublimity, apocalypse, or both. As a result, even when Lowell writes directly about personal experiences, as he does in a number of these poems—including "Buttercups," "In Memory of Arthur Winslow," "Mary Winslow," "Rebellion," and "In the Cage"—the elevated, highly metaphorical language tends to distance both reader and speaker from the experience at hand. This is not surprising, of course, since the primary effect of the sublime, as Henry Hart points out in *Robert Lowell and the Sublime,* is to lift us above mundane experience.

In addition to the "original" poems in *Lord Weary's Castle,* the volume also contains six poems identified as being "after" the work of earlier writers, including Paul Valéry, Arthur Rimbaud, Rilke, and Sextus Propertius. Lowell tells the reader in his introductory note that each of these is "not a translation but an imitation which should be read as though it were an original English poem." Throughout his career, Lowell turned to these loose translations or "imitations" of other writers, particularly when he was stymied in his own "original" work. Over the years he published two separate collections of these poems, *Imitations* (1961) and *The Voyage and Other Versions of Poems by Baudelaire* (1968), as well as versions of three dramatic works—Racine's *Phèdre* (1961) and Aeschylus' *Prometheus Bound* (1969) and *Oresteia* trilogy (1978)—and dramatic adaptations of two short stories by Nathaniel Hawthorne— "My Kinsman, Major Molineux" and "Endicott and the Red Cross"—along with Herman Melville's novella "Benito Cereno," under the collective title *The Old Glory* (1965). His poetic translations have been both praised and criticized for their originality.

Lowell's next book, *The Mills of the Kavanaughs* (1951), contains only seven poems, but the title poem of the book is a 600-line narrative written in heroic couplets. It is a complex, convoluted poem, full of nightmare sequences, that explores the relationship between a husband and wife, Harry and Anne Kavanaugh. The story is set in Maine, where Lowell and Stafford had a summer house, and it draws heavily on autobiographical materials, but distances and disguises them as fictional. Reviewers of the book found the characters unconvincing and the narrative chaotic. Lowell himself had difficulty writing the poem and was never fully satisfied with it. In his *Selected Poems,* he cut the poem down to a mere eighty lines. Another poem in *The Mills of the Kavanaughs,* "Her Dead Brother," also makes use of biographical materials, but from Stafford's life rather than Lowell's; and Stafford's distress over this invasion of her privacy prefigured Hardwick's response to Lowell's use of her letters and conversations in *The Dolphin.* The best-received poems in the book were "Falling Asleep over the Aeneid," which describes an old man in Concord, Massachusetts, missing church to drowse over a copy of Virgil's epic poem; and "Mother Marie Therese," a monologue in the manner of Robert Browning, memorializing a drowned abbess.

Then, in 1959, Lowell published *Life Studies,* almost certainly his most influential, groundbreaking work, for which he won the National Book Award. The book is in four parts—the first, third, and fourth are verse; the second is a long prose memoir, "91 Revere Street." It was particularly influential in several ways: in form, in subject matter, and in voice. The four poems in the first section are rhymed and in regular meter (if somewhat looser than Lowell's previ-

ous poems). The four poems in the third section display a wider range of form, from the sonnet, "Words for Hart Crane"; through the broken and haphazardly rhymed iambic pentameter of "Ford Madox Ford"; to the chopped lines (including, most dramatically, "-'s web-") of "To Delmore Schwartz." Finally, the fourth part—which is itself titled "Life Studies" and which is also by far the longest poetry section—continues the "free verse" of "To Delmore Schwartz." *Life Studies,* therefore, embodies a movement from formal verse to free verse. Yet the appearance of freedom is somewhat misleading, for although it may be said that the free verse "triumphs" in the book, the overall structure and effect of *Life Studies* would not be possible without the inclusion of the formal poems of the first section or the mixed poems of the third.

Furthermore, even the poems in the fourth section are not as "free" as they appear at first. For one thing, Lowell originally wrote many of these poems (including "To Delmore Schwartz") in strict form and then purposefully broke them in revision. In addition, a number of these poems derive from autobiographical prose pieces, and so they represent further instances of the kind of crafting and adapting of prose that he undertook in *Lord Weary's Castle.* Also, these poems regularly make use of rhythmical patterns, intermittent (or even regular) rhyme, and regular stanzas. In fact, the last two poems in the book are perhaps the most "formal" of the section. "'To Speak of Woe That Is in Marriage'" prefigures the fourteen-liners, or loose sonnets, Lowell would begin to write in the mid-1960s, except that its form is even more strict, being written entirely in heroic couplets, except for the first two lines, which are alexandrines. Likewise, "Skunk Hour" is written in six-line stanzas, and most of the lines are end-rhymed. Therefore, if free verse triumphs in the book as a whole, formal verse stages a comeback at the end.

While Lowell's move into free verse surprised and either delighted or alienated readers, his subject matter was equally shocking to those familiar with his earlier work. Suddenly this author of abstract, intellectual verse, this Roman Catholic poet who had attributed even the behavior of the family cat to transcendental forces, was writing confessional poetry that focused on the intensely personal, sometimes humiliating details of his marriage, his relatives' lives, and his own mental disease. Now, rather than searching for sublimity in daily life, he was deflating hopes for greater meaning, exposing the sordid ironies of human aspirations, and focusing on the absurd and seemingly trivial details that surround even the most serious, elevated experiences, such as death. So he notes in "Sailing Home from Rapallo" that "In the grandiloquent lettering on Mother's coffin, / Lowell had been misspelled LOVEL"; and in "Terminal Days at Beverly Farms," he chooses to describe his father's death in these terms: "After a morning of anxious, repetitive smiling, / his last words to Mother were: / 'I feel awful'"; and in "My Last Afternoon with Uncle Devereux Winslow," he portrays his dying uncle in the following way:

> . . . as brushed as Bayard, our riding horse.
> His face was putty.
> . . . .
> like a ginger snap man in a clothes-press.

Along with Lowell's shift in subject matter went a shift in voice. The speakers in Lowell's previous poems had been either highly educated, disembodied voices or personae employed in the service of a larger conceptual vision. But the speakers in the final section of *Life Studies* are not distinguishable from Lowell. Likewise, the language Lowell used had been thick, metaphorical, and allusive, whereas in *Life Studies* he turns to a more transparent, literal, immediate style. There are, of course, many reasons for a shift of this sort, but as Paul Mariani emphasizes in *Lost Puritan,* one of these

was the influence of William Carlos Williams' insistently American idiom, which was now balancing Lowell's earlier indebtedness to T. S. Eliot's and Ezra Pound's more European, academic styles. In this move, Lowell was part of a larger development in American poetry, coming closer to the work of his friend Elizabeth Bishop (see David Kalstone, *Becoming a Poet*), and his student W. D. Snodgrass.

Lowell's next volume of original poems, *For the Union Dead* (1964), does not present any radical surprises. It continues in the confessional vein with the same literal, direct voice, though a number of the poems are spoken by personae who are quite clearly distinct from Lowell. The main difference in these poems is that their tone is on the whole more moderate and less bitter (though there are exceptions, notably the title poem that ends the volume). Their forms are also generally more regular: most are written in consistent stanzas with one or two pairs of rhymes per stanza, as though with "Skunk Hour," the poem that ends *Life Studies,* Lowell had found a comfortable level of formal constraint into which he settles in *For the Union Dead.* Finally, it is worth recalling that despite the personal, confessional nature of these poems, they remain strongly committed to the exploration of political and historical themes. This can be seen clearly, for example, in "For the Union Dead," which addresses the degeneration of Boston by centering on the construction of a parking garage under Boston Common, near Augustus Saint-Gaudens' memorial to the Civil War colonel Robert Shaw and his African-American regiment.

In *Near the Ocean* (1967), Lowell returns to a more formal verse, this time tetrameter couplets modeled after Andrew Marvell. The volume is thin, though it was expensively (some critics said ostentatiously) produced with illustrations by Sidney Nolan, and once again a number of the poems are loose translations of other poets' work. At their best, however, the poems in this volume have a linguistic vitality that lives up to the energy and effectiveness of Lowell's previous work:

> O to break loose, like the chinook
> salmon jumping and falling back,
> nosing up to the impossible
> stone and bone-crushing waterfall—
> raw-jawed, weak-fleshed there, stopped by ten
> steps of the roaring ladder, and then
> to clear the top on the last try,
> alive enough to spawn and die.

These lines from the opening of "Waking Early Sunday Morning" introduce a new attitude in Lowell's verse. Though the language remains vigorous, the tone is at once more celebratory of life and more exhausted. The book was published as Lowell turned fifty, and a distinct note of nostalgia had begun to sound in his poems.

In 1969 Lowell published *Notebook 1967–68,* a collection of fourteen-line poems, or loose sonnets. Although he wrote these poems almost daily over the course of a year, beginning, as the title suggests, in 1967, and although they incorporate a great deal of autobiographical material, they do not constitute a journal. The word "notebook" is entirely appropriate here, for the poems resemble notes Lowell wrote to himself in an associative shorthand about subjects ranging from Rembrandt to Margaret Fuller to the Vietnam War to visiting his dentist. The poems are fragmentary, allusive, and elusive: as Lowell wrote in an "Afterthought" to the collection, "I lean heavily to the rational, but am devoted to surrealism." The poems are, therefore, difficult to interpret, and at their worst they seem like the disjointed jottings of a self-involved eccentric; yet the collection has a tremendous power as a whole, and the verse is generally compelling, energetic, even daring. If "one wants words meat-hooked from the living steer," as Lowell writes in "The Nihilist as Hero," these poems will reward a patient reader, though they will resist exegesis.

Lowell recognized the inherent arbitrariness of these poems, and he struggled to find an organizing principle that would help them to cohere. In 1970 he published a revised and expanded edition of the book, titled simply *Notebook.* In both these editions, Lowell tries to make the poems hold together in two ways: first, through their temporal organization, which (sometimes loosely) follows the passage of one season to the next; and second, by virtue of the unifying consciousness of their speaker. In an important sense, these poems can be read as a remarkable attempt to construct a persona in verse, along lines very different from the narrative-driven monologues of Robert Browning. These poems more closely resemble the fragmented consciousness of Eliot's *The Waste Land* (1922); yet where Eliot's famous poem constructs an abstract persona—a spirit of the age—out of multiple voices, Lowell uses a single voice to build a fuller, richly realized individual persona. Though Lowell's may seem the more modest endeavor, it is in the end at least as ambitious and just as much a synthesis of the historical and political issues of the age.

Yet Lowell remained unsatisfied with the organization of these volumes, and in 1973 he published two further revisions and extensions: *History* and *For Lizzie and Harriet.* The first of these books arranges Lowell's more overtly historical poems in chronological order. The second gathers the more obviously personal poems in a volume named for Lowell's wife, Elizabeth Hardwick, and his daughter, Harriet—even though he had just divorced Hardwick the year before. When he assembled his *Selected Poems* (1976), these were the volumes from which he excerpted his fourteen-liners, rather than from *Notebook 1967–68* or *Notebook,* an indication that he believed the later volumes superseded the earlier.

Lowell published a third volume of poems in 1973, titled *The Dolphin.* Of his three books published that year, *The Dolphin* is generally considered the most important, and it earned him his second Pulitzer Prize. In some ways, though, this judgment is curious, since the poems in *The Dolphin* are indistinguishable from those in *History* and *For Lizzie and Harriet* in form or voice. What seems to differentiate *The Dolphin* from its companion volumes is its (sometimes elusive) narrative structure: the book recounts, though in fictionalized form, Lowell's experience of falling in love with Caroline Blackwood, the dolphin of the title; leaving Hardwick; and having a son with his new love. When the book was first published, it received many hostile reviews, primarily from critics who believed that Lowell's treatment of these personal matters was not an appropriate poetic subject. These critics, notably Adrienne Rich, who had formerly been a friend of Lowell's, disparaged Lowell's behavior and, in particular, his use in the poems of extensive quotations from Hardwick's letters and conversations.

Lowell's final book of poetry, *Day by Day,* published in 1977, the year of his death, is the least formal of all his verse. Yet this time, the shift to free verse may have been involuntary. As he writes in "Epilogue," the final poem in the book (with the exception of three translations gathered in an appendix):

> Those blessèd structures, plot and rhyme—
> why are they no help to me now
> I want to make
> something imagined, not recalled?

Throughout his career, Lowell believed that a poem "*is* an event, not a record of an event," as Helen Vendler recalls in her essay "Lowell in the Classroom," collected in Jeffrey Meyers' *Robert Lowell* (1988). Although his verse is consistently filled with details culled from memory and history, it is never meant as a mere record of the events it invokes. For Lowell, poems were made—willful creations that transformed the raw materials of memory and his-

tory into imaginative events—and formal techniques were essential tools in that making.

Yet here, at the end of his life, he seems to feel that those techniques were failing him, that he was losing the ability to transform or transcend the experiences of mundane life:

> But sometimes everything I write
> with the threadbare art of my eye
> seems a snapshot,
> lurid, rapid, garish, grouped,
> heightened from life,
> yet paralyzed by fact.

The young Lowell would have burned and raved in response to such a feeling of helplessness, but the mature Lowell demonstrates more humility. In the face of his own limitations, he writes, "Yet why not say what happened? / Pray for the grace of accuracy / Vermeer gave to the sun's illumination." This is not an admission of defeat—for he is still reaching for the artistry of a Vermeer, not settling for a snapshot—but it does signal a new level of acceptance of the constraints of human life and art. So *Day by Day* strikes many readers as a falling-off, a less vigorous and crafted collection. But if *Life Studies* took advantage of looser form to avoid the abstraction that sometimes makes the poems in Lowell's first volumes seem remote from human experience, *Day by Day* extends that effort, seeking a more direct engagement with life as it is lived every day, and so it makes a fitting conclusion to a career devoted to searching for more effective ways to transform personal experience and historical incident into lasting art.

Selected Bibliography

WORKS OF ROBERT LOWELL

POETRY

Land of Unlikeness. Cummington, Mass.: Cummington Press, 1944.

Lord Weary's Castle. New York: Harcourt, Brace, 1946.

The Mills of the Kavanaughs. New York: Harcourt, Brace, 1951.

Life Studies. New York: Farrar, Straus and Cudahy, 1959.

Imitations. New York: Farrar, Straus and Cudahy, 1961.

For the Union Dead. New York: Farrar, Straus and Giroux, 1964.

Near the Ocean. New York: Farrar, Straus and Giroux, 1967.

The Voyage and Other Versions of Poems by Baudelaire. New York: Farrar, Straus and Giroux, 1968.

Notebook 1967–68. New York: Farrar, Straus and Giroux, 1969.

Notebook. New York: Farrar, Straus and Giroux, 1970.

The Dolphin. New York: Farrar, Straus and Giroux, 1973.

For Lizzie and Harriet. New York: Farrar, Straus and Giroux, 1973.

History. New York: Farrar, Straus and Giroux, 1973.

Selected Poems. New York: Farrar, Straus and Giroux, 1976.

Day by Day. New York: Farrar, Straus and Giroux, 1977.

PLAYS

Phaedra: Racine's "Phèdre" in an English Version by Robert Lowell. New York: Farrar, Straus and Cudahy, 1961.

The Old Glory. New York: Farrar, Straus and Giroux, 1965.

Prometheus Bound. New York: Farrar, Straus and Giroux, 1969.

The Oresteia of Aeschylus. New York: Farrar, Straus and Giroux, 1978.

PROSE

Collected Prose. New York: Farrar, Straus and Giroux, 1987.

CRITICAL AND BIOGRAPHICAL STUDIES

Axelrod, Steven Gould. *Robert Lowell: Life and Art.* Princeton, N.J.: Princeton University Press, 1978.

————, ed. *The Critical Response to Robert Lowell.* Westport, Conn.: Greenwood Press, 1999.

Axelrod, Steven Gould, and Helen Deese. *Robert Lowell: A Reference Guide.* Boston: G. K. Hall, 1982.

————, eds. *Robert Lowell: Essays on the Poetry.* Cambridge: Cambridge University Press, 1987.

Bell, Vereen M. *Robert Lowell, Nihilist as Hero.* Cambridge, Mass.: Harvard University Press, 1983.

Bloom, Harold, ed. *Robert Lowell.* New York: Chelsea House, 1987.

Cooper, Philip. *The Autobiographical Myth of Robert Lowell.* Chapel Hill: University of North Carolina Press, 1970.

Cosgrave, Patrick. *The Public Poetry of Robert Lowell.* London: V. Gollancz, 1970.

Crick, John. *Robert Lowell.* Edinburgh: Oliver and Boyd, 1974.

Doreski, William. *The Years of Our Friendship: Robert Lowell and Allen Tate.* Jackson: University Press of Mississippi, 1990.

————. *Robert Lowell's Shifting Colors: The Poetics of the Public and the Personal.* Athens: Ohio University Press, 1999.

Fein, Richard J. *Robert Lowell.* New York: Twayne, 1970.

Hamilton, Ian. *Robert Lowell: A Biography.* New York: Random House, 1982.

Hart, Henry. *Robert Lowell and the Sublime.* Syracuse, N.Y.: Syracuse University Press, 1995.

Heep, Hartmut. *A Different Poem: Rainer Maria Rilke's American Translators Randall Jarrell, Robert Lowell, and Robert Bly.* New York: Peter Lang, 1996.

Hobsbaum, Philip. *A Reader's Guide to Robert Lowell.* London: Thames and Hudson, 1988.

Kalstone, David. *Becoming a Poet: Elizabeth Bishop with Marianne Moore and Robert Lowell.* Ann Arbor: University of Michigan Press, 2000.

London, Michael, and Robert Boyers, eds. *Robert Lowell: A Portrait of the Artist in His Time.* New York: D. Lewis, 1970.

Mackinnon, Lachlan. *Eliot, Auden, Lowell: Aspects of the Baudelairean Inheritance.* London: Macmillan, 1983.

Mariani, Paul L. *Lost Puritan: A Life of Robert Lowell.* New York: Norton, 1994.

Martin, Jay. *Robert Lowell.* Minneapolis: University of Minnesota Press, 1970.

Matterson, Stephen. *Berryman and Lowell: The Art of Losing.* Basingstoke, Eng.: Macmillan, 1988.

Mazzaro, Jerome. *The Poetic Themes of Robert Lowell.* Ann Arbor: University of Michigan Press, 1965.

Meyers, Jeffrey. *Manic Power: Robert Lowell and His Circle.* London: Macmillan, 1987.

————, ed. *Robert Lowell: Interviews and Memoirs.* Ann Arbor: University of Michigan Press, 1988.

Parkinson, Thomas Francis, ed. *Robert Lowell: A Collection of Critical Essays.* Englewood Cliffs, N.J.: Prentice-Hall, 1968.

Perloff, Marjorie. *The Poetic Art of Robert Lowell.* Ithaca, N.Y.: Cornell University Press, 1973.

Price, Jonathan, ed. *Critics on Robert Lowell.* Coral Gables, Fla.: University of Miami Press, 1972.

Procopiow, Norma. *Robert Lowell: The Poet and His Critics.* Chicago: American Library Association, 1984.

Raffel, Burton. *Robert Lowell.* New York: Ungar, 1982.

Rudman, Mark. *Robert Lowell: An Introduction to the Poetry.* New York: Columbia University Press, 1983.

Smith, Vivian Brian. *The Poetry of Robert Lowell.* Sydney: Sydney University Press, 1974.

Staples, Hugh. *Robert Lowell: The First Twenty Years.* New York: Farrar, Straus and Cudahy, 1962.

Stuart, Sarah Payne. *My First Cousin Once Removed: Money, Madness, and the Family of Robert Lowell.* New York: HarperCollins, 1998.

Tillinghast, Richard. *Robert Lowell's Life and Work: Damaged Grandeur.* Ann Arbor: University of Michigan Press, 1995.

Travisano, Thomas J. *Midcentury Quartet: Bishop, Lowell, Jarrell, Berryman, and the Making of a Postmodern Aesthetic.* Charlottesville: University Press of Virginia, 1999.

Vendler, Helen. *The Given and the Made: Strategies of Poetic Redefinition.* Cambridge, Mass.: Harvard University Press, 1995.

Wallingford, Katharine. *Robert Lowell's Language of the Self.* Chapel Hill: University of North Carolina Press, 1988.

Williamson, Alan. *Pity the Monsters: The Political Vision of Robert Lowell.* New Haven, Conn.: Yale University Press, 1974.

Witek, Terri. *Robert Lowell and* Life Studies: *Revising the Self.* Columbia: University of Missouri Press, 1993.

Yenser, Stephen. *Circle to Circle: The Poetry of Robert Lowell.* Berkeley: University of California Press, 1975.

—JOHN CANADAY

Norman Mailer

1923–

ONE WAY TO understand the diversity of the career of Norman Mailer, its complex relationship with his personal life, and the sharply divided opinion of the merit of his achievements is to see all of these as reflections of Mailer's effort to stay alive spiritually, artistically, even physically. "Repetition kills the soul" is a favored mantra of Mailer's even if, in mid-career, he was guilty of it. But for the great majority of his writing life he has moved back and forth through the literary genres, rotating his crops, so to speak, among the novel (always the favored form), novellas, short stories, every sort of essay, sports and political reportage, screenplays, film and book reviews, the interview, plays, the nonfiction novel, newspaper and magazine columns, a bit of science fiction, a few scraps of memoir, philosophical dialogues, brief and extended biographies and poems. Speaking in the voice of Jesus, he has even retold the Gospels. He has put his hand to virtually every form, everything but autobiography, which he has avoided in the belief that such a volume would be a tombstone. Mailer's Emersonian belief in the infinitude of the self, a self energized by new ventures, precludes the sort of summing up that a full-scale autobiography demands.

Mailer is one of the most well-known living American authors; his renown is due first of all to the length of his career and his many different and important works. But there are other factors: his forays into public life; his attempts to delineate the art in politics and the politics in art; his fights, causes, underground films, divorces, and other legal problems; and his relentless appearances in the media. He has been on the cover of every major American magazine and has appeared on nearly every talk show in existence. It is safe to say that he has been interviewed on radio, television, and in print more than any other author, well over five hundred times. Although he has little use for the Internet, his presence there is also large. He has been tremendously productive, publishing forty books from 1948 to 2003, but he has also been a provocateur, a performer, and a regular in gossip columns. His life, especially after the 1950s, has alternated between monkish labor—when he is working, he writes almost every day—and heralded appearances at literary events, protest meetings, intellectual forums, fund-raising receptions, college campuses, and, of course, on television. He is the prototypical public artist–intellectual of the last half of the twentieth century. In his essay "Prolegomenon to a Biography of Mailer," collected in *Critical Essays on Norman Mailer* (1986), the dean of Mailer critics, Robert F. Lucid, says Mailer "may seem finally to have embodied our time."

No discussion of the modern American novel would be complete without reference to his novels, several of which have become classics; no record of the "new journalism" and the nonfiction novel (Mailer dislikes the term) could pass over his contributions to the form, which some critics believe he, more than anyone else, invented; no examination of several post–World War II events, movements, and phenomena—the cold war, the rise of feminism, the Kennedy assassination, the moon shot, the great prize fights, presidential campaigns and elections (he has covered six), capital punishment, and the compacted miseries of urban life—could eschew his commentary. In the unlikely event that plastic is ever banned for its ill effects, Mailer will be credited for his strident warnings; any consideration of the role of the postwar author as celebrity hero in opposition to the deadening effects of modern technology, bureaucracy, and the corporation will have to begin with Norman Mailer.

EARLY YEARS

Mailer's mother's family ran small resort hotels on the Jersey Shore, and he was born there, in Long Branch, on January 31, 1923. He grew up in Brooklyn, where his parents moved in 1925. He was the first child of Isaac Barnett "Barney" Mailer, who emigrated from South Africa after World War I, and Fanny Schneider Mailer, whose family came from Lithuania a generation earlier. His sister, Barbara Jane, was born on April 6, 1927. His parents had lifelong professional occupations: he was an accountant, and she managed a series of small businesses. In 1933 the family moved to Crown Heights, a bastion of the Jewish middle class. Mailer attended public schools, skipping two half-year terms, and in 1939, at sixteen, graduated with high grades from Boys High School. He applied to Harvard and the Massachusetts Institute of Technology, choosing the former partly because an older cousin had gone there. Intending to major in aeronautical engineering, he immediately became entranced with his creative writing classes, reviving the interest he had had as a young boy.

Mailer wrote scores of stories and took every available writing class while at Harvard, and in April 1941, one of them, "The Greatest Thing in the World," won *Story* magazine's college contest. The influence of three writers—John Dos Passos, James T. Farrell, and John Steinbeck—was apparent in the story, a fast-paced, naturalistic tale of violence and hustling set in Chicago. The story's success convinced him

that he was launched as a writer, and in the summer of 1941 he began his first novel, "No Percentage," which is still unpublished. When he graduated in June 1943 with a degree in engineering sciences (with honors), World War II was raging, and he wondered, as he told the story later in *Advertisements for Myself* (1959), whether "a great war novel would be written about Europe or the Pacific." He was already carefully planning his literary career.

THE ARMY AND THE ARMY NOVEL

Before shipping out to the Pacific as an artillery trainee, Mailer married his college sweetheart, Beatrice "Bea" Silverman, and completed a second apprentice novel, *A Transit to Narcissus*, which remained unpublished until 1978. He arrived in Leyte in the Philippines in late December 1944 and shortly after was reassigned to the 112th Regimental Combat Team, a Texas outfit, serving first as a clerk and then as a rifleman in a reconnaissance squad. Mailer went on patrols, dug foxholes, got into a few firefights, and carefully observed his fellow soldiers, the landscape, the weather, and the ways in which the army shaped behavior. His lifelong interest in the permutations of power began with his study of the "fear ladder" of the army. He sent hundreds of letters to Bea describing daily incidents that would be used in the war novel he planned to write after the war. The central action of the novel was to be a long patrol, one that resembled in many ways an actual patrol behind enemy lines that his platoon had undertaken. The patrol ended disastrously, as he later recounted in an interview with Steven Marcus (collected in J. Michael Lennon, *Conversations with Norman Mailer*, 1988), when someone in his unit kicked over a hornet's nest and half of the men ran ingloriously down the mountain. "War is disproportions," he told Marcus, "and the hornet's nest seemed a perfect disproportion to me. We were ready to lose our lives but we weren't up to getting stung by a hornet."

After the war ended in August 1945 Mailer was sent to Japan, where he served as a cook. He was discharged on May 2, 1946, and in June began work on what was to become *The Naked and the Dead* (1948) in a rented apartment in North Truro, Massachusetts, near Provincetown, the town in which he would spend most of his summers for the next half-century. In November of the same year, he signed a contract with Rinehart and Company, and in September 1947, he turned in a completed manuscript. Then he and Bea, also a veteran, left for Paris to study at the Sorbonne on the GI Bill. When the book came out, on May 6, 1948, Mailer was still in Europe. The reviews were overwhelmingly enthusiastic, and one of the most dazzling careers in postwar American literature was launched. *The Naked and the Dead* was aided by timing: immediately after the war readers wanted to forget about it, but then there was a resurgence of interest. Mailer's novel rode the crest of this wave. It jumped to the top of the *New York Times* best-seller list, where it remained in first position for eleven straight weeks, aided by continuing strong reviews, award nominations, and praise from Sinclair Lewis, who called Mailer "the greatest writer to come out of his generation," a comment publishers used on his books for years. All told, the novel was on the *New York Times* best-seller list for sixty-two weeks from its publication through the summer of 1949.

The novel is set on the fictional Pacific island of Anopopei, where an American division commanded by General Cummings seeks to defeat a Japanese force entrenched behind the Toyaku Line. The struggle against the Japanese, however, is secondary to the one among the Americans. The key power struggle takes place among the officers and among the enlisted men, and along two different, but related, plotlines. The first half of the novel focuses on Cummings' ef-

fort to marshal his troops and so rout the stubborn Japanese forces. The division is sluggish and recalcitrant, and he is frustrated by his inability to mold it to his will. The tide of the war in the Pacific is beginning to turn, and Cummings (the first of several Machiavellian power-seekers in Mailer's work) knows he must be quickly victorious if he is to rise to the pinnacle in the postwar army, which, he believes, may have to fight the Soviet Union—something that Americans, including Mailer, began to fear in the years right after the war. His aide, Lieutenant Hearn, is fascinated by the general's intelligence and foresight but ultimately opposes his semi-fascistic methods, his use of the fear ladder, on which every officer and soldier must torment the man on the next lower rung, passing down the punishment and looking up for the occasional reward.

On the enlisted level, Sergeant Croft, a masochistic, whipcord Texan, leads a fourteen-man platoon of lower- and middle-class soldiers from every part of the United States. This cross-section enables Mailer to juxtapose a member of every major ethnic group (except African Americans—the army was still segregated) with every other one, and capture a representative range of dialects, biases, and values. His ability to orchestrate so many characters and themes in this 721-page novel foreshadows his later efforts to handle even more complex materials. So Jews and southerners, Swedes, Poles, Irish, and Italians, Mexican Americans and WASPs cooperate and oppose one another even as they fight the Japanese. To illuminate the motivations of his characters, Mailer inserts ten "Time Machine" sketches of the soldiers—including Cummings, Croft, and Hearn—in their prewar lives. This technique, adapted from John Dos Passos's 1936 novel *U.S.A.*, gives pace and balance to the narrative by juxtaposing domestic scenes with battle scenes and sex with violence, linkages Mailer will explore many times during his career.

In the early part of the novel, Hearn and Cummings debate the nature and uses of power, with Hearn ultimately siding with those on the lower rungs. Their discussions are the beginning of Mailer's lifelong study of the totalitarian mentality and are a notable display of intellect by the twenty-five-year-old author. Indeed, it is clear that Mailer admires the Faustian energies of Cummings, his "unique ability to extend his thoughts into immediate and effective action," as much as he dislikes the half-baked liberalism of Hearn. The discussions lead finally to a confrontation, and Hearn is forced to back down, to "crawfish," after which the General reassigns him to lead Croft's reconnaissance platoon. Thus Hearn becomes the link between officers and enlisted men, as well as between the two major plotlines.

The second part of the novel centers on the platoon's long patrol, which is intended to determine if the Toyaku Line can be attacked from the rear, something that Croft believes can only be accomplished by climbing Mount Anaka, the tallest mountain on the 150-mile-long island. The mountain and the assault on it are symbolic—much like Herman Melville's white whale and Ahab—of nature's power and human desire to dominate it. This is especially true for Croft, who "felt a thrill of anticipation at the thought that by the following night they might be on the peak. Again, he felt a crude ecstasy. He could not have given the reason, but the mountain tormented him, beckoned him, held an answer to something he wanted. It was so pure, so austere."

But before the assault can be made two things happen that demonstrate Mailer's ideas about the nature of war. First, Wilson, a member of the platoon, is gut shot in a Japanese ambush. Four soldiers are detailed to carry the suffering, increasingly incoherent Wilson on a litter back to the beach, an exhausting journey down and away from the mountain that parallels the platoon's journey up the flank of Anaka. The

second event is Hearn's murder. He is killed by a Japanese machine gun, but only because Croft has suppressed information about Japanese positions. This surprising event has generated much critical comment, with some believing that Mailer eliminates Hearn to discredit his ineffectual liberalism, and others seeing it as a realistic event that underlines the disproportions of war. It also reveals that Cummings' power lust is equaled by that of Croft. Together they dominate the action of the novel, although in the end both are defeated. Croft's unit is driven off the mountain by the hornets, demonstrating that nature has its own tricks and is not easily subjugated. As for Cummings, he is denied the self-aggrandizing pleasure of wielding his division like a fine sword and slicing through the Toyaku Line. When he is away from the island attempting to secure naval firepower to blast the Japanese, his dull understrapper, Major Dalleson, unimaginatively penetrates the line and crushes the Japanese, who are found to be sick, starving, and dispirited. It is a fluke victory, not a military masterstroke, and the star of General Cummings will now decline.

Some readers, while lauding Mailer's powerful ability to describe men in action, and to capture the obscene lingo of soldiers (using the word "fug" for the commonest four-letter obscenity), concluded that the defeats and defaults in the novel amount to a bleak depiction of the human condition, something that Mailer disputed. He said in an interview with Lillian Ross that the novel "offers a good deal of hope," and that even in the novel's "corruption and sickness" there are "yearnings for a better world." Such a yearning can be seen in the portage of Wilson by Goldstein and Ridges, the novel's odd couple, Brooklyn Jew and southern sharecropper. Heroically and stoically, they carry on after the other two soldiers fall away in exhaustion. Wilson groans and hallucinates obscenely as they carry him through jungle, field, and stream. When he dies, they never consider leaving him; they labor on, only to lose him in a surging jungle stream. This memorable sequence, coming near the end of the novel, balances the cold-blooded murder of Hearn and the novel's other acts of violence and treachery.

In what is generally considered to be the finest essay on *The Naked and the Dead*, Donald Pizer calls it "a work in which Mailer has successfully created a symbolic form to express the naturalistic theme of the hidden recesses of values in man's nature despite his tragic fate in a closely conditioned and controlled world." For the remainder of his career Mailer will continue to show us the most abominable in human nature, while continuing to endorse the merits of courage—the essential virtue for Mailer—leading to growth and a hint of transcendence.

THE CHALLENGES OF FAME

In the middle of the twentieth century, American writers were more celebrated than at century's end, and *The Naked and the Dead* was a huge success, selling millions of copies. This success, Mailer later explained in *Advertisements for Myself*, cut him off from his past; he called it "a lobotomy." He was twenty-five and famous. Microphones were thrust in his face; the option of being a detached observer was gone. In Paris, under the influence of Jean Malaquais, his French translator, Mailer had begun a new novel about leftists and an FBI agent living in a Brooklyn rooming house much like the one where he had finished *The Naked and the Dead*. But his success unsettled him, and he shelved his new novel and went to Hollywood, where he eventually worked on screenplays for the Hollywood producer Samuel Goldwyn. He moved to California with his family (his daughter Susan was born in 1949) and Malaquais and met the famous actors and actresses who were eager to meet the newly

famous author. After a year of accomplishing little in collaboration with Malaquais (but soaking up material about Hollywood), he returned east and finished his novel, titled *Barbary Shore*. It came out in May 1951.

Mailer wanted his second novel to be radical and radically different from his first; it was both. He shifted from third- to first-person narration, worked with a smaller number of characters, and all but eliminated descriptions of physical activity of the kind that he was so highly praised for in his first novel. *Barbary Shore* takes place in several closed rooms where the five chief characters talk a blue streak about the collision of the two "colossi," the United States and the Soviet Union, and about the past and future of Marxism, its mistakes, horrors, promise, and ruling ideas. Sometimes the debates are engaging, sometimes not. Mailer was, in a sense, continuing his education with this novel, learning from his characters as he did in the Cummings-Hearn dialogues.

The five chief characters of *Barbary Shore* are Mrs. Guinevere, the sexy landlady; her husband, McLeod, a former high functionary for the Soviets; his nemesis, Hollingsworth, a sadistic FBI agent; Lannie Madison, a mad Cassandra; and Mickey Lovett, a war veteran who has only fragmentary memories of his youth and war experiences. Lovett is writing a novel and, like everyone else, wants to have sex with Guinevere. Besides the tracing of sexual desire, the only discernible plot thread is Hollingsworth's continuing interrogation of McLeod concerning his Stalinist affiliations and secrets. Despite the tedium of much of the talk, there are many bright moments, including Lovett's surreal memories and visions of an Orwellian future, and the very different fantasies of Guinevere and Lannie. Guinevere, the novel's most genuinely felt character, has a hilarious idea for a tabloid-type, murder-love story, which she presents in detail to Lovett (Mailer's comic gifts have not always been appreciated). Lannie's dark, Holocaust visions anticipate Marion Faye, the hipster in his next novel, *The Deer Park* (1955), and show, as Mailer told Steven Marcus, his unconscious interest in "murder, suicide, orgy, psychosis, all the themes I discuss in *Advertisements.*" Lovett, who is tutored in Marxism and its offshoot, Trotskyism, by McLeod, is both the narrator and the chief protagonist, but except for his dreams and visions, he is a dull tool. McLeod, a pontificator of leftist thought, wishes to pass on the remnants of a viable Marxist program, his hope for a just world, to Lovett's generation. Mailer will use this sort of father-son relationship in every one of his future novels to clarify their philosophical underpinnings. McLeod gives Lovett the symbolic but unnamed object sought by Hollingsworth as the novel closes with Lovett's flight and McLeod's murder. The torch has been passed, it seems, but Lovett's future is ambiguous at best.

Barbary Shore is a bold, claustrophobic, somewhat Kafkaesque narrative that never succeeds in merging a river of abstract argument (which is evidence of Mailer's lifelong admiration for the dialectics of Marxist thought) with the development of characters or plot. One important reason for the lack of integration is that he did not have a line of action. *Barbary Shore* received the worst reviews of any of Mailer's books but intellectually represented a genuine advance. The novel also transmitted something of the zeitgeist, always one of Mailer's cardinal virtues. As he put it in *Advertisements,* "It has in its high fevers a kind of insane insight into the psychic mysteries of Stalinists, secret policemen, narcissists, children, Lesbians, hysterics, revolutionaries—it has an air which for me is the air of our time, authority and nihilism stalking one another in the orgiastic hollow of this century." Today the novel is seen as a seedbed of ideas, one to which Mailer would return many times.

THE HOLLYWOOD NOVEL

One of the commonplaces of Mailer criticism is that his first three novels deal, respectively, with violence, politics, and sex. Certainly there is a good deal of sexual content in *The Deer Park,* material considered salacious by the prudish conventional standards of the time. The novel created a stir in the publishing world and presented Mailer with a completely new set of narrative challenges and opportunities. Turned down by Rinehart, he went to six publishing firms before Putnam's accepted it. Originally, Mailer conceived the novel as the first in a cycle of eight interlocking novels that would each explore a different reach of modern life—pleasure, business, crime, church, working-class life, and so forth—but he gave up the ambitious scheme after he had written the prologue, a long short story titled "The Man Who Studied Yoga," and the first draft of the "pleasure" novel, *The Deer Park.* (Mailer has on two other occasions projected serial novels but only written the first; it seems to be a method of jump-starting new work.)

The protagonist of "The Man Who Studied Yoga," Sam Slovoda, was supposed to have a dream that laid out the eight-part scheme and introduced the hero, Sergius O'Shaugnessy. But Mailer, as always, followed the new flow he discovered at the point of his pencil. Still, the story, one of his two finest, was a success, and Slovoda stands as a negative exemplum, the timid opposite of Mailer's hipster heroes. O'Shaugnessy survived as one of the chief characters of the "pleasure" novel and later shows up as a Greenwich Village bullfighting instructor and sexual athlete in "The Time of Her Time," Mailer's most erotic, polished, and provocative short story, published in 1959 in *Advertisements for Myself.*

The chief protagonist of *The Deer Park* is Charles Francis Eitel. O'Shaugnessy, a former U.S. Air Force jet pilot, stands, roughly, in the same relation to him as Nick Carraway does to

Jay Gatsby. He narrates the novel, and, as Robert Merrill astutely points out, Mailer "counterpoints Sergius's development and Eitel's moral decline," again, very roughly paralleling *The Great Gatsby*. The novel is set in Desert D'Or, a resort community modeled after Palm Springs where the Hollywood community comes for recreation. Sex and other illicit pleasures are for sale there, and a river of booze runs through it.

Eitel is a blacklisted director, banned from making films because of his leftist connections in the 1930s, who is unwilling to testify about these associations before a congressional committee. Middle-aged, divorced, handsome, and cultivated, he is trying to write an ambitious film script while living on the last of his savings. His former boss, Herman Teppis, the head of Supreme Studios, and Teppis' son-in-law, the producer Collie Munshin (another small comic masterpiece), would like to have Eitel produce more of the money-making, sentimental films he made before the war, but first he must tell what he knows. And he will not. He wants to get back to the kind of honest social realism films he made when he first came to Hollywood, but he misses the action, the fame, the high life. Like *Gatsby*, the novel details the effects of corrupt money. There are other parallels, but Eitel differs greatly from Jay Gatsby in that his goal is not to regain a lost love but to recover his artistic integrity.

O'Shaugnessy is young and handsome and has $14,000 that he won in a Tokyo poker game, but he is also uncertain and impotent as a result of his war experience, most of which, as he explains in the long, beautiful opening of the novel, was spent dropping firebombs on Korean villages. He becomes part of the bar-party scene at the resort and makes friends with Eitel, a pimp named Marion Faye, and a beautiful, zany movie star named Lulu Meyers, one of the biggest attractions of Teppis' studio. As O'Shaugnessy falls in love with Meyers, Eitel

picks up with Elena Esposito, a former mistress of Munshin's. The course of their two affairs, especially Eitel's, make up the heart of the novel. Mailer's clear intention is to show the arc of Eitel's attempt to regain his moral-artistic stature and the role Esposito (based loosely on Mailer's new love, Adele Morales) plays in this quest. It is one of the most brilliantly depicted affairs in modern literature. As Robert Merrill, one of the finest critics of this novel, notes in his study *Norman Mailer Revisited,* "Nowhere else in Mailer's fiction is a love relationship developed so fully."

Mailer's problem in the novel was that by choosing the first-person point of view, he made it impossible to present the most important aspects of the Eitel-Esposito affair. Mailer's narrator can report on the machinations of Teppis and Munshin to get Eitel to testify, return to the fold, and make more sappy films; he can tell us what Faye, the Baudlairean pimp who functions as Eitel's good angel, is saying and doing; he can report the gossip of the barflies, call girls, and flunkies; and he can, of course, give us Lulu Meyer's take on things. He is a marvelous narrator in the first half of the book, far superior to Lovett, but he cannot take us into the bedroom, cannot be privy to the intimate conversations between the passionate, uneducated Esposito and the older man who is teaching her about life just as she is inspiring him, at least at the beginning of their relationship. Mailer's solution was to use O'Shaugnessy less and less as narrator as the novel progresses and shift to an omniscient perspective. He does this at the beginning of the novel's third part (of six), noting only that Sergius will use his "imagination" to present the affair from the inside. The shift is jarring. The narrative focus moves from Eitel and Esposito (she is only seen from the outside) to O'Shaugnessy's parallel affair with Lulu, and later to Faye, a total of some thirty shifts in point of view. Henry James would be appalled, but in truth, the fascinating love affair of Eitel and Elena more than compensates for the split perspective. Readers feel an urgency to return to the private place where the couple struggle with each other in an effort to locate their deepest identities.

Some critics believe *The Deer Park* to be a satire of Hollywood Babylon, a not unreasonable position, but others argue that the novel is really about a great, tragic love affair. Both are right, but there is no debating the fact that the rising action of the novel culminates in Eitel's decision to shed Elena, name names to the House Un-American Activities Committee (his name is pronounced "I-tell"), and "make some more crud," as Faye puts it. She is the moral winner in the battle, and her long letter to Eitel is strong evidence of Mailer's power to create character—always his strong suit. She is one of his most memorable characters. Mailer's instinct when revising the novel in early 1955 (it came out in October 1955) was to make O'Shaugnessy stronger, tougher, more believable, even as he worked to make the affair more vibrant. But although O'Shaugnessy develops muscles, as it were, he is unable to lift us into a vantage point on the affair. Eitel's love affair and his battle with the greedy forces of commercialism comprise the novel's morality play, and O'Shaugnessy's new stubbornness and belligerence, which represent, Mailer says in *Advertisements,* "an implicit portrait of myself," have only tangential importance. Eitel sells his integrity and splits with Esposito, who then is sorely but successfully tested when she moves in with Faye, who ends up in prison. Sergius goes off to Mexico and later New York to run his bullfighting school and write "this novel," an admission that weakens its pretensions to reality. The novel is, after all, the only form that tries to convince us that it is something else.

NEW YORK CITY AND THE HIPSTER

The Deer Park made the best-seller list, but it was not the big success Mailer badly needed.

Its reception made him angry at the establishment in a more intense way; an outlaw mentality surged up in him. Now divorced from Bea and living in New York City with Adele (whom he married in 1954), he began to soak up jazz and the nightlife and get involved in new ventures such as *Dissent,* a leftist journal of ideas. With Daniel Wolf and Edwin Fancher, he cofounded the *Village Voice,* which he named. The first issue appeared on October 26, 1955, just as his novel was climbing the best-seller list. He devoted much of the next eight months to the paper and contributed a weekly column, titled "Quickly: A Column for Slow Readers," the first of his many journalistic forays.

But Mailer's most important effort immediately after *The Deer Park* was his 1957 essay for *Dissent,* later collected in *Advertisements.* Titled "The White Negro," the essay presents his emerging view of the challenges of life in a post-Holocaust world threatened by the atomic bomb. This dense, beautifully written piece is Mailer's most important polemical essay and one of the most anthologized of the postwar period. In its emphasis on the primacy of inner promptings, it is a key to all of Mailer's later work. The essay presents a prospectus for a new hero, the hipster, an urban, jazz-soaked sexual adventurer whose closest parallel are the blacks who live on the dangerous edge in America's cities. The hipster believes that "the only life-giving answer is to accept the terms of death, to live with death as immediate danger, to divorce oneself from society, to exist without roots, to set off on that uncharted journey into the rebellious imperatives of the self."

The essay's celebration of personal violence, among other things, created a great stir, and it was often linked, with some justification, to the Beat movement, which took off at about the same time. What made Mailer's argument different from those of the Beats and other extreme romantic programs is that the search for growth, aided by a variety of risk-taking ventures, most notably the release of damned-up sexual energy, is never-ending. No one has explained this better than Robert Solotaroff. In his study *Down Mailer's Way,* he says that Mailer's prescription for growth "in its ideal or natural movement describes a spiral—a man grows by freeing energy, but this energy must be put to the task of freeing still more energy." Mailer's "endlessly spiraling dialectic" is ultimately "the quest for the infinite."

MAILER'S MISCELLANIES

Mailer's next novel, *An American Dream,* would not appear until 1965, over nine years after *The Deer Park.* In the work published in the interim, and in interviews, he often referred to the "big novel" he was writing. *Advertisements* contained two excerpts, and *The Presidential Papers,* a 1963 miscellany focused on the Kennedy administration, offered another. Between these two books came Mailer's only extended foray into poetry, *Deaths for the Ladies (and Other Disasters)* (1962). In 1966 he published his third miscellany, *Cannibals and Christians,* although the great majority of this collection was written before *An American Dream.* The bulk of Mailer's activity between his third and fourth novels was not directed at the "big novel" but consisted of a series of narrative ventures and experiments in several literary forms, as well as a reconsideration and consolidation of all his previous work.

The content of these three miscellanies includes a majority of Mailer's columns from the *Village Voice, Esquire,* and *Commentary,* a generous sampling from his second and third novels, short stories, reviews, interviews, dialogues, dramatic fragments, speeches, political commentary, a clutch of essays, a long piece on the Floyd Patterson–Sonny Liston fight (titled "Ten Thousand Words a Minute"), "The White Negro," some poems and literary criticism. Each of the three miscellanies is linked,

respectively, by a series of "advertisements," "postscripts," and "arguments" that federate a narrative thrust, especially in *Advertisements,* where they are often more important than the work they frame. Like Henry James in the prefaces to his novels, Mailer broods and muses over the context of each separate piece, telling the story of the story. Together the miscellanies comprise a comprehensive sourcebook of Mailer's wide-ranging concerns. The tone is by turns wry, edgy, angry, sardonic; the content is rich with social observation, now-or-never fulmination, jeremiads, pointed comments on his own career and future possibilities and life in these American states. But they contain little new fiction. Nevertheless, the reader gets the sense of a man very much in motion.

Now the father of two daughters by Adele (Danielle in 1957 and Elizabeth Anne in 1959), Mailer was considering running for mayor of New York, but after he stabbed Adele with a penknife at a drunken party in November 1960 (an event that continues to resonate in Mailer's life), he had to shelve the idea. Adele recovered quickly and refused to press charges, but their marriage was effectively over. They were divorced in 1962, and shortly thereafter Mailer married Lady Jean Campbell, an Englishwoman who gave him his fourth daughter, Kate, also in 1962. This third marriage also failed, and they were divorced in 1963. Mailer then married Beverly Bentley, an actress, who became the mother of his first two sons (Michael, born in 1964, and Stephen, in 1966). Mailer's roiled psychic state is apparent in the miscellanies, especially in *Advertisements for Myself,* the most powerful of the three, and the most autobiographical. Many who came of age after World War II shared Mailer's rage at American moderation, compromise, and conformity. In *Advertisements* he forged his distinctive style, a fierce, frank, agile, self-reflective, and often humorous voice; his angry cry, "the shits are killing us," became a rallying point for a second generation of Mailer readers. *The Presidential Papers* has a similar tone, focusing on the politics of the early 1960s. It includes one of the prototypes of the "new journalism," his report on the 1960 Democratic political convention in San Francisco, titled "Superman Comes to the Supermarket." The tenor of the piece, the first of many profiles of presidential candidates, can be gauged by the fact that Mailer calls John F. Kennedy the first "hipster" candidate for president. The third in the series, *Cannibals and Christians,* focuses, in part, on the Johnson administration. Among its many items of continuing interest are Mailer's assessment of nine of his novelistic colleagues, "Some Children of the Goddess," two long philosophical dialogues on matters such as form, spirit, beauty, and soul, and some strong criticism of the Vietnam War. Mailer was among the earliest and most thoughtful critics of the war.

GOD AND THE DEVIL

Constantly tempted to write nonfiction about the tumultuous events of the period, Mailer knew he must find a way to commit himself to a new novel, his first in over eight years. His solution was to up the ante by writing a serialized novel, following the same frantic pace of earlier novelists such as Charles Dickens and Fyodor Dostoyevsky. He announced *An American Dream* in his final "Big Bite" column in *Esquire* in December 1963, a magazine that was on the stands when John F. Kennedy was killed in Dallas. The *Esquire* version appeared in eight parts, from January to August 1964, and the final, much-revised version, the following March. Barry Leeds, in his study *The Enduring Vision of Norman Mailer* (2002), aptly summarizes the novel as "a pilgrimage by protagonist Stephen Richards Rojack from imminent alcoholism, damnation and madness to salvation and sanity."

Rojack, a television talk-show host, former congressman, and professor of existential psychology, says he holds "the not inconsiderable thesis that magic, dread and the perception of death were the roots of motivation." His compromises and failures have made him suicidal; he receives emanations from the moon and smells cancer and carnality in people. In fact, he has perhaps the finest olfactory intuition in modern literature. A war hero like John F. Kennedy, Rojack meets Deborah Kelly, whom he later marries and murders, on a double date with Kennedy during their term together in Congress after World War II. Rojack's murder of the hateful Deborah (which he claims is suicide); a love affair with Cherry Melanie, the former mistress of Deborah's father, Barney Oswald Kelly, the "solicitor" for the Devil; and a series of physical and psychic confrontations with the police, the Mafia, Shago Martin (Cherry's former lover, a black jazz artist), and Kelly—all taking place within thirty-six hours in New York City—make up the external action of the story. But the novel is really an account of a battle between God and the Devil. Rojack's internal war both mirrors and partakes of the struggle between good and evil.

An American Dream is the first fully developed depiction of Mailer's Manichaean cosmology, which holds that the universe is a dialectical process with the final synthesis unknown. God is limited, imperfect in the same way humans are, and locked into combat with a powerful, wily Devil. Human beings are participants in this war, usually unknowingly, and fight on both sides. The outcome is uncertain; the Devil could win. Rojack is aware of the nature of this struggle, but he does not always know which side his actions will benefit. "The moral consequences of this," Mailer said in a 1958 interview with Richard G. Stern and Robert F. Lucid, "are not only staggering, but they're thrilling; because moral experience is intensified rather than diminished."

As in *The Deer Park,* the primary linkages between the characters are sexual. A web of infidelity and incest links the mob with high society, Harlem with the small-town South, black with white, father with daughter, and sister with brother. Cherry, who is murdered at the end of the novel, sleeps with almost every important male character. While it is clear that Mailer intends her love for Rojack to be of a higher order, she is not developed enough for this to be completely convincing.

By far the best analysis of the novel is Tony Tanner's in his essay "On the Parapet," collected in Harold Bloom's *Norman Mailer: Modern Critical Views* (1986). He points out that although initially many critics found the novel to be an outrageous study of how to murder your wife and get away with it, such views miss the deeper moral dimensions of the novel. It is, he says, "a vivid exploration of a man's relationship to the different orders of American reality." Tanner notes the extraordinary use of metaphors of "pre-social reality— the jungle, the forest, the desert, the swamp, the ocean-bed" and how these metaphors contrast with the realistic depictions of New York City. The novel presents a series of oppositions between nature and civilization, the supernatural and the rational, the demonic and the angelic, and, ultimately, between the forces of life and death. Rojack must contend with these dualisms, Tanner explains, aided by not much more than the voices he hears in his head, his sense of smell, and the talismanic umbrella of Shago Martin, which trembles portentously in his hands. In the novel's climax, high up in the Waldorf Towers, where Rojack has been summoned by Kelly to answer questions about Deborah's death, he resists the carnal temptations of his host and then, in a self-imposed test, walks the parapet around Kelly's terrace, smashing Kelly with the umbrella when Kelly attempts to push him off the edge and then throwing the umbrella over the parapet. Tanner

concludes his brilliant discussion by noting that Rojack has "to prove that he can negotiate that edge where the worlds meet," succumbing neither to the fixed and rational nor to the formless and irrational. He shows that he can, at least for a time, "hold on to his identity between two threatening realms."

Mailer was pleased with the achievement of *An American Dream.* He imbued the novel with his dynamic belief system; melded, for the first time with Rojack, the narrative consciousness and the main protagonist, the teller and the chief character; and his style was now fully mature—it has never been more lyrical, energetic, and richly metaphoric. The novel sold well and made the best-seller list, although the reviews were mediocre at best. Reviewers have often been unable to appreciate Mailer's bold vision and experiments in form.

After *An American Dream* he was again uncertain which way to move and how much energy to expend on various projects. But he knew, as he says in *Cannibals,* that "repetition kills the soul" and that he must tackle new projects. In 1967 his solution was to move in several directions simultaneously. His play *The Deer Park* opened in New York in January and had a successful four-month run. He published four books: *The Short Fiction of Norman Mailer; The Deer Park: A Play;* his fifth novel, *Why Are We in Vietnam?;* and *The Bullfight,* a long nonfiction essay about a Mexican bullfighter. He also made two experimental films, *Wild 90* and *Beyond the Law* (and the following year *Maidstone,* his most ambitious film) and appeared at several antiwar protests. In October at the March on the Pentagon, Mailer was arrested, and before the year was over he was at work on his nonfiction narrative about the march, *The Armies of the Night: History as a Novel, The Novel as History* (1968).

Why Are We in Vietnam? his most linguistically innovative work, follows a party of Texans hunting big game in Alaska and is narrated by the son of the party's leader, Ranald Jethroe, an eighteen year old known to all as D. J. Part Huck Finn and part William Burroughs, D. J. talks, as he himself notes, like a wired disc jockey. His rapid-fire recounting of the high-tech hunts in the Brooks Range of Alaska, recollected two years later on the eve of his departure for Vietnam, crackles with obscene merriment. The novel does not directly consider American involvement in Vietnam. Rather, it accounts for American militarism by depicting the Texans as nature-defiling louts. It is Mailer's most extended meditation on nature after *Naked*. But the descriptions in *Vietnam* are superior to those in *Naked* because its natural world is the incarnation of a prodigious and divided anima. The forests and mountains of Alaska vibrate with supersensory messages from heavenly and demonic forces, much as the forests of Lebanon do in his later novel, *Ancient Evenings*. Passages of description of caribou and wolves alternate with unforgiving portraits of the Texans (all employed by a huge corporation) competing for the biggest trophy animals. The rams and grizzly bears are shot, in some instances, from a helicopter. The novel was generally reviewed well and was nominated for a National Book Award, the first of five nominations for Mailer.

NONFICTION NARRATIVES

From 1967 through 1979 Mailer published twenty-two books. Only one of them—*Vietnam*—was a novel. During this tumultuous period in American life, especially the late 1960s and early 1970s, history seemed to be accelerating. As Mailer put it in *Of a Fire on the Moon* (1971), "the real had become more fantastic than the imagined." In response, Mailer interrupted his novelistic mission in order to chronicle these events and to challenge them with his imagination. Some of the books he wrote during this period were just sparks from

the wheel, but several of them are among his major achievements. Perhaps the most important of these are the five nonfiction narratives he published from 1968 to 1972: *The Armies of the Night: History as a Novel, The Novel as History* (1968), a depiction of the October 1967 anti-war protest March on the Pentagon; *Miami and the Siege of Chicago* (1968), a report on the violent 1968 political conventions; *Of a Fire on the Moon* (1971), a long analysis of the American space program and the first landing on the moon; *The Prisoner of Sex* (1971), an account of his debate with the women's liberation movement, which earned the movement's enmity; and *St. George and the Godfather* (1972), a report on the 1972 political conventions.

In his glowing review of *Armies*, Alfred Kazin concluded by stating, "Mailer's intuition in this book is that the times demand a new form. He has found it." Each of the five nonfiction narratives attempts to bridge what Mailer in *The Presidential Papers* calls the "double life" of Americans: "the history of politics which is concrete, factual, practical and unbelievably dull" and "a subterranean river of untapped, ferocious lonely and romantic desires, that concentration of ecstasy and violence which is the dream life of the nation." Whether Mailer is writing about astronauts or feminists, athletes or presidents, protestors or FBI agents, he is always attempting to bridge outer and inner, public and private in the national experience. It is his deepest narrative aspiration. To capture the complexities of a nation poised between the malevolent and the heroic, he was obliged to break down the walls between narrative genres. A work like *Armies* accomplishes this by employing the techniques of both the modern psychological novel and the historical narrative.

The narrative is divided into two parts. The first "novelistic" part is three times the length of the second "historical" overview, the latter serving as factual ballast for the first, which traces Mailer's involvement in the protest activities, the events leading up the march, his arrest and incarceration, and, two days later, his release. He does not divide the other four narratives in the same way; instead, he shuttles between outer and inner, the events and his participation and his mercurial, often humorous responses to them. But he does employ the same unusual point of view; he describes himself in the third person, a technique used by some classical historians and, in the twentieth century, most notably, by Henry Adams and Gertrude Stein. Here is an example, a description of the scene just before his arrest at the Pentagon.

> It was not unlike being a boy about to jump from one garage roof to an adjoining garage roof. The one thing not to do was wait. Mailer looked at Macdonald and Lowell. "Let's go," he said. Not looking again at them, not pausing to gather or dissipate resolve, he made a point of stepping neatly and decisively over the low rope. Then he headed across the grass to the nearest MP he saw.
>
> It was as if the air had changed, or light had altered; he felt immediately more alive—yes, bathed in air—and yet disembodied from himself, as if indeed he were watching himself in a film where this action was taking place. He could feel the eyes of the people behind the rope watching him, could feel the intensity of their existence as spectators. And as he walked forward, he and the MP looked at one another with the naked stricken lucidity which comes when absolute strangers are for the moment absolutely locked together.

It reads like a modern novel, which is precisely what Mailer wanted. In *Barbary Shore* and *The Deer Park,* he used first-person narrators who resembled him in some ways, but not too much. It was not permitted; a modicum of distance between narrators and authors was required. Authors were supposed to be invisible and powerful, everywhere and nowhere, like God. But Mailer wanted to use himself, explore himself, watch himself winning, losing, being bold, being a fool, performing, as he says in the quoted passage, as if he were in a movie, and

above all searching for congruence between himself and the republic in peril. So he took the step of describing himself in the third person, which, in effect, divided him into teller and told, narrating and narrative selves. It is only an apparent paradox that this division of self by aesthetic fiat came as a result of his growing awareness of the desirability of no longer attempting to separate the private and public hemispheres of his life. To harness both selves, use them simultaneously, he was, in effect, taking seriously Ralph Waldo Emerson's injunction in his essay "Fate": "A man must ride alternately on the horses of his private and his public nature, as the equestrians in the circus throw themselves nimbly from horse to horse, or plant one foot on the back of the one and the other foot on the back of the other." This is Mailer's narrative stance in the five nonfiction narratives, as well as in his 1975 account of the Muhammad Ali–George Foreman boxing match in Zaire, *The Fight.*

He is even a bit more nimble than Emerson's metaphor allows in that he also explores the many sides and pockets of his character. He uses many names to describe himself: Brute, Ruminant, Reporter, Aquarius (a favorite, used in both *Fire* and *St. George*), Acolyte, Novelist, Director, Prisoner, Prospector, and Participant. In addition, Mailer has placed himself over the years everywhere on the political spectrum from the left of Robespierre to the right of William F. Buckley, from Marxian anarchist in *Advertisements* to "*grand conservateur*" in *Armies.* During his quixotic race for mayor of New York in 1969, his campaign literature said he was to the left and right of everyone else in the race, and by the time of *Armies,* he regularly described himself as a "Left Conservative." From his cosmology to his politics and everywhere in between, Mailer is a thoroughgoing dualist, but one whose two sides are themselves often divided. Richard Poirier, in perhaps the most intelligent full-length study of Mailer, *Norman*

Mailer, pointed out that Mailer "is quite unable to imagine anything except in oppositions, unable even to imagine one side of the opposition without proposing that it has yet another opposition within itself," or "the minority within."

FAMOUS AMERICANS

Mailer received the best reviews of his career for *Armies*; it won a Pulitzer Prize and the National Book Award and is generally seen to be one of the finest achievements of the "new journalism." His other nonfiction narratives fared almost as well, garnering awards, plaudits from reviewers, and strong sales. He was widely seen as Aquarius-in-charge-of-construing-America, but he recognized that he had all but used himself up as a reference. There were also personal problems: his marriage with Beverly Bentley failed in 1969, and he never seemed to earn enough to pay alimony and expenses for his seven children (Maggie, his seventh, was born to Carol Stevens, his fifth wife, in 1971). By the early 1970s he felt an urgent desire to get back to his first love, the novel. Even before *St. George and the Godfather* appeared in late 1972, he was at work at what was initially called "the Egyptian novel." Shortly thereafter, he signed a contract with Little, Brown for a three-part novel and a large advance. But there were distractions, obligations, opportunities to be dealt with along the way to the novel's completion.

All through the 1970s—which might be called his biographical decade—Mailer alternated between work on the Egyptian novel and a series of portraits of famous and infamous Americans, twin lines of artistic enterprise that necessarily overlapped. The first biography was of Marilyn Monroe, which was also the first of several collaborative efforts with the entrepreneurial photographer and producer Lawrence Schiller. *Marilyn: A Biography* (1973) was originally to have been a 25,000-word preface to a selection of photographs by Schiller and other photographers, but it grew into a 95,000-word, full-scale biography that concluded with the suggestion that Monroe had been murdered. Controversy surrounded the book, which only increased sales; 400,000 copies were in print by the end of 1973. It was Mailer's biggest bestseller since *Naked*.

His next outing, *The Fight* (1975), is a portrait of Muhammad Ali in Africa. Mailer again complained in the narrative that using himself as a lens, describing himself in the third person, was tedious, and the book is most successful in its depiction of Ali's improvisations in the ring. He then returned to the Egyptian novel, pausing in 1976 to publish a collection of his political writings, *Some Honorable Men: Political Conventions, 1960–1972,* and, later the same year, a collection of excerpts from the work of an author he admired. *Genius and Lust: A Journey through the Major Writings of Henry Miller* contains eighty pages of commentary on Miller, making it Mailer's lengthiest piece of literary criticism. The cover drawing of Miller is by Barbara Norris (later Norris Church Mailer), whom Mailer met in Arkansas in 1975. He later married her after she and her son from an earlier marriage, Matthew, moved to New York. In 1978 she gave birth to their son John Buffalo. This marriage, Mailer's sixth and last, brought a large measure of stability to his life. Norris Church Mailer is an actress, painter, novelist, and theatrical artistic director in Provincetown, Massachusetts, the Mailers' permanent home since the mid-1980s.

A NEW AUDIENCE

Gary Gilmore was a convicted murderer who gained national attention by insisting that his death sentence by firing squad be promptly carried out. Shortly after his execution in early 1977, Lawrence Schiller contacted Mailer to ask if he would collaborate with him on

Gilmore's story, to which he owned the rights. Mailer dropped work on his novel and spent six months in Utah with Schiller interviewing hundreds of people who had known Gilmore, including convicts, lawyers, prison guards, members of the media, his mother, and his girlfriend, Nicole Barrett, and poring over 15,000 pages of interviews and court transcripts. He was excited by Gilmore's story; it seemed to embody many of the ideas that had preoccupied him for years, ideas about existential violence, the good in bad people, and the efficacy of dying in a state of grace, as well as the whole issue of capital punishment and Americans' fascination with outlaws. After the relatively quiet years of the middle and late 1970s, Mailer was also eager for another victory; he wanted a new audience. The narrative had several working titles: "Violence in America," "The Saint and the Psychopath," and "American Virtue." He finally settled on *The Executioner's Song.* Choosing a title was a small difficulty. Mailer had another problem: point of view. Inserting himself in the narrative and then describing himself in the third person would not work; he had never met Gilmore and much of his material was secondhand. He needed to be a central eye but could not be a character in the story himself. Mailer's solution was to revert to the omniscient, anonymous point of view of *Naked,* which appropriately eliminated him from the story. He chose a style as flat as the Utah landscape and relied heavily on the actual words of those involved. Here and there a careful reader can find some of Mailer's characteristic locutions, but not enough to weigh on the narrative, which accelerates as it progresses. He divided the book into two parts, "Western Voices" and "Eastern Voices." The first part tells the story of Gilmore's life up to his incarceration for two senseless murders and is told mainly by women, as Joan Didion noted in her highly laudatory review (reprinted in J. Michael Lennon, *Critical Essays on Norman Mailer*). In contrast, the "Eastern Voices" in book 2, Didion states, "are largely those of men—the voices of the lawyers, the prosecutors, the reporters, the people who move in the larger world and believe that they can influence events. The 'Western' book is a fatalistic drift, a tension. . . . The 'Eastern' book is the release of that tension, the resolution, the playing out of the execution." Mailer boldly resolves the problem of how to situate Schiller by making him the chief figure of part 2 and, after Gary and Nicole, the most important in the book. Schiller is both Gilmore's executor and a journalist struggling to assemble the raw materials of the story with integrity. The effort of compiling the massive documentary cache is the main line of action in part 2, although Gilmore's execution (four bullets through the heart from a firing squad), autopsy, and cremation ends the narrative.

Mailer subtitled *The Executioner's Song* "a true life novel," even though it was scrupulously factual, out of his debatable conviction that its scope, form, characters, and themes made it a novel. Published in 1979, the book became another best-seller and won Mailer another cadre of admirers. The reviews were mainly quite positive, and the book was nominated for the National Book Critics Circle Award and won the 1980 Pulitzer Prize for fiction, bearing out Mailer's belief in its fundamental novelistic identity. He was the only writer in the twentieth century to win the Pulitzer in both fiction and nonfiction.

FROM AMERICA TO EGYPT

As soon as *The Executioner's Song* was completed Mailer returned to the Egyptian novel, although he broke from the effort twice more: in 1980 for a novella titled *Of Women and Their Elegance,* which is narrated entirely by Marilyn Monroe, his only female narrator; and in 1982 for *Pieces and Pontifications,* his sixth miscellany. The first half consisted of his essays from the 1970s; the second half of twenty of his most important interviews from 1958 to 1981. There was one other interruption. In 1981 Mailer supported the parole request of Jack Henry Abbott (who had been imprisoned for a series of robberies) and wrote the introduction to Abbott's book, *In the Belly of the Beast: Letters from Prison.* Abbott was released and Mailer supported him generally. But within a month of his release Abbott killed a waiter in a New York restaurant during a petty dispute. Mailer was accused of being blind to Abbott's violent nature and was pilloried in the tabloid press, while others who had helped Abbott out of prison went relatively unnoticed. Mailer admitted his culpability, but the tragic situation haunted him. Abbott was convicted and, after his later parole attempts failed, committed suicide in 2002.

The novel *Ancient Evenings* was published with unusual fanfare in April 1983. It is Mailer's most ambitious, complex work and, by his estimate, his finest. Set in Egypt over a 180-year span (1320–1100 B.C.E.), it is also his most unread major work. Readers have complained of getting bogged down in what one critic, Michael Glenday, called the novel's "involutions," its memories of memories of the magical moments of Menenhetet I, who has learned from a Jewish slave how to father himself and lives four lives in the course of the novel. The process of re-creating himself, like much of the magic in the book, is obscure. Glenday goes on to say that the critical community, not to mention the common reader, remains baffled by the novel because it "is still regarded as both *outre* and so resistant to category as to subvert any substantial critical appraisal of it."

The violent, carnal, and magical religiosity of the Egyptians is not presented in any symbolic or metaphorical way, as Robert Begiebing points out in his study *Toward a New Synthesis* (1989). When Mailer chose ancient Egypt, a time and place saturated in magic, he was automatically released from "the restrictions of fictional real-ism," as well as from "twentieth-century rationalism and scientism." He was free to indulge his gnostic impulses to the fullest, free to re-create a society unaffected by Western culture's ruling beliefs—Judaic monotheism, Christian compassion and distrust of the body, Faustian progress, romantic love, and Freudian guilt. Mailer attributes telepathy and reincarnation to the Egyptians, but, apart from these, he does not depart from the available evidence on the nature of Egyptian culture, including its burial customs, which fascinated him. Unable to narrate a novel except in the first person, Mailer uses telepathy as a substitute for omniscience; reincarnation allows him to explore Menenhetet's four very different lives as charioteer-general and harem master, high priest, wealthy businessman, and, finally, tomb robber—note the trajectory—thus providing views of different levels and corners of Egyptian life without shifting from one consciousness to another, and then two more (Menenhetet remembers his previous lives). The first of his lives is the most impressive by far; depiction of the others, according to Harold Bloom in his review, gives "every sign of truncation." Almost all reviewers and critics agree that the account of the Egyptians' great chariot battle against the Hittites at Kadesh—an actual battle—is one of the strongest expositions in Mailer's work and, for many, in modern literature.

Perhaps the high point of the novel is Mailer's account of the rape and butchery during the drunken celebration before the gates of the Hittite capital, which he contrasts with the majestic aplomb of Ramses receiving through the long night the severed hands of slain Hittites from thousands of his troops. The pharaoh deftly tosses each hand into a perfectly pyramidal pile, never moving his feet, as his scribe records the soldiers' names and gory trophies. In addition to this luminous account, there are other wonderful runs of prose in the novel. The opening offers a remarkable retelling of the myths of the Egyptian gods by Menenhetet I to his grandson, Menenhetet II, after their deaths, one ghost to another, inside the great pyramid of Khufu as they prepare for a final journey and final judgment. Meni II is the actual narrator, although he is displaced from most of the action, much like O'Shaugnessy in *The Deer Park*. The narrative's involuted provenance is often confusing, but the chief criticism of the novel centers on the languorous Book of the Queens, a 130-page account of Meni I as harem master. Future consideration of the novel may focus on its complex epistemology, its spiraling narrative skeins and inlaid perspectives, and their relationships with the four narratives Mailer wrote during the same period as *Ancient Evenings,* those on Marilyn Monroe, Muhammad Ali, Henry Miller, and Gary Gilmore. Certainly the blend of their cardinal vices and virtues are manifested in both Menenhetet I and Ramses II.

BACK TO THE COLD WAR

Mailer's next book was an "entertainment," to use Graham Greene's phrase, a murder mystery set in Provincetown. It was published in 1984, the same year Mailer was elected president of the international writers' organization PEN and inducted into the American Academy of Arts and Letters. *Tough Guys Don't Dance* (1984) is notable mainly for its evocations of the drear winter landscapes of lower Cape Cod and its portraits of the eccentrics, artists, and criminals who live there. It was written in sixty-one days to fulfill a contract with his publisher at the time, Little, Brown, although it was ultimately published by Random House, his continuing publisher. *Tough Guys* was also a way of winding down after the decade-long effort to complete *Ancient Evenings.* Mailer went on to direct a feature film based on the novel, a film that has gained something of a cult reputation.

But the bulk of Mailer's effort during the 1980s was focused on a very long novel that deals with the cold war. The novel's length may be an American record. *Harlot's Ghost* is 1,310 pages long and ends with the words "To be continued." The sequel, Mailer said when the novel was published in October 1991, will continue the story of Herrick "Harry" Hubbard; his father, "Cal"; his godfather, Hugh Montague (code name "Harlot"); and Montague's wife, Kittredge, all CIA agents. After Kittredge divorces Harlot, she marries Harry, who might be seen as Harlot's ghost, or one of them. He ghostwrites spy novels favorable to the CIA and shadows Harlot in several ways, most notably with Kittredge. But Harlot's ghost refers chiefly to the spirit of the dead Harlot, if he is indeed dead. A body resembling his washes up on the shores of Chesapeake Bay with the face blown away and fingertips missing. Mailer's eighth novel is crammed with questions about the CIA, the cold war, the cosmic war of God and the Devil, and the fundamental loyalties of all the characters, including Harlot, who is loosely based on the American master spy James Jesus Angleton. In *Harlot's Ghost,* Mailer bends over backward to present the CIA fairly, making clear the contradictory impulses of selfless patriotism and Faustian arrogance that motivate its agents and leaders. One critic of the novel, John Whalen-Bridge, in his essay "Adamic Purity as Double-Agent," calls it an "obsessively dualistic novel," where "the coexistence and interdependence of good and evil . . . receive supreme expression."

Harlot's Ghost is of course divided into two parts, "Alpha" and "Omega," both manuscripts written by Harry, who narrates the story from Moscow in 1984. "Omega," about 100 pages, begins the novel and is set in Harry's island home in Maine on a day in 1983. It is a riveting opening, replete with sex, murder, an icy road and a stormy sea, double agents, a dank cellar, and, of course, ghosts. It ends with the revelation of the body washed ashore, the disappearance of Kittredge (with Dix Butler, a bisexual professional rival of Harry's), and Harry's flight from his burning house. "Alpha," at 1,200 pages, is the story of Harry's early life and includes his youth in the 1930s and 1940s, Yale education, and tours of duty abroad and in the United States, up to 1965, where the narrative ends. Presumably, the period between 1965 and 1984 dealing with Vietnam, Watergate, the impeding collapse of the Soviet Union, and the marriage of Hubbard and Kittredge will be in the sequel, although Mailer seems to have abandoned it. *Harlot's Ghost* was Mailer's eighth best-seller, although reviews, as usual, were mixed. Praised for the interweaving of fiction and fact, his extraordinary anatomy of the agency, and the authoritative portraits of so many prominent figures (Kennedy, Castro, Allen Dulles, J. Edgar Hoover, Kim Philby), the novel was also criticized for the length of some episodes, especially the nearly 300 pages devoted to Hubbard's years in Uruguay, and for his protracted correspondence with Kittredge. In an attempt to reveal Kittredge—who never comes completely into focus—within the limitations imposed by a first-person narrator, Mailer was forced to create an awkward, epistolary relationship. Finally, many reviewers contrasted the fast-paced opening with the tedium of some of the South American material. This counterpoint, like that in *Ancient Evenings,* not to mention *Moby-Dick* and other ambitious novels, was undoubtedly intentional; Mailer has always believed that the parts of a narrative should clarify and complicate other parts. Given the novel's length and ambition, and its saturation in the horrors and glories of the American Century, it seems more likely than any of Mailer's other works to be measured by his 1959 statement in *Advertisements* that he wanted to "try to hit the longest ball ever to go up into the accelerated hurricane air of our American letters."

MORE BIOGRAPHIES AND A CONSOLIDATION

No event in twentieth-century American life has resonated longer or stronger for Mailer than John F. Kennedy's assassination. In 1992 he decided to tackle it head on via a biography of the much-despised but poorly understood Lee Harvey Oswald, the man arrested for shooting the president and then executed by a small-time Dallas mobster, Jack Ruby. The opportunity was presented to him by his collaborator on *The Executioner's Song* and *Marilyn,* Lawrence Schiller, who had gained access to KGB archival material and operatives in Belarus, where Oswald had lived in 1960 after marrying Marina Prusakova. Mailer and Schiller spent six months there, interviewing everyone available who had known Lee and Marina or spied on them and poring over the verbatim transcripts of the couple's life in the bleak city of Minsk. Characteristically, Mailer divides the resulting 828-page narrative, *Oswald's Tale* (1995), into two parts. The first, "Oswald in Minsk with Marina," is devoted to Oswald's two and a half years in the Soviet Union; the second, "Oswald in America," moves back to his childhood and U.S. Marine Corps service, skipping his Russian years and continuing up to the day of Kennedy's assassination in Dallas. Mailer's subtle analysis of Jack Ruby's enigmatic motives follows his unmatched re-creation of the assassination, which he concludes was 75 percent likely to be the sole work of Oswald. The full narrative, equal if not superior to *The Executioner's Song,* ends with wrenching portraits of three widows: Jacqueline Kennedy, Marina Oswald, and her mother-in-law, the nattering, narcissistic Marguerite Oswald, who Mailer says "is worthy of Dickens."

The portrait of Oswald is the fairest hearing he might ever receive. Mailer attempts the Herculean task of generating, if not sympathy, then understanding of the dyslexic, nerdy Oswald. A failure at almost everything to which he put his hand but possessed of the ambition of the young Hitler or Lenin, Oswald comes across as much victim as monster. Reviewers favored the first part of the narrative, which presented fascinating material theretofore unavailable on the domestic life of Lee and Marina. For the second part of his narrative, Mailer relied on the twenty-six-volume *Warren Commission Report* and a large number of biographies and investigative reports. Many readers are still not ready to fully appreciate Mailer's portrait of Oswald, but one hundred years from now it might stand as definitive, worthy of Leo Tolstoy in its severity and compassion.

Never one to let the grass grow under his feet, Mailer had all but completed a biography of Pablo Picasso by the end of 1992, but because of various difficulties in obtaining permissions, *Portrait of Picasso as a Young Man* was not published until late 1995, some months after *Oswald's Tale.* Without referring to himself, Mailer uses his own fifty years of artistic success, failure, and experimentation to measure Picasso's career from his birth in 1881 to the end of his early manhood and the flowering of cubism at the beginning of World War I. Mailer's biography is premised on the notion that Picasso was a self-created artist who "gambled on his ability to reach into mysteries of existence that no one else had even perceived." His insights in this rather comradely biography vibrate with fellow-feeling. Picasso was "doomed," Mailer says, "to relive his obsessions through all of ninety-one years of life," to continue to paint until the end "as if work itself could hold death off."

Picasso received terrible reviews, especially from members of the professional art community, which was not eager to sanction a somewhat iconoclastic portrait of the central figure of twentieth-century art. Mailer toyed with the idea of publishing his next book, *The*

Gospel According to the Son, anonymously, but finally did not. When it appeared in 1997, it fared only slightly better than *Picasso,* with some reviewers castigating Mailer for daring to speak in the first person as Jesus. Others saw his gospel-as-autobiography as another example of his brilliance at integrating narrative forms. His motive, he explained in various interviews, was to improve on the committee prose of the Gospels, to place the wisdom and agony of Jesus in a narrative without the contradictions, lacunae, and weak transitions of Matthew, Mark, Luke, and John. As Mailer put it in an interview with Sean Abbott in *At Random,* "If I can write about Isis and Osiris and Ra, then certainly the New Testament is not going to be that difficult to do." With his plot in hand (always a worry for Mailer), he expended his creative energies on depictions of Judas, Pilate, Mary, John the Baptist, and, especially, Satan, who comes across as a devious, Middle Eastern playboy-prince. Mailer's other important achievement in *Gospel* is the voice of Jesus, who, according to John Updike in his *The New Yorker* review, speaks in "a direct, rather relaxed English that has yet an eerie, neo-Biblical dignity."

On May 6, 1998, fifty years to the day after the publication of *The Naked and the Dead,* Mailer published *The Time of Our Time,* a massive consolidation of all his previous work. Searching for an organizing principle for the 1,286-page anthology containing 139 excerpts from 26 previous books, Mailer decided that each piece would appear "in accordance with the year it refers to rather than the year it was written." So it opens with a short sketch describing a 1929 boxing match between Ernest Hemingway and Morley Callaghan and works its magnificent way, event by chronological event, to the 1996 presidential race between Bill Clinton and Bob Dole, although Mailer then violates his own scheme by ending with several excerpts from *Ancient Evenings* and *The Gospel According to the Son.* The true heart of the collection, however, is those pieces that treat World War II and the cold war, taken from both Mailer's fiction and nonfiction. Mailer rigorously excluded his own presence from the book. The preface and acknowledgments make up the only original material apart from "The Shadow of the Crime: A Word from the Author," a one-page reflection on the 1960 stabbing of his second wife, Adele. The collection sold well and was generally praised by reviewers.

In the years immediately following *The Time of Our Time,* Mailer collaborated with Schiller on television scripts dealing with O. J. Simpson and the FBI spy Robert Hanssen. He continued to write, and a compilation of his comments and insights on being a professional writer for more than fifty years, titled *The Spooky Art: A Book about Writing,* was scheduled to be published on his eightieth birthday.

In a career of length and achievement, full of awards and fights, mistakes and masterpieces, Mailer has challenged, angered, and amazed three generations of readers worldwide. Perhaps no life in modern American literature has been at once so brilliant, varied, controversial, public, provocative, and misunderstood. When asked by the *New York Times* to describe himself in one word, he answered "improvisational," providing a key to his protean identity and achievements. But he is improvisational by design rather than by default or happenstance. Metaphorically speaking, he always keeps a bag packed on the chance he will hear the train whistle of new opportunity that may result in new energy, new success, new growth. Consequently, he is predisposed—sometimes erroneously—to sense turning points and sea changes in America's health and identity, and in his own. Constant anticipation of a new plot for American lives is for him the price, and the reward, of the liberty of his consciousness. Norman Mailer can lay fair claim to being the chief narrative chronicler and interpreter of the American Century.

Selected Bibliography

WORKS OF NORMAN MAILER

NOVELS AND SHORT STORIES

The Naked and the Dead. New York: Rinehart, 1948. (Fiftieth anniversary reprint with author's introduction; New York: Henry Holt, 1998.)

Barbary Shore. New York: Rinehart, 1951.

The Deer Park. New York: Putnam's, 1955.

An American Dream. New York: Dial, 1965.

The Short Fiction of Norman Mailer. New York: Dell, 1967.

Why Are We in Vietnam? New York: Putnam's, 1967.

A Transit to Narcissus. New York: Fertig, 1978. (Facsimile of manuscript of previously unpublished 1942–1943 novel; limited edition of 1,000 copies.)

Of Women and Their Elegance. New York: Simon & Schuster, 1980.

Ancient Evenings. Boston: Little, Brown, 1983.

Tough Guys Don't Dance. New York: Random House, 1984.

Harlot's Ghost. New York: Random House, 1991.

The Gospel According to the Son. New York: Random House, 1997. (First-person retelling of the Gospels by Jesus Christ.)

ESSAYS, NONFICTION NARRATIVES, BIOGRAPHIES

The White Negro: Superficial Reflections on the Hipster. San Francisco: City Lights, 1958. (Reprinted in *Advertisements for Myself.*)

The Bullfight: A Photographic Narrative with Text by Norman Mailer. New York: Macmillan, 1967. (Reprinted in *Existential Errands.*)

The Armies of the Night: History as a Novel, the Novel as History. New York: New American Library, 1968.

Miami and the Siege of Chicago: An Informal History of the Republican and Democratic Conventions of 1968. New York: New American Library, 1968.

King of the Hill: On the Fight of the Century. New York: New American Library, 1971.

Of a Fire on the Moon. Boston: Little, Brown, 1971.

NORMAN MAILER / 215

The Prisoner of Sex. Boston: Little, Brown, 1971.

St. George and the Godfather. New York: New American Library, 1972.

Marilyn: A Biography; Pictures by the World's Foremost Photographers. Produced by Lawrence Schiller. New York: Grosset and Dunlap, 1973.

The Faith of Graffiti. New York: Praeger, 1974. (Reprinted in Mailer's *Pieces and Pontifications.*)

The Fight. Boston: Little, Brown, 1975.

Some Honorable Men: Political Conventions, 1960–1972. Boston: Little Brown, 1976.

The Executioner's Song. Boston: Little, Brown, 1979.

Oswald's Tale. New York: Random House, 1995.

Portrait of Picasso as a Young Man: An Interpretive Biography. New York: Atlantic Monthly Press, 1995.

MISCELLANIES

Advertisements for Myself. New York: Putnam's, 1959.

The Presidential Papers. New York: Putnam's, 1963.

Cannibals and Christians. New York: Dial, 1966.

The Idol and the Octopus: Political Writings on the Kennedy and Johnson Administrations. New York: Dell, 1968.

Existential Errands. Boston: Little, Brown, 1972.

Pieces and Pontifications. Boston: Little, Brown, 1982. (Essays and twenty interviews, 1958–1991).

The Time of Our Time. New York: Random House, 1998. (Best overall collection of Mailer's work, with selections from twenty-six of his books.)

The Spooky Art: A Book on Writing. Edited by J. Michael Lennon. New York: Random House, 2003.

OTHER WORKS

Deaths for the Ladies (and Other Disasters). New York: Putnam's, 1962. (Poems.)

The Deer Park: A Play. New York: Dial, 1967.

Maidstone: A Mystery. New York: New American Library, 1971. (Screenplay.)

Genius and Lust: A Journey through the Major Writings of Henry Miller. New York: Grove, 1976. (Excerpts from Miller's works accompanied by critical commentary.)

COLLECTED WORKS

Running against the Machine: The Mailer-Breslin Campaign. Edited by Peter Manso. Garden City, N.Y.: Doubleday, 1969. (Articles, debates, interviews, and position papers concerning Mailer's campaign for the Democratic nomination of mayor of New York.)

The Long Patrol: Twenty-five Years of Writing from the Work of Norman Mailer. Edited by Robert F. Lucid. New York: World, 1971. (Selections from the major works through *Of a Fire on the Moon.*)

BIBLIOGRAPHIES

Adams, Laura. *Norman Mailer: A Comprehensive Bibliography.* Metuchen, N.J.: Scarecrow, 1974.

Lennon, J. Michael. "Norman Mailer." In *Bibliography of American Fiction: 1919–1988.* Edited by Matthew J. Bruccoli and Judith S. Baughman. New York: Facts on File, 1991. Pp. 306–310.

Lennon, J. Michael, and Donna Pedro Lennon. *Norman Mailer: Works and Days.* Preface by Norman Mailer. Shavertown, Pa.: Sligo Press, 2000. (Comprehensive, annotated, chronological list of all Mailer works, including interviews, symposia contributions, letters to the editor, and ephemera— 1,110 entries. Also contains life chronology, 91 photographs, and largest annotated secondary bibliography—387 entries.)

CRITICAL AND BIOGRAPHICAL STUDIES

Adams, Laura, ed. *Will the Real Norman Mailer Please Stand Up.* Port Washington, N.Y.: Kennikat, 1974. (Fourteen essays, reviews, and one interview.)

———. *Existential Battles: The Growth of Norman Mailer.* Athens: Ohio University Press, 1976.

Aldridge, John W. *The Devil in the Fire: Retrospective Essays on American Literature and Culture, 1951–1971.* New York: Harper's Magazine Press, 1972.

Anderson, Chris. *Style as Argument: Contemporary American Nonfiction.* Carbondale: Southern Illinois University Press, 1987.

Begiebing, Robert J. *Acts of Regeneration: Allegory and Archetype in the Works of Norman Mailer.* Columbia: University of Missouri Press, 1980.

———. *Toward a New Synthesis: John Fowles, John Gardner, Norman Mailer.* Ann Arbor, Mich.: UMI Research Press, 1989.

Bloom, Harold, ed. *Norman Mailer: Modern Critical Views*. New York: Chelsea House, 1986. (Sixteen essays and reviews.)

Braudy, Leo, ed. *Norman Mailer: A Collection of Critical Essays*. Englewood Cliffs, N.J.: Prentice-Hall, 1972. (Thirteen essays.)

Bufithis, Philip M. *Norman Mailer*. New York: Ungar, 1978.

Dearborn, Mary. *Mailer: A Biography*. New York: Houghton Mifflin, 1999.

Dickstein, Morris. *Leopards at the Gate: The Transformation of American Fiction, 1945–1970*. Cambridge, Mass.: Harvard University Press, 2002.

Flaherty, Joe. *Managing Mailer*. New York: Coward-McCann, 1970. (Account of Mailer's campaign for mayor of New York by his campaign manager.)

Glenday, Michael K. *Norman Mailer*. New York: St. Martin's Press, 1995.

Kazin, Alfred. *Bright Book of Life: American Novelists and Storytellers from Hemingway to Mailer*. Boston: Little, Brown, 1973.

Kaufmann, Donald L. *Norman Mailer: The Countdown (The First Twenty Years)*. Carbondale: Southern Illinois University Press, 1969.

Leeds, Barry H. *The Structured Vision of Norman Mailer*. New York: New York University Press, 1969.

———. *The Enduring Vision of Norman Mailer*. New York: Pleasure Boat Studio, 2002.

Lennon, J. Michael. *Critical Essays on Norman Mailer*. Boston: G. K. Hall, 1986. (Ten essays and ten reviews; introduction with summary of critical and popular responses to Mailer's work.)

———. "Norman Mailer." In *Contemporary Authors Bibliographical Series*. Vol. 1, *American Novelists*. Edited by James J. Martine. Detroit: Gale, 1986. Pp. 219–260. (Includes extended commentary on reviews and criticism.)

Lounsberry, Barbara. *The Art of Fact: Contemporary Artists of Nonfiction*. New York: Greenwood Press, 1990.

Lucid, Robert F. *Norman Mailer: The Man and His Work*. Boston: Little, Brown, 1971. (Thirteen essays on Mailer's work, four on his life, and an interview.)

Manso, Peter. *Mailer: His Life and Times*. New York: Simon & Schuster, 1985. (Oral biography based on interviews with over 150 people.)

Merrill, Robert. *Norman Mailer Revisited*. New York: Twayne, 1992.

Millett, Kate. *Sexual Politics*. Garden City, N.Y.: Doubleday, 1970.

Millgate, Michael. *American Social Fiction: James to Cozzens*. Edinburgh: Oliver and Boyd, 1964.

Mills, Hilary. *Mailer: A Biography*. New York: Empire Books, 1982.

Olster, Stacey. *Reminiscence and Re-Creation in Contemporary American Fiction*. Cambridge: Cambridge University Press, 1989.

Pizer, Donald. *Twentieth-Century American Literary Naturalism*. Carbondale: Southern Illinois University Press, 1982.

Poirier, Richard. *Norman Mailer*. New York: Viking, 1972.

Solotaroff, Robert. *Down Mailer's Way*. Urbana: University of Illinois Press, 1974.

Tabbi, Joseph. *Postmodern Sublime: Technology and American Writing from Mailer to Cyberpunk*. Ithaca, N.Y.: Cornell University Press, 1995.

Whalen-Bridge, John. *Political Fiction and the American Self*. Urbana: University of Illinois Press, 1998.

INTERVIEWS

Abbott, Sean. "America's Obsessions: Norman Mailer Talks about Lee Harvey Oswald, JFK, the KGB, O. J. Simpson, and the Nasty Nineties." *At Random* 11:12–19 (summer 1995).

———. "Mailer Goes to the Mountain." *At Random* 17:48–55 (spring–summer 1997). (On *The Gospel According to the Son*.)

Hamill, Pete. "Kindred Spirits: Mailer and Picasso." *Art News*:208–213 (November 1995).

Hitchens, Christopher. "A Minority of One: An Interview with Norman Mailer." *New Left Review* 222:115–128 (March–April 1997).

Lennon, J. Michael, ed. *Conversations with Norman Mailer*. Jackson: University Press of Mississippi, 1988. (Thirty-four interviews, 1948–1987, including three self-interviews).

———."A Conversation with Norman Mailer." *New England Review* 20:138–48 (summer 1999). (On *The Time of Our Time*.)

Mailer, Michael. "Mailer on Mailer." *Time Out* (New York), October 11–18, 1995, pp. 20–21, 23. (On *Picasso.*)

———."Black and White Justice." *New York,* October 16, 1995, pp. 28–32. (On O. J. Simpson.)

McInerney, Jay. "Author to Author: Norman Mailer Talks to Jay McInerney." *Providence Phoenix,* November 10, 1995, pp. 10–11, 15. (On *Picasso.*)

Ruas, Charles. *Conversations with American Writers.* New York: Random House, 1985.

Solomon, Barbara Probst, "Callow Young Genius." *New York,* September 11, 1995, pp. 81–84. (On *Picasso.*)

———. "Struggling with God: A Conversation with Norman Mailer." *Culturefront* 6:36–41 (winter 1997–1998). (On *The Gospel According to the Son.*)

Spencer, Scott. "The Old Man and the Novel." *New York Times Magazine,* September 22, 1991, pp. 28–31, 40, 42, 47. (On *Harlot's Ghost.*)

FILMS BASED ON THE WORKS OF NORMAN MAILER

An American Dream. Screenplay by Mann Rubin. Directed by Robert Gist. Warner, 1966.

Beyond the Law. Screenplay by Mailer. Directed by Mailer. Supreme Mix/Evergreen Films, 1968.

Maidstone. Screenplay by Mailer. Directed by Mailer. Supreme Mix, 1971.

The Naked and the Dead. Screenplay by Denis and Terry Sanders. Directed by Raoul Welsh. RKO, 1958.

Tough Guys Don't Dance. Screenplay by Mailer. Directed by Mailer. Cannon Films, 1987.

Wild 90. Directed by Mailer. Supreme Mix, 1968.

—*J. MICHAEL LENNON*

Flannery O'Connor

1925–1964

"*I* HAVE NEVER been anywhere but sick," wrote Flannery O'Connor, in June 1956, to her Atlanta friend Betty Hester, the "A" of her collected letters. "In a sense sickness is a place, more instructive than a long trip to Europe, and it's always a place where there's no company, where nobody can follow. Sickness before death is a very appropriate thing and I think those who don't have it miss one of God's mercies." Eight years later O'Connor died in the Baldwin County Hospital, Milledgeville, Georgia, of complications from acute disseminated lupus erythematosus, the same disease that claimed her father at age forty-two. When O'Connor died at the age of thirty-nine, she had struggled against the debilitating blood disease for almost fourteen years. From 1950, when she was twenty-five and on the threshold of authorship, just after moving from her New York City apartment to the Connecticut countryside, until her death in 1964, she had coped with and managed, haltingly though uncomplainingly, the disease that at first seemed a forbidding specter and then became a vehicle for both personal grace and a creative source for her fiction.

Writing again to "A" on November 25, 1955, O'Connor connected the completion of her first novel, *Wise Blood,* with her lupus. "I was five years writing that book," she remembered, "and began to take cortisone in large doses and cortisone makes you think night and day until I suppose the mind dies of exhaustion if you are not rescued." Somehow she survived both this initial bout with lupus and the work of finishing her book, but she adds, "I was more or less living my life and H. Moats too and as my disease affected the joints, I conceived the notion that I

would eventually become paralyzed and was going blind and that in the book I had spelled out my own course, or that in the illness I had spelled out the book." Thus, like one of the characters of her stories, O'Connor seized the transfiguring quality of a tragic and cruel personal event and found through it a kind of salvation that would not have been possible otherwise. Had O'Connor not, because of the illness, left the North to return first to Milledgeville and then to live on her mother's dairy farm, Andalusia, on U.S. highway 441 four miles north of town, she would not have become the particular storyteller that we know, nor have achieved the unique genius she did.

Mary Flannery O'Connor was born in Savannah, Georgia, on March 25, 1925, the only child of Edward Francis and Regina Cline O'Connor. She grew up in a three-story row house on Charlton Street at Lafayette Square in Savannah, where her family lived until she was thirteen. Across the moss-draped, oak-shaded square was the imposing gothic structure of the Cathedral of St. John the Baptist—an extraordinary edifice that still dominates the square and the city—where O'Connor attended mass and grade school. The O'Connor home actually belonged to a cousin on her mother's side of the family, the Clines being a tight-knit clan with kin and property in Savannah, Augusta, and Milledgeville (the capital of Georgia from 1803 to 1868). O'Connor's great-grandfather Cline had emigrated from Ireland in the nineteenth century, as had her great-grandfather O'Connor on her father's side of the family. The O'Connors had established themselves in Savannah in the wagon-making business before the Civil War, while her mother's family had made a considerable fortune in dry goods in Milledgeville during Reconstruction. Her grandfather Peter James Cline became Milledgeville's first Catholic mayor in 1888. O'Connor's father owned the prosperous Dixie Realty in Savannah, which he expanded into a construction company prior to the Great Depression. Young Mary Flannery's summers were spent in Milledgeville, at the imposing Cline mansion on West Greene Street, and her school days were spent in Savannah.

After the Great Depression hit the South, Edward O'Connor's business ventures declined to the point that he sought a position with the Federal Housing Administration, a job that carried him in 1938 to Atlanta, where O'Connor briefly went to school. Edward O'Connor's health began steadily declining as well, with a mysterious, arthritis-like disease that was eventually diagnosed as lupus. Adjusting to the city proved difficult for both O'Connor and her mother, so within a few months mother and daughter moved to the Cline family home in Milledgeville, with Edward commuting on weekends. O'Connor was fond of saying, with typically exaggerated humor, that she grew up on a street where at one end was the insane asylum and at the other the prison. As a teenager, O'Connor for the first time was not attending parochial schools, but the creative young woman found an encouraging environment in the Peabody Lab School, attached to Georgia State College for Women, located in the center of town and two blocks from Cline House. With the Cline gift for gab, a wicked sense of humor, and considerable artistic talent, O'Connor found herself a pleasant space on the second floor of the antebellum house, where she drew cartoons and wrote for the school paper. She also enjoyed the support of an extended family amid the gregarious, storytelling Irish-Catholic Clines, who encouraged her precocious talent.

By 1940 Edward O'Connor's health had declined to the point that he was no longer able to work at his Atlanta job with the FHA. He joined the family in Milledgeville, and he died the following year—a loss that profoundly affected his daughter. Finding solace in her writing and developing some notoriety in conservative Milledgeville for what, in polite southern social circles, would be referred to as a "creative flair," O'Connor became more and more enamored with literature, reading the work of Edgar Allan Poe and other southern and local color writers who would later influence her fiction. After high school graduation, she remained in Milledgeville to attend Georgia State College for Women, graduating in just three years and majoring in sociology and English—fields, along with psychology, that do not fare well in her satire.

During O'Connor's college years, Cline House became a colorful gathering place for an array of family members, boarders connected with GSCW, and visitors. O'Connor began rendering satiric sketches of the "folks" and family who came to visit, sketches that served to enhance her developing powers of observation and keen ear for dialogue. By 1943 she was regularly writing for the campus literary journal, *The Corinthian,* and she served as art editor for the yearbook. Her obvious talent attracted the support of her teachers at GSCW, in particular her English professor George Beiswanger, who encouraged her to apply to graduate school at State University of Iowa, where she received a scholarship in journalism and eventually entered the Writers' Workshop. Mentored there by Paul Engle, O'Connor began submitting her work for publication and working on her master's thesis, a collection of stories. In fiction writing classes at the Writers' Workshop, her work was critiqued by the likes of John Crowe Ransom (the editor of the *Kenyon Review*), Andrew Lytle, and Robert Penn Warren.

During this time she began to read and write in a more structured fashion, setting aside a particular number of hours each day to write, a habit that she retained throughout her life; she also began studying the fiction style of such writers as James Joyce, William Faulkner, Nathaniel Hawthorne, and Franz Kafka. Her first story accepted for publication, "Geranium" (later reworked as "Judgement Day"), appeared in March 1946 in *Accent*. That same year she began work on a novel that would become *Wise Blood,* and Engle encouraged her to submit her work (often stories excerpted from *Wise Blood*) to literary journals and established publishing houses, including Rinehart. Shortly before obtaining her master of fine arts degree in 1947, O'Connor won the Rinehart-Iowa Fiction Award for a first novel, which made her the recipient of $750 in prize money and gave Rinehart first option to publish *Wise Blood* when she finished the book to the publisher's satisfaction.

Although O'Connor wrote to her mother daily and enjoyed keeping up with the local news from back home (by this point, her mother had inherited partial ownership in a dairy farm near Milledgeville, later christened Andalusia by O'Connor), she had little desire to return to Georgia, as she launched into her career as a writer. She understood too well that talent alone would not find her publishers and readers, so after graduation she returned to Iowa as a postgraduate student in the Writers' Workshop, where she met and became friends with the visiting poet Robert Lowell. In the following year, 1948, Andrew Lytle, who was regularly teaching at the workshop, began working with her on the novel, and with Lowell's and Lytle's encouragement, she accepted an invitation from the Yaddo Artist Colony near Saratoga Springs, New York, to live and work. After a short trip home to Georgia in September 1948, O'Connor settled into a writing routine at Yaddo and a fellowship of artists that proved invaluable. Lowell was also living there at the time, as well as the critic Malcolm Cowley and the writer Elizabeth Fenwick. O'Connor applied for and won a Guggenheim Fellowship and worked through that winter and then through February 1949.

By this time, O'Connor had a literary agent, Elizabeth McKee, and was beginning to have serious conflicts with her Rinehart editor John Selby as *Wise Blood* took shape. She found Selby to be rigid and inflexible; she wrote to him in February 1949: "I would not like at all to work with you as do other writers. . . . I feel that whatever virtues the novel may have are very much connected with the limitations you mention. I am not writing a conventional novel." She added that she was "amenable to criticism but only within the sphere of what I am trying to do." By the end of February, O'Connor and Elizabeth Hardwick, who had only just arrived at the artist colony, left Yaddo for New York, in the wake of a controversy that hit the colony when several of the artists were accused of being Communists. In the ensuing controversy, O'Connor, Lowell, and Hardwick, and others with apolitical views, publicly criticized Yaddo's director, Elizabeth Ames, who was being investigated by the FBI for endangering the colony through her involvement with a political movement. After a great deal of hoopla, culminating in a vote to retain Ames as director, Lowell left the colony for good, and O'Connor moved into Hardwick's New York apartment on 10th Street before finding a room at the YWCA and then a furnished apartment at 255 West 108th Street.

After moving to New York, O'Connor met Sally and Robert Fitzgerald, with whom she established a close friendship that lasted for the rest of her life. Robert Fitzgerald was a translator and a poet whose advice O'Connor greatly valued. By September 1949, at the Fitzgeralds' invitation, O'Connor had ensconced herself in a garage apartment at their Ridgefield, Connecticut, home, offering baby-sitting services and paying a nominal amount in exchange for bed and board and a quiet morning each day of uninterrupted writing. That same fall, O'Connor's agent Elizabeth McKee was negotiating a contract with Harcourt Brace and a release from the Rinehart contract. It was a stressful time for O'Connor, and she was often incensed by the patronizing attitude of John Selby, who had called her "dishonest," said that she was "working in a vacuum," and implied that she could not accept criticism. She wrote to a friend in September 1949: "I am on a tightrope somewhere between Rinehart & Harcourt-Brace." By the end of the year, she had been released from Rinehart and had officially signed with Harcourt Brace, but not without considerable worry and frustration.

In early 1950, at the age of twenty-five, O'Connor began to suffer from symptoms that she called in a letter to a friend "AWRTHRITUS." During the next year, as she plodded along trying to finish her novel, pain in her joints and a general malaise plagued her. By the end of the year, on a train trip home to Georgia for Christmas, she developed a high fever and arrived home more dead than alive. In February 1951 her doctors transferred her to Emory University Hospital in Atlanta, where she received blood transfusions and began cortisone treatments, and where her symptoms were diagnosed as lupus. Her family decided to withhold the lupus verdict until she had regained her health, and during the spring and summer of 1951, O'Connor was in and out of the hospital while she continued to work on *Wise Blood.* She mailed McKee a draft of the completed novel in March, but a verdict would not come until the middle of summer. Meanwhile, knowing that she would have some rewriting to do, and at the recommendation of Robert Fitzgerald, O'Connor sent the manuscript to the novelist Caroline Gordon. Gordon would become a principal literary confidant and critic

throughout O'Connor's life, and the young Georgia writer learned much about the art of fiction from Gordon's suggestions and comments.

Despite a worsening of her condition, O'Connor continued to work on the novel throughout the summer. When it became evident that she could not climb the stairs to her room at Cline House, she and her mother moved to the dairy farm that the latter had inherited with a brother. There a room on the first floor was arranged for O'Connor so that she could work a portion of each day, though her energy was virtually depleted. Writing to Sally and Robert Fitzgerald in September 1951, O'Connor relied on her characteristic humor and sense of irony to parody her new country life at Andalusia: "Me & maw are still at the farm and are like to be, I perceive, through the winter." Her mother, she declares in the letter, "is nuts about it out here, surrounded by the lowing herd and other details." In another letter to the Fitzgeralds at this time, she recounts a conversation with her mother, who, though not literary by any means, was fiercely loyal to her daughter, rearranging her life in order to nurture both O'Connor's health and her talent: "Regina is getting very literary. 'Who is this Kafka?' she says. 'People ask me.' A German Jew, I says, I think. He wrote a book about a man that turns into a roach. 'Well I can't tell people that,' she says." Undaunted and eager to find some literary commonality with her daughter, O'Connor's mother continues the conversation: "Who is this Evalin Wow [Evelyn Waugh]?" Though, for a time, O'Connor was eager to return to New England, she began to develop her own interests on the farm, which included raising an array of geese and ducks and eventually peacocks. She also read and studied—the religious meditations of Søren Kierkegaard and St. Thomas Aquinas, T. S. Eliot's *Murder in the Cathedral,* J. D. Salinger's *Catcher in the Rye,* the stories of Ring Lardner and Joseph Conrad. She found

Samuel Johnson's *Life of Dryden* and his account of Dryden's conversion to Catholicism especially fascinating.

By early 1952 O'Connor had corrected the proofs of *Wise Blood,* which finally came out in May, and sold the paperback rights of the book to New American Library. Feeling well enough to return to Connecticut in early June, she remained in New England little more than a month before the lupus flared up again, following a virus infection. After returning to Georgia, receiving two blood transfusions, and having her medication adjusted, she sent for the books and belongings she had left with the Fitzgeralds and reconciled herself to spending the rest of her life at Andalusia. After her return, she was told by her family that she had lupus. They had kept the knowledge from her for more than a year, fearing that to know would only make her condition worse, but O'Connor was relieved when she learned at last what was wrong with her. "I saw my doctor as soon as I got to Atlanta," she wrote to Robert Fitzgerald. "I know that [it] is lupus and am very glad to so know." In all the voluminous letters O'Connor wrote to friends and confidants, she never complained, questioned, or lamented the lot she had drawn. Even when she was desperately ill, she avoided self-pity, in large part through her wry wit and extraordinary humor, and she adjusted to and coped with the disease that continually wore away at her energy and mobility for the next twelve years.

THE ART OF FICTION SOUTHERN-STYLE

In the finely crafted short story "The Real Thing," Henry James dramatizes his theory of fiction writing, which he also articulates in "The Art of Fiction." Both works provide an extraordinary road map and reading of James's critical ideas, which, in essence, portray his impressionistic theory that art can only represent rather than reproduce life. O'Connor, who admired James's writing, also provides a clear and careful guidebook to understanding her fiction in a series of nonfiction essays, including "The Fiction Writer and His Country," "The Church and the Fiction Writer," "Some Aspects of the Grotesque in Southern Fiction," "The Regional Writer," and "The Catholic Novelist in the Protestant South" (all in *Collected Works* and initially edited by the Fitzgeralds and published in 1969 as *Mystery and Manners*). Like James, O'Connor also articulates her ideas about fiction writing, in an extraordinary short story called "The Crop."

"The Crop" opens with a remarkable first sentence: "Miss Willerton always crumbed the table," a mind-catching image firmly grounded in the concrete, one of the absolutes in O'Connor's fiction writing. The specific "burden of the fiction writer," O'Connor says in "The Fiction Writer and His Country," is to evoke a vivid setting "through the concrete particulars of a life that he can make believable." So in the case of "The Crop" she employs a third-person limited omniscient point of view, with Miss Willerton, a writer and one of four elderly siblings who share household chores, going about her morning tasks before settling down for a "day's write." The life of the Willerton siblings is regular and eminently conventional, yet "Willie," the narrator, has a rich interior life, an imaginative writer's life. She weaves a stream-of-consciousness reality throughout her morning chores as she dusts and "crumbs" and simultaneously constructs a work of fiction. A writer's world is both "inside as well as outside him," O'Connor writes in "The Fiction Writer and His Country." "Art requires a delicate adjustment of the outer and inner worlds, in such a way, without changing their nature, they can be seen through each other." For O'Connor and Miss Willerton the hardest part of writing is thinking: Miss Willerton laments that she spends "more time thinking of something to write about" than she does writing.

Attempting to settle on some characters for a new story, Miss Willerton considers writing about teachers, or perhaps bakers, musing to herself: "Hmmmmm. Bakers. No bakers wouldn't do. Hardly colorful enough. No social tension connected with bakers." Finally, she settles on sharecroppers, despite her lack of familiarity: "Miss Willerton had never been intimately connected with sharecroppers, but, she reflected, they would make as arty a subject as any, and they would give her that air of social concern." As she struggles to achieve just the right opening sentence, she rejects any sounds "displeasing to the ear": "Miss Willerton was a great believer in what she called, 'phonetic art.' She maintained that the ear was as much a reader as the eye." O'Connor herself maintained in "The Catholic Novelist in the South" that the particular strength of southern writers was in their acute sensitivity to the sounds of their region. "The Southern writer's greatest tie with the South," she writes, "is through his ear, which is usually sharp but not too versatile outside his own idiom." Thus, southern characters retain a colorfulness and verisimilitude for the southern writer that emanates from the region itself.

In "The Crop" O'Connor satirizes those critics who lament her tendency toward characters that are "freaks." Miss Willerton thinks, "But a sharecropper, she knew, might reasonably be expected to roll over in the mud. Once she had read a novel dealing with that kind of people," and she remembers how her sister Lucia had thrown the story in the furnace. O'Connor addresses her use of "freaks" in "The Grotesque in Southern Fiction." "Whenever I'm asked," she admits, "why Southern writers particularly have a penchant for writing about freaks, I say it is because we are still able to recognize one. To be able to recognize a freak, you have to have some conception of the whole man." Yet, she says of the critic's preoccupation with the "grotesque" in her fiction: "I have written several stories which did not seem to me to have any grotesque characters in them at all, but which have immediately been labeled grotesque by non-southern readers." The difficulty, she adds, is "finding something that is not grotesque and of deciding what standards we would use in looking."

Miss Willerton continues to lay out her story's action in her mind, noting that there "would have to be some quite violent, naturalistic scenes." However, like Virginia Woolf, who was continually plagued by the Victorian "angel" forever looking over her shoulder censoring what she wrote, Miss Willerton too is concerned about the violence her imagination conjures in her stories, wondering "what the family would say when they read them." So she rejects a roll in the mud for her character, "Lot Motun," and opts for his sitting down to morning grits while his nemesis, a female character, runs at him with a kitchen knife. At this point in the story that runs through her imagination, Miss Willerton has second thoughts about any violence to Lot, and she strikes down the enraged woman with a blow from behind and turns to Lot Motun herself, offering some more hot grits.

The character thanks Miss Willerton, saying, "You always know how I feel," which of course she does, and they sit together for some time, character and author in a kind of Pirandello moment of surrealism, basking contentedly in how well they understand each other. The two continue in each other's company all day, with Lot reminding Miss Willerton that next week the rain would probably start and if they do not get "the crop" in by then (finish the story), they will lose it. The next day Willie and Lot work tirelessly, and by evening, "pregnant" with her narrative, she finds herself in the throws of "labor" and "gives birth" to a daughter, not exactly what she had planned when she began this collaboration with her character. Nonetheless, grateful that the narrative has at least taken some shape, Miss Willerton asks her character

Lot what she can do for him, and he replies that she can go to the grocers.

At this point, Miss Willerton puts away the typewriter and tucks Lot away as well, just as one of her siblings reminds her it is Miss Willerton's turn to go to the grocery store. Having little interest in such a mundane chore and inept to boot, she nonetheless complies, finding her way to the store, where an array of tired and short-tempered men and women juggle busy lives with shopping. Miss Willerton thinks as she watches a woman with a child on a leash, "pulling, jerking him, dragging him away from a window with a jack-o-lantern in it," that she "would probably be pulling and jerking him the rest of her life." Shopping done, Miss Willerton hurries back home and to her room, anxious to return to Lot Motun, for whom she promptly writes a fictional "roll in the mud" with his dog. Dissatisfied with the progress of her story, however, she determines she needs "something more colorful—more arty." After staring lamely at the typewriter for a while, she suddenly finds a moment of inspiration. "The Irish!" she shouts. Of course! They are "full of spirit—red-haired, with broad shoulders and great, drooping mustaches."

Thus O'Connor imbues Miss Willerton with each of the characteristics she admires most in a writer: keen observation; the propensity to find fodder for her art in an experience that at least begins in the realm of the everyday; and her proclivities for the unusual, the bizarre, and the downtrodden or the distasteful. She also communicates in "The Crop" the importance of place. She writes in "The Fiction Writer and His Country": "The country that the writer is concerned with . . . is, of course, the region that most immediately surrounds him, . . . with its body of manners." The South, in particular, has that necessary "body of manners" that will create good fiction because "we have had our Fall," O'Connor writes in "The Regional Writer." She contends, as well, that "good and evil appear to be joined in every culture at the spine, and, as far as the creation of a body of fiction is concerned, the social is superior to the purely personal." The South, with its rigid religious strictures and complex and contradictory social ideals, is unusually fertile soil for the writer. "Somewhere," she writes, "is better than anywhere. And traditional manners, however unbalanced, are better than no manners at all." Just as Miss Willerton ambles between the real and the extraordinary, the imaginative and the mundane, the writer of fiction must operate, O'Connor concludes, "at a peculiar crossroads where time and place and eternity somehow meet. His problem is to find that location." That peculiar "location" was explored in abundance in O'Connor's first novel, *Wise Blood*.

WISE BLOOD AND THE WAY TO REDEMPTION

Looking back on her first book two years after its publication, O'Connor recalled in a March 1954 letter: "I wrote [*Wise Blood*] just like Enoch would have, not knowing too well why I did what but knowing it was right. I think everything in the book is right and I am astounded by it." When the book appeared in May 1952, parts had already been published as a variety of short stories: "The Train" in *Sewanee Review*, "The Heart of the Park" and "The Peeler" in *Partisan Review*, and "Enoch and the Gorilla" in *New World Writing*. However, when all the parts were put together into the book, Rinehart, certainly, appeared unable to appreciate or fully comprehend the whole, as did, unfortunately, many of O'Connor's contemporary critics, who missed the satire and were shortsighted in understanding the religious allegory of the story.

O'Connor's first book is best understood if read as a Christian morality play or allegory. It is, as O'Connor herself wrote, about "a Protestant saint, written from the point of view of a Catholic." The saint is Hazel Moats, a young man raised in a fundamentalist tradition that he comes to reject as a young soldier just returned from World War II and who, on his way "home" (both spiritually and literally), passes through a variety of emblematic experiences before he comes to "see" that "there was a fall, has been a Redemption, and will be a judgment," as O'Connor writes in a March 21, 1954, letter. O'Connor explains that Haze "does not want to have been redeemed. He most wants man to be shut of God," but despite the "free choice" that God has given human beings, Hazel Moats discovers that the undeniable truth of redemption cannot be obscured. O'Connor continues, "The Redemption simply changes everything. The fact is that try as he will Haze cannot get rid of his sense of debt and his inner vision of Christ." Thus Hazel Moats is "Everyman" on his way down the path toward salvation.

Margaret Earley Whitt, in *Understanding Flannery O'Connor* (1995), explains the symbolic significance of Haze's name, which comes from the biblical "Hazael," a Syrian king who attempts to reject God through violence to his people and whose name literally means "God has seen." Hazel's surname "Motes" comes from Matthew 7:3–5:

And why seest thou the mote that is in thy brother's eye, but seest not the beam that is in thy own eye? Or how sayest thou to thy brother: Let me cast the mote out of thy eye; and behold a beam is in thy own eye? Thou hypocrite, cast out first the beam out of thy own eye; and then shalt thou see to cast out the mote out of thy brother's eye.

Hazel Motes' name further suggests the "fog" or "haze" that he finds himself in as he painfully wends his way toward salvation.

Moats' journey begins with a train ride through the South, his destination, he explains, Taulkinham. "Don't know nobody there," he tells the inquisitive Mrs. Hitchcock, whom he meets on the train and who coaxes him into conversation, "but I'm going to do some

things." His only belongings are a new suit of clothes, a few dollars in his pocket, and a pair of silver-rimmed glasses and black Bible that both belonged to his mother. So Haze enters the tale with the "baggage" of his mother's beliefs and the skepticism of a young man at twenty-two just back from four years of war. He may look like a preacher in his new black suit, but, as he insists to the taxi driver who carries him to the house of Mrs. Watts, the local prostitute, he is a nihilist in his heart. "Listen," he insists, "get this: I don't believe in anything."

Yet Haze's denial, like the apostle Peter's, is superficial, and even the carnal and corpulent Mrs. Watts, who introduces Haze to her lascivious pleasures, sees the redemptive potential in Hazel's eyes. In answer to her charged question, "You huntin' something," Haze insists again, "I'm no goddam preacher." As he explores Taulkinham, a modern-day Sodom with its crass commercialism, hedonistic pleasures, and shallow, materialistic values, he meets a variety of grotesque and emblematic characters who function unknowingly to direct his journey. First, there is Enoch Emery, whose fundamental, intuitive knowing—his wise blood—gives the novel its title. Enoch, representative of a kind of ignorant, misdirected faith, is an eighteen-year-old working at the zoo, who helps Haze find the blind street preacher, Asa Hawks, whom he thinks can work "miracles."

O'Connor explains in a 1954 letter, "Enoch, with his wise blood, unerringly lights on what man looks like without God and obligingly brings it for Haze to have a look at." At one point in the story, Enoch absconds with a mummified man from the local museum that he tries to set up as an "icon" for Hazel's Church without Christ. It is also Enoch who, later in the story, trades his real clothes for a gorilla suit and prances off into the countryside in sheer animal bliss. "No gorilla in existence," explains the narrator, "whether in the jungles of Africa or California . . . was happier at that moment than this one," and Enoch discovers, quite by accident, "what man looks like without God." O'Connor explains the "wise blood" of both Hazel Motes and Enoch Emory in this way:

> Enoch's [wise blood] gets him inside an ape suit and Haze's gets him further & further inside himself where one may be supposed to find the answer. When I say he negates his way back to the cross I only mean that complete nihilism has led him the long way (or maybe it's really the short way) around to the Redemption again.

Haze becomes obsessed with finding Asa Hawks, the blind prophet whom he eventually discovers is no more blind than he—and every bit as "blind" at this point in the story. Haze confesses to Hawks that he does not believe in sin: "They ain't nothing but words," he insists. "If I was in sin I was in it before I ever committed any." Motes further insists that he is perfectly "clean" and needs no saving from anybody. Hawks and his bastard daughter Sabbath Lily are charlatans and blasphemers, and when Haze discovers the deception, he subconsciously charts his own route toward accepting Christian grace. However, his penance and salvation do not come before he has crossed paths with Onnie Jay Holy (pig latin for John the Baptist, the prophet who announced Christ's coming). Onnie Jay, however, is a radio preacher and every bit as phony as Hawks. His real name is Hoover Shoats, a "shoat" being a young pig and "Hoover" a reference to a popular brand of vacuum cleaners, able to suck the dirt from a carpet and leave a room cleansed and spotless. Hazel rejects Shoats by literally slamming his car door on the man's thumb and sending the false prophet howling into the streets of Taulkinham.

The turning point for Hazel Moats's strange journey toward redemption comes when he meets Solace Layfield, Shoats's hired associate who helps work the crowds. One night Hazel follows Solace home and rams the prophet's car with his own newly purchased, "rat-colored"

Essex, a representation of the liberty and free choice we have to accept or reject salvation. When Solace confronts him to question this action, Hazel replies simply, "You ain't true." Then he orders Layfield to strip off his trousers and shirt, and as Layfield bends down to untie his shoes, Haze runs over him with the Essex, declaring, "Two things I can't stand . . . a man that ain't true and one that mocks what is." Leaving Layfield appropriately "lying in the field," Hazel drives back toward town. On the way, he is stopped by a policeman who pushes the Essex off an embankment, punishing Motes for driving without a license, unaware that he has run over a man. When Hazel finally reaches Mrs. Flood's rooming house, where he lives, he opens a sack of lime and commences to blind himself—an act of penance that, at last, allows him "to see" and understand the truth of redemption. After this act, Mrs. Flood wonders at the grace that shows on his face: "To her, the blind man had the look of seeing something. His face had a peculiar pushing look, as if it were going forward after something it could just distinguish in the distance."

At length, Mrs. Flood determines to have this strange preacher-man for a husband. She asks Hazel, upon discovering gravel and broken glass in his shoes, what such self-flagellation means. "To pay," he answers sternly. Later, she discovers three strands of barbed wire wrapped around his chest, which he explains by saying, "I'm not clean," having now come full circle in recognizing the redemptive power of Christ. Mrs. Flood is fascinated by her boarder, wanting nothing better than "to penetrate the darkness behind" his face and the odd light emanating from those blank, sightless eyes, which now appear strangely enlightened. When she announces to Motes that she plans to marry him, he takes his hat and walks out of the house. "Nobody ought to be without a place of their own to be," she calls to him as he goes out the door. Two days later two young policemen return Motes to Mrs.

Flood. "I knew you'd come back," she says to him, but Hazel Motes is dead, redemption found, grace secured. "She had never observed his face more composed," says the narrator. Mrs. Flood looks at the "deep burned eye sockets," which seem to lead "into the dark tunnel" where he had disappeared. For a moment she closes her own eyes and sees "the pin point of light" herself, suggesting the possibility of her own grace. Her eyes still closed, "she saw him moving farther and farther away, farther and farther into the darkness until he was the pin point of light."

Hazel Motes may seem repulsive to the reader, but O'Connor's own admiration, if not affection, for her character is obvious. She wrote three years after the publication of *Wise Blood,* in a July 1955 letter: "Of course, I think of Haze Motes as a kind of saint. His overwhelming virtue is integrity." Although O'Connor was perplexed by the public's reaction to the book and the critics' lack of understanding, she insisted in a letter to Robie Macauley as she answered to the erroneous charge that she was a "hillbilly nihilist": "I'm a hillbilly Thomist." And of her grotesque and darkly comic portrayal of the Church, she explained in December 1958, to her friend Cecil Dawkins: "Christ never said that the Church would be operated in a sinless or intelligent way." A perfect Church would not "teach error." To those critics who were offended by Hazel Motes's long-suffering and offensive denial of the true Church, the "Church with Christ," she said: "All human nature vigorously resists grace because grace changes us and the change is painful."

A LITERARY COMING OF AGE

Toward the end of 1952, between blood transfusions, O'Connor applied for a *Kenyon Review* fellowship at the urging of John Crowe Ransom. In December of that year she wrote to Sally and Robert Fitzgerald to say she had been awarded the fellowship. "My mamma is getting a big bang out of notifying all the kin who didn't like the book," she wrote the Fitzgeralds, "that the Rockerfeller Foundation, etc, etc,—this very casual like on the back of Christmas cards. Money talks, she says, and the name of Rockerfeller don't hurt a bit." O'Connor added, however, with wry humor, "It don't, except that all they'll think is that the Foundation is going to pot. I reckon most of this money will go to blood and ACTH [her lupus prescription] and books, with a few sideline researches into the ways of the vulgar." A month later, on January 25, 1953, after receiving a thousand-dollar check from *Kenyon,* she was qualifying her cynicism to the Fitzgeralds:

> My kin folks think I am a commercial writer now and really they are very proud of me. My uncle Louis is always bringing a message from somebody at the King Hdw. Co. who has read *Wise Blood.* The last was: ask her why she don't write about some nice people. Louis says, I told them you wrote what paid.

As O'Connor strained at the reins imposed by her lupus, she began receiving offers of speaking engagements and enjoying some of the celebrity that comes with a successful first book; however, her precarious health often kept her on the back porch of Andalusia. She confessed in January 1953 to the Fitzgeralds, who had invited her for a visit, that "mamma is none too favorable toward any kind of travel for me or at least nothing longer than two weeks she says because you know who has to do the nursing when you get sick; and I do." At times she thought the cortisone treatment was worse than the disease, adding in her letter, "I am practically bald-headed on top and have a watermelon face." Yet she was learning to adjust to the confinement the lupus imposed, as she shared in a March 17, 1953, letter to Elizabeth Hardwick and Robert Lowell: "I manage well enough to live with both [lupus and its treatment]. Lupus is one of those things in the rheumatic department; it comes and goes, when it comes I retire and when it goes, I venture forth." She added that she had "enough energy to write with and as that is all I have any business doing anyhow, I can with one eye squinted take it all as a blessing. What you have to measure out, you come to observe closer or so I tell myself."

It is at this time that O'Connor purchased her famous peafowl and, as she reported to Hardwick and Lowell, she enjoyed "sitting on the back steps a good deal studying them. I am going to be the World Authority on Peafowl, and I hope to be offered a chair some day at the Chicken College." An enforced anchorite now, O'Connor had more to study than just the peacocks. She wrote in 1953 to the Fitzgeralds to thank them for sending her an inspirational sonnet by Shakespeare, adding: "My mamma asked me the other day if I knew Shakespeare was an Irishman. I said no I didn't. She said well its right there in the Savannah paper." As O'Connor's health slowly improved in 1953, she began to correspond with the Tennessee writer Brainard Cheney. Cheney paid a visit to Andalusia in June of that year, and O'Connor returned the visit a few months later, feeling well enough to travel to the Cheney's Cold Chimneys home near Smyrna, Tennessee.

By 1953 O'Connor was also working hard on a series of short stories to be published by Harcourt Brace, some of them originally published independently in literary magazines and journals such as the *Sewanee Review* ("The River"), *Kenyon Review* ("The Life You Save May Be Your Own"), and *Shenandoah* ("A Stroke of Good Fortune"). She also began a friendship and ultimately fell in love with Erik Langkjaer, a Danish-born Harcourt Brace textbook representative, who became a frequent guest at Andalusia. At the end of 1953 she was notified that she had won second prize in the O. Henry Award fiction competition for "The Life You Save May Be Your Own," and shortly after, she learned that the *Kenyon Review* fellowship had been renewed. It was also about this time that her mother brought to work at Andalusia an immigrant Polish family and O'Connor began writing "The Displaced Person," an extraordinary story that became one of "nine stories about original sin" that she planned for her new collection *A Good Man Is Hard to Find and Other Stories*.

As O'Connor began to refine the stories that would go into her new volume, she worked ever more closely with Caroline Gordon, whose creative advice had become a sustained and marked influence on her work. The next year, 1954, saw publication of "A Circle in the Fire" and "The Artificial Nigger" in *Kenyon Review*. As her deadline for the new collection grew closer, Harcourt Brace told her that she was exceeding the agreed upon length. She wrote to Robert Giroux, her editor, saying that she had just finished a story called "Good Country People," which "Allen and Caroline [Tate and Gordon] both say is the best thing I have written and should be in this collection," so she agreed to cut out something else in order to include this short story gem. She found also that, increasingly, her work was influenced by Catholic doctrine, writing in another 1954 letter: "The truth is my stories have been watered and fed by Dogma. . . . I see everything as beginning with original sin, taking in the Redemption, and reckoning on a final judgment." However, the stress of her work, the disappointment of hearing that Erik Langkjaer had decided to return to Denmark (by the end of the year she would hear that he was to be married), all took a toll on her health. A limp that she had attributed to rheumatism gradually worsened, and by the end of 1954, she could not get around without a cane. Her doctors at Emory discovered that the bone in her hip was rapidly degenerating and speculated that she would probably be on crutches for the duration of her life. To friends she did not despair, however: "Naw, I don't think life is a tragedy," she wrote in June 1955. "Tragedy is something that can be explained by the professors. Life is the will of God and this cannot be defined by the professors."

Despite her weakness and lack of mobility, O'Connor accepted a May 1955 television interview with Harvey Breit to be followed by a dramatization of the opening scene of "The Life You Save May Be Your Own." She admitted dreading the experience and watching her story "translated" for mass consumption by television writers and given a happy ending. In O'Connor's version the deluded drifter-handyman, Mr. Shiftlet, marries the retarded daughter of a woman "ravenous for a son-in-law," yet he callously leaves her behind on their honeymoon in a roadside diner. "I know it will be a mess," she wrote to Langkjaer of the television play adaptation, "actors without shoes, New Jersey hillbilly voices, etc. etc." During the interview part of the show with Breit, O'Connor's answers to the mundane interview questions were curt, though polite. Toward the end of the interview, Breit asked if she would summarize the story for the viewers: "Flannery, would you like to tell our audience what happens in that story?" O'Connor responded bluntly: "No I certainly would not. I don't think you can paraphrase a story like that. I think there's only one way to tell it and that's the way it is told in the story." When the whole experience was over, she wrote: "The television was mildly ghastly and I am very glad to be back with the chickens who don't know I have just published a book."

A GOOD MAN IS HARD TO FIND AND OTHER STORIES

Few readers or critics understood the point behind O'Connor's stories, behind her use of grotesque characters and particularly her use of violence. O'Connor dreaded reviews of her stories, writing in July 1959 that "sometimes the most you can ask is to be ignored." She also disliked the negative associations between her work—which she looked at as basically allegorical—her southern settings and herself. Making a distinction between her rural Georgia home and the dark humor of her stories, she wrote in a January 1, 1955, letter: "I know about violence only from hearsay. I come from very careful people who lock their doors at night and look under all the beds and never find anything." *A Good Man Is Hard to Find and Other Stories* (1955), dedicated to the Fitzgeralds, continues O'Connor's tendency toward an emblematic style that exposes the hypocrisy and valueless mores of contemporary American life. Again, her work has more in common with the medieval morality play and allegorical storytelling than it does with the gothic designation that she has been assigned by most critics. The violence and grotesque details of the stories have perplexed some: ten characters in the volume die, some in shocking fashion. However, "violence," O'Connor writes in *Mystery and Manners,* "is strangely capable of returning my characters to reality and preparing them to accept their moment of grace." Violence and grace are juxtaposed throughout the collection, as this odd assortment of characters stumbles toward redemption and salvation.

"A Good Man Is Hard to Find" is representative of most of the stories in the volume, particularly in terms of purpose and method of narration. O'Connor favors a limited omniscient point of view, which generally focuses on a particular character's flawed perception of reality—in this case, that character is the grandmother. Dramatic irony throughout adds a dimension of poignancy to the piece, and the tinge of dark humor gives the story an element of surrealism. O'Connor's compact prose style is sparing but masterfully sufficient with details. The contentious, dysfunctional family dynamic in the story reveals itself from the opening line:

"The Grandmother didn't want to go to Florida." From there readers are introduced to two rude children, John Wesley and June Star, names flavored with irony and satire, and to their short-tempered, disengaged parents. Both children are disrespectful to their grandmother and to strangers they meet on their way to Florida from Atlanta, and their parents are generally uninterested in disciplining them.

When the grandmother, steeped in a plethora of romantic, *Gone with the Wind* illusions, convinces her son Bailey to detour off the highway in search of an old plantation house near Toombsboro, where they hope to find a secret panel with silver hidden away, the car, in a hilariously comic scene, runs off the road after the grandmother's stowaway cat escapes and springs upon Bailey's shoulder, disrupting his driving. "Nobody's killed," shouts June Star "with disappointment" after they pile out of the badly damaged car. Almost immediately a carload of strangers pulls up, who turn out to be a notoriously brutal gang led by a man the papers refer to as "The Misfit." Instantly, the grandmother recognizes the politely sinister stranger, as the group stops to "help." The recognition is unfortunate, and The Misfit tells her so: "Yes'm . . . but it would have been better for all of you, lady, if you hadn't of reckernized me."

One by one, the family is led off into the woods and shot, with the grandmother last. Bailey utters his first kind word in the story to his mother as he is led off by one of the men, his usually petulant son, John Wesley, clinging subdued to his hand. The grandmother keeps insisting as she strikes up a conversation with The Misfit, who dons her son's shirt, that he is "a good man." With disarming courtesy, The Misfit tells her that he is not a good man. The grandmother's unconscious expletive, "Jesus. Jesus," as her daughter-in-law, the baby, and June Star are led off to join her son and grandson, elicits a remarkable response from

The Misfit: "Yes'm . . . Jesus thrown everything off balance." We have the choice, O'Connor suggests, to accept Christ's redemptive power or lead meaningless, nominal lives void of value and love, which the grandmother and her cantankerous brood have obviously chosen. When the grandmother insists that he could have been "one of my babies. You're one of my own children!" the Misfit shoots her.

At the point where the Misfit shoots her, the grandmother, who until this time has not uttered a serious word in the story, appears to come to a realization that they are indeed connected, and through a horrible act of violence she has received a moment of understanding, if not grace. O'Connor makes it quite clear in an April 14, 1960, letter that the "old lady" is actually a "medium for grace" for The Misfit himself, who shoots her at that instant "she recognizes him as her own child." "His shooting her is a recoil, a horror at her humanness," O'Connor explains, "but after he had done it and cleaned his glasses, the Grace has worked in him and he pronounces his judgment"—as the malfeasant and motley gang stares at the old lady, reclining against the ditch in a puddle of her own blood, "her face smiling up at the cloudless sky." "She was a talker, wasn't she?" one of the gang says to The Misfit, who answers the thoughtless comment with knowing profundity and the point of the story: "She would of been a good woman . . . if it had been somebody there to shoot her every minute of her life." And the reader is left to ponder this assertion and the fact that in such a world as ours both good women and good men are indeed hard to find.

All of the other stories in the collection offer some variation of O'Connor's insights about grace, redemption, and the hollow and shallow society that supports the human journey toward these ends. In each of the stories illusions are stripped away and characters discover truth, if not satisfaction. A child drowns in "The River," searching for meaning and grace in his young life that has neither. A woman who has denied her pregnancy, in "A Stroke of Good Fortune," comes to an epiphany when she recognizes the burden she has imagined a child brings can also become a stroke of good fortune in terms of growth and creative sacrifice. In "A Temple of the Holy Ghost" both Protestant and Catholic values are satirized when a child learns that even a perceived "freak," in this case a carnival hermaphrodite, is also a "temple of the Holy Ghost." In "A Circle in the Fire," "Good Country People," and "The Displaced Person," three characters that O'Connor portrays as self-satisfied, arrogant, or self-righteous come to an understanding of their true weaknesses and misplaced delusions. In "A Late Encounter with the Enemy" O'Connor wrestles with those southern delusions of past grandeur, of an "heroic" Confederacy and the myth of a grandiloquent Old South (fostered everywhere in the South by a book that she could barely tolerate, *Gone with the Wind*), in a story about the 104-year-old General Flintrock Sash. On a day he is being honored merely for staying alive all these years, General Sash dies at the Coca-Cola machine while his thoughtless Boy Scout nephew and his prideful, arrogant granddaughter are obliviously unaware. General Sash is a symbol for an Old South O'Connor thankfully puts to rest.

One of O'Connor's favorite stories in the collection was "The Artificial Nigger" (the story whose title was chosen for the British edition of the collection, published by Spearman in 1957). Here the allegorical journey toward redemption of a backwoods white racist, Mr. Head, and his grandson Nelson rests with the emblematic suffering of the African American race, which O'Connor associated with Christ's Passion. O'Connor writes in a May 4, 1955, letter: "What I had in mind to suggest with the artificial nigger was the redemptive quality of the Negro's suffering for us all." Mr. Head takes his grandson, Nelson, to the city, both as a rite of pas-

sage and "to humble him"; their journey is cloaked in the mythical and ironic symbolism of Virgil's leading Dante through the bowels of Hell, with Nelson as Dante and Mr. Head as Virgil. The allegorical journey, however, offers as much enlightenment for Mr. Head as for Nelson, whose arrogance is apparent but overshadowed by his grandfather's racism and selfish need to "master" and humble the boy.

When Mr. Head and Nelson lose their way and spend an exhausting afternoon wandering through the all-black Vining Street, or "colored" district of Atlanta, it is an "artificial nigger," a plaster figure of a Negro sitting on a fence holding a watermelon—a symbol of southern bigotry—that points the way to the train station and home. Nelson has experienced his first colored folk on their journey, and their individuality and humanity have emerged in contrast to the impersonalized, prejudiced portrait that his grandfather has tried to instill in him. By now, the roles of grandfather and grandson are reversed, as Mr. Head, like Peter denying Christ, betrays his grandson in a moment of fear and ignorance: "Mr. Head looked like an ancient child and Nelson like a miniature old man," writes O'Connor, as the two metaphorically exchange roles and stand before the curious icon and remain transfixed by their epiphany.

> They stood gazing at the artificial Negro as if they were faced with some great mystery, some monument to another victory that brought them together in their common defeat. They could both feel it dissolving their differences like an action of mercy. Mr. Head had never known before what mercy felt like because he had been too good to deserve any, but he felt he knew now.

ON BEING FAMOUS AND BEING CATHOLIC

After the publication of *A Good Man Is Hard to Find and Other Stories* in 1955, O'Connor received, despite her despairing of literary critics, rave reviews, and the volume went into three printings by September of the same year. Her work began regularly to receive the kind of acclaim that would place her solidly in the canon. She won an O. Henry first prize for "Greenleaf" in 1956. In 1957, after a CBS production of "The Life You Save" had aired in March (with Gene Kelly incongruously cast in the role of Mr. Shiftlet), she wrote, tongue in cheek to her Atlanta friend "A": "My mother has been collecting congratulations all week like eggs in a basket. Several children have stopped me on the street. . . . Dogs who live in houses with television have paused to sniff me. The local city fathers think I am a credit now to the community." And she added ruefully, "One old lady said, 'That was a play that really made me think!' I didn't ask her what."

During these years of almost intrusive success, a number of literary and personal friendships began to flourish, mostly through correspondence: Elizabeth Bishop, Cecil Dawkins, James Dickey, and Katherine Anne Porter. While she was working on a new novel in 1957, which she decided to title *The Violent Bear It Away,* O'Connor received an offer from her cousin in Savannah, Mrs. Semmes, to make a pilgrimage to Europe during April and May 1958, with the central destination being the spring at Lourdes, France, whose waters were claimed to have miraculous healing powers. Although O'Connor's letters are filled with wit and sarcasm describing their travels (she was on crutches for the whole of the trip but content that they served, in most cases, as entrée to the front of the line), it is evident that the experience meant a great deal to her, and though the journey was physically exhausting, she credited her hipbone regeneration to Lourdes. She wrote to Caroline Gordon on her return about the "recalcifying" of her hipbone, adding hopefully, at the end of the November 16 letter, that she had put away her crutches: "Maybe this is Lourdes. Anyway, it's something to be thankful to the same Source for."

O'Connor's Catholicism was central to her life and work, her idea of religion being neither nominal nor abstract. Writing to Cecil Dawkins on July 16, 1957, a year before her trip, she had said: "Catholicity has given me my perspective on the South and probably gives you yours. I know what you mean about being repulsed by the Church when you have only the Jansenist-Mechanical Catholic to judge it by." She adds, clarifying her disdain of nominal, casual believers: "I think that the reason such Catholics are so repulsive is that they don't really have faith but a kind of false certainty. They operate by the slide rule and the Church for them is not the body of Christ but the poor man's insurance system." Writing more pointedly on the subject in a 1959 letter to a friend, she asserted: "What people don't realize is how much religion costs. They think faith is a big electric blanket, when of course it is the cross." To those who criticized her Catholicism and its presence in her fiction, she wrote in "The Church and the Fiction Writer": "When people have told me that because I am a Catholic, I cannot be an artist, I have had to reply, ruefully, that because I am a Catholic I cannot afford to be less than an artist." Although O'Connor did not believe that Church dogma should, by any means, be an end to fiction, she did feel that it added "a dimension to the writer's observations" and enhanced, certainly, her own fiction. She summarized the religious quality of her writing in this way:

> It is when the individual's faith is weak, not when it is strong, that he will be afraid of an honest fictional representation of life, and when there is a tendency to compartmentalize the spiritual and make it resident in a certain type of life only, the sense of the supernatural is apt gradually to be lost. Fiction . . . is an antidote to such a tendency, for it renews our knowledge that we live in the mystery from which we draw our abstractions.

On her return from Europe on May 9, 1958, O'Connor not only felt physically better but also quickly made progress on her new book, finishing the first complete draft of *The Violent Bear It Away* by January 1959. About this time, she received an $8,000 grant from the Ford Foundation, which meant that she would not have money worries for the next few years, and before the end of 1959, she had signed a contract with Longmans, Green for the British publication rights to her book. On February 8, 1960, *The Violent Bear It Away* was published in the United States by Farrar, Straus and Cudahy, and, as she had suspected, initial reviews made it clear that, once again, few understood what she had attempted in the story.

THE VIOLENT BEAR IT AWAY

The book's donnée comes from Matthew 11:12: "From the days of John the Baptist until now, the kingdom of heaven suffereth violence, and the violent bear it away"—the "it" being the "kingdom of heaven," as O'Connor wrote to Elizabeth Bishop in April 1959. The book tells the story of young Francis Marion Tarwater's struggle to resist grace, as presented through the vision of his Great-uncle Tarwater, a crusty, unappealing country prophet living in the backhills of middle Georgia, an old man whom O'Connor clarified as "not typical of the Southern Baptist or the Southern Methodist . . . [but essentially] a crypto-Catholic." Tarwater has raised the boy to follow in his path, trying to accomplish with Frank what he failed with his nephew, Frank's uncle, Rayber, whom Tarwater had long ago attempted to seduce unsuccessfully to religion. When the story opens, Rayber, who has rejected grace for shallow, intellectual pursuits (though he bears a cross of sorts and serves penance by having to care for Bishop, his retarded son from a failed marriage), is a college professor bent on "reclaiming" his nephew from the old man's fundamentalist clutches. Old Tarwater, likewise, deeply resents his nephew for trying to use his life as a sociological study of southern "religious fanati-

cism" and dysfunction. "The modern reader will identify himself with the school teacher," O'Connor wrote in a September 1959 letter to John Hawkes, "but it is the old man who speaks for me."

The book is essentially, as O'Connor explains, a struggle "for the boy's soul between the dead uncle and the school teacher." It is a struggle that takes on almost mythic proportions, as old Tarwater's presence lingers in the boy's psyche, and on the pages of the book, long after he has fallen suddenly dead sitting at the breakfast table, on the first page of the story. Although Tarwater had schooled the boy and expected him willingly to accept the call, Frank has exerted his free choice to resist—symbolized early in the story by his disconcerted glare toward "the dark blue treeline" that stretched between sky and earth, an emblem for the divide between the material and the mystery. The "treeline" in O'Connor's stories is an important image associated with that vital moment when grace is offered and we have the power either to accept or reject. "Grace to the Catholic way of thinking," wrote O'Connor to John Hawkes in April 1960, "can and does use as its medium the imperfect, purely human, and even hypocritical." She goes on to explain, "Cutting yourself off from Grace is a very decided matter, requiring a real choice, act of will, and affecting the very ground of the soul."

Francis Tarwater's struggle against grace unfolds in the course of O'Connor's most ambitious and organically rich narrative yet. Employing multiple points of view and interweaving a brilliant stream-of-consciousness narrative—particularly in chapter 5, where Rayber goes back in time to portray his own struggle against grace—O'Connor utilizes a nonlinear narrative progression. Literally, there are five days that evolve in the story, but two generations are covered in the brief time frame. Often O'Connor repeats a scene from another character's point of view (for example, the fountain scene in chapter 6), thrusting the burden of choice and clarity of perception on the reader's shoulders as well as on the character's. If Francis Tarwater's resistance of grace precipitates cruel tragedies in the story—and certainly his drowning of Rayber's retarded son and his own cruel rape are tragic—he at least rises above his uncle's effete nominalism in that, as he asserts again and again in the story, he "can act."

Throughout the book, and particularly at the end, Francis' face has the look of "someone starving who sees a meal he can't reach laid out before him." His "hunger" for spiritual food (an image persistent throughout O'Connor's canon) is a replay of his uncle's own spiritual hunger, but Rayber's choices have led him to a sterile life where his only hope for salvation might have been found in graciously accepting the burden of raising his retarded son, a burden or penance he struggles to resist, as violently as does his nephew his own burden and penance. In the end, Francis accepts his penance, and, wounded physically and emotionally, he also accepts the hunger of his heart, "no longer as a pain but as a tide." Smearing on his forehead the sign of penance, he turns once again "toward the treeline," in the center of which is seen "a red-gold tree of fire" that lights up the dark sky, and he begins the slow walk toward the "dark city, where the children of God lay sleeping." Like Moses in the desert or Jonah in the belly of the whale, Francis Tarwater's dark night of the soul is ended, and he is ready to sacrifice himself for the cross.

The Violent Bear It Away did not sell well and both her British and American publishers were disappointed. O'Connor was not surprised, writing to Robert Giroux in November 1960 that the Longmans edition had "only sold 1500 copies. That was about 1500 more than I would have expected." To her friend Elizabeth Bishop she confessed, however, her despair over the critics' misunderstanding of the novel: "My book has received considerable attention, most all of it simple-minded—a revolting review in *Time*, . . . the usual snide paragraph in the *New Yorker* & some very funny items from newspapers. The funniest to date was in the Savannah paper . . . [which] called the hero 'Tarbutton' throughout." But O'Connor was encouraged by the reviews that counted—the praise she received from literary friends like Lowell, Lytle, and Penn Warren.

O'Connor was not encouraged, however, by her health, which began again to deteriorate. She had suffered necrosis in her jaw in the summer of 1959 while working on the galley proofs of her novel, learning by the end of the year that the bone disintegration in her hips and jaw was the result of the steroid drugs she was taking to keep the lupus in check. Her doctors considered an operation to insert steel hip joints, but the idea was rejected for fear that an operation would reactivate the lupus, still in drug-induced remission.

Despite her health problems, O'Connor was actively writing and speaking at colleges and universities. One speaking occasion at nearby Wesleyan College found her on a panel with Caroline Gordon, Katherine Anne Porter, and Madison Jones (see Rosemary M. Magee's *Conversations with Flannery O'Connor,* 1987); another speaking engagement at Converse College in Spartanburg, South Carolina, gave her the opportunity to meet for the first time Eudora Welty and Cleanth Brooks. In an effort to manage her busy life and her increasing health problems, O'Connor worked out a writing schedule of at least two hours a day of uninterrupted work, and she bought an electric typewriter to save her energy. The writing regimen allowed her to begin a new novel, tentatively titled "Why Do the Heathen Rage?" By 1963 she was also putting together another collection of stories, which would be published in 1965 under the title *Everything That Rises Must Converge,* the title story of the collection having received an O'Henry first prize at the end of 1962. Meanwhile, O'Connor gave her friend Cecil Dawkins permission to develop stage adaptations of several of her stories, with "The Displaced Person" finally produced in 1966.

Throughout the early 1960s, O'Connor tended her garden, raised her peafowl, wrote her stories, and tried to live as structured a life as she could at Andalusia. As the accolades poured in—even an honorary doctor of letters degree from the University of Notre Dame, St. Mary's College—O'Connor was not without self-doubt, writing to her friend Sister Mariella Gable in May 1963: "I've been writing eighteen years and I've reached the point where I can't do again what I know I can do well and the larger things that I need to do now, I doubt my capacity for doing." She had, however, "done very well" indeed in her final published collection, *Everything That Rises Must Converge* (1965).

EVERYTHING THAT RISES MUST CONVERGE

Everything That Rises Must Converge is an extraordinary collection of stories, addressing many motifs to which O'Connor was drawn in these later years: race relations in the South, the disjoint or disconnect between generations, the conflict between the Old South and the New, and the hypocrisy, nominalism, and effetism of a plethora of good country folk who are content to live their illusions until happenstance indecorously shatters them. In the volume's title story, most of these themes conjoin to produce a stinging indictment of the Old South, embodied in a character who comes from an illustrious old southern family, the Chestnys, long fallen from economic and social glory. The woman's son, Julian, a failed writer of pseudo-liberal sentiments, currently a typewriter salesman, is in constant warfare with his hypocritical mother, whom he criticizes relentlessly, oblivious of his own shortcomings: "She lived according to the laws of her own fantasy world," he thinks,

"outside of which he had never seen her set foot. . . . All of her life had been a struggle to act like a Chestny without the Chestny goods."

Yet the son is little better in his judgmental, ill-natured, self-righteous attitude, unable to recognize his own latent racism. On a day when the two are riding a bus, the mother attempts to strike up a somewhat condescending yet friendly conversation with a heavyset black woman who is wearing an identical hat as she. When she tries to give the woman's son a penny as she leaves the bus, the woman rages that her son "don't take nobody's pennies!" and hits the white woman with her handbag. Julian's mother is astounded, shocked, as well as physically wounded. "That was your black double," her son tells her, implying that racism in the New South is coming from both sides of the racial divide. "The old manners are obsolete and your graciousness is not worth a damn." Far more interested in gloating than consoling, Julian tells his mother, "Buck up . . . it won't kill you." However, the incident does precisely that, as the woman crumbles to the pavement and succumbs to a stroke.

A similar situation arises in "The Enduring Chill," in which another unappreciative, pseudo-liberal son, angry and self-righteous, comes home to his mother's dairy farm, thinking he is dying. He, however, finds that he has temporarily succumbed to bovine fever after drinking unpasteurized milk from the dairy (which his mother had cautioned him against) in an unsuccessful effort to have communion with the black farmhands as he gathers material for "a play about the Negro." The two Negro hands think that his efforts are curious and clumsy, and they wonder, "Howcome he talks so ugly about his ma."

In "Judgement Day," a revision of O'Connor's prize-winning story "Geranium," old man Tanner decides to join his daughter in New York rather than be forced to go to work for the local colored doctor, who tells him prophetically, "The day coming . . . when the white folks IS going to be working for the colored and you might's well to git ahead of the crowd." Unhappy and lost in the city, Tanner tries clumsily and with obvious racist bravado to initiate a friendship with a black man in his daughter's apartment building. He ends up having his hat pulled down over his head and being slammed against the wall. "I don't take no crap . . . off no wool-hat red-neck son-of-a-bitch peckerwood old bastard like you," the man tells him. Although the old Tanner is a hopeless, oblivious racist, O'Connor leaves the reader with some doubt as to whether the new world order will be much of an improvement over the old.

In these stories O'Connor has little patience with the self-absorbed children of the New South ("The Comforts of Home") or the self-righteous, hypocritical, and tyrannical old men and women of the Old South ("Greenleaf" and "A View of the Woods"). She is equally hard on superficial "do-gooders" ("The Lame Shall Enter First") and all species of hypocrites. Some of these characters have revelations of sorts but none to the degree of Mrs. Turpin in "Revelation." Mrs. Turpin thinks she is a paragon of good nature and virtue, though her thoughts often dwell on the social status of everyone around her and hover in the realm of racial and social bigotry. When she and husband, Claud, must wait in the doctor's office prior to an appointment to take care of Claud's ulcerated leg, the waiting room becomes a microcosm of every type on the social strata of the South, from "redneck white trash" to "stylish lady."

Mrs. Turpin's amiable, self-satisfied nature dominates the group, as she moves the conversation from grocery store green stamps to the quality of the shoats on her farm. When finally the graceless Mary Grace, fresh from the hallowed halls of Wellesley College, can tolerate her no more, she throws a book at Mrs. Turpin and lunges for her throat. The young woman is

at last subdued, and Mrs. Turpin demands, by way of apology, "What you got to say to me?" The girl locks eyes with her and whispers hoarsely, "Go back to hell where you came from, you old wart hog." This "revelation," that she has been judged in the same way she passes judgment on others, will not leave Mrs. Turpin's consciousness, and she accepts it defeated and "aware" as she has never been before, asking God, "What do you send me a message like that for." As the sun slips behind the treeline, a "visionary light settled in her eyes"—an apocryphal vision of the sorriness of human nature, and her own.

O'Connor was working on the collection in early February 1964 when her doctors told her that she would have to undergo an operation for a fibroid tumor found to be the cause of chronic anemia. Despite her physicians' concern that an operation would reactivate her lupus, the tumor was removed on February 25. Afterward, she was treated for an infected kidney and high blood pressure; as she spent time in and out of the hospital in March and April, it was obvious that her lupus had returned. As summer approached, she continued to work on her stories and engaged herself, at least through letters, with friends. Her letters are upbeat, despite extraordinary fatigue and pain from her kidney infection. On July 8, she asked for a priest, who gave her Communion and performed the sacrament of the sick, Extreme Unction. On July 25 she learned that she had won another O. Henry first prize for "Revelation." The last letter that she wrote was to her friend Maryat Lee on July 28, in which she wondered when she would feel well enough to retype her stories. She signed the short note, "Cheers Tarfunk," a cheerful reference to herself and her willing acceptance of God's will and grace. A few days later, on August 2, 1964, she slipped into a coma, and on the following day Mary Flannery O'Connor died of kidney failure.

Selected Bibliography

WORKS OF FLANNERY O'CONNOR

NOVELS AND COLLECTED SHORT STORIES

Wise Blood. New York: Harcourt, Brace, 1952.

A Good Man Is Hard to Find and Other Stories. New York: Harcourt, Brace, 1955.

The Violent Bear It Away. New York: Farrar, Straus and Cudahy, 1960.

Everything That Rises Must Converge. New York: Farrar, Straus and Giroux, 1965.

The Complete Stories. New York: Farrar, Straus and Giroux, 1971.

COLLECTED ESSAYS, CORRESPONDENCE, BOOK REVIEWS

Mystery and Manners. Edited by Sally Fitzgerald and Robert Fitzgerald. New York: Farrar, Straus and Giroux, 1969.

The Habit of Being: Letters. Edited by Sally Fitzgerald. New York: Farrar, Straus and Giroux, 1979.

The Presence of Grace and Other Book Reviews by Flannery O'Connor. Edited by Carter W. Martin. Athens: University of Georgia Press, 1983.

The Correspondence of Flannery O'Connor and the Brainard Cheneys. Edited by C. Ralph Stephens. Jackson: University Press of Mississippi, 1986.

Flannery O'Connor: Collected Works. Edited by Sally Fitzgerald. New York: Library of America, 1988. (Includes collected essays and letters.)

MANUSCRIPTS

Flannery O'Connor's papers are housed at the Georgia College and State University at Milledgeville, Georgia.

BIBLIOGRAPHY

Driggers, Stephen S., and Robert J. Dunn. *The Manuscripts of Flannery O'Connor at Georgia College*. Athens: University of Georgia Press, 1989.

Farmer, David. *Flannery O'Connor: A Descriptive Bibliography*. New York: Garland, 1981.

CRITICAL AND BIOGRAPHICAL STUDIES

Asals, Frederick. *Flannery O'Connor: The Imagination of Extremity*. Athens: University of Georgia Press, 1982.

Bacon, Jon Lance. *Flannery O'Connor and Cold War Culture*. Cambridge: Cambridge University Press, 1993.

Baumgaertner, Jill P. *Flannery O'Connor: A Proper Scaring*. Wheaton, Ill.: Harold Shaw, 1988. Rev. ed., Chicago: Cornerstone Press, 1999.

Brinkmeyer, Robert H., Jr. *The Art and Vision of Flannery O'Connor*. Baton Rouge: Louisiana State University Press, 1989.

Browning, Preston M. *Flannery O'Connor*. Carbondale: Southern Illinois University Press, 1974.

Cash, Jean W. *Flannery O'Connor: A Life*. Knoxville: University of Tennessee Press, 2002.

Coles, Robert. *Flannery O'Connor's South*. Baton Rouge: Louisiana State University Press, 1980.

Desmond, John F. *Risen Sons: Flannery O'Connor's Vision of History*. Athens: University of Georgia Press, 1987.

Di Renzo, Anthony. *American Gargoyles: Flannery O'Connor and the Medieval Grotesque*. Carbondale: Southern Illinois University Press, 1993.

Driskell, Leon V., and Joan T. Brittain. *The Eternal Crossroads: The Art of Flannery O'Connor*. Lexington: University Press of Kentucky, 1971.

Eggenschwiler, David. *The Christian Humanism of Flannery O'Connor*. Detroit: Wayne State University Press, 1972.

Feeley, Kathleen. *Flannery O'Connor: Voice of the Peacock*. New Brunswick, N.J.: Rutgers University Press, 1972. 2d ed., New York: Fordham University Press, 1982.

Fickett, Harold, and Douglas R. Gilbert. *Flannery O'Connor: Images of Grace*. Grand Rapids, Mich.: Eerdmans, 1986.

Friedman, Melvin J., and Lewis A. Lawson, eds. *The Added Dimension: The Art and Mind of Flannery O'Connor*. New York: Fordham University Press, 1977.

Gentry, Marshall Bruce. *Flannery O'Connor's Religion of the Grotesque*. Jackson: University Press of Mississippi, 1986.

Getz, Lorine M. *Flannery O'Connor: Her Life, Library, and Book Reviews*. New York: Edwin Mellen, 1980.

———. *Nature and Grace in Flannery O'Connor's Fiction.* New York: Edwin Mellen, 1982.

Giannone, Richard. *Flannery O'Connor and the Mystery of Love.* Urbana: University of Illinois Press, 1989.

Gordon, Sarah. *Flannery O'Connor: The Obedient Imagination.* Athens: University of Georgia Press, 2000.

Grimshaw, James A. *The Flannery O'Connor Companion.* Westport, Conn.: Greenwood, 1981.

Hawkins, Peter S. *The Language of Grace: Flannery O'Connor, Walker Percy, and Iris Murdoch.* Cambridge, Mass.: Cowley, 1983.

Hendin, Josephine. *The World of Flannery O'Connor.* Bloomington: Indiana University Press, 1970.

———. *The Otherness Within: Gnostic Readings in Marcel Proust, Flannery O'Connor, and Francois Villon.* Baton Rouge: Louisiana State University Press, 1983.

Hyman, Stanley Edgar. *Flannery O'Connor.* Minneapolis: University of Minnesota Press, 1966.

Kessler, Edward. *Flannery O'Connor and the Language of the Apocalypse.* Princeton, N.J.: Princeton University Press, 1986.

Kinney, Arthur F. *Flannery O'Connor's Library: Resources of Being.* Athens: University of Georgia Press, 1985.

McFarland, Dorothy Tuck. *Flannery O'Connor.* New York: Frederick Ungar, 1976.

McKenzie, Barbara. *Flannery O'Connor's Georgia.* Athens: University of Georgia Press, 1980.

Martin, Carter W. *The True Country: Themes in the Fiction of Flannery O'Connor.* Kingsport, Tenn.: Vanderbilt University Press, 1969.

May, John R. *The Prunning Word: The Parables of Flannery O'Connor.* Notre Dame, Ind.: University of Notre Dame Press, 1976.

Montgomery, Marion. *Why Flannery O'Connor Stayed Home.* La Salle, Ill.: Sherwood Sugden, 1981.

Muller, Gilbert H. *Nightmares and Visions: Flannery O'Connor and the Catholic Grotesque.* Athens: University of Georgia Press, 1972.

Orvell, Miles. *Invisible Parade: The Fiction of Flannery O'Connor.* Philadelphia: Temple University Press, 1972.

———. *Flannery O'Connor: An Introduction.* Jackson: University Press of Mississippi, 1991.

Paulson, Suzanne Morrow. *Flannery O'Connor: A Study of the Short Fiction.* Boston: Twayne, 1988.

Rath, Sura P., and Mary Neff Shaw, eds. *Flannery O'Connor: New Perspectives.* Athens: University of Georgia Press, 1966.

Shloss, Carol. *Flannery O'Connor's Dark Comedies: The Limits of Inference.* Baton Rouge: Louisiana State University Press, 1980.

Stephens, Martha. *The Question of Flannery O'Connor.* Baton Rouge: Louisiana State University Press, 1973.

Walters, Dorothy. *Flannery O'Connor.* New York: Twayne, 1973.

Westarp, Karl-Heinz, and Jan Nordby Gretlund, eds. *Realist of Distances: Flannery O'Connor Revisited.* Aarhus, Denmark: Aarhus University Press, 1987.

Westling, Louise. *Sacred Groves and Ravaged Gardens: The Fiction of Eudora Welty, Carson McCullers, and Flannery O'Connor.* Athens: University of Georgia Press, 1985.

Whitt, Margaret Earley. *Understanding Flannery O'Connor.* Columbia: University of South Carolina Press, 1995.

Wood, Ralph C. *The Comedy of Redemption: Christian Faith and Comic Vision in Four American Novelists.* Notre Dame, Ind.: University of Notre Dame Press, 1988.

INTERVIEWS

Conversations with Flannery O'Connor. Edited by Rosemary M. Magee. Jackson: University Press of Mississippi, 1987.

—SYLVIA BAILEY SHURBUTT

Sylvia Plath

1932–1963

SYLVIA PLATH WAS born on October 27, 1932, at Robinson Memorial Hospital in the Jamaica Plain section of Boston, Massachusetts. She was the first child of Otto and Aurelia Plath. Her parents were of German and Austrian derivation. Otto Plath, who had relatives already in the United States, emigrated at the age of sixteen from Grabow, a Prussian town in the Polish corridor, to New York, where he initially worked in an uncle's delicatessen. Financed by his grandparents, who had settled in Wisconsin, he studied languages at Northwestern University and the University of Washington, Seattle. He went on to teach languages at the University of California where he also studied biology. He began work in biology at Johns Hopkins University in 1920 and in entomology at Harvard University in 1925, receiving his doctorate from Harvard in 1928. He met his future wife, Aurelia Schober, at Boston University in 1929. They were married in Carson City, Nevada, on January 4, 1932, Otto having obtained a divorce from a previous marriage. He was forty-five; Aurelia was twenty-four.

Aurelia gave up a teaching job to become a full-time housewife, and she helped her husband in developing for publication the manuscript of his major work, *Bumblebees and Their Ways*. It was published in 1934. The couple had originally settled in Jamaica Plain, near Boston, but eventually moved to a frame house on Johnson Avenue in Winthrop, near Boston city center. Aurelia's parents, Frank and Aurelia Schober, lived nearby, and this first grandchild, Sylvia, was close to them emotionally. A second child, Warren, was born on April 27, 1935, but he was sickly in comparison with his sister. Otto Plath's health deteriorated as a result of undiagnosed diabetes. Eventually his leg was amputated and he died of an embolism on November 5, 1940. Aurelia Plath went back to teaching in order to support her family.

In 1942 Aurelia was given the task of developing a course for medical students at the Boston University College of Practical Arts and Letters. She moved with her parents and the two children to Wellesley, an area a dozen miles west of Boston, which she deemed to be healthier than her previous domicile and that in any case was more convenient for her work. "The little white house," 26 Elmwood Road, was where Sylvia Plath grew up.

JUVENILIA

Sylvia Plath's earliest written works, mostly short stories, refer to the father as a power figure in various shapes but also suggest what seem to have been racial incidents that had taken place at school—first the Annie F. Warren Grammar School in Winthrop, and then the Marshall Livingstone Perrin School in Wellesley: it was wartime, and the family had foreign antecedents. Sylvia kept diaries, wrote poems published in the school magazine, and always attained high grades in her studies. She was an exemplary pupil, anxious to please, and graduated in 1950 from Gamaliel Bradford Senior High School, Wellesley. There she had especially impressed an English teacher, Wilbury Crockett, who placed emphasis on European as well as modern American literature. Sylvia had become coeditor of the high school newspaper, *The Bradford,* and took active part in the compiling of a yearbook about the school's alumni. A story, "And Summer Will Not Come Again," was published in *Seventeen* magazine in August 1950, the year before she entered Smith College. She also had work accepted by the *Boston Globe* and the *Christian Science Monitor.*

Her story in *Seventeen* brought about a correspondence which developed into a five-year friendship with Ed Cohen, four years older than herself and a student at Roosevelt University. She entered Smith College in September 1950 equipped with scholarships from the Olive Higgins Prouty fellowship and the local Smith club but did not make friends there easily. She dated Dick Norton, who was to be the model for Buddy Willard in her future novel *The Bell Jar,* and she maintained a somewhat stormy relationship with Ed Cohen. She did well in her university courses, though not so spectacularly as she had done at school. Another story, "Den of Lions," appeared in *Seventeen,* and she wrote up her summer experiences as a baby-sitter for the *Christian Science Monitor.* Yet another story, "Sunday at the Mintons," won a prize in a competition sponsored by the magazine *Mademoiselle* and was published in August 1952. In her junior year at Smith she specialized in English, studying writing with Elizabeth Drew and even meeting W. H. Auden, who was an occasional visitor to the college. She encountered Gordon Lameyer, a senior at Amherst who had already heard of her from various sources, and she also dated Myron Lotz, a Yale athlete who had been the roommate of one of the boys she had known back home. In the fraught social atmosphere of the time, when well-brought-up girls were expected to retain their virginity until marriage, these and other relationships with the opposite sex, were not the easy triumphs that they may seem now. Further, there was always the fear of being caught out with an unwanted pregnancy, to the detriment of one's reputation and career.

One result of her success with *Mademoiselle* was that she was chosen with nineteen other girls to spend a month in New York in June 1953, to learn about editorial processes. The effect on her is of one driven by her extracurricular activities, her social relationships, and the demands of her academic work. She returned home from New York very depressed. Her condition was intensified when she learned that she had not been accepted into the Harvard summer school fiction course taught by the great Irish writer and critic Frank O'Connor. She tried electroconvulsive therapy, but without the context of counseling, this proved to be a mistake.

One hot August day Plath crept into a space under the porch of the little white house, equipped with a great many pills, and swallowed them. Fortunately she took too many and vomited them up. She was found still breathing within two days. When physically recovered, at least in part, she was transferred to the psychiatric wing of the Massachusetts General Hospital, thereafter receiving treatment at the McLean Hospital, Belmont, at the expense of Mrs. Olive Prouty, a well-known Smith benefactress.

Under the care of a sympathetic psychiatrist, Dr. Ruth Beuscher, Plath learned to trust herself a little more. During the next year she started an all-out sexual affair with Richard Sassoon, three years younger than herself, who was a junior at Yale and a distant relative of the World War I poet Siegfried Sassoon. Her previous experiments in lovemaking had hardly prepared her for the attention of this sophisticate brought up on the European continent. Over the same period of time Smith voted her the largest scholarship ever given to an undergraduate, and *Harper's* published one of her poems, "Doomsday." She was set to graduate from Smith at the top of her class.

That summer, Plath and a friend, Nancy Hunter, attended Harvard Summer School together and took an apartment on Massachusetts Avenue, Boston, where she seems to have indulged in a bout of mild promiscuity. On returning to Smith in September for her final year, she began a thesis concerned with studying the concept of the double as acted out in the fiction of Fyodor Dostoevsky—not the easiest of topics. She turned out several short stories for a class taught by Alfred Kazin and was the sole pupil in a course on poetics taught by Alfred Fisher. It was at that point that she really got going as a poet, producing what at least may be termed brilliant juvenilia. Her early poems, such as "Female Author," were highly formal in technique and very accomplished:

> All day she plays at chess with the bones of the
>   world:
> Favored (while suddenly the rains begin
> Beyond the window) she lies on cushions curled
> And nibbles an occasional bonbon of sin.
>
> Prim, pink-breasted, feminine, she nurses
> Chocolate fancies in rose-papered rooms
> Where polished highboys whisper creaking curses
> And hothouse roses shed immoral blooms.
>
> The garnets on her fingers twinkle quick
> And blood reflects across the manuscript;
> She muses on the odor, sweet and sick,
> Of festering gardenias in a crypt,
>
> And lost in subtle metaphor, retreats
> From gray child faces crying in the streets.

Though devoid of literary merit, there is enough in this apprentice piece to excite the interest of a teacher of creative writing. For one thing, it is conscientiously formal: it is couched in the form of the English or Shakespearean sonnet. The rhymes are full and the rhythms, save for that odd extra syllable in line four, iambic. It is an example of the conventional alternating light beat and heavy beat stretching over ten syllables per line that is the basis of most traditional poetry in English, be it the sonnet or blank verse itself. True, the subject is highly conventional, in that it expresses the isolation of the female author from that which ought to be her subject matter. It is self-reflexive; it characterizes itself. But again, the poem in effect ironizes this position by representing the idyllic posture of the young poet as one open to moral objection. Only someone determined to learn her craft could have written this, and that "someone" was clearly an apprentice earnestly seeking the approbation of a master.

In May 1955, still heavily involved with Richard Sassoon, Plath heard that she had been successful in her application for a Fulbright grant and that, supported by references from Mary Ellen Chase, Elizabeth Drew, and Alfred Kazin—on whom she had published an article—she would be enrolling as a foreign student at Cambridge University. She also tied for first place in the Glascock Poetry Contest at Mount Holyoke College; the *Atlantic Monthly* accepted her poem "Circus in Three Rings"; her thesis tied for the Marjorie Hope Nicolson Prize; she was photographed with the poet Marianne Moore for the *Christian Science Monitor;* and she graduated summa cum laude.

CAMBRIDGE

By October 2, 1955, Plath was in Cambridge. She was to read for part 2 of the Tripos, the main qualifying examination for the bachelor of arts degree. Her lectures included those of Basil Willey on the English Moralists, David Daiches on the modern English novel, and F. R. Leavis on literary criticism. She showed no sign of recognizing the intellectual distinction of the latter, preferring in later years to consort with such heroes of the Sunday press as Stephen Spender and John Lehmann. Dorothea Krook, who befriended her and became her favorite don, taught her Henry James. Plath stood out among the dowdy English girls of that period; with her five feet, nine inches of height, her model's figure, and her brightly casual American clothes, she seemed akin to a character from a film by Paul Bogart or Richard Alan Roth.

All the attractive men in Cambridge, where the male students outnumbered the female students ten to one, could not cure Plath of Richard Sassoon. She went to Paris to see him in December, and they traveled together by train down to Nice and by motor scooter to Venice. Back in Cambridge by January 10, 1956, she was tormented by the achingly damp weather but made contact with the local literati, especially the editors of *Delta, Chequer,* and *Granta,* in all of which magazines her poems were published. But even with such easy conquests she was in danger of sinking into another depression. The launching party of yet another magazine, *St. Botolph's Review,* however, attracted her attendance. It was held at the Women's Union in Falcon Yard, and it was there that Sylvia Plath met Ted Hughes.

Cambridge parties of those days were somewhat rough affairs, with no pretensions other than copious drink, a plethora of cigarettes, and occasionally some noisy jazz music on record. *St. Botolph's Review* had been started in opposition to an imagined Cambridge establishment of writers, and was named after the disused rectory in which several of the contributors lived, among them Daniel Huws and Lucas Myers.

Some of these characters were distinctly uncouth, as if in revolt against the state education they were receiving from the ancient university of Cambridge. Ted Hughes, despite his masculine good looks, characteristically dressed in shabby corduroy trousers and frayed jerseys, with uncombed hair flaked unbecomingly with dandruff. He had already graduated and was up on a visit from London. Towering at six feet, two inches over the crowd present, he instantly drew Plath's notice. She confronted him about his poems in the magazine, in honor of which the party was ostensibly being held. He tried to kiss her and, in return, she bit him on the cheek. It was clear that she was casting

this quiet, somewhat awkward youth in the role of Emily Brontë's Heathcliff. As Marie Singer, a distinguished Cambridge psychiatrist of the day, said, "Sex is nine-tenths fantasy."

The acquaintance was continued with the help of Luke Myers, a compatriot poet whom Plath already knew. She had a drink with him and Hughes in London at the beginning of the Easter vacation, going on to Paris to see Richard Sassoon. He, however, had gone away. After some desultory wandering, she returned to Cambridge where, in May 1956, Hughes left his dead-end job in London and joined her, taking work as a teacher at Coleridge Road Secondary School.

Hughes and Plath decided to marry, and the ceremony took place by special license, a device to deal with emergencies and those in a hurry, on June 16, 1956, at the church of St. George the Martyr in Bloomsbury, London. Their honeymoon was spent in Benidorm, Spain, then a fishing village rather than the holiday resort into which it later developed. They visited Hughes's parents in Heptonstall, on the verge of the Brontë country. Plath returned to Cambridge to continue her studies and found that the *Atlantic Monthly* had accepted another poem while *Poetry* (a Chicago magazine) had accepted six. She revealed her marriage to the Fulbright commissioners, who supplied her grant as a single student, and secured their approval. The married couple could now openly cohabit, which they did from mid-November at Eltisley Avenue. Plath had heard of a competition for a best first book of poems, sponsored by Harper Brothers through the New York Poetry Center. It was judged by Marianne Moore, W. H. Auden, and Stephen Spender. She entered a sheaf of poems by Hughes with the title *The Hawk in the Rain.* In February 1957 a telegram arrived from New York informing them that Hughes had won. From 1957, when this collection was published by Faber and Faber, until his death forty years later, Hughes was probably the most highly regarded poet in Great Britain, his only rival being the much younger Seamus Heaney.

Through the good offices of Mary Ellen Chase, Plath achieved an instructorship at Smith and, with a respectable but not dazzling degree from Cambridge, traveled with her husband to the United States and set up house in August 1957 at 337 Elm Street in Northampton, Massachusetts. At Smith, Plath taught three freshman English classes three times a week, introducing her mass audiences to such writers as Nathaniel Hawthorne, Henry James, D. H. Lawrence, and Virginia Woolf. She became increasingly discontented with the regime, largely because of its emphasis on literary criticism, and left Smith in May 1958. It is not recorded whether any student was significantly helped by her ministrations.

The couple remained at first on Elm Street, composing frenetically and seeking to establish themselves as professional writers. Plath achieved her first acceptance from *The New Yorker*. In September 1958, the couple moved to a tiny apartment on Beacon Hill in Boston, a city full of poets. Plath met, among many others, Robert Lowell and his then wife Elizabeth Hardwick, Adrienne Rich and her then husband Alfred Conrad. She took a job, typing records in the psychiatric clinic of Manhattan General Hospital and turned this to account in her story "Johnny Panic and the Bible of Dreams" (1958):

> On the blackest days, when I've scarcely time to squeeze one dream out of the old books and my copywork is nothing but weepy college sophomores who can't get a lead in *Camino Real*, I feel Johnny Panic turn his back, stony as Everest, higher than Orion, and the motto of the great Bible of Dreams, "Perfect love casteth out fear" is ash and lemon water on my lips.

She abandoned the job some time before May of the next year, 1959, but not before it had afforded her further material.

THE COLOSSUS

During this period Plath began to attend the poetry workshops of Robert Lowell, then the most highly regarded poet in the United States. Other participants were George Starbuck and Anne Sexton, whose first book, *To Bedlam and Part Way Back* (1960), had been accepted by Houghton Mifflin. Hughes and Plath spent part of the fall of 1959 in a writers' retreat called Yaddo. Here she turned twenty-seven and started a book of poems to be called *The Colossus,* the title poem of which was based on her father. Soon after, she discovered that she was pregnant. The couple decided to move to England. Once there, they stayed with Hughes's friend from Cambridge, Daniel Huws, and his wife, Helga.

Eventually Plath and Hughes found a flat on the third floor of a house in Chalcot Square, not too far away from the Huws's flat and from Regent's Park. It was cramped, with one bedroom and no room that could serve as a study. Plath claimed the sitting room and bedroom while Hughes worked on a small card-table in a cupboard off the hallway. He was able, at times, to use the study of his rich friends, W. S. and Dido Merwin, who lived nearby. The British Broadcasting Corporation (BBC) provided a source of income; both Hughes and Plath were accomplished readers and broadcasters. Hughes's second book, *Lupercal* (1960), freshly out, consolidated his already formidable reputation.

The social pattern of the Hugheses' household tended to consist of visits from a male friend of Hughes, Luke Myers or Peter Redgrove being perennial, and the two men going off to a public house while Plath cooked dinner. Sometimes they were back late, and there was, if not a row, a certain frostiness. Plath was not one for pubs, and that was why several of Hughes's friends and acquaintances scarcely knew her. She did not manage much by way of writing in these early months in London, but she signed a contract with Heinemann, not a noted publisher of poetry, to bring out *The Colossus.*

The Hugheses's first child, Frieda, was born on April 1, 1960, a month after Hughes won the Somerset Maugham Award. *The Colossus* came out in October 1960. It is an accomplished college-girl sort of book, without much in the way of emotional pressure, but exhibiting signs that the author had read all the best writers, especially John Crowe Ransom and Theodore Roethke. The earliest poems in it are probably "Two Sisters of Persephone" and "Strumpet Song," dating from 1956. The two latest are probably "The Burnt-out Spa" and "Mushrooms," dating from 1959.

One of the better poems is "The Eye-Mote." A day is darkened by a splinter flying into the speaker's eye: "I dream that I am Oedipus." However, she is not Oedipus; she is just one well-read young woman with a mote in her eye. In another promising piece, "Lorelei," Plath envies her spiritual sisters, those nymphs that float romantically down the reaches of the river. The river is necessarily culled from mythology, and the poem is all prettily done, but there is a certain lack of depth. In yet other pieces, there are various English views, and exhibitions in museums that attract the young author's attention. They are rendered felicitously in her adroit verse, with its neat pararhyming ("back"/ "gimcrack") and its sprung rhythms. Notice the habit of inversion that allows most lines to begin with a recurring stress, also called an ictus, leaping forward—"Rigged," "Lies," "Relics"—in "All the Dead Dears":

Rigged poker-stiff on her back
With a granite grin
This antique museum-cased lady
Lies, companioned by the gimcrack
Relics of a mouse and a shrew
That battened for a day on her ankle-bone

The point is, as a helpful note tells us, that the ankle-bone of the woman has been slightly gnawed. It is not clear that either of the exhibits displayed with her, the mouse and the shrew, had anything to do with the gnawing. This is just an odd circumstance, displayed for our (mild) interest.

Possibly the author's recent childbearing has had some influence over her work. Another poem, "I want, I want," begins

Open-mouthed, the baby god
Immense, bald, though baby-headed,
Cried out for the mother's dug.

But any comment on this poem would need to relate it to the eccentric lyricism of Theodore Roethke, in those days an immense influence over young poets. It seems to derive from literature rather than from any very sharp apprehension of life. Insofar as "life" exists as an entity in this book, it is there (as her writing teacher, Kazin, said of Plath's early work) to be written about.

There is enormous talent in *The Colossus,* but it lies mostly in potential. Here is a capacity for expression looking for a subject. Only twice in this volume does the subject of a poem press upon readers. One of these examples, "The Beekeeper's Daughter," is proleptic to later writing. It is part of a series of poems that runs through Plath's work and which should certainly be recognized as a sequence concentrating on bees. Here is the budding of an idea in rich imagery, although at this juncture existing almost for its own sake:

A garden of mouthings. Purple, scarlet-speckled, black
The great corollas dilate, peeling back their silks.
Their musk encroaches, circle after circle,
A well of scents almost too dense to breathe in.
Hieratical in your frock coat, maestro of the bees,
You move among the many-breasted hives. . . .

It could all have come out of a fairy story, yet there is a sense of impending pressure here.

One finds it in the verbs, rather too heavy for their purpose: "dilate," "peeling," "encroaches." It intensifies and becomes adult poetry in the final stanza:

>   . . . Kneeling down
> I set my eye to a hole-mouth and meet an eye
> Round, green, disconsolate as a tear.
> Father, bridegroom, in this Easter egg
> Under the coronal of sugar roses. . . .

There is poignancy in that "disconsolate as a tear." The eye-to-eye contact is doing far more than the mote-to-eye contact in the earlier poem, "The Eye-Mote."

Plath's father wrote a standard book, *Bumblebees and Their Ways,* based on hours of observation and curiosity, though it is unlikely that his daughter ever read it. Here, in the title poem of *The Colossus,* the polite mask comes off, and readers catch a glimpse of what this collection of poems should have been about. An acute reviewer would have started with this poem, and, in this poem, with the key moment, the dominant—in which the author is diminished to a humble little creature seeking to repair the fabric of a ruined masterpiece:

> Scaling little ladders with gluepots and pails of
>   lysol
> I crawl like an ant in mourning
> Over the weedy acres of your brow
> To mend the immense skull-plates and clear
> The bald white tumuli of your eyes.

Lysol was not only a cleansing agent but a well-known way of committing suicide—used, for example, by that forceful predecessor of Plath's, Charlotte Mew, whose sexually explicit poems Sir Edward Marsh would not permit into his anthology, *Georgian Poetry.* Lysol is also alluded to in a fragmentary poem by T. S. Eliot, which Plath would certainly have known, *Sweeney Agonistes.*

The key poem in *The Colossus* does not have to do with the passive viewing of effigies in museums but with the active attempt to renovate one of them. The author wants the image of her dead father, kept in the recesses of her memory, back, restored, alive. Anyone interested in Plath's development from this promising first book would expect the future to be built upon this structure. The reviewers were not so acute as that. One of the shrewder ones, A. E. Dyson, wrote in the *Critical Quarterly* of "her occasional sense of being teased by glimpses of better worlds, also lurking just behind the surfaces of things."

Plath's reputation in this period, however, was nothing compared with that of Hughes. He was feted, interviewed, quoted; he was the cynosure of all eyes. The effect of this upon Plath, who had a miscarriage in February 1961, was a tendency to jealousy concerning the numerous women editors and producers who commissioned Hughes's work. After an especially successful session with the radio producer Moira Doolan, Hughes returned to the flat in Chalcot Square to find that Plath had destroyed all his writing in progress and also torn up a number of books. There had already been incidents of conflict with his family. Plath was proving to be a difficult person to live with.

COUNTRY MATTERS

Pregnant again, and with the baby due in January, the Hugheses decided to move to the country. After some searching in the west of England, they discovered Court Green, a place in Devon, which had nine or ten rooms. Court Green was surrounded by more than two acres of grounds and placed near a village, and the village itself was on a main railway line that led to London, so that they need not feel cut off. They sublet the flat at Chalcot Square to David Wevill, a Canadian poet whom Hughes had met through his Cambridge connections.

Plath and Hughes moved into Court Green on August 31, 1961. During this period of removal and resettlement, Plath completed a spate of poems including some of her best work, much of which is included in a posthumous volume, *Crossing the Water* (1971). The title poem dates from April 1962. It is a lyrical appreciation of the delights incident upon being where one is. There is also, however, the feeling that a change is being made; that the two people who seem to be involved in the poem are crossing some such river as Acheron over which, it was said in classical mythology, the souls of the dead were conveyed:

> A little light is filtering from the water flowers.
> Their leaves do not wish us to hurry:
> They are round and flat and full of dark advice.

This quietude is characteristic of the poems gathered in *Crossing the Water*. They mostly occur after the apprentice work of *The Colossus* and before the Sturm und Drang represented in *Ariel*.

A singularly beautiful poem included in *Crossing the Water* was written before the move from London. It dates from October 1960 and is called "Candles." It sustains throughout, both in terms of subject and expression, a gentle romanticism that gives us a good idea of what Plath could have accomplished if she had spared herself. It plays upon both the physical appearance and the history of candles to give some idea of a more arbitrary, more easygoing, more compassionate world:

> It is touching, the way they'll ignore
>
> A whole family of prominent objects
> Simply to plumb the deeps of an eye
> In its hollow of shadows, its fringe of reeds,
> And the owner past thirty, no beauty at all.

Cunningly, the fact of the newborn baby is woven in. Readers get the picture of the young mother nursing her child in a world that can be censorious, and thinking of herself as being ephemeral, like these same candles, more retrospective in vision as the years pass by. The poem ends, not quite addressing either the candles or her baby, on a sustained falling cadence:

> I watch their spilt tears cloud and dull to pearls.
> How shall I tell anything at all
> To this infant still in a birth-drowse?
> Tonight, like a shawl, the mild light enfolds her,
> The shadows stoop over like guests at a
>   christening.

Plath later made a recording of this poem. To hear it is to undergo one of the most poignant experiences modern literature has to offer. It is hard to believe that there was anything that an artist of this distinction would have been unable to accomplish.

Of a kindred quality is a poem of October 1961, "Mirror." The plotting in "Mirror" is meticulous, and the form is that of a perfect dramatic monologue. In some ways, the poem is like one of those remarkable Anglo-Saxon riddles that give the body of a text and demand that the reader supply the title. There is little here which is not true of a looking-glass, except that it speaks: "I am silver and exact," "I am not cruel, only truthful":

> Most of the time I meditate on the opposite wall.
> It is pink, with speckles. I have looked at it so
>   long
> I think it is part of my heart. But it flickers.
> Faces and darkness separate us over and over.

The subtext of the poem is a disquisition on time and growing older, accomplished through the running metaphor of that other reflective entity, a lake. The second half tells of a woman looking into the mirror, "searching my reaches for what she really is," then turning back to the more flattering images revealed by "those liars," the candles or the moon. To that extent "Mirror" is a companion-poem to "Candles." The poem ends with a revelation in keeping with its naturalistic candor throughout:

In me she has drowned a young girl, and in me an
old woman
Rises toward her day after day, like a terrible fish.

The poem is written in a blank verse for our time, which has learned both from Robert Frost and from Wallace Stevens. It gives one the sense that, had Plath lived to something like the years reached by those masters, she might well have rivaled them in technique.

THE BELL JAR

Some months earlier, during the spring of 1961, Knopf accepted *The Colossus* for American publication, and, elated by this, Plath began her one completed novel, *The Bell Jar* (1963). It is through this novel, rather than through her poems, that most readers have come to know of Sylvia Plath. In many ways, it is the ideal student novel, as *Catcher in the Rye* (1951) by J. D. Salinger had been a generation before.

Plath's novel is based on her stay in New York in June 1953. On June 19 of that year, Ethel and Julius Rosenberg had been executed for spying. Hence the striking start of the novel: "It was a queer sultry summer, the summer they electrocuted the Rosenbergs, and I didn't know what I was doing in New York." The novel reads like a first-person journal in all its rawness and apparent artlessness. What art there is inheres in a well-trained ear, that rejects anything vague or specious. But there is little plot to hold all this together, although there are many incidents: clumsy passes being made at the protagonist, a good deal of ill health through injudicious eating and drinking, a leg broken in skiing, a suicide attempt. What binds these together, if anything, is a persistent sense of loss, focused on the memory of a father. One key incident is a visit to the graveyard where he lies buried:

At the foot of the stone I arranged the rainy armful of azaleas I had picked from a bush at the gateway of the graveyard. Then my legs folded under me, and I sat down in the sopping grass. I couldn't understand why I was crying so hard.

Then I remembered that I had never cried for my father's death.

My mother hadn't cried either. She had just smiled and said what a merciful thing it was for him he had died, because if he had lived he would have been crippled and an invalid for life, and he couldn't have stood that, he would rather have died than had that happen.

I laid my face to the smooth face of the marble and howled my loss into the cold rain.

There is no accurate sense of the father's character here. All is centered on the feelings of the girl-narrator. So it is through the book. There are certainly areas of distinguished writing— notice the internal rhyme patterns in the prose of the extract just quoted—but the narrative achieves its effects because of vivid rendition of the protagonist's feelings, not through any perceptive recording of other characters or of the external world. Be that as it may, this is exactly what an adolescent audience was waiting for, and *The Bell Jar* became the key book for at least two generations of college students.

Heinemann accepted the novel in October 1961. However, in view of its autobiographical content, it was decided to publish it under the pseudonym Victoria Lucas—Lucas possibly because of the full name of Hughes's old friend, Luke Myers. Only a few month later, on January 17, 1962, the new baby, Nicholas, was born.

The rural habitat at Court Green deprived the couple of their big-town associations. It was better for Hughes, who could slip away to a publishers' meeting or a rendezvous with writers, than for Plath, who was tied up with the two babies. They had visitors, but these were as likely to be irritants to Plath, with her duties as hostess, as alleviations. Among those visitors were David and Assia Wevill, who arrived for a short weekend on May 19, 1962. There is no doubt that Hughes and Assia, who was an exceptionally beautiful woman, were attracted to each other. After this visit, during which there was a degree of tension, Plath began a cycle of poems in which Hughes became a kind of replacement of Otto, the dreaded father figure.

During a visit from her mother in July, and while Hughes was briefly absent in London, Plath made a bonfire of his papers and insisted that he leave the house. Though he returned, the couple began discussing a trial separation. They stayed together long enough for them both to take an Irish holiday in Cleggan, on the Connemara coast, domicile of the poet Richard Murphy, whose entry Plath, together with other judges, had just placed first in a competition organized by the Cheltenham Literary Festival. The couple arrived in Cleggan together but split up soon afterward. Plath returned via Dublin to Court Green. Hughes went to London where he continued to see Assia.

ARIEL

Upon her return Plath filled her intervals of insomnia by writing the poems through which she is best known. Forty of them were produced between the end of September and the first day of December. These were mostly to appear in a collection, published posthumously, called *Ariel* (1965). Those who were acquainted with Plath chiefly through the accomplished college-girl work assembled in the previous book were astonished by the new poems spat at them furiously over the air in a Radio 3 broadcast organized by her longtime producer, George MacBeth. The characteristic diction of the poems is drawn from folk song and nursery rhyme. A good deal of the imagery derives from fairy stories, especially the darker ones like those of the Grimm Brothers: gold rings, flapping bats, spider-men, yew trees, witches, balloons. Yet the tone is manic, almost approaching that of a frenetic kind of light verse. The content, however, is far from light.

The poems that drew most attention were "Daddy" and "Lady Lazarus," and no wonder. Though they may lose something of their surprise quality by frequentation, there is no doubt that their direct force shook the preconceptions of many listeners and, subsequently, readers. In "Daddy" the male figure looms so malevolently that the poem has become the banner of many an aggressive feminist:

> You do not do, you do not do
> Any more, black shoe
> In which I have lived like a foot
> For thirty years, poor and white,
> Barely daring to breathe or Achoo.

> Daddy, I have had to kill you.
> You died before I had time——
> Marble-heavy, a bag full of God,
> Ghastly statue with one grey toe
> Big as a Frisco seal

> And a head in the freakish Atlantic
> Where it pours bean green over blue
> In the waters off beautiful Nauset.
> I used to pray to recover you.
> Ach, du.

This poem is basically a continuation of "The Colossus." In part, the father figure is seen as a statue, a monument. It may be questioned how the symbol of the shoe got into the poem. In fact, it could have been any image capable of bearing a reference to masculinity: a penis, say, or a column. But Plath's education forbade undue explicitness, and "shoe" has the advantage of permitting a great deal of rhyming words congruent with it.

The poem would collapse into a scream of hysteria were it not for the unshakable craft Plath had forged in her schooldays. As it is, the form derives from the stepped verse of William Carlos Williams, who wrote movingly about women in distressed situations. Also, more immediately, it is inspired by the poem "Roosters," in which Elizabeth Bishop, one of the poets Plath most respected, deprecates male pretensions. In "Daddy" Plath is linking the early death of her father, which she sees as a betrayal, with her growing up as a woman in a male-controlled world, and with being married to a husband whom she suspects of betraying her with another woman.

Alongside this howl of rage is "Lady Lazarus." Hints regarding German and Jewish ancestry in "Daddy" are here developed into an identification with the victims who perished in the Nazi prison camps during the war. The protagonist of "Lady Lazarus" manages to resurrect herself every ten years. Thus, the plot of the poem seems to depend on some imagined death soon after Plath's father died, the attempted suicide at home when she was twenty-one, and the suicide she is now contemplating. From each of these she seems to rise:

> I have done it again.
> One year in every ten
> I manage it——
>
> A sort of walking miracle, my skin
> Bright as a Nazi lampshade,
> My right foot
>
> A paperweight,
> My face a featureless, fine
> Jew linen.
>
> Peel off the napkin
> O my enemy.
> Do I terrify? ——

In draft, excised from the finished version of this poem, the next stanza runs: "Yes yes Herr professor / it is I / Can you deny. . . ." And then the poem goes on, in the next printed line, "The nose, the eye pits, the full set of teeth?" This ratifies the notion one might have had anyway that this poem is addressed in hysterical reproach to Plath's father. One can say this: that the poem in question would certainly have horrified the industrious, conformist figure of Otto Plath, had he been unfortunate enough to have lived to see it.

"Lady Lazarus" is a shriek of hatred against men, succumbing to misery even through its air of triumph which so sorely brings no relief. The poem ends, however, anything but wearily:

> Ash, ash—
> You poke and stir.
> Flesh, bone, there is nothing there——
>
> A cake of soap,
> A wedding ring,
> A gold filling.
>
> Herr God, Herr Lucifer
> Beware
> Beware.
>
> Out of the ash
> I rise with my red hair
> And I eat men like air.

It is hard, though one must try, to read this poem as a work of literature. One's first reaction is, necessarily, "how dreadful to feel like that." It is tempting to consign it to the psychiatrist rather than to the reader of literature. Yet the force, which it undoubtedly directs outward, is also controlled. The poem may even, through the agony it displays, have earned the right to draw upon imagery stemming from the most terrible events in the world. For the Nazis not only slaughtered their victims by the millions, but some Nazis even extracted the gold fillings from their victims' teeth to make jewelry and peeled off their skin to make lampshades.

How Plath got herself into this state is a matter of clinical inquiry. One may infer a severe dislocation between two aspects of personality: that which seeks, as an artist does, to plough out a furrow of one's own, and that which seeks to please an already existing establishment. The two attitudes are contradictory and hence incompatible. Plath was highly accomplished and attempted to be everything at once: poet, novelist, student, journalist, broadcaster, housewife, mother. Nobody could do all that, and, above all, nobody could do it at the pitch of perfection she sought.

The structure of *Ariel* appears to be somewhat arbitrary. Poems may have been omitted that should have been included, and the arrangement may not have been what the author intended. Nevertheless, in its present shape it has taken its place among the classics of the time and, until some superior form of publication is agreed upon, it is better to consider this and other books by Sylvia Plath as we have them.

Other poems that require notice in this remarkable book of 1965 include, in order of appearance: "Morning Song," "The Applicant," "Tulips," "Cut," "Berck-Plage," "The Rival," and four items that belong in the much longer Bee Sequence, "The Bee Meeting," "The Arrival of the Bee Box," "Stings," "Wintering"— though there are others with which one would not wish to dispense. What is chiefly noticeable is the strength with which the poems are plotted, the decisive onsets at the various beginnings, and the charismatic quality of the linguistic texture. These are not poems that lie flat on the page.

"Morning Song" is one of the happier pieces, announcing the arrival of a baby. It is only after further acquaintance that one notices a certain glib romanticizing in the writing: "Love set you going like a fat gold watch." There is only a tenuous relationship between a baby's heart starting to beat and the ticking of a gold watch; indeed, the appropriateness of comparing a living being with a mechanical artifact itself may be held in question. The dominant of the poem, that which gives it persuasiveness and intensity, comes rather late: "One cry, and I stumble from bed, cow-heavy and floral / In my Victorian nightgown." The clumsiness of the speaker's movements disperse what romanticism lingers from the beginning, but it is noticeable that this realistic verse refers to the mother, not the child. The poem succeeds, if at all, through afflatus: its striking beginning and the recovery of that exuberance at the end:

> . . . And now you try
> Your handful of notes;
> The clear vowels rise like balloons.

"The Applicant" is more a sort of joke-poem. Plath is not remarkable for her humor, and the humor here savors of cartoon; it is two-dimensional. The applicant in question is a man, and he is being offered a female with all working parts, somewhat after the pattern of the figures portrayed in popular songs of Plath's epoch, such as "Paper Doll," as sung by the Mills Brothers, and "Living Doll," associated with Cliff Richard. The doll in question is guaranteed to be obedient. The key lines are:

> Naked as paper to start
>
> But in twenty-five years she'll be silver,
> In fifty, gold.
> A living doll, everywhere you look.
> It can sew, it can cook,
> It can talk, talk, talk.

"The Applicant" contains at once a compendium of the chauvinistic references to women in popular song and also a caricature version of what takes place in a bourgeois marriage, with its silver wedding anniversary of twenty-five years, golden wedding anniversary of fifty years, and so on. Behind the jocose rhythms, there is a good deal of bitterness—expressed chiefly through the gap between perception of a civilized life and the macabre "reality" that Plath envisages.

"Tulips" shows Plath at her most verbally charismatic. The poem begins with characteristic bite: "The tulips are too excitable, it is winter here. / Look how white everything is, how quiet, how snowed-in." This contrast between the sensual warmth of the tulips and the pale remoteness of the speaker, who is a hospital patient, is maintained throughout the poem. Any other writer might have rested with the whiteness, the numbness, the washed-out quality, the sheer emptiness of the patient. It could have been managed. There is plenty of room for play upon words:

> They have propped my head between the pillow
>   and the sheet-cuff
> Like an eye between two white lids that will not
>   shut.
> Stupid pupil. . . .

The last phrase is a pun to delight William Empson, analyst of ambiguity, and all other students of the metaphysicals. The pun is obvious enough once Plath has made it. But all this paleness and whiteness is disturbed throughout the poem by the almost anthropomorphic activity of the tulips: "The tulips are too red in the first place, they hurt me"; "Their redness talks to my wound"; "they weigh me down, / Upsetting me with their sudden tongues and their colour, / A dozen red lead sinkers round my neck"; "The vivid tulips eat my oxygen." The set of contrasts achieves closure with an astonishing synthesis between the internal organs of the patient and the troubling entry of the tulips:

> And I am aware of my heart: it opens and closes
> Its bowl of red blooms out of sheer love of me.
> The water I taste is warm and salt, like the sea,
> And comes from a country far away as health.

"Cut" works through an expressionist exaggeration of a household event. Plath's mastery of the excessively short line is exemplary. It is managed by a jerkily energetic rhythm wholly consonant with a jokey treatment of the subject matter. The speaker's thumb, which has just been cut, is transformed into a scalped pilgrim, a turkey wattle, a bottle of pink fizz, and then weirdly expanded to a gap out of which run a million soldiers—"redcoats, every one." Plath must have been one of the first poets to use the word "kamikaze" in her verse, which is all part of the expansion of the cut thumb into apparently universal warfare. But then Plath, with equal skill, shuts the whole venture down, and what readers see at the end is

> Trepanned veteran,
> Dirty girl,
> Thumb stump.

"Berck-Plage" is the most obscure of Plath's major poems, partly because it is a conflation of two apparently unrelated experiences that bring in a third which is not spelled out. The year

before it was written, 1961, the Hugheses had set off to spend time on a holiday with W. S. and Dido Merwin in Lacan in southern France. On the way, they motored through Berck-Plage on the Normandy coast, which contained sanatoria for men wounded in the Algerian war. The sufferers sunned themselves on the beach intermingled with the vacationers. A year later Plath was to witness the decline through cerebral hemorrhage of their neighbor in Devon, Percy Key, himself resettled from London with his wife, Rose. Plath attended Percy's funeral on June 29, 1962, and she seems to some extent to have associated it with the funeral of her father, Otto, which of course she had not attended. It is from this last that the black boot–black shoe symbolism seeps in. In an imaginative synthesis, Plath has an Otto/Percy figure buried on Berck-Plage. Clearly, the admixture of wounded men and vacationers had deeply affected her.

Thus the poem depicts a priest in funereal garb walking slowly up a beach stretching past a hotel and itself populated by mackerel gatherers, children with their hooks and cries, invalids in tubular steel wheelchairs. All of this serves as a backdrop to the funeral of "an old man . . . vanishing. / There is no help in his weeping wife." The speaker, through whose surrealistic vision all this flourishes, denies the necessity for her own presence there—"I am not a nurse, white and attendant"—at the same time as having to admit her attendance in another capacity, that of mourner: "dark-suited and still, a member of the party." The beauty of the hinterland—"The natural fatness of these lime leaves"—forms an ironic comment on the whole vista.

Behind it all is not only guilt at failure to mourn the father properly—without a funeral ceremony, there is no closure—but resentment at being expected to attend at all, probably tinctured by a sense of duty in having reluctantly visited the dying Percy Key and a feeling of disgust at the old man's physical deterioration. The poem ends, maintaining its slow dignity:

And the priest is a vessel,
A tarred fabric, sorry and dull,

Following the coffin on its flowery cart like a
beautiful woman,
A crest of breasts, eyelids and lips

Storming the hilltop.
Then, from the barred yard, the children

Smell the melt of shoe-blacking,
Their faces turning, wordless and slow,

Their eyes opening
On a wonderful thing——

Six round hats in the grass and a lozenge of wood,
And a naked mouth, red and awkward.

For a minute the sky pours into the hole like
plasma.
There is no hope, it is given up.

"The Rival" is a straightforward hate poem. The other woman is compared with the moon, which borrows light but creates nothing, and is stripped when seen without her mysteries: "in the daytime she is ridiculous." The rival also has the qualities of the medusa, a species of Gorgons or sub-women found in classical mythology. Though renowned for her beauty, especially that of the locks of her hair, the medusa has the property of reducing everything at which she looks to stone. The speaker of the poem holds her in contempt, yet feels harassed by her: "Your dissatisfactions, on the other hand, / Arrive through the mailslot with loving regularity." The poem, which in tone and emphasis is a dramatic monologue, suggests that the dreaded rival is as obsessed by the speaker of the poem as the speaker is by her rival: "No day is safe from news of you, / Walking about in Africa maybe, but thinking of me."

"Lesbos," included in the U.S. edition of *Ariel,* may be assumed, with no undue emphasis on biography, as Plath's reaction to her rival, Assia Wevill. The poem begins with a highly sibilant diatribe. Its positioning of the "-s" and "-z" words will bear a degree of attention:

Viciousness in the kitchen!
The potatoes hiss.
It is all Hollywood, windowless,
The fluorescent light wincing on and off like a
terrible migraine,
Coy paper strips for doors—
Stage curtains, a widow's frizz.

What characterizes this utterance is not the sibilant consonants only, but the preference for short vowels high in pitch: "viciousness," "kitchen," "windowless," "wincing." "strips," "frizz," and so on. All this makes for a highly distinctive tone of voice. It is a voice utterly self-absorbed, addressing the reader with peremptory force, an eruption such as a manic journal-entry proclaiming, with undeniable sincerity, pain.

The Bee Poems make up an identifiable sequence. Four of them occur in *Ariel.* "The Bee Meeting" pitches tone against subject-matter. The tone is excited, as though anticipating a party, but it is soon clear that the central figure, who speaks the poem, is an object of sacrifice:

I am nude as a chicken neck, does nobody love
me?
Yes, here is the secretary of bees with her white
shop smock,
Buttoning the cuffs at my wrists and the slit from
my neck to my knees.

Swathed in the smock, she is now not only clothed but imprisoned. This does not prevent an identification with the queen bee: "The villagers open the chambers, they are hunting the queen. / / She is old, old, old, she must live another year, and she knows it." The villagers, from initially welcoming figures, change into a concourse of threats. They include a rector in black, identifiable as Otto Plath, a midwife who consigns one to domesticity, and also a mysterious apparition in a green helmet that seems to combine the functions of surgeon and executioner. By the end of the poem, the victim is unquestionably dead—still in that exuberant, bustling verse: "The villagers are untying their disguises, they are shaking hands. / Whose is that long white box in the grove, what have they accomplished, / why am I cold?" The bustle is maintained through the plethora of light syllables in relation to the stresses on the relatively fewer strong ones.

"The Arrival of the Bee Box" is altogether a simpler poem. It does not involve the villagers; the activity has been sparked off by the protagonist herself. She has ordered a box that might almost be a small coffin, and certainly it is the potential agency of death, for it contains a swarm of bees that are angry, as can be inferred by the sound they make:

> It is the noise that appals me most of all,
> The unintelligible syllables.
> It is like a Roman mob,
> Small, taken one by one, but my god, together!

Opening the box could prove certain death. She wishes she were a tree—"the laburnum, its blond colonnades"—but pictures herself as she is, in her beekeeper's gear: "my moon suit and funeral veil." It is a simple story, simply told, but deftly expressed almost beyond criticism.

"Stings" is a bee version of "Lady Lazarus." As in "The Bee Meeting," there is a degree of duality in the poem. The speaker hands the combs of honey to a man in white, but she is conscious of the brood cells and, somewhere within them, the queen:

> . . . she is old,
> Her wings torn shawls, her long body
> Rubbed of its plush——
> Poor and bare and unqueenly and even shameful.

The speaker identifies with the old queen, and says she has been worn out by household drudgery. It is clear that this is a fate she expects for herself, and her blame settles upon "a third person" who ostensibly "has nothing to do with the bee-seller or with me." He seems to be identified with the surgeon in the green mask who features in "The Bee Meeting." "The sweat of his efforts," sweet in its time, has reduced the queen to this decrepitude after an orgy of child-bearing. But the queen, with whom the speaker of the poem now explicitly identifies, will avenge herself:

> Now she is flying
> More terrible than she ever was, red
> Scar in the sky, red comet
> Over the engine that killed her——
> The mausoleum, the wax house.

"The Swarm," published in the U.S. edition of *Ariel,* comes next in the Bee Sequence. In this poem the bees are symbols of the aggression of Napoleon's Grand Army and of the resistance that it encounters. The poem is intensely graphic, and also onomatopoeic in its insistence on a synthesis of sound, vision, and emotion: "Somebody is shooting at something in our town—— / A dull pom, pom in the Sunday street." The bees shoot up into the boughs of trees seventy feet from the ground. They are the very quintessence of anger: "The bees argue, in their black ball, / A flying hedgehog, all prickles." The speaker of the poem claims that her reason for shooting at the angry bees is that "They would have killed *me.*" As well as being part of Plath's bee mythology, the poem is an allegory of war.

"The Swarm" is logically followed by "Wintering," another of the *Ariel* poems. Here the bees are surviving under artificial conditions: they have no contact with flowers. In other words, they have rid themselves of the men and are all women—"Maids and the long royal lady"—but they are slowed down, and there is some question as to whether the swarm will survive. However, the poem ends on a hopeful note—"The bees are flying. They taste the spring"— an unusual occurrence in this threatening sequence.

LETTING GO

The *Ariel* poems were written in a state of mania. There is no doubt that Plath received an uplift from a sense that she was free to be a poet and had shed the bourgeois expectation of her youth that had cast her in the role of housewife. It was a time of dramatic decisions. After abandoning a previous plan to settle in Ireland, she acquired a five-year lease on a rented flat in a house, 23 Fitzroy Road, in Primrose Hill, an area that she had considered several years before she went to live, first in Chalcot Square, then in Court Green. She moved in, with the children, on December 12, 1962.

By January a terrible winter had started, the worst London had known for many years. Plath and the children were ill. She had hired a Belgian au pair to help her with the children, but this arrangement did not last. Plath claimed to be helpless and penniless and stayed with various friends who noticed her mood swings. Her antipathy to Hughes, who had been for several months conducting an open affair with Assia Wevill, meant that he was limited in what he could do to help her on the domestic side. By February 10 Plath was back in the Fitzroy Road flat. Early on the morning of February 11, she turned on the gas of her oven and put her head in it. She had left cups of milk beside the childrens' beds and had stuffed towels under the doors of their rooms to protect them from escaping gas.

Plath had arrived at the flat with nearly all the *Ariel* poems already written. The ones produced at Fitzroy Road include "The Munich Mannequins," "Totem," "Paralytic," "Balloons," "Kindness," "Contusion," "Edge," and "Words." Of these, at least "The Munich Mannequins," "Kindness," and "Edge" are fully up to anything she had written previously. The manic quality has intensified; and indeed there is a sense in which many of these final poems could be read as a controlled hysteria, a sensitized black

comedy. Take, for example, "Kindness" with its mocking tone:

> Kindness glides about my house.
> Dame Kindness, she is so nice!
> The blue and the red jewels of her rings smoke
> In the windows, the mirrors
> Are filling with smiles.

The *faux-naïf* geniality, the effect produced by an apparently childlike tone, imperfectly serves to hide the subterranean anger; again, it is the anger of a poet put into the position of a housewife. Dame Kindness stands for the usual sort of well-wisher, who asks you how you are as a matter of form. The end of the poem is especially poignant, in which Dame Kindness presents the speaker with the usual kind of present, flowers, and these turn out to be something tangible but also, under the charming surface, an entrapment: the speaker's own children. It is a controlled *simplesse*—a false simplicity—and the effect is scalding:

> And here you come, with a cup of tea
> Wreathed in steam.
> The blood jet is poetry,
> There is no stopping it.
> You hand me two children, two roses.

Another *Ariel* poem written in London is "Edge," clearly the latest poem in *Ariel* because it is very probably the last poem Plath ever wrote, dated February 5, 1963. It is, in form, a kind of epitaph, but a very sinister one. For example, the speaker declares her children to be dead:

> Each dead child coiled, a white serpent,
> One at each little
>
> Pitcher of milk, now empty.
> She has folded
>
> Them back into her body . . .

It is clear that Plath was in a dangerous state of mind.

The final volume of Plath's poems before the collected edition of 1981 is called *Winter Trees* (1971). It is essentially an overflow from *Ariel,* with "Gigolo" and "Mystic" being written in that final London sojourn. The beginning of each poem is particularly startling: "The wet dawn inks are doing their blue dissolve" ("Winter Trees"); "It was a place of force— / The wind gagging my mouth with my own blown hair" ("The Rabbit Catcher"); "The air is a mill of hooks—" ("Mystic"). And if one replies to this last, "No it isn't," the likely response comes upon one like a shriek of self-justification: "Yes it is, to me. . . ."

FINAL THINGS

Poetry requires no such agony to be born. Ted Hughes, in that eventful October of 1962, instead of packing his clothes and leaving for London, should have had the wearied and frenetic Plath certified and placed in a nursing home under heavy sedation. What she needed was a good long rest: nobody could have done as many things as she tried to do, at such a pitch. If the poems were going to come, they would have come without hysterical behavior and endless battening upon the waning patience of friends. Plath's condition had become pathological. Poems such as "Candles" and "Mirror" show what Plath could do under minimum conditions of stress. There was no need for that defiant gesture of suicide.

As it is, the work of Sylvia Plath is inextricably bound up with her life. Her predicament to no small degree resembles that of F. Scott Fitzgerald, a victim of alcoholism. We shall never be able to read their work in the same way we read, say, Wallace Stevens or Robert Frost. It lacks the classical quality of detachment. However, because the public tends to prefer life to letters, and in any case delights on this side of prurience in a good story, Sylvia Plath is likely to continue as an icon and a cynosure, as well as one of the more flawed and wayward of classic American writers.

Selected Bibliography

WORKS OF SYLVIA PLATH

POETRY

The Colossus and Other Poems. London: Heinemann, 1960; New York: Knopf, 1962.

Ariel. London: Faber and Faber, 1965; New York: Harper & Row, 1966.

Crossing the Water. London: Faber and Faber, 1971; New York: Harper & Row, 1971.

Winter Trees. London: Faber and Faber, 1971; New York: Harper & Row, 1972.

COLLECTED POETRY

The Collected Poems. Edited by Ted Hughes. London: Faber and Faber, 1981; New York: Harper & Row, 1981.

Sylvia Plath's Selected Poems. Edited by Ted Hughes. London: Faber and Faber, 1985.

Plath: Poems. Edited by Diane Wood Middlebrook. New York: Knopf, 1998.

Sylvia Plath: Poems. Edited by Ted Hughes. London: Faber and Faber, 2000.

PROSE

The Bell Jar. London: Heinemann, 1963, Faber and Faber, 1966; New York: Harper & Row, 1971.

The Bed Book. London: Faber and Faber, 1976; New York: Harper & Row, 1976.

COLLECTED PROSE

Letters Home: Correspondence, 1950–1963. Edited by Aurelia Schober Plath. London: Faber and Faber, 1975; New York: Harper & Row, 1975.

Johnny Panic and the Bible of Dreams: Short Stories, Prose and Diary Excerpts. Edited by Ted Hughes. London: Faber and Faber, 1977; New York: Harper & Row, 1979.

The Journals of Sylvia Plath. Edited by Frances Mc-Cullough and Ted Hughes. New York: Dial Press, 1982.

The Journals of Sylvia Plath, 1950–1962. Edited by Karen V. Kukil. London: Faber and Faber, 2000.

Collected Children's Stories. London: Faber and Faber, 2001.

MINOR EDITIONS

Wreath for a Bridal. Frensham, Eng.: Sceptre Press, 1970.

Crystal Gazer and Other Poems. London: Rainbow Press, 1971.

Lyonnesse: Poems. London: Rainbow Press, 1971.

Pursuit. London: Rainbow Press, 1973.

Two Poems. Knotting, Eng: Sceptre Press, 1980.

Voices and Visions. New York: New York Center for Visual History, 1988. (Videotape of Plath in an interview and reading many of her poems.)

The It-Doesn't-Matter Suit. London: Faber and Faber, 1996; New York: St. Martin's Press, 1996.

Mrs Cherry's Kitchen. London: Faber and Faber, 2001.

BIBLIOGRAPHIES

Brennan, Claire, ed. *The Poetry of Sylvia Plath: A Reader's Guide to Essential Criticism.* Duxford, Eng.: Icon, 1999; New York: Columbia University Press, 2001.

Homberger, Eric, ed. *A Chronological Checklist of the Periodical Publications of Sylvia Plath.* Exeter, Eng.: University of Exeter, 1970.

Hughes, Ted. "Notes on the Chronological Order of Sylvia Plath's Poems." In *The Art of Sylvia Plath.* Edited by Charles Newman. Bloomington: Indiana University Press, 1970.

Meyering, Sheryl L., ed. *Sylvia Plath: A Reference Guide 1973–88.* Boston: G. K. Hall, 1990.

Tabor, Stephen, ed. *Sylvia Plath: An Analytical Bibliography.* Westport, Conn.: Greenwood Publishing, 1987; London: Mansell, 1987.

CRITICAL AND BIOGRAPHICAL STUDIES

Aird, Eileen. *Sylvia Plath: Her Life and Work.* New York: Harper & Row, 1973.

Alexander, Paul. *Rough Magic: A Biography of Sylvia Plath.* New York: Viking, 1991.

———, ed. *Ariel Ascending: Writings about Sylvia Plath.* New York: Harper & Row, 1985.

Alvarez, A. "Sylvia Plath." *The Review* 9:20–26 (October 1963). Reprinted, with postscript, in *Triquarterly* 7:65–73 (fall 1966). Reprinted in A. Alvarez, *Beyond All This Fiddle.* London: Allen Lane, 1968.

———. *The Savage God: A Study of Suicide.* London: Penguin, 1971.

Ames, Lois. "Notes towards a Biography." *Triquarterly* 7:95–107 (fall 1966). Reprinted in *The Art of Sylvia Plath.* Edited by Charles Newman. Bloomington: Indiana University Press, 1970. Pp. 155–173.

Axelrod, Steven Gould. *Sylvia Plath: The Wound and the Cure of Words.* Baltimore: Johns Hopkins University Press, 1990.

Bassnett, Susan. *Sylvia Plath.* London: Macmillan, 1987.

Becker, Jillian. *Giving Up: The Last Days of Sylvia Plath.* London: Ferrington, 2002.

Bloom, Harold, ed. *Sylvia Plath.* New York: Chelsea House, 1989.

———. *Sylvia Plath: Comprehensive Research and Study Guide.* Bloom's Major Poets series. Broomall, Pa.: Chelsea House, 2001.

Bonnefoy, Yves, Audrey Jones, Daniel Weissborth, and Anthony Rudolf, eds. *Theme and Version: Plath and Ronsard.* London: Menard Press, 1995.

Britzolakis, Christine. *Sylvia Plath and the Theatre of Mourning.* Oxford: Clarendon, 1999.

Butscher, Edward. *Sylvia Plath: Method and Madness.* New York: Seabury Press, 1976.

———, ed. *Sylvia Plath: The Woman and the Work.* New York: Dodd Mead, 1977.

Campbell, Wendy. "Remembering Sylvia." In *The Art of Sylvia Plath.* Edited by Charles Newman. Bloomington: Indiana University Press, 1970. Pp. 182–187.

Connell, Elaine. *Sylvia Plath: Killing the Angel in the House.* Hebden Bridge, West Yorkshire, Eng.: Pennine Pens, 1993.

Decker, Sharon D. *I Have a Self to Recover: Sylvia Plath's "Ariel."* Ann Arbor: Michigan Feminist Studies, 1980.

Dickie-Uroff, Margaret. *Sylvia Plath and Ted Hughes.* Urbana: University of Illinois Press, 1979.

Dyson, A. E. "Sylvia Plath: 'The Colossus and Other Poems.'" *Critical Quarterly* 3:181–185 (summer 1961).

Faas, Ekbert. "Chapters in a Shared Mythology: Sylvia Plath and Ted Hughes." In *The Achievement of Ted Hughes.* Edited by Keith Sagar. Athens: University of Georgia Press, 1983. Pp. 107–124.

Gardner, Philip. "'The Bland Granta': Sylvia Plath at Cambridge." *Dalhousie Review* 60:496–507 (autumn 1980).

Gilbert, Sandra M. "A Fine White Flying Myth: The Life/Work of Sylvia Plath." In *Shakespeare's Sisters: Feminist Essays on Women Poets.* Edited by Sandra M. Gilbert and Susan Gubar. Bloomington: Indiana University Press, 1979. Pp. 245–260.

Hall, Caroline King Barnard. *Sylvia Plath.* Rev. ed. New York: Twayne, 1998.

Hardy, Barbara. "Sylvia Plath: Enlargement or Derangement?" In *The Survival of Poetry.* Edited by Martin Dodsworth. London: Faber and Faber, 1970. Pp. 164–187.

Hargrove, Nancy Duvall. *The Journey toward* Ariel. Lund, Sweden: Lund University Press, 1994.

Hayman, Ronald. *The Death and Life of Sylvia Plath.* London: Heinemann, 1991.

Heaney, Seamus. "The Indefatigible Hoof-Taps." *Times Literary Supplement,* February 5–11, 1988, pp. 134, 143–144. Reprinted in Seamus Heaney, *The Government of the Tongue: The 1986 T. S. Eliot Memorial Lectures and Other Critical Writings.* London: Faber and Faber, 1988. Pp. 148–170.

Hobsbaum, Philip. "The Temptation of Giant Despair." *Hudson Review* 25:597–612 (winter 1972–1973).

Holbrook, David. *Sylvia Plath: Poetry and Existence.* London: Athlone Press, 1976.

Kendall, Tim. *Sylvia Plath: A Critical Study.* London: Faber and Faber, 2001.

Kroll, Judith. *Chapters in a Mythology: The Poetry of Sylvia Plath.* New York: Harper & Row, 1976.

Krook, Dorothea. "Recollections of Sylvia Plath." In *Sylvia Plath: The Woman and the Work.* Edited by Edward Butscher. New York: Dodd, Mead, 1977. Pp. 49–60.

Lane, Gary, ed. *Sylvia Plath: New Views on the Poetry.* Baltimore: Johns Hopkins University Press, 1979.

Lehrer, Sylvia. *The Dialectics of Art and Life: A Portrait of Sylvia Plath.* Salzburg: Universtät Salzburg, 1985.

Lowell, Robert. "Sylvia Plath's Ariel." In *Robert Lowell, Collected Prose.* Edited by Robert Giroux. New York: Farrar, Straus and Giroux, 1987. Pp. 122–125.

Malcolm, Janet. *The Silent Woman: Sylvia Plath and Ted Hughes.* New York: Knopf, 1994.

Markey, Janice. *A Journey into the Red Eye: The Poetry of Sylvia Plath—A Critique.* London: Women's Press, 1993.

Marsack, Robyn. *Sylvia Plath.* Buckingham, Eng.: Open University Press, 1992.

Matovich, Richard M. *A Concordance to the Collected Poems of Sylvia Plath.* New York: Garland, 1986.

Meyers, Jeffrey. "Epilogue: Sylvia Plath." In his *Manic Power: Robert Lowell and His Circle.* New York: Arbor House, 1987. Pp. 139–179.

Murphy, Richard. *The Kick: A Memoir.* London: Granta, 2001.

Newman, Charles Hamilton, ed. *The Art of Sylvia Plath.* Bloomington: Indiana University Press, 1970.

Northhouse, Cameron, and Thomas P. Walsh. *Sylvia Plath and Anne Sexton: A Reference Guide.* Reference Guides in American Literature, No. 13. Boston: G. K. Hall, 1974.

Peel, Robin. *Writing Back: Sylvia Plath and Cold War Politics.* Madison, N.J.: Farleigh Dickinson University Press, 2002.

Rose, Jacqueline. *The Haunting of Sylvia Plath.* London: Virago, 1991.

Rosenthal, M. L. "Other Confessional Poets: Sylvia Plath." In his *The New Poets: American and British Poetry since World War II.* London and New York: Oxford University Press, 1967.

Simpson, Louis. *A Revolution in Taste: Studies of Dylan Thomas, Allen Ginsberg, Sylvia Plath, and Robert Lowell.* New York: Macmillan, 1978.

Steiner, Nancy Hunter. *A Closer Look at Ariel: A Memory of Sylvia Plath.* New York: Harper's Magazine Press, 1973.

Stevenson, Anne. *Bitter Fame: A Life of Sylvia Plath.* Boston: Houghton Mifflin, 1989.

————. "The Biographer as Fiction Maker: Writing on Sylvia Plath." In her *Between the Iceberg and the Ship: Selected Essays.* Ann Arbor: University of Michigan Press, 1998. Pp. 29–38.

————. "Sylvia Plath's Word Games." *Poetry Review* 86, no. 4 (winter 1996). Reprinted in Anne Stevenson, *Between the Iceberg and the Ship.* Ann Arbor: University of Michigan Press, 1998. Pp. 39–51.

Tennant, Emma. *Sylvia and Ted.* New York: Henry Holt, 2001.

Thomas, Trevor. *Sylvia Plath: Last Encounters.* Bedford, Eng.: T. Thomas, 1989.

Van Dyne, Susan R.. *Revising Life: Sylvia Plath's Ariel Poems.* Chapel Hill: University of North Carolina Press, 1993.

Wagner, Erica. *Ariel's Gift: Ted Hughes, Sylvia Plath and the Story of* Birthday Letters. New York: W. W. Norton, 2001.

Wagner-Martin, Linda. *Sylvia Plath: A Biography.* New York: Simon & Schuster, 1987.

————. *The Bell Jar: A Novel of the Fifties.* New York: Twayne, 1992.

————, ed. *Critical Essays on Sylvia Plath.* Boston: G. K. Hall, 1984.

————, ed. *Sylvia Plath: The Critical Heritage.* London: Routledge, 1988.

Yorke, Liz. *Impertinent Voices: Subversive Strategies in Contemporary Women's Poetry.* London: Routledge, 1991.

—PHILIP HOBSBAUM

Edgar Allan Poe

1809–1849

ROMANTICISM IS UNTIDY and imprecise. The concept is almost as difficult to define as the exact dates of its history. Because the movement was attracted to subjectivity and the unconscious, mystery and the imagination, the romantic sensibility tended to embrace the contradictions and complications of human nature. Under the Romantic umbrella we thereby find art that embodies spiritual tranquillity and inner poetic beauty while also containing elements of restless distortion and the macabre, a plaintive yearning for the sublime in spite of the suspicion that perhaps the quest for tranquillity and beauty is forever beyond the human ability to grasp.

It is helpful to keep these dualisms in mind when considering the art of Edgar Allan Poe. For while he often yearned to dwell in the realm of ideality, particularly in his poetry, he also understood that untainted by dream or drug, the world we normally inhabit is a decidedly unpoetic one. True to his Romantic yearnings and following precisely the sentiments expressed by one of his greatest literary influences, the poet John Keats in "Ode to a Nightingale," Poe may have claimed art as a vehicle for transcendence to a better place. But in most of his poems and stories this quest was ephemeral and frequently futile, leaving the poet/prose narrator in a state of even greater spiritual torment. This is a partial explanation for why Poe was so adored by the nineteenth-century French symbolists, whose translations and influential commentary on Poe helped to rescue him from literary obscurity and the scurrilous lies of his literary executor and first biographer, Rufus Griswold. The symbolists saw in Poe a kindred spirit, a sensitive artist struggling to survive in a merciless, mercantile environment that valued neither art nor the artist. From the very beginning, the French, particularly the poet Charles Baudelaire, were stunned by Poe. Baudelaire did not read Poe as many modern critics have, as a psychologically unstable or even shallow genius. Instead, he saw in Poe the consummate figure of the modern artist struggling against bourgeois culture: "literary spites, terrors before the infinite, domestic griefs, the insults of poverty—from all these Poe sought refuge in the darkness of drunkenness, as though it were a preliminary tomb."

While his nineteenth-century American contemporaries and many of the authors who immediately followed him knew of his work, Poe's reputation as a great writer was initially forged in Europe. Despite the artistic obscurity and personal struggles that plagued him during his lifetime, Poe has emerged as one of the great figures in the American literary canon. The titles of his stories have varied over the years, as most were initially published in East Coast newspapers and journals and then sometimes revised, retitled, and reprinted elsewhere in order for Poe to make additional money. The first printing of "Ligeia," for example, in 1838, did not include the poem "The Conqueror Worm," which would appear for the first time when the tale was reprinted in 1848.

Poe was the first American writer esoteric and talented enough to impress the literati of Europe. As Lois Davis Vines documents country by country in her edited volume *Poe Abroad: Influence, Reputation, Affinities,* no American artist has exerted—and continues to exert—an influence over the international world of visual art, music, and literature that has been equal to the stature of Poe. He stands simultaneously as a figure at the center of modernism—the line that stretches from Charles Baudelaire (who spent twenty years translating Poe's short stories into French) and the symbolist movement to T. S. Eliot and the rise of New Criticism—and as the inventor or innovator of several popular genres, including science fiction, the detective tale (which Poe invented), and the psychological horror thriller.

It was not until the twentieth century that the United States began to bestow upon Poe the artistic status that he had garnered in Europe and Russia since his death. His nineteenth-century countrymen, concerned with documenting explorations into the North American wilderness, may have found Poe's weird tales and haunting poems too claustrophobic, too introverted, perhaps even too European. Some were dissuaded from taking Poe seriously because of the success of Rufus Griswold in associating Poe posthumously with drug addiction, immoral sexual acts, and insanity. But the degree of separation between Poe and his nineteenth-century American contemporaries may come down to a fundamental philosophical difference. Poe's decadent pessimism contrasts sharply with the spirit of American optimism, most notably articulated by the transcendental philosopher Ralph Waldo Emerson and the poet Walt Whitman, and appears to be much more at home within the European villages and decayed aristocratic mansions inhabited by many of his characters. As the America of the nineteenth century looked brightly into a future of limitless possibilities, Poe's work counterpointed the general spirit of the age by revealing the human propensity to seek pain rather than transcendence. Poe offered a constant rebuttal to the doctrines of self-reliance and a faith in the future by asserting that we inhabit a universe unfavorably disposed toward humankind and that human nature itself was ultimately unpredictable. Harold Bloom has observed, "Self-reliance, the Emersonian answer to Original Sin, does not exist in the Poe cosmos, where you necessarily start out damned, doomed, and dismal."

In our own time, Poe's reputation makes him at once a tremendously significant literary icon and a refugee from a salacious Halloween costume party. He may have been the first American writer embraced by the international literati, but he is also the progenitor of a line that includes a whole genre of Hollywood B-grade movies that have gone directly from screening room to late-night television cable and videocassette. Each week the newspapers herald the release of a new book or film that explores the bizarre, the mysterious, or the supernatural. An obsession with the fantastic and all things Gothic occupies a central place in contemporary popular culture. As Mark Edmundson persuasively insists in his book *Nightmare on Main Street,* "1990s Gothic modes are beholden to the genius of American terror, to Edgar Allan Poe. Poe's . . . spirit, like a specter from one of his own tales, has risen up to brood over the fin de siècle."

Indeed, Poe might have felt much more at home in the contemporary epoch than he ever was in his own. He would have witnessed his vision of life treated not as an aberration but as reality. He would have found his poetic embrace of surreal worlds and his literary propensity for perverse pleasure derived from the "beautiful," the "wanton," the "bizarre," and "something of the terrible" (as he put it in "The Masque of the Red Death") translated into haute couture fashion, urban nightclub life, cinematography, advertisements, video games, record lyrics and cover designs, magazine art, and Internet websites. In its fascination with all things Gothic, our age continually references the very pathological symptoms Poe once described, as the serial killer has emerged from police blotters and psychological profiles to become an emblem of our cultural moment and the monster of the postmodern age. There is an unmistakable line of connection between Poe's murderers, whose bloody crimes have resulted in the narrating of personal histories by the condemned from prison cells and asylums, and the powerful, highly intelligent, and utterly deranged killers who stalk our streets as well as our movie and television screens. The sensual attraction to the forbidden and its consequential guilt; the paranoiac anxiety that attends an acute awareness of cosmic absurdity and emptiness; the urge toward self-destruction as a state of being; the self locked in restive combat with itself; the concurrent fear of, and desire for, death—these elements in Poe's work represent both his most significant contributions to literature and the intimate nexus he has come to share with the postmodern reader.

LIFE AND TIMES

Romantic elements in Poe's literature are omnipresent—from his creation of mysterious atmospheres as the backdrops for his poems and tales to characters that are deeply troubled and motivated by highly subjective demons. Poe's Romantic predilection is further evinced by the manner in which his art was shaped by the distressing events of his personal life. Poe helped to establish the image of the Romantic artist as a being who not only created art from the essence of his personal suffering but also came to define himself through this suffering. Many of Poe's protagonists suffer from "the fever called 'Living,'" as Poe described it in his poem "For Annie," the same fever that Poe knew intimately in his lifelong struggles against poverty, alcoholism, and despair. His biological father, David Poe, was a New York City actor who abandoned his two sons and wife when Edgar was two years old. None of Poe's biographers have been able to trace where he went,

exactly why he left, or whatever became of him. Edgar would come to share several unfortunate characteristics with his biological father: most notably, a propensity for drunkenness and the inability to ever reach a level of financial stability. His mother, Eliza, also an actor, struggled to keep the family together for more than a year after her husband's disappearance. Eliza gave birth to a daughter before she herself died when Poe was three years old. The young Poe children then were dispersed to different surrogate parents, and Poe never saw his siblings again.

Poe's loss of both parents in early childhood; his tempestuous relationship with his foster father, John Allan; and the successive deaths to tuberculosis or pneumonia of the most important women in his life—his mother; his foster mother, Frances Allan; and his wife, Virginia Clemm—left their mark on a body of work that prompted Freud to call Poe "a great writer with pathological trends." The actual death ordeals these three women underwent were both prolonged and particularly gruesome; their graphic images of death and dying probably would have been enough to animate a lifetime of nightmares for anyone. For Poe, however, they would translate into obsessive components of his art.

Born in Boston on January 19, 1809, Poe was raised by surrogate parents, John and Frances Allan. His foster father was a Scottish immigrant who established the Richmond firm of Ellis and Allan to market Virginia tobacco for European commodities. During Edgar's adolescence, the two men grew mutually estranged; Allan came to resent the decadent "Byronic tendencies" he saw emerging in Poe's fascination with the life of the artistic imagination, while it was Poe's conviction that Allan was parsimonious in his response to his foster son's financial needs. John Allan's psychological presence in Poe's troubled life is perhaps as significant as the psychological void caused by David Poe's early abandonment. Later, with other men, Poe generally maintained contentious relationships, reenacting the dramatic hostilities engendered from his two father figures. The bitterness that Poe harbored toward these two central authority figures extended well beyond the death of John Allan in 1834, to the point where Poe may well have re-created these men in his portraits of the dark fathers and judgmental authority figures that populate his tales. Examples are the oppressive representatives of the Inquisition in "The Pit and the Pendulum" and the sadistic king and his obsequious ministers in "Hop-Frog."

If the absence of a positive father-figure role model dogged Poe through all his relationships with male authority figures, particularly fellow writers, reviewers, and the East Coast editors of periodicals with whom he had to interact professionally, the lack of a stable maternal figure influenced his romantic relationships with women. His psychobiographer Marie Bonaparte was first to note that Poe maintained a lifelong fixation on women as mother surrogates. She concluded that because Poe was always searching for a mother replacement in the romantic relationships he established with women, he was never able to develop healthy or "normal" bonds with a female, and consequently all his romantic efforts were doomed to failure. In her treatment of Poe's story "The Black Cat," for example, Bonaparte identifies the hostility of Poe's male narrator toward his wife and cat with Poe's own enduring ambivalence toward the mother for whom he yearned but also simultaneously abhorred because of her "abandonment" of him at an early age. Bonaparte speculated that Poe was probably impotent and that his marriage to his second cousin, Virginia, was never consummated. Whether this speculation is true (the Poe marriage remained childless), Poe's attitude toward Virginia appeared to border upon the reverential. She was his muse and friend, sister and lover. Thus, when Virginia began to exhibit signs of physical deterioration occasioned by the onset of tuberculosis, Poe's own corporeal condition also weakened. After a protracted struggle with the disease, she died on January 30, 1847.

Poe lived another two years after the death of Virginia, electing to dress entirely and exclusively in black, and they were perhaps the most miserable years of his life. Poe may have written in the poem "Ulalume" the ultimate private allegory of his own conflict of mind after his wife's death over whether he should seek the love of another woman or remain faithful to his wife's memory. In the summer of 1848, the tension at the heart of "Ulalume" was paralleled in Poe's own life as he began romantic courtships with at least three different women. He proposed to one of these women, Sarah Helen Whitman, in a graveyard in Providence, Rhode Island. Their relationship reached its pinnacle when, after agreeing to marry Poe, Sarah decided to terminate the engagement in December 1848 when his drinking alarmed her.

The issue of how Poe died in a Baltimore hospital at 5 A.M. on Sunday, October 7, 1849, is a matter that continues to inspire controversy among Poe biographers. On September 27, 1849, Poe set out from Richmond on a planned trip to New York City. From that point on, it is pure conjecture how and why he ended up wandering aimlessly for nearly a week through the streets of the tavern district of Baltimore wearing clothes that were not his own. The most recent speculation, posited by an American physician named R. Michael Benitez in the *New York Times,* is that Poe's hospital symptoms—cold perspiration, delirium, trembling, general confusion, and loss of memory—suggest that he was experiencing an advanced case of rabies poisoning. But Poe's death could have been caused just as well by complications associated with various illnesses he may have been suffering for a long time. It remains this author's belief that Poe's association with "demon gin"—his lifelong struggle with alcoholism—coupled with an advanced state of pneumonia brought on by an inadequate diet and a weakened immune system is probably the most plausible explanation for the delirium and semiconscious state that precipitated his demise.

In his long-suffering efforts to become a critically acclaimed and financially independent writer, Poe traveled up and down the East Coast. He lived for varied periods of time in Philadelphia, New York City, Providence, Richmond, Baltimore, and Charleston, often working as an editor or book reviewer for periodicals published in these major cities. Nearly all of Poe's work was published initially in popular household journals and magazines, such as the *Broadway Journal, Southern Literary Messenger, Graham's Magazine, Godey's Lady's Book,* and *Burton's Gentleman's Magazine.* Unfortunately, Poe was not much more successful as a writer than he was as a lover. The fact that he continued to write at such a prodigious pace is all the more impressive, given the fact that he never achieved anything more than subsistence payment for the work he published in his lifetime.

There are many Poes. Several years ago, Daniel Hoffman published *Poe Poe Poe Poe Poe Poe Poe,* a book whose title managed to highlight at least seven of the possible Poes. But there are more Poes than even the Hoffman title recognizes. Although Poe saw himself primarily as a poet, his omnipresent need to make money with his writing forced him to pursue work in other genres. Poe became, for example, the first American to make literary criticism a rigorous discipline rather than the appreciative ruminations of a leisurely reader. His reputation for authoring scathing reviews of work that failed to live up to his rigorous literary expectations were not matched in savagery until the arrival of the critic H. L. Mencken on the literary scene. Many commentators on Poe's reviewing techniques have noted that in his detailed explications he was one of the first of the "New Critics," who, a century later, would formulate the methodology for examining and judging an individual work of art on its own merits, existing in a sphere of its own creation. He reviewed books on a host of variegated subjects, from nostrums and medicine to technical works and economics. But outside the coterie of Poe scholars, few people are aware of the impressive number of reviews Poe produced as a book critic for a variety of periodicals. The world remains most interested in Poe the creative artist, who wrote poetry, grotesquely comic sketches, fantasies, hoaxes, a wide range of psychological horror tales, several stories of ratiocination, and a single, uneven novel entitled *The Narrative of Arthur Gordon Pym of Nantucket* (1850). Given the prodigious size and scope of the literary canon he managed to put out during essentially a twenty-year writing span, it is truly remarkable that Poe ever found the time or the energy to get drunk.

THE POETRY

As a poet, Poe has never quite achieved the fame and recognition associated with his prose narratives; our own age tends to identify him poetically as the author of "The Raven" and not much else. But this was not always the case. In the latter part of the nineteenth century, Poe was known internationally and respected posthumously for his poetry. Perhaps his poetry is less appreciated in our time because it so clearly embodies the spirit of his age: too often sentimental, overly derivative, redundant in theme, and obsessed with metrical rules and formulations. All his life Poe studied other poets meticulously, modeling his own verse after theirs; as a consequence, his own corpus of work often fails to distinguish itself (unlike his short stories) in terms of either subject matter or radically inventive forms of expression. Furthermore, Poe left us very little of it—sixty-three poems total.

On the other hand, Poe thought long and hard about what constitutes the essence of true poetic sentiment. His lengthy ruminations of genre criticism on poetry, written in the 1840s—"Fifty Suggestions," "The Philosophy of Composition," "The Rationale of Verse," "The Poetic Principle"—indicate that he believed that beauty, unity, and brevity were core components of any good poem. An element of the bizarre or strange, even an "exquisite sense of Deformity or disproportion" ("Fifty Suggestions") only added to and heightened the appreciation of beauty. To enrich these sensibilities, Poe argued that poetry, while inferior to music in the evocation of a desired melancholic mood, must endeavor to approximate its melodies in the rhythmic music of word pairings, repetition, and rhyme. The musical analogy inherent in a poem such as "The Bells" represents a distinguishing characteristic of Poe's verse. Each section of the poem relies heavily upon alliteration, alternating interior rhythms, assonantal rhyme, and monosyllabic rhyme to produce a different musical effect, whether it is associated with the "molten-golden notes / And all in tune" of a wedding or the "clamorous appealing" of fire alarm bells ringing. Consequently, his poetic diction frequently has been arranged to music, and Poe always has exerted a special influence over musicians—from the nineteenth-century composer Claude Debussy, who wrote two operas based upon Poe stories, to contemporary rock artists such as Lou Reed, who, in 2001, authored and performed a special musical production entitled POEtry, a collection of original songs based upon Poe's life and work.

Marie Bonaparte recognized qualities of obsessive adoration in the descriptions of women by Poe's many first-person narrators; additionally, she identified a genuine element of fear surrounding the objects (women) of their adoration. The Poe male narrator is an adorer "who dares not approach the object of his adoration, since he feels it surrounded by some fearful, dangerous mystery." Poe's treatment of females in his poetry and prose would appear to support a certain ambivalence toward women on the part of the writer. A guiding principle for his poetry and one of Poe's core literary obsessions, as outlined in the 1846 essay "The Philosophy of Composition," was the tenet that "the death . . . of a beautiful woman is, unquestionably, the most poetical topic in the world—and equally is it beyond doubt that the lips best suited for such topic are those of a bereaved lover." While it is clear that this subject haunted Poe personally, a consequence of his own biographical tragedies, it is also important to note that Poe wished to create poetry of feeling, to put the reader in a situation where identification with the bereaved narrator was unavoidable. In the destruction of a beautiful woman, the beauty of the world is diminished and all of us are correspondingly affected, but none more deeply than "a lover lamenting his deceased mistress." Contemplating the death of a beautiful woman provides the opportunity for creating an appropriately self-enclosed world replete with the necessary evocation of melancholia, the element Poe viewed as "the most legitimate of all the poetical tones." Readers enter the mind of the narrator–bereaved lover in "The Raven," "Annabel Lee," "Ulalume," "Alone," and other poems only to find themselves trapped in the stifling atmosphere of a funeral home from which there is neither escape nor modulation. The majority of Poe's poems can be characterized as short ballads and lyrics—deeply personalized love songs rendered from the perspective of a solitary and melancholic male—that are both brief and intensely emotional.

Certainly Poe's most famous poem remains "The Raven," which was published in 1845 and earned Poe the nickname "Raven" for the remainder of his life. The poem is a quintessential illustration of the death of a beautiful woman and the subsequent bereavement of her abandoned male lover. Additionally, "The Raven" highlights the constituent atmospheric effects that Poe felt were crucial: midnight of a bleak night in December, the poem's grieving narrator sits alone in his dreary chamber reading books in an effort to distract himself from thinking about his "lost Lenore." When he allows a "stately" raven to join him in this room, however, his mourning strategy backfires, as the bird's mindless repetition of the word "Nevermore" to each of the narrator's questions creates an ever more frustrating awareness of the narrator's recent loss. Real raven or narrator's enclosed hallucination, good or evil, prophetic omen or tormenting demon—it is never confirmed exactly what this intrusive bird represents, but it is clear that its presence helps to reveal a human mind that is unraveling and that finally descends completely into the realm of madness.

In the tale "The Imp of the Perverse" Poe posits that human beings, despite their best efforts at self-preservation, also possess a counter urge toward self-torture and even self-destruction: "In the case of that something which I term *perverseness,* the desire to be well is not only not aroused, but a strongly antagonistical sentiment exists." The concept of perverseness is a central element in many of Poe's most famous stories. It is, for instance, the explanation for why the narrators in "The Tell-Tale Heart," "The Black Cat," and "The Imp of the Perverse" feel compelled to discourse so unnecessarily and extensively that they end up revealing their criminal actions to officious policemen. In "The Raven," Poe's perversity principle is a major component of the poem. While the narrator is shown suffering the attendant pain of human heartbreak, a careful reader also appreciates the fact that Poe's speaker is *cultivating* his interaction with the raven to the point where he is actively indulging and even heightening the level of his romantic melancholia. As Poe reminds us in "The Philosophy of Composition," the narrator of the poem "is impelled, as I have before

explained, by the human thirst for self-torture . . . to propound such queries to the bird as will bring him, the lover, the most of the luxury of sorrow." He sits alone in a dimly lit room, where he perversely intensifies and covets his pain. When it becomes clear that the raven's presence serves only to increase the narrator's anguish, he does nothing to force the bird into leaving. In fact, his questions regarding the ultimate destiny of the dead Lenore and his own urge to be with her again are constructed rhetorically to end with the bird's sad refrain: "Nevermore." Poe's narrator clings with a desperate zeal to his own self-punishment; his masochism is all that he has left in the absence of Lenore. At the conclusion of the poem, we are led to believe that the raven has become a permanent resident of the poet's chamber and soul and that the narrator appears to gain a perverse pleasure in the additional gloom afforded by the raven's presence: "And my soul from out that shadow that lies floating on the floor / Shall be lifted—nevermore!"

THE PSYCHOLOGICAL HORROR TALE

Poe's poetry centers upon the creation of static tableaus of beauty mixed with pain in the mind of the poetic narrator. Since so many of the themes in his poems revolve around the consequences of death or dying, there is very little "dramatic action" in Poe's ballads. His poems maintain a highly subjective and internalized vision of the world. Similarly, very little action takes place in Poe's short tales of terror and suspense, the genre he helped to define and perfect. The real energies are mental: the self tearing against the self. When we turn to Poe's tales of terror, however, it is not merely the sadness of lost love or the abrupt transition from or to a visionary landscape that inspires his deepest contemplation, but rather the complex spectrum of aberrant psychological motivation that ranges from sadomasochistic representations and object fixations to delusions of grandeur and the perversity of self-loathing. Poe is America's Shakespeare of the lunatic asylum. He writes of a compressed world populated by men out of control. By depicting unstable minds unable to discipline their darkest urges, his horror stories thrust even the reluctant reader into the demented psyches of his first-person male narrators. Poe was the first to tell the tale of terror from the monster's first-person narrative point of view—to shift the perspective from Gothic victim to victimizer. He pressed the relationship between the monster and the reader to the point where it became simultaneously unbearable and pleasurable.

One of the most important elements that Poe inherited from his Gothic forefathers—from whom emerged the dominant literary form in the last two decades of the eighteenth century—and went on to sharpen to the point of near suffocating exactitude was an emphasis on the biology of place. Poe's horror tales are set in an architecture that is invigorated with an infernal energy of its own. But in Poe, the machinery of the haunted castle or mansion always becomes a semiotic parallel to the tortured psyche of the main character; place, in other words, mirrors personality. Poe's tales of terror generally progress toward a downward spiral: the action of the narrative becomes ever more circumscribed, descending into the basement or under the floorboards or into the darkness of a crypt or pit. Since journeys in Poe are always spiritual and psychological as much as they are actual voyages, the movement away from the objective, social realm and into the sequestered world of psychological obsession finds important correspondences in the narrowing physical space that Poe employs in the course of his storytelling.

For example, the physical journey that Montressor entices Fortunato to undertake in "The Cask of Amontillado" is a descent into an underground wine cellar. As Fortunato follows Montressor deeper into the vault, both men move further away from the world of the living, further from Fortunato's wife and all normal social life and into the solipsistic structure of Montressor's repressed urge for revenge. By the time the two men reach the deadly cul-de-sac at the end of a corridor littered with the bones of Montressor's ancestors, Fortunato has entered unwittingly into the symbolic landscape of Montressor's mind. The narrowing passageway that descends deeper into the earth, the chains that are employed to immobilize Fortunato, even the act of sealing his victim into a dark and airless crypt underscore the obsessive and corrosive nature of Montressor's quest for revenge. The sterile, circumscribed space that becomes Fortunato's final repose is an ironic metaphor for Montressor's soul; in his need to revenge an insult with impunity, Montressor buries his victim in a place that is devoid of companionship and light. This murderous, self-enclosed crypt poses an apt parallel to the psychological space where all men who are unable to forget or to forgive must necessarily reside.

"The Cask of Amontillado," "The Masque of the Red Death," and "Hop-Frog" highlight Poe's fascination with elaborately costumed characters, surreal atmospheres, and illicit conduct. These tales present an environment of licentious freedom that reaches its climax precisely at midnight. The stories embody "the supreme madness of the carnival season," where excess is indulged without much attention to consequences (as Poe says in "The Cask of Amontillado"). The mad party atmosphere of these narratives appears as a metaphor that underscores the extreme choices and penalties of the central characters. While each tale paints elaborate color portraits of decadent behavior, it is also a critique of this activity, of individuals who have lost sight of reality in the confusion of an intoxicating fog.

In "The Masque of the Red Death" Poe informs us through the voice of a third-person narrator that in the creation of a sequestered ambiance inside his castle, Prince Prospero has combined "much of the beautiful, much of the wanton, much of the *bizarre,* [and] something of the terrible." Since this artificial world comes at the expense of the Prince's kingdom, however—the disenfranchised who are abandoned to take care of themselves amidst the ravages of the plague—Poe adds an important concluding clause that there was also "not a little of that which might have excited disgust." Similarly, in "The Cask of Amontillado," Montressor takes the flagrant flaunting of moral law and codes of misconduct that characterize carnival season to their obscene extremes. And in the story "Hop-Frog," the exotic masquerade party, in which a king and his ministers—whose particular brand of comedy always requires an object of ridicule, a "jester to laugh with and a dwarf to laugh at"—are transformed into apes, is an ironic externalization of the king's true nature. Poe himself, who was never one for moderation in either his drinking or his pursuit of self-indulgent behavior, understood, perhaps better than most people, the lure of personal excess. Yet by the time he wrote these three stories in the 1840s, Poe also had learned that such arrogance comes at a heavy price and that what often appears to be real—whether it be the deathless revelry inside Prospero's castle, the "Hop-Frog" king's obscene need to be elaborately entertained at the expense of others, or the perspective induced by a brain immersed in alcohol—is, in reality, a dangerous illusion that often ends up tragically parodying itself.

Poe produced a range of tales that established his reputation as America's first great horror writer. They are best characterized as tales of intrusion—whether culminating in the act of violent murder or in the physical or psychological violation of another person or in describing the internal war of a divided self. "The Cask of Amontillado," "William Wilson," "Hop-Frog," "The Pit and the Pendulum," "The Masque of the Red Death," "The Black Cat," and "The Tell-Tale Heart" feature internalized elements of anxiety and fear pushed to an unrelenting extreme. All these tales employ various acts of violence and cruelty that indicate their affinity to the well-worn equipment of the Gothic romance that preceded their writing, yet each induces a degree and quality of horror that is unique to Poe alone. For no writer before Poe was capable of producing an atmosphere of terror that is as palpable to the reader.

In "The Pit and the Pendulum" the victimized narrator must struggle against the frantic madness that literally presses in against him in the blackness of his prison; the "sweep of the fearful scimitar" that threatens to split him in two; the disgusting rats that are the only other living organisms that share his chamber; and the bottomless pit in the center of the room that symbolizes the abandonment of reason, the capitulation to suicidal despair. Such a horrific environment forces the narrator into a battle that is as much centered inside his own head as it is in the excruciating tortures designed by his jailers, as the goal of the Inquisition torturers is to drive their victim mad rather than simply to ensure his execution. Poe's tale relies heavily upon the Gothic apparatus of sadistic torture—faceless anonymity; the blurring of nightmare and reality; a shape-changing, unstable environment; and the omnipresent sense of personal violation—but then transforms the experience from that of purely sensual and empirical description to one that attains metaphysical implications.

While the story remains a persuasive example of the power of physical description to evoke terror and fear in the reader, its real achievement is philosophical: "The Pit and the Pendulum" is the ultimate allegory of an anguished soul confronted by the blackness of existence in an absurd and meaningless universe whose shape and meaning can never be ascertained. This represents one of Poe's greatest and most enduring literary achievements: the ability to elevate the Gothic tale from an experience of heightened sensual titillation into an expression of the isolated individual's existential lament. As Poe remarked in the preface to the first volume of *Tales of the Grotesque and Arabesque* (1840), when confronted with accusations of plagiarism from the imported German *Schauer-romantik* ("shocker tale") that was popular during his lifetime: "I maintain that terror is not of Germany, but of the soul." According to the scholar Donald Ringe, "Poe was . . . much too serious a thinker to make his stories merely the source of meaningless titillation. . . . Until Poe's time, no American writer had managed to forge so organic a bond between Gothic device and symbolic meaning."

THE MARRIAGE GROUP

Unlike the dead and dying female muses that mark his poetry, the women in Poe's prose tales cannot and do not stay dead. The female protagonists in "Morella," "Ligeia," "Berenice," "The Oval Portrait," "The Premature Burial," and "The Fall of the House of Usher," which constitute the love stories—or what some Poe scholars refer to as "the marriage group"—metamorphose into female vampires who come back to life in an aggressive search for the men they once loved. Unlike the traditional vampire story, however, in Poe the vampire-victim relationship is forever shifting while the usual need for blood is replaced with a gendered quest for power. Also, while the vampiric consumption of blood in the typical vampire text is simultaneously and complexly a sexual act, the core issue in Poe's vamping tales is less concerned with sexual eroticism or physicality itself and more with psychic domination. His tales revolve around interpersonal relationships between men and women, their respective struggles for control over the relationship, and the gender polarities and antagonisms that

distinguish these interactions. Unlike the arrogant criminals and murderers in "The Tell-Tale Heart," "The Cask of Amontillado," or "The Black Cat," Poe's love stories feature emasculated and melancholic males who wait and watch for the return of the women they both loved and tortured in some way or another. The male's need to destroy the female—either through an overbearing adoration or a literal premature burial—violates her psychic and physical being. In turn, she returns from the dead to consume him. Female transformations into revenging vampires in Poe should be read as the upshot of an unholy tryst between the narrator's neurotic guilt and the compulsion of a pre-feminist spirit to rise up from passivity to revenge.

Each of the tales in "the marriage group" centers upon a blood relative or wife-lover who dies mysteriously, often in a way that implicates, however obliquely, the central male character in her death. As Joan Dayan posits, "In Poe's tales about women, marriage turns what was cherished into what is scorned." Nothing in Poe's world is ever completely sentient; buildings as well as people—and especially entombed women—retain an animation that defies both rational logic and biology. In "The Fall of the House of Usher," for example, Roderick buries his sister in spite of the fact that there remains "a faint blush upon [her] bosom and . . . face, and that suspiciously lingering smile upon the lip." When she escapes her crypt and climbs three flights of stairs to collapse upon her brother, she bears "him to the floor a corpse, and a victim to the terrors he had anticipated." Despite the narrator's efforts to help Roderick compose himself, the latter anticipates the return of the repressed in his dead sister's reanimation almost immediately after her entombment.

Poe's programmatic elimination of women in these tales has come under increasing scrutiny in light of feminist criticism applied to his work, and understandably so, for this pattern, in the words of J. Gerald Kennedy, "raises troubling questions about an inherent misogyny." Typically, Poe's males force women to cohabit deliberately constructed worlds of decadent isolation and antisocial activities that would make it difficult for even the healthiest female to remain sane, much less free of life-debilitating disease. Once a Poe woman succumbs to an illness that drains away her vitality, the male, who often harbors a not so subtle ambivalence toward his love object, is plunged immediately into guilt and remorse.

In "Ligeia," the story's theme of a man's longing for his deceased dark-haired soul mate merges with his obsessive need to bring her back to life, even at the possible expense of another woman's life. The negative feelings that the narrator demonstrates toward his innocent second wife, the blond Lady Rowena, however, indicate that his attitude toward women in general borders on the pathological. Poe's male lovers are typically consumed in a blaze in which ecstasy and horror are identical. Although he professes that his love for his first wife is so overwhelming that Rowena's mere presence in his life serves only to highlight his loss of Ligeia, the truth is that the narrator takes out on Rowena all the unresolved feelings of hostility he harbors against women in general—and Ligeia specifically. The reanimated Rowena-Ligeia corpse that is used to complete "this hideous drama of revivification" literally shrinks from the narrator's touch even as he moves toward it. The narrator may have won his wish to be reunited with Ligeia, but the "vamped" creature that rises from the dead at the end of this tale appears to be less than appreciative toward the man who, at least in part, is responsible for orchestrating this macabre situation.

TALES OF RATIOCINATION

In sharp contrast to the intensely emotional and irrational moments that frequent Poe's poetry and his tales of murder and vampirism, Poe's invention of the detective tale highlights the opposite side of his authorial consciousness. Indeed, Poe's tales of ratiocination—which employ the rational powers of an enlightened mind—strive to place the dark forces that motivate destructive acts such as murder and perverseness under control. These two distinct compositions suggest the hemispheric specialization of a single human brain, as the right hemisphere supports the mathematical and reasoned acts of cognition associated with acts of deduction and detection, while the poetical (and musical) dreamers and bombastic criminals in Poe's fiction are best aligned with the left hemisphere. In Poe's tales of psychological horror and vampirism, the sensational nature of crime and its aftermath give rise to energies that always verge out of control. And while the world's first literary detective, C. Auguste Dupin, enters into situations that are similarly charged with confusion and violent mayhem, he never loses his cool, electing instead to conduct his investigations according to a plan that is guided by reason and a highly developed intuitive sense. In the tales of psychological terror and suspense, Poe's protagonists relinquish whatever remains of their self-discipline and rational faculties. In the detective tales, however, it is the discipline of logic and reason that sustains the narrative.

In his essay "The Philosophy of Composition," Poe insisted that a successful work of literature must contain nothing superfluous to its plot; that is, its themes must proceed, "step by step, to its completion with the precision and rigid consequence of a mathematical problem." The detective tales—"The Murders in the Rue Morgue," "The Purloined Letter," and "The Mystery of Marie Rogêt"—are the best illustrations of this precept in Poe's entire canon. All of Poe's detective tales feature a problem or a puzzle that must be solved, a pattern that must be deciphered. A series of clues are brought into juxtaposition with one another, and from this a discernible pattern begins to take shape. But this pattern is discernible only to a logical mind capable of creating an associative web that links together separate pieces of evidence.

In "The Purloined Letter" and "Murders in the Rue Morgue," Dupin solves criminal situations that baffle the police. The latter's investigative abilities prove too narrowly defined because the police are unable to think beyond the details and facts supplied by the evidence. They remain hamstrung by their expectation that criminal activity is historically predicable and shaped by decipherable events—for example, motive and recognizable patterns of criminality. Dupin, on the other hand, operates on the theory that the extraordinary is always manifesting itself in the ordinary. This open-minded approach to criminology enables him to create a bond with the criminal and to conceptualize a crime that has never before occurred:

> It is by these deviations from the plane of the ordinary, that reason feels its way, if at all, in its search for the true. In investigations such as we are now pursuing, it should not be so much asked "what has occurred" as "what has occurred that has never occurred before."

Thus, the police remain dumbfounded in "The Murders in the Rue Morgue" by the evidence that a double homicide of particular brutality has been committed without apparent motive—"two bags, containing nearly four thousand francs in gold" are recovered on the floor—and without forced entry. These facts, coupled with the broken nail in what was thought to be a locked window and the strange language used by the murderer that no one in the apartment building understands, point the way for Dupin to reach his conclusion that the killer was not human but an escaped "Ourang-Outang."

Similarly, in "The Purloined Letter," the meticulous police investigators overlook the pursued literary object because they become obsessed in their search for a clever hiding place. Dupin, on the other hand, notices the stolen letter, which has been left out in the open by Minister D—, because it is noticeably different—that is, crumpled and dirty—from the other objects on the minister's desk and his usual methodical habits. Dupin pays attention to what others cannot see, to the significance of the easily overlooked. He is the one figure who brings together the imaginative capacities of Poe's poet-narrators and homicidal masterminds and the analytical intelligence of the mathematician to solve insoluble crimes. Minister D— also possesses the unique combination of a poetic imagination and analytic abilities, and this transports him into the sphere where Dupin himself resides. Even the choice of the letter "D" to begin the minister's last name is meant to suggest his close connection—perhaps "doubling" is even more accurate—to Dupin. Dupin's identification with the criminal—his ability to enter into his thought processes—makes the art of solving a crime an intellectual and intuitive exercise, something akin to the creation of a beautiful poem. As in "Murders in the Rue Morgue," Dupin solves this case by looking for the extraordinary to manifest itself in the mundane, by paying attention to what everyone else overlooks, and by training his mind to think in the manner of a criminal.

THE COMIC GROTESQUE

Although Poe's reputation as the king of the macabre was established by virtue of tales and poems that appear at first glance to be far removed from any appreciation of the comedic, he wrote many stories that while they may constitute a lesser-known aspect of his canon are nonetheless important to a full appreciation of his art. The American short-story writer Flannery O'Connor, for example, read all of Poe's humorous tales early in her career, and her inimitable fusion of the grotesque and the horrible with the darkly comic and ludicrous is deeply indebted to Poe's artistry. In Frederick S. Frank's critical assessment, published in *Gothic Writers*, "Gothic comedy depicting absurd death, ridiculous punishments, odd revenges, and demonic chicanery forms a significant portion of Poe's output. These comic tales are often tinged with a sarcastic and gruesome wit." But even a "serious" story such as "The Cask of Amontillado" possesses wonderful moments of comic misrepresentation that tend to counterpoint the horror of premature burial and the dire consequences of a grisly revenge. As the two men proceed along toward Fortunato's ultimate resting place, Montressor's sarcastic commentary and behavior—from toasting his victim's health and long life to revealing his mason trowel when Fortunato mentions that he is a member of the secret Mason society to toying with the chained Fortunato by telling him that he intends to provide him "all the little attentions in my power"—makes this narrative one of Poe's darkest comedies.

Poe's comic formulations anticipate the theory of the *carnivalesque* as it would be formulated nearly a century later by the Russian literary theorist Mikhail Bakhtin in his book *Rabelais and His World*. Bakhtin's analysis of the medieval carnival draws comedy and horror together, since, in their most excessive forms, they both emphasize grotesque exaggerations of the body, particularly its degradation. Poe's comic art dramatizes what Bakhtin first noticed about the tradition of the pre-Lenten carnival: that mocking and misrule reign in undermining the routine of established authority and accepted definitions of reality.

If Poe's psychological horror tales push pathological issues and self-destruction toward the point of obsessive madness, his comedies take slapstick and absurdity to their furthest extremes. Horror and hilarity merge when Poe's protagonists find themselves fatally entrapped in situations that provoke humor in public humiliation and the jeopardizing of their physical well-being. Poe's horror tales tend to focus upon the acute psychological conditions of his characters—their internal distress—while his comedies are based almost exclusively upon the predicaments of the physical body under duress. Tales such as "King Pest," "The Devil in the Belfry," "A Predicament," "How to Write a Blackwood Article," and "Never Bet the Devil Your Head" often blur the line separating horror from ludicrousness, the grotesque and the sublime, to the point where his characters find themselves inhabiting a universe they can neither control nor comprehend. In the story "A Predicament," the main character finds herself trapped in the belfry of cathedral tower clock. While attempting to obtain a superior view of the world below, Signora Psyche Zenobia extends her head out a convenient aperture in front of the clock, and gets her own face stuck in the face of the clock itself. Suddenly aware of her predicament, she anticipates her own beheading as the clock's giant minute hand slowly descends simulating the action of a guillotine. It is a moment similar to that described by the bound prisoner in "The Pit and the Pendulum." But whereas that story speaks of unmistakable terror during the descent of the razor pendulum, "A Predicament" renders the experience comical as Zenobia provides a calm, analytical, and "disembodied" description of her own decapitation. To make her plight even more ridiculous, she continues a philosophical discourse on the dichotomy of body and soul while gazing up at the remains of herself after her head has been severed from her neck.

THE NARRATIVE OF ARTHUR GORDON PYM

Although the majority of Poe's prose works are set in increasingly circumscribed environments—houses, phantasmagoric corridors, crypts, chambers, that is, all manner of typical Gothic dwellings—his only novel, *Pym* (1837) is set upon the open ocean in a thriller that conveys his hero to the very ends of the earth. While Poe's short stories are, at their best, brilliant studies of the internal working of the mind's aberrant psychology, *Pym* continually expands its narrative scope outward. It focuses less upon the inner psychological states found in the typical Poe tale and more upon the fantastic and exaggerated visionary landscapes of poems such as "The City in the Sea" and "Dream-Land." Indeed, Pym has no psychological underpinnings; he does not work, and he has neither history nor personality with which the reader can identify or engage. Throughout the novel, but especially in the opening chapters, realistic details are subordinate to an overall dreamlike atmosphere and horrific effects. The reader learns, for example, that after cannibalizing Richard Parker, a fellow sailor and shipwreck survivor, Pym can barely recall the experience. When sharks devour his best friend and like-minded adventurer, Augustus Barnard, Pym never mentions him again. These specific events lose their reality, as Pym remains virtually unconscious of anything that he is not immediately experiencing.

Like the other two tales in Poe's saltwater trilogy, "MS. Found in a Bottle" and "A Descent in the Maelström," *Pym* is a first-person reminiscence of an imaginary and dangerous sea voyage structured and unified by a series of highly episodic adventures. Strongly influenced by Daniel Defoe's *Robinson Crusoe* (1719–1720), a book Poe greatly admired, *Pym* is actually less a novel than a series of action scenes involving Pym traveling in and out of dangerous situations. Poe was to emerge as a great theoretician and practitioner of the short-story genre, arguing for the importance of keeping the narrative *short* and centered upon a single climax. In this light, *Pym* resembles more a series of short stories in which many minor climaxes occur than a truly organized and unified piece of extended fiction.

With its mysterious and much debated ending and its confluence of bizarre and life-threatening events, it is appropriate to think of *Pym* as a Gothic novel gone afloat. Aboard the various boats and ships where Pym is variously sequestered, shipwrecked, rescued, and kidnapped, he experiences nearly every variety of Gothic shock. In fact, it is helpful to read Pym in the role of the typical Gothic maiden under siege as he is projected into horror after horror by his thirst for adventure and is forced to endure a series of awful events. These disturbing sequences include cannibalism, savage natives, a boat collision and shipwreck, near starvation while hiding in a large box on board the *Grampus* for four days, a mutiny in which Pym is forced to defend himself by killing the remaining mutineers, and several near-death experiences in sea storms of such violence that it is a wonder how he summons the courage to sail again. The ordeal once reserved for the prototypical eighteenth-century Gothic maiden in flight from some masculine entrapment or perceived threat becomes the pattern of Pym's existence en route to an absolute south of no return. Poe essentially creates a series of floating Gothic castles and haunted houses, replete with the misadventures that would typically befall a Gothic heroine confined within its walls, by sending Pym on a downward journey of hemispheric proportions and having him grope his way toward freedom—through a combination of good fortune, a singularly unreflective mind that immediately forgets its most recent interaction with horror, and fantastic survival skills.

The novel, then, hovers continually upon the edge of nightmare, a flow of horrific occurrences that tend to wash over and overwhelm both Pym and the reader. The journal narrative concludes as Pym makes his way via canoe toward the southern polar cap, where he discovers an albino world where "white ashy material fell now continually around us . . . and began to assume more distinctness of form. I can liken it to nothing but a limitless cataract." There, a final confrontation takes place between Pym and an enormous "shrouded human figure, very far larger in its proportions than any dweller among men." This figure "of the perfect whiteness of the snow" dwarfs the novel's final scene, as it rises up in front of Pym's little boat. Many critics have endeavored to explain this moment, some linking it to the white whale in Herman Melville's own haunted sea tale, *Moby-Dick* (1851), but none has yet produced a totally satisfying explanation of the book's final figure of white.

THE POSTMODERN POE

The boundless energies that characterize the work of Edgar Allan Poe are often contradictory, both in the manner of their expression and in the meanings that they ultimately signify. Poe's coterie of bereaved male suitors are drawn to women either dead or dying—women who have been put into the grave prematurely by men who, like the narrator in "Ligeia," await anxiously their return, "a helpless prey to a whirl of violent emotions, of which extreme awe was perhaps the least terrible, the least consuming." One moment his psychotic criminals perform cold-blooded murders and hideous acts of evisceration while "the guilt of [their] dark deed disturbed [them] but little" ("The Black Cat"), and then, in the next heartbeat, they give themselves over to the police and to *perversity,* exercising the compulsion to confess their secreted crime and experience the exquisite pain of self-punishment. Even his most rational and logical character, the detective Dupin, owes at least a part of his professional success to the fact that he is a social outsider, a man who is as strangely alienated from the mainstream as the criminals he pursues. Within the tormented and tormenting psyches of Poe's protagonists, Romanticism's emphasis on a contradictory and divided self is omnipresent.

Poe's genius was to remind us always that human beings are devilishly complex individuals who are pulled simultaneously toward acts of beauty and violence and that oftentimes violence translates itself strangely into an act of beauty. How else is a reader to comprehend the desperately compulsive revelry of Prospero's glitterati or appreciate the ironic brilliance inherent in Montressor's narrative of vicious revenge? Poe explored continually the de Sadean tenet that pain and pleasure are inextricably linked and that the human psyche craves them both. In the end, his personal torments and contradictory aesthetics might have made Poe the quintessential nineteenth-century Romantic, but his insight into human nature and its infinite capacity for—and attraction to—evil suggest that he is also one of our own.

Selected Bibliography

WORKS OF EDGAR ALLAN POE

COLLECTED WORKS
The Works of the Late Edgar Allan Poe. 4 vols. Edited by Rufus Wilmot Griswold. New York: J. S. Redfield, 1850–1856.
The Works of Edgar Allan Poe. 10 vols. Edited by Edmund Clarence Stedman and George Edward Woodberry. Chicago: Stone & Kimball, 1894–1895.
The Complete Works of Edgar Allan Poe. 17 vols. Edited by James A. Harrison. New York: Thomas Y. Crowell, 1902; New York: AMS Press, 1965.
Selected Writings of Edgar Allan Poe. Edited by Edward H. Davidson. Boston: Houghton Mifflin, 1956.
The Letters of Edgar Allan Poe. 2 vols. Edited by John Ward Ostrom. New York: Gordian Press, 1966.
Selected Writings of Edgar Allan Poe: Poems, Tales, Essays, and Reviews. Edited by David Galloway. Baltimore: Penguin, 1967, 1975.

The Narrative of Arthur Gordon Pym of Nantucket. Edited by Harold Beaver. Baltimore: Penguin, 1975.

Portable Edgar Allan Poe. Edited by Phillip V. Stern. New York: Viking Penguin, 1977.

The Collected Writings of Edgar Allan Poe. 5 vols. Edited by Burton R. Pollin. Boston: Twayne, 1981 (vol. 1); New York: Gordian Press, 1985–1997 (vols. 2–5).

Selections from the Critical Writings of Edgar Allan Poe. Edited by Frederick C. Prescott. New York: Gordian Press, 1981.

Edgar Allan Poe: Essays and Reviews. Edited by Gary Richard Thompson. New York: Library of America, 1984.

Edgar Allan Poe: Poetry and Tales. Edited by Patrick F. Quinn. New York: Library of America, 1996.

BIBLIOGRAPHIES, CONCORDANCE, AND OTHER REFERENCE SOURCES

Carlson, Eric W., ed. *A Companion to Poe Studies.* Westport, Conn.: Greenwood Press, 1996.

Dameron, J. Lasley, and Louis Charles Stagg. *An Index to Poe's Critical Vocabulary.* Hartford, Conn.: Transcendental Books, 1966.

Frank, Frederick S., and Anthony Magistrale. *The Poe Encyclopedia.* Westport, Conn.: Greenwood Press, 1997.

Gale, Robert L. *Plots and Characters in the Fiction and Poetry of Edgar Allan Poe.* Hamden, Conn.: Archon, 1970.

Hammond, J. R. *An Edgar Allan Poe Companion.* New York: Barnes and Noble, 1981.

Hyneman, Esther F. *Edgar Allan Poe: An Annotated Bibliography of Books and Articles in English, 1827–1973.* Boston: G. K. Hall, 1974.

Pollin, Burton Ralph. *Word Index to Poe's Fiction.* New York: Gordian Press, 1982.

Robbins, J. Albert. *A Checklist of Edgar Allan Poe.* Columbus, Ohio: Charles E. Merrill, 1969.

Smith, Don G. *The Poe Cinema: A Critical Filmography of Theatrical Releases Based on the Works of Edgar Allan Poe.* Jefferson, N.C.: McFarland, 1999.

Smith, Ronald L. *Poe in the Media: Screen, Songs, and Spoken Word Recordings.* New York: Garland, 1990.

Wiley, Elizabeth. *Concordance to the Poetry of Edgar Allan Poe.* Selinsgrove, Pa.: Susquehanna University Press, 1989.

CRITICAL AND BIOGRAPHICAL STUDIES

Bakhtin, Mikhail. *Rabelais and His World.* Translated by Helene Iswolsky. Bloomington: Indiana University Press, 1984.

Baudelaire, Charles. *Baudelaire on Poe.* Translated and edited by Lois Hyslop and Francis E. Hyslop Jr. State College, Pa.: Bald Eagle Press, 1952.

———. *The Painter of Modern Life, and Other Essays.* Translated and edited by Jonathan Mayne. London: Phaidon Press/Da Capo Press, 1964.

Bloom, Clive. *Reading Poe/Reading Freud: The Romantic Imagination in Crisis.* New York: St. Martin's Press, 1988.

Bloom, Harold, ed. *Edgar Allan Poe.* New York: Chelsea House, 1984.

Bonaparte, Marie. *The Life and Works of Edgar Allan Poe: A Psycho-analytic Interpretation.* Translated by John Rodker. London: Imago, 1949.

Carlson, Eric W., ed. *Critical Essays on Edgar Allan Poe.* Boston: G. K. Hall, 1987.

Dayan, Joan. *Fables of Mind: An Inquiry into Poe's Fiction.* New York: Oxford University Press, 1987.

Edmundson, Mark. *Nightmare on Main Street: Angels, Sadomasochism, and the Culture of the Gothic.* Cambridge, Mass.: Harvard University Press, 1997.

Fiedler, Leslie. "The Blackness of Darkness: E. A. Poe and the Development of the Gothic." In her *Love and Death in the American Novel.* New York: Stein and Day, 1982. Pp. 370–382.

Frank, Frederick S. "Edgar Allan Poe." In *Gothic Writers: A Critical and Bibliographical Guide.* Edited by Douglass H. Thomson, Jack G. Voller, and Frederick S. Frank. Westport, Conn.: Greenwood Press, 2002. Pp. 330–343.

Hoffman, Daniel. *Poe Poe Poe Poe Poe Poe Poe.* Baton Rouge: Louisiana State University Press, 1998.

Kennedy, J. Gerald. *Poe, Death, and the Life of Writing.* New Haven, Conn.: Yale University Press, 1987.

Lovecraft, H. P. "Edgar Allan Poe." In *Supernatural Horror in Literature.* Edited by E. F. Bleiler. New York: Dover, 1973. Pp. 52–59.

Magistrale, Anthony, and Sidney Poger. *Poe's Children: Connections between Tales of Terror and Detection.* New York: Peter Lang, 1999.

May, Charles E. *Edgar Allan Poe: A Study of the Short Fiction.* Boston: Twayne, 1991.

Muller, John P., and William J. Richardson, eds. *The Purloined Poe: Lacan, Derrida, and Psychoanalytic Reading.* Baltimore: Johns Hopkins University Press, 1988.

Ringe, Donald. *American Gothic: Imagination and Reason in Nineteenth-Century Fiction.* Lexington: University Press of Kentucky, 1982.

Rosenheim, Shawn, and Stephen Rachman, eds. *The American Face of Edgar Allan Poe.* Baltimore: Johns Hopkins University Press, 1995.

Silverman, Kenneth. *Edgar A. Poe: Mournful and Never-Ending Remembrance.* New York: Harper-Collins, 1991.

———, ed. *New Essays on Poe's Major Tales.* New York: Cambridge University Press, 1998.

Thomas, Dwight, and David J. Jackson. *The Poe Log: A Documentary Life of Edgar Allan Poe, 1809–1849.* Boston: G. K. Hall, 1987.

Veler, Richard, ed. *Papers on Poe: Essays in Honor of John Ward Ostrom.* Springfield, Ohio: Chantry Music Press, 1972.

Vines, Lois Davis, ed. *Poe Abroad: Influence, Reputation, Affinities.* Iowa City: University of Iowa Press, 1999.

Walker, I. M. *Edgar Allan Poe: The Critical Heritage.* London and New York: Routledge and Kegan Paul, 1986.

FILMS BASED ON THE WORKS OF EDGAR ALLAN POE

Since 1908 no fewer than ninety films from thirteen countries have been based on or inspired by Poe's writings. What follows is a selected chronological listing of some of the major cinemagraphic adaptations.

The Avenging Conscience. Screenplay by D. W. Griffith. Directed by D. W. Griffith. MUT/Reliance-Majestic, 1914. (Based on "The Tell-Tale Heart.")

The Fall of the House of Usher. Screenplay by Jean Epstein. Directed by Jean Epstein. Jean Epstein Films, 1928.

The Murders in the Rue Morgue. Screenplay by John Huston, Tom Reed, and Dale VanEvery. Directed by Robert Florey. Universal, 1932.

The Fall of the House of Usher. Screenplay by Richard Matheson. Directed by Roger Corman. American International, 1960.

The Pit and the Pendulum. Screenplay by Richard Matheson. Directed by Roger Corman. American International, 1961.

The Raven. Screenplay by Richard Matheson. Directed by Roger Corman. American International, 1963.

The Masque of the Red Death. Screenplay by Charles Beaumont and Robert Wright Campbell. Directed by Roger Corman. American International, 1964.

The Tomb of Ligeia. Screenplay by Robert Towne. Directed by Roger Corman. American International, 1965.

Spirits of the Dead; Tales of Mystery. Screenplay by Daniel Boulanger, Pascal Cousin, Federico Fellini, Louis Malle, Roger Vadim, Clement Biddle Wood, and Bernardino Zapponi. "Metzengerstein," directed by Roger Vadim; "William Wilson," directed by Louis Malle; "Never Bet the Devil Your Head," directed by Federico Fellini. Films Marceau/Concinor/Cinematografica, 1968.

The Pit and the Pendulum. Screenplay by Dennis Paoli. Directed by Stuart Gordon. Full Moon Entertainment, 1991.

—TONY MAGISTRALE

Adrienne Rich

1929–

ADRIENNE CECILE RICH was born on May 16, 1929, in Baltimore, Maryland. She was the first daughter of Arnold Rice Rich and Helen Rich, née Jones. Arnold Rich was Jewish, of Austro-Hungarian origins, and became a pathologist at the Johns Hopkins Medical School. He seems to have had a domineering propensity, determined to make Adrienne into a poet and her sister, Cynthia, into a novelist. The children did not enter Roland Park Country School until the fourth grade but were encouraged to read in the well-stocked library of Dr. Rich. Each child was supposed to write something each day and show such work to their father. Their mother, a Protestant from the South, seems to have had less influence. She was a musician who gave up a career as a pianist to be a housewife.

Adrienne was at Roland Park Country School between 1938 and 1947. Her father's regime paid off, to this extent. She was admitted to Radcliffe College in 1947. This was entry into a wider world. Encouraged by her Radcliffe tutors, she entered some of her poems for the 1951 Yale Series of Younger Poets competition, which was to be judged that year by W. H. Auden. She won the first prize, and Auden wrote the preface to the resultant 1951 publication, *A Change of World*. In his preface Auden stressed the craftsmanship of the poems and spoke of "a determination to ensure that whatever she writes shall, at least, not be shoddily made." From the first, then, Rich was aware of the medium through which her thoughts were transmitted.

A Change of World is certainly a beautifully written book. It is like a filigree mask or an oriental fan, using craft to disguise rather than to convey attitude and meaning. Nobody could doubt the promise it conveyed. The key lines of several poems—"Storm Warnings," "Aunt Jennifer's Tigers," and "A Clock in the Square"—suggest this: "Time in the hand is not control of time, / Nor shattered fragments of an instrument / A proof against the wind"; "When Aunt is dead, her terrified hands will lie / Still ringed with ordeals she was mastered by"; "Time may be silenced but will not be stilled." There is a preoccupation with time and its passing, an attachment to the five-beat or pentametric line, an evocation of scenes and atmosphere akin to Auden's own "walking together in the windless orchard" and "the clock-towers tell the gardens day and night." Without doubt, Adrienne Rich conned such copies of Auden's poems as were in her possession with extra care before going in for the Yale Younger Poets competition. She was eager to please, determined to succeed, and motivated to make her way in the world.

Rich graduated cum laude and Phi Beta Kappa from Radcliffe with a bachelor of arts degree in 1951 and was awarded a Guggenheim Fellowship to study at Oxford, having already placed poems in *Poetry* and *Atlantic Monthly*. She made less impact socially at Oxford than her near-contemporary Sylvia Plath would at Cambridge some years later. However, in 1952 she was placed as the twelfth in a prestigious series of poetry pamphlets issued by the Fantasy Press and edited by her fellow countryman Donald Hall and the proprietor of the press, Oscar Mellor. The poems contained therein were reprinted from *A Change of World* and *Atlantic Monthly*, in which they had previously appeared. She did not return to Oxford after the Easter vacation and spent some time traveling, especially in Italy, and writing verse. In 1953 she returned to Massachusetts and married a Harvard economist, Alfred Conrad, whom she had met as an undergraduate. This may well have been a way of distancing herself from her father. They were resident for a time in Boston.

She must have found married life restrictive, partly because she bore three sons in quick succession: David in 1955, Paul in 1957, and Jacob in 1959. The writing from early in her marriage, eked out with pieces based on her European impressions, was published in 1955 in a collection called *The Diamond Cutters and Other Poems*. She herself was much more severe on this book than any of the reviewers or subsequent critics have been. In the foreword to her *Collected Early Poems, 1950–1970* (1993) she writes, "Too many of the poems were, at best, facile and ungrounded imitations of other poets—Elinor Wylie, Robert Frost, Elizabeth Bishop, Dylan Thomas, Wallace Stevens, Yeats, even English Georgians—exercises in style." To her credit, however, Adrienne Rich neither revised nor suppressed these poems, thus giving her readers a chance to make their own minds up about the matter. After all, no less a critic than Randall Jarrell wrote of this book, "The poet whom we see behind the clarity and gravity of Miss Rich's poems cannot help seeming to us a sort of princess in a fairy tale."

What one can say is that *The Diamond Cutters* is a substantial volume. It contains forty-five poems, compared with the forty of the previous collection. At least two of these, "Autumn Equinox" and "The Perennial Answer," considerably outrun the length of any of their predecessors. With this bulk of verse, the quality of the poems may be expected to vary. One could suggest that some of the longer poems go on a good deal for what they have to express, somewhat in the manner of the laxer and more garrulous Robert Frost. There is an even greater attachment to the iambic norm than that which is found in the previous volume. The rhymes, too, are perhaps unvaryingly full, creating an effect of sonority that sometimes verges on monotony.

Nevertheless, these characteristics play their part when genuine explosions of delight occur, as in the poem "Bears":

Wonderful bears that walked my room all night,
Where are you gone, your sleek and fairy fur,
Your eyes' veiled imperious light?

Brown bears as rich as mocha or as musk,
White opalescent bears whose fur stood out
Electric in the deepening dusk,

And great black bears who seemed more blue than
 black,
More violet than blue against the dark—
Where are you now? upon what track

Mutter your muffled paws, that used to tread
So softly, surely, up the creakless stair
While I lay listening in bed?

When did I lose you? whose have you become?
Why do I wait and wait and never hear
Your thick nocturnal pacing in my room?
My bears, who keeps you now, in pride and fear?

This can be taken as a child's poem or, more precisely, as the poem of an adult recollecting the fantasies of childhood. It has energy as well as charm and, like a number of the earlier poems of Adrienne Rich, draws upon sources formed before adulthood.

Similar in some respects, and certainly popular with older schoolchildren, is "Living in Sin." The poem progresses in a leisurely fashion through its unrhymed yet still quite formal lines. Gradually the more squalid aspects of the bohemian life obtrude. The speaker appears to be a young woman who has left her home to live with a painter or composer wholly concerned with his art.

She had thought the studio would keep itself;
No dust upon the furniture of love.
Half heresy, to wish the taps less vocal,
The panes relieved of grime. A plate of pears,
A piano with a Persian shawl, a cat

Stalking the picturesque amusing mouse
Had risen at his urging.
Not that at five each separate stair would writhe
Under the milkman's tramp; that morning light
So coldly would delineate the scraps
Of last night's cheese and three sepulchral bottles;
That on the kitchen shelf among the saucers
A pair of beetle-eyes would fix her own—
Envoy from some village in the moldings . . .
Meanwhile, he, with a yawn,
Sounded a dozen notes upon the keyboard,
Declared it out of tune, shrugged at the mirror,
Rubbed at his beard, went out for cigarettes;
While she, jeered by the minor demons,
Pulled back the sheets and made the bed and found
A towel to dust the table-top,
And let the coffee-pot boil over on the stove.
By evening she was back in love again,
Though not so wholly but throughout the night
She woke sometimes to feel the daylight coming
Like a relentless milkman up the stairs.

What is clever about this poem is the way the ordered previous life of the speaker is implied, without a word ever being said about it explicitly. One can infer, however, that this was not a life where towels were used to dust table-tops or where coffee-pots boiled over.

The next few years were difficult. This is marked by the fact that no new volume of verse appeared until 1963. One catches a glimpse of Rich as she was at this time in Boston in a journal entry from Sylvia Plath (*The Journals of Sylvia Plath,* 1982), who regarded her as a dangerous rival: "little, round and stumpy, all vibrant short black hair, great sparkling black eyes and a tulip-red umbrella: honest, frank, forthright & even opinionated." During her third pregnancy Rich decided to have herself sterilized. More and more she seems to have resented the fact that her life was governed by her husband's promotions and peregrinations. In 1962 he received a Guggenheim Fellowship and used this to work at the Netherlands Economic Institute. This meant that she lived in Holland for a time, but scarcely on her own terms. Rich had three sons under the age of seven. She

would have met only her husband's associates and their wives and the mothers of other young children. The effect must have been claustrophobic.

When they returned to the United States, Rich began spending more time with her relatives in Vermont and also met such litterateurs resident there as Hayden Carruth and Galway Kinnell. In 1966 the family moved to New York when her husband took up a post at City College. Rich began teaching a graduate poetry course at Columbia University and two years later herself started to teach at City College, in a program designed to reach underprivileged students. During this period she became highly politicized, joining several radical groups and societies and becoming especially active in the women's liberation movement, and her prose began appearing in radical and feminist journals. It had become difficult for her husband to keep up with her. She continued to write verse, though her style and metric changed fundamentally. Her work of these years crystallized in the title poem of her 1963 collection, *Snapshots of a Daughter-in-Law: Poems, 1954–1962.*

A daughter-in-law is both formally connected to and a step removed from a senior figure, a person of another epoch who is, nevertheless, to be treated with respect. There may be fear that this is the kind of person one will grow into. Perhaps one key line of this poem is an unattributed quotation from Samuel Johnson: "Not that it is done well, but / that it is done at all." Johnson was thinking of a woman preaching a sermon, but Rich is applying this notion to the activity of women in art, science, politics, and indeed any human enterprise.

The whole poem is a major statement on behalf of feminism. Rich had been reading Emily Dickinson, Mary Wollstonecraft, and Simone de Beauvoir. The importance of such authors to "Snapshots of a Daughter-in-Law" is that in Rich's poem we have, as related fragments rather than a sustained narrative, the portraits of women whose lives have not been taken up and lived. These are images as seen in shards of a mirror. Section 4, in which Dickinson herself is reflected, is a key to the whole:

Knowing themselves too well in one another:
their gifts no pure fruition, but a thorn,
the prick filed sharp against a hint of scorn . . .
Reading while waiting
for the iron to heat,
writing, *My Life had stood—a Loaded Gun—*
in that Amherst pantry while the jellies boil and
    scum,
or, more often,
iron-eyed and beaked and purposed as a bird,
dusting everything on the whatnot every day of
    life.

Rich has taken the first line of Dickinson's poem 754, beginning "My Life had stood—a Loaded Gun— / In Corners—till a Day," a poem later analyzed in her book *On Lies, Secrets, and Silence: Selected Prose, 1966–1978* (1979). Even for Dickinson, poem 754 is strange. In it a woman appears to turn from inanimate weapon to something like a hunting hawk. Her life has been inert—stuck in a corner—until the arrival of the Owner, for whom the hawk kills. In its weird way, this is a poem of release, and in Rich one finds a claustrophobic sense of powers unused. The "Owner" may be taken to represent not so much a conquering male as the powers pent up in the woman and now released. One is reminded of yet another poem of frustration, George Herbert's "The Collar":

I struck the board and cry'd, No more.
I will abroad.
What? shall I ever sigh and pine?
My lines and life are free, free as the rode,
Loose as the winde, as large as store.
Shall I be still in suit?
Have I no harvest but a thorn
To let me bloud, and not restore
What I have lost with cordiall fruit?

The woman in section 4 of "Snapshots of a Daughter-in-Law" is surrounded by the equiva-lent of cordial fruit—"the jellies boil and scum"—but it does not appear to afford much by way of refreshment. Rich creates an intense pressure of anger held back by social decorum. This is done through images related to Dickinson's loaded gun: the iron heating up, the woman herself "iron-eyed," ceaseless repetitive dusting. This is a calamity building up to break loose.

The poem's title, "Snapshots," is appropriate. Image after image indicates frustration held in by self-discipline. These are respectable middle-aged women restraining fury. The line "Your mind now, mouldering like wedding-cake," recalls the character Miss Havisham, the super-annuated bride of Charles Dickens' *Great Expectations* (1860–1861). The image of the woman "Banging the coffee-pot into the sink" indicates that anger takes its revenge on the domestic objects with which she is surrounded because "nothing hurts her anymore." "Two handsome women, gripped in argument," suggests powers perverted into pointless antago-nism—pointless especially given the women in question are mirror images of each other.

Some words—"*ma semblable, ma soeur*"—are adapted from T. S. Eliot's *The Waste Land* (1922) and, beyond that, from Baudelaire's "Au lecteur" in *Les Fleurs du mal* (1857), in which the poet addresses the reader as an equal, almost as a counterpart. Rich's poem, therefore, is a tissue of allusions. But what they amount to is a protest against the low status of women.

The poem begins with an oddly dehumanized doll-like aspect of femininity: "You, once a belle in Shreveport, / with henna-colored hair." It proceeds with an image of a woman dehuman-izing herself by shaving the natural hair off her legs "until they gleam / like petrified mammoth-tusk." It ends with a prophetic image of the woman freed, "at least as beautiful as any boy / or helicopter," delivering the promised cargo—"palpable / ours." This is an adaptation from de

Beauvoir's *The Second Sex* (1953): "She comes down from the remoteness of ages . . . she is a helicopter and she is a bird." "Snapshots of a Daughter-in-Law" is a tissue of such carefully chosen quotations that it might well be termed Rich's *Waste Land*. And, like Eliot's poem, it proceeds by qualitative progression rather than through direct narrative. The allusive nature of Rich's poetry might well form the basis for a thorough inquiry into her verse, if indeed such an inquiry has not already been made.

This poem, with its flexible play of free verse, says goodbye not only to earlier modes of writing but also to a previous way of life. There are poems in *Snapshots of a Daughter-in-Law* that look backward to the old formalism, and very attractively, too: "At Majority," for example, and "Rural Reflections."

> This is the grass your feet are planted on.
> You paint it orange or you sing it green,
> > But you have never found
> A way to make the grass mean what you mean.

That poem was written in 1956. Here, from 1962, is a poem called "Novella":

> Two people in a room, speaking harshly.
> One gets up, goes out to walk.
> (That is the man.)
> The other goes into the next room
> and washes the dishes, cracking one.
> (That is the woman.)
> It gets dark outside.
> The children quarrel in the attic.
> She has no blood left in her heart.

Between those two dates, 1956 and 1962, "Snapshots of a Daughter-in-Law" was composed. Its nervous and, on the whole, free verse is something new. The poetry is stripped down, left bare—though, in years to come, further meanings were to accrete.

Out of this verse, some written in Leiden and simmering with angst, came *Necessities of Life: Poems, 1962–1965* (1966). Temporarily, per-haps, something of texture was lost. But the poems look forward, with an accession of pain and self-recognition. They are at their strongest when the poet has some image to seize and to hang on to. That is what renders "Moth Hour" outstanding among its coevals:

> I am gliding backward away from those who knew
> > me
> as the moon grows thinner and finally shuts its
> > lantern.
> I can be replaced a thousand times,
> a box containing death.
> When you put out your hand to touch me
> you are already reaching toward an empty space.

This poem was written in 1965, and it is fair to say that, at that period, Rich was more effective at images of death and decay than at anything more welcoming.

Take, for example, a portrait of someone who can be identified with her father, whose mind, she declared in *Blood, Bread, and Poetry: Selected Prose, 1979–1985* (1986), had gone by 1968, the year in which he died. In "After Dark" he arouses disgust as he grows more decrepit:

> You are falling asleep and I sit looking at you
> old tree of life
> old man whose death I wanted
> I can't stir you up now.
>
> Faintly a phonograph needle
> whirs round in the last groove
> eating my heart to dust.
> That terrible record! how it played
>
> down years, whenever I was
> in foreign languages even
> over and over, *I know you better*
> *than you know yourself   I know*
>
> *you better than you know*
> *yourself   I know*
> *you*   until, self-maimed,
> I limped off, torn at the roots . . .

Everything depends on that image of the phonograph and its ingenious way of suggesting a parent's tireless repetition. At the same time the image suggests that, at this late stage, the repetition is winding down. However, the reader might like to have had the parent's opinion on record. Rich is uncomfortably near confessional verse here, where self-pity, that most sincere of emotions, tends to run rampant. However, there is a degree of control evinced in this particular verse. The quatrains impose a measure of constraint that precludes shrillness. Further, the quietness of tone—even though *King Lear* is evoked later in the poem—precludes any undue buttonholing of the reader's emotions.

Somewhat less control is evinced in *Leaflets: Poems, 1965–1968,* which was published in 1969. The poems therein are uncomfortably near therapy. Rich herself indicates how they are to be taken when she writes in the title poem, "I want to hand you this / leaflet streaming with rain or tears." And again: "the leaflet then merely something / to leave behind, a little leaf." The comments are shrewd, but is this really enough?

Leaflets contains many shards of experience, seen in poems such as "Orion" and "In the Evening":

Three hours chain-smoking words
and you move on. We stand in the porch,
two archaic figures: a woman and a man.

The old masters, the old sources,
haven't a clue what we're about,
shivering here in the half-dark 'sixties.

As with the previous volume, the poems are best when shaped by a concrete image, as in "Women":

My three sisters are sitting
on rocks of black obsidian.
For the first time, in this light, I can see who they
     are.

My first sister is sewing her costume for the
     procession.
She is going as the Transparent Lady
and all her nerves will be visible.

Too many of the poems, however, tend toward the arbitrariness of journal entries. They are sharp in immediate particulars but lacking in context, and the reader might well surmise why they are being offered at all.

Rich is a prolific poet. One has the sense that these specific pieces are part of a larger program, incompletely spelled out. *The Will to Change: Poems, 1968–1970,* from 1971, and 1973's *Diving into the Wreck: Poems, 1971–1972* are really fragments of a journal, full of discrete particulars but lacking works that have the shape of poems, as witness "Planetarium" from the earlier of these two books:

I am bombarded yet . . .
. . . .
     . . . I am an instrument in the shape
of a woman trying to translate pulsations
into images   for the relief of the body
and the stimulation of the mind.

It depends on how one wishes to read. Many of these pieces, derived from prose, are near to prose. Possibly one would wish them in fact to declare themselves as prose—especially because, during this period, a turbulent one in her life, Rich was pouring out a stream of articles for *College English,* the *New York Review of Books,* the *American Poetry Review, Parnassus: Poetry in Review, Sinister Wisdom,* and *Chrysalis,* among others. Notice the mix of literary journals with frankly feminist ones. To understand Rich at this juncture, it is to her prose that we must look, and it is probably in her prose that, at this juncture, her creative strength is found.

Of Woman Born: Motherhood as Experience and Institution came out in 1976. It is a study of maternity, patriarchy, and gender—values at once learned and searching—and is also far more cohesive than the poems of the period. Its influence has been pervasive, and much of what it says is now accepted in a wide variety of circles. Drawing upon her own journals, Rich begins, in her chapter "Anger and Tenderness," by showing how demanding the care of young children is:

> From the fifties and early sixties, I remember a cycle. It began when I had picked up a book or began trying to write a letter, or even found myself on the telephone with someone toward whom my voice betrayed eagerness, a rush of sympathetic energy. The child (or children) might be absorbed in busyness, in his own dreamworld; but as soon as he felt me gliding into a world which did not include him, he would come to pull at my hand, ask for help, punch at the typewriter keys. And I would feel his wants at such a moment as fraudulent, as an attempt moreover to defraud me of living even for fifteen minutes as myself. My anger would rise; I would feel the futility of any attempt to salvage myself, and also the inequality between us: my needs always balanced against those of a child, and always losing.

This has a powerful and concerted quality that makes one ask why the poet did not attempt to render her feelings in verse. The answer is given in this same volume: "Once in a while someone used to ask me, 'Don't you ever write poems about your children?' The male poets of my generation did write poems about their children—especially their daughters. For me, poetry was where I lived as no-one's mother, where I existed as myself."

Of Woman Born is the most cohesive prose work Rich has produced. It is a kind of bible of the new feminism. What is said about encroachments on femininity gains support from the author's strictures on paternalism. Many of these may be found in the chapter "The Kingdom of the Fathers." The value of the arguments here is that Rich exposes as special many attitudes that have been accepted through the sheer force of convention as normal. For example:

> A crucial moment in human consciousness, then, arrives when man discovers that it is he himself, not the moon or the spring rains or the spirits of the dead, who impregnates the woman; that the child she carries and gives birth to is *his* child, who can make *him* immortal, both mystically, by propitiating the gods with prayers and sacrifices when he is dead, and concretely, by receiving the patrimony from him. At this crossroads of sexual possession, property ownership, and the desire to transcend death, developed the institution we know: the present-day patriarchal family with its supernaturalizing of the penis, its division of labor by gender, its emotional, physical, and material possessiveness, its ideal of monogamous marriage until death (and its severe penalties for adultery by the wife), the "illegitimacy" of a child born outside wedlock, the economic dependency of women, the unpaid domestic services of the wife, the obedience of women and children to male authority, the imprinting and continuation of heterosexual roles.

Some part of the power here comes from the use of accretion, as in the lists and catalogs found so frequently in the work of highly masculine writers such as Walt Whitman and John Dos Passos.

It is backed up, moreover, by the substantial collection of Rich's various essays and articles gathered together in 1979's *On Lies, Secrets, and Silence*. For example, take the essay "Husband-Right and Father-Right." It was originally written as the introduction to *Legal Kidnapping* by Anna Demeter (1977). Rich argues against the historic concept that women should occupy a role in the domestic sphere while men belong in the public arena of power. She sees motherhood as a political institution that is the keystone to the domination in every sphere of women by men. Her arguments are based on Demeter's casebook history, concerning a woman whose two youngest children were held as hostages by her husband—whom she wished to divorce—as a means of forcing her back into the marriage. This may be seen as an extreme case, but Rich uses it to illustrate the fact that the law is strongly on the side of the male in matters such as this. She pleads for a new psychology of male behavior in order to prevent male antagonism against a woman seeking divorce: "Beyond the issues of marriage and divorce, beyond the issue of motherhood, lies the implacable political necessity for women to gain control of our bodies and our lives." She sees the future in terms of mothers who are able to take their lives in hand and confront the institutions that oppress them.

Forceful though this argument is, it begs several questions. There is the biological fact that it is women who bear children, thus rendering themselves far more vulnerable than men. There is the economic fact that a mother looking after her children is able to work less and earn less than a man. There is the social fact that a single mother may have difficulty in gaining financial support from a husband from whom she is separated and who may well have started another family with another woman. This is not meant to deny either Rich's arguments or her conclusions, but to indicate certain built-in difficulties in marital situations that need to be addressed.

However, *On Lies, Secrets, and Silence* is a thought-provoking volume. It contains penetrating essays on Anne Sexton, Anne Bradstreet, and Charlotte Brontë, the last indicating the existence of a sliding scale employed to evaluate female as distinct from male writers. Especially effective is an essay on Emily Dickinson—"Vesuvius at Home"—that would not only convince a skeptical reader of that poet's distinction but also provide a remarkable insight into her presumed mental processes. Rich lays especial emphasis on the probability that Dickinson saw herself as a professional writer and that any apparent eccentricities, such as her reclusiveness, were a means of safeguarding her art. An experienced academic herself by now, Rich also included an essay that should be required reading for every university teacher, "Taking Women Students Seriously." Here, as elsewhere in this valuable book, she indicates the need to remember that the institutions under

whose domination women seek to survive are male-constructed.

The reputation of Adrienne Rich continued to grow. Prizes and awards were showered upon her. She received National Endowment for the Arts grants in 1968 and 1969, along with the Academy Fellowship awarded by the Academy of American Poets (1960), the Amy Lowell Travelling Scholarship (1962), a Bollingen Foundation grant (1962), the Bess Hokin Prize (1963), the Eunice Tietjens Memorial Prize (1968), a National Translation Center grant (1968), the Shelley Memorial Award (1971), an Ingram Merrill Foundation grant (1973), the National Book Award (1974), and the Fund for Human Dignity Award (1981). Her career built up. From 1968 to 1974, she was in turn lecturer, instructor, assistant professor, and professor at the City College of New York. Subsequently, she was professor of English at Douglass College, New Jersey, from 1976 to 1979, then became the A. D. White Professor-at-Large at Cornell University in 1981.

What of her personal life in all this? In the later 1960s, her marriage to Alfred Conrad continued to deteriorate. There were extramarital affairs on both sides. The couple separated in 1970, with Rich leaving the marital home and moving into a small apartment nearby. After a period of grave uncertainty, Conrad left on what he told his children was a trip. In fact he drove up to Vermont, to the woods, and shot himself dead.

It is said that at this point Rich cut off her contacts with most of her male friends. Her various interviews thereafter cloak much of her life under a decent reticence. For example, it is not known how her three sons, at this point aged fifteen, thirteen, and eleven, were affected by this event. Nor is there much by way of information as to how they were subsequently brought up during their mother's busy and indeed hectic professional life as a full-time academic as well as a writer. There is much here to be pondered by some future biographer.

It must have been at about this time that Rich recognized she was a lesbian. The signs of this orientation, in retrospect, had been apparent in her poems before this period. But the explicit statement appeared in 1976 in *Twenty-one Love Poems*, reprinted in what is probably her best book, *The Dream of a Common Language: Poems, 1974–1977* (1978).

It is safe to say that nothing like these poems had ever appeared before. Though they are traditional in their antecedents, the subject matter is original to Rich and marks a turning point for all young women poets. For one thing, the Love Poems are explicitly directed to a woman. She seems to have been Jewish, but her exact identity is as important or as unimportant as that of the Young Man of Shakespeare's sonnets. Indeed, most audaciously, the poems are an answer to Shakespeare's sonnets. It takes a remarkable writer to look Shakespeare straight in the eye, but many will feel that Rich has managed it.

In his Sonnet 27 Shakespeare writes:

Weary with toil, I haste me to my bed,
The dear repose for limbs with travail tired,
But then begins a journey in my head
To work my mind, when body's work's expired.
For then my thoughts, from far where I abide,
Intend a zealous pilgrimage to thee,
And keep my drooping eyelids open wide,
Looking on darkness which the blind do see;
Save that my soul's imaginary sight
Presents thy shadow to my sightless view,
Which like a jewel hung in ghastly night
Makes black night beauteous, and her old face new:
   Lo, thus by day my limbs, by night my mind,
   For thee, and for myself, no quiet find.

A modern reader notes the formal structure of the poem. There may be deep emotion here, but it is held in check by the full rhymes, the formal quatrains, the careful attention to the iambic beat. The notation of feeling, too, is deliberate: "I haste" comes with, so to speak, due preparation and is followed by "then begins a journey in my head." Weight is gained at the expense of spontaneity; the poem is held in retrospect. The present tense—"then begins a journey," "my thoughts . . . / Intend a zealous pilgrimage"—has the effect of a narrative in the past.

In Rich's Love Poem II one finds a very different use of the present tense. Here, everything is immediate, recorded at the moment it is happening. There are dreams, but they are far nearer to present experience than Shakespeare's somber "my soul's imaginary sight / Presents thy shadow." Rich writes:

I wake up in your bed. I know I have been dreaming.
Much earlier, the alarm broke us from each other,
you've been at your desk for hours. I know what I dreamed:
our friend the poet comes into my room
where I've been writing for days,
drafts, carbons, poems are scattered everywhere,
and I want to show her one poem
which is the poem of my life. But I hesitate,
and wake. You've kissed my hair
to wake me. *I dreamed you were a poem,*
I say, *a poem I wanted to show someone . . .*
and I laugh and fall dreaming again
of the desire to show you to everyone I love,
to move openly together
in the pull of gravity, which is not simple,
which carries the feathered grass a long way down the upbreathing air.

Paraphrased, Shakespeare's poem says something like: "I go to bed tired and sleep but find no rest because I dream of you, and that dream, contrasted with the surrounding darkness, provokes desire and creates disturbance. And so I find no peace." Paraphrased, Rich's poem says: "You kissed my hair and woke me from a dream in which a friend who is a poet comes into my room, and I want to show her a poem, and the poem is you, who have just woken me. I fall once more asleep and dream that I want to show my poem, yourself, to everyone." The final metaphor takes the meaning almost beyond the argument, suggesting that their two beings are as unresisting as the feathered grass that is pulled by love, which itself has the mighty force of gravity.

Rich has taken the essence of Shakespeare's poem, deformalized it, and stood it on its head. Shakespeare finds weariness in being reminded of the love for which he longs. Rich finds fulfillment in displaying the love that she possesses and is possessed by.

The undertaking is audacious. It would have been unfortunate had it not come off. Rich has taken on a man, the greatest of men in his own art, and feminized him. One could almost say that this is how Shakespeare would have written if he had lived in the twentieth century and been a woman. That is the undertaking of *Twenty-one Love Poems.* They are not sonnets in the Elizabethan sense, but they have taken the Elizabethan form and buckled it, so to speak, to accommodate the freer thoughts of the twentieth century. Shakespeare, in his Sonnet 73, writes:

> That time of year thou mayst in me behold,
> When yellow leaves, or none, or few do hang
> Upon those boughs which shake against the cold,
> Bare ruined choirs, where late the sweet birds sang;
> In me thou seest the twilight of such day
> As after sunset fadeth in the west,
> Which by and by black night doth take away,
> Death's second self that seals up all in rest.
> In me thou seest the glowing of such fire,
> That on the ashes of his youth doth lie,
> As the deathbed, whereon it must expire,
> Consumed with that which it was nourished by;
>   This thou perceiv'st, which makes thy love more strong,
>   To love that well, which thou must leave ere long.

This draws upon the Italian sonnet as promulgated by Petrarch and adapted into English by Sir Thomas Wyatt and the Earl of Surrey—and, after them, by Sir Philip Sidney. English being

short of rhymes, this form is simpler than that of Petrarch, but it is still not easy to write. The problem is a constant fight between the sense of the poem and the form in which it is expressed. On the one hand, one must not become a slave to rhyme and write ungracefully. On the other hand, it is a matter of technique to observe as far as possible the rhyme scheme that has already been laid down.

As Shakespeare draws upon the technique of his predecessors and so writes in something of a preset form, so Adrienne Rich in Love Poem III draws upon Shakespeare to express her sense of a lover growing older:

> Since we're not young, weeks have to do time
> for years of missing each other. Yet only this odd warp
> in time tells me we're not young.
> Did I ever walk the morning streets at twenty,
> my limbs streaming with a purer joy?
> did I lean from any window over any city
> listening for the future
> as I listen here with nerves tuned for your ring?
> And you, you move toward me with the same tempo.
> Your eyes are everlasting, the green spark
> of the blue-eyed grass of early summer,
> the green-blue wild cress washed by the spring.
> At twenty, yes: we thought we'd live forever.
> At forty-five, I want to know even our limits.
> I touch you knowing we weren't born tomorrow,
> and somehow, each of us will help the other live,
> and somewhere, each of us must help the other die.

Shakespeare sees growing older in terms of death, which he evokes most movingly—the lover is expiring, like a spent fire, upon "the ashes of his youth." Rich, however, answers this joyously; she is no burned-out case: "Did I ever walk the morning streets at twenty, / my limbs streaming with a purer joy?" The implication is that this is what she is doing now, though she is "not young."

The Shakespeare sonnet is charged with a controlled melancholy, a self-reflexive recognition of the speaker as part of a decline in all the seasons. The speaker in the Rich poem is exuberant, and her images stem from the earlier and more fertile part of the year—"the green spark / of the blue-eyed grass of early summer, / the green-blue wild cress washed by the spring." These are images of life, of abundance. Even so, the poem ends with a grave recognition of impermanence: "somewhere, each of us must help the other die."

A further coupling, of Shakespeare's Sonnet 30 and Rich's Love Poem IX, dwells on memories, mostly sad ones, recognizing that, whatever happens in the present, it carries a burden of the past. Shakespeare realizes this in a series of mournful generalizations that, nevertheless, are moved by the pressure of specific implication:

> When to the sessions of sweet silent thought
> I summon up remembrance of things past,
> I sigh the lack of many a thing I sought,
> And with old woes new wail my dear time's
>   waste;
> Then can I drown an eye, unused to flow,
> For precious friends hid in death's dateless night,
> And weep afresh love's long since cancelled woe,
> And moan th' expense of many a vanished sight.
> Then can I grieve at grievances foregone,
> And heavily from woe to woe tell o'er
> The sad account of fore-bemoanèd moan,
> Which I new pay as if not paid before.
>   But if the while I think on thee, dear friend,
>   All losses are restored, and sorrows end.

The counters—"many a thing I sought," "precious friends," "vanished sight"—are rendered specific largely because of the pressure of the verse. The plethora of weighty syllables—"summon," "sigh," "drown"—insist upon the emotion behind the words, even though the words remain themselves generalized.

Adrienne Rich, however, deals in particulars. It is noticeable that she takes over from Shakespeare's sonnet the sense of memory as a pool in which items are drowned; the images of liquidity persist throughout Shakespeare's poem.

But with Rich these memories, drowned as they are, are nevertheless highly specific, as in Love Poem IX:

> Your silence today is a pond where drowned things
>   live
> I want to see raised dripping and brought into the
>   sun.
> It's not my own face I see there, but other faces,
> even your face at another age.
> Whatever's lost there is needed by both of us—
> a watch of old gold, a water-blurred fever chart,
> a key . . . Even the silt and pebbles of the bottom
> deserve their glint of recognition. I fear this
>   silence,
> this inarticulate life. I'm waiting
> for a wind that will gently open this sheeted water
> for once, and show me what I can do
> for you, who have often made the unnameable
> nameable for others, even for me.

Shakespeare has "grievances foregone"; Rich has "a watch of old gold, a water-blurred fever chart, / a key." Clearly the latter stand for much the same entities as are indicated in the Shakespearean implication. In Shakespeare the resolution comes from the beloved one being recollected: "if the while I think on thee, dear friend." In Rich it comes from the loved one's silence being broken.

It is noticeable that the basis of the metric in the Rich poems, here as elsewhere, is a species of five-stress line. Yet syllables are added, as in the first line here, or subtracted, as in the fourth, in a manner that is free, though not wayward. It varies considerably according to what the speaker is saying, being to that extent less framed by a preset form than the Shakespeare sonnets are. At the same time, it is clear that Rich is drawing upon Shakespeare much as Shakespeare himself drew upon his Italian and his English Tudor predecessors.

Shakespeare, in his Sonnet 87, writes:

> Farewell, thou art too dear for my possessing,
> And like enough thou know'st thy estimate.
> The charter of thy worth gives thee releasing;

My bonds in thee are all determinate.
For how do I hold thee but by thy granting,
And for that riches where is my deserving?
The cause of this fair gift in me is wanting,
And so my patent back again is swerving.
Thyself thou gav'st, thy own worth then not know-
  ing,
Or me, to whom thou gav'st it, else mistaking;
So thy great gift, upon misprision growing,
Comes home again, on better judgment making.
  Thus have I had thee as a dream does flatter:
  In sleep a king, but waking no such matter.

The meter is variegated in rather a curious way here, with a great many final syllables displaying what is called a feminine ending, thus: "possessing," "releasing," "granting," "deserving," "wanting," "swerving." This has the effect of placing great emphasis on the only two-line endings that are not feminine, thus: "estimate," "determinate." The effect is to create a kind of sinuous rhythm, not on the whole settling on any line ending as being definitive, other than the two already instanced. This goes along with the subject matter, which treats the love existing between the lovers as a kind of lease or pledge. This lease was granted at a time when either the value of the love was not known or when the state of the lover, who speaks the poem, was exaggerated. The love being later on found to be of great value and the person to whom it was given to be of lesser value than previously thought, necessarily the lease is withdrawn, the original grounds of ceding it having been discovered to be mistaken. The poem concludes by suggesting that the whole contract was illusory anyway.

Rich's version of this in her Love Poem XX suggests that the conversation that would have established the basis of the relationship never took place. At this point, much earlier than in the Shakespeare poem, the belief that the bond was illusory begins:

That conversation we were always on the edge
of having, runs on in my head,

at night the Hudson trembles in New Jersey light
polluted water yet reflecting even
sometimes the moon
and I discern a woman
I loved, drowning in secrets, fear wound round
  her throat
and choking her like hair. And this is she
with whom I tried to speak, whose hurt, expressive head
turning aside from pain, is dragged down deeper
where it cannot hear me,
and soon I shall know I was talking to my own
  soul.

Here, as in the Shakespeare sonnet, the lover is felt to be unworthy, but here, unlike the sonnet, it is the loved one who suffers. Both the Shakespeare poem and that by Rich depend upon the concept of a dream, but, as previously indicated, in the Rich poem the dream starts much earlier. The illusion of the overestimated lease in Shakespeare is represented by Rich as the water of the Hudson River, which, because it is polluted, reflects all the better. Rich picks up and complicates the idea of "reflection" that is found in Shakespeare. He is reflecting upon the misprized lease; she sees the misunderstanding with her lover as that which is reflected in the Hudson—in her case, a woman choked, it would seem, because of the crucial conversation that never took place. In lieu of Shakespeare's sinuous feminine endings, Rich's free verse is alert to nuances of speech. She breaks down the Shakespearean metric, setting aside formality in favor of what might be termed expressive or operative form—that which follows the cadences of speech and is precarious, running the risk of collapsing into fragmentation or, indeed, mere prose.

If this collapse does not happen in Rich's verse, that is a tribute to her sure way of matching subject to utterance. These frequently blithe love poems are answered in *The Dream of a Common Language* by that rarity in the English language, a major elegy upon a woman. This is the poem entitled "A Woman Dead in Her Forties."

Here, there is no very obvious model. The verse of the poem is akin to the various journal entries utilized in such a book as *Of Woman Born,* yet there is never any danger of it fragmenting into prose. It is rescued from any such degeneration by the underlying rhythm of three heavy stresses per line. These act as a binding agent. Unlike the elegies in English written by male poets about men—"Lycidas" (John Milton, 1638), "Adonais" (Percy Bysshe Shelley, 1821), "Thyrsis" (Matthew Arnold, 1866)—the tone is subdued. Rather than being proclaimed from the heights, this poem is hushed, couched in the second person, a letter to a friend who happens to be dead.

The key to the poem, which begins by admitting the cancer and the scars from the surgery attempting to treat it, comes early on:

I want to touch my fingers
to where your breasts had been
but we never did such things

The poem turns on the reticence between the two women: "What did I hide from her," "How can I reconcile this passion / with our modesty," "I never told you how I loved you."

Structurally, the poem begins in the present as an attitude of mourning; reverts in sections 3 and 4 to their mutual childhood—"you fought a girl / who said she'd knock me down"; comments, in section 5, on the bereavement; and then, in section 6, broadens out to a general threnody refracting, in section 7, to the dream imagery already made familiar in the Love Poems:

Time after time in dreams you rise
reproachful

once from a wheelchair pushed by your father
across a lethal expressway

A final summing up appears in section 8, with the Hudson once more as a familiar backcloth, the speaker seeking to understand the meaning of death: that, in the end, the body makes its own decision—"the body tells the truth in its rush of cells." The poem finishes with a reminiscence of its own key lines, tuned down to a minor key, so to speak, put into the past tense:

I would have touched my fingers
to where your breasts had been
but we never did such things

This epoch-making book was succeeded in 1981 by *A Wild Patience Has Taken Me This Far: Poems, 1978–1981,* which seeks to historicize Rich's personal predicament by relating it to the lives of other women—for example, Susan B. Anthony, Jane Addams, Elizabeth Barrett Browning, and Mary E. J. Colter. Outstanding in this book are such poems as "Culture and Anarchy," "Mother-in-Law," Heroines," and "Grandmothers," especially "Hattie Rice Rich":

Your sweetness of soul was a mystery to me,
you who slip-covered chairs, glued broken china,
lived out of a wardrobe trunk in our guestroom
summer and fall, then took the Pullman train
in your darkblue dress and straw hat, to
  Alabama. . . .

The first poem in the book, "The Images," is a key to the whole:

I can never romanticize language again
    never deny its power for disguise for
mystification
  but the same could be said for music
or any form created
    painted ceilings beaten gold worm-worn
Pietàs
  reorganizing victimization   frescoes translating
violence into patterns so powerful and pure
    we continually fail to ask are they true forus

The next collection, *Your Native Land, Your Life: Poems,* published in 1986, develops the themes of the previous book. In the first section, "Sources," Rich looks at her own upbringing, placing it in historical context. The second section, "North American Time," a near-documentary in verse, takes in current affairs as well as the past. The third sequence, which concludes the book, is a series of buckled sonnets—at times freer even than those in *Twenty-one Love Poems*—that are poignantly personal yet also feminist in attitude, as though Rich is attempting to present herself as an archetype of womanhood. A good deal in this book and the previous one concerns her struggle with her father. In a most moving poem, number 14, she reverts from the buckled sonnet to a remarkably formal rendition of the genre and acts out the problems involved in the language of patriarchy:

> Lately in my dreams I hear long sentences
> meaningless in ordinary American
> like, *Your mother, too, was a missionary of poets*
> and in another dream one of my old teachers
> shows me a letter of reference
> he has written for me, in a language
> I know to be English but cannot understand,
> telling me it's in "transformational grammar"
> and that the student who typed the letter
> does not understand this grammar either.
> Lately I dreamed about my father,
> how I found him, alive, seated on an old chair.
> I think what he said to me was,
> *You don't know how lonely I am.*

All this time, of course, Rich was pouring out prose in the form of articles that appeared in such periodicals as *Freedomways, Signs, Women's Studies Quarterly,* the *Boston Review,* and the *Massachusetts Review.* These were collected in *Blood, Bread, and Poetry* (1986). Perhaps the tone in this volume is more strident than in the earlier prose. Certainly the attitudes are, understandably, more partisan. Rich seems to have in mind the creation of a women's community. There is certainly an apparently closed canon of women's writing, involving such authors as Mab Segrest, Jan Clausen, Gloria T. Hull, Alice Walker, Gloria Anzaldúa, and Irena Klepfisz. These authors are not in addition to but instead of those on which Rich herself was brought up, such as William Wordsworth, Samuel Taylor Coleridge, T. S. Eliot, and William Empson. Behind this new canon is the concept

that heterosexuality is a condition imposed upon women. One could suggest—as indeed is made clear in an autobiographical essay, "Split at the Root"—that a good deal of the argument stems from Rich's own heavily patriarchal upbringing by parents who would not even attend her wedding because she was marrying the wrong kind of Jew. However, one cannot help but feel that there is a coarsening in the grain. In lieu of the perceptive Emily Dickinson essay, for example, is one on Elizabeth Bishop that is singularly critic-centered and not very helpful.

What Is Found There: Notebooks on Poetry and Politics (1993) continues the propaganda found in the previous prose book. Despite its subtitle, the essays are in fact no more and no less rough-hewn than some of the earlier prose pieces. Through everything runs a social concern: how the poet earns her living, for example, and how the white male Protestant tradition of American literature is changing—and how it needs to change. The prose gathered in *Arts of the Possible: Essays and Conversations* (2001) maintains a stance that, for all one feels one is being assailed by feminist propaganda, is unfailingly serious. Her essay "Defining the Space That Separates" proclaims, "I believe that poems are made of words and the breathing between them." In a world of extrapolation, that demands to be the critic's slogan. She—or he—must never forget the text.

However, Rich's main claim to attention is—as probably she would feel herself—her verse. *Time's Power: Poems, 1985–1988* (1989) draws heavily on the past. For example, "Letters in the Family" utilizes the voices of three women: a girl who went to the Spanish Civil War, a Jewish woman on a mission behind Nazi lines, and a mother on the run in the South Africa of the period of writing. In this way Rich links personal predicament to history.

An Atlas of the Difficult World: Poems, 1988–1991 (1991) was written during Operation Desert Storm and shows the pressure of contemporary events during the Gulf War. At times Rich seems to be answering Whitman or even succumbing to his hortatory style, as in the second section of the title poem:

> This is the desert where missiles are planted like
>   corms
> This is the breadbasket of foreclosed farms
> This is the birthplace of the rockabilly boy
> This is the cemetery of the poor
> who died for democracy

This ranging between rhetoric and journalism is especially manifest in *Dark Fields of the Republic: Poems, 1991–1995* (1995). The title comes from F. Scott Fitzgerald at his most thrasonic and is not propitious. The book in question emanates genuine concern about contemporary America, but one could wish the concern had been hewn more formally. The poems, such as "To the Days," leap out at one in an excited way:

> From you I want more than I've ever asked,
> all of it—the newscasts' terrible stories
> of life in my time, the knowing it's worse than
>   that,
> much worse—the knowing what it means to be
>   lied to.
>
> Fog in the mornings, hunger for clarity,
> coffee and bread with sour plum jam.
> Numbness of soul in placid neighborhoods.
> Lives ticking on as if.

Yet even when one knows that this poem depends in part upon the *Letters of Rosa Luxemburg* (1993), as translated by Stephen Eric Bronner, one cannot help feeling that the poet should be doing rather more of the work.

Midnight Salvage: Poems, 1995–1998 (1999) is named after a yard where an old craftsman was killed:

> He was walking in the road which was always
>   safe
> The young driver did not know that road
> its curves or that people walked there

> or that you could speed yet hold the curve
> watching for those who walked there
> such skills he did not have being in life unpracticed

This poem is the sixth in a sequence that gives the book its name. There are flashes of defining imagery, often culled from Whitman, but one misses a sense of narrative. There is immediacy, yes, but where is the context?

Fox: Poems, 1998–2000, the next book of verse, was published in 2001. Even its longer poems, "Veterans Day" and "Terza Rima," proceed in jerks. One can certainly salvage individual lyrics such as "For This," though the title could be more helpful. Still, there is a hushed elegiac quality in the writing that has considerable appeal:

> If I've reached for your lines (I have)
>   like letters from the dead that stir the nerves
> dowsed you for a springhead
>   to water my thirst
> dug into my compost skeletons and petals
>   you surely meant to catch the light

Rich says, in the same poem, that this is a "lighthouse keeper's ethics," and that is true. She has turned into a prophetic figure, relying substantially on the past. She is drawing, one might say, upon the ashes of her youth. There is not the sense of self-renewal one finds in major poets as diverse as Wallace Stevens and Peter Redgrove.

Still, this is certainly an oeuvre. And it has been recognized, and not only at home. Rich's work has been translated into German, Spanish, Swedish, Dutch, Hebrew, Greek, Italian, and Japanese. From 1976 to 1979 Rich occupied a professorship at Douglass College; she later coedited the magazine *Sinister Wisdom.* Subsequently she held teaching positions at Swarthmore, Columbia, Brandeis, Rutgers, San Jose State, and Stanford. Perhaps as an alleviant to her chronic malady of arthritis, she is currently domiciled in California. Since 1976 she has lived with the writer and editor Michelle Cliff, to whose help in her work she has paid generous tribute in several books. In addition to her earlier awards Rich has gained the Ruth Lilly Poetry Prize, the Lenore Marshall/Nation Poetry Prize, the Lambda Literary Award, the Los Angeles Times Book Prize for Poetry, the Poet's Prize, a MacArthur Fellowship, the Dorothea Tanning Prize of the Academy of American Poets, the Lannan Foundation Lifetime Achievement Award, and the National Poetry Association Award for Distinguished Service to the Art of Poetry. Rich created a sensation when in 1997 she refused the National Medal for the Arts at the hands of President William Jefferson Clinton on the grounds that the meaning of art was incompatible with the cynical politics of the administration.

Such a career should indicate that the odds are not so overwhelmingly against a woman, especially a woman writer, as Rich's prose polemic would indicate. In particular, her work as both poet and polemicist has had its impact in helping to reshape a good many preset attitudes of an essentially patriarchal society. One would have to say, as was the case with Wordsworth two hundred years before her, that the world is not the same as it was when she started writing and that she has been directly responsible for much of the difference. In strictly literary terms, she has opened up areas of subject matter that were not approachable by women poets before her time. Her influence especially upon younger women poets is incalculable. Adrienne Rich is generally respected, in some quarters revered, and certainly ranks as one of the foremost writers of either sex in her time.

Selected Bibliography

WORKS OF ADRIENNE RICH

POETRY

A Change of World. New Haven, Conn.: Yale University Press, 1951.

Poems. Eynsham, Oxon, Eng.: Fantasy Press, 1952.

The Diamond Cutters and Other Poems. New York: Harper, 1955.

The Knight: After Rilke. San Francisco: Poems in Folio, 1957.

Snapshots of a Daughter-in-Law: Poems, 1954–1962. New York: Harper & Row, 1963; London: Chatto and Windus, 1970.

Focus. Cambridge, Mass.: Lowell-Adams House Printers, 1966.

Necessities of Life: Poems, 1962–1965. New York: W. W. Norton, 1966.

Leaflets: Poems, 1965–1968. New York: W. W. Norton, 1969; London: Chatto and Windus, Hogarth Press, 1972.

The Will to Change: Poems, 1968–1970. New York: W. W. Norton, 1971; London: Chatto and Windus, 1972.

Diving into the Wreck: Poems, 1971–1972. New York: W. W. Norton, 1973.

Twenty-one Love Poems. Emeryville, Calif.: Effie's Press, 1976.

The Dream of a Common Language: Poems, 1974–1977. New York: W. W. Norton, 1978.

A Wild Patience Has Taken Me This Far: Poems, 1978–1981. New York: W. W. Norton 1981.

Sources. Woodside, Calif.: Heyeck Press, 1983.

Your Native Land, Your Life: Poems. New York: W. W. Norton, 1986.

Time's Power: Poems, 1985–1988. New York: W. W. Norton, 1989.

An Atlas of the Difficult World: Poems, 1988–1991. New York: W. W. Norton, 1991.

Dark Fields of the Republic: Poems, 1991–1995. New York: W. W. Norton, 1995.

Midnight Salvage: Poems, 1995–1998. New York: W. W. Norton, 1999.

Fox: Poems, 1998–2000. New York: W. W. Norton, 2001.

PROSE

Of Woman Born: Motherhood as Experience and Institution. New York: W. W. Norton, 1976.

Women and Honor: Some Notes on Lying. Pittsburgh, Pa.: Motheroot Publications, 1977; London: Onlywomen Press, 1979.

On Lies, Secrets, and Silence: Selected Prose, 1966–1978. New York: W. W. Norton, 1979.

Compulsory Heterosexuality and Lesbian Existence. London: Onlywomen Press, 1981; Denver, Colo.: Antelope Publications, 1982.

Blood, Bread, and Poetry: Selected Prose, 1979–1985. New York: W. W. Norton, 1986.

What Is Found There: Notebooks on Poetry and Politics. New York: W. W. Norton, 1993.

Arts of the Possible: Essays and Conversations. New York: W. W. Norton, 2001.

POETRY COLLECTIONS

Selected Poems. London: Chatto and Windus, 1967.

Poems: Selected and New, 1950–1974. New York: W. W. Norton, 1975.

The Fact of a Doorframe: Poems Selected and New, 1950–1984. New York: W. W. Norton, 1984.

Collected Early Poems, 1950–1970. New York: W. W. Norton, 1993.

CRITICAL AND BIOGRAPHICAL STUDIES

Altieri, Charles. *Self and Sensibility in Contemporary American Poetry.* New York: Cambridge University Press, 1984.

Boyers, Robert. "Adrienne Rich." In his *Contemporary Poetry in America: Essays and Interviews.* New York: Schocken Books, 1974.

Caris, Jane. "Body as Metaphor in the Poetry of Adrienne Rich." *Pleiades* 16, no. 2:105–115 (spring 1996).

Cooper, Jane Roberta, ed. *Reading Adrienne Rich: Reviews and Re-visions, 1951–81.* Ann Arbor: University of Michigan Press, 1984.

Díaz-Diocaretz, Myriam. *Translating Poetic Discourse: Questions on Feminist Strategies in Adrienne Rich.* Amsterdam and Philadelphia: J. Benjamins, 1985.

Eckstein, Barbara. "Iconicity, Immersion, and Otherness: The Hegelian 'Dive' of J. M. Coetzee and Adrienne Rich." *Mosaid* 29, no. 1:57–77 (March 1996).

Erickson, Peter. "Singing America: From Walt Whitman to Adrienne Rich." *Kenyon Review* 17, no. 1:103–119 (winter 1995).

Estrin, Barbara L. "Space-Off and Voice-Over: Adrienne Rich and Wallace Stevens." *Women's Studies* 25, no. 1:23–46 (November 1995).

Flowers, Betty S. "The 'I' in Adrienne Rich: Individuation and the Androgyne Archetype." In *Theory and Practice of Feminist Literary Criticism.* Edited by Gabriela Mora and Karen S. Van Hooft. Ypsilanti, Mich.: Bilingual Press, 1982.

———. "Wrestling with the Mother and the Father: 'His' and 'Her' in Adrienne Rich." In *Private Voices, Public Lives: Women Speak of the Literary Life.* Edited by Nancy Owen Nelson. Denton: University of North Texas Press, 1995.

Gelpi, Barbara Charlesworth, and Albert Gelpi, eds. *Adrienne Rich's Poetry.* New York: W. W. Norton, 1975.

Gilbert, Roger. "Framing Water: Historical Knowledge in Elizabeth Bishop and Adrienne Rich." *Twentieth Century Literature* 43, no. 2:144–161 (summer 1997).

Greenwald, Elissa. *"The Dream of a Common Language*: Vietnam Poetry as Reformation of Language and Feeling in the Poems of Adrienne Rich." *Journal of American Culture* 16, no. 3:97–102 (fall 1993).

Herzog, Anne. "Adrienne Rich and the Discourse of Decolonization." *Centennial Review* 33, no. 3:258–277 (summer 1989).

Jarrell, Randall. "Five Poets." *The Yale Review* (autumn 1956). Reprinted in *Randall Jarrell, Kipling, Auden and Co.: Essays and Reviews, 1935–64.* New York: Farrar, Straus and Giroux, 1980.

Johnson, Jeri. "Unfolding the Folded Lie." *Times Literary Supplement,* July 8, 1994.

Keyes, Claire. *The Aesthetics of Power: The Poetry of Adrienne Rich.* Athens: University of Georgia Press, 1986.

Klein, Karen W. "Adrienne Rich: 'Stuck to Earth.'" In *Daughters of Valor: Contemporary Jewish American Women Writers.* Edited by Jay L. Halio and Ben Siegel. Newark: University of Delaware Press, 1997. Pp. 194–208.

Lindroth, James. "Tropes of Discovery: Adrienne Rich and *Diving into the Wreck.*" *CEA Critic: An Official Journal of the College English Association* 47, no. 3:69–78 (spring 1985).

McCorkle, James. "Adrienne Rich: A Common Language of Self-Definition." *Notes on Modern American Literature* 9 (winter 1985, item 15).

McGuirk, Kevin. "Philoctetes Radicalized: *Twenty-one Love Poems* and the Lyric Career of Adrienne Rich." *Contemporary Literature* 34, no. 1:61–87 (spring 1993).

Markey, Janice. *A New Tradition? The Poetry of Sylvia Plath, Anne Sexton, and Adrienne Rich.* New York: Peter Lang, 1985.

Martin, Wendy. *An American Triptych: Anne Bradstreet, Emily Dickinson, Adrienne Rich.* Chapel Hill: University of North Carolina Press, 1984.

Matson, Suzanne. "Talking to Our Father: The Political and Mythical Appropriations of Adrienne Rich and Sharon Olds." *American Poetry Review* 18, no. 6:35–41 (November–December 1989).

O'Mahoney, John. "Adrienne Rich: Poet and Pioneer." *The Guardian,* June 15, 2002.

Ratcliffe, Krista. *Anglo-American Feminist Challenges to the Rhetorical Traditions: Virginia Woolf, Mary Daly, Adrienne Rich.* Carbondale: Southern Illinois University Press, 1996.

Shreiber, Maeera. "'Where Are We Moored?': Adrienne Rich, Women's Mourning, and the Limits of Lament." In *Dwelling in Possibility: Women Poets and Critics on Poetry.* Edited by Yopie Prins and Maeera Shreiber. Ithaca, N.Y.: Cornell University Press, 1997. Pp. 301–317.

Sielke, Sabine. "Snapshots of Marriage, Snares of Mimicry, Snarls of Motherhood: Marianne Moore and Adrienne Rich." *Sagetrieb* 6, no. 3:79–97 (winter 1987).

Slowick, Mary. "The Friction of the Mind: The Early Poetry of Adrienne Rich." *Massachusetts Review* 25, no. 1:142–160 (spring 1984).

Spender, Dale. *Women of Ideas and What Men Have Done to Them: From Aphra Behn to Adrienne Rich.* Boston: Routledge and Kegan Paul, 1982.

Spiegelman, Willard. "Voice of the Survivor: The Poetry of Adrienne Rich." *Southwest Review* 60:370–388 (autumn 1975).

Stimpson, Catharine. "Adrienne Rich and Lesbian/Feminist Poetry." *Parnassus* 12–13, nos. 2–1:249–268 (spring–winter 1985).

Strine, Mary S. "The Politics of Asking Women's Questions: Voice and Value in the Poetry of Adrienne Rich." *Text and Performance Quarterly* 9, no. 1:24–41 (January 1989).

Walker, Jeffrey A. "Remapping Freudian America: Adrienne Rich and the Adult Son." *North Dakota Quarterly* 62, no. 3:76–93 (summer 1994–1995).

Werner, Craig. *Adrienne Rich: The Poet and Her Critics.* Chicago: American Library Association, 1988.

Winterson, Jeanette. "Poets Should Not Be Cuddly." *The Times,* July 4, 2001.

Yorke, Liz. *Impertinent Voices: Subversive Strategies in Contemporary Women's Poetry.* New York and London: Routledge, 1991.

Zimmerman, Lee. "An Eye for an I: Emerson and Some 'True' Poems of Robinson Jeffers, William Everson, Robert Penn Warren, and Adrienne Rich." *Contemporary Literature* 33, no. 4:645–664 (winter 1992).

—PHILIP HOBSBAUM

Philip Roth

1933–

*F*OR MORE THAN four decades Philip Roth's fierce satirical wit, unflagging transgressive spirit, and daring narrative structures have made him one of America's most accomplished and controversial writers. With the exception of the Nobel Prize, he has been honored with every literary award of consequence. These include, among others, National Book Awards for *Goodbye, Columbus and Five Short Stories* in 1960 and *Sabbath's Theater* in 1995; National Book Critics Circle Awards for *The Counterlife* in 1987 and *Patrimony: A True Story* in 1992; PEN/Faulkner Awards for *Operation Shylock: A Confession* in 1993 and *The Human Stain* in 2001; the Pulitzer Prize for *American Pastoral* in 1998; the National Jewish Book Award in 2000 and the Koret Jewish Book Award in 2001, both for *The Human Stain;* and in 2001 the Edward MacDowell Medal for artistic achievement.

Roth is a tireless explainer and defender of his work, but two quotations stand out as particularly revealing. The first can be found in a 1960 essay written when he was twenty-seven years old and just beginning to get wide public attention. In "Writing American Fiction" he declares that "the American writer in the middle of the twentieth century has his hands full in trying to understand, describe, and then make *credible* much of American reality. It stupefies, it sickens, it infuriates, and finally it is even a kind of embarrassment to one's one meager imagination." Roth may have been more prescient than even he realized. American reality continues to upstage American fiction writers despite the best efforts of established figures such as Norman Mailer, John Updike, Susan Sontag, and younger ones such as Thomas Pynchon, Don DeLillo, David Foster Wallace, and Jonathan Franzen.

Roth has tried to separate himself from this early remark but for better or worse, his estimate of the American writer's essential condition continues to stick. The second quotation can be found in a 1994 essay titled "Juice or Gravy," a playful account of his early years as a struggling writer at the University of Chicago: "A couple of stories had already appeared in literary quarterlies, and one had even gained some national recognition, but these stories were not dazzling, they were derivative, and I wished to dazzle in my very own way and to dazzle myself no less than anyone else."

"Dazzling" is as good a way as any of describing Roth's style. Like other Jewish American writers of his generation and also from an older generation, such as Saul Bellow or Bernard Malamud, Roth thinks of himself as a strictly *American* writer, despite the fact that the bulk of his work is about his ongoing quarrel with the limitations of Jewish tribalism. The result is yet another instance of an American writer's insistence that the self is always in an uneasy tension with its society. "Dissent" is one way to describe this posture, and in Roth's case it is this abiding critique of American morals, rather than his personal tirades, that has made him a writer of cultural importance. Roth *matters,* not only because he could always write rings around most of his competitors, but also because what he says, especially from the 1990s onward, probes toward the very heart of the American experience in the latter half of the twentieth century.

Philip Roth was born on March 19, 1933, making him a near contemporary of John Updike. Each writer later imagined a protagonist—Harry ("Rabbit") Angstrom for Updike and Nathan Zuckerman for Roth—who reflects the place of his upbringing. Updike was raised in Shillington, Pennsylvania, while Roth spent his childhood in Newark, New Jersey. Rabbit Angstrom is an extended portrait of an American Everyman, someone who depends on AM radio and the evening news for his information. By contrast, Nathan Zuckerman is influenced by FM radio and heavy reading in the modernist classics. While Rabbit unsuccessfully struggles to make good on his sense of specialness amid limiting circumstances and a series of bad choices, Nathan finds himself continually surprised by the ways that a life of seriousness has made him singularly unprepared for the surprises, the curve balls, that quotidian life throws at him.

Roth has retained a career-long obsession with his birthplace in ways that other Newark-born writers such as Allen Ginsberg, LeRoi Jones (now Amiri Baraka), and Leslie Fiedler have not. Moreover his novels—more than two dozen of them—have caused their share of grief, both for thin-skinned readers from Newark and for Roth himself. The clash between the writer and his native ground began in 1959 with the smart-alecky nastiness of *Goodbye, Columbus* (1959) and grew even more intense when *Portnoy's Complaint* (1969) burst onto the scene ten years later.

Meanwhile Roth's books kept coming out, with a regularity—and often a brilliance—that is virtually unparalleled in contemporary letters. Not surprisingly, easily offended readers remained suspicious. They simply could not understand—much less agree with—Roth's insistence that a writer must be free to have a perspective larger, deeper, and, yes, comically darker than that of a son, lover, or citizen. Roth, often through the character of Nathan Zucker-

man, tries to explain—and thus to justify—how he came to write the fictions that made him simultaneously famous and infamous. In each work, Newark occupies an important part of the arithmetic, for it was Newark, populated by immigrant Jews, that set into motion the very tensions Roth's art would explore. Granted, Roth would later find himself attracted to other locations—Prague in *The Prague Orgy* (1985); Israel in *The Counterlife* (1986) and *Operation Shylock* (1993); cities such as London and New York; as well as an upscale farmhouse retreat in Connecticut. But it is finally Newark where his muse is most at home, and it is Newark where he continues (imaginatively) to return.

To gauge the depths of Newark's grip one need only read *The Facts: A Novelist's Autobiography* (1988), Roth's effort to talk about his Newark upbringing and in the process to separate Bess (Finkel) Roth's "nice Jewish" son from the monster many associate with his fictional characters. In addition, *Patrimony* (1991) is a moving, nonfictional account of his father's slow, agonizing death from the ravages of cancer. Memory is a potent force because, as Roth's father, Herman Roth, liked to say, "If a man's not made of memory, he's made of nothing." His literary son added sizable measures of the necessary requisites for fiction writing—an eye for detail, an ear for the rhythms of language, and a talent for wise-guy mimicry—but it is memory (and often a protracted memory of Newark) that is essential to understanding the writer Philip Roth became.

Roth received his B.A. degree in 1954 from Bucknell University, a small liberal arts college located in Lewisburg, Pennsylvania, and his M.A. from the University of Chicago in 1955. As a graduate student Roth began publishing short stories that were filled with promise, even though they seem tame—that is, socio-realistic—when compared with his later fiction. He was an instructor at the University of Chicago after completing his study, moving to the University of Iowa as a visiting lecturer from 1960 until 1962. In the years that followed, Roth taught at a variety of colleges and universities, including SUNY at Stony Brook, Hunter College, Princeton University, and the University of Pennsylvania. He was twice married: to Margaret Martinson on February 22, 1959 (she died from an automobile crash in 1968), and to the actress Claire Bloom on April 29, 1990 (they were divorced in June 1994). The first marriage is chronicled, with minor adjustments, in *My Life as a Man* (1974), whereas the second is the subject of Claire Bloom's insider account, *Leaving a Doll's House: A Memoir* (1996). Roth currently resides in a restored farmhouse in Connecticut, where he leads what has been described as a "monastic life" as he writes one book after another.

NEWARK AS SEEN THROUGH A DARKLY COMIC LENS

Goodbye, Columbus was published at a moment conveniently wedged between the innocence that (perhaps unfairly) characterized the 1950s and the permissiveness that was to dominate American culture from the late 1960s onward. In retrospect, Roth's stories are a remarkably accurate barometer of this radical shift in consciousness, one that changed the very ground rules for writing about Jewish American life. Theodore Solotaroff, a classmate of Roth at the University of Chicago and later the editor of *New American Review,* records in *The Red Hot Vacuum* (1970) that when he first read the opening paragraphs of *Goodbye, Columbus,* whatever resistance he might have had "toppled like tenpins":

> It was like sitting down in a movie house and suddenly seeing there on the screen a film about the block on which I had grown up: the details of place, character, incident all intimately familiar and yet new, or at least never appreciated before for their color and interest. This story of Neil

Klugman and Brenda Patimkin was so simple, direct, and evident that it couldn't be "art," and yet I knew that art did advance in just this way.

If an older generation of Jewish American writers had insisted, in Bernard Malamud's words, that "all men are Jews!" (he went on to add, "except they don't know it"), Roth's early stories seemed bent on proving that all Jews were also men—vulnerable, fallible, and comically frail. He not only turned the local into *art,* but also into a significant comment about how the postwar suburbs had changed the ways Jewish characters saw themselves and were seen by others.

Roth's gallery of these new meretricious types includes the comfortably well-off Patimkins and their spoiled Jewish daughter, Brenda, of *Goodbye, Columbus;* a pint-sized rebel who disrupts his Hebrew school class in "The Conversion of the Jews" (1958); a Jewish adulterer in "Epstein" (1958); and Grossbart, the unsavory, gold-bricking Jewish soldier of "Defender of the Faith" (1959). Jewish war veterans were particularly upset over the last story, which they regarded (perhaps understandably) as an ugly slur against their patriotism and sacrifice. But it was also clear that they had not read the story closely and had missed the moral rectitude it in fact reflected. When they asked the Anti-Defamation League to do what it could to stop this subversive writer in his tracks, the organization, to its credit, refused.

The bruised feelings and outrage, however, kept rolling in. During a panel discussion about contemporary writing held at Yeshiva University, a group of students angrily accused Roth of being a Christian writer while also labeling him a self-hating Jew. Never mind the contradictions built into their catcalls or the fact that Roth was simply trying to write well-crafted paragraphs and tightly structured stories. For them, Brenda Patimkin was little more than a stereotypical Jewish American Princess (JAP), just as characters from the other stories were so vulgar, so unlikable, that they gave succor to anti-Semites everywhere.

What mattered—and this feeling was shared by many of Roth's early, conservatively inclined readers—was that dirty linen about the Jews was being hung out on public lines. True, there was no indication, then or now, that a single Jew anywhere had been physically abused because a Philip Roth story appeared in the pages of *Commentary* or *The New Yorker* magazines. Nonetheless, rabbis gave sermons denouncing Roth's unfair representation of Jewish American life (many more would follow the publication of *Portnoy's Complaint*), and leaders of the official Jewish community reminded their followers that with a pen in his hand Roth was a dangerous man. Such criticism wounded Roth into writing about other, less volatile subjects: the sorrows of graduate school in *Letting Go* (1962) and the Midwest in *When She Was Good* (1967). These novels, however, were at best only moderately successful, largely because Roth strayed from the material that, for better or worse, unleashed his most vivid writing.

PORTNOY'S COMPLAINT AND WHAT IT WROUGHT

Portnoy's Complaint remains Roth's most widely known and certainly most controversial novel, largely because in this book he first liberated himself from cultural guilts and embraced freewheeling comedy. Roth has always believed that his prose on the page was more genuinely subversive, and flat-out funnier, than anything that a stand-up comedian, such as Lenny Bruce, ever performed behind a nightclub microphone. *Portnoy's Complaint* is a nonstop performance on the psychoanalyst's couch, a way of finally letting out all his neuroses and his cultural angst. Subsequent Roth novels found other ways to afford characters the same unbridled pleasure. The result is a long study in transgression, one

that uses humor as a way to deflect the punishments that will surely come to those artists who tell the truth.

Alexander Portnoy is instrumental in Roth's ongoing complaint against the edifice of law that separates foods into meat, dairy, and the forbidden; divides the upper, more intellectual portions of the body from the lower, baser ones; and—perhaps most of all—places uncompromising distinctions between superego and id. Portnoy's battle cry is "LET'S PUT THE ID BACK IN YID!" He wants to be bad and to enjoy it in the bargain. That his extended bout of comic rebellion ends, as it surely must, in impotence and rage is not surprising.

In an essay included in *Reading Myself and Others* (1975), Roth asserts that it was Franz Kafka who provided the inspiration necessary to write *Portnoy's Complaint*; Kafka showed him how it is that guilt could be a "comic idea." There are, however, important differences between Kafka and Roth: if Kafka is all mystery, Roth seems all explanation—not only in his series of self-justifying essays, collected first in *Reading Myself and Others* and then in *Shop Talk* (2001), but also as a compulsion embedded in the very fabric of his fiction. In this sense Roth's brilliantly imaginative rumination on Kafka, "'I Always Wanted You to Admire My Fasting'; or, Looking at Kafka," may finally tell us more about Roth than it reveals about Kafka, for it suggests that, despite the obvious instances of Kafka worship, Roth prefers the antics of the closer-to-home Henny Youngman ("Take my wife, please!") as a foil to the severe aestheticism of writers such as Henry James. What one most notices in the trajectory of a typical Roth novel is the neurotic zig-zagging between cultural brows—the high one exemplified by studiousness and Jamesian decorum while the middle and lower ones are at once earthier and more playful. Henny Youngman stands both for the Newark street corner and the patter that postimmigrant sons learned to perfect as they negotiated their way between the restrictions of one's home and the giddy possibilities of the streets.

Roth often seems at his most adventurous when he gives himself over to the Henny Youngman voice rattling around in his head. Without this generous dose of serious playfulness Roth might have continued the dreary, heavy-water melancholia of *Letting Go* and *When She Was Good;* with it, however, books such as *The Great American Novel* (1973) and vivid characters such as the Alvin Pepler of *Zuckerman Unbound* (1981) became possible. *Portnoy's Complaint* pointed the way by demonstrating that excess could lead to art and that comic exaggeration could become more than social satire. Roth's title works on at least three levels: as Portnoy's "complaint" in the legalistic sense of an indictment handed down against those cultural forces that have created him; as a complaint in the old-fashioned sense of illness, one that Doctor Spielvogel, Portnoy's psychoanalyst, comically describes as "a disorder in which strongly-felt ethical and altruistic impulses are perpetually warring with extreme sexual longings, often of a perverse nature"; and finally as a complaint in the more ordinary existentialist sense of the word.

We first meet Alexander Portnoy, a thirty-three-year-old "Momma's boy" and "Assistant Commissioner for The City of New York Commission on Human Opportunity," as he sprawls across his therapist's couch and launches into a prolonged litany of his accumulated grief. The result is at once a parody and an extension of Sigmund Freud's "talking cure," one in which Portnoy alternates between blaming his mother and wallowing in self-pity. There are moments of self-awareness—or at least inklings in that direction, such as when Portnoy wonders, "Is this truth I'm delivering up, or is it just plain *kvetching* [complaining]? Or is *kvetching* for people like me a *form* of truth?" But most of the time his fractured monologue comes tumbling out in a desperate rush, as if a lifetime of repression and guilt had made it impossible until now for him to air the sordid details of his compulsive masturbation as an adolescent and his later adventures as a sexual outlaw.

Portnoy is a world-class *kvetcher,* just as his mother is a world-class worrier. But his uninterrupted tirade is a "form of truth," especially if one sees it as an essential truth about Jewish ethnicity in the post–World War II suburbs, greatly distorted for comic effect. In traditional Yiddish humor, one's quarrel is with God, as is the case when Sholem Aleichem's character Tevye satirically notes that "with God's help he starved three times a day," or when Yiddish-speaking wags point out that it would be better if God "chose" another people next time. By contrast, in much of Jewish American humor—and here *Portnoy's Complaint* can serve as the prime example—one's quarrel is with one's mother. Spring me out of the shopworn Jewish joke about a mother wailing that her son, the doctor, is drowning, Portnoy pleads, because such jokes "*hoit.*" There is genuine human pain being felt just beneath the folds of what too easily passes as humor. Thus he recalls dozens of incidents in which his mother, the all-powerful, all-knowing Sophie Portnoy, stands over him with a knife if he is a finicky eater or positions herself just outside the bathroom door to gather intelligence about his bowel movements. Such humiliations, only slightly altered, follow him into what should have been his adulthood but instead becomes a prolonged adolescence. As Sophie declares without the slightest trace of irony, her only crime is that she is "too good." Meanwhile it is her son who is headed toward the psychiatrist's couch from the moment he first realizes that masturbation can be an act of rebellion and that eating French fries on the way home from school is a dagger aimed at his mother's heart.

Portnoy's deepest wish, however, is to live not only beyond Sophie's smothering control but also outside the grip of history itself. Everything that Jewish law once represented has been altered for Portnoy into an assortment of "thou shalt nots," some originating on Sinai, but most emanating from the watered-down culture of the Portnoy household. What Portnoy "learns" about Judaism comes down to this: Jews do not believe in Christmas, athletics in general, junk food consumed outside the house, or hunting, and the list goes on with countless other examples of ethnicity gone amuck. At one point Portnoy recalls that he "turned from the window out of which I was watching a snowstorm, and hopefully asked, 'Momma, do we believe in winter?'"

Thus is Portnoy's world neatly divided into that which is "Jewish" and that which is not. Small wonder that he rails against everything that he now regards as products of ignorance and evidence of fear:

> Because I am sick and tired of *goyische* this and *goyische* that! If it's bad it's the *goyim,* if it's good it's the Jews! Can't you see, my dear parents, from whose loins I somehow leaped, that such thinking is a trifle barbaric? That all you are expressing is your *fear?*

Small wonder, given his version of growing up under his parents' wings, that he balances castigating the gentiles ("These are the people for whom Nat 'King' Cole sings every Christmastime, 'Chestnuts roasting on an open fire, Jack Frost nipping at your nose'") with berating the Jews ("What in their world was not charged with danger, dripping with germs, fraught with peril?").

Rampant sexuality becomes Portnoy's weapon of choice in his ongoing war against instilled repression. From the imaginary Thereal McCoy of his adolescent fantasies at the Empire Burlesque house through his sordid history of private masturbation to the fleshly embodiment of kinky sex known as The Monkey (whose actual name is Mary Jane Reed), Portnoy seems more hyperactive than ineffectual. He scores big, and often.

At the same time however, Portnoy operates under the long shadow cast by Sigmund Freud's seminal essay, "The Most Prevalent Form of Degradation in Erotic Life." What Freud argues—and what Roth cites in a chapter bearing the essay's title— is that "where such men love they have no desire, and where they desire they cannot love." The underlying cause, Freud goes on to explain, is the oedipal conflict: an obsessive love for the mother that turns subsequent women into versions of either the madonna or the prostitute. As Portnoy reviews his respective affairs with The Monkey, Kay Campbell (also known as The Pumpkin), and Sarah Abbott Maulsby (whose alias is The Pilgrim), his mother's warning rings (ironically) in his ears: "DON'T RUN FIRST THING TO A BLONDIE, *PLEASE. . . .* A BRILLIANT INNOCENT BABY BOY LIKE YOU, SHE'LL EAT YOU UP ALIVE!" Portnoy has no trouble making dirty jokes from such straight lines, but the deep-seated guilts he rehearses never stray far from home.

In the case of The Monkey, an illiterate note to her cleaning lady ("dir willa polish the flor") is at least as telling as her orgasm at first hearing William Butler Yeats's poem "Leda and the Swan." Portnoy is moved by the latter but deeply disturbed by the former. He may be a professional defender of the downtrodden, but he is also a bit of a snob: "This woman is ineducable and beyond reclamation. By contrast to hers, my childhood took place in Brahmin Boston."

Kay Campbell, on the other hand, is "hard as a gourd on matters of moral principle, beautifully stubborn in a way I couldn't but envy and adore." Best of all, "*she never raised her voice in an argument.*" Unlike the middle-class screamers of *When She Was Good,* the Campbells are gentiles at their most genteel. When Portnoy visits their midwestern Norman Rockwellesque house during a college vacation, he realizes for the first time that the English language can be "*a form of communication.*" Things are otherwise in Newark, New Jersey. But the polite can also be the lifeless, the bland, and Portnoy prefers those special revenges all paranoids gleefully imagine: "If someone [in the Campbell household] starts in with 'the pushy Jews,' or says 'kike' or 'jewed him down'—Well, I'll jew them down all right. . . . I will shame and humiliate them in their bigoted hearts! Quote the Declaration of Independence over their candied yams!" Portnoy's worst fears about the anti-Semitic Campbells go unrealized; however, when Kay thinks she is pregnant, Portnoy assumes (wrongly as it turns out) that she will convert to Judaism. His shocked disappointment makes it clear that, rebellious postures aside, he is still Sophie's dutifully Jewish son.

Sarah Abbott Maulsby has an even longer string of WASP credentials than The Pumpkin: New Canaan, Foxcroft, Vassar. As a member of the House subcommittee investigation into television quiz show scandals, Portnoy had attacked people like "Charlatan" Van Doren (the "ur-WASP") with all the zeal of a biblical prophet. Ms. Maulsby is thrilled by the energy of Portnoy's rough edges, but finally she too is *unsatisfactory:* "Then there were the nicknames of her friends; there were the friends themselves! Poody and Pip and Pebble, Shrimp and Brute and Tug, Squeek, Bumpo, Baba—it sounded, I said, as though she had gone to Vassar with Donald Duck's nephews."

All these doomed relationships can be chalked up to Portnoy's tragicomic Oedipus complex, but the pain runs deeper than his explanations, Freudian or otherwise. Guilt is the energizing force that makes a culture of sons like Portnoy possible. What he resists without quite knowing it is the fatherhood that is both his destiny and his deepest fear. At one level of consciousness he desperately wants "to grow up to *be* one of those men"; at another, he is afraid that he will become the mirror image of his constipated, altogether emasculated father.

If perversion is Portnoy's ambivalent response to Jewish American life, Israel alters the situation as radically as it exhausts it comically. In Israel even the bus drivers and policemen are Jewish; thus, his ongoing battle between the *goyische* world and the Jewish one no longer makes sense. Moreover, in Israel, there are no *shikses.* They have been replaced by Naomi, a militant Israeli, as tough in her Marxism as she is confident about her Jewishness, "a Jewish Pumpkin!" Portnoy happily declares, "*I am being given a second chance.*" However, the cunning revealed in his psychic history indicates that he should know better. Impotence—what he later dubs as "The Monkey's Revenge"—becomes his seriocomic fate.

Even more important, Naomi's tough-minded assessment of Portnoy's self-lacerating humor (in passages that prove that Roth can give adversarial positions nearly equal weight) suggests yet another face of the ubiquitous Sophie. Naomi cuts through Portnoy's whining with the sharp edge that statehood—rather than comic "exile"—saves for its wayward Jewish sons: "You seem to take some special pleasure, some pride, in making yourself the butt of your own peculiar sense of humor. . . . Everything you say is somehow always twisted, some way or another, to come out 'funny.' . . . In some little way or other, everything is ironical, or self-depreciating." Does this unflinching assessment hit Portnoy's confessional nail on the head? Perhaps. But Roth knows full well how valuable built-in criticisms can be. They beat would-be critics to the punch by alternating the distances he keeps from his nervous protagonist. Portnoy becomes the comic vehicle by which Roth controls the humiliation and, yes, pain (however much exaggerated) of a largely assimilated generation of Jewish American males.

In the final analysis, however, Naomi's critique may tell us more about the novel's limitations than it does about its protagonist. *Portnoy's Complaint* is a minor classic, "minor" in that it chooses to examine a highly selected segment of human experience. Taken together, Portnoy's freewheeling rants turn the novel into a stylistic tour de force, but also into one that exhausts itself in a string of gags. As Irving Howe insisted, "The cruelest thing anyone can do with *Portnoy's Complaint* is to read it twice." The remark, taken from a 1972 essay titled "Philip Roth Reconsidered," so stuck in Roth's craw that he later singled Howe out for special satiric revenge in *The Anatomy Lesson* (1983). Therein appear snippets from Howe's essay as Nathan Zuckerman fumes about the moral smugness they represent and then turns its author into a czar of pornography.

Other critics found it easier to admit, in public print, that the novel was, well, *funny*. In a 1971 essay, "The Earthly City of the Jews," Alfred Kazin, long regarded as the dean of American literary criticism, put it this way: "Portnoy's howls of rage, love and anguish were so concentrated that this made them funny." Walter Blair and Hamlin Hill, coauthors of *America's Humor: From Poor Richard to Doonesbury* (1978), argued that "Portnoy, for the most part, is a traditional schlemiel; but even when he isn't one, he comically pretends to be." Meanwhile, the controversy—and the sales—that the novel generated became a sociological phenomenon quite apart from the book's literary merits.

If it is true that *Portnoy's Complaint* exhausts its limited (and delimiting) material, it is also true that Roth's extended riffs on the tribal constraints of ethnic Jewishness provided, as no novel had before, a guidebook to the *kvetching* that characterized the new steerage. Portnoy insists:

I am not in this boat alone, oh no, I am on the biggest troop ship afloat . . . only look in through the portholes and see us there, stacked to the bulkheads in our bunks, moaning and groaning with such pity for ourselves, the sad and watery-eyed sons of Jewish parents, sick to the gills from rolling through these heavy seas of guilt . . . and oh sick, sick as dogs, we cry out intermittently, one of us or another, "Poppa, how could you?" "Momma, why did you?" and the . . . vying we do—who had the most castrating mother, who the most benighted father, I can match you, you bastard, humiliation for humiliation, shame for shame.

Portnoy is the clear winner in this high-stakes contest. It is a novel that had to be written as much as it is the novel Roth had to write. Portnoy bravely—and, of course, comically—tears from his mattress the tag reading "Do Not Remove under Penalty of Law" and, with the bravado of a gangster from a 1930s Warner Brothers movie, prepares to die ("while I lived, *I lived big!*"). At this point Portnoy's self-destructive monologue comes to an end (*imp*loded, as it were), and his analyst can, at long last, begin what will surely be a long, protracted "cure."

Circular and nonconclusive, *Portnoy's Complaint* laid out all the psychic pieces in a rush of comically verbal pyrotechnics. More important, it was the culmination of an urban, Jewish American idiom that remains Roth's most congenial turf. He would not return to it until *My Life as a Man*, and then with a bitterness that makes Portnoy's complaints look like kid stuff. *Portnoy's Complaint* has managed to survive and even transcend the angry noises that surrounded its original publication because, for better or worse, with this novel Roth provides both a chronicle and an epitaph for those times, that place.

ROTH BETWEEN ALEXANDER PORTNOY AND NATHAN ZUCKERMAN

For Roth, the late 1960s and early 1970s were an interim period, one in which he cast around for subjects large enough to match his considerable talent. But hindsight suggests that until he hit upon Nathan Zuckerman as mouthpiece, al-terego, and the character who made his most inventive fictions possible, Roth spent his time writing books that are longer on playful gim-micks than genuine substance. *Our Gang* (1971) is such a novel—at once a satire of the Richard Nixon White House during the war in Vietnam and an extended exercise in self-indulgence. The risks of such overtly political writing are obvious: those who agreed with his anti-Nixon tirade found much to admire, whereas those on the other side of the aisle were not amused. Two literary models were at work: "A Modest Proposal," Jonathan Swift's savage satire of how cheaply the English counted Irish life; and George Orwell's "Politics and the English Language," a seminal essay on the ways that politicians consciously manipulate language. Nixon, then and now, makes for an easy target, and a post-Watergate reading of Roth's slim novel suggests that, however much white heat may have gone into its composition, he was more prescient than paranoid. If anything, Roth's outrageous parody of Nixon was not out-rageous enough for the post-impeachment era.

Our Gang takes Nixon's position about abortion-on-demand as its starting point, quot-ing from his San Clemente ("San Dementia" in Roth's version) statement:

UNRESTRICTED ABORTION POLICIES, OR ABORTION ON DEMAND, I CANNOT SQUARE WITH MY PERSONAL BELIEF IN THE SANCTITY OF HUMAN LIFE—INCLUD-ING THE LIFE OF THE YET UNBORN. FOR, SURELY, THE UNBORN HAVE RIGHTS ALSO.

And here is Trick E. Dixon, as he sounds in Roth's send-up:

And let me make one thing more perfectly clear: I am not just talking about the rights of the fetus. I am talking about the microscopic embryos as well. If ever there was a group in this country that was "disadvantaged," in the sense that they are utterly without representation or a voice in our national government, it is not the blacks or the Puerto Ricans or the hippies or what-have-you, all of whom have their spokesmen, but these infinitesi-mal creatures up there on the placenta.

The bromides of political rhetoric, as Orwell knew full well, make a virtuoso performance such as Roth's both possible and a bit too easy.

History has not been kind to *Our Gang*, largely because it was so tied to a political mo-ment that passed, only to be replaced by the lat-est political indignation. Unlike Swift's biting satire, which long outlived its occasion, Roth's effort seems bound to the cultural moment that gave rise to the absurdities that he so dutifully chronicles.

Our Gang was followed by *The Breast* (1972), another slim volume that often seems more an exercise than a sustained novel. That time, however, Roth turned his attention to liter-ary symbolism—whether taken comically, seri-ously, or on an ironic level somewhere in between—rather than to current events. David Kepesh, a comparative literature professor and the subject of what would later become a tril-ogy of novels, is a man who *becomes* the characters he teaches. But the long shadow of Kafka's *The Metamorphosis* (1915), about a thoroughly ordinary man who wakes up one morning to find himself turned into a cockroach, is too self-conscious and insisted upon. Kepesh is surprised to discover that he has been metamorphosed into a six-foot female breast, with all the comic consequences that bespeak Roth's sense of the absurd.

Gregor Samsa, the protagonist of Kafka's hilariously eerie tale, made a cameo appearance earlier in the Roth canon when Alex Portnoy imagines his mother chasing him "with a broom, trying to sweep my rotten carcass into the open. Why, shades of Gregor Samsa! Hello Alex, goodbye Franz!" With *The Breast*, however, Roth turns fabulist, giving his kinship with Kafka full comic rein. Thus his version of the Kafa story translates the angst of one age into the stridently flip postures of another. The result is an insider joke about a literature professor who wonders if turning into a giant breast "might well be my way of being a Kafka, being a Gogol, being a Swift. They could envision the incredible, they had the words and those relentless fictionizing brains. But I had neither. . . . So I took the leap. Made the word flesh. Don't you see, I have out-Kafkaed Kafka."

Kepesh ends up crying out for more sex, more ingeniously performed. This refrain, with certain alterations, continues in the next installments of the Kepesh saga: *The Professor of Desire* (1977) and *The Dying Animal* (2001). Thus Kepesh joins others in Roth's gallery of sexual outlaws, from the relatively tame Neil Klugman through the sadomasochistic Alexander Portnoy to the seriously filthy Mickey Sabbath of *Sabbath's Theater* (1995).

In *A Hazard of New Fortunes* (1889), William Dean Howells, probably the most influential American man of letters during the late nineteenth century, creates a gingerly would-be writer who "wondered if it would do to put her [another character] into literature just as she was, with all her slang and brag"; he concludes that he cannot and, furthermore, that "the great American novel, if true, must be incredible." Roth knows that the very idea of the "G.A.N." (great American novel) is a mug's game, and in his *Great American Novel* he means to give it a comic burial. Nonetheless Roth's thick novel was not only the "big book" his critics kept demanding, but it was also a genuinely comic look at our national literature as seen through the special prism of baseball. Here Roth is working simultaneously in two great traditions: one, the skeptical irony that characterizes twentieth-century answers to the continuing demand for a G.A.N.; and the other, a metaphorical use of baseball that had provided a structure for such novels as Bernard Malamud's *The Natural* (1952).

Roth's fascination with our national pastime was foreshadowed early in Alexander Portnoy's lyrical descriptions of the freedom that baseball represented:

> Thank God for center field! . . . Because center field is like some observation post, a kind of control tower, where you are able to see everything and everyone, to understand what's happening the instant it happens, not only by the sound of the struck bat, but by the spark of movement that goes through the infielders in the first second that the ball comes flying at them; and once it gets beyond them, "It's mine," you call, "it's mine," and then after it you go. For in center field, if you can get to it, it *is* yours.

For the usually hassled Portnoy, center field is a zone of safety, a place where he is free to move at the crack of the bat and make the all-important catch—all without the worry of being Jewish and Sophie Portnoy's son.

In *The Great American Novel,* however, such pastoral visions quickly turn into paranoid fantasies. Rather than the turf of center field over which Portnoy can both scamper and feel supreme, there is a sinking feeling in *The Great American Novel* that someone—or something—is controlling our lives. This conspiratorial vision is what makes Word Smith tick. He is an eighty-seven-year-old former sports reporter and the novel's narrator. "Call me Smitty," he declares in the novel's opening salvo, thereby giving fair warning that even more outrageous literary parodies are to come. It is Smitty's general opinion that evil forces are out to change our national history, and his particular obsession is that they have singled out baseball's defunct Patriot League for special abuse. It is this tale of the Patriot League, told by a senile crusader, full of comic sound and fury, that makes *The Great American Novel* such a sustained and at times delicious romp.

Smitty is a man enamored of alliteration, the compiler of Rabelaisian lists that run the comic gamut from one end of the alphabet to the other.

A partial listing of those who once called him Smitty include:

the boxers, the Brahmins, the brass hats, the British (*Sir* Smitty as of '36), the broads, the broadcasters, the broncobusters, the brunettes, the black bucks down in Barbados (*Meestah* Smitty), the Buddhist monks in Burma, one Bulkington, the bullfighters, the bullthrowers, the burlesque comics and the burlesque stars, the bushmen, the bums, and the butlers. And that's only the letter B, fans, only *one* of the Big Twenty-Six!

As Smitty's doctor suggests, this "orgy of alliteration . . . strikes me as wildly excessive . . . and just a little desperate." Many of Roth's critics agree—not only about Smitty but also about Roth's novel itself. Writing in the pages of the autumn 1973 issue of the *Hudson Review,* Marvin Mudrick took aim against literary swingers, "who in their so-called comic novels invent monsters merely as laboriously disagreeable as themselves." Smitty certainly qualifies as a member of this tribe, but he is small potatoes when compared with the rants of the darkly comic Mickey Sabbath.

After Smitty's long-winded introduction the bulk of the novel is given over to his testy desire to have the truth about the Patriot League be known, to make it the mythological subject of his alliterative epic. When well-meaning people suggest that he act his age, Smitty replies with a tough-minded, self-righteous stance that bears more than a few similarities to that of Roth himself: "What I want is for them to admit THE TRUTH!" Smitty, in short, constitutes a majority of one, a sentiment that puts him in good American company. Each year at Cooperstown he casts his ballot for Luke Gofannon, the greatest slugger in Patriot League history, but the forces aligned against Smitty are so insidious that no Patriot player is ever elected to the Hall of Fame, nor are his votes ever recorded.

Smitty's tale gives over-the-top parody whole new meanings as chunks of classic American literature strut across the stage: Herman Melville's *Moby-Dick,* Nathaniel Hawthorne's *The Scarlet Letter,* Edgar Allan Poe's "The Raven," and Mark Twain's *The Adventures of Huckleberry Finn.* Thus is *The Great American Novel* top heavy with academic jokes, even as it tries to turn the Ruppert Mundys, a comically ill-fated baseball team, into a metaphor for the wandering Jews or perhaps into a symbol of generalized rootlessness. The point, however, is that nobody believes Smitty's long chronicling of the Patriot League, despite the fact that Roth has threaded dozens of baseball anecdotes (comically retold) into the novel's fabric. As one of Smitty's many rejection letters puts it: "Several people here found portions of it entertaining, but by and large the book seemed to most of us to strain for its effects and to simplify for the sake of facile satiric comment the complex realities of American political and cultural life." *The Great American Novel* is guilty as charged. Not until Roth wrote his trilogy about the sweep of American history— *American Pastoral* (1997), *I Married a Communist* (1998), and *The Human Stain* (2000)— did he have the requisite tools and understanding to give the "complex realities of American political and cultural life" their due.

THE ZUCKERMAN CHRONICLES: PART 1

As the well-traveled quip would have it, Roth wrote one novel about masturbation (*Portnoy's Complaint*) that made him rich and famous, followed by a half-dozen novels about how terrible being rich and famous turned out to be. Most of the books that detail this grief are narrated by Nathan Zuckerman, a fictional creature who bears a strong resemblance to Roth himself. Zuckerman, in turn, was "born" in the head of the fictional fictionist Peter Tarnopol, yet another writer, this one suffering from writer's block. In *My Life as a Man,* we learn that Tarnopol cannot tell the story of how he was tricked into a disastrous marriage and how nothing in his wide reading seems applicable to his case. What works, however, are the "useful fictions" he writes from the more liberated perspective of Nathan Zuckerman. These stories—"Salad Days" and "Courting Disaster"—bristle with imaginative energy and bounce. Most of all, they have a distinctive *voice,* a quality that makes the early stories of *Goodbye, Columbus* so memorable. With Zuckerman, Roth discovered the ingredient necessary to tongue a number of sore teeth in public print.

In *The Ghost Writer* (1979), Zuckerman reconstructs a fateful visit he had made twenty years earlier to the New England hideaway of E. I. Lonoff, a legendary writer and the one person who might give Zuckerman the large measures of sympathy and understanding he badly needs. When Nathan's father reads "Higher Education" (Nathan's latest story and his most ambitious and accomplished to date), he cannot disguise his disapproval. Such a story, he tells his son, is an accident waiting to happen, not because it is poorly constructed (aesthetic niceties are not at issue here) but because Nathan has been too sheltered to realize how ordinary people will respond to a tale about a Jewish family squabbling over money: "From a lifetime of experience I happen to know what ordinary people will think when they read something like this story. . . . Nathan, your story, as far as Gentiles are concerned, is about one thing and one thing only. . . . It is about kikes. Kikes and their love of money."

The accusations sting, but they also serve to stiffen Nathan's resolve. If his benighted, podiatrist father is incapable of appreciating the story, perhaps Lonoff will. After all, the Lonoff he finally meets has been captivated by what he calls Nathan's fictive voice ("something that begins at around the back of the knees and reaches well above the head"); but, alas, Lonoff is decidedly uninterested in applying for the open position as Nathan Zuckerman's surrogate father.

The Ghost Writer makes no apologies about its deep debt to the tradition of the bildungsroman, and among the many things that constitute Nathan's education as an artist is the specter of Lonoff's life itself—at once lonely and uneventful, disciplined to the core, and supremely confident in its ability. Most of all, however, it is a life, as Lonoff puts it, devoted to "turning sentences around" and then to turning them around again. Nathan is alternately attracted and repulsed by the costs such a bloodless existence exacts. On one hand, Nathan's life and art requires the very turbulence (sentences ending in exclamation points and hands roiling in the air) that Lonoff so rigorously eschews; on the other, the imagination has the power to engineer victories not readily available in actual life.

Amy Bellette, Lonoff's hauntingly enigmatic former student, provides the raw material necessary for Nathan to make the spectacular case that he is a nice Jewish boy after all. By first transmogrifying Amy into Anne Frank, the "Jewish saint," and then by fantasizing that he *marries* her, Nathan constructs the ultimate vindication of the misunderstood writer:

> This is my Aunt Tessie, this is Frieda and Dave, this is Birdie, this is Murray . . . as you see, we are an enormous family. This is my wife, everyone. She is all I have ever wanted. If you doubt me, just look at her smile, listen to her laugh. Remember the shadowed eyes innocently uplifted in the clever little face? Remember the dark hair clipped back with a barrette? Well, this is she. . . . Anne, says my father—the Anne? Oh, how I have misunderstood my son. How mistaken we have been!

Nathan's need to be accepted, indeed to be *loved,* by his parents is at least as powerful as is his desire to write stories that are "true," regardless of the social consequences. His dream of bringing home no less a Jewish girl than Anne Frank, like his later decision in *The Anatomy Lesson* to chuck fiction writing altogether and become a Jewish doctor, is a shameless bid for approval. In the case of *The Ghost Writer*, appropriating Anne Frank by turning her writerly rebellion into a mirror image of his own was even more daring, more subversive, than anything Roth had done in *Portnoy's Complaint.*

Such imagined victories are balanced by another Roth technique: incorporating devastating self-criticism into the body of his work itself, as if Roth is aware of what hostile critics might say and how he might beat them to the punch. Second-rate writers turn their adversaries into straw men, but Roth knows better: Doc Zuckerman's worries about the consequences of his son's story are not silly. He has a *point,* one Roth wrestles with throughout *The Ghost Writer* and, indeed, throughout the saga of grief that follows Nathan Zuckerman after he publishes *Carnovsky,* a novel with a strong resemblance to *Portnoy's Complaint.*

In addition, the prefix "counter-" begins showing up regularly in Roth's work as a way of complicating the relationship between illusion and reality, between what we *think* we know about a character and what we later discover. No longer the conventional social realist, Roth begins a series of postmodernist experimentations in which characters, and sometimes whole plots, resemble a kaleidoscope. Henry Zuckerman, Nathan's brother, is at the center of *The Counterlife,* Roth's most successful effort in turning his fictional cylinder a quarter turn and watching the pieces inside the kaleidoscope's tube rearrange themselves. In one chapter, "Basel," Henry undergoes a heart operation and dies on the table; in "Judea," however, he survives, chucks his wife, and makes his way to Israel, where he falls under the spell of a charismatic, right-wing Zionist. The shape-shifting was too much for Christopher Lehmann-Haupt, a reviewer for the *New York Times,* who wrote that "it's as if the novelist were saying, since I don't make you believe in anything, the ultimate challenge is to make you believe in nothing." By contrast the novel-

ist Richard Stern, writing in *Chicago Tribune Books,* praised the novel as "an equivalent of action painting" and, moreover, as a work that avoids the "claustrophobia which oppresses so many self-reflexive novels."

ROTH ON ROTH

Although *The Facts* means to be a straightforward, autobiographical account of Roth's childhood in Newark and his years at Bucknell, Nathan Zuckerman, in a letter to Roth advising him not to publish the book, steals the show. Zuckerman's point is that Roth is miserable when he writes about himself and magnificent when he writes about Zuckerman. Moreover, without Roth there is no Zuckerman, and without Zuckerman there is no Roth.

In something of the same playful spirit, *Operation Shylock* tries to convince us that Roth himself is plagued by a doppelgänger who has been giving lectures in Israel on Diasporism, urging Jews of east European ancestry to return to Poland. The idea is wacky at face value but also precisely the kind of over-the-top material Roth likes to explore. Add a subplot in which Roth presumably aids the Mossad (the Israeli secret police) in foiling a plot against Israel (dubbed "Operation Shylock"), and the result is yet another instance of bidding for tribal approval, this time by saving Israel itself.

Sometimes, as with *Deception* (1990), all readers get is postmodernist smoke and mirrors, followed by more smoke and mirrors; but with a novel such as *Operation Shylock,* the blurred line between fiction and fact is tied (as the solipsistic musings in *Deception* are not) to the problematics of the Arab-Israeli conflict and the passions aroused by the trial of John Demjanjuk, an especially vicious concentration camp guard suspected of being Ivan the Terrible. By contrast, *Patrimony,* the unflinching chronicle of Herman Roth's cruel death, is a richer book, at once more honest and more satisfying aesthetically. What might have been an exercise in sentimentality becomes a way of coming to grips with a difficult parent and a lifetime of tension. Granted, Roth's canon is dotted with gently—even lovingly—portrayed fathers, but none of them holds a candle to Roth's extended depiction of his own father in vulnerable old age. The result is a book written with equal measures of compassion and love, and it is one of Roth's best.

THE ZUCKERMAN CHRONICLES: PART 2

In novel after novel Nathan Zuckerman is a character doomed to tell his story repeatedly. However, beginning with *American Pastoral,* Zuckerman became the teller of other people's tales. Like the Marlow of Joseph Conrad's *Lord Jim* (1900) and "Heart of Darkness" (1902), he becomes an ersatz detective, piecing together bits of information he gathers and, most important of all, adding imaginative elements to the chronicle of the person he tries to understand and whose complicated story he tries to tell.

American Pastoral is at once a story of Newark, Roth's most congenial fictional turf, and of Seymour ("Swede") Levov, a blond-haired, square-jawed protagonist who lived and died within the giddy possibilities and tragic coils of the American dream. In outline the subject looks for all the world like an oft-told tale, for who has not experienced the subtle ways that dreams can turn inexorably into nightmares or recognized that cultural assimilation brings as many liabilities as assets? But Roth infuses his chronicle of cultural disintegration with such raw, unflinching power that it is safe to say that we have never before encountered its sheer ferocity.

Swede Levov is everything that the immigrant Jewish world of Newark regards as success incarnate: a legendary high school athlete, a devoted family man, a hard worker, and the prosperous inheritor of his father's glove fac-

tory. Levov, in short, appears to have it all, even if some elements of his charisma raise certain skeptical eyebrows:

> The Swede starred as end in football, center in basketball, and first baseman in baseball. Only the basketball team was ever any good—twice winning the city championship while he was its leading scorer—but as long as the Swede excelled, the fate of our sports teams didn't matter much to a student body whose elders, largely undereducated and overburdened, venerated academic achievement above all else. . . . Nonetheless, through the Swede, the neighborhood entered into a fantasy about itself and about the world, the fantasy of sports fans everywhere: almost like Gentiles (as they imagined Gentiles), our families could forget the way things actually work and make an athletic performance the repository of all their hopes. Primarily, they could forget the war.

The narrative voice belongs to the now-familiar Nathan Zuckerman. This time, however, he plays second banana to the fabulous Swede, unrolling a shivery tale that pits the social tapestry of the 1950s (affluence, assimilation, and optimism) against the darker story of what undermined and ultimately destroyed all this during the countercultural 1960s.

Swede Levov is not only a man more sinned against than sinful, he is also a good man of the sort that Roth had not really previously explored. Mickey Sabbath, the sexually hyperactive death-haunted protagonist who preceded the Swede, is more typical of Roth's ranting at everything that restricts a character's freedom. *American Pastoral* is a second look, one filled with "second thoughts," about the turbulent 1960s and the heartbreak it caused for an innocent like the Swede.

In yet another demonstration that character is fate, Roth holds the Swede's large athletic feet to the fire, balancing his slow but steady climb toward assimilation (he marries a former Miss New Jersey and sets up housekeeping in gentile Old Rimrock) against a mentally unbalanced daughter, Merry, hell-bent on punishing capitalist America—and her father— for the war in Vietnam. When she blows up a local post office, four people die.

Zuckerman pieces together the Levov family tragedy from snippets he garners from the Swede's younger brother as well as from his uncanny knack for allowing a part to stand for the cultural whole. In the process we are given as good a revisionist portrait of the chaos the late 1960s unleashed as we are likely to get, as well as a lively emblem of why the dreams of several generations of immigrant Jews ended in "the vandalization of their world." When Merry's long disquisitions about politics and the hippie life and her foray into Jainism have run their course, Zuckerman suddenly realizes that "everything she could not achieve with a speech therapist and a psychiatrist and a stuttering diary she had beautifully realized by going mad." Furthermore, as the Swede's no-nonsense brother puts it:

> Look, are you going to break with appearances and pit your will against your daughter's or aren't you? Out on the *field* you did it. That's how you scored, remember? You pitted your will against the other guy's and you *scored*. Pretend it's a game if that helps. . . . [Or] admit her contempt for your life and bail out. Admit that there is something very personal about you that she hates and bail . . . out and never see the bitch again. Admit that she's a monster, Seymour. Even a monster has to be from somewhere— even a monster needs parents. But parents don't need monsters.

But as the Swede knows all too well, the father-daughter relationship is more complicated than his much divorced brother can imagine; furthermore, to have a daughter so shrilly, so self-righteously call everything about your life into question turns the novel's title into a cruel joke.

As we watch, horror stricken, the pains deepen because what unfolds is the very essence of the tragic mode: that which cannot be, must be; and that which must be, cannot be. At the end, one is rocked to the core and left with the feeling that Roth has finally found a cultural subject large enough for his considerable talents. As the novel's final lines would have it:

> Yes, the breach had been pounded in their fortification, even out here in secure Old Rimrock, and now that it was opened it would not be closed again. They'll never recover. Everything is against them, everyone and everything that does not like their life. All the voices from without, condemning and rejecting their life!
>
> And what is so wrong with their life? What on earth is less reprehensible than the life of the Levovs?

Seldom has an apparently rhetorical question packed such resonance or raised more questions about the choices and destiny of American Jewish life in the middle decades of this century. To all the adjectives we usually apply to Roth's fiction—satiric, sexy, stylistically brilliant—*American Pastoral* bids us to add yet another: wise.

In much the same way that Zuckerman pieces together the rise and fall of Seymour Levov in *American Pastoral* and then ruminates about how the innocence of the 1950s was rudely overturned by an anarchic 1960s, *I Married a Communist* pushes the cultural time line back to the days of red scares and Joseph McCarthy witch hunts. About these matters much has been written in an effort to get the facts straight and the meaning clear. What Roth does—and does superbly—is give a literary spin to love and betrayal, blacklists and naming names. In effect this novel probes more deeply into the consciousness (and complications) of individual lives than standard histories usually do, and as a result it gives the turbulent 1950s a human face.

When he was a high school student, Zuckerman's favorite teacher had been Murray Ringold—and it is this Ringold, now in his ninetieth year, who comes clean about how his younger brother, the celebrated radio actor Iron

Rinn (born Ira Ringold), was framed by his aptly named, elegant, vindictive wife, Eve Frame (born Chava Fromkin). Her ghostwritten exposé titled *I Married a Communist* ruins Rinn's public career, but Roth complicates the tale of martyrdom that usually surrounds such scenarios. Before he landed his posh job in radio, Iron Rinn had been a ditchdigger, an Abraham Lincoln impersonator, and a believing communist. That he returns to the proletarian life a sadder but wiser man is true enough; that he remains a true believer and a proletarian in good standing is even truer. Murray recounts all this in a six-day recitation that strains credulity, but one must keep in mind that Murray is recalling an era in which Zuckerman was in the grip of communism at its most idealistic. At fifteen he tried his hand at radio plays that were agitprop of the first order. What Murray makes clear, all these years later, is how deluded Nathan had been—not only about American communists who parroted the Moscow line, but also about the dark secret at the bottom of Iron Rinn's life. In his roustabout youth he had bashed a fellow worker to death, and it is this, rather than the melodramatic shambles of his once glamorous marriage, on which much of Iron Rinn's subsequent life hangs.

Murray Ringold, who lost his teaching job when he refused to cooperate with a government-sponsored investigation of Newark subversives, has little patience with those on either side of the cultural coin. Communism was a disaster waiting to happen, just as the witch hunters of the House Un-American Activities Committee were zealots wielding a political stick. But to focus merely on all this, Murray hastens to add, is to miss the human dimensions of the tragedy—and that is where Roth's novel is particularly noteworthy. It adds a significant dimension to our cultural understanding of those times, those places.

During Nathan's freshman year at the University of Chicago, an English professor read him the riot act for penning a radio play that flies its political colors and little else: "Politics is the great generalizer," he begins, "and literature the great particularizer, and not only are they in an inverse relationship to each other—they are in an *antagonistic* relationship." What follows is a disquisition on the literary imagination that turned Zuckerman into the serious young fictionist in *The Ghost Writer*, and that is worth serious consideration in our own politically contentious age:

> As an artist the nuance is your *task*. Your task is *not* to simplify. Even should you choose to write in the simplest way, à la Hemingway, the task remains to impart the nuance, to elucidate the complication, to imply the contradiction. Not to erase the contradiction, not to deny the contradiction, but to see where, within the contradiction, lies the tormented human being. To allow for the chaos, to let it in. You *must* let it in. Otherwise you produce propaganda, if not for a political party, a political movement, then stupid propaganda for life itself—for life as it might itself prefer to be publicized.

It would be hard to find a better description of Roth's more than forty years at the writing desk. Like E. I. Lonof, he turns sentences around and then turns them around again. The difference is that Roth writes about Newark in roughly the same way that a self-exiled James Joyce wrote about Dublin—that is, from a distance and with the details of youth filtered through the prism of an adult imagination.

The Human Stain continues the beat, with Zuckerman now piecing together the enormously complicated story of Coleman Silk, a classics professor who watches as his long, distinguished career goes up in politically correct smoke because of an offhand remark. What he uttered was the word "spooks," referring (at least in his mind) to the specters, the *ghosts,* of two students who had not been present when he called role during the opening session of his class. As it turns out, the students in question are black and are much offended by the remark—no matter how much Professor Silk tries to explain that he meant the word in its primary, more precise definition. But it is the late 1990s and nobody at Athena College (the same Athena College where E. I. Lonoff once taught) is willing to risk his or her career by speaking up in Silk's behalf—even those (or perhaps *especially* those) whom Silk had hired when he was dean.

The incident leads to Silk's resignation and, in his mind, to his wife's death. Silk becomes a bitter man who seeks retribution in the form of a memoir he cannot write. When the seventy-one-year-old Silk asks a slightly younger Zuckerman—neighbor, professional writer, and friend—to be his ghostwriter, the two become what Joseph Conrad called "secret sharers."

The Human Stain is the book resulting from this collaboration, but at the same time it is much more than the tale of a man presumably more sinned against than sinful. As Zuckerman discovers, each of the characters he runs across in his research has a hidden secret. Indeed one of the things he comes to realize is that we all have lives hidden from ourselves and, moreover, that the neat formulations of, say, classical tragedy are never so nicely defined in life. Coleman Silk, for example, is not the Jewish professor he passed himself off as being but, instead, is an extraordinary black man from an extraordinary black family. He simply refuses to let race define either his limits or his possibilities. Given the classroom incident that led to his downfall, the resulting ironies multiply in ways that could only happen in a Roth novel.

Set against the background of President Bill Clinton's impeachment trial, the age of Viagra, and the cultural warfare that plays itself out on talk shows and in the halls of Congress, *The Human Stain* takes a provocative, often disturbing look at the contemporary world. Granted, the vision at work here is finally Roth's—as penetrating and uncompromising as ever about

sexuality, race, Jewishness, and the complicated ways that all these (and others) are fashioned by forces that simply *are:*

> We leave a stain, we leave a trail, we leave our imprint. Impurity, cruelty, abuse, error, excrement, semen—there's no other way to be here. Nothing to do with disobedience. Nothing to do with grace or salvation or redemption. It's in everyone. Indwelling. Inherent. Defining. The stain that is there before its mark.

Roth's version of original sin has little to do with biblical explanations of evil and even less with John Milton's efforts to justify "the ways of God to man." Rather Roth explores our fate as flawed and fallible human beings as well as our capacity for love in all its multiple combinations.

It is hard to predict the path Roth's subsequent writing will take because the only safe prediction is that it will be *un*predictable. But, whatever form it takes, his last books suggest that the next ones will be subversive, darkly funny, gorgeously written, and—most of all—important. Philip Roth has found a wide variety of ways to take on the incredible aspects of American life and make them imaginatively credible.

Selected Bibliography

WORKS OF PHILIP ROTH

FICTION
Goodbye, Columbus and Five Short Stories. Boston: Houghton Mifflin, 1959.

Letting Go. New York: Random House, 1962.

When She Was Good. New York: Random House, 1967.

Portnoy's Complaint. New York: Random House, 1969.

Our Gang (Starring Tricky and His Friends). New York: Random House, 1971.

The Breast. New York: Holt, Rinehart and Winston, 1972.

The Great American Novel. New York: Holt, Rinehart and Winston, 1973.

My Life as a Man. New York: Holt, Rinehart and Winston, 1974.

The Professor of Desire. New York: Farrar, Straus and Giroux, 1977.

The Ghost Writer. New York: Farrar, Straus and Giroux, 1979.

A Philip Roth Reader. New York: Farrar, Straus and Giroux, 1980.

Zuckerman Unbound. New York: Farrar, Straus and Giroux, 1981.

The Anatomy Lesson. New York: Farrar, Straus and Giroux, 1983.

The Prague Orgy. London: Cape, 1985; New York: Vintage, 1996.

Zuckerman Bound: A Trilogy and Epilogue. New York: Farrar, Straus and Giroux, 1985. (Includes *The Ghost Writer, Zuckerman Unbound, The Anatomy Lesson,* and *Epilogue: The Prague Orgy.*)

The Counterlife. New York: Farrar, Straus and Giroux, 1986.

Deception: A Novel. New York: Simon & Schuster, 1990.

Operation Shylock: A Confession. New York: Simon & Schuster, 1993.

Sabbath's Theater. Boston: Houghton Mifflin, 1995.

American Pastoral. Boston: Houghton Mifflin, 1997.

I Married a Communist. Boston: Houghton Mifflin, 1998.

The Human Stain. Boston: Houghton Mifflin, 2000.

The Dying Animal. Boston: Houghton Mifflin, 2001.

NONFICTION

Reading Myself and Others. New York: Farrar, Straus and Giroux, 1975.

The Facts: A Novelist's Autobiography. New York: Farrar, Straus and Giroux, 1988.

Patrimony: A True Story. New York: Simon & Schuster, 1991.

"Juice or Gravy: How I Met My Fate in a Cafeteria." *New York Times Book Review,* September 18, 1994, p. 3.

Shop Talk. Boston: Houghton Mifflin, 2001.

BIBLIOGRAPHY

Rodgers, Bernard F., Jr. *Philip Roth: A Bibliography.* Metuchen, N.J.: Scarecrow Press, 1974.

CRITICAL AND BIOGRAPHICAL STUDIES

Baumgarten, Murray, and Barbara Gottfried. *Understanding Philip Roth.* Columbia: University of South Carolina Press, 1990.

Berryman, Charles. "Philip Roth and Nathan Zuckerman: A Portrait of the Artist as a Young Prometheus." *Contemporary Literature* 31:177–190 (summer 1990).

Blair, Walter, and Hamlin Hill. "*The Great American Novel.*" In their *America's Humor: From Poor Richard to Doonesbury.* New York: Oxford University Press, 1978. Pp. 472–486.

Bloom, Harold, ed. *Philip Roth.* New York: Chelsea House, 1986.

Budick, Emily Miller. "Philip Roth's Jewish Family Marx and the Defense of Faith." *Arizona Quarterly* 52, no. 3:55–70 (autumn 1996).

Cooper, Alan. *Philip Roth and the Jews.* Albany: State University of New York Press, 1996.

Cooperman, Stanley. "Philip Roth: 'Old Jacob's Eye' with a Squint." *Twentieth-Century Literature* 19:203–216 (July 1973).

Crews, Frederick. "Uplift." *New York Review of Books,* November 16, 1972, pp. 18–20.

Dickstein, Morris. "Black Humor and History: The Early Sixties." In his *Gates of Eden: American Culture in the Sixties.* New York: Basic Books, 1977. Pp. 91–103.

Donaldson, Scott. "Philip Roth: The Meanings of *Letting Go.*" *Contemporary Literature* 11:21–35 (winter 1970).

Goodheart, Eugene. "Writing and the Unmaking of the Self." *Contemporary Literature* 29:438–453 (fall 1988).

Guttmann, Allen. "Philip Roth and the Rabbis." In his *The Jewish Writer in America: Assimilation and the Crisis of Identity.* New York: Oxford University Press, 1971. Pp. 64–76.

Halio, Jay L. *Philip Roth Revisited.* New York: Twayne, 1992.

Howe, Irving. "Philip Roth Reconsidered." *Commentary* 54:69–77 (December 1972).

Isaac, Dan. "In Defense of Philip Roth." *Chicago Review* 17:84–96 (1964).

Jones, Judith Paterson, and Guinevera A. Nance. *Philip Roth.* New York: Ungar, 1981.

Kauvar, Elaine M. "This Doubly Reflected Communication: Philip Roth's' Autobiographies.'" *Contemporary Literature* 36:412–446 (fall 1995).

Kazin, Alfred. "The Earthly City of the Jews." In his *Bright Book of Life.* New York: Little, Brown and Co., 1973. Pp. 144–149.

Kellman, Steven G. "Philip Roth's Ghost Writer." *Comparative Literature Studies* 21:175–185 (summer 1984).

Landis, Joseph C. "The Sadness of Philip Roth: An Interim Report." *Massachusetts Review* 3:259–268 (winter 1962).

Lee, Herminone. *Philip Roth.* London: Methuen, 1982.

Lehmann-Haupt, Christopher. "The Counterlife." *New York Times,* December 29, 1986, pp. 19ff. (Review of *The Counterlife.*)

McDaniel, John N. *The Fiction of Philip Roth.* Haddonfield, N.J.: Haddonfield House, 1974.

Meeter, Glenn. *Bernard Malamud and Philip Roth: A Critical Essay.* Grand Rapids, Mich.: Eerdmans, 1967.

Milbauer, Asher Z., and Donald G. Watson, eds. *Reading Philip Roth.* New York: St. Martin's Press, 1988.

Mudrick, Marvin. "Who Killed Herzog? Or Three American Novelists." *University of Denver Quarterly* 1, no. 1:61–97 (spring 1966).

O'Donnell, Patrick. "The Disappearing Text: Philip Roth's *The Ghost Writer.*" *Contemporary Literature* 24:365–378 (fall 1983).

Pinsker, Sanford, ed. *The Comedy That "Hoits": An Essay on the Fiction of Philip Roth.* Columbia: University of Missouri Press, 1975.

———, ed. *Critical Essays on Philip Roth.* Boston: G. K. Hall, 1982.

Podhoretz, Norman. "Laureate of the New Class." *Commentary* 54:4–7 (December 1972).

Rodgers, Bernard F., Jr. *Philip Roth.* Boston: Twayne, 1978.

Rubin-Dorsky, Jeffrey. "Honor Thy Father." *Raritan* 11:137–145 (spring 1992).

Searles, George J. *The Fiction of Philip Roth and John Updike.* Carbondale: Southern Illinios University Press, 1985.

Shechner, Mark. "Philip Roth." *Partisan Review* 41, no. 3:410–427 (1974).

———. "The Road of Excess: *Philip Roth.*" In his *After the Revolution: Studies in the Contemporary Jewish American Imagination.* Bloomington: Indiana University Press, 1987. Pp. 196–238.

Siegel, Ben. "The Myths of Summer: Philip Roth's *The Great American Novel.*" *Contemporary Literature* 17:171–190 (spring 1976).

Solotaroff, Theodore. "The Journey of Philip Roth." *Atlantic,* April 1969, pp. 64–72.

Stern, Richard. "Philip Roth Lets Go: Zuckerman Revisited in Style." *Chicago Tribune Books,* January 11, 1987, pp. 1, 5. (Review of *The Counterlife.*)

Tanner, Tony. "Fictionalized Recall—or, 'The Settling of Scores: The Pursuit of Dreams.'" In his *City of Words: American Fiction 1950–1970.* New York: Harper & Row, 1971. Pp. 295–321.

Wilson, Matthew. "Fathers and Sons in History: Philip Roth's *The Counterlife.*" *Prooftexts* 11:41–56 (January 1991).

Wirth-Nesher, Hana. "The Artist Tales of Philip Roth." *Prooftexts* 3:263–272 (September 1983).

Wisse, Ruth R. "Language as Fate: Reflections on Jewish Literature in America." In *Literary Strategies: Jewish Texts and Contexts.* Edited by Ezra Mendelsohn. New York: Oxford University Press, 1996. Pp. 129–147.

INTERVIEWS

Rubin, Stephen. "Dialog: Philip Roth." *Chicago Tribune Magazine,* September 25, 1977, pp. 74–75.

Searles, George J., ed. *Conversations with Philip Roth.* Jackson: University of Mississippi Press, 1992.

"A Symposium: Jewishness and the Younger Intellectuals." *Commentary* 31:306–359 (April 1961).

—SANFORD PINSKER

Isaac Bashevis Singer

1904–1991

*I*N HIS 1978 speech accepting the Nobel Prize in literature, Isaac Bashevis Singer proclaimed, "Yiddish has not yet said its last word." At least in terms of the impact of his own work on readers in English and other languages, his statement has proven true. For the first seventy-four years of his life, the author wrote primarily for a small but loyal following of Yiddish readers. Although much of Singer's work was available in English at the time he was awarded the Nobel Prize, his stories, novels, and memoirs have continued to appear, including posthumously published translations of volumes from the original versions published decades before in serial form in Yiddish. Singer has been controversial, but his contribution to world literature needs to be understood in the wide scope of his range and depth. He was famously resistant to categorization, but it may be possible to sum up his achievement in terms of a category of his own, "cabalistic realism."

Not that Singer's work invites pedantic or esoteric analysis. A master storyteller above all, Singer believed literature should provide enjoyment and entertainment to the reader. He eschewed the difficulties of Franz Kafka, James Joyce, and other favorites of academic critics in favor of the straightforward narrative style of traditional literary classics. In addition to the influences of Yiddish masters, such as I. L. Peretz and Sholem Asch, he drew inspiration from novelists, such as Leo Tolstoy and Fyodor Dostoyevsky, and short story masters, such as Guy de Maupassant and Anton Chekhov, and hearkened back to Shakespeare, Homer, and the Hebrew Bible as models of character, plot development, and style. Singer's popularity has depended to a great extent on the accessibility of his prose. He had a knack for descriptions that whet the reader's appetite for details, and he created vivid characters that arrest the distracted attention of the contemporary mind.

But if Singer is a literary realist in his narrative technique, his subject matter and authorial perspective are derived from the tales and legends of Jewish mysticism. He is known for his portrayals of demonic possession by dybbuks, lost souls from the nether worlds, who can invade the body usually of an innocent young woman or girl. He also dabbles in occult manifestations of unseen imps and demons that can cause havoc in otherwise normal situations. Singer indulges in expositions on the names of angels and other lore of esoteric texts. But the serious basis of all these fictional techniques is the author's concern with the eternal struggle against the forces of evil, an ongoing battle in which humanity can never ultimately triumph except for brief periods of happiness and pleasure in this world and, perhaps, in some hidden but uncertain final reckoning in worlds beyond our own. For Singer, a lingering doubt that any Higher Power has humanity's interests at heart always remains. But he conveys absolute certainty about the cosmic forces of darkness and an imperative to resist the subtle tendencies and overt compulsions toward corruption, degradation, and brutality. Paradoxically, Singer's consistent message is that, despite any rational explanations, in a way that can only be understood through experience as reflected in his stories and novels, Death is the great illusion and Life is eternal.

Without attempting to systematize his beliefs, Singer evoked the sanctity of life and the mystery of the human condition. In his *Nobel Lecture* (1979), Singer acknowledged the mystic influences of the Hasidic Rabbi Nachman of Breslov side by side with the rationalism of Baruch Spinoza. Along with Hasidic mysticism, Singer inherited a talmudic tradition as a way of life in which he was raised in his formative years. But within this tradition, he also found a validation for arguing with the deity, in protest against the vagaries of Providence. This form of holy protest against the Creator hearkens back to Abraham, Moses, and Job as well as the fiery, fierce Rabbi Menachem Mendel of Kotzk. From Spinoza and the European philosophers, Singer derived respect for skepticism and logic as an antidote to what he called in his Nobel lecture "the lies, the cliches, and the idolatries of the human mind." Yet Spinoza's *Ethics* also opened the door to a pantheistic embrace of all the phenomena of nature as being direct manifestations of the divine. Together, the mystical and rational sides of Singer's worldview formed his belief in a deity "who speaks in deeds, not in words, and whose vocabulary is the universe," as he put it in his Nobel lecture. For the Yiddish storyteller I. B. Singer, as for the visionary poet William Blake, everything that exists, from the pebble in the street to the star in the sky, belongs to and with the deity.

Never, however, does Singer allow himself to sermonize or preach to the reader. Instead, he seduces us to the joys and thrills of vicarious experience through literary representations of worlds that reflect our own. Above all, he wins the interest of even the casual browser through his work with his wild flights of imagination. To read one Singer short story is to feel almost an irresistible desire to read at least two more. Yet the pleasure of reading him depends on more than an impulse to escape from humdrum experience to adventurous excursions into the paranormal. To quote again from his Nobel lecture, the Yiddish in which he wrote is "a language of exile, without a land, without frontiers, not supported by any government, a language which possesses no words for weapons, ammunition, military exercises, war tactics. . . . The truth is that what the great religions preached, the Yiddish-speaking people of the ghettos practiced day in and day out."

Paradoxically, Singer's reputation has been more subject to criticism among Yiddish readers than among those who know his work only in translation. For some of his critics, he is guilty of misrepresenting the Jewish world, putting too much emphasis on sexuality and the outer fringes of mystical lore rather than on the solid foundations of Jewish morality. Others have taken him to task because he rejects stances based on Marxism, Zionism, or any other modern ideology. Singer was both a conservative defender of traditional Jewish values and, at the same time, a provocative gadfly who challenged any and all assumptions of orthodoxy of any sort. A prolific writer, with many guises and changing identities, he wrote under various Yiddish pseudonyms, including Isaac Bashevis for his poetic prose, Isaac Warshavsky for memoirs and occasional pieces, and D. Segal for other journalistic articles. He was also able to apply his particular brand of observation to stories set in modern New York and Florida as well as in the eastern Europe of the past. Far from a naive or sentimental folk artist, Singer expressed the inner divisions of the author's own spirit in a style that reflects the divisions of a global culture in crisis and transition. In his work, "in a figurative way," Yiddish became a universal language expressing "the idiom of frightened and hopeful humanity."

IN MY FATHER'S COURT

Singer grew up in a strictly religious Jewish home during the first decades of the twentieth century in Poland, as he describes in his memoir *In My Father's Court* (1966). His father, a Hasidic rabbi without an established congregation of his own, served within the family's neighborhood in Warsaw as judge and jury on a variety of issues, ranging from the minutiae of Talmudic law to affairs of both the heart and the pocketbook. The author recalls in dramatic detail how, as a young boy, he eavesdropped on his father and an endless parade of advice seekers who came to trust their problems to the rabbi. The central gist of the roughly chronological collection of vignettes is the author's reverence for the "heroic code" inherited from centuries of Yiddish culture based on the "ability to endure suffering for the sake of spiritual purity." At the same time, however, this first-person, nonfiction collection of experiences recounts the author's early growth away from the pious tradition of his ancestors and his introduction, through intellectual exploration and historical necessity, into the secular culture of European modernism.

Singer was born on July 14, 1904, in the miniscule village of Leoncin, Poland. He was the son of Pinchos Menachem Singer and Bathsheba Zylberman Singer, both of whom traced their lineage to prominent rabbinical ancestry. Singer and his family moved in 1907 to the slightly larger village of Radzymin, and about a year later, they moved once again to No. 10 Krochmalna Street in Russian-occupied Warsaw. Populated largely by Orthodox Jews, the neighborhood "bordered on the ill-famed Krochmalna Square," where petty gangsters and prostitutes congregated. Serving as messenger to his father's rabbinical tribunal, Singer was sent into the dark corners and crannies of the poverty-stricken dwellings. As witness to the proceedings in his father's private study, even if he had to listen through a crack in the door, the child who would grow up to write about the mysteries of man and woman observed the tragedies of broken-hearted lovers and families in conflict. Within the narrow realm of the Jew-ish ghetto, Singer discovered the vast, unmapped territories of the human heart. Singer later attended a rabbinical seminary in Warsaw, Poland, but his Talmudic and mystical studies as well as his knowledge of literature and philosophy came mainly from home schooling and self-education. *In My Father's Court* includes hidden saints, like the Jewish dairyman who saved the Singer family from famine and fire, and open scoundrels, such as a sham scholar and wandering confidence artist who made his living by auctioning off his share in the world to come. Here are also the eccentrics, the schemers, the simpletons, and the ordinary Jews who came to receive the formal wisdom of the Torah from Singer's father while informally educating the young Singer in the complexities of character. From earliest childhood, the author notes, he learned the deep ambivalence of the emotions and how "for most people there is only one small step" between love and hate, "between blows and kisses, between spitting at one's neighbor's face and showering him with kindness."

Without a regular salary, Singer's father depended on the generosity of the community he served. The grim realities of living in poverty affected not only his less-fortunate neighbors but Singer's own family as well. The family income sometimes sank below even the modest material needs of the family for food and clothing. Others had even less. The author recounts examples of extreme deprivation, such as the widower with no bed to sleep in because his wife died on the Sabbath and rats in his apartment make it impossible to put the corpse on the floor. He also recalls instances of noble sacrifice, such as the gentile washerwoman who will not allow herself to die until she finishes the laundry she promised to deliver before her final sickness.

Into this anachronistic world of traditional piety, modern materialism intrudes in the form of secular ideas and world war. The author's older brother rebels against the rabbinical faith of their father and espouses the rationalism of Enlightenment philosophy and the culture of modern art. For years, Isaac Bashevis Singer developed intellectually and artistically in the shadow of his brother, Israel Joshua Singer. He often refers to him, even in the prefaces to his later works, as his master in the art of writing. As an author of realistic fiction, the elder Singer blazed the trail and served as mentor and guide for his younger brother. But in terms of intellectual development, the younger Singer did not as decisively reject traditional Jewish scholarship in favor of unencumbered rationalism. Where I. J. Singer seems to have become an avowed disbeliever in revealed religion, I. B. Singer neither accepted fully nor repudiated totally the faith of previous generations. Instead, he clung to the mystical and imaginative inspiration of the Jewish past, even though he could not in good conscience espouse the religious practices of his ancestors. As a result, Isaac Bashevis Singer developed as a hybrid still rooted in the fundamental Torah of timeless tradition yet grafted to the restless skepticism of the modern world.

I. B. Singer describes the upheaval his brother's rebellion caused in the family. Their mother partly agrees and partly argues with influences of science and rationalism, while their father renounces secular learning as a desecration of the sacred. Meanwhile, World War I rages around them, pushing the family's circumstances down the slope of genteel poverty toward the danger of starvation. To escape, the family separates, and the mother takes the younger children, Isaac and his little brother, to her family's rural village. For Isaac, the trip is an adventure. Until then, he had rarely explored the world beyond the ghetto, except when he rode on the milk wagon of the family friend or when he and another boy dared to ride a Warsaw streetcar to the end of the line. The experience of his mother's village opens his mind to a

world of timeless innocence unchallenged by the complexities of historical flux. At the other end of the spectrum, he visits his brother, who has forged false identity papers to avoid being drafted into the army while living among freethinkers and artists in the Warsaw equivalent of Greenwich Village. It becomes apparent that I. B. Singer fully belongs in neither the world of the believers nor the world of the skeptics yet has deep connections with both.

LOVE AND EXILE

This inner struggle is developed in *Love and Exile* (1984). Picking up where the earlier volume leaves off, with some minor repetitions, Singer in this book adopts a more discursive style rather than the focused vignettes of *In My Father's Court*. The result may be less successful in artistic terms, but it is more frankly revealing as a confessional record of the author's conflicted faith in a personal deity, his struggle to define himself as an artist, and his tangled and problematic relationships with women. Describing himself as torn between the Hasidic teachings of Rabbi Nachman of Breslov and the philosophical rationalism of Spinoza's *Ethics*, drawn to both and yet unable to find conclusive satisfaction in either, he develops his own, improvised "ethic of protest" against the suffering and injustice of the human condition, expressed by a determination to avoid doing evil insofar as possible and refusing to accept evil whether done to oneself or to others by agents natural, human, or divine. In a convoluted process of internal dialectic, his determination to live a life of spiritual protest against the omnivorous forces of cruelty and destruction seems to have crystallized in his decision, only fully implemented years later, to become a strict vegetarian. Vegetarianism meant many things to Singer. It substituted for Jewish dietary laws, since all fruits and vegetables are by definition kosher. It also seems to have been the result of his aversion to participating in the drama of predators and victims, whether in natural or cosmic terms.

He refused, however, to join the protest of others in his generation, especially all of those who sought idealistic social improvement for the suffering masses whether through Communist, Socialist, Zionist, or other popular movements. Although he was in the swirling center of all these political controversies and included many followers of various persuasions among his closest acquaintances, Singer remained aloof from any party or ideology. By instinct, he rejected historical materialism as a less-believable creed than the historical spiritualism on which he had been raised. Among his fellow writers, he often found himself on the defensive in debates about the progressive hope for the future of humanity, but he insisted that his pessimism was the opposite of cynicism or abject surrender to despair. "The pessimism of the creative person" he argued in his Nobel lecture, "is not decadence but a mighty passion for the redemption of man." He was fascinated by all forms of occult spiritual investigation, but in the end he refused to give credence to anything other than the evidence of his own senses. If his inquiries into the puzzle of existence left him with more questions than answers, he resolved to use the ambiguities of his immediate experience for artistic expression rather than to defend abstract principles that he could not prove to his own satisfaction.

In 1935, with Adolf Hitler already in power and the future of European Jewry under a cloud of doom, Singer departed Warsaw for New York, leaving behind the Poland of his birth to find refuge in an adopted America in which, as a Yiddish writer, he would always be an anomaly if not simply an outcast. In Poland, he had achieved a measure of success with his first novel *Satan in Goray* (1935), and he had established an identity as a member of the Warsaw Yiddish Writers Club, which served as a

cultural and intellectual sanctuary. Also he had begun to carry on a complicated series of simultaneous love affairs with women of various backgrounds. One of these lovers, a Communist activist, had become his common law wife and had given birth to the author's only son. Still, he continued to involve himself with other women. No sense of family obligation or domestic responsibility prevented him from leaving his young son and his son's mother—as well as the author's own mother and younger brother—while he immigrated to the United States.

It was evidently only through the assistance of his older brother that I. B. Singer managed to obtain the precious visa that allowed him to escape from the impending storm that would wipe out the world of European Jewry. Harshly criticized by his detractors for putting his own survival above those closest to him, he paid a high price in psychic suffering. The issue of survivor's guilt runs as a red thread through his work, most prominently in novels that were translated and published posthumously. Twenty years after he immigrated, Singer met and reconciled with his son, Israel Zamir, an Israeli journalist. In the meantime, he wrestled with his own inner demons and created a distinctive perspective bridging the reality of a lost world of Yiddish culture with a post-Holocaust awareness.

The transition was difficult for Singer economically, creatively, and personally, leaving him, as he says in *Love and Exile,* "lost in America, lost forever." For a number of years, he lost the ability to create, living a meager existence as a stringer for the Yiddish press. The awesome indifference of the world to the plight of Yiddish culture almost extinguished his impulse to keep writing. After the devastating impact of World War II had sunk in, however, Singer seems to have rediscovered his inspiration, based on a determination to resurrect the world that had been wiped out except in his own cultural memory. His first literary achievement in the United States was *The Family Moskat* (1950), an epic novel about Polish Jewry in the early twentieth century written with the awareness that the world described had been doomed to extinction. A critical if not a financial success, Singer continued to write mainly for the Yiddish press while his previous novel, *Satan in Goray,* found its way into English translation.

SATAN IN GORAY

Set in a tiny Jewish village "in the midst of the hills at the end of the world," *Satan in Goray* reveals the formative background of Singer's creative genius. This mosaic of poetic-prose vignettes paints in graphic detail the nightmare of Jewish history, from which the author as a young man wished to awaken. Its chief flaw is the lack of a central point of view around which the story can unfold. Its strength, however, may be the kaleidoscopic quality achieved by the shifting perspective from one vividly drawn character to another, with seemingly evil characters becoming good and vice versa, in the psychodrama of a community of forsaken outcasts suffering the crushing depths of Jewish Exile. What it lacks as a well-constructed novel, the book makes up for by illuminations of the fine line between prophecy and perversion, piety and superstition, sincere devotion to human salvation and grotesque betrayal of that ideal.

The narrative begins in 1648 with "the wicked Ukrainian hetman, Bogdan Chmelnicki," the seventeenth-century forerunner of Hitler. Decimating Polish Jewry as a sidelight to their failed uprising against the reigning aristocracy, Chmelnicki's followers invade Goray along with the surrounding larger villages:

They slaughtered on every hand, flayed men alive, murdered small children, violated women and afterward ripped open their bellies and sewed cats inside. Many fled to Lublin, many underwent

baptism or were sold into slavery. Goray, which once had been known for its scholars and men of accomplishment, was completely deserted. . . . The handful who survived left the town and wandered away. It seemed as though Goray had been erased forever.

Slowly, painfully, this devastated shtetl reconstructs itself in a truncated and diminished version of its former prosperity and high repute. By the time of the main action of the story, from October 1666 until the following year, the surviving remnant has fallen into a collective frenzy of mixed despair and expectation inspired by the word of mouth accounts of one of the most controversial and bizarre figures of Jewish history, the false messiah Sabbatai Zevi. The inhabitants of Goray first hear of this newly proclaimed Jewish savior from a rabbinical legate from Yemen. In reaction, the old Rabbi Benish, who led the community in the years before 1648, expels this messianic messenger. Rabbi Benish is unable, however, to uproot the heresy, which spreads quickly, even among his own family, and soon takes over almost the entire congregation. Raising up leaders of their own, followers of the new movement, with the help of dark invisible forces, drive Rabbi Benish himself from their midst. What follows is a shocking portrayal of mass psychosis on a miniature scale. Briefly, the community seems to ascend heights of spiritual ecstasy, but the redemption never comes.

At first, the news trickles down to these distant followers that the man on whom they have pinned their hopes, Sabbatai Zevi, has gone to Istanbul to confront the caliph, declare his messianic identity, and lead the Jews from the dark corners of their dispersion back to Jerusalem:

The holy kingdom would be revealed when the last spark was returned whence it had come. Then the ritual ceremonies would no longer hold. Bodies would become pure spirit. From the World of Emanations and from the Throne of Glory new souls would descend. There would be no more eating and drinking. Instead of being fruitful and multiplying, beings would unite in combinations of holy letters. The Talmud wouldn't be studied. Of the Bible only the secret essence would remain. Each day would last a year, and the radiance of the holy spirit would fill all space.

Instead of converting the caliph in Istanbul, however, the self-declared messiah Sabbatai Zevi converts to Islam under threat of death. The resulting upheaval discredits him and his followers with the masses but leaves true believers still claiming that this pseudo-conversion was part of an esoteric messianic plan to raise up the appearances of evil betrayal to the higher reality of true goodness and devotion. For these determined messianists, the secret teachings require the inversion of all values. Everything forbidden must be commanded and vice versa to bring redemption. Reflected in the microcosm of Goray, the effects are represented as the victory of Satan and his evil hosts over the forces of light and the ultimate perversion of humble faith.

At the heart of this struggle, the orphan Rechele endures the consequences of the twisted aspirations and doomed desires of the community within her own body and soul. She becomes the embodiment of an oppressed people lost in the labyrinth of Exile. Born shortly before the Chmelnicki massacre, Rechele is rescued by her mother, even as her older sister is raped and murdered by the mob. She is still a little girl when her mother dies. Her father, formerly a respected rabbi, becomes a wandering beggar and abandons her to a widowed uncle and a crazed, superstitious grandmother, who terrorizes Rechele with tales of goblins and witches. After her grandmother's death, haunted by the old woman's spirit, Rechele curls up in a frozen catatonic trance from which she is aroused by the most primitive treatment. The psychological shocks of her childhood leave her physically crippled with a lame left foot. Yet she retains some of the qualities of her once wealthy and powerful background, receiving more than the usual level of education for a woman in Hebrew and growing up eerily attractive to men and mysterious to all. Living almost totally isolated within the community, suffering strange maladies that some attribute to epilepsy and others to demonic possession, she seems like "one apart."

In the midst of the Sabbatean enthusiasm, Rechele suddenly begins to prophesy. She hears a voice in the night instructing her to dress in her Sabbath clothes, go to the synagogue, and declare the imminent redemption, to coincide with the coming New Year. Her utterances set the community into a frenzy of expectation. When the redemption fails, it becomes evident that Rechele is possessed by a dybbuk, an evil spirit from the world of the dead. The novel ends with an exorcism that, though successful, leaves both Rechele and the community of Goray condemned to oblivion. In this novel, the author dramatizes the plight of the Shekinah, the Indwelling Divine Presence symbolic of the Jewish people, represented in the character Rechele, driven to despair. Without reducing the psychological subtlety of *Satan in Goray* to political allegory, Singer creates a historical metaphor for both the apocalypse and false ideologies of his own time.

THE SLAVE

In *The Slave: A Novel* (1962), Singer returns to the aftermath of the Chmelnicki horrors. In many ways, Singer's two novels about seventeenth-century Jews complement each other. Rechecle, the central consciousness of *Satan in Goray*, poses the problem of historical evil. Jacob, the protagonist of *The Slave*, suggests Singer's solution. From early childhood, as recorded in his memoirs, Singer foraged in books of traditional Jewish mysticism known as the cabala. From these esoteric works, he drew a number of his favorite fictional devices, including the whole realm of unseen powers playing tricks and doing favors for unaware mortals. But Singer found more than imps, dybbuks, and demons in these mystical teachings. Singer based much of his work on the cabalistic concepts of Exile and Redemption. Exile, the primal manifestation of evil, is rooted in the alienation of the soul. Rechele represents the embodiment of Jewish Exile. The purpose of cabalistic teachings is to repair the fragmentation of this Exile. When all souls return to their spiritual home, Redemption will be achieved. Jacob shows the path to this Redemption and demonstrates the hidden purpose of the Exile by uniting with Wanda/Sarah, raising the fallen sparks of holiness from the darkest corners of Creation.

One of the few really heroic figures in Singer's work, Jacob is not without fault. He is a mortal man with desires of the flesh too strong for him to overcome, despite his spiritual strength. But his self-confessed sins serve the purpose of a higher holiness. Unlike the false messiahs and hypocritical leaders of *Satan in Goray*, Jacob is a simple, humble, but sincerely devoted individual who refuses to surrender his soul to bondage. As the novel opens, however, he has escaped from Chmelnicki's hordes only to be abducted by robbers who literally sell him to a peasant in a distant mountain village. The villagers work together to make sure that Jacob does not escape from the remote ranges where he is sent, like his biblical namesake, to herd the flocks of his master. After several years of this forced servitude, Jacob fears he has already forgotten his religious training. Unable to observe the rituals and holidays of the Jewish calendar in the context of communal life, Jacob makes intense efforts to remain aware of his origins. He keeps as many of the commandments as possible, praying without ritual fringes or phylacteries and avoiding any forbidden foods. Forcing his memory to respond, he uses a metal hook to try to engrave each one of the

613 commandments of the Torah on a rock on the mountainside. Meanwhile, the Polish peasants of the village, though nominally Christian, continue to serve the pagan deities and nature spirits of their own ancient traditions. Most of them are shamelessly amoral, drunken louts, including the priest and the local bailiff. Yet Jacob's master happens to be a simple but good-hearted man. And his master's daughter, Wanda, loves Jacob.

With all his spiritual might, Jacob resists the temptation of Wanda's love, but the force of natural desire overcomes the strictures of eternal faith. Although their love is forbidden by both Polish and Jewish authorities, Jacob and Wanda transcend legal and religious barriers. But what nature grants them, nature also takes away. When his wife dies in childbirth, Jacob must find within himself the strength to rebel against the forces that want to take his child from him. Seeking refuge in a perilous trip to the Holy Land, Jacob becomes a kind of reincarnated embodiment of his biblical namesake:

> Everything remained the same: the ancient love, the ancient grief. Perhaps four thousand years would again pass; somewhere, at another river, another Jacob would walk mourning another Rachel. Or who knew, perhaps it was always the same Jacob and the same Rachel. Well, but the Redemption has to come. All of this can't last forever.

In *The Slave* Singer comes as close as he ever allows himself to portraying his own concept of a messianic redemption. But rather than emphasizing the otherworldly aspects of salvation, the author stresses the need for a humanistic interpretation of traditional teachings. Through his protagonist, the author criticizes a religious tradition that punctiliously "observed the laws and customs involving the Almighty, but broke the code regulating man's treatment of man with impunity." Instead, Jacob develops his own religion based on an abiding faith in a deity who hides his face and keeps his silence, leaving humanity to resolve its problems with only its own heart as a guide. While he remains a sinner in his own eyes, it is clear to the reader that Jacob represents as close to a human redeemer as Singer's intellectual skepticism can allow.

THE COLLECTED STORIES

Perhaps the best introduction to Isaac Bashevis Singer, the tales in *The Collected Stories of Isaac Bashevis Singer* (1982) range across the worlds and issues that concerned the author. Yet each story tends to be a world unto itself, with its own rules and definitions of the mysterious relationships between imagination and reality. In "Gimpel the Fool," one of the first of Singer's works to attract a wider audience, partly thanks to the translation by Saul Bellow, the first-person narrator, who is considered by others to be a fool, reveals a deeper awareness of the problems in perception for sages as well as for simpletons. On the surface, the story is an extended folktale about a man who marries a village harlot. His wife presents Gimpel with a series of suspiciously fathered children, yet she insists, in spite of appearances, that she remains a faithful wife. In some implicit bargain with Providence, the more Gimpel seems to play the fool, the more successful he becomes as a tradesman, until his little bakery becomes a small gold mine. Ultimately, Gimpel discovers the truth about his own deception and the deception of the world in general. First, he claims, there really are no lies, since everything happens eventually to someone, somewhere, if only in a dream. And then, on the deepest level of all, the aged Gimpel confronts his own imminent death with joyful anticipation, for only there, beyond this world of betrayal and heartbreak, can a true reality "without complication, without ridicule, without deception" exist.

In "The Spinoza of Marketstreet," the author creates another kind of alternative reality through the character of an aged and impoverished scholar, who has devoted his entire life to the study of philosophy, especially Spinoza's *Ethics,* only to discover in old age—but not too late to be appreciated—that wisdom requires more than book learning. Lonely and decrepit, Dr. Fischelson finds comfort in the unsolicited care and concern of an equally old and neglected spinster who happens to live in the garret next to his. The romance that blossoms between these two solitary souls, the streetwise but uneducated old woman who sells broken eggs in the market and the intellectually sophisticated yet unworldly scholar, transcends the seemingly grotesque nature of their mutual attraction. According to the story's omniscient narrator, the marriage of the ancient Black Dobbe and Dr. Fischelson "could be called a miracle" of humanistic dimensions.

Something about the concentrated form of the short story brought out the author's genius. Many of the stories deal with life in the lost world of the Jewish communities of eastern Europe. Others are set in America, in New York City, or Miami Beach. Some deal with demonic possession, others with strange happenings involving unforeseen and inexplicable coincidences. The narrator sometimes appears to be the alter ego of the author, but almost as often introduces himself as "the Primal Snake, the Evil One, Satan." In "The Destruction of Kreshev," once again the followers of Shabbatai Zevi take center stage, undermining the peaceful town of Kreshev and leaving it in ruins. In this text, the author makes clear the distinction between his own brand of messianic humanism and the antinomianism of the perverters of true faith. Among the many miniature masterpieces of Singer's short fiction are tales of spiritual inspiration, such as "Joy"; historical dramas, such as "Grandfather and Grandson"; tragic romances, such as "Taibele and Her Demon" and "Old Love"; as well as gothic horror stories, such as "The Unseen." Readers will choose their own favorites from an astonishing array of powerful selections.

In "A Friend of Kafka," for example, the central character is drawn from an individual the author recalls, in his memoirs, having known from the Warsaw Yiddish Writer's Club. A former actor in Yiddish theater, Jacques Kohn, as he is called in the story, is described as a dilettante and hanger-on. Although he has accomplished nothing himself, he claims to be on intimate terms with the great minds of his generation, especially Franz Kafka, whose genius he discovered before anyone else had heard of him. He recalls the great man as sexually and creatively inhibited. "He craved love and fled from it. He wrote a sentence and immediately crossed it out." He dismissively recalls the young Kafka as "sunk to the neck in the bourgeois swamp." But to another member of the club who questions Kafka's style, he responds: "A master does not have to follow the rules."

With world-weariness and condescending nobility, Jacques Kohn describes his life in terms of a game of chess "with Fate as partner." All of humanity plays this game, he says, and though we know we cannot defeat the opponent, Death, we keep fighting for the sake of the game itself. For his part, the struggle is personal, with an angelic adversary who "sits up there in an office in the third or seventh heaven, in that department of Providence that rules our little planet, and has just one job—to trap Jacques Kohn." This scenario keeps him barely alive, while one day miraculously follows another. One night, for instance, a violent banging on his door turns out to be a beautiful countess wearing only an expensive fur coat, trying to escape her murderously jealous lover who lives in a downstairs apartment. Another time, Jacques Kohn has lost his key but discovers it again on a dark stairway at night in another part of town. The odds of finding a key this way he calls "one in a billion, but it seems that my op-ponent was afraid I might give up the ghost before he was ready." Is there a divine plan to all this? Perhaps not. But "if there isn't, who is playing all these games with Jacques Kohn?"

A central theme of all of Singer's work is spiritual return, which is the literal translation of the Yiddish and Hebrew word for repentance. But although the author seeks return to his spiritual origins, he does not promise an easy path. As much as the characters of Singer's work yearn for simplicity and sincerity, they find their way barred by the complex realities of the world and, even more troubling, by their own inner contradictions and conflicts. If he holds up simplicity and truthfulness as virtues, Singer himself was far from simple, and it would be a misconception to see him as a secular saint without sophistication or cunning. Rather, he invoked a mischievous imagination to create wild, provocative situations, and he could be a cutting critic of the modern world.

THE MAGICIAN OF LUBLIN

One of Singer's recurring scenarios is the man faced with the dilemma of three women who love him and for each of whom he feels a mixture of affection and moral dread. In *The Magician of Lublin* (1960) Yasha Mazur is a high-wire prestidigitator. He makes his living performing for audiences at the Alhambra Theater in Warsaw for extended runs and spends the rest of the year traveling an endless circuit of circuses, county fairs, and provincial carnivals in his native Poland. Crowds pay to see him risk life and limb. Meanwhile, he juggles relationships with various women. His faithful Orthodox Jewish wife, Esther, keeps his home and anchors him in the Jewish community, from which Yasha has otherwise become alienated. Though, "like his father and grandfather," he had been born in Lublin, Yasha feels as much a stranger there as when he is on the road. Esther accepts his absences and regrets only that she has not been able to give birth. But Yasha is filled with doubts bordering on despair:

> Was there such a thing as a soul? And what happened to it after it left the body? Since early childhood he had listened to tales of dybbuks, ghosts, werewolves, and hobgoblins. He himself had experienced events unexplained by natural law, but what did it all mean? He became increasingly confused and withdrawn. Within him, forces raged; passions reduced him to terror.

Although she suspects him of infidelity, Esther remains unaware of the intimacy between Yasha and his young Polish assistant, Magda, who is also devoted to him with a fierce passion. In his way, Yasha feels responsible for Magda and depends on her professionally. Yasha's own romantic obsession, however, is with Emilia, an aristocratic widow in Warsaw who wants him to convert to Christianity and escape with her to western Europe, where his artistry will be appreciated. In the interim, Yasha dallies with Zeftel, a local harlot whose husband is in prison. Yasha also enjoys the company of her underworld friends. He derives a special satisfaction in being able, as a performer, to prove the master of opening every lock with nothing more than a pin or a simple pick.

Whatever his doubts about the meaning of existence, Yasha's confidence in his own ability seems unlimited. At the crisis, however, he finds he is unable to break free of the religious convictions and training of his Jewish origins. He decides on an impulse to commit one act of intentional theft to free himself from the circumstances that bind him to obscurity. But when he tries to commit a crime, he fumbles badly, failing to steal anything while both injuring and implicating himself as he tries to get away from the scene of the bungled attempt. All at once, his multiple affairs come crashing down on him. Magda kills herself in brokenhearted despair. Emilia rejects him when he confesses his failed robbery. Only his wife, Esther, stays with him to the end. But, filled with

self-loathing and remorse, the magician retreats into utter solitude, building a brick hut for himself and sealing all the entrances. Nevertheless, full repentance is not and evidently cannot be achieved by Yasha Mazur. Although he longs to return to the religion of his ancestors, he is too filled with inner doubts to attain real faith. And the world remains too tempting to him to allow him to leave his self-imposed isolation.

The legend of Yasha the Penitent circulates among Jews from the surrounding areas, who begin to come to him for advice, trusting him as a holy sage. But to the end, Yasha cannot trust himself.

> No, peace of mind was not to be found in this world. There is no tomorrow without sorrow, as the philosophers say. But even more powerful than the temptations from without were those born within man himself, in his brain, his heart. No hour passed without Yasha's being besieged by every sort of passion. No sooner did he forget himself for a moment than they gathered about him; empty fancies, daydreams, repulsive desires.

As much as Yasha struggles for true faith, he never really attains it.

THE PENITENT

In *The Penitent* (1983), Singer presents a quite different, yet related, perspective on the return to traditional faith. The opening pages portray Joseph Shapiro as "a little man in a long gaberdine and a velvet hat," externally indistinguishable from the crowd of Orthodox Jews from which he emerges to introduce himself to the author during his first visit as a tourist to the Wailing Wall in Jerusalem. Describing himself as a loyal reader, Shapiro approaches the author with the desire to tell his story. Through the mouth of its protagonist, this novella blasts the poisonous depravity and hypocrisy of modern life and offers traditional religion as the antidote.

The narrator tells the tale of his own spiritual odyssey. From the depths of suffering as a Jewish survivor of the Holocaust, Joseph Shapiro rises to the heights of materialistic success as a new immigrant to New York. Then, however, he falls to new depths of despair after finding himself betrayed by both his wife and his mistress; the hypocritical irony of this predicament is not lost on either the narrator or the reader. Without any clear guide to rescue himself from the dark thicket of confusion in his midlife crisis, Shapiro finds himself drawn by a combination of conditioned predilection and seemingly uncanny coincidences to the ultraorthodox Judaism still preserved in the Meah Shearim neighborhood of Jerusalem. For Joseph Shapiro, life is an eternal struggle of good and evil, symbolized for him by the contrast between the faithful wife of pious orthodoxy and the liberated woman of modern relativism. The ultimate test of his new faith comes in the form of a woman passenger next to whom he happens to sit in an airplane on his first trip to Israel. The temptress assails him with her glib philosophy and her promiscuous caresses. Though he is tried, Joseph Shapiro reaffirms his faith.

To maintain an objective distance from his narrator, however, the author uses the device of a prologue and epilogue. The narrative continues with minor interruptions through the main character's voice until the final few pages, where the authorial presence resumes control to comment obliquely on the content of this short but powerful morality tale. Joseph Shapiro is portrayed as an "angry man" with whom the author disagrees in his conviction that there can be a "final escape from the human dilemma." Singer, in his own voice, however, depicts the "lack of dignity and degradation of modern man, his precarious family life, his greed for luxury and gadgets, his disdain of the old, his obeisance before the young, his blind faith in psychiatry, his ever growing tolerance of crime" as the symptoms of a general spiritual illness. For his part, Singer declares his protest not just against society and its lack of morality but against the Almighty himself for allowing the cruelty and violence of the world to exist. In this context, the declaration of faith by Joseph Shapiro becomes more than a pious reactionary credo. It does not, however, provide answers for the fundamental conundrums of life, nor will it be likely to satisfy either liberals or conservatives, except as lovers of good stories.

ENEMIES: A LOVE STORY

As subjects of literary interest, Singer does not usually favor strong moral characters but, rather, moral weaklings who cannot give up yearning for morality. The man wound up in a web of conflicting relationships typifies Singer's central character, whether in his first-person or third-person narratives. He seems especially obsessed with the problems of a man with three women, each of whom he loves and to none of whom he is willing to commit. Perhaps the best-known version of this plot device is *Enemies: A Love Story* (1972), which succeeded both as a Hollywood film and as a novel.

Herman Broder, the central character, is a Polish Jew living in Brooklyn. His current wife, Yadwiga, is a peasant woman who saved his life by hiding him in a hayloft during the terrible years of World War II. His former wife, Tamara, was shot by the Nazis, and according to eyewitnesses, she perished along with their two children in the horrors of the Holocaust. Yadwiga, formerly the servant to the family, still takes a servile and humble posture before Herman. Though she is willing to convert to Judaism, Herman insists they have only a civil marriage. In fact, their marriage is a legal fiction, since Herman maintains a second dwelling place with his mistress Masha, also a Holocaust survivor, who lives with her aged mother at the other end of the subway line in the Bronx. Together, they are all unforgivably guilty of the sin of having survived "when so many innocent men and women had been martyred."

Obsessed by Masha's sexuality and neurotic intelligence, Herman nurtures his deception by telling Yadwiga that he is a traveling salesman who must spend days or even weeks at a time on the road. Actually, Herman earns his underground income working for a wheeler-dealer American rabbi who is primarily occupied with various real estate deals. Rabbi Lampert "played the stock market, gambled, and raised money for all sorts of charitable causes. He was over six feet tall, had a potbelly, and weighed two hundred and sixty pounds. . . . He ate two-pound steaks, smoked Havana cigars, drank champagne." To keep up appearances, the rabbi contracts to give lectures and write books on Jewish subjects. Herman, the ghostwriter for these projects, uses his traditional European upbringing and philosophical training to maintain the rabbi's learned front.

Unable to abandon Yadwiga, to whom he owes his existence, and unwilling to break with Masha, Herman realizes he is living a lie. Plagued by guilt, he expects any moment to be caught by the authorities and deported to Europe for crimes ranging from tax evasion to bigamy. He avoids anyone who might have known him in the past. "Every human contact was a potential danger to him," since somebody might connect his double identity. In effect, he continues to hide from the world as he did throughout the war. In fact, Herman realizes, all his life he has been alienated from humanity. "He was not a victim of Hitler. He had been a victim long before Hitler's day."

Into this ongoing life of inherent contradiction, Herman's former wife, Tamara, arrives one day as if raised from the dead. Despite everything, she has survived the war. During their years together, Herman had been unfaithful to Tamara and considered her a bothersome nag. Now, however, he desires her all over again. She seems to reaffirm his wish to believe in the immortality of the soul. As if controlled by a force other than his own will, he becomes again intimately involved with Tamara despite his already overly complicated love life. He knows that a psychiatrist or any other outside observer would tell him to decide to settle down with the one woman he truly loves. But Herman cannot decide to settle down. He simultaneously loves all three and perhaps loves none. "As for love, these professionals used the word as if it were capable of clear definition–when no one had yet discovered its true meaning." Herman's problems mount until the edifice of interlocking deceptions comes crashing down. In the end, despite his unworthiness, all three women continue to love him. There is no resolution. Herman simply disappears.

SHADOWS ON THE HUDSON

In *Shadows on the Hudson* (1998), the author covers much of the same ground in greater detail and with more psychological depth. Published in Yiddish between January 1957 and January 1958 in twice-weekly installments in *The Jewish Daily Forward,* the entire novel first appeared in English translation in 1998. It reads as a sort of rough draft for *Enemies: A Love Story,* which was also first published in serial installments in Yiddish in 1966, then translated into English in 1972. Both books deal with European Jewish immigrants in New York City during the early cold war era of the late 1940s. Both novels focus on the tangled personal relationships of characters trying to put together the pieces of a fragmented post-Holocaust reality. The central character of *Shadows on the Hudson,* like the womanizing protagonist of *Enemies: A Love Story,* also juggles intimate relations with three different women while seeking the answers to the eternal questions of his anguished Jewish soul. Hertz Dovid Grein is an earlier version of Herman Broder.

The women in both books are also notably similar. The beautiful and neurotic Masha in *Enemies* is virtually identical to Esther in *Shadows,* except that Esther does not live with her aged mother and her apartment is in Brooklyn, not the Bronx. Yadwiga, the loyal and long-suffering peasant wife of *Enemies,* is a more interesting character than the pathetic Leah of *Shadows,* but Leah also fills the role of the wife who will not divorce her philandering husband no matter how outrageous his betrayals. Although she has not suffered as much as Tamara, the first wife of Herman Broder in *Enemies,* Anna Makaver in *Shadows* is in many ways a more complex character. As the brilliant and talented daughter of the rabbinical capitalist Boris Makaver, Anna rivals Singer's male protagonists by marrying three different men and betraying them with each other. Anna and Tamara both represent the serious intellectual and moral female counterpart to the charismatic but unreliable Hertz/Herman. As if to clue the reader to similarities in the two books, the author even includes one minor character with the same name in both. Yasha Kotik, a Yiddish actor and comedian, plays a cameo part in *Enemies: A Love Story,* where he is described as having "told jokes while digging his own grave and the Nazis had been so amused by him that they let him go." In a more fully developed role in *Shadows on the Hudson,* the same Yasha Kotik is Anna's first husband who returns, as Tamara reappears in *Enemies: A Love Story,* to haunt the other characters and provide bitter wisdom from the depths of his own suffering and moral compromise.

Artistically, *Enemies: A Love Story* is a more effective novel, tightly structured and focused on one central point of view throughout the plot. But the meandering and explorative prose of *Shadows on the Hudson* reveals the author's own consciousness, especially in comparison and contrast. One similarity of both Hertz Dovid Grein and Herman Broder is their double standard for the sexual behavior of men and women. Hertz and Herman have some qualms about their own infidelities, but each seems to accept male promiscuity as an understandable and unremarkable weakness of the species. In reaction to the mere possibility of one of their multiple partners having multiple lovers of her own, however, both Hertz and Herman express moral outrage and condemnation. Hertz Dovid Grein is described as "one of those men who, out of the house, throw off every restraint, but at home long for chasteness." He is unapologetically jealous of his dishrag of a wife and justifies his double standard with citations from the Bible. In the same way, Herman Broder would never forgive Tamara if she had slept with another man—though she swears she did not—during the long years of the war and its aftermath. For Herman to sleep with Tamara is considered merely an incident, but for Masha to have sexual relations with her former husband puts an indelible stain on her character.

The differences between the two protagonists, less pronounced than their similarities, suggest a changing authorial perspective. Hertz Dovid Grein is taller, more handsome, and successful in worldly terms. But Herman Broder has a greater talent for suffering. Even after surviving the war and arriving in America, Herman continues to hide in the hayloft of his own soul. Small, dark, and feckless, he seems to have nothing to offer the women who love him except his shameless need for them. Hertz Dovid Grein is both more capable of introspection as well as better equipped to make his way in the world. Described as a child prodigy who never found any serious focus for his many talents, Hertz seems to succeed at everything without effort. His suffering is all within himself, in twisted paradoxes of self-consciousness philosophical and psychological conundrums. Herman is as much an alienated intellectual as Hertz but seems more at home in the underworld and less connected to normal society. The narrator in

Enemies: A Love Story neither explains nor apologizes for Herman Broder's behavior. At the conclusion of *Shadows on the Hudson,* Hertz Dovid Grein returns to the religion of his ancestors and escapes from the complexities of modern life to the cloistered ultraorthodox community in the Jeruasalem neighborhood of Meah Shearim—exactly as Joseph Shapiro does in *The Penitent.* For Herman Broder, there is no such resolution, however tentative. At the conclusion of *Enemies: A Love Story,* he vanishes as if the earth had swallowed him up.

In *Shadows on the Hudson,* the authorial point of view shifts from chapter to chapter, giving insight to Singer's own preoccupations. Perhaps the central thesis of the novel comes from the mouth of an unnamed Hasidic rebbe whom Boris Makaver follows as his spiritual guide. In contrast to the magnanimous but cowboy-like American rabbi of *Enemies: A Love Story,* Boris is closely connected to the Old World. On Rosh Hashanah, the Jewish New Year, Boris visits the old and ailing zaddik in Williamsburg, just as Boris's father visited the rebbe's own father in Narczew. In a parable, the dying rebbe sums up the mysticism of Singer's work as a whole. Basing his comments on the text "Because of our sins we were exiled from the land," the sage declares, "When the soul is pure, it sees no blemish in the earthly or physical." Only the artificial distinction between body and soul has alienated the minds and hearts of humanity. "For the truly righteous man, a stone is as valuable as a sacred book. There is no distinction between the fruit and the blessing one makes over it." Thus, "Our Father Abraham had no need to climb up to heaven. For him, heaven was on this earth. He even set food before the angels. For in truth, everything is spirit: the tent, the sun, the ox, the dust on men's feet." But, when man imagines a separation between the physical and the spiritual, he creates a false consciousness that alienates him from himself. The only remedy is in sanctification of this mortal world, with its imperfections, "for the physical and the spiritual are one."

Although Singer eschews any declaration of faith, his writing points toward a reality that is either hidden or lost forever from the appearances of modern life. This preoccupation with the lost wholeness of Jewish life is more than an exercise in nostalgia, just as it is less than a call for return to a tradition discredited by history. For Singer, it seems the world of the spirit still exists, if only in his own imagination, and he dedicated his creative life to making that world of the spirit real for his readers.

SHOSHA

In *Shosha* (1978), Singer adopts the first-person point of view of Aaron Greidinger, a struggling young Yiddish writer in Warsaw during the years leading up to World War II. First published in 1974 in serial form in Yiddish under the title *Soul Expeditions,* the novel concerns a small group of friends and acquaintances, with the narrator at the center, who are trying to live normally even while the threat of imminent Nazi invasion looms over them as a certainty of doom. Like the author, Aaron Greidinger recalls with nostalgia his childhood on Krochmalna Street. Unlike the author, the narrator's memories center around a girl, Shosha, with whom he fell in love while still a little boy. With her, he finds a refuge from both the austere religiosity of his own family and the outside courtyard "controlled by rough boys with sticks." Shosha represents the private world of unfettered make-believe. As Shosha and her family move to another building, however, the narrator grows up to become a freethinking member of the Warsaw Yiddish Writer's Club, where he meets the freelance philosopher Dr. Morris Feitelzohn and a supporting cast, including Betty Slonim, a Yiddish actress, and Sam Dreimann, an American millionaire who wants to finance a play with Betty as the star. With Feitelzohn's encouragement, Betty and Sam agree to hire the narrator to provide a script. He admits, with self-deprecating reluctance, that he has been working on a closet drama based on a Hasidic prophetess possessed by a dybbuk. Betty feels sure that this is the vehicle she has been looking for, and Sam immediately bestows the impoverished young writer with a cash advance. Suddenly, he has enough money to live on.

Meanwhile, Aaron continues a furtive love affair with a woman who is active in the Communist Party. Despite Aaron's warnings, Dora plans to smuggle herself into the Soviet Union. Whenever he spends the night with her, Aaron is afraid they will both be arrested by the secret police. As much as he disagrees with her ideologically, however, he finds her compatible sexually. At the same time, Aaron becomes intimately involved with Celia, the intelligent but bored wife of Haiml Chentshiner, who inherited a fortune. Celia and Haiml provide Aaron with unconditional love, which he finds hard to accept. Aaron, inevitably, also falls into a sexual entanglement with Betty Slonim, who says she wants to rescue him from himself. While showing Betty his old neighborhood one day, he is reunited with Shosha, his childhood sweetheart. Strangely, Shosha has remained a child. Neither her mind nor her body has developed normally. Even more strangely, Aaron falls in love all over again and determines to marry her. His friends and family think he has lost his mind. But, as he explains to Betty, Shosha "is the only woman I can trust."

For Aaron, Shosha represents an innocence that can never be lost, a world of sheer imagination that provides Aaron an antidote to the corrosive realties of both the political and the artistic realms of society. Deeply moving even in its inherent lack of verisimilitude, the relationship of the intellectual writer and the illiterate dwarf creates a metaphor of yearning for love as the essential nature of human existence. As Feitelzohn theorizes, according to cabalistic teachings, before the Infinite created the universe, "He first dimmed His light and formed a void. It was only in this void that the Emanation commenced. This divine absence may be the very essence of creation."

But if inchoate longing is the basis of all existence, how can that nameless yearning be reconciled with desire for order and purpose and civilized self-expression? Aaron Greidinger, like the author who created him, does not claim to have any answers. Instead he lives his life of conflicting loves and dreams. Aaron realizes that the "Jews in Poland are trapped" between Adolf Hitler and Joseph Stalin. In his view, neither Communism nor Zionism in any variation offers hope of salvation. His grandiose plans for a triumph of the Yiddish theater also never materialize, while his multiple sexual affairs continue with a mechanism of their own. Only his attachment to the freakish but adored Shosha seems to offer hope of redemption. Only with her can he share his wildest fantasies and dreams as well as his doubts and fears. To Shosha, Aaron suggests that world history is a book that continues even as the page of each day is turned forward. Humanity can "never turn the pages of this world book backward. But everything that had ever been still existed." In this sense, the world of the Polish Jews who perished in the hells of the Holocaust still live, as does Shosha herself, in an eternal life of the soul, not in a hypothetical world-to-come but in an omnipresent here and now that includes all that is past, present, and future.

THE CERTIFICATE

In *The Certificate* (1992), another first-person narrator named David Bendiger serves as the author's fictional alter ego. Like Aaron Greidinger of *Shosha,* David Bendiger is an aspiring writer in Warsaw who feels self-conscious about frequenting the Writer's Club because he has so far published nothing worthy of note. But *The*

Certificate is set in the 1920s, a decade earlier than *Shosha*. While it is already assumed that Poland has no future for its Jewish inhabitants, the central conflicts of *The Certificate* concern the inner struggle of a young man in search of love. The plot closely parallels Singer's autobiographical account of his own experiences. To obtain certificates from the ruling British authorities allowing Jews to enter Palestine, the Zionist organization arranges fictional marriages between wealthy young women and impoverished young men to allow both of them to immigrate quasi-legally. Once in the Holy Land, they can divorce. "We know that it's not exactly right," admits the official Zionist representative Dov Kalmenzohn, "but is it right for England to dictate to half the world and control the certificates that permit us to go back to our own land?"

For his part, David Bendiger is concerned neither with legalities nor ideological justifications. He simply wants to escape from the dead end he is up against. His intended partner in this subterfuge, Minna Ahronson, the pampered daughter of a wealthy Warsaw Jewish family, also is not really a committed Zionist. Minna wants to get away from her overly protective parents and reunite with her real fiancé, a shadowy adventurer who had to leave Poland to evade a military tribunal. The chief obstacle to David and Minna's departure seems to be the bureaucracy that requires numerous documents and permissions before David can obtain an exit visa. To facilitate the process, David hires a "fixer" who may or may not be bilking him. Meanwhile, David pursues half-hearted love affairs with Edusha, the daughter of his Communist landlady, and with Sonya, a poor shop assistant he knows from the provinces.

Miss Minna, as the narrator calls her even after their wedding ceremony, evolves into the central figure of the book. Her beloved fiancé marries another woman. Her father loses his fortune. David Bendiger tries to propose turning their fictive marriage into a real marriage, but neither of them can suspend his or her disbelief. Minna's life seems to unravel in utter despair. Comparing *The Certificate* to the events in *Love and Exile,* the novel closely follows the author's own experience, except that the woman he had planned to marry was pregnant with her former lover's child. In the novel, Minna seeks out her former lover and becomes part of a ménage à trois, even agreeing to become the governess to the stepchild of his wealthy new wife in order to remain somehow connected to him. She and David Bendiger erase their fictive marriage with a real divorce. The certificate to emigrate never materializes. Everything and everyone remains fixed in a kind of suspended animation, neither quite living nor yet really dead. Well-educated, sensitive, elegant, and utterly doomed, Minna has become alienated from her Jewishness as well as from humanity, the embodiment of a soul in limbo. For his part, David Bendiger ends as he begins, hanging by his fingernails to a tenuous existence in a Warsaw that is both a sophisticated European capital and a graveyard of history.

MESHUGAH

In *Meshugah* (1994), Singer returns to Aaron Greidinger, but the plot is now set in the post-Holocaust world of Jewish survivors. Again, the central figure is not the narrator but a woman he both loves and loathes. Unlike Singer's other heroines, however, Miriam holds the upper hand in her relations with the men in the book. The story begins one day when Max Aberdam, "the Warsaw patron of painters and writers, the well known glutton, guzzler, womanizer," appears almost like a ghost rising from the grave in the office of the Yiddish newspaper where Aaron works. The year is 1952, and the narrator had assumed his old friend perished during the war. But it seems, anything is possible in a world that has turned, as Max declares, meshugah, crazy.

The plot develops gradually, with Max Aberdam leading the narrator into an interlocking labyrinth of survivors, mostly elderly women. Max serves these aging widows as both investment adviser and male companion, delivering their dividend checks in person, eating their heavy old-fashioned cooking, and sometimes sharing their beds. One of these women, otherwise indistinguishable from the rest, is Max's wife, Priva. Eventually, however, it becomes clear that the real focus of the action is a much younger woman, also a survivor, who is both Max's lover and surrogate daughter. Twenty years younger than the narrator and forty years younger than Max, Miriam becomes Aaron's lover as well; she is also still married to an estranged husband, Stanley. Presenting herself as the narrator's most loyal reader, Miriam casts a spell of seductive enchantment. When she proposes that he and Max should both be her husbands, though she makes clear from the start that the narrator must play second fiddle to the primal father figure, Aaron agrees almost as if he has been hypnotized by her allure. The spell is broken, however, when her still jealous husband, Stanley, wildly waving a loaded revolver, bursts in and discovers Miriam and Aaron in bed together.

Part saint and part villain, Miriam seems like a stereotype of Otto Weininger's misogynist definition of The Feminine: "a creature without ethics, without memory or logic, the purveyor of sex, the affirmation of materiality, the denial of the spirit." Yet, she is devoted to Max and nurses him through his last years of fatal illness with loving care. She is also the embodiment of the lost world the narrator Aaron Greidinger wishes to re-create through his writing. She becomes his creative muse. If the book romps through scenes of farcical comedy, the underlying tone is deeply disturbing. Unlike other Singer characters who suffer from survivors'

guilt, Miriam may have committed real crimes. It is alleged, but not quite proven, that she not only used her sexual favors to help her through the nightmare of the war years but that she became a Nazi collaborator.

Serialized in Yiddish from April 1981 to February 1983 under the title *Lost Souls* and published posthumously in 1994 in English, *Meshugah* is creative and unsettling. Miriam recalls the heroine of one of Singer's most haunting stories, "The Cafeteria." Both Miriam in the novel and Esther in the short story are still young and attractive women who have returned from the depths of hell unable to impart the full range of their suffering. The derangement of Esther's point of view is focused on a nightmare vision of Hitler and his henchmen returning to a Broadway cafeteria in the middle of the night. In contrast, *Meshugah* makes readers wonder if even the so-called rational and sane perspective can be defined as such. In an exploratory and open-ended style, the author pushes the limits of his own imagination to pose questions about loyalty and betrayal, good and evil, love and hate that he cannot answer. Miriam seems more alive than Esther, yet she is perhaps less successful as a representation of a woman of eternal sorrows. "The Cafeteria" is tightly constructed and leaves the reader with the realization that the unimaginable actuality of the Holocaust will always defy any rational explanation, that the insanity of human evil can never be defined in sane language.

SCUM AND THE KING OF THE FIELDS

In *Scum* (1991) and *The King of the Fields* (1988), Singer continues to invent fictions that reflect his puzzlement and wonder. In *Scum,* the author makes his strongest statement on the nature of fatalism. Set in Warsaw in 1906, the plot revolves around a Polish Jew returning from Argentina, where he has made his fortune. Cut in the mold of Singer's fast-talking wheeler-dealers, Max Barabander is rich, strong, and still good-looking at forty-seven. In his heyday, he once won a bet that he could "eat three dozen eggs and drink twelve bottles of beer." And "what he could do with women no one, except the women involved, would believe." A former thief and denizen of the underworld, Max had become a respectable businessman and member of the Buenos Aires community. But all is not well with him. Since the sudden death of his only son, Arturo, the fabric of his life has begun to unravel. In a word, he has become impotent. His fabled sexual prowess has vanished. He thinks constantly of death, and he is afraid to be alone for even an hour. The real purpose for his return to Poland is to find a woman who will rejuvenate him.

Driven to compulsive activity, Max works his way into one situation after another, with a glib response and an open wallet to deal with any eventuality. With unlimited funds at his disposal, Max can gain the attention of anyone he wishes to impress, from the daughter of a poor rabbi to the queen of the Warsaw underworld. But even though Max is a brutal exploiter who invents lies as easily as he breathes, he is also, at heart, a suffering Jew who wishes to do good deeds and help others. Capable of any crime, he still carries a guilty conscience in his subconscious mind, just below the surface of his primal lust and fear. Blond, blue-eyed, and physically powerful, he seems like an atypical Jew, yet Max remains quintessentially Jewish. He cannot write a letter without errors, but he is an avid reader of the Yiddish press and is fluent in both Polish and Russian. Pathetic and disgusting as he can be, it is almost impossible not to like him. On a whirlwind tour of the Warsaw of his childhood, the author provides a gripping tale of a man who cannot give up hope of redemption in this world. Even in the best of times, however, Max has been haunted by one recurring nightmare. For years, he has awakened in the middle of the night from a dream that he is locked up in the Warsaw prison known as the

Arsenal. All the complicated circumstances of the plot combine to make Max's nightmare come true. Hypothetically, Max could have made choices to evade the inevitable. But Max did not make those choices simply because he is Max.

A similar fatalism pervades *King of the Fields,* but here the terror is in the historical reality of tenth-century Poland, populated by characters combining the primitive qualities of Beowulf and the comic possibilities of Yiddish theater. In this context, rape, pillage, and violent conquest are the norm. The fascination of the book is in the author's deft irony, portraying the worst of the barbarians as strangely human and the few redeeming characters as equally limited by circumstances beyond their control. Fatalism is assumed as reality, Singer implies. Free choice is possible, but only through the human miracle of dreams, hopes, and stifled spiritual aspirations. Although he is careful to avoid esoteric analyses or mystical exegeses, Singer acknowledges that he hopes and prays for the redemption of his characters, and he insists that in "literature, as in our dreams, death does not exist."

After he received the Nobel Prize in 1978, Singer published more books for English-language readers than he did during the years leading up to that prize. Novels in translation and children's stories have been published posthumously in various editions. Critical studies have worked toward evaluating his whole contribution. A psychoanalytical biography written by Janet Hadda (1997) went out of print. Memoirs such as Israel Zamir's *Journey to My Father, Isaac Bashevis Singer* (1995) and Dvorah Telushkin's *Master of Dreams: A Memoir of Isaac Bashevis Singer* (1997) offer glimpses into the author's personality. But an authoritative critical biography requires a scholar who can combine the knowledge of Yiddish with the insights of world literature. One of a kind, as are all great authors, Isaac Bashevis Singer speaks to readers in the unique language he created for his expression, through the most specific and particular details, of the most universal truths. In his hands, Yiddish became "the wise and humble language of us all, the idiom of frightened and hopeful humanity."

Selected Bibliography

WORKS OF ISAAC BASHEVIS SINGER

NOVELS AND SHORT STORIES

Satan in Goray. Translated by Jacob Sloan. Warsaw, 1935; New York: Noonday, 1955.

The Family Moskat. Translated by A. H. Gross. New York: Knopf, 1950.

Gimpel the Fool, and Other Stories. Translated by Saul Bellow, Isaac Rosenfeld, and others. New York: Noonday, 1957.

The Magician of Lublin. Translated by Elaine Gottlieb and Joseph Singer. New York: Noonday, 1960.

The Spinoza of Market Street. Translated by Martha Glicklich and others. New York: Farrar, Straus and Cudahy, 1961.

The Slave: A Novel. Translated by the author and Cecil Hemley. New York: Noonday, 1962.

Short Friday, and Other Stories. Translated by Joseph Singer, Roger Klein, and others. New York: Farrar, Straus and Giroux, 1964.

The Manor. Translated by Joseph Singer and Elaine Gottlieb. New York: Farrar, Straus and Giroux, 1967.

The Séance, and Other Stories. Translated by Roger H. Klein, Cecil Hemley, and others. New York: Farrar, Straus and Giroux, 1968.

The Estate. Translated by Elaine Gottlieb and Joseph Singer. New York: Farrar, Straus and Giroux, 1969.

A Friend of Kafka, and Other Stories. Translated by the author and others. New York: Farrar, Straus and Giroux, 1970.

Enemies: A Love Story. Translated by Aliza Shevrin and Elizabeth Shub. New York: Farrar, Straus and Giroux, 1972.

A Crown of Feathers, and Other Stories. Translated by the author and others. New York: Farrar, Straus and Giroux, 1973.

Passions, and Other Stories. Translated by the author and others. New York: Farrar, Straus and Giroux, 1975.

Shosha. Translated by Joseph Singer and Dvorah Menashe. New York: Farrar, Straus and Giroux, 1978.

Old Love. New York: Farrar, Straus and Giroux, 1979.

The Penitent. Translated by Joseph Singer. New York: Farrar, Straus and Giroux, 1983.

The Image, and Other Stories. New York: Farrar, Straus and Giroux, 1985.

The Death of Methuselah, and Other Stories. New York: Farrar, Straus and Giroux, 1988.

The King of the Fields. Translated by the author. New York: Farrar, Straus and Giroux, 1988.

Scum. Translated by Rosaline Dukalsky Schwartz. New York: Farrar, Straus and Giroux, 1991.

The Certificate. Translated by Leonard Wolf. New York: Farrar, Straus and Giroux, 1992.

Meshugah. Translated by the author and Nili Wachtel. New York: Farrar, Straus and Giroux, 1994.

Shadows on the Hudson. Translated by Joseph Sherman. New York: Farrar, Straus and Giroux, 1998.

More Stories from My Father's Court. Translated by Curt Leviant. New York: Farrar, Straus and Giroux, 2000.

MEMOIRS

In My Father's Court. Translated by Channah Kleinerman-Goldstein and others. New York: Farrar, Straus and Giroux, 1966.

Love and Exile. Translated by Joseph Singer. Garden City, N.Y.: Doubleday, 1984. Reprinted as *Love and Exile: An Autobiographical Trilogy.* New York: Noonday, 1997.

CHILDREN'S STORIES

Mazel and Shlimazel; or, The Milk of a Lioness. Illustrated by Margot Zemach. New York: Farrar, Straus and Giroux, 1966.

The Fearsome Inn. Illustrated by Nonny Hogrogian. New York: Scribner, 1967.

When Schlemiel Went to Warsaw, and Other Stories. Illustrated by Margot Zemach. New York: Farrar, Straus and Giroux, 1968.

Elijah the Slave: A Hebrew Legend Retold by Isaac Bashevis Singer. Illustrated by Antonio Frasconi. New York: Farrar, Straus and Giroux, 1970.

Joseph and Koza; or, The Sacrifice to the Vistula. Illustrated by Symeon Shimin. New York: Farrar, Straus and Giroux, 1970.

Alone in the Wild Forest. Illustrated by Margot Zemach. New York: Farrar, Straus and Giroux, 1971.

The Topsy-Turvy Emperor of China. Illustrated by William Pène Du Bois. Translated by J. Singer and Elizabeth Shub. New York: Harper & Row, 1971.

The Wicked City. Illustrated by Leonard Everett Fisher. New York: Farrar, Straus and Giroux, 1972.

The Fools of Chelm and Their History. Illustrated by Uri Shulevitz. New York: Farrar, Straus and Giroux, 1973.

Why Noah Chose the Dove. Illustrated by Eric Carle. New York: Farrar, Straus and Giroux, 1974.

A Tale of Three Wishes. Illustrated by Irene Lieblich. New York: Farrar, Straus and Giroux, 1975.

Naftali the Storyteller and His Horse, Sus, and Other Stories. Illustrated by Margot Zemach. New York: Farrar, Straus and Giroux, 1976.

The Power of Light: Eight Stories for Hanukkah. Illustrated by Irene Lieblich. New York: Farrar, Straus and Giroux, 1980.

The Golem. Illustrated by Uri Shulevitz. New York: Farrar, Straus and Giroux, 1982.

COLLECTED WORKS

The Collected Stories of Isaac Bashevis Singer. New York: Farrar, Straus and Giroux, 1982.

Stories for Children. New York: Farrar, Straus and Giroux, 1984.

OTHER WORKS

Nobel Lecture. New York: Farrar, Straus and Giroux, 1979.

CRITICAL AND BIOGRAPHICAL STUDIES

Allentuck, Marcia, ed. *The Achievement of Isaac Bashevis Singer.* Carbondale: Southern Illinois University Press, 1969.

Allison, Alida. *Isaac Bashevis Singer: Children's Stories and Memoirs.* New York: Twayne, 1996.

Biletzky, Israel Ch. *God, Jew, Satan in the Works of Isaac Bashevis-Singer.* Lanham, Md.: University Press of America, 1995.

Buchen, Irving H. *Isaac Bashevis Singer and the Eternal Past.* New York: New York University Press, 1968.

Farrell, Grace, ed. *Critical Essays on Isaac Bashevis Singer.* New York: G. K. Hall, 1996.

Gibbons, Frances Vargas. *Transgression and Self-Punishment in Isaac Bashevis Singer's Searches.* New York: Peter Lang, 1995.

Goran, Lester. *The Bright Streets of Surfside: The Memoir of a Friendship with Isaac Bashevis Singer.* Kent, Ohio: Kent State University Press, 1994.

Hadda, Janet. *Isaac Bashevis Singer: A Life.* New York: Oxford University Press, 1997.

Kazin, Alfred. *Bright Book of Life: American Novelists and Storytellers from Hemingway to Mailer.* Boston: Little, Brown, 1973.

Kresh, Paul. *Isaac Bashevis Singer: The Magician of West 86th Street.* New York: Dial, 1979.

Madison, Charles A. *Yiddish Literature: Its Scope and Major Writers.* New York: Ungar, 1968.

Malin, Irving. *Isaac Bashevis Singer.* New York: Ungar, 1972.

————, ed. *Critical Views of Isaac Bashevis Singer.* New York: New York University Press, 1969.

Perl, Lila. *Isaac Bashevis Singer: The Life of a Storyteller.* Illustrated by Donna Ruff. Philadelphia: Jewish Publication Society, 1994.

Ran-Moseley, Faye. *The Tragicomic Passion: A History and Analysis of Tragicomedy and Tragicomic Characterization in Drama, Film, and Literature.* New York: Lang, 1994.

Telushkin, Dvorah. *Master of Dreams: A Memoir of Isaac Bashevis Singer.* New York: Morrow, 1997.

Tuszyanska, Agata. *Lost Landscapes: In Search of Isaac Bashevis Singer and the Jews of Poland.* Translated from the Polish by Madeline G. Levine. New York: William Morrow, 1998.

Wirth-Nesher, Hana. *City Codes: Reading the Modern Urban Novel.* New York: Cambridge University Press, 1996.

Zamir, Israel. *Journey to My Father, Isaac Bashevis Singer.* Translated by Barbara Harshav. New York: Arcade, 1995.

INTERVIEWS

Singer, Isaac Bashevis, and Richard Burgin. *Conversations with Isaac Bashevis Singer.* New York: Farrar, Straus and Giroux, 1986.

FILMS, PLAYS, AND OPERAS BASED ON THE WORKS OF ISAAC BASHEVIS SINGER

The Mirror. Adapted for the stage. Produced in New Haven, Conn., 1973.

Schlemiel the First. Produced in New Haven, Conn., 1974.

Yentl, the Yeshiva Boy. Adapted for the stage with Leah Napolin. Produced in New York City on Broadway, 1974.

The Magician of Lublin. Film starring Alan Arkin, produced by Mehahem Golan and Yoram Globus, directed by Mehahem Golan. N. F. Geria III, 1978.

Teibele and Her Demon. Adapted for the stage with Eve Friedman. Produced in Minneapolis at Guthrie Theatre, 1978.

Gimpel the Fool. Adapted for the stage by David Schechter. Produced by the Bakery Theater Cooperative of New York City, 1982.

Yentl. Film starring Barbra Streisand, directed and produced by Barbra Streisand. United Artists, 1983.

A Play for the Devil. Adaptation for the stage of "The Unseen." Produced in New York City at Folksbiene Theatre, 1984.

Enemies: A Love Story. Film by Paul Mazursky and Roger L. Simon. Twentieth Century Fox, 1989.

—*JAMES A. LEWIN*

Nathanael West

1903–1940

NATHANAEL WEST IS the pseudonym of Nathan Weinstein and a byword for satiric genius. West's reputation rests on four short and devastatingly funny, bleakly surrealist novels: *The Dream Life of Balso Snell* (1931), a virtuoso parody of the cult of high modernism; *Miss Lonelyhearts* (1933); *A Cool Million* (1934); and *The Day of the Locust* (1939), all anticapitalist, antifascist satires. West died, however, before his work met with critical acclaim. "Somehow or other I seem to have slipped in between all the 'schools,'" he confided to F. Scott Fitzgerald in 1939: "My books meet no needs except my own, their circulation is practically private and I'm lucky to be published." In his 1934 preface to a reissue of *The Great Gatsby,* Fitzgerald identified West as a young writer indeed "being harmed . . . for lack of a public." Newspaper reports of the motor accident that killed West in fact focused mainly on the apparently more significant loss to the world of his wife, Eileen, the famous model for Ruth McKenney's highly successful *New Yorker* sketches, 1938 novel, and later play, *My Sister Eileen.* But while he struggled for wider public recognition, West was during his lifetime a much admired and internationally respected "writers' writer." In American circles Fitzgerald considered him "a potential leader in the field of prose fiction," and he was a close friend and colleague to William Carlos Williams, with whom he coedited *Contact* magazine and in whose epic experimental poem *Paterson* appear choice moments from West's life; he was lifelong friend to the writer S. J. Perelman (his brother-in-law); and he was greatly admired by Edmund Wilson. West was equally *au fait* with the European avant-garde—he was befriended, for example, by the French surrealist Philippe Soupault, and he met Max Ernst and Louis Aragon on a formative trip to Paris in 1926; he also knew the exiled German dadaist George Grosz and contributed to his short-lived magazine, *Americana.* As did many of his contemporaries, West served in Hollywood as a screenwriter, which gave him a second education in the production of fantasy and escapism for mass consumption, providing the material for his last novel, *The Day of the Locust* (a satire on the Hollywood dream factory), and eventually enabling, as well, some financial stability to support his art.

West's writing eluded widespread acclaim during his lifetime because it defied ready critical categorization. "While many people whose opinion I respect are full of sincere praise," he wrote to Edmund Wilson in 1939, "the book reviewers disagree, even going so far as to attack the people who do praise my books, and the public is completely apathetic." The critical antagonisms over his work have only escalated and further polarized in the decades following his death. For some time orthodox criticism was keen to interpret West as an aesthete turned absurdist, a misanthrope turned nihilist, whose final novel, *The Day of the Locust,* marks a turn away from his more tightly constructed earlier (and equally bleak and savage) works. Above all West and his work were characterized as "apolitical." But like so many of his avant-garde heroes, he issued two or three terse manifestos, and these are helpful in understanding his position among the critics through the decades: "Through the Hole in the Mundane Millstone"

(1931), "Some Notes on Violence" (1932), and "Some Notes on Miss L." (1933).

Inspired by Edgar Allan Poe and Charles Baudelaire and despising the "muddle-class" realism of Sinclair Lewis and Theodore Dreiser, West championed the formally experimental, short "lyric novel," which he recognized as a potently "distinct form" particularly appropriate for American use. "Forget the epic, the master work," he advises in "Some Notes on Miss L.," a defense of his second novel, *Miss Lonelyhearts:*

> In America fortunes do not accumulate, the soil does not grow, families have no history. Leave slow growth to the book reviewers, you only have time to explode. Remember William Carlos Williams' description of the pioneer women who shot their children against the wilderness like cannonballs. Do the same with your novels.

In West's writing European modernism combusts with the violence of the American comic strip, a technique perfected in *Miss Lonelyhearts.* In "Some Notes on Miss L." he explains, "each chapter instead of going forward in time, also goes backward, forward, up and down in space like a picture. Violent images are used to illustrate commonplace events. Violent acts are left almost bald."

West wrote "Though the Hole in the Mundane Millstone" as an advertisement for his debut novel, *The Dream Life of Balso Snell,* a fast-moving, scatological, and collagistic narrative, the fruit of his formative trip to the Parisian avant-garde. The novel tells the story of the protagonist Balso's penetration and tour of the Trojan horse, which, according to the advertisement, he finds to be "inhabited solely by authors in search of an audience" whose numerous "tales are elephantine close-ups of various literary positions and their technical methods." West's advertisement boasts his surpassing Kurt Schwitters' definition, "Tout ce'que l'artiste crache, c'est l'art," which sounds even more

graphic in the original alliterative, onomatopoeic German—"Alles was ein Künstler spuckt ist Künst"—but perhaps less so translated into English: "Everything that the artist expectorates [or spits or spews or gobs up] is art." As well as pointing out the influence of the maverick dadaist Schwitters, West's advertisement also makes clear his debt to French avant-garde sources, declaring himself "much like Guillaume Apollinaire, Jarry, Ribemont-Dessaignes, Raymond Roussel, and certain of the surrealistes."

Just as his own joyous pretensions as aesthete and connoisseur are simultaneously celebrated and lampooned in the bookplate his friend Perelman designed for him—which sports a motto from Goethe, "Do I love what others love?"—so West's fantastic parodic strategies in *The Dream Life of Balso Snell* and his lampooning of the Parisian art scene in the short story "The Impostor" (posthumously published in *The New Yorker*) suggest a gloriously well-qualified ambivalence toward high modernist aesthetics. His contributions to the magazine *Americana,* under the sobriquet of "the laughing morticians of the present," may have sharpened his satiric vision, but West's achievement lies primarily in adapting European avant-garde techniques to American traditions for distinctively American use, as emphasized by the task he and William Carlos Williams defined for their literary magazine, *Contact:* "to cut a trail through the American jungle without the use of a European compass." West told Williams in 1932, however, that their work would be "not only in but against the American grain and yet in idiomatic pain." The all-American rags-to-riches fantasies of Horatio Alger became his target in his third novel, the antifascist satire *A Cool Million,* whose hero literally falls apart in his attempt to become president. Toothless, eyeless, thumbless, bald, and one-legged, Lemuel Pitkin eventually dies a fascist martyr. During one episode American consumerism is memorably figured as "a surfeit of shoddy" in the scathing invective of Chief Satinpenny, who scalps Pitkin and leaves a young brave to loot his "bloody head of its store teeth and glass eye." In such scenes, West brings the American dream face to face with the Cabaret Voltaire, and Mark Twain goes Dada.

In "Some Notes on Violence," West defends the excessive violence in his work as an accurate reflection of American experience:

> In America violence is idiomatic. Read our newspapers. To make the front page a murderer has to use his imagination, he also has to use a particularly hideous instrument. Take this morning's paper: FATHER CUTS SON'S THROAT IN BASEBALL ARGUMENT. It appears on an inside page. To make the first page, he should have killed three sons and with a baseball bat instead of a knife. Only liberality and symmetry could have made this daily occurrence interesting.

This position earned him the postwar reputation of nihilist, which was enhanced by his writing's refusal of psychological depth. In keeping with the avant-garde experimentalism he admired, West's characters are grotesquely dehumanized and semi-reified, often resembling "mechanical drawing." Earle Shoop, the stock cowboy in *The Day of the Locust,* for example, has "a two-dimensional face that a talented child might have drawn with a ruler and a compass." Another character is described as "a badly made automaton." West nevertheless mined psychology as mythic resource:

> Psychology has nothing to do with reality nor should it be used as motivation. The novelist is no longer a psychologist. Psychology can be something much more important. The great body of case histories can be used in the way the ancient writers used their myths. Freud is your Bullfinch; you cannot learn from him.

This sort of narrative strategy apparently baffled a generation of 1950s critics who looked in vain for depth of character and signs of

spiritual redemption and whose fears culminated in W. H. Auden's lasting diagnosis of "West's Disease." "Nathanael West is not, strictly speaking, a novelist," Auden finds, or even a satirist:

> There are many admirable and extremely funny satirical passages in his books, but West is not a satirist. Satire presupposes conscience and reason as the judges between the true and the false, the moral and the immoral, to which it appeals, but for West these faculties are themselves the creators of unreality. . . .

> All his main characters suffer from the same spiritual disease which, in honor of the man who devoted his life to studying it, we may call West's Disease. This is a disease of consciousness which renders it incapable of converting wishes into desires. . . .

> There have, no doubt, always been cases of West's Disease, but the chances of infection in a democratic and mechanized society like our own are much greater than in the more static and poorer societies of earlier times.

Norman Podhoretz, in an essay of 1957, typifies cold war criticism of West in finding his humor "profoundly unpolitical" and West himself so "anti-'radical'" as to be "almost un-American" (a novel use of the term, in the era of Senator Joseph McCarthy). In assessing his uneasy relationship with his Jewish background, critics have tended either to denounce him as self-hating or, more constructively, to attempt to read West's work in relation to Jewish prophetic traditions.

West himself thought of his work as "moral satire," and although he was politically sympathetic with the left (he attended meetings of the John Reed Club, for example, but was never a member of the Communist Party), his writing was in fact deplored by his Communist friends, who were all by the mid-1930s exponents of socialist realism, as the Marxist writer Michael Gold explains: "His writing seemed to me symbolic rather than realistic and that was, to me, the supreme crime." West certainly recognized he was doomed to be misunderstood by his contemporaries on the left and right alike. "The radical press, although I consider myself on their side, doesn't like my particular kind of joking, and think it even Fascist sometimes," he wrote in letters to his friends, "and the literature boys whom I detest, detest me in turn. The high brow press finds that I avoid the big significant things and the lending library touts in the daily press think me shocking."

Later interpretations from such critics as Rita Barnard and Matthew Roberts have moved beyond the previous despondency over West's bleak and absurd vision and dark irony to offer more sophisticated readings of his negative critique of consumerism and the culture industry. There has been a similar shift in feminist criticism of West. Accusations of misogyny, following on from Leslie A. Fiedler, characterized initial feminist responses to West's depiction of violence or violent intent toward women, particularly his portrayal of Faye Greener in *The Day of the Locust*: "Her self-sufficiency made him squirm and the desire to break its smooth surface with a blow, or at least a sudden obscene gesture, became irresistible." West's brilliantly subversive accounts of cross-dressers, homosexuals, and androgynes, encapsulated for many critics by the textual masquerade of the man known only as "Miss Lonelyhearts," have met with the far-reaching disapproval of Sandra M. Gilbert and Susan Gubar, who place West in the company of T. S. Eliot, D. H. Lawrence, Ernest Hemingway, and William Faulkner—all literary men who "record their horror at a battle they fear men are losing." West and the other male modernists are for Gilbert and Gubar misogynist and homophobic. Whereas "literary women generally persisted in seeking an ontological 'wild free thing,' a third sex beyond gender," these men "continued for the most part to express anxieties about . . . sex change in texts focusing on transvestism and transsexualism." Gilbert and Gubar simplistically place West's work among male-authored texts in affinity with Oswald Spengler's protofascist, polemical vision, texts that "in various ways express a nausea associated with the blurring of gender boundaries." Later readings have offered more positive explorations of West's disruption of gender boundaries and categories and even an apologia for his apparent misogyny.

The rocky trajectory of West's critical reception might be summarized as occurring in three phases: West's work was misunderstood and rejected in the 1930s largely because of the dogmatic influence of the Soviet enforcement of socialist realism to which West's left-wing friends had converted; it was further traduced as absurd and nihilistic by American cold war criticism in the 1950s and after; and later it was condemned as misogynist by a fundamentalist feminism. But in all this time there have been writers and critics who have understood West's originality, his witting and sophisticated position within the avant-garde tradition he worshiped, perpetuated, and, in turn, shaped. The most illuminating criticism on West has been that which explores his engagement with European and American dadaism and surrealism. There has also been an increasingly rich seam of criticism exploring his film work, his Hollywood experiences and material, as well as the various film adaptations of his work. More important, West's brief oeuvre has been recognized for its enormous effect on later twentieth-century writers, including Carson McCullers, Flannery O'Connor, Joseph Heller, Saul Bellow, Thomas Pynchon, and Ishmael Reed. Soupault's 1946 French edition of *Miss Lonelyhearts* (translated by Marcelle Sibon) is also considered a significant landmark in European postwar fiction. While critics such as Malgorzata Sikora have frequently picked up on the continuities with West in O'Connor's gothic grotesque or in the comedic Jewish American writing of Heller, there has been little response to the acknowledgment by the African American writer Ishmael

Reed of West as his primary, most formative, literary influence.

West's work no longer languishes out of print. Picador and Penguin have reprinted the novels in the United Kingdom, and Sacvan Bercovitch's Library of America edition of West's novels offers an extensive selection of his other writings, including short stories, scripts, and letters, and provides a welcome opportunity for renewed critical interest.

LIFE

In *Novels and Other Writings,* Bercovitch provides a helpful and informative chronology of West's life, but the fullest and most intelligent account remains Jay Martin's excellent critical biography, *Nathanael West: The Art of His Life* (1970). Prior to this, West's friend, the writer Josephine Herbst, published in 1954 a fictionalized portrait of West titled "Hunter of Doves." Herbst's story is a melancholic memoir veiled in a third-person account of a rather jaded woman's recollections of "a dead man, Alec Barber," and "the dead author, Noel Bartram," her nom à clef for Weinstein/West. Barber/Bartram is a friend whose "cipher concealed a further enigma" and who "had triply buried himself and behind his several masks had slipped on the final mask that dying bestowed." In her later, and brief, straight memoir, "Nathanael West" (1961), Herbst finds the past just as impenetrable, expressing disquiet at the then-orthodox views on West (she is talking of James F. Light in particular) which tend

> to reflect more of the climate of the '50s than of the era in which West lived, felt, created. The penitents of that earlier decade have poured lava over some of the living elements which should once again be seen in their original verdure to make sense of the time and the place. . . . To see what West used and discarded one must return to the *Then* and strip away the *Now.*

More refreshing, and probably the most lava-free (and also the funniest and most succinct) introduction to West's person and personality, it should be acknowledged, is S. J. Perelman's magnificent surrealist portrait of his friend, which appeared in *Contempo* magazine, endorsing the publication of *Miss Lonelyhearts:*

> Picture to yourself a ruddy-cheeked, stocky sort of chap, dressed in loose tweeds, a stubby briar in his teeth, with a firm yet humorous mouth, generous to a fault, everready for a flagon of nut-brown ale with his cronies, possessing the courage of a lion and the tenderness of a woman, an intellectual vagabond, a connoisseur of first editions, fine wines, and beautiful women, well above six feet in height and distinguished for his pallor, a dweller in the world of books, his keen grey eyes belying the sensual lip, equally at home browsing through the bookstalls along the Paris quais and rubbing elbows in the smart literary salons of the Faubourg St. Honore, a rigid abstainer and non-smoker, living entirely on dehydrated fruits, cereals, and nuts, rarely leaving his monastic cell, an intimate of Cocteau, Picasso, Joyce and Lincoln Kirstein, a dead shot, a past master of the foils, dictating his novels, plays, poems, short stories, epigrams, aphorisms, and sayings to a corps of secretaries at lightning speed, an expert judge of horseflesh, the owner of a model farm equipped with the latest dairy devices—a man as sharp as a razor, as dull as a hoe, as clean as a whistle, as tough as nails, as white as snow, as black as the raven's wing, and as poor as Job. A man kind and captious, sweet and sour, fat and thin, tall and short, racked with fever, plagued by the locust, beset by witches, hagridden, cross-grained, a fun-loving, serious-minded dreamer, visionary and slippered pantaloon. Picture to yourself such a man, I say, and you won't have the faintest idea of Nathanael West.

There are, however, many grains of truth in Perelman's celebration of his friend's predilections for the life of an American flaneur-writer in Paris; and from early youth, West was indeed steeped in the hyper-aesthetics and sartorial elegance of a fin de siècle bibliophile and sensualist. He was also an enthusiastic hunter and a "damned good shot," according to William Faulkner (quoted in an article by William White), and he did in fact at one time have a share in a farm.

It comes as no surprise to learn of West's experimentation with a number of different names and personae before settling on Nathanael West. Nicknamed "Pep" and sometimes known as Nathaniel, he adopted various permutations of his family names, the most extravagant of which was Nathaniel Von Wallenstein Weinstein. He was born Nathan Weinstein on October 17, 1903, into a Russian Jewish immigrant family in New York. His parents, Anna Wallenstein Weinstein and Max Weinstein, were married in May 1902, and Nathan was their first child. His father was a wealthy man in the construction and real estate business, but his fortune was largely wiped out in the crash of 1929. West took advantage of his family's wealth, when they had it, to educate himself in literature and art. He was well read in classical and contemporary literature and was an enthusiastic collector of fine books and avant-garde "little magazines" such as transition, The Egoist, and The Criterion. He loved the work of the yellow period and was particularly fond of Oscar Wilde and Walter Pater, Baudelaire, Arthur Rimbaud, Paul Verlaine, as well as Alfred Jarry and J. K. Huysmans. He was very familiar with modernist and contemporary writing—Guillaume Apollinaire, James Joyce, Gertrude Stein, Ezra Pound, William Carlos Williams, Wallace Stevens, Eliot, and James Russell Lowell—and was particularly influenced by Fitzgerald. He was also very knowledgeable about modern visual arts.

But although his self-education shows impeccable avant-garde credentials, his official academic career, it is recorded, was fraudulent (in itself another impeccable avant-garde credential). In 1922 he transferred from Tufts College to Brown University using the superior grades of another student also called Nathan

Weinstein: "Having failed to graduate from high school or to pass any courses at Tufts," Martin notes, "he would arrive in Providence with a year and a half advanced standing . . . with 57 credits in scientific subjects, German, and economics," and further, he passed himself off as a veteran of the United States Navy. At Brown he met and befriended S. J. Perelman. In the same year he published some accomplished Beardsleyesque cartoons in Brown's humor magazine, The Brown Jug, and in 1923, under the name of Nathaniel v. W. Weinstein, he published the hoax essay "Euripides—A Playwright" in Casements, the university magazine in which he later published some apprentice poems. As a Jew he was excluded from the university's fraternities, and so he founded the "Hanseatic League," a society satirically named after the Baltic provinces where his ancestors had flourished until the tsarist oppression of the 1880s. His biographer notes: "West regarded himself and his friends as similar to the free towns, centers of enlightenment and modernism set in the midst of the medieval barbarism of the Bacchanalian sensualists." Martin goes on to characterize the esoteric interests and activities, the mystical, ritual, and magical obsessions of this self-styled intellectual elite, as West's "dadaist willingness to experiment with the absurd." His sexual adventurism led him to contract gonorrhea, the treatment for which left him with recurrent prostate problems. Another anecdote from West's college days encapsulates the divide between style and politics that later played out in critical responses to his work: West claimed to have taken part in a violent coal strike in the 1920s when he was still a student. Martin casts doubt on this tale of political activism, saying, "The truth was his car broke down [on the way back from a football game in Pennsylvania] near a coal town . . . and while waiting for it to be repaired he . . . briefly eyed the idle miners, then bought hunting clothes, boots, and buffalo plaid shirts in the local general store. The fashion they thus began at Brown was interest not in labor problems but in clothes, for the whole college began to imitate them and the rural fashion held brief sway in the Ivy League."

West graduated from Brown in June 1924 and worked for a while in his father's construction business as he had done during his vacations. In October 1926, financed by his relatives, he went to Paris for a few months, where he began his first novel, *The Dream Life of Balso Snell*. It was in anticipation of this trip that he officially changed his name on August 16, 1926, to Nathanael West. He chose "West" as a surname, he told William Carlos Williams, because "Horace Greeley said, 'Go West young man.' So I did." Going to Paris was the launch of his identity as a writer and a pilgrimage to the shrine of his modernist and avant-garde heroes. He stayed near Montparnasse; bought copies of Joyce's *Ulysses* at Sylvia Beach's legendary bookshop, Shakespeare and Co.; toured the cafés, bars, and brothels of the literary and bohemian scene; met a number of surrealists; and was able to boast of having glimpsed or rubbed shoulders with the likes of Jean Cocteau, André Gide, Ernest Hemingway, T. S. Eliot, and others. He also met the American writer Henry Miller, who was introduced to West by his closest companion in Paris, the painter Hilaire Hiler.

West in later accounts fantastically (and typically) exaggerated the length of time he spent in Paris as well as the sort of life he led there, sometimes embroidering on true experiences, sometimes plain inventing others. He both celebrates and satirizes such subterfuge in "The Impostor," which gives an account of Paris in the 1920s and of Beano, a young man who has no artistic talent except for his ability to masquerade as a brilliant avant-garde sculptor: "Here was a man who could talk a whole gallery full of art works and who looked like a genius yet couldn't draw worth a damn." The desperate Beano has a moment of revelation when he realizes or decides

> that all the anatomy books were wrong because they used a man only five feet ten inches tall for their charts. Some used a man even shorter. They should have used a man six feet tall because the perfect, modern man is six feet tall. . . . A new anatomy book had to be written, and not until he had written it could he even think of drawing or sculpture.

Later Beano joins the expatriate Americans drinking at the Dôme. He has acquired from the morgue the corpse of a six-foot sailor "fished from the Seine," which is sitting wrapped in paper in the back of his taxi, and the story relates the dadaist events that follow. "The Impostor" was never published in West's lifetime, but as Martin observes, "parts of it West later told as true stories about himself." He was enticed home in January 1927 by his anxious family whose fortunes, like many others, were taking a turn for the worse.

Over the next few years West worked in the hotel business, first on the night desk of a cheap hotel called the Kenmore, where he was able to entertain fellow writers, including Perelman, and allow his friends to stay free of charge in rooms with unchanged linen. At this time he also met, through Perelman who had joined them, *The New Yorker* writers and infamous wits George S. Kaufman, Dorothy Parker, and Alexander Woollcott. West continued his hospitality in the fall of 1930, when he became the manager of the Sutton Club Hotel, a depression-era refuge for writers, including Perelman (who by then was married to West's sister Laura), Dashiell Hammett, Lillian Hellmann, James T. Farrell, and Edmund Wilson. At this time West worked on a series of short stories for which he was unable to secure publication and some of which remain unfinished. West kept a close eye on the people living in his hotel—prostitutes, no-hopers, occasional suicides—and he would even read their mail. A thinly fictionalized sampling of the Sutton clientele populate West's later novels, critics have suggested; and a personal anecdote concerning West's life there appears in Book IV of William Carlos Williams' poem *Paterson:*

> a tall and rather beautiful young woman came to his desk one day to ask if there were any interesting books to be had on the premises. He, being interested in literature, as she knew, replied that his own apartment was full of them and that, though he couldn't leave at the moment—Here's my key, go up and help yourself.

When he later returned to his room, forgetting about the woman who had his key,

> the door was unlatched and as he entered, a girl was lying naked on the bed. It startled him a little. So much so that all he could do was to remove his own clothes and lie beside her. Quite comfortable, he soon fell into a heavy sleep. She also must have slept.

They awoke later, at the same time, "much refreshed."

It was Williams who recommended *The Dream Life of Balso Snell* to Contact Editions, the prestigious small press that in the 1920s published some of the best experimental writing by authors such as Gertrude Stein and Ernest Hemingway. West's novel was issued in the summer of 1931 in a deluxe edition of five hundred.

West began writing his novel *Miss Lonelyhearts* while working at the Sutton, and at Williams' invitation he became an associate editor of a new version of *Contact* magazine, which Williams had previously coedited with Robert McAlmon. *Contact* magazine, in its new manifestation, attempted to reorient international avant-garde aesthetics toward the development of a new, local, in this case American, aesthetic. *Contact* saw itself in 1931 as the "legitimate successor" (in the words of Martin) to Eugene Jolas's Paris-based journal, *transition,* which

was possibly the most important and influential little magazine of the period. West published extracts from *Miss Lonelyhearts* in *Contact* as well as work by Williams, Perelman, e. e. cummings, and others.

By the time *Miss Lonelyhearts* was published in April 1933 as a book, West's father had died and his fiancée, Alice Shepard, the dedicatee of his first novel, had broken off their engagement (over West's infidelity with Lillian Hellman). Although constantly complaining of poverty, West was able to buy, along with the Perelmans, a farm in Erwinna, New York, not far from his friends the novelists Josephine Herbst and John Herrmann. His ill luck continued when Liveright, the publisher of *Miss Lonelyhearts,* went bankrupt, and only a few hundred copies of the novel survived the printer's seizure of stock. It was republished in June by Harcourt, Brace, but the disruption slowed sales considerably. Nevertheless West sold the movie rights to Twentieth Century Pictures for four thousand dollars, and some time later his novel was unrecognizable as the film adaptation *Advice to the Lovelorn.* In July 1933 West joined the Perelmans in Los Angeles, having been contracted as a writer to Columbia Pictures, but after intensive labor on a number of unproduced scripts, he was out of work and back hunting in Erwinna by the fall.

West's third novel, *A Cool Million,* was published by Covici, Friede in 1934, and the movie rights went this time to Columbia Pictures. This apparently premature antifascist novel failed to please reviewers, and his collaborative attempt with Perelman at a play, *Even Stephen,* attracted no interest. West's application in the same year for a Guggenheim Fellowship also failed despite his having Fitzgerald as his most prominent referee. In 1935, after a disastrous love affair with a married woman, West threw himself into political activities. He was arrested and jailed for picketing with strikers at a department store. He also joined the newly formed League of American Writers, whose revolutionary manifesto he signed.

Back in Los Angeles, unemployed and suffering another bout of gonorrhea, West was supported by the Perelmans until January 1936, when he got a decent contract with Republic Productions. And for the remaining years of his life he worked as a screenwriter, with stints at Republic, Columbia, R.K.O., and Universal Studios.

At Republic, West collaborated on screenplays such as *Ticket to Paradise,* his first produced film; *Follow Your Heart,* which he worked on with Lester Cole; *The President's Mystery,* which West and Cole worked up from an idea of President Franklin Delano Roosevelt's; *Gangs of New York; Jim Hanvey—Detective; Rhythm in the Clouds; It Could Happen to You;* and many more. For Universal he worked on *The Spirit of Culver* and Lester Cole's story *I Stole a Million,* his first major solo credit. For R.K.O. he worked on *Five Came Back* and had solo credits for *Men against the Sky* and *Let's Make Music.* In an appendix to his biography Jay Martin gives a thoroughly researched, itemized account of West's film writing. Edmund Wilson's 1930s journal, in a different vein, offers an invaluable glimpse of West actually at work in Hollywood and shows him capable of employing avant-garde techniques in the screenwriting he largely considered hack work, treating it with joyful irreverence, something that did not appear to impress his employers:

—They told West they wanted a scenario with a little perversity in it—he had written them a sentimental reminiscence (he supposed) of some old movie he had seen and had carefully stuck in so many clichés as to make it practically unreadable, so that the movie man had said, I want you to write it so that if we don't use it, you can print it as a short story.—His idea for scenario involving D. H. Lawrence stallion (shot of white arms around his neck), clean scientific steely doctor whom woman corrupts (she dances the lewd Martinique dance and beat of drum repeats hoofbeats of stallion—she is in dope ring to keep up stud farm because she loves the stallion so)—but finally the doctor's son turns up, the only lover who has been able to compete with the stallion, she saves the doctor on account of him (wonderful photo montage of hypodermic, the machine, against her white leg)—stallion finally tramples her to death.—West tolerant, Perelman intolerant.—West had sold movie rights of *Lonelyhearts* for $4,000.—Their names!—Gimfel—Lastvogel—West had gotten in wrong for saying to him, And the Lastvogel shall be Firstvogel.

In a letter of April 1939 West wrote to Wilson on the sort of demands made to him by Hollywood producers and the crude measure of their aesthetic expectations:

I've just come back from a story conference in which I was told that the picture I'm writing lacks significance and sweep—or, as the producer put it—"Why, tell me why, I dare you, we should spend half a million dollars on it, what fresh ideas have we got to sell—it isn't funny enough to make them piss their seats—it isn't sad enough to make them snuffle, and there's no message for them to carry away. Go back and put a message in it."

West continued his political activity in Hollywood. He spoke on "Makers of Mass Neuroses" at the Western Writers Congress of 1936, and between 1937 and 1938 worked for the Spanish Refugee Relief Campaign. A year later, when Hollywood hosted a fund-raising exhibition of Picasso's *Guernica,* West was one of its sponsors, and he pays homage to this painting in his last novel, *The Day of the Locust,* which was published in May of 1939 by Random House, again a different publisher from his previous novels. (West once mordantly noted that he had "never had the same publisher twice.") West's fourth novel was criticized by the left because its depiction of the Hollywood dream factory did not acknowledge or mention any of the oppositional political forces with which even West himself was involved. But to do so would have skewed West's entire satiric method, as he explained in a 1939 letter to Malcolm Cowley:

> I'm a comic writer and it seems impossible for me to handle any of the "big things" without seeming to laugh or at least smile. Is it possible to contrive a right-about face with one's writing because of a conviction based on a theory? I doubt it. What I mean is that out here we have a strong progressive movement and I devote a great deal of time to it. Yet, although this new novel is about Hollywood, I found it impossible to include any of those activities in it. . . . Take the "mother" in Steinbeck's swell novel—I want to believe in her and yet inside myself I honestly can't. When not writing a novel—say at a meeting of a committee we have out here to help the migratory worker—I do believe it and try to act on that belief. But at the typewriter by myself I can't.

West met Eileen McKenney in October 1939, and they were married in April 1940. In the following months his career as a screenwriter was beginning to turn around. His screen story "A Cool Million," which he wrote with Boris Ingster, was bought for ten thousand dollars by Columbia, and West and Ingster's treatment "Bird in Hand" went for twenty-five thousand dollars to R.K.O. By the spring of 1940 he was talking about a new book: "I have the entire story clearly in my mind and know just what I intend to do with it," he told Bennett Cerf at Random House. "The more I think about it, the more certain I am that it can be a hell of a book." Bercovitch has published an "Untitled Outline" by West from this time that sketches "a story about a racket"—the friendship clubs found in personal columns of newspapers. It may well be his notes for this new book. But on December 22, 1940, returning from a hunting trip in Mexico, West and his wife died as a result of a car crash at an intersection near El Centro, California, and modern American prose fiction was robbed of a leader.

THE DREAM LIFE OF BALSO SNELL

West's debut book—for which his favorite inscription was "From one horse's ass to another"—begins in imitation of Dante, as a descent into Hell, except that for the protagonist Balso the journey is though the anus and intestines of the Trojan horse. At the "lips of the mystic portal" Balso finds graffiti:

> Engraved in a heart pierced by an arrow and surmounted by the initial N, he read, "Ah! Qualis . . . Artifex . . . Pereo!" Not to be outdone by the actor-emperor, Balso carved with his penknife another heart and the words "O Byss! O Abyss! O Anon! O Onan!" omitting, however, the arrow and his initial.

Aside from Dante, Balso's graffiti might be compared with Nick Carraway's custodianship of Gatsby's myth in Fitzgerald's novel, where, at the close he carefully erases the graffiti he finds on the white steps of Gatsby's house. West, on the contrary, sets up mythic symbols only to vandalize them. The citation of Nero's dying words, "What an artist is lost with me!" is rhythmically supplemented by Balso's playful celebration of the lyric exclamation, "O," as arsehole and on this orifice as portal of death ("Abyss"). "O Byss" puns on the Latin verb *obire,* to die, as well as almost suggesting bliss; and the move from "Anon" to "Onan," links the oblivion of authorial anonymity with the erotic oblivion of masturbation (as the novel closes with an account of Balso's masturbatory ejaculation, onanism may well be the novel's alpha and omega).

Like many students and readers of avant-garde texts, Balso becomes angry and confused on entering the horse, and, just as Dante is guided through the Inferno by the spirit of Virgil, he feels obliged to hire "a philosophic guide who insists on discussing the nature of art," as West explains in his advertisement for the novel. Balso's guide, however, turns out to be a cryptically ranting, name-dropping bore: "After all, what is art? I agree with George Moore. Art is not nature, but rather nature digested. Art is a sublime excrement." By the time his guide begins to prose on about the formative influence of Cézanne, Balso manages to escape: "With a violent twist, Balso tore loose and fled." He continues on his journey alone, and, unassisted by the guide, he manages to survive being buttonholed along the way by various other—more entertaining—authors as he explores what lies beyond the portal.

The novel ends, as mentioned, not with the poet's expectoration, as might be suggested by West's initial choice of epigraph (the dictum of the collagist Kurt Schwitters that West cites in his advertisement for the novel, "Tout ce'que l'artiste crache, c'est l'art ["Everything that the artist expectorates is art"]) but in Balso's own masturbatory ejaculation. The antagonistic energies of the historical avant-garde resonate in West's choice of military metaphor for his account of Balso's final ejaculation: "The army that a moment before had been thundering in his body retreated slowly—victorious, relieved." Balso's orgasmic release of an army of sperm is not only charged with the mythopoeisis of the Trojan War, then, but is also an homage to more recent avant-garde celebrations of bodily fluids, such as the dictum by Schwitters, and to more visual examples such as the dadaist Francis Picabia's blasphemous 1920 ink splash titled *La Sainte Vierge,* which was published in his notorious international review, *391* (a publication West, as a disciple of the avant-garde, would probably have been familiar with).

The novel is packed with additional literary allusions, starting with its Proustian epigraph—"'After all, my dear fellow, life, Anaxagoras has said, is a journey'—Bergotte." Bergotte, himself a fictional construct, "a novelist and Marcel's hero in Proust's *A la recherche de temps perdu,*" cites the ancient philosopher Anaxagoras, whose concept of the universe as a "mixture" of spermata—"seeds"—"of every qualitatively distinct natural substance, organic and inorganic" (according to the *Oxford Classical Dictionary*)—seems particularly apt for West's onanistic text. If such arcane and obscurantist humor, coupled with West's bizarre and disorienting narration, his Eliotic allusions to classical mythology, and his Joycean wit and sordidity, has not already alerted the reader to the fact that he is writing in the new, avant-garde manner, then Balso's following invocation would surely do so: "O Beer! O Meyerbeer! O Bach! O Offenbach! Stand me now as ever in good stead." This synthetic bacchic (so to speak) invocation of drink and operatic song also clearly echoes Stephen's famous invocation of Dedalus in the concluding lines of one of the major founding avant-garde texts, *A Portrait of the Artist as a Young Man* (1916) by James Joyce: "Old father, old artificer, stand me now and ever in good stead." One might also note that *Portrait of the Artist* begins in a conflation of fairy tale, baby talk, colloquialism, and song. Just as Joyce's text is punctuated by song, so West has Balso break into song as he enters the "foyer-like lower intestine" of the Trojan horse:

> To keep his heart high and yet out of his throat, he made a song.
>> Round as the Anus
>> Of a Bronze Horse
>> Or the Tender Buttons
>> Used by Horses for Ani. . . .

Here West parodies, among other things, the sparse syntax of imagism, the compressed lyric symbolism of the poet William Butler Yeats, the perverse somatic humor of Joyce, and the cryptic poetics of Gertrude Stein's 1915 volume of cubist poetry, *Tender Buttons.* Farther down the digestive tract of the Trojan horse, Balso encounters parodies of Fyodor Dostoyevsky, the Marquis de Sade, Rainer Maria Rilke, Arthur Rimbaud, J. K. Huysmans, Yeats, Joyce, Proust, Williams, Pound, Perelman, Dashiell Hammett, Maksim Gorky, James Branch Cabell, François Rabelais, Voltaire, Aldous Huxley, D. H.

Lawrence. Snell, incidentally, was the name of West's college basketball coach.

MISS LONELYHEARTS

In West's second novel, which explores the role of the Hearst papers in the construction of oppressive gender and class positions in depression-era America, the author of a newspaper advice column, Miss Lonelyhearts, masquerades as a female subject and a Christian yet is manifestly at odds with his assignment. The novel's humor not only exploits the gap between Miss Lonelyhearts' imaginary and real experience but also his role in the ideological indoctrination of his readers. But Miss Lonelyhearts, a man for whom no other name is given, dubbed a latter-day Christ by his feature-editor, cannot cope with his messianic designation. His gruesome dream in the chapter "Miss Lonelyhearts and the Lamb" belies the religious sentiments he is daily obliged to purvey in his column. In the dream Miss Lonelyhearts and friends sacrifice a lamb to the Lord, only to be confronted with a gory scene of non-transcendence which prompts Miss Lonelyhearts to violence: "He went back alone and found it under a bush. He crushed its head with a stone and left the carcass to the flies that swarmed around the bloody altar flowers." The novel exposes its hero as the self-loathing vector of an ideology that promises salvation but brings only squalid devastation to its victims. The founding rationale of the column is economic, not pastoral (Miss Lonelyhearts cannot recommend suicide because it means a drop in circulation). Yet Miss Lonelyhearts is "overwhelmed by the desire to help" his readers escape the misery of their lives, misery that his journalism helps to bring about. This complicity is signaled in the novel's pervasive references to newspapers and magazines in images of cultural despair: "He saw a ragged woman with an enormous goiter pick a love story magazine out of a garbage can and

seem very excited by her find." Doyle, the crippled man cuckolded by Miss Lonelyhearts, and who later shoots the columnist through a newspaper (appropriately enough), appears as an assemblage of disparate elements: "like one of those composite photographs used by screen magazines in guessing contests."

Originally the story was told in the first person, and Miss Lonelyhearts' real name made known. In the final version, every time Miss Lonelyhearts is referred to in the third-person masculine, readers are reminded of the constructs of gender or what are seen as male and female roles and of Miss Lonelyhearts' own crisis of gender categorization. Miss Lonelyhearts, uncomfortably clothed in a feminine name, recognizes how clothes themselves designate gender roles—and not just for their wearers:

> He begged the party dress to marry him, saying all the things it expected to hear, all the things that went with strawberry sodas and farms in Connecticut. He was just what the party dress wanted him to be: simple and sweet, whimsical and poetic, a trifle collegiate yet very masculine.

By personifying the party dress, West exposes conventional gender roles as consumerist constructions. The dress is worn by Miss Lonelyhearts' sweetheart, Betty, as a rhetorical device articulating what she desires from a relationship with a man. "She dressed for things, he realized": she dresses for a marriage proposal and the commodities she expects to go with it. Additionally, the title of this scene, "Miss Lonelyhearts and the Party Dress," seems to promise, though does not deliver, his transition from textual to literal transvestism, and this prospect haunts the exchange.

Yet Miss Lonelyhearts does not give up his feminine persona ("He was not deliberately lying"), thus deferring the party dress's construction of him as "very masculine." The incident provides a metaphor for Miss Lonelyhearts' professional function. Just as the party dress establishes both Betty's and his gender roles, so the guise of Miss Lonelyhearts in effect constructs both him and his correspondents: they write what Miss Lonelyhearts, like the party dress, wants to read. With his assistance they become society's victims in need of his quasi-Christian succor. But like Miss Lonelyhearts, himself, each letter is also a site of ideological conflict.

Significantly, the letters from "Sick-of-it-all," "Desperate," "Broken-hearted," "Disillusioned-with-tubercular-husband," "Broad Shoulders," and so on are not the inventions of Nathanael West, but real letters. They were sent to the "Susan Chester" column of the *Brooklyn Eagle* and were originally offered as material to Perelman; but it was his brother-in-law, West, who saw their potential. One of the first letters in *Miss Lonelyhearts* is from "Desperate," a sixteen-year-old girl who writes about her lack of a nose as some teenagers might worry over a mild crop of blackheads. She blames herself for her missing appendage:

> I would like to have boy friends like the other girls and go out on Saturday nites, but no boy will take me because I was born without a nose— although I am a good dancer and have a nice shape and my father buys me pretty clothes. . . .
>
> What did I do to deserve such a terrible bad fate? . . . I asked Papa and he says he doesnt know, but that maybe I did something in the other world before I was born or that maybe I was being punished for his sins. . . . Ought I commit suicide?

The crippled Peter Doyle, earlier cuckholded by Miss Lonelyhearts, furtively hand-delivers his letter. He has a more complicated, and materialist, response to his predicament than the superstition and self-blame of "Desperate":

> What I want to no is why I go around pulling my leg up and down stairs reading meters for the gas company for a stinking $22.50 per while the bosses ride around in swell cars living off the fat of the land. Dont think I am a greasy red. . . . But thats not what I am writing you about. What I

want to no is what is it all for my pulling my god damed leg along the streets and down in stinking cellars with it all the time hurting fit to burst so that near quitting time I am crazy with pain and when I get home all I here is money money which aint no home for a man like me.

Doyle's desires for an end to bodily suffering, a change in social relations, a sexual relationship free of financial implications, emerge through the jostling discourses of the journalese he avidly consumes. Significantly, he opens his letter by remarking on his difficulties, as a *man,* in articulating his feelings: "I am kind of ashamed to write you because a man like me dont take stock in things like that but my wife told me you were a man and not some dopey woman so I thought I would write to you after reading your answer to Disillusioned." Doyle cannot broach these matters with a fellow male or raise them with "some dopey woman," but a man textually masquerading as a woman wins his confidence. Miss Lonelyhearts' very transvestism, then, opens up a space for Doyle's articulation:

> While Miss Lonelyhearts was puzzling out the crabbed writing, Doyle's damp hand accidentally touched his under the table. He jerked away, but then drove his hand back and forced it to clasp the cripple's. After finishing the letter, he did not let go, but pressed it firmly with all the love he could manage. At first the cripple covered his embarrassment by disguising the meaning of the clasp with a handshake, but he soon gave in to it and they sat silently hand in hand.

The "meaning of the clasp" remains ambiguous. It may be interpreted partly as a Christian gesture—the implementation of Miss Lonelyhearts' messianic fantasies—and partly as a sexual one. Miss Lonelyhearts repeats the gesture in the next scene, "Miss Lonelyhearts Pays a Visit," when he gets mixed up in the sexual conflict of the Doyles' marriage (after "Doyle tore open Miss Lonelyhearts' fly"). Mrs. Doyle remarks, "What a sweet pair of fairies you guys are." Miss Lonelyhearts, suppressing the possibilities of a relationship with Doyle himself, chooses this moment to enforce his newspaper's message of traditional, oppressive gender roles for the married couple: "You have a big, strong body, Mrs. Doyle. Holding your husband in your arms, you can warm him and give him life." The scene closes with Miss Lonelyhearts' brutal assault on Mrs Doyle's face: "He kept hitting her until she stopped trying to hold him, then he ran out of the house." Miss Lonelyhearts' Christian mission ends in the further oppression of those he seeks to help. His brutality toward Mrs. Doyle is bound up with her voicing of his unspoken sexual feelings. Mrs Doyle earlier in the scene "rolled a newspaper into a club and struck her husband on the mouth." This time Miss Lonelyhearts violently implements the oppressive ethos of his newspaper column.

This scene might be compared with an earlier one, "Miss Lonelyhearts and the Clean Old Man," in which Miss Lonelyhearts and a drinking pal pretend to be scientists to humiliate an old man taking refuge in a public toilet. The encounter makes Miss Lonelyhearts feel "as he had felt years before, when he had accidentally stepped on a small frog. . . . When its suffering had become real to his senses, his pity had turned to rage and he had beaten it frantically until it was dead." Using the quasi-scientific discourse of sexologists, Miss Lonelyhearts and his companion consciously inflict a similar sense of suffering: "'Aw, come off,' Gates said. 'We're scientists. He's Havelock Ellis and I'm Krafft-Ebing. When did you first discover homosexualistic tendencies in yourself?'" To their barrage of further questions the old man retorts:

"By what right do you ask?"

"Science gives me the right" [Miss Lonelyhearts said.]

"Let's drop it," Gates said. "The old fag is going to cry."

"No, Krafft-Ebing, sentiment must never be permitted to interfere with the probings of science."

Miss Lonelyhearts put his arm around the old man. "Tell us the story of your life," he said, loading his voice with sympathy.

When Miss Lonelyhearts turns to inflicting bodily violence on the old man, he feels that he is "twisting the arm of all the sick and miserable, broken and betrayed, inarticulate and impotent. He was twisting the arm of Desperate, Broken-hearted, Sick-of-it-all, Disillusioned-with-tubercular-husband." In authoritarian mode Miss Lonelyhearts equates homosexuality with social decline and poverty and punishes it as a register of all he despises (and feels threatened by).

William Carlos Williams, in "Sordid? Good God!" a defense of West's novel published in *Contempo* magazine in 1933, invokes the powerful image of the war veteran when he asks of Miss Lonelyhearts' correspondents:

Should such lives as these letters reveal never have been brought to light? Should such people, like the worst of our war wounded, best be kept in hiding?

The characters in West's book, these people whom the newspapers make a business of deceiving, are the direct incentive to his story, the seriously injured of our civic life—although the cases occur everywhere, even worse, perhaps in the rural districts. . . .

When writing is well made it enlivens and elevates the whole reader—without sweetening or benumbing the sense—while he plunges toward catastrophe.

The letters reveal the sad complicity of these people in their own oppression. As economic casualties of the depression, they wage war on each other. The letters are "counterpointed" (in Williams' phrase) with the scenes of Miss Lonelyhearts' turbulent exploration of his intersecting professional and sexual lives. Miss

Lonelyhearts never literally cross-dresses, but his textual cross-dressing nevertheless is a constant reminder of the constructedness of gender categories and exposes even as it enforces their ideological framing. If alternatives to oppressive gender codes are glimpsed, the main focus of the novel is to satirize the enforcement of conventional expectations.

In "A New American Writer," an article originally published in Ezra Pound's literary page of *Il Mare* (1931), Williams sums up West's achievement in *Miss Lonelyhearts* in terms of subject matter and method:

> The special strength of West, apart from his ability to maneuver words, is that he has taken seriously a theme of great importance so trite that all of us thought there would be no life in it; I mean the terrible moral impoverishment of our youth in the cities.
>
> But to do that he has discovered that the way to treat this theme is to use the dialect natural to such a condition. Since the newspapers are the principal corruptors of all that has value in language, it is with the use of this very journalistic "aspect" and everyday speech that language must be regenerated. West has taken as his material the idiom of the reporters, the tough men of the newspapers, and has counterpointed it with the pathetic letters and emotions of the poor and ignorant city dwellers who write to the newspapers to obtain counsel for their afflictions and poverty.

Williams identifies West's brilliant combination of powerful political satire and erudite avant-garde experimental technique as the factors that mark out this work as significant:

> After all, what is the urban population made up of? Of seduced and corrupted, nothing more. They have been gathered together so that they may be better exploited, and this is West's material. But no, his "material" is writing itself—he has invented a new manner. . . . "Don't be deceived" could be West's motto. Don't think yourself literate merely because you write long books and use correct English. Here are the problems, do something with them that will not be a lie. Don't deceive yourself: you don't see because you don't look. These things are there just the same. And if you think you can write poems while you live in a sewer, and at the same time think you're lying in a bed of roses—well, go ahead and be happy!
>
> The cities are rotten and desperate—so is most polite, "literary" literature.

A COOL MILLION

Like Miss Lonelyhearts' readers, the central character in *A Cool Million* steadfastly remains loyal to the ideology that is actually destroying him piece by piece. The deluded Lemuel Pitkin, faced with repossession, is duped by the Horatio Alger plowboy-to-president rhetoric of Shagpoke Whipple into a life of vagrancy and even greater poverty. The gap between his imaginary and his real experiences, as he doggedly sticks to his dangerous beliefs in the face of exploitation, is the source of the satire here. Promised the ultimate in unified subjective and sovereign power (the presidency), Lemuel Pitkin literally falls apart. In the course of *A Cool Million*, significantly subtitled "or, The Dismantling of Lemuel Pitkin," "our hero" Pitkin is almost entirely dismantled (he loses all his teeth, one eye, a thumb, a leg, and is scalped to the bone), and continually reassembled with the aid of various prostheses (false teeth, glass eye, wooden leg, and wig). Generally Pitkin is obliviously happy with his lot, and not surprisingly, he ends up a stooge in a comedy act:

> At this both actors turned on Lem and beat him violently over the head and body with their rolled-up newspapers. Their object was to knock off his toupee or to knock out his teeth and eye. When they had accomplished one or all of these goals, they stopped clubbing him. Then Lem, whose part it was not to move while he was being hit, bent over and with sober dignity took from the box at his feet, which contained a large assortment of false hair, teeth and eyes, whatever he needed to replace the things that had been knocked off or out.

Pitkin never seems to achieve a sense of complete identity, physically or mentally. He has become a site of identity in process. His fragmenting body puts into question not only his dignity as an individual but also the very possibility of individual somatic integrity (bodily wholeness). The prostheses indicate his partial and fluctuating commodification: Pitkin is continually being made and remade (but never finally completed) with commercially manufactured goods (wig, false teeth, glass eye, and so on). He resembles the wizard's description of the tin woodsman in the film of the *Wizard of Oz:* "a clinking, clanking, clattering collection of colligenous junk." His grotesque body stands also as a metaphor for mass experience. For when "our hero's employers congratulated him on his success," he piously reverts to the dominant depression ideology: "although he had a headache from their blows he was made quite happy by this. After all, he reasoned, with millions out of work he had no cause to complain."

Lemuel Pitkin, needless to say, does not become president. He dies a fascist martyr:

"Alas, Lemuel Pitkin himself did not have this chance, [Whipple says] but instead was dismantled by the enemy. His teeth were pulled out. His eye was gouged from his head. His thumb was removed. His scalp was torn away. His leg was cut off. And, finally, he was shot through the heart.

"But he did not live or die in vain. Through his martyrdom the National Revolutionary Party triumphed, and by that triumph this country was delivered from sophistication, Marxism and International Capitalism. Through the National Revolution its people were purged of alien diseases and America became again American. . . ."

"Hail, Lemuel Pitkin!"

"All hail, the American Boy!"

But Pitkin's flight through the various somatic and sartorial changes that are inflicted upon him also help him to resist gender roles in ways that other characters cannot. His sweetheart, Betty Prail, for example, is imprisoned in a brothel for most of the novel, and although she suffers a couple of transformations of her own, they are nowhere near to the extent of Pitkin's.

At first Betty is the sole American representative in Wu Fong's "House of All Nations" where, like the other inmates, she is forced to wear a costume "especially designed to go with her surroundings" ("colonial" in Betty's case). But later:

when the Hearst papers began their "Buy American" campaign [Wu Fong] decided to get rid of all the foreigners in his employ and turn his establishment into an hundred per centum American place.

Although in 1928 it would have been exceedingly difficult for him to have obtained the necessary girls, by 1934 things were different. Many respectable families of genuine native stock had been reduced to extreme poverty and had thrown their female children on the open market.

Asa Goldstein, in whose store window is exhibited Pitkin's family house, is hired to redecorate the brothel in a series of American interiors (Betty keeps her original costume). Betty remains trapped in this fixed, commodified gender category (the pun on "stock" suggesting America as warehouse-cum-whorehouse), but Pitkin, in a comparable situation, manages to evade the role marked out for him by virtue of his dismantling body. In one scene he is forced "to don a tight-fitting sailor suit" and is offered to a client in a brothel, but the disappointed customer withdraws bewildered: "What kind of a pretty boy was this that came apart so horribly?"

Dedicated to S. J. Perelman, *A Cool Million,* with its fast-change vaudeville humor, is certainly in keeping with that of the Marx brothers for whom Perelman worked as a scriptwriter, but it also pays homage to the equally fast-moving collagistic art of Schwitters (cited by West in "Through the Hole in the Mundane Millstone"). The accumulation of detritus, clichés, the secondhand, and so on, is certainly an organizing principle in both men's work. Indeed, Chief Israel Satinpenny, shortly before scalping Lemuel Pitkin, memorably itemizes some basic materials of the collagist:

> The land was flooded with toilet paper, painted boxes to keep pins in, key rings, watch fobs, leatherette satchels. . . .
>
> The day of vengeance is here. The star of the paleface is sinking and he knows it. Spengler has said so; Valéry has said so; thousands of his wise men proclaim it.
>
> O, brothers, this is the time to run upon his neck and the bosses of his armor. While he is sick and fainting, while he is dying of a surfeit of shoddy.

West's satire attempts to transform America's "surfeit of shoddy," or as he phrases it elsewhere, "the apocalypse of the Second Hand." But the timing of his antifascist gesture was premature, as he remarked in a 1939 letter to Saxe Commins on the reprinting of *A Cool Million:*

> Did you ever read a book called "A Cool Million"? . . . A lot of people think it is a pretty good one and that the reason it flopped is because it was published much too soon in the race toward Fascism. It came out when no one in this country except a few Jeremiahs like myself, took seriously the possibility of a Fascist America. . . . I feel that at the present time it might have a very good chance of arousing some interest.

THE DAY OF THE LOCUST

West's somewhat checkered experience as a screenwriter in Hollywood formed the basis for his last and, for some, his most successful work, *The Day of the Locust.* Often compared with F. Scott Fitzgerald's *The Last Tycoon,* this coruscating satire on the Hollywood dream factory (originally titled *The Cheated*) is a kind of *künstlerroman* because it has an artist, Tod Hackett, at its center and, like Virginia Woolf's

1927 novel *To the Lighthouse,* closes with the (visionary) execution of a painting. The subjects in this painting also form the focus of the novel: a seedy panorama of the grotesque, displaced, and marginalized—the losers at Hollywood's fringes rather than the success stories at its center. This is the California of prostitution, violence, and sleaze, where people "come to die." Commodity fetishism as masquerade features too:

> The fat lady in the yachting cap was going shopping, not boating; the man in the Norfolk jacket and Tyrolean hat was returning, not from a mountain, but an insurance office; and the girl in slacks and sneaks with a bandanna around her head had just left a switchboard, not a tennis court.

The influence of dadaist collage technique can be seen again, for example in West's description of the cultural dumping ground of a Hollywood film lot:

> There were bridges which bridged nothing, sculpture in trees, palaces that seemed of marble until a whole stone portico began to flap in the light breeze. And there were figures as well. A hundred yards from where Tod was sitting a man in a derby hat leaned drowsily against the gilded poop of a Venetian barque and peeled an apple. Still farther on, a charwoman on a stepladder was scrubbing with soap and water the face of a Buddha thirty feet high.

A phrase from Picasso may resonate at this point: he referred to his painting technique as "a hoard of destructions." West transforms here the traditional American list, as itemized by such writers as Ralph Waldo Emerson and Walt Whitman, into a catalog of detritus, a theatrical version of Eliot's *Waste Land.*

The machismo of Hemingway's fiction is sent up in one of the most violent scenes in the book, a description of a cockfight that also suggests the surrealist violence of a Louis Bunuel film:

> The red thrust weakly with its broken bill. Juju went into the air again and this time drove a gaff

through one of the red's eyes into its brain. The red fell over stone dead. . . . Juju pecked at the dead bird's remaining eye.

Such bloody scenes are woven into the story of Tod Hackett's courtship of Faye Greener, whose name seems to swipe at Daisy Fay (of the "green light" at the end of her dock) in *The Great Gatsby,* as well as Fay Doyle in *Miss Lonelyhearts.* And West continues his undermining of gender categories in, for example, this moving depiction of a transvestite:

All three of them turned to watch a young man in a tight evening gown of red silk sing a lullaby.

"Little man, you're crying,

I know why you're blue,

Someone took your kiddycar away;

Better go to sleep now,

Little man, you've had a busy day. . ."

He had a soft, throbbing voice and his gestures were matronly, tender and aborted, a series of unconscious caresses. What he was doing was in no sense parody; it was too simple and too restrained. It wasn't even theatrical. This dark young man with his thin, hairless arms and soft, rounded shoulders, who rocked an imaginary cradle as he crooned, was really a woman.

When he had finished, there was a great deal of applause. The young man shook himself and became an actor again. He tripped on his train, as though he weren't used to it, lifted his skirts to show he was wearing Paris garters, then strode off swinging his shoulders. His imitation of a man was awkward and obscene.

Homer and Tod applauded him.

"I hate fairies," Faye said.

"All women do."

In the final apocalyptic chapter, the artist-hero Tod Hackett in the midst of a mindless and bloody mob riot imagines completing his painting, "The Burning of Los Angeles." Intertextual links between Tod's painting and West's poem "Burn the Cities," a strange celebration of the

ascendancy of Marxism over Christianity, have been acknowledged, but the significance of the connections for readings of West's work remains a vexed point of debate. The first part of the poem was published in 1933 as "Christmass Poem" in *Contempo,* but it was only printed in its entirety after West's death. In the final mob scene, West offers not a vision of *all* humanity but a depiction of a certain social sector. West himself acknowledges this as a deliberate satiric strategy: his target is the proto-fascist middle-class mob. He confesses to the impossibility of including in his new novel the activities of Hollywood's left wing "progressive movement" with which he sympathized: "I tried to describe a meeting of the Anti-Nazi League, but it didn't fit and I had to substitute a whorehouse and a dirty film. The terribly sincere struggle of the League came out comic when I touched it and even libelous." West alerts readers both to his glorious resistance of the techniques of socialist realism (by then de rigeur on the left) and to his own selective, and highly effective, method of satire.

Selected Bibliography

WORKS OF NATHANAEL WEST

NOVELS

The Dream Life of Balso Snell. Paris and New York: Contact Editions, 1931.

Miss Lonelyhearts. New York: Liveright, 1933.

A Cool Million. New York: Covici, Friede, 1934.

The Day of the Locust. New York: Random House, 1939.

Mademoiselle Coeur-Brisé. Translated by Marcelle Sibon, with a preface by Philippe Soupault. Paris: Le Sagittaire, 1946.

COLLECTED WORKS

The Complete Works of Nathanael West. Introduction by Alan Ross. Farrar, Straus and Cudahy, 1957.

The Writings of Nathanael West. Edited by Alistair Wisker. Basingstoke, Eng.: Macmillan, 1990. (Includes all the works published in Bercovitch's *Novels and Other Writings.*)

Novels and Other Writings: Includes The Dream Life of Balso Snell; Miss Lonelyhearts; A Cool Million; The Day of the Locust; Other Writings; Unpublished Writings and Fragments; Letters. Edited by Sacvan Bercovitch. New York: Library of America, 1997. (Includes West's proposal to the Guggenheim Foundation, "The Adventurer," "The Impostor," "Mr. Potts of Pottstown," "Untitled Outline," and "Western Union Boy.")

OTHER WORKS

"Rondeau." *The Brown Jug* 2:24 (December 1922).

"Euripides—A Playwright." *Casements* 1:2–4 (July 1923).

"Through the Hole in the Mundane Millstone." Advertisement for *The Dream Life of Balso Snell.* Paris and New York: Contact Editions, 1931.

"Some Notes on Violence." *Contact* 1:132–133 (October 1932).

"Christmass Poem." *Contempo* 3:23 (February 21, 1933).

"Some Notes on Miss L." *Contempo* 3:1–2 (May 15, 1933).

"Business Deal." *Americana* 1:14–15 (October 1933).

"Soft Soap for the Barber." *New Republic,* November 14, 1934, p. 23. (Review of Gene Fowler, *Father Goose: The Story of Mack Sennett.* New York: Covici, Friede, 1934.)

STAGE DRAMA AND SCREENPLAYS

"Before the Fact, a Screen Play." In *Novels and Other Writings.* Edited by Sacvan Bercovitch. New York: Library of America, 1997. Pp. 621–744.

"'A Cool Million': A Screen Story." In *Novels and Other Writings.* Edited by Sacvan Bercovitch. New York: Library of America, 1997. Pp. 745–754.

Good Hunting, A Play in Three Acts. Written with Joseph Schrank. In *Novels and Other Writings.* Edited by Sacvan Bercovitch. New York: Library of America, 1997. Pp. 467–620.

BIBLIOGRAPHIES

Vannatta, Dennis P. *Nathanael West: An Annotated Bibliography of the Scholarship and Works.* New York: Garland, 1976.

White, William. *Nathanael West: A Comprehensive Bibliography.* Kent, Ohio: Kent State University Press, 1975.

CRITICAL AND BIOGRAPHICAL STUDIES

Aaron, Daniel. "The Truly Monstrous: A Note on Nathanael West." *Partisan Review* 14:98–106 (January–February 1947).

Abrahams, Roger D. "Androgynes Bound: Nathanael West's *Miss Lonelyhearts.*" In *Seven Contemporary Authors: Essays on Cozzens, Miller, West, Golding, Heller, Albee, and Powers.* Edited by Thomas B. Whitbread. Austin: University of Texas Press, 1966.

Auden, W. H. "Interlude: West's Disease." In *The Dyer's Hand, and Other Essays.* New York: Random House, 1962. Pp. 238–245.

Barnard, Rita. *The Great Depression and the Culture of Abundance: Kenneth Fearing, Nathanael West, and Mass Culture in the 1930s.* Cambridge: Cambridge University Press, 1995.

Bloom, Harold, ed. *Nathanael West.* New York: Chelsea House, 1986.

———. *Modern Critical Views: Nathanael West's "Miss Lonelyhearts."* New York: Chelsea House, 1987.

Budniakiewicz, Therese. *Fundamentals of Story Logic: Introduction to Greimassian Semiotics.* Amersterdam: Benjamins, 1992.

———. "The Value of the Notion of Contract to Literary Interpretation: Greimas, Propp, and West's *Miss Lonelyhearts.*" In *Semiotics around the World: Synthesis in Diversity: Proceedings of the Fifth Congress of the International Association for Semiotic Studies.* 2 vols. Edited by Irmengard Rauch and Gerald F. Carr. Berlin: Mouton de Gruyter, 1997.

Comerchero, Victor. *Nathanael West, the Ironic Prophet.* Syracuse, N.Y.: Syracuse University Press, 1964.

Daniel, Carter A. "West's Revisions of *Miss Lonelyhearts.*" *Studies in Bibliography* 16:232–243 (1963).

Dardis, Tom. *Some Time in the Sun*. New York: Scribners, 1976.

Edenbaum, Robert I. "Dada and Surrealism: A Literary Instance." *Arts in Society* 5:114–125 (1986).

Fiedler, Leslie A. *Love and Death in the American Novel*. Rev. ed. New York: Stein and Day, 1966.

Gilbert, Sandra M., and Susan Gubar. *No Man's Land: The Place of the Woman Writer in the Twentieth Century*. Vol. 1, *The War of the Words;* Vol. 2, *Sexchanges*. New Haven, Conn.: Yale University Press, 1988, 1989.

Goldman, Jane. "'Miss Lonelyhearts and the Party Dress': Cross-dressing and Collage in the Satires of Nathanael West." *Glasgow Review* 2:40–54 (autumn 1993).

———. "Dada Goes West: Re-Reading Revolution in *The Day of the Locust*." *Imprimatur* 2, nos. 1–2:20–36 (autumn 1996).

Gottlieb, Sidney. "The Madding Crowd in the Movies." In *The Modern American Novel and the Movies*. Edited by Gerald Peary and Roger Shatzkin. New York: Ungar, 1978. Pp. 95–106.

Herbst, Josephine. "Hunter of Doves." *Botteghe Oscure* 13:310–344 (1954).

———. "Nathanael West." *Kenyon Review* 23:611–630 (autumn 1961). Reprinted in Jay Martin, ed., *Nathanael West: A Collection of Critical Essays*. Englewood Cliffs, N.J.: Prentice-Hall, 1971.

Hyman, Stanley Edgar. *Nathanael West*. Minneapolis: University of Minnesota Press, 1962.

Jackson, Thomas H., ed. *Twentieth Century Interpretations of Miss Lonelyhearts*. Englewood Cliffs, N.J.: Prentice-Hall, 1971.

Light, James F. *Nathanael West: An Interpretative Study*. Evanston, Ill.: Northwestern University Press, 1971.

Long, Robert Emmet. *Nathanael West*. New York: Ungar, 1985.

Madden, David, ed. *Nathanael West: The Cheaters and the Cheated: A Collection of Critical Essays*. Deland, Fla.: Everett/Edwards, 1973.

Malin, Irving. *Nathanael West's Novels*. Carbondale: Southern Illinois University Press, 1972.

Martin, Jay. *Nathanael West: The Art of His Life*. New York: Farrar, Straus and Giroux, 1970.

———, ed. *Nathanael West: A Collection of Critical Essays*. Englewood Cliffs, N.J.: Prentice-Hall, 1971.

Mesher, David R. "A Note on Nathanael West Bibliographies." *American Notes & Queries* 20, nos. 5–6:79–80 (January–February 1982).

Perelman, S. J. "Nathanael West: A Portrait." *Contempo* 3:1, 4 (July 25, 1933). Reprinted in Jay Martin, ed., *Nathanael West: A Collection of Critical Essays*. Englewood Cliffs, N.J.: Prentice-Hall, 1971.

Podhoretz, Norman. "A Particular Kind of Joking." *The New Yorker*, May 18, 1957, pp. 156–165. Reprinted in Jay Martin, ed., *Nathanael West: A Collection of Critical Essays*. Englewood Cliffs, N.J.: Prentice-Hall, 1971.

Pogel, Nancy, and William Chamberlain. "Humor into Film: Self-Reflections in Adaptations of Black Comic Novels." In *Black Humor: Critical Essays*. Compiled and edited by Alan R. Pratt. New York: Garland, 1993.

Prasad, Suman Prabha. "The Sympathetic Misogynist: A Consideration of the Treatment of Women in N. West's *Miss Lonelyhearts*." In *Modern Studies and Other Essays: In Honour of Dr. R. K. Sinha*. Edited by R. C. Prasad and A. K. Sharma. New Delhi, India: Vikas, 1987. Pp. 72–79.

Reid, Randall. *The Fiction of Nathanael West: No Redeemer, No Promised Land*. Chicago: University of Chicago Press, 1967.

Roberts, Matthew. "Bonfire of the Avant-Garde: Cultural Rage and Readerly Complicity in *The Day of the Locust*." *Modern Fiction Studies* 42:61–90 (spring 1996).

Scott, Nathan A., Jr. *Nathanael West: A Critical Essay*. Grand Rapids, Mich.: Eerdmans, 1971.

Siegel, Ben, ed. *Critical Essays on Nathanael West*. New York: G. K. Hall, 1994.

Sikora, Malgorzata. "Discovering the Grotesque in the South." In *Approaches to Fiction*. Edited by Leszek S. Kolek. Lublin, Poland: Folium, 1996.

Strychacz, Thomas F. *Modernism, Mass Culture, and Professionalism*. Cambridge: Cambridge University Press, 1993.

Veitch, Jonathan. *American Superrealism: Nathanael West and the Politics of Representation in the 1930s*. Madison: University of Wisconsin Press, 1997.

Wadlington, Warwick. *The Confidence Game in American Literature*. Princeton, N.J.: Princeton University Press, 1975.

Walden, Daniel. "Nathanael West: A Jewish Satirist in Spite of Himself." In Ben Siegel, ed., *Critical Essays on Nathanael West.* New York: G. K. Hall, 1994.

Ward, J. A. "The Hollywood Metaphor: The Marx Brothers, S. J. Perelman, and Nathanael West." In *S. J. Perelman: Critical Essays.* Edited by Steven H. Gale. New York: Garland, 1992. Pp. 659–672.

White, William. "Unpublished Faulkner: Reply to a Nathanael West Questionnaire." *American Book Collector* 17:27 (September 1966).

Widmer, Kingsley. *Nathanael West.* Boston: Twayne, 1982.

Williams, William Carlos. "A New American Writer." Translated into Italian by E. Dodsworth. *Il Mare* XI (January 21, 1931). Reprinted in Jay Martin, ed., *Nathanael West: A Collection of Critical Essays.* Englewood Cliffs, N.J.: Prentice-Hall, 1971. (Williams's original was lost.)

———. "Sordid? Good God!" *Contempo* 3, no.11 (July 25, 1933). Reprinted in Jay Martin, ed., *Nathanael West: A Collection of Critical Essays.* Englewood Cliffs, N.J.: Prentice-Hall, 1971.

Wilson, Edmund. *The Thirties.* Edited by Leon Abel. New York: Farrar, Straus and Giroux, 1980.

Wyrick, Deborah. "Dadaist Collage Structure and Nathanael West's *Dream Life of Balso Snell.*" *Studies in the Novel* 11:349–359 (1979).

—*JANE GOLDMAN*

Index

Arabic numbers printed in bold-face type refer to extended treatment of a subject.

Supp. IV Part 2: 681, 682; Supp. VIII: 40; Supp. X: 187

Gideon Planish (Lewis), II: 455

Gielgud, John, I: 82; Supp. XI: 305

Gierow, Dr. Karl Ragnar, III: 404

Gifford, Bill, Supp. XI: 38

"Gift, The" (Creeley), Supp. IV Part 1: 153

"Gift, The" (Doolittle), Supp. I Part 1: 267

Gift, The (Nabokov), III: 246, 255, 261–263; Retro. Supp. I: 264, 266, **268–270,** 273, 274–275, 278

"Gift from the City, A" (Updike), Retro. Supp. I: 320

"Gift of God, The" (Robinson), III: 512, 517, 518–521, 524

Gift of the Black Folk, The: The Negroes in the Making of America (Du Bois), Supp. II Part 1: 179

"Gift of the Magi, The" (O. Henry), Supp. II Part 1: 394, 406, 408

"Gift of the *Osuo,* The" (Johnson), Supp. VI: 194

"Gift of the Prodigal, The" (Taylor), Supp. V: 314, 326

"Gift Outright, The" (Frost), II: 152; Supp. IV Part 1: 15

"Gigolo" (Plath), Retro. Supp. II: 257

"Gila Bend" (Dickey), Supp. IV Part 1: 185–186

Gilbert, Jack, Supp. IX: 287

Gilbert, Peter, Supp. IX: 291, 300

Gilbert, Roger, Supp. XI: 124

Gilbert, Sandra M., Retro. Supp. I: 42; Retro. Supp. II: 342; Supp. IX: 66

Gilbert, Susan. *See* Dickinson, Mrs. William A.

Gilbert and Sullivan, Supp. IV Part 1: 389

Gil Blas (Le Sage), II: 290

Gilded Age, The (Twain), III: 504; IV: 198

"Gilded Six-Bits, The" (Hurston), Supp. VI: 154–155

Gilder, R. W., Retro. Supp. II: 66; Supp. I Part 2: 418

Gildersleeve, Basil, Supp. I Part 1: 369

Giles, H. A., Retro. Supp. I: 289

Giles, James R., Supp. IX: 11, 15; Supp. XI: 219, 223–224, 228, 234

"Giles Corey of the Salem Farms" (Longfellow), II: 505, 506; Retro. Supp. II: 166, 167

Giles Goat-Boy (Barth), I: 121, 122–123, 129, 130, 134, 135–138; Supp. V: 39

Gill, Brendan, Supp. I Part 2: 659, 660

Gillette, Chester, I: 512

Gillis, Jim, IV: 196

Gillis, Steve, IV: 195

Gilman, Charlotte Perkins, Supp. I Part 2: 637; Supp. V: 121, 284, 285; Supp. XI: **193–211**

Gilman, Daniel Coit, Supp. I Part 1: 361, 368, 370

Gilman, Richard, IV: 115; Supp. IV Part 2: 577

Gilmore, Eddy, Supp. I Part 2: 618

Gilpin, Charles, III: 392

Gilpin, Laura, Retro. Supp. I: 7

Gilpin, Sam, Supp. V: 213

Gilpin, William, Supp. IV Part 2: 603

"Gil's Furniture Bought & Sold" (Cisneros), Supp. VII: 61–62, 64

"Gimpel the Fool" (Singer), IV: 14; Retro. Supp. II: 22, 325

Gimpel the Fool and Other Stories (Singer), IV: 1, 7–9, 10, 12

"Gin" (Levine), Supp. V: 193

"Gingerbread House, The" (Coover), Supp. V: 42–43

Gingerbread Lady, The (Simon), Supp. IV Part 2: 580, 583–584, 588

Gingerich, Willard, Supp. IV Part 2: 510

Gingertown (McKay), Supp. X: 132, 139

Gingrich, Arnold, Retro. Supp. I: 113

Ginna, Robert, Supp. IX: 259

Ginsberg, Allen, I: 183; Retro. Supp. I: 411, 426, 427; Retro. Supp. II: 298; Supp. II Part 1: 30, 32, 58, **307–333;** Supp. III Part 1: 2, 91, 96, 98, 100, 222, 226; Supp. III Part 2: 541, 627; Supp. IV Part 1: 79, 90, 322; Supp. IV Part 2: 502; Supp. V: 168, 336; Supp. VIII: 239, 242–243, 289; Supp. IX: 299; Supp. X: 120, 204; Supp. XI: 135, 297; Supp. XII: 118–119, 121–122, 124, 126, 130–131, 136, 182

Gioia, Dana, Supp. IX: 279; Supp. XII: 209

Giotto di Bondone, Supp. I Part 2: 438; Supp. XI: 126

Giovanni, Nikki, Supp. I Part 1: 66; Supp. II Part 1: 54; Supp. IV Part 1: 11; Supp. VIII: 214

Giovanni's Room (Baldwin), Retro. Supp. II: 5, 6, **6–7,** 8, 10; Supp. I Part 1: 51, 52, 55–56, 57, 60, 63, 67; Supp. III Part 1: 125

Giovannitti, Arturo, I: 476

"Giraffe" (Swenson), Supp. IV Part 2: 651

Giraldi, Giovanni Battista. *See* Cinthio

"Girl" (Kincaid), Supp. VII: 182–183

"Girl, The" (Olds), Supp. X: 207

"Girl from Red Lion, P.A., A" (Mencken), III: 111

"Girl of the Golden West" (Didion), Supp. IV Part 1: 195, 208, 211

Girl of the Golden West, The (Puccini), III: 139

"Girl on the Baggage Truck, The" (O'Hara), III: 371–372

Girls at Play (Theroux), Supp. VIII: 314, 315, 316, **317**

"Girls at the Sphinx, The" (Farrell), II: 45

Girl Sleuth, The: A Feminist Guide (Mason), Supp. VIII: 133, 135, **139,** 142

"Girl's Story, A" (Bambara), Supp. XI: 10–11

"Girl the Prince Liked, The" (Z. Fitzgerald), Supp. IX: 71

Girl Who Loved Tom Gordon, The (King), Supp. V: 138, 152

Girl with Curious Hair (Wallace), Supp. X: 301, **305–308**

"Girl with Curious Hair" (Wallace), Supp. X: 306

"Girl with Silver Eyes, The" (Hammett), Supp. IV Part 1: 344, 345

"Girl with Talent, The" (Z. Fitzgerald), Supp. IX: 71

Girodias, Maurice, III: 171; Supp. XI: 297

Giroux, Robert, Retro. Supp. II: 177, 229, 235; Supp. IV Part 1: 280; Supp. VIII: 195

Gish, Dorothy, Retro. Supp. I: 103

Gissing, George, II: 138, 144

Gittings, Robert, II: 531

"Give Us Back Our Country" (Masters), Supp. I Part 2: 472

"Give Way, Ye Gates" (Roethke), III: 536

"Give Your Heart to the Hawks" (Jeffers), Supp. II Part 2: 433

"Giving Blood" (Updike), IV: 226; Retro. Supp. I: 332

Giving Good Weight (McPhee), Supp. III Part 1: 307

"Giving Myself Up" (Strand), Supp. IV Part 2: 627

Glackens, William, Retro. Supp. II: 103

Gladden, Washington, III: 293; Supp. I Part 1: 5

Gladstone, William Ewart, Supp. I Part 2: 419

A Complete Listing of Authors in
American Writers

Henry, O.   Supp. II
Hijuelos, Oscar   Supp. VIII
Hoffman, Alice   Supp. X
Hogan, Linda   Supp. IV
Holmes, Oliver Wendell   Supp. I
Howe, Irving   Supp. VI
Howe, Susan   Supp. IV
Howells, William Dean   Vol. II
Hughes, Langston   Supp. I
Hughes, Langston   Retro. Supp. I
Hugo, Richard   Supp. VI
Humphrey, William   Supp. IX
Hurston, Zora Neale   Supp. VI
Irving, John   Supp. VI
Irving, Washington   Vol. II
Jackson, Shirley   Supp. IX
James, Henry   Vol. II
James, Henry   Retro. Supp. I
James, William   Vol. II
Jarrell, Randall   Vol. II
Jeffers, Robinson   Supp. II
Jewett, Sarah Orne   Vol. II
Jewett, Sarah Orne   Retro. Supp. II
Johnson, Charles   Supp. VI
Jones, James   Supp. XI
Jong, Erica   Supp. V
Justice, Donald   Supp. VII
Karr, Mary   Supp. XI
Kazin, Alfred   Supp. VIII
Kennedy, William   Supp. VII
Kenyon, Jane   Supp. VII
Kerouac, Jack   Supp. III
Kincaid, Jamaica   Supp. VII
King, Stephen   Supp. V
Kingsolver, Barbara   Supp. VII
Kingston, Maxine Hong   Supp. V
Kinnell, Galway   Supp. III
Knowles, John   Supp. XII
Kosinski, Jerzy   Supp. VII
Kumin, Maxine   Supp. IV
Kunitz, Stanley   Supp. III
Kushner, Tony   Supp. IX
LaBastille, Anne   Supp. X
Lanier, Sidney   Supp. I

Lardner, Ring   Vol. II
Lee, Harper   Supp. VIII
Levertov, Denise   Supp. III
Levine, Philip   Supp. V
Levis, Larry   Supp. XI
Lewis, Sinclair   Vol. II
Lindsay, Vachel   Supp. I
London, Jack   Vol. II
Longfellow, Henry Wadsworth   Vol. II
Longfellow, Henry
    Wadsworth   Retro. Supp. II
Lowell, Amy   Vol. II
Lowell, James Russell   Supp. I
Lowell, Robert   Vol. II
Lowell, Robert   Retro. Supp. II
McCarthy, Cormac   Supp. VIII
McCarthy, Mary   Vol. II
McClatchy, J. D.   Supp. XII
McCourt, Frank   Supp. XII
McCullers, Carson   Vol. II
Macdonald, Ross   Supp. IV
McGrath, Thomas   Supp. X
McKay, Claude   Supp. X
MacLeish, Archibald   Vol. III
McMurty, Larry   Supp. V
McPhee, John   Supp. III
Mailer, Norman   Vol. III
Mailer, Norman   Retro. Supp. II
Malamud, Bernard   Supp. I
Marquand, John P.   Vol. III
Marshall, Paule   Supp. XI
Mason, Bobbie Ann   Supp. VIII
Masters, Edgar Lee   Supp. I
Mather, Cotton   Supp. II
Matthews, William   Supp. IX
Matthiessen, Peter   Supp. V
Maxwell, William   Supp. VIII
Melville, Herman   Vol. III
Melville, Herman   Retro. Supp. I
Mencken, H. L.   Vol. III
Merrill, James   Supp. III
Merton, Thomas   Supp. VIII
Merwin, W. S.   Supp. III
Millay, Edna St. Vincent   Vol. III

Sontag, Susan   Supp. III
Southern, Terry   Supp. XI
Stafford, William   Supp. XI
Stegner, Wallace   Supp. IV
Stein, Gertrude   Vol. IV
Steinbeck, John   Vol. IV
Stern, Gerald   Supp. IX
Stevens, Wallace   Vol. IV
Stevens, Wallace   Retro. Supp. I
Stone, Robert   Supp. V
Stowe, Harriet Beecher   Supp. I
Strand, Mark   Supp. IV
Styron, William   Vol. IV
Swenson, May   Supp. IV
Tan, Amy   Supp. X
Tate, Allen   Vol. IV
Taylor, Edward   Vol. IV
Taylor, Peter   Supp. V
Theroux, Paul   Supp. VIII
Thoreau, Henry David   Vol. IV
Thurber, James   Supp. I
Toomer, Jean   Supp. IX
Trilling, Lionel   Supp. III
Twain, Mark   Vol. IV
Tyler, Anne   Supp. IV
Updike, John   Vol. IV
Updike, John   Retro. Supp. I
Van Vechten, Carl   Supp. II
Veblen, Thorstein   Supp. I
Vidal, Gore   Supp. IV
Vonnegut, Kurt   Supp. II
Wagoner, David   Supp. IX

Walker, Alice   Supp. III
Wallace, David Foster   Supp. X
Warren, Robert Penn   Vol. IV
Welty, Eudora   Vol. IV
Welty, Eudora   Retro. Supp. I
West, Nathanael   Vol. IV
West, Nathanael   Retro. Supp. II
Wharton, Edith   Vol. IV
Wharton, Edith   Retro. Supp. I
White, E. B.   Supp. I
Whitman, Walt   Vol. IV
Whitman, Walt   Retro. Supp. I
Whittier, John Greenleaf   Supp. I
Wilbur, Richard   Supp. III
Wideman, John Edgar   Supp. X
Wilder, Thornton   Vol. IV
Williams, Tennessee   Vol. IV
Williams, William Carlos   Vol. IV
Williams, William Carlos   Retro. Supp. I
Wilson, August   Supp. VIII
Wilson, Edmund   Vol. IV
Winters, Yvor   Supp. II
Wolfe, Thomas   Vol. IV
Wolfe, Tom   Supp. III
Wolff, Tobias   Supp. VII
Wright, Charles   Supp. V
Wright, James   Supp. III
Wright, Richard   Vol. IV
Wylie, Elinor   Supp. I
Yates, Richard   Supp. XI
Zukofsky, Louis   Supp. III